The United States *and the* World Economy

FOREIGN ECONOMIC POLICY FOR THE NEXT DECADE

INSTITUTE FOR INTERNATIONAL ECONOMICS

The United States *and the* World Economy

FOREIGN ECONOMIC POLICY FOR THE NEXT DECADE

C. Fred Bergsten and the
Institute for International Economics

Washington, DC
January 2005

C. Fred Bergsten has been the director of the Institute for International Economics since its creation in 1981. He is also chairman of the "Shadow G-8," which advises the G-8 countries on their annual summit meetings, and the TransAtlantic Strategy Group, created by the Bertelsmann Foundation. He was chairman of the Competitiveness Policy Council, which was created by Congress, throughout its existence from 1991 to 1995 and chairman of the APEC Eminent Persons Group throughout its existence from 1993 to 1995. He was assistant secretary for international affairs of the US Treasury (1977–81); assistant for international economic affairs to Dr. Henry Kissinger at the National Security Council (1969–71); and a senior fellow at the Brookings Institution (1972–76), the Carnegie Endowment for International Peace (1981), and the Council on Foreign Relations (1967–68). He is the author, coauthor, or editor of 34 books on a wide range of international economic issues, including *Dollar Adjustment: How Far? Against What?* (2004), *Dollar Overvaluation and the World Economy* (2003), *No More Bashing: Building a New Japan–United States Economic Relationship* (2001), *Global Economic Leadership and the Group of Seven* (1996), and *The Dilemmas of the Dollar* (2d ed. 1996).

INSTITUTE FOR INTERNATIONAL ECONOMICS
1750 Massachusetts Avenue, NW
Washington, DC 20036-1903
(202) 328-9000 FAX: (202) 659-3225
www.iie.com

C. Fred Bergsten, *Director*
Valerie Norville, *Director of Publications and Web Development*
Edward Tureen, *Director of Marketing*

Typesetting by BMWW
Printing by United Book Press, Inc.

Printed in the United States of America
07 06 05 5 4 3 2 1

Library of Congress Cataloging-in-Publication Data

The United States and the world economy : foreign economic policy for the next decade / C. Fred Bergsten.
p. cm.
Includes bibliographical references and index.
ISBN 0-88132-380-2
1. United States—Commercial policy. 2. United States—Commerce. 3. United States—Economic policy—2001–4. 4. United States—Foreign economic relations. I. Bergsten, C. Fred, 1941– . II. Institute for International Economics (U.S.)

HF1455.U483 2005
337.73—dc22 2004062540

Contents

Tables

Figures

Boxes

Preface

This book proposes an agenda for the foreign economic policy of the United States for the next decade. It was motivated most immediately by the presidential and congressional elections of 2004 in the belief that those chosen to govern the United States over the coming years would benefit from an analysis of the issues they would be facing in this area and from recommendations for addressing them. This might be especially true because many of the central topics discussed here are barely considered in US political campaigns and are poorly understood by the broader public.

The book argues that several of the key problems facing the United States in the international economic arena in fact need to be addressed with considerable urgency. Those issues are exceedingly complex and deep-seated, however, and even a speedy initiation of policy responses to them will necessarily play out over a number of years. At the same time, many of the problems (including some of the same ones) reflect fundamental changes in both global economic relationships and domestic political attitudes within the United States itself. We suspect that the suggested policy agenda will thus prevail over a fairly lengthy period and can accurately be characterized as a medium-term, or even longer-term, program.

The book hopes to serve a second purpose as well: to present a comprehensive analysis of the international economic picture that will help a much broader audience understand the set of issues facing the United States (and the world as a whole) in this domain over the next five to ten years. Regardless of reactions to our policy proposals, and whether or not they are adopted by the US authorities, we hope and believe that our appraisals of these topics may provide useful background for those contemplating the whole range of international economic topics and geographical regions of the world.

The technique chosen for the volume was to deploy the considerable resources of the Institute to address each of the international economic issues that we believe will be of highest priority to the United States and to the world economy over the coming period. Each chapter was prepared by one of our senior fellows (joined in 4 of the 13 chapters by one or more Institute colleagues) on her or his own topic of particular expertise. I wrote the overview chapter, which seeks to present an integrated strategy for US foreign economic policy for the coming period, drawing on each of the subsequent chapters as well as other previous research and some of my own earlier work.

As with every Institute project, the final result derived enormous benefit from vigorous debate within the Institute, reflecting the fact that the different authors do not always agree with every word of the chapters written by others. We also greatly appreciate the extensive comments of Professor Richard N. Cooper of Harvard University, the chairman of our advisory committee, and other outside commentators. Our particular thanks go to the numerous high officials of the US government, members of Congress, Chairman Alan Greenspan and other governors of the Federal Reserve, IMF Managing Director Rodrigo de Rato, and others to whom we presented prepublication copies of the book in November-December 2004 and who were extremely generous in conveying their reactions to it. I want to particularly express my deep personal gratitude to all of my colleagues who made this effort possible and my hope that this publication of "the best of the Institute" will be helpful to the conduct of the foreign economic policy of the United States in 2005 and beyond.

The Institute for International Economics is a private, nonprofit institution for the study and discussion of international economic policy. Its purpose is to analyze important issues in that area and to develop and communicate practical new approaches for dealing with them. The Institute is completely nonpartisan.

The Institute is funded by a highly diversified group of philanthropic foundations, private corporations, and interested individuals. Major institutional grants are now being received from the William M. Keck Jr. Foundation, the New York Community Trust, and the Starr Foundation. About 18 percent of the Institute's resources in our latest fiscal year were provided by contributors outside the United States, including about 8 percent from Japan.

The Board of Directors bears overall responsibilities for the Institute and gives general guidance and approval to its research program, including the identification of topics that are likely to become important over the medium run (one to three years), and which should be addressed by the Institute. The director, working closely with the staff and outside

Advisory Committee, is responsible for the development of particular projects and makes the final decision to publish an individual study.

The Institute hopes that its studies and other activities will contribute to building a stronger foundation for international economic policy around the world. We invite readers of these publications to let us know how they think we can best accomplish this objective.

C. Fred Bergsten
Director
January 2005

Executive Summary

The United States derives substantial benefits from open trade and other manifestations of globalization. We estimate that

- US incomes are $1 trillion per year higher due to the country's increased integration with the world economy since 1945;
- US incomes could rise by a further $500 billion per year by moving all the way to global free trade;
- offsetting adjustment costs amount to only about $50 billion per year; but
- the country spends only $1 billion to $2 billion annually to address directly these costs of adjusting to globalization.

Hence the United States has an overwhelming national interest in maintaining and expanding its integration with the world economy. However, it needs to do a much better job of addressing the downsides of globalization and thus restoring a sustainable domestic foundation for continued proglobalization policies. In the short run, the United States faces three significant risks with major international dimensions that could mutually reinforce their negative effects on its economy:

- *the essential substantial correction of the large and growing current account deficit*, which is already approaching $700 billion annually and is on a trajectory toward $1 trillion within the next few years and which will require slower growth of US domestic demand in any event, could trigger much higher interest rates and a sharp growth slowdown if the orderly decline of the dollar that has prevailed in 2002–04 were to accelerate into a free fall (especially as the economy is moving closer to full employment);

- *renewed increases, perhaps to $60 to $70 per barrel, in the world oil price* with severely adverse effects on inflation, interest rates, and growth; and
- *increased trade protectionism*, especially against China in light of a bilateral trade deficit approaching annual rates of $200 billion, due importantly to the inadequacies of US domestic programs to cushion the impact of trade-induced dislocation and to equip American workers to compete successfully in a globalized economy.

Over the longer run, the United States also faces three structural international economic challenges:

- the advent of *an expanded European Union* with an economy as large as America's and a single money that provides the first rival to the dollar since it became the world's key currency;
- the meteoric *rise of China* (with India perhaps coming in its wake); and
- the evolution toward an *East Asian economic bloc* that could create a tripolar world economy, with significant geopolitical as well as economic implications for the United States.

Several major new policy initiatives, including domestic as well as international measures, are thus needed in the near future. The most urgent would aim

- to correct the current account deficit in an orderly manner without severely disrupting US or global economic growth by:
  - launching a credible program to *reduce the budget deficit substantially* over the next few years and move it back into surplus over time, thus raising domestic savings, cutting the need for capital inflows, and boosting confidence in the US economic outlook and policies;
  - *accelerating multilateral pressure on China to revalue its currency by 20 to 25 percent*, through direct intervention if necessary to counter their market manipulation via massive intervention in the foreign exchange markets, enabling the other Asian countries to let their currencies appreciate further as well and thus achieving a geographically balanced as well as qualitatively adequate correction of the continuing overvaluation of the dollar (about 15 percent on a trade-weighted basis at the end of 2004);

- aggressively encouraging the *other major economies (especially in Europe) to boost domestic demand* to offset the coming declines in their trade surpluses, through both structural reforms and more expansionary macroeconomic policies, perhaps via a "new Plaza" or "new Bonn summit" agreement.

- to reduce and stabilize global energy prices through:
  - *sales from the Strategic Petroleum Reserve,* in the short run to avoid dangerously high prices and, in the long run, as a component of coordinated market intervention by consuming countries, to counter the continuing price manipulation of the Organization of Petroleum Exporting Countries (OPEC);
  - enactment of a *substantial gasoline tax* (perhaps $1 per gallon), to be phased in as market prices decline, to cut US demand and strengthen its international negotiating position; along with
  - development of *a North American energy strategy* that promotes greater investment in energy production and distribution channels in all three NAFTA countries; and
  - pursuit of a *producer-consumer agreement,* with the other main consuming countries, to hold the world oil price within the range of $22 to $28 per barrel traditionally espoused by OPEC, implemented through a stabilization stock built on the strategic reserves (1.5 billion barrels) currently held by the United States and other consuming countries.

- to focus trade policy on:
  - *heightened priority for liberalization of services and sharp cuts in agricultural supports* and import restrictions in the Doha Round, to exploit US comparative advantage and help reduce the US budget deficit as well as to credibly maintain the forward momentum of opening markets;
  - *initiation of new negotiations for free trade agreements (FTAs)* with several countries with significant economic size, foreign policy importance, and potential for major economic reform, including *Egypt, India, Korea, and/or Japan,* as soon as they indicate a readiness to liberalize sufficiently; and
  - strong support for the *Asia Pacific Economic Cooperation (APEC) forum's pursuing a Free Trade Area of the Asia Pacific* to consolidate the proliferation of FTAs in the region (over 40 by 2007, of a global total of about 300), to avoid "drawing a line down the middle of the Pacific," in the wake of the likely creation of an Asia-only economic bloc, and to energize the Doha Round by suggesting to the Euro-

pean Union and others that the United States and the Asians have a credible alternative.

- to address the costs of globalization and strengthen domestic resistance to the backlash against it, substantial further expansion of Trade Adjustment Assistance (TAA) including:
  - *eligibility for services workers*, who are affected by a growing share of US trade and are the focus of most of the new concerns over "outsourcing";
  - *qualification of trade-impacted industries* rather than individual groups of workers, to simplify and speed the delivery of all available TAA remedies;
  - *revival of community adjustment* programs, to counter the broader impact of trade-related dislocations; and
  - a *Human Capital Investment Tax Credit*, like the traditional tax credits for investment in physical and in research and development, to encourage adoption of worker training programs by private companies, who can do it much more effectively than the government.

The conduct of US foreign economic policy will require substantial modification at both the multilateral and bilateral levels to pursue two new approaches effectively:

- at the multilateral level, new emphasis on the large emerging-market economies (especially Brazil, India, Russia, and South Africa, along with China) with the *G-20 steadily replacing the G-7* as the informal steering committee for the world economy; and
- at the bilateral level, special*("G-2") relationships with the European Union* (for macroeconomic, monetary, and some other issues), *China* (inter alia for global growth, exchange rates, and energy), *Japan* (for trade and to counter China's rise), and *Saudi Arabia* (for energy).

I

FOREIGN ECONOMIC POLICY FOR THE UNITED STATES

1

A New Foreign Economic Policy for the United States

C. FRED BERGSTEN

The United States faces a series of intense challenges, acute threats, and promising opportunities from its interaction with the world economy. These challenges, threats, and opportunities confront both the US economy, as it seeks to sustain growth and stability at satisfactory levels, and overall US foreign policy and the country's place in the world. Some are immediate and require urgent response. Others reflect structural changes in global economics and politics that will play out over a number of years and even decades.

A number of the threats are immediate. The most important and most likely is the substantial economic adjustment that will be required to correct the unprecedented and rapidly growing US current account deficit. If this includes a crash of the dollar within the next year or so, when the US economy is nearing full employment and full capacity utilization, the result could be a sharp rise in US inflation and interest rates along with a rapid fall in trade surpluses and economic growth in other countries. These events could produce a very hard landing for the US and entire world economies.

A second major risk is even higher energy prices. The global price of oil could return to the late-2004 level of $55 per barrel and climb even further to $60 to $70 per barrel. Sharp disruptions in global energy supplies could make the situation even worse. Such developments, especially if they were to occur simultaneously with a sharp fall of the dollar, would add to

C. Fred Bergsten is the director of the Institute for International Economics.

the likelihood of both higher inflation and economic downturn (as well as carry wide-ranging repercussions for US foreign policy).

A third risk is a retreat from globalization and trade liberalization, driven mainly by domestic opposition to these trends within the United States. Such a retreat would severely affect US economic interests, over both the short and longer runs, by disrupting a major source of US income enhancement and productivity growth. In light of the widespread international identification of globalization with the United States, such a retreat would have major adverse consequences for US foreign policy as well.

Beyond these immediate threats, a second set of major foreign economic policy issues relates to profound changes in the structure of the global economy that are altering the framework within which the United States will operate for the foreseeable future. Completion of the process of European unification has created an economy roughly equal in size to the United States, with a single money (the euro) that provides the first potential competition to the dollar since it became the world's key currency in the early part of the 20th century. China is rapidly becoming a third global economic superpower and, in some vital senses, an even larger driver of the world economy than the United States. Regional economic cooperation in East Asia, in both the trade and monetary arenas, is likely to create over time an even more powerful entity in that part of the world. These developments could usher in a three-bloc global construct that would carry major national security as well as economic implications for the United States, requiring wholesale reconsideration of the United States' basic foreign policy as well as economic strategies.

International economic issues must be viewed in the context of overall US foreign policy as well as overall US economic policy. Events of recent years, including the Iraq war but going well beyond it, have raised fundamental questions in many parts of the world (and much of American society) about the posture of the United States with respect to international, especially multilateral, cooperation. A restoration of strong US relations with many of its disenchanted friends and allies will obviously require new US policies outside the economic realm. Given the high(est) priority that virtually all countries attach to their international economic interests, however, the stance of the United States on those topics will go far to shape attitudes toward the United States across an array of issues far broader than the economic agenda itself. For foreign policy as well as economic reasons, unilateralism is simply not an option for the United States in the 21st century.

This book concludes that the United States needs to undertake, with considerable urgency, a series of major policy initiatives to head off the immediate international economic risks just cited. As is usually the case with foreign economic policy, those responses must start at home. The United States will need a credible program to substantially reduce its budget deficit over the next few years, and then to return it to modest surplus over time, to help correct the current account imbalance, and to sustain confidence in US economic policy and the economy's long-term prospects. It will need an effective new strategy to cut US energy consumption and boost domestic production. It will need much stronger and more effective assistance for US workers who are now hurt by globalization, or fear that they will be in the future, so that they will become able to take advantage of that phenomenon rather than feel victimized by it, restoring in the process a more stable domestic foundation for a constructive international economic policy.

Each of these steps must be complemented by important initiatives in other key countries. The other major economies, especially China and elsewhere in Asia, will have to cooperate in achieving an orderly adjustment in the exchange rate of the dollar to avoid a subsequent crash and resulting hard landing. The countries that will experience declines in their trade surpluses to accommodate the correction in the US trade deficit, especially the largest ones in Europe and Asia, will have to stimulate growth in domestic demand to maintain their own and global prosperity. Oil-importing and oil-exporting countries must come together to work out a global energy regime that will support rather than constantly jeopardize the world economy. Rich and poor countries must cooperate to further open international markets, via both multilateral and regional trade agreements, to obtain the huge benefits that are available from additional globalization, including its enormous payoff for reducing poverty in developing nations.

These initiatives must be launched promptly but will take some time to implement and to produce the desired results. At best, it will take several years to correct the US external and internal deficits and to install new domestic and global energy regimes. Hence the reforms proposed in this book constitute a medium-term strategy that will have to be pursued with perseverance as well as vigor over a prolonged period. Moreover, none of the suggested measures will be costless. Their adoption will be strongly in the national interest of the United States, however, and they should be pursued as matters of very high priority.

Our proposed strategy rests on this volume's clear conclusion that the prosperity and stability of the United States depend heavily on events and activities that take place outside its borders and over which it has limited control. The share of international trade in the US economy has almost tripled over the past 40 years and now exceeds the same ratio for the European Union or Japan. The United States must attract about $4 billion of foreign capital inflow every working day to finance its current account deficits and outward foreign investments.[1] It relies on foreign sources for

1. The current account deficit exceeds $600 billion per year and US capital outflows have been averaging about $300 billion per year. Both must be offset by capital inflows to balance the international books. There are about 240 working days in a year.

more than half its oil supplies and, even if it could cut that ratio substantially, would still depend on prices set largely abroad for the world's most important commodity. The United States has long since passed the point where economic isolationism would be feasible despite its continuing status as the world's largest national economy.

Another clear conclusion of this study must also be emphasized at the outset: that the United States benefits substantially from globalization and can reap large additional benefits from the further spread of that phenomenon. As estimated conservatively in chapter 2, the US economy is now richer by about $1 trillion per year as a result of its further integration with the world economy since 1945. This translates into higher average incomes of about $9,000 per year for every American household. The average US citizen is thus about 10 percent more prosperous as a result of globalization. Indeed, well over 10 percent of Americans' income gains over the past half century have resulted from the country's increased internationalization. All income groups, and small and medium-sized enterprises as well as larger firms, share in these benefits.

These economic gains could be increased by at least $500 billion annually for the entire country, and another $4,500 per year per household, by adopting wholly free trade on a global basis, and it should be feasible to move a considerable distance in that direction over the coming years. Some of the other policy proposals in this volume, such as limiting the volatility of world energy prices and reducing their long-term average toward levels that would prevail under more market-related conditions, would also bring large benefits for the US economy. Still others, such as achieving gradual rather than abrupt correction of the country's huge external imbalances, would prevent sizable costs that could otherwise subtract substantially from its well-being.

In addition, US foreign policy and indeed national security gain enormously from the benefits of globalization to *other* countries. Major economic and trading partners have not gone to war with each other for over half a century. No country has ever achieved successful economic development without integrating with the world economy, a historical fact of great importance as we seek to combat the security (including terrorist) implications of mass unemployment in poor countries and failed states around the world. At this point in time, with relations between the United States and many of its traditional (especially European) allies so frayed by disagreements over Iraq and "US unilateralism" more generally, successful new international economic cooperation even could help restore America's overall international ties to an important extent.

To be sure, there are costs to globalization as there are for any dynamic economic process. Chapter 2 suggests that these costs total only a small fraction, perhaps 5 percent, of the gains from globalization to the overall US economy. But some workers—perhaps 100,000 to 200,000 annually in recent years out of a total labor force of 130 million and annual net job creation that averages at least 1 million to 2 million (chapter 2, Baily and Lawrence, forthcoming)—become unemployed as a result of changes in trade, most for temporary periods but a few more permanently. Manufacturing workers dislocated in trade-impacted industries also experience average wage declines of about 13 percent in their new jobs (Kletzer 2001), losses that may be offset only partially by the lower prices they pay for imports. Chapter 3 concludes that globalization has also added modestly to the increasing income inequality that has characterized the United States over recent decades, increasing the dispersion of American incomes at the same time it raises both their mean and the income *level* of all groups.

A major theme of this book is that the *foreign* economic policy of the United States must embrace a wide-ranging set of *domestic* measures to address the costs of globalization. Its overall benefits for the United States, both to date and prospectively for the future, are far too important to roll back or forgo. Those gains are indeed so large that the United States can readily afford to deploy a modest fraction of them to effectively address the costs of globalization and to help the losers both cushion their transition periods and become qualified to take advantage of the opportunities it provides. Despite the need for aggregate fiscal tightening, it will be essential to do so if the United States is to maintain a sustainable domestic base for the conduct of an effective foreign economic policy over both the shorter and longer runs.

Short-Run Agenda

The United States and world economies were advancing smartly as this book was completed in late 2004. Global growth approximated 5 percent in 2004, its fastest pace in over 20 years. Continued if somewhat less rapid expansion seemed likely for 2005. The world's two chief locomotives, the United States and China, continued to lead the advance despite modest slowdowns in both.

The breadth of the global expansion has been impressive as well. Japan, after a decade of stagnation, has been a major "upside surprise" with growth exceeding 4 percent in 2004. East Asia outside Japan is expanding at 7 percent. Regions with small economic impact but sizable populations, including Africa and Latin America, are recording their best performance in two decades or more.

Can this synchronized global expansion continue? Many of the underlying portents are promising. Inflation and interest rates remain low almost everywhere. Productivity continues to rise rapidly in the United States. China could experience another decade or two of impressive growth. India may become a new source of major expansion. Many emerging-market economies have adopted floating exchange rates, sharply reducing the risk of crises à la Mexico, East Asia, Russia, and Brazil that derailed large parts of the world economy during the 1990s.

Unfortunately, there is a substantial possibility that this scenario could be shattered by a combination of five international economic developments within the next few years. Three of these risks center on the United States itself but are substantially exacerbated by their extensive international dimensions: renewed sharp increases in the trade and current account deficits, requiring an early and substantial reversal that may include a crash of the dollar; a rising budget deficit; and a retreat from open trade policies. A fourth relates to the other growth locomotive, China, where a sharp slowdown due to its recent overheating is likely and a hard landing is possible. Fifth, oil prices could climb to $60 to $70 per barrel, or much more in the event of a major political or terrorist disruption, and stay there for a while. Any one of these events could substantially reduce US and world growth. A combination of two or three of them, let alone all five, could radically reverse the prospects and bring a sharp turndown at home and abroad.

There remains time to head off each of these risks. Preventive policy actions could avoid at least their worst consequences and preserve a positive outlook. Hence the United States, in its own self-interest, must address them effectively as a matter of urgency. Moreover, the United States has an enormous international responsibility to act constructively in light of its sizable share of the world economy and its central role in, if not responsibility for, most of the global problems. But each of these issues has major worldwide components and cooperative international action will also be essential. US policy over the next year or so must be devoted both to making the necessary policy changes at home and to providing international leadership to forge their essential international complements.

The most alarming prospect is renewed sharp deterioration in the US trade and current account imbalances. These deficits have been growing again since early 2004 and already exceed annual rates of $600 billion, well above 5 percent of the economy. As a result, America's net foreign debt has reached $2.5 trillion and the country must attract about $4 billion of foreign capital every working day (to finance the current account deficits and America's own foreign investments). These present levels are almost certainly unsustainable. New scenarios by Institute senior fellow Catherine L. Mann, moreover, suggest that the current account deficit could now be rising again by a full percentage point of the economy per year (about $100 billion annually) as it actually did in 1997–2000. If this were to occur, the deficit would rise well beyond $1 trillion per year and 10 percent of GDP by 2010 (figure 1.1).[2]

2. There are five reasons for this dismal prospect. First, the fall of the dollar from its peak in early 2002 through 2004 amounted to a trade-weighted average decline of only 15 percent, taking only about $150 billion off the annual imbalances that would otherwise exist and being swamped by the other factors cited here. Second, the current US baseline is highly un-

Figure 1.1 Current account versus trade balance (assumes no further dollar depreciation)

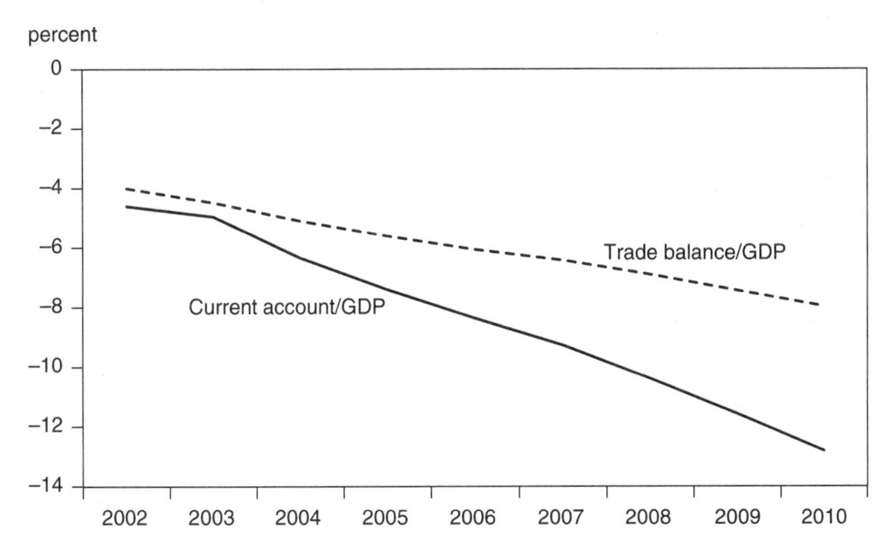

Source: Figure obtained from Catherine L. Mann.

This prospect poses three major risks for the United States and other countries. One, to be discussed shortly, is a further escalation of trade protectionism in the United States. Dollar overvaluation and the huge external deficits it spawns have traditionally been the primary precursors of such domestic political swings, which would carry large costs for both the US economy and foreign policy.

The second major risk is a disorderly crash of the dollar. If this were to occur in late 2005 or beyond, when much of the slack will probably have disappeared from US product and labor markets as the economy approaches full employment, inflation pressures would shoot up and standard macroeconomic models show that US interest rates could hit double digits (Baily 2003). The stock market would almost surely tank in response. Economic growth would drop sharply and perhaps fall into recession.

favorable: Merchandise imports are now almost twice as large as merchandise exports, so the latter have to grow about twice as fast as imports grow, an unprecedented relationship except in the late 1980s after the trade-weighted dollar had fallen by over 30 percent during 1985–87, just to halt the deterioration. Third, US economic growth is likely to be faster than growth in its major markets, even on conservative assumptions for the United States and optimistic assumptions about the others. Fourth, the income elasticities of trade are much higher for merchandise imports in the United States (about 1.7) than in the rest of the world for American merchandise exports (1.0). Fifth, the large debtor position of the United States means that its net investment income payments to the rest of the world will probably be increasing steadily, especially as interest rates rise. See Mann (2004a).

The third risk stems from the negative impact on other countries from correction of the US deficits, especially if triggered by a sharp fall of the dollar. As described by Michael Mussa in chapter 6, their trade surpluses must decline as a counterpart of the US improvement and their economic growth would fall correspondingly unless they could reorient their policies to generate offsetting increases in domestic demand. In some surplus countries, this would call for expansionary fiscal policies. In others, including some of the largest such as Germany and Japan, long overdue structural reforms would be required. Lower interest rates would be in order virtually everywhere although Japan cannot cut rates below zero, where they have stood for several years, and the European Central Bank resisted much easing despite a rise of 40 percent in the euro against the dollar by late 2004.

The difficulties of achieving the needed global response, especially if the dollar's fall is precipitate and the foreign adjustments need to take place quickly, suggest that the results could be very costly for world growth. The United States would also be hurt by the slowdowns elsewhere (though it would benefit from a declining current account deficit over a period of several years). The situation would be worse if future increases in energy prices and the US budget deficit push in the same direction of higher inflation and interest rates, and then slower growth or even recession.

Fears of a hard landing for the dollar, and for the US and world economies, are of course not new. It is certainly true that the United States derives short-run benefits from the additional consumption and investment permitted by its current account deficit, and surplus countries like the job creation that results for them, creating considerable resistance from both sides of the imbalances to any substantial reduction of them (Mann 2004a). Even if further substantial dollar correction eventuates, moreover, it could do so in a gradual and orderly manner as in fact occurred throughout 2002–03 and when the decline resumed in late 2004.

The unsustainability of the situation is much more ominous now, however, because of the record levels of the current account deficit and America's international debtor position, and the high probability of further sharp deterioration in both. The risk of renewed escalation of world oil prices at the same time suggests a parallel with the dollar declines of the 1970s, which were associated with the two oil shocks of that decade and subsequent stagflation, rather than the 1980s, when a sharp fall in energy costs (and thus inflation) cushioned dollar depreciation.

It is impossible to foresee when this renewed deterioration of America's international financial position might produce a sharp fall in the dollar. The deficits have already been in uncharted terrain for several years, and US economic performance may be sufficiently attractive to keep the foreign capital coming in at the requisite levels at current prices for a while longer. Foreign monetary authorities could step in to keep the dollar from falling much (or at all) against their currencies, as several of the major Asian countries did through much or all of the period of dollar decline in 2002–03. This is where the two other US-centered risks enter the picture: the budget deficit and a retreat from open trade policies.

Objective projections score the US budget deficit at $5 trillion over the next decade. Even they, however, ignore possible or even likely future increases in overseas military costs and homeland security expenditures, further extension of the recent tax cuts and necessary fixes for the tax system (especially concerning the alternative minimum tax), and proposed new entitlement increases. The retirement of the baby boomers that begins in five years will make the picture much worse over succeeding decades by steadily increasing transfer payments to the elderly. It is not difficult to foresee a budget deficit that also approaches $1 trillion per year. Yet there is little serious discussion in the United States of how to restore fiscal responsibility let alone an agreed strategy for reining in the runaway entitlement programs, especially Medicare (Peterson 2004).

The budget and current account deficits are not "twin" in any rigid sense. The budget in fact improved dramatically throughout the 1990s, moving into surplus in the early part of this decade, while the external imbalance soared anew. But additional increases in the fiscal shortfall, with the economy nearing full employment, will further reduce national saving in the United States and intensify the need for foreign capital. Hence such increases will promote further increases in the current account deficit, increasing the prospects of a dollar crash. Former Federal Reserve Chairman Paul Volcker predicts with 75 percent probability that America's internal and external imbalances will produce a financial crisis within five years (Peterson 2004).

Former Secretary of the Treasury Robert Rubin has also stressed the psychological importance for financial markets of expectations concerning the medium-term trajectory of the US budget position (Rubin and Weisburg 2003). If that deficit is viewed as likely to rise steadily and substantially, confidence in America's financial instruments and currency could crack. The dollar could fall sharply as it has about once per decade over the last 40 years (in 1971–73, 1978–79, 1985–87, and 1994–95). Market interest rates would rise immediately and the Federal Reserve would probably have to push them higher to limit the escalation of inflation. Given the timing, such risks are exacerbated in this case by the presumed change in leadership at the Federal Reserve Board in early 2006, inevitably creating new uncertainties after 25 years of superb leadership by Volcker and Alan Greenspan. A very hard landing is not inevitable, but neither is it unlikely. Preventing it, through decisive action on both the budget and the exchange rate, must rank very high on the overall US policy agenda and head the agenda for foreign economic policy.

The third risk to US economic and foreign policy interests is a retreat from open trade policies. The risk at present takes new as well as traditional forms. The spate of trade actions already initiated against China represent traditional protectionism, with greatest impact in the historically sheltered sectors of textiles and apparel but extending as well into color television sets, furniture, shrimp, and other products of declining US competitiveness (Hufbauer and Wong 2004). So did the hike in steel tariffs in 2001 and the new subsidies included in the 2002 farm bill. Sugar managed to win total exclusion from the United States–Australia free trade agreement (and minimal quota increases in other FTAs).

The hubbub over outsourcing, however, has led to a "new approach": proposals to deter foreign direct investment by altering the taxation of foreign income accruing to American multinationals (Hufbauer and Grieco 2004) and to limit government procurement (at both the federal and state levels) from companies that "offshore." The tax bill passed by Congress in late 2004, in addition to much unrelated pork, cut tax rates on "domestic US production" in an effort to strengthen American competitiveness. The US move to launch a World Trade Organization (WTO) case against Airbus, after 25 years of acceptance of its subsidies, may reignite transatlantic trade conflict.

The trade policy problem could come to a head in early 2005 when Congress will vote on at least three contentious bills. It must extend Trade Promotion Authority (TPA) to 2007 or neither the Doha Round of multilateral negotiations in the World Trade Organization nor any other meaningful international trade talks can be completed. It must address the mandated five-year reauthorization of US membership in the WTO. And it will have to vote on the FTAs that have already been negotiated with Central America and the Dominican Republic, and with Bahrain, the former of which will almost certainly produce a pitched battle over how to treat labor and environmental standards in all US trade pacts.

The projected escalation of the external imbalance would also make it harder to bring the Doha Round to a successful conclusion and pilot it through Congress. Failure of the Round, or even a substantively minimal outcome, could halt the momentum of trade liberalization and further open the door for protectionism and mercantilism. Under contemporary circumstances, such outcomes would also be likely to further accelerate the negotiation of new bilateral FTAs and regional economic blocs, especially in East Asia, and hasten the advent of a potentially dangerous three-bloc world. All this would place the current multilateral trading system in extreme jeopardy.

These trade policy concerns add further to the case for strong and urgent action to correct the US fiscal position and the currency misalignment. Indeed, it was domestic political rather than international financial pressure that induced previous US administrations (Nixon in 1971, Reagan in 1985) to aggressively seek dollar depreciation to avoid severe disruption of the global trading system. These concerns also underline the case, to be developed shortly, for a major effort by the United States to restore the momentum of trade liberalization by ensuring a successful outcome to the Doha Round.

The fourth global economic risk centers on China, the second locomotive of the present and potential global expansion. Nicholas Lardy notes in chapter 4 that it became the third largest trading nation in the world in 2004, has already become the second largest importer of a wide range of commodities from cement to oil, and accounted for over 20 percent of the entire increase in world trade during 2000–03. China's worldwide impact derives not only from its size and rapid growth but also from its openness to the global economy; its ratio of trade to GDP is double that of the United States, European Union, or Japan, and its ratio of inward foreign investment to GDP is even larger by comparison.

It is thus of great global consequence that China faces the risk of a substantial slowdown of its own economy. The country must rein in its recent runaway credit expansion and unsustainable levels of investment, with growth slowing as a result. The new political leadership that took office in late 2002 refused to address the problem for more than a year. It finally did so via a peculiar mix of market-related policies, such as higher reserve requirements for the banks and modest interest rate increases, and traditional command-and-control directives such as sectoral ceilings on increases in bank lending.

Under the best of circumstances, China's growth will have to drop for a while from the 9 to 10 percent pace of recent years. When the country cooled its last excessive boom, after 1993, the rate of growth declined for six straight years (figure 1.2). A truly hard landing, due to the delay in addressing the problem and the half-measures initially adopted, could be much more abrupt and severe. Either outcome will dampen growth in all of East Asia (including Japan) and, via commodity markets and other trade effects, significantly affect the rest of the world.

The fifth threat to US and global prosperity and stability is energy prices. The rapid growth of world demand, lagging investment in new production, shortages of refining and other infrastructure (particularly in the United States, due partly to its environmental requirements and other regulatory decisions), and fears of new supply disruptions have vastly outstripped any possibility for increased production from either Organization of Petroleum Exporting Countries (OPEC) or non-OPEC sources in the short run. Hence prices rose steadily throughout much of 2004 and hit record highs in nominal terms before falling back at the end of the year. The global economic effects are extremely significant since every sustained rise of $10 per barrel in the world price takes $250 billion to $300 billion (about half a percentage point) off annual global growth for several years, of which about one-third occurs in the United States.

Philip Verleger concludes in chapter 7 that this lethal combination could become much worse before it gets better on a lasting basis, pushing the price into the range of $60 to $70 per barrel over the next year or two and

Figure 1.2 China's GDP growth, 1992–2004Q3

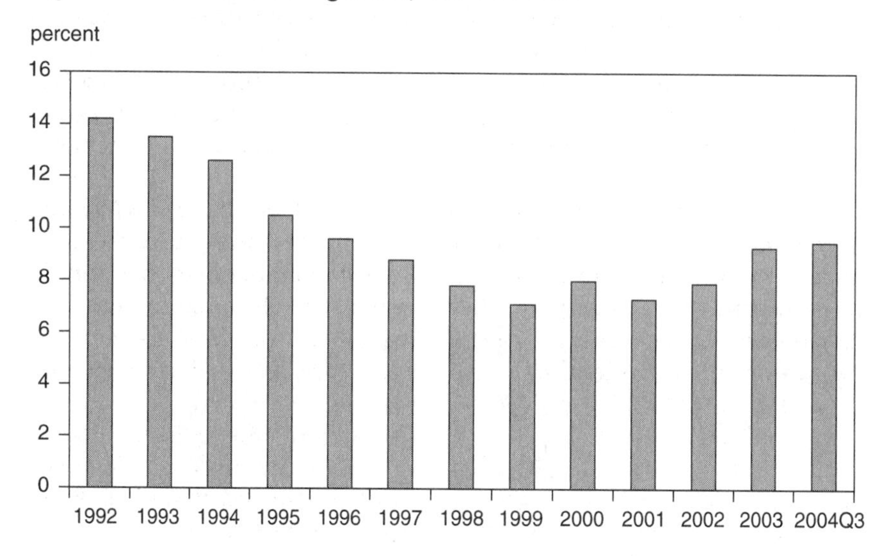

Source: China Statistical Yearbook 2003, 57, National Bureau of Statistics of China, www.stats.gov.cn.

reaching the previous record high of 1981 in real terms, even without any political or terrorist events to actually impede production for a prolonged period in the Middle East, the former Soviet Union, or elsewhere. Both the likelihood of this outcome and its costs increase significantly as the US and world economies move closer to full employment and full capacity utilization. As Chairman Greenspan frequently reminds us, the three largest postwar recessions were triggered by sharp increases in the price of oil.

The more fundamental problem of the global energy system, however, is the oligopolistic nature of the world oil market. The OPEC cartel in general, and dominant supplier Saudi Arabia in particular, restrict supply in the short run and output capacity in the long run in order to preserve prices far higher than would occur under market conditions. Recent prices of $40 to $55 per barrel compare with production costs of $15 to $20 per barrel in even the highest-cost locales. These problems also look likely to get worse before they get better as OPEC has talked openly about increasing its target price range from the traditional $22 to $28 per barrel to $30 to $40 per barrel or even higher. The lack of "surge capacity" exhibited by OPEC in 2004 suggests that such a hike might indeed be viable for some time unless explicitly countered by consuming countries. Whatever the short-run outcome, this could dampen global growth substantially for some time.

OPEC and Saudi Arabia do not always succeed in controlling the energy market. Indeed, they have suffered several sharp price falls over the past three decades. They have been unable (due to their lack of additional capacity) to counter the recent price rise. But their actions would violate most national antitrust laws if they occurred within countries and should be totally unacceptable to both the United States and the international community.

The United States must address these five problems, three of which are largely homegrown but all of which (including the budget, because of its impact on the external imbalance) carry substantial international dimensions, urgently and decisively. They alone justify elevating foreign economic policy to the top of the overall national agenda. They also emphasize the need to consider the international aspects of seemingly domestic issues such as the budget and gasoline prices.

As important as these immediate problems are, however, they understate considerably the salience of the world economy for US policy over the coming years. Structural changes both at home and abroad underlie the more immediate problems and intensify their impact on US society. Responses to the short-term agenda require an understanding of these more fundamental underpinnings.

Domestic Foundations of Foreign Economic Policy

The foreign economic policy of every country of course derives from its national interests, which attach high priority to the success of its own economy. These interests include the creation of stable and well-paying jobs, the maintenance of reasonable price stability, the achievement of maximum economic growth, and the presence of social safety nets to provide "shock absorbers" against the inevitable disruptions that occur in all economies.

In a highly interdependent world, these national goals can seldom be achieved unless the global economy as a whole is functioning effectively. This requires the foreign economic policy of each country to take serious account of both the international repercussions of its own policies and the impact on it of developments emanating from abroad. Such considerations are particularly crucial for a global economic superpower, certainly the United States, since the external effects of its own initiatives (e.g., large tax cuts leading to larger trade deficits and ultimately a sharp fall in the dollar, as in the mid-1980s and prospectively again now) can come back to affect its own economy with great force.

The domestic political base for foreign economic policy is nevertheless shaped largely by popular perceptions of the impact of the country's international involvement on the key domestic variables, which may or may not accurately reflect objective reality. Here too there has been a sea change in the United States over the past couple of decades, producing an unprecedented paradox. As the globalization of the US economy and the benefits from it have expanded dramatically, so too has the backlash against globalization. Both phenomena reached their postwar zeniths in the late 1990s: Just as US productivity growth and thus economic prosperity surged, importantly due to the gains from globalization, the negative reactions surged as well due to the increased adjustments that it required. Hence much of US foreign economic policy stalemated just when the issues it addresses reached the high degree of salience outlined earlier, significantly complicating the ability of the administration and Congress to effectively promote American interests across the entire range of global economic topics.[3]

The gains to the US economy as a whole from globalization are clear and impressive, as noted earlier and explained in detail in chapter 2. These gains have been achieved through two main channels. On one side of the trade equation, increased imports—and the competition they have levied on domestic producers—have reduced costs and increased variety across a wide range of goods and services to American consumers and American firms using imported inputs. On the other side, increased exports have expanded total US output in sectors where it is most efficient and competitive, greatly expanding economies of scale and producing real wages for American workers that are 15 to 20 percent above the national average.

The sharp increase in US economic growth over the past decade owes a great deal to these benefits of globalization. The acceleration of US output growth derived directly from the sharp pickup of growth in labor productivity, which jumped from 1½ percent during 1973–95 to 2½ percent in 1996–2000 and to 4 percent in 2001–04. When the normal annual expansion of the US labor force (about 1 percent) is added to the likely future course of these numbers, the result is that US output potential is now probably rising by at least 3 to 4 percent per year. This (or more) was indeed the rate of realized growth in the late 1990s and again in the second half of 2003 and 2004, when the unemployment rate dropped below 4 percent for a prolonged period and back down to 5.5 percent, respectively—well below the "full employment" floor of 6 percent that was thought to exist before the productivity boom set in. This is an impressive performance for a rich and mature industrial country like the United States and will continue as long as productivity continues to expand at anything like its pace of the past decade.

3. The most dramatic examples were the three failures to win congressional support for new trade negotiating authority (1994, 1997, and 1998) and the tiny margins (majorities of one and three in the critical House votes in 2002) when TPA was finally restored. Congress also significantly delayed passage of new International Monetary Fund (IMF) funding legislation (1997–98) at the height of the Asian financial crisis.

The increase in US productivity derives largely from the interaction between widespread adaptation of the new technologies, particularly in information and communications, across much of the economy and the simultaneous globalization of those technologies. It is difficult to disentangle these two closely related developments, but as much as half of the jump in total productivity may stem from their globalization alone. For example, globalization of the information technology (IT) hardware sector in the 1990s is estimated to have reduced the costs of such products by a further 10 to 30 percent and thereby added a full 0.3 percentage points per year to US economic expansion. Going forward, similarly sizable benefits—leading perhaps to further acceleration of overall US productivity growth—can be anticipated from the globalization of IT services and software that is now under way. Major sectors that have not yet globalized much, such as health care and construction, along with small and medium-sized enterprises more generally, could reap substantial benefits from greater internationalization and thereby provide a further boost to US productivity and overall economic growth (Mann 2003).

A hypothetical elimination of all remaining barriers to international trade in goods and services would provide substantial further benefit to the US economy and to American citizens. Such "completion of the globalization process" could perhaps add another $500 billion (or roughly 5 percent) to the annual level of national income. This would amount to an additional $4,500 annually per household. Hence US policy should continue to seek liberalization of the sizable remaining barriers to world commerce. Such liberalization would help the United States more on the export side of the trade equation than the import side because it has already eliminated most of its own import restrictions while many other countries, especially some of the rapidly growing large economies of the developing world (such as Brazil and India), retain much higher restraints.

As with any dynamic economic change, there have been costs to the extensive adjustments required by the globalization process. That process has created losers as well as winners among individual workers and firms. The salience of these costs has become greater in recent years for three reasons: the overvalued dollar and growing trade deficit have greatly exacerbated the breadth and intensity of the adjustment problems; the increasing pace of globalization has forced more rapid change on all those affected; and the final barriers to be eliminated are, by definition, those maintained in sectors that face the most difficult adjustment burdens (e.g., apparel in the United States).

The number of Americans adversely affected by increased US trade is modest but not insignificant. Kletzer (2001) estimates that there are perhaps 100,000 workers per year who lose jobs due to increased imports *and* whose replacement work reduces their pay by 30 percent or more. (There are perhaps twice as many workers who also lose their jobs due to imports but find new work at the same or, in many cases, even a higher wage.) These numbers of course cumulate over time and, even more importantly from a social and political standpoint, instill concerns across a much larger share of the labor force that "there but for the grace of God go I." A recent summary of polling and other public opinion data shows that American workers are in fact evenly divided over the results of further globalization even though only a small minority are adversely affected themselves (Scheve and Slaughter 2001). Hence the United States must devote priority attention to this domestic adjustment problem, especially as the magnitude of the national gain from globalization is so large as to easily provide adequate financing to do so.

The United States, unlike most rich industrial countries, has relied primarily on market forces to manage this problem. To be sure, rapid growth and relatively full employment provide the best possible environment within which displaced workers can find remunerative new jobs. But growth is not always rapid and employment is not always full, and neither workers nor their unions are willing to rely on such benign circumstances. Moreover, there are important disconnects between the skill mix of the American labor force and the job opportunities that are created in the United States as globalization continuously pushes the economy toward the high-skill end of the spectrum. The concern over outsourcing is the latest case in point: The expansion of trade in IT services and software will almost certainly create more jobs than it exports, indeed jobs that pay considerably better, but it is not clear whether Americans with the requisite skills will be available to assume these positions (see chapter 9).

Hence two types of policy responses are required, both to deal with the real problems of adjustment and to provide a stable new political foundation for a constructive foreign economic policy for the United States. One is the creation of adequate social safety nets to cushion the short-term transition periods faced by displaced workers. The second is better education and training programs to equip US workers to take advantage of globalization rather than feel victimized by it. Both steps will be crucial in forging a new domestic consensus in support of further opening of the world economy: The polls and worker surveys show that the ambivalence over the issue yields to a substantial proglobalization majority when the government is perceived as providing effective adjustment programs, and that every year of additional education for the labor force as a whole adds a full 10 percentage points to the share of the population that supports further opening (Scheve and Slaughter 2001).

Since 1962, the United States has taken tepid steps in both directions through the program of Trade Adjustment Assistance (TAA). As outlined in chapter 10, however, TAA—despite steady improvements over the past four decades, most notably in the TPA legislation in 2002—remains too small, too restrictive, too unimaginative, and too poorly administered to achieve either purpose effectively in substantive and thus political terms.

The needed reforms will clearly have to broaden the scope of eligibility for TAA to include the services sector and perhaps entire trade-impacted communities and sectors (such as apparel); substantially increase benefit levels, especially for training programs; provide the innovations of the 2002 legislation, wage insurance and a health care tax credit, to all eligible workers rather than a restricted subset thereof; develop further innovations, such as homeowner insurance and a human capital investment tax credit, to address more effectively the practical problems of displaced workers; and administer the program aggressively to bring its benefits to as large a number of trade-impacted workers as possible.

The US government must embrace this wholly domestic program as an integral component of its foreign economic policy. If it fails to do so, there is a severe risk that much of its effort to maintain an open and constructive stance toward the rest of the world will fail for lack of internal support. Such a specter was already raised to a large extent in the late 1990s when, despite the strength of the economy, domestic resistance to further globalization produced a political stalemate that denied the president new trade negotiating authority and thus blocked any substantial new initiatives. The debacle at Seattle in 1999, when the United States failed to convince WTO members to launch a new multilateral trade round, occurred largely due to doubts that the United States would be able to reduce any of its own remaining trade barriers in the future and hence was simply seeking one-sided concessions from other countries. It will be essential to sharply expand and improve TAA as part of any successful new foreign economic policy in the United States.

The New Global Context

Just as the domestic foundations of foreign economic policy have been changing dramatically, so has the international context within which that policy must be pursued. Fundamental shifts are occurring in both the composition of global economic power and the distribution of global economic performance—sometimes (as with China) in the same direction, sometimes (as with the European Union) in opposite directions. The United States must reprioritize its international economic ties and institutional commitments at the same time that it reforms its policies at home to provide a firm foundation for those international linkages.

Throughout the postwar period, the United States could safely assume that the other major players in the world economy were essentially like-minded: Western Europe, Japan, Canada, and a few others on specific issues. To be sure, there were often bitter and prolonged disputes (especially with Japan). But the similarities dominated: All the major players were market-based high-income economies and political democracies that had huge stakes in a flourishing world economy and were dependent on the United States for their security. Hence, in a crunch, they could usually be relied on as dependable supporters.

The composition of the global economic elite for the next few decades looks likely to be quite different. The United States is no longer the world's dominant economic entity in view of the creation, and now expansion, of the European Union. Europe's new single currency (the euro) is the first potential rival to the dollar's global financial dominance in the century since the dollar replaced the pound sterling as the world's key currency.[4] European attitudes toward basic economic and social preferences may increasingly diverge from those of the United States (Baily and Kirkegaard 2004). As the dispute over Iraq has displayed so brutally, much of Europe is no longer the reliable US ally of Cold War days.

Even more dramatically, China has become the new growth pole and chief driver of global trade expansion. As described by Nicholas Lardy in chapter 4, China has already become the world's third largest trading country and provided the largest stimulus to world trade of any country (even the United States) during 2000–03. Its economy has expanded ninefold since its adoption of outward-oriented economic reforms in 1978 and, with exchange rates measured at purchasing power parity, it is already the world's second largest economy. (With currencies converted at market rates, it ranks sixth but will move up to fourth—after only the United States, Japan, and Germany—within the next couple of years.) Its trade *increase* in 2003 was more than double India's total trade *level*. It accounted for almost half the increase in total global demand for oil in 2002–03. It already has the third largest stock of inward foreign direct investment (FDI) in the world, surpassing the United States as the leading destination for such investment flows in 2003 and amassing an inflow in that year alone larger than the cumulative flow of FDI to India since its independence in 1947.

China, however, differs radically from the United States on at least four counts. First, it remains a poor country and will still be relatively poor, with per capita incomes one quarter of the United States' or less, even if it again becomes the world's largest economy by the middle of the century. Second, the privatization of its economy has proceeded only part way, and the state is likely to play a much more central role indefinitely than in any of the "western" countries including Japan (though China's remarkable openness to the world economy and conscious strategy of globalization are likely to align it with the United States on a number of international trade and other issues). Third, political democracy, while making limited strides at the local level, remains a distant dream in Com-

4. This development is likely to be beneficial, if occasionally painful, for the United States as the euro makes it more difficult for the United States to fund and thus run excessive external and internal deficits. See Posen (forthcoming).

munist China, and one-party government seems likely to prevail there for the foreseeable future. Fourth, far from being an ally, China is viewed as a potential threat by many Americans, and the view from the Chinese side is clearly reciprocal; the uneasiness of the present (albeit substantially improved) relationship provides a far different foundation for economic cooperation than the close cultural, historic, and ideological ties that have underlain US relations with the rest of the G-7.

An additional possibility, which is still far less important but whose potential nevertheless merits consideration, is India. With its rapid population growth and consistent economic expansion of 5 to 6 percent over the past decade, which could rise to China-type levels of 8 to 10 percent for the next decade or so with the adoption of plausible if difficult additional reforms (Srinivasan and Tendulkar 2003), India is projected by some to become the world's third largest economy by 2050 (Goldman Sachs 2003). Like China, it too would remain a poor country even with such an impressive aggregate. It would be a more market-oriented economy, however, with a vibrant democratic polity. Though not an ally of the United States, it carries none of the threatening implications of resurgent China—and its inherent rivalry with China naturally orients it toward the United States in a world where both Asian giants are becoming important players. India is unlikely to become nearly as large a global economic factor as China, because of the relatively closed nature of its economy, but could still become a very important player on the world scene.

The situation in Asia, whose economic growth is likely to remain the world's most dynamic at the same time these huge changes in relative positions are occurring, will also be affected by the decline of Japan. Demographics alone point to a continuing reduction in Japan's global role—the country never assumed much international leadership even during its miracle growth period—even if it proves able to restore a reasonable degree of economic progress as now seems likely (Posen 2004).

Major differences in current and prospective economic performance further intensify the complexities of these tectonic changes in the structure of global economic power. America's closest traditional partners in Western Europe and Japan, while still the wealthiest countries in the world, have been laggards for the past decade and could maintain that dubious distinction for the foreseeable future. There are a few exceptions to this generalization: the United Kingdom has fared far better than continental Europe; a few of the smaller Europeans (notably Ireland, the Netherlands, and Scandinavia) have done better than the "big three" (France, Germany, and Italy); Canada has led the G-7 in growth in some years; and there are a few bright spots in Latin America (notably Chile and Mexico).

The world's best economic performers, however, except for the United States itself, have been largely elsewhere: especially China, India, and others in East and Southeast Asia. If the United States wants to align itself with the changing pattern of world trade and investment expansion, it is likely to be pulled in very different geographical directions than over the past five or six decades.[5]

Some of the world's new economic powerhouses, including China and India, will nevertheless remain developing countries for the foreseeable future. Moreover, virtually the entire net increase in world population during the years ahead will occur in the poor countries. Despite dramatic reduction in both global poverty and inequality over the past two or three decades (Bhalla 2002), half the world still lives on less than $2 per day. Much of the African continent has experienced deterioration in its economic conditions in recent years. Many of these poor countries, in part because of their poverty, represent security threats to the United States because of their susceptibility to becoming safe havens for terrorists, drugs, and crime. The United States will therefore also have to strengthen its commitment to address development issues as a priority within its overall foreign economic policy.

These shifts also carry potentially profound institutional implications. It is already clear that the G-7 must either alter its own membership or give way to the relatively new G-20 (or some other more representative group) as the chief steering committee for the world economy (Bergsten 2004a). The creation of the "non-G-5"—including Brazil and India along with the European Union, the United States, and Australia—which restored life to the Doha Round and thus the WTO in 2004 is already a step in that direction. But the United States must prod the formal multilateral institutions to alter their ways as well if they are to become more effective and thus continue to serve US interests. The entrenched incumbents in the International Monetary Fund (IMF) and World Bank, especially from grossly overrepresented Europe, have fiercely resisted the wholesale reallocation of "chairs and shares" that will be needed to reflect the objective changes, and has thereby undermined the legitimacy of those organizations (see chapter 5).

The United States will need to reorient its foreign economic policy priorities accordingly. It will need to further develop and nurture special ("G-2") relationships in at least four directions: with the European Union, the world's largest economy and home of its other key currency; with China, the other chief locomotive of the world economy and the leader of a potential East Asian economic bloc; with Japan, to provide a counterweight to China and ensure its ties with a central player in any new Asian grouping; and with Saudi Arabia, because of its continued dominance of the world energy picture for at least the next couple of decades.

---

5. Henry Kissinger ("America's Assignment," Special Report in *Newsweek*, November 8, 2004) has recently concluded that "China's renaissance, the rapid growth in India, and the globalization in every corner of the world . . . [will] bring about massive issues of policy that can be postponed only at peril to the world economy. . . . These issues must be addressed with great urgency by the newly elected president—in concert with directly affected trading and financial partners."

Some of this essential evolution has already begun. The United States and the European Union have maintained a functioning "G-2" on trade policy for several decades. The United States and Saudi Arabia have conducted a "special relationship" that includes oil for even longer, although its orientation has focused on "security of supply" rather than price. The United States and China have for some time had intergovernmental committees on economic and monetary issues, but their meetings have been largely perfunctory, and most serious business, like WTO entry, has been pursued on an ad hoc basis. On the multilateral front, the United States played a major role in the creation of the forward-looking G-20 of finance ministers and central bank governors in the late 1990s and, in a much earlier period, took the lead in engaging Japan in the global leadership structure in an effort to avoid repeating the tragic historical errors through which new economic powers in earlier periods (especially Germany during the late 19th century) were held at bay.

The United States, however, has not to date adopted a strategy that recognizes, and responds to, the fundamental changes in both economic structure and economic performance just outlined. The case for new initiatives is clearest with China, which is rapidly becoming a global economic superpower (despite maintaining an inconvertible currency) as well as the world' s leading growth pole. But the European Union, especially with enlargement and the inevitable expansion of the global role of the euro, must be viewed as an essential partner due to its size and wealth and—with China and the possible emergence of an East Asian bloc—as a continuing ally in a tripartite global system. The complexities are even greater with respect to Saudi Arabia, but its central importance to the global energy picture, and the critical importance of that picture to the entire world economy, are so great that the major initiatives proposed later in that issue area will require an intensification as well as reorientation of the traditional relationship.

These new international requirements for US foreign economic policy will of course interact extensively with the need for new domestic foundations for that policy as addressed in the previous section. Increasingly close cooperation with China, for example, will be a tough sell for workers who view it as a threat to be confronted rather than an essential collaborator. Explicit links with Saudi Arabia may run counter to other US foreign policy goals in the region as they have in the past. Tighter ties with "old" as well as "new" Europe may be disparaged in some quarters, perhaps more thoughtfully for Europe's recent lack of economic dynamism than for its disagreements with other aspects of US foreign policy. Presidential leadership will be required on a consistent basis to reconcile these potential conflicts and maintain the priority attention that the issues deserve.

With both the domestic and international contexts in place, it is time to lay out a "foreign economic policy for the next decade." These proposals are directed most immediately to the administration and Congress that assume office in early 2005. They address deep problems that will take some time to resolve, however, even under the best of circumstances. They also hope to set out an agenda for at least the medium term, given their incorporation of underlying forces both at home and abroad as well as the immediate focus that will be required of any government. A major challenge will be in choosing priorities from the list of issues already noted and the even longer list addressed in subsequent chapters of this book.

Proposals for Policy

Five issues would seem to deserve priority attention for US foreign economic policy over the coming period:

- restoring the *US current account and foreign debt positions* to levels that will be sustainable in both international financial and domestic political terms;
- conducting a *trade policy* that will both preserve the enormous gains that globalization has already brought to the United States and pursue the substantial further benefits that are clearly available;
- constructing and implementing a comprehensive program of *domestic supports* to cushion the losses that some Americans will suffer from continued and further globalization of the economy, through substantial improvements in both social safety nets and education/training programs;
- creating a new strategy for *energy policy,* combining major changes in domestic consumption and production patterns with a fundamental reorientation of our international approach to the issue; and
- making further improvements in *development policy* to support growth and poverty reduction in the poorer countries of the world.[6]

Correcting the Current Account Deficit

The highest priority for foreign economic policy—and perhaps overall US economic policy—must be to correct the large and rapidly growing

6. The foreign economic policy of the United States will of course have to address a number of issues that are not addressed in this book, for reasons of both space and priority. The most notable omission is probably international environmental policy, which the Institute has considered previously in Esty (1994) and Cline (1992). Other exclusions include sanctions policy, which has been covered extensively by Hufbauer, Schott, and Elliott (1982, 1990, and forthcoming 2005), and the important role of US government corporations in foreign economic policy (see Hufbauer and Rodriguez 2001 on the Export-Import Bank and Moran 2003 on the Overseas Private Investment Corporation).

deficits in the US current account and international debtor positions. Those imbalances are already far above previous record levels and on a trajectory that will take them increasingly into even more clearly unsustainable territory. It would be risky to the point of irresponsibility to base policy on a hope that a sharp adjustment can be avoided over the next four or five years.

An effective response to this problem has both short-term and long-term dimensions and must be supported by other countries though the United States must of course take the lead. The goal should be to cut the US current account deficit roughly in half, to 2 to 3 percent of GDP. Depending on how fast the adjustment can be achieved, this could stabilize the country's net international investment position ("net foreign debt") at about 50 percent, an uncomfortable level but the *best* the United States can hope for at this juncture. By contrast, Mussa shows in chapter 6 that current account deficits even holding at the present level of 5 to 6 percent of GDP would take the net foreign debt ratio beyond 50 percent in five to eight years and reach a clearly unsustainable 100 percent in less than 20 years.

The most constructive remedy in the short term is a three-part package that includes credible and sizable reductions in the US budget deficit, expansion of domestic demand in major economies outside the United States, and a gradual but substantial realignment of exchange rates. The key initial step would be a commitment by the United States to achieve sharp reduction in its budget deficit over the next few years. By reducing the dissaving of the federal government, such a US step would reduce the savings/investment imbalance that requires huge capital inflows, strengthens the dollar, and is thus a key underlying cause of the US external deficit. By compressing the growth of domestic demand within the United States, it would make room for improvement in the trade balance without generating higher inflation and interest rates. By restoring confidence in US fiscal management and the country's economic outlook, it would enhance the prospect for an orderly currency adjustment.

This is not the place to provide details of the needed US budget correction. The goal, however, should be a reduction of the deficit by at least 50 percent over the new presidential term. That progress will need to be sustained thereafter and preferably extended to the achievement of a surplus so that the federal government would begin to make a positive contribution to the abysmally low national saving rate.[7]

7. There are several possible steps to help correct the budget deficit that would also be quite helpful, or even essential, in pursuing US foreign economic policies that will be discussed later. Sharp cuts in US agricultural subsidies might provide $5 billion to $10 billion annually in budget savings while making a major contribution to the Doha Round negotiations. A substantial increase in carbon or gasoline taxes, a necessary ingredient in any serious new US energy policy, could contribute importantly to higher revenue levels. The substitution for

As outlined by Mussa in chapter 6, however, budget correction will not by itself restore a sustainable US current account position. A decline of about 30 percent in the trade-weighted average exchange rate of the dollar from its peak at the outset of 2002, implying a fall of another 15 percent or so from its level at the end of 2004, will be required to achieve that outcome. It is vital that this depreciation occur in a gradual and orderly manner, at the rate of the decline of 10 to 15 percent actually recorded in 2002–03 or even the additional 5 percent in October–November 2004, to avert the risk of a crash landing.

The euro, Canadian dollar, and a few other unmanaged floating currencies will need to appreciate further to permit this adjustment to take place. Their rates rose substantially in 2002–03, however, and they have thus already made a substantial contribution to the necessary outcome. A major part of the remaining dollar correction needs to take place against the currencies of the East Asian countries (Bergsten and Williamson 2003, 2004). Their surpluses and foreign exchange buildups are the chief counterparts of the US deficits and debt buildup. Moreover, their rapid economic growth enables them to "afford" modest reductions in their trade surpluses more than the sluggish Europeans.

To date, however, these countries have permitted very little appreciation of their currencies. China is the key because its continued peg to the dollar means that its currency has actually depreciated, by a trade-weighted average of more than 10 percent over the past three years, as it rode the dollar down and further increased the competitiveness of one of the world's most competitive countries. This has blocked direct US adjustment against the world's fastest growing economy and second largest holder of currency reserves. It has taken virtually all of Asia largely out of the international adjustment process because other countries in the region, from Japan to India, are very reluctant to countenance losses in their competitiveness against China and hence resist letting their currencies rise against the renminbi and perforce against the dollar. It violates China's international obligations to avoid manipulating its currency for competitive purposes, as analyzed by Morris Goldstein in chapter 12.

China should revalue its currency by 20 to 25 percent, while maintaining its fixed exchange rate system and capital controls for the time being,[8]

---

direct taxes of new indirect taxes, which would be rebatable at the border and thus help correct the current account imbalance, could also contribute to budget correction if their rates were set at levels to increase revenues. Elimination of the deferral of US taxation on overseas profits of US companies until they are repatriated, as proposed by Senator John Kerry in the 2004 presidential campaign, could also contribute a modest amount of revenue to the budget (Hufbauer and Grieco 2004).

8. The US administration, the G-7, and the IMF have mistakenly asked China to adopt a floating exchange rate and progressively eliminate its capital controls. These are worthy goals for the longer run, which China has adopted long ago. They are totally infeasible for at least the next several years, however, because of the continued weakness of the Chinese

for both internal and external reasons. Such a move would simultaneously promote all three of its priority domestic economic goals: slowing its growth rate to 7–8 percent by cutting demand for its exports; reducing inflation, which has been rising rapidly and now exceeds 5 percent, by cutting import costs directly; and halting the inflow of speculative capital, which has made it more difficult to control the expansion of the monetary base. On the international side, a substantial revaluation would be by far the most effective response to the protectionist measures that are escalating so rapidly against China in the United States (and will rise in a number of other importing countries as well if their currencies have to accept a disproportionate share of the counterpart appreciations against the dollar's correction because China and other Asians continue to resist doing their part).

A substantial Chinese revaluation would enable the other Asian surplus countries to let their currencies appreciate by at least a large fraction of the Chinese move. The main contributions need to come from Japan, Korea, Taiwan, Malaysia, Singapore, and India. All these currencies are nominally floating, but their authorities have intervened heavily in recent years to resist market pressures for appreciation. If they were all to move more or less simultaneously against the dollar, along with China, the appreciations in their own trade-weighted average rates—which is what counts for trade and economic impact—would be substantially mitigated. If the other Asians moved by 10 to 15 percent in response to a Chinese move of 20 to 25 percent, the US current account would improve by an estimated $50 billion to $60 billion per year (Goldstein 2003, Hufbauer and Wong 2004).

The contours of this short-term adjustment package are broadly similar to those worked out in the Plaza Agreement of 1985, which sought to correct the previously largest international imbalances in history through a coordinated realignment of floating exchange rates among the G-7 countries. The main question, now as then, is how to implement the required changes. The best outcome would be a continued gradual dollar depreciation in the markets, as occurred in 2002–03 and again in late 2004, *and* a willingness by all the important surplus countries (especially in Asia) to permit that adjustment to play out against their currencies. In the absence of such a fortuitous development, the dollar decline could either stall out far short of completion, storing up even larger problems for the future, or accelerate into a free fall with very adverse effects on the US and world economies.

---

banking system and hence the risk of capital flight. Indeed, early Chinese acceptance of the US/G-7/IMF proposal could produce a substantial capital outflow due to portfolio diversification by Chinese investors and thus lead to a *weaker* renminbi, which would *intensify* the international imbalances and protectionist problems. See Goldstein (2004).

Hence the United States should take several policy initiatives to ensure the necessary correction. The most important, as already noted, is early initiation of a credible program to reduce its own budget deficit substantially over the next few years. With respect to implementing the currency adjustment, there are two basic options. The preferable course would be a "second Plaza Agreement" through which the world's major economies, including China and several of the other key Asians, publicly announce that they would promote a substantial realignment.[9] They would presumably then indicate their readiness both to intervene in the markets to achieve such an outcome (in the case of the Asians, beginning with a cessation of interventions to prevent it) and to implement measures to expand their domestic demand if needed to offset the adverse impact on their (and thus world) growth of the induced cuts in their trade surpluses.[10] There is ample justification for launching such an international initiative in light of the clear-cut manipulation of their currencies by China, Japan, and other Asian countries in violation of their obligations under the IMF's Articles of Agreement—which the United States, the G-7, and the IMF itself have to date conspicuously failed to insist upon (see chapter 12).

The United States could achieve at least some of the impact of such a multilateral agreement by indicating unilaterally that it wanted to see a weaker dollar. Such a US declaration (or simply leaking of such an intent), reversing the "strong dollar policy" of the past decade, would have considerable impact on the foreign exchange markets (see Fratzscher 2004 on the effectiveness of "oral intervention"). However, the results would be much less certain than under an agreed international compact. Moreover, the effect on world growth would be much more problematic given the absence of any commitment by the surplus countries to make appropriate adjustments in their economic policies to cushion the global impact.

In addition, some countries in Europe as well as in Asia might seek to counter such a unilateral US move by intervening directly or indirectly

9. A more modest variant of this idea would be an "Asian Plaza Agreement" in which the Asian countries, perhaps prompted by the United States, agreed to stop intervening to block dollar adjustment and worked out to some extent the relative appreciation of their respective currencies and thus the trade-weighted change in each. China, once it has decided to revalue the renminbi, might want to lead such an initiative to make sure that it had company in the region. However, the Asians would justifiably want to know what Europe, Canada, and other major countries were planning to contribute to the overall global adjustment, so an agreement with broader participation would be more likely to succeed.

10. It is of course quite possible that such an initiative would be "too successful" and that the dollar's fall would become too rapid and/or overshoot on the downside at the conclusion of its adjustment. If such outcomes were appearing to eventuate, the cooperating countries could then intervene on the other side of the market to stop it—as the G-7 in fact did with its Louvre Agreement in 1987 when the correction agreed at the Plaza threatened to become disruptive (Funabashi 1988).

(e.g., via monetary policy) to block substantial dollar depreciation—thus triggering "currency wars" that would make the global financial situation worse for a while. Hence the United States might have to employ aggressive tactics to achieve the needed currency correction: threatening to sell dollars in the currency markets, as it actually did after the Plaza Agreement and as recently as 1998 against the yen and 2000 against the euro, or to impose new trade barriers against noncooperating countries as done by the Nixon administration with its import surcharge in 1971.

With a US budget commitment and international agreement to realign exchange rates, the other major countries would be much more likely to adopt the measures needed to offset the resultant declines in their trade surpluses by expanding domestic demand.[11] The precise nature of these measures should be left to the individual countries though they would be expected to adopt some combination of more expansionary macroeconomic policy (especially monetary policy, taking advantage of the anti-inflationary impact of their currency appreciations) and needed structural changes (especially in Europe and Japan). Indeed, the need to expand domestic demand in these countries to offset anticipated currency appreciations should have the desirable effect of strengthening the prospects for successful implementation of the policy reform efforts already undertaken by some governments (à la Schröder in Germany). Domestic political resistance, which has blocked such efforts, might be overcome in the new circumstances and especially if they were part of an international compact worked out with the United States, China, and other key countries.

Dollar depreciation, while essential to the needed correction, will nevertheless provide only a temporary (albeit prolonged) respite for the external financial problems of the United States. Excessive current account deficits have consistently reappeared despite repeated and sizable dollar declines. Prior to the sharp pickup in productivity growth and robust US output growth over the past decade, many analysts believed that the United States faced fundamental problems of international competitiveness. With that strong pickup in economic performance in recent years, the puzzle is even greater.

A substantial part of the underlying problem is clearly macroeconomic, centered on the low national saving rate (since it would be foolish to cut investment spending on a lasting basis to resolve the external deficit problem). Hence the United States should aim to run budget surpluses in prosperous economic periods to contribute positively to the domestic availability of capital. Serious consideration should likewise be given to measures that promote private saving but, since all manner of tax and

11. China, which has set an official goal of reducing its overall output growth to 7 to percent from 9 to 10 percent in order to cool recent overheating, would not need to take such measures. It should simply let the cut in its external surplus translate into a cut in total output growth for at least the next couple of years.

other incentives have been attempted and failed, this would probably require mandatory savings requirements à la Singapore.

Foreign economic policy could pursue at least two major initiatives in this context that would strengthen the US current account position over the longer run and thus reduce the need to rely on periodic depreciations of the dollar.[12] One would be to alter the current international trading rules that permit most other countries to rebate their indirect taxes on exports and impose those taxes on imports, while prohibiting the United States from doing so on its direct taxes. In theory, these across-the-board differences in tax systems between the major trading countries should be neutralized by changes in exchange rates. In practice, the dollar has experienced prolonged periods of overvaluation during the past 50 years (as at present) rather than the undervaluation that would be needed to counter the trade impact of the tax differences. Hence the United States should seek a change in the global tax rules in future multilateral trade negotiations and be prepared to make offsetting concessions (for example, in its implementation of antidumping duties) to win foreign acceptance thereof.

Alternatively, or as a lever to promote such international agreement, the United States could reform its own tax system to comport with the existing international rules. Possibilities include a national retail sales tax or a corporate activity tax (CAT) to replace the corporate income tax for this and other purposes (Hufbauer and Grieco, forthcoming). Such a shift could improve both the efficiency and simplicity of the US tax code, and the new tax could reasonably be set at a level that would raise additional revenue as a contribution to cutting the budget deficit. Such a tax would clearly be rebatable at the border under the current international rules, so the United States could either match other countries' practices or, without then having to offer any quid pro quo, much more easily negotiate a cessation of all border rebate practices.

The US current account position could also be improved by further increasing US emphasis, in international trade negotiations, on liberalization of other countries' barriers to imports of services. The United States runs a sizable surplus in its trade in services, which partially offsets a huge gap in merchandise trade. Moreover, it appears that foreign income elasticities of demand for US services exports are higher than the US income elasticity of demand for services imports—the reverse of the Houthakker-Magee phenomenon that applies to merchandise trade (Mann 2004b).

Liberalization of their services sectors by other major trading countries, especially the rapidly growing developing countries, would have doubly beneficial effects for the United States. On the one hand, the share of ser-

12. To do so on a lasting basis, they would have to contribute to a reduction in the underlying savings/investment imbalance. Both strategies proposed here would achieve that goal by boosting corporate profits and thus business saving.

vices in these countries' overall economies would grow more rapidly; those shares remain very low by international standards and, though they will inevitably rise to a dominant position as in all other mature high-income countries, an acceleration of that trend would be very helpful for US exports. At the same time, reduction of those countries' barriers to services imports, including domestic regulations that have such restrictive effects, would enable the United States (and other competitive exporters) to secure a growing share of a rapidly expanding market. Some studies of the future gains to the US economy from moving to global free trade indicate that three-quarters of those benefits would accrue in the services sector (Brown, Deardorff, and Stern 2003).

The US current account deficit and external debt are macroeconomic problems that require primarily macroeconomic responses, notably a sizable and lasting increase in the domestic saving rate and a competitive exchange rate for the dollar. Import restrictions would be an ineffective and indeed counterproductive policy response because they would impair American productivity and trigger retaliation and/or emulation by other countries. But it is perfectly appropriate, indeed imperative, for the United States to seek long-run improvement in its export performance by adding reform of the international tax rules and liberalization of foreign services markets to its priority goals in international trade negotiations, especially multilateral talks in the WTO like the current Doha Round. Trade policy can thus play a helpful role in reinforcing US efforts to restore stability to the country's economic and external financial positions over both the long and short runs.

International Monetary Reform

There is one other implication for US foreign economic policy of the major problem, and potential crisis, surrounding the current account deficit and overvaluation of the dollar. This is not the first time that such a situation has confronted the United States. Indeed, it is at least the fifth cycle in the postwar period with similar characteristics: a sharp rise in the dollar leading to a substantial deterioration in the current account, producing in turn domestic protectionist pressures and growing fears of a dollar crash, resolved via more or less disorderly realignments of exchange rates and ad hoc policy measures among the major countries. Such patterns emerged in the early 1970s and led to both the first serious protectionist threats in the postwar period and the termination of the Bretton Woods system of fixed but adjustable exchange rates, in the late 1970s surrounding double-digit inflation in the United States and elsewhere, in the mid-1980s with such an outbreak of US protectionism that the United States had to seek international help to weaken the dollar via the Plaza Agreement, and more mildly in the mid-1990s leading to the all-time lows for the dollar in 1995.

The international monetary system has nevertheless stubbornly resisted any reforms that would reduce the prospect of repeated misalignments among the major currencies. The entire debate over strengthening the "international financial architecture" in recent years has centered on problems surrounding emerging-market economies, which were indeed the chief systemic problem in the second half of the 1990s,[13] while ignoring the countries and currencies at the center of the system (and the large increase in the imbalances among them that was building up while this debate transpired). It should be a major goal of US foreign economic policy in the coming years to develop, propose, and negotiate improvements in the international monetary system to reduce the likelihood that huge misalignments and imbalances will continue to recur, with the adverse effects on the United States seen so many times over the past 30 years.[14]

Trade Policy

As noted earlier and elaborated in chapter 2, the United States has gained enormously from the dramatic reduction of its own and other countries' trade barriers over the past 50 years. The total benefit to the US economy totals about $1 trillion, or almost 10 percent of GDP, per year. The annual standard of living of the average US family is about $9,000 higher as a result. Complete elimination of all remaining barriers, at least those that can now be identified and quantified, would augment these aggregates by perhaps another 50 percent.

There is of course no prospect of moving to completely free world trade in the near future. However, US policy has been approaching that ultimate

13. A number of highly desirable further reforms with respect to these issues are analyzed and proposed by Morris Goldstein in chapter 12.

14. One possibility would be to install at least a weak version of the target zone idea (Bergsten and Williamson 1983, updated in Bergsten and Henning 1996), perhaps the "monitoring zone" variant recently developed by John Williamson (Williamson 1998, 2000). Such an approach would seek to keep currencies from deviating too far from equilibrium levels, thus producing sustainable current account positions over the longer run in both financial and trade policy terms. The key countries, probably initially through the G-7 (or its successor) and institutionally through the IMF, would agree on the ranges for their currencies that would meet the "sustainability" test. They would then agree to take no actions that would push their exchange rates away from those levels or keep them from moving toward those levels, such as intervening in the markets either financially (as Japan, China, and others have done in recent years to block appreciation of their currencies against the dollar) or rhetorically (as the United States has done in recent years to support continued overvaluation of the dollar). If experience with such an approach proved to be effective and useful, it could subsequently be strengthened to incorporate explicit cooperation to stop rates from moving away from their equilibrium levels and even to push rates toward their equilibrium levels as with the Plaza Agreement in 1985. The chief policy instrument would be sterilized intervention in the currency markets, which has been shown to be a successful tool in numerous episodes over the past 20 years (Fratzscher 2004, Kubelec 2004).

goal via three channels of negotiation: bilateral FTAs with individual countries or small groups thereof, megaregional FTAs with Latin America (and, though only rhetorically so far, with the Asia Pacific), and multilateral reductions to trade barriers at the global level through the WTO (currently via the Doha Round). The strategic underpinning of this threefold approach is the concept of "competitive liberalization," under which negotiations at each level create new incentives and pressures for nonparticipating countries to join the process (Bergsten 1996a, 1996b; Zoellick 2001). For example, US FTAs with Central America and the Andean countries create new discrimination against the South American countries in some of their important markets; this should help induce them to agree to a continentwide Free Trade Area of the Americas (FTAA), which generates important new discrimination against the Europeans and Asians throughout this hemisphere; this in turn should pressure the non-FTAA participants to agree to a substantial global reduction of all barriers via the WTO. The shoe can of course be on the other foot: A meaningful free trade pact between the European Union and Mercosur (Mercado Común del Sur, or the Southern Cone Common Market) should quicken US willingness to complete an FTAA, and the creation of an East Asian Free Trade Area, like the steady movement toward a single market within Europe before it, could represent an enormous inducement to others to reach ambitious multilateral agreements to reduce barriers at the global level.

The chief objective of US trade policy over the next few years should be to implement this strategy in a way that will most effectively promote US economic and foreign policy interests. This will require several changes in both the substance of the US negotiating agenda and the list of countries with which talks are conducted.

As noted earlier, three major changes in the US approach to trade negotiations would advance US budgetary as well as trade objectives. One is a complete elimination of agricultural protection by all countries, which would enable the United States to cut $20 billion in farm payments from its annual budget as well as eliminate distortions that severely limit world trade in this sector and hence lift 200 million people out of poverty in the poorest countries (Cline 2004 and chapter 13). Such a goal is unrealistic for the Doha Round because of the continued resistance of the European Union, the world's largest farm subsidizer, and others (including within the United States). But the United States should redouble its efforts in this direction in Doha, by offering to reduce its own trade-distorting subsidies as close to zero as reciprocity from others will permit and by continuing to pursue the ultimate objective in megaregional and future multilateral negotiations after the Doha Round is completed (presumably in 2007).

Second, the United States should raise worldwide liberalization of barriers to services trade to the top of its priority agenda. US comparative advantage is both clear and particularly constrained by policies in other countries in many services sectors. Hence substantial services liberalization might make an important contribution to reducing the US current account deficit, especially over the longer run, as well as generating a large number of high-paying domestic jobs.

Such negotiations on services will not be easy, however. Most of the offending policies derive from domestic regulatory regimes in other countries, rather than tariffs or other border measures, and are thus harder to identify and negotiate away (as the long-running US efforts with Japan through the 1980s and 1990s demonstrated so vividly). Moreover, the United States would presumably have to liberalize some of its own barriers to imports of services as part of such a deal. Some of these—as on maritime services (including the venerable Jones Act) and especially on labor services, which will almost certainly be demanded by some of the developing countries whose services markets the United States is most eager to pry open—would entail domestic adjustment that would be politically if not economically painful. The potential payoff is nevertheless substantial and should be pursued aggressively at all three levels of negotiation.

A third, more radical, addition to the future global agenda would be to tackle the WTO rules governing the relationship between taxes and trade. The current rules discriminate badly against the United States (and the few other countries that rely on direct, mainly income, taxes as revenue sources) in favor of countries that use indirect (including value-added and sales) taxes. Those rules permit indirect taxes to be rebated on exports and added to imports but bar similar treatment for direct taxes. The theoretical offset to this structural difference via changes in exchange rates obtains only over the very long run, if at all, and the persistent overvaluation of the dollar (in trade terms) throughout the postwar period suggests that this particular component of the invisible hand is nowhere to be seen.

The United States can counter this particular distortion in two ways: join 'em or fight 'em. The United States could convert its direct taxes to indirect taxes, perhaps a national retail sales tax or corporate activity tax for the key corporate sector, for revenue as well as competitiveness reasons (Hufbauer and Grieco, forthcoming). It could then emulate the border adjustments of other countries and subsequently negotiate from an equal starting point to end that entire practice.

However, it may be difficult to reform US tax policy in this direction. Objections would be raised to the allegedly regressive effects (and sizable transition costs) of the proposed changes and, for some variants of the approach, to "letting companies go tax-free," and to relations between the US federal and state governments. Hence the United States may want to pursue the alternative course of seeking elimination of the archaic distinction in the WTO rules. This would carry a very high payoff for the United States, along with services liberalization probably bringing the biggest benefit it could obtain from multilateral trade negotiations.

However, most other countries would stoutly resist such a reform since the current rules favor them so substantially. Hence it would probably be impossible to add it to the agenda for the Doha Round at this late date, when major efforts will be needed simply to achieve the goals already agreed (in principle) for that initiative. The United States should thus use the next few years to try to alter its tax code to conform to the WTO rules and, if that route fails, seek to place the issue on the agenda for whatever multilateral trade negotiation follows Doha.

In addition to these modifications in the US agenda for future multilateral trade negotiations, changes are needed in the regions and countries with which it is pursuing the other components of the "competitive liberalization" strategy. In particular, new approaches are needed with respect to Asia, and particularly northeast Asia, the largest gap in the network of trade agreements that have been pursued in recent years (Baucus 2004). Another reason to devise new strategies toward that region is that the East Asians are contemplating major new trade (and financial) agreements among themselves, ranging from bilateral deals between significant pairs like Japan-Korea and China-ASEAN (Association of Southeast Asian Nations) to a full East Asian Free Trade Area (including ASEAN, China, Japan, and Korea), which would carry substantial trade (and perhaps foreign policy) diversion costs for the United States.[15]

The United States faced similar issues in the late 1980s and early 1990s, when Asia was booming and Prime Minister Mahathir bin Mohamad of Malaysia attracted considerable attention with his proposal for an East Asian Economic Group. The United States responded firmly against "drawing a line down the middle of the Pacific," in Secretary of State James Baker's memorable phrase, and insisted on full membership in the new Asia Pacific Economic Cooperation (APEC) forum that was originally contemplated as an Asia-only grouping (Funabashi 1995). The United States and others were subsequently able to use the initial APEC summit meeting in 1993, which raised the prospect of a potentially huge Asia-Pacific trade bloc, to induce the European Union to agree to a successful conclusion of the Uruguay Round and creation of the WTO after they had stalled for three years and threatened total failure of the exercise (Bergsten 1994).

After a promising start in the mid-1990s, however, APEC has achieved very little actual liberalization. It did lead the negotiations toward the eventually global Information Technology Agreement in 1996, which freed $500 billion of trade in high-technology goods and services, but its subsequent pursuit of the agreed goal of "free and open trade and investment in the region by 2010 (for its developed members) and 2020 (for its developing members)" has stalled out. The group's private-sector arm, the

15. Scollay (2001) implies that US exports would decline by $25 billion annually as an immediate effect of the creation of an East Asian Free Trade Area.

APEC Business Advisory Council, attempted to restart the process in 2004 by proposing serious study of a Free Trade Area of the Asia Pacific (FTAAP) that, like all other FTAs, would extend its liberalization only to members of the group. APEC has never explicitly confronted the need to proceed on such a preferential basis, which is obviously essential to win domestic support for the idea in the United States and indeed virtually all member economies, opting instead for vague calls for "open regionalism" that implied extending the benefits of its liberalization on a most-favored-nation basis to nonmembers.

The United States should strongly support this initiative. It is the best way to head off the risk of Asia-only regionalism that could severely hurt US economic and foreign policy interests. Building on APEC's halting but promising results to date, it would begin to forge serious institutional ties across the Pacific that could over time emulate the enormously successful (if currently frayed) transatlantic ties that have been so vital to the United States for half a century. It would enable the United States to engage directly with the most dynamic economies in the world.

From the perspective of trade policy, US participation in the credible launch of an FTAAP would represent the most potent next step in the "competitive liberalization" process. Brazil and the other Latin American countries would realize that their potential megaregional agreement with the United States, the FTAA, had a serious and potentially more lucrative rival for US attention. The European Union and other non-APEC countries would immediately see the huge trade diversion they would suffer if an FTAAP were to eventuate and would almost surely "sue for peace" by making sure that the Doha Round, and perhaps early successors in the WTO, reasserted the centrality of global liberalization. APEC might never need to actually create an FTAAP if it offered a credible prospect of doing so in the near future. Such an arrangement could also be viewed, however, as a potential fallback in case the Doha Round were to fail or even produce a disappointing result (Bergsten 2004b).

Perhaps in addition to an FTAAP, or certainly if it failed to proceed because other APEC members resisted the idea, the United States should pursue comprehensive bilateral FTAs with key countries in the region, especially Japan and Korea. The reasons are similar to those just noted: to preempt discrimination from the FTAs those countries are working out among themselves and with others in the region, to engage directly with some of the world's largest and most rapidly growing economies and traders, and to apply meaningful "competitive liberalization" pressures to others. Moreover, FTAs with larger countries of this type would attract substantial political interest in Congress (Baucus 2004) and the business community (US Chamber of Commerce 2003) and thus provide support for an open trade policy that is sorely needed. Agriculture would of course have to be fully included for these FTAs to achieve this purpose, and indeed for them to be acceptable to Congress.

A refocus of negotiating attention on larger countries should go well beyond East Asia (Schott 2004 and chapter 8 in this book). Many of the smaller agreements pursued in recent years have been of limited economic or even foreign policy benefit to the United States, and their pursuit diverts the limited trade policy resources of the US government from more important targets. In addition to Japan and/or Korea in East Asia, two other candidates offer the most promise.

The most intriguing possibility is India (Lawrence and Chadha, forthcoming 2004). A US FTA with India would link the world's two largest (by population) democratic states and offer major foreign policy benefits in a crucial and difficult part of the globe. It could also induce meaningful liberalization in a country that may be the world's next economic superpower, after China, but that remains highly protected (on investment as well as trade). Just as a US offer to negotiate free trade with Japan or Korea might be enough to induce those countries to finally overcome their agricultural protectionism, given its enormous payoff to them in foreign policy as well as economic terms, such an offer to India might enable a reform-minded government there (such as the current regime) to strengthen the economy on a much broader scale.

Another candidate would be Egypt (Galal and Lawrence, forthcoming 2005). FTAs with Jordan, Morocco, Bahrain, and possibly Oman and the United Arab Emirates in the near future are useful beginnings toward a trade agreement with the entire Middle East, which would be of great value in overall foreign policy and national security terms. Egypt, however, is both by far the largest country in the region and the center of influence on many far-reaching issues. It has also been pursuing economic reform, albeit fitfully, and encompasses a substantial number of reformers in key positions (in both government and business) who could use an FTA negotiation with the United States to promote such an agenda. Success in those efforts would have important spillover effects throughout the Middle East, in terms of both economic policies and the benefits from working closely with the United States.

US trade policy for the next four years should thus pursue a multiple agenda as at present but with significant modifications. Highest priority should continue to be attached to a successful conclusion of the Doha Round in the WTO because of its large economic payoff to the United States ($164 billion in the aggregate per Brown, Deardorff, and Stern 2003), its major foreign policy benefits (especially with the developing countries), and its huge systemic significance (by restoring confidence in a multilateral system that is more important than ever in a world of accelerating regionalism). But the United States should substantially amend its agenda for those talks to give priority to reducing agricultural subsidies and barriers to services trade as much as possible. Second priority should be given to the megaregional possibilities, especially the addition of an FTAAP as well as renewed efforts to complete the FTAA. Large changes should also be made in the determination of potential partners for bilateral FTAs: Japan and/or Korea should head the list as part of a new lineup that also includes India and Egypt.

To achieve any of these goals, the US administration and Congress in early 2005 will have to surmount several legislative hurdles:

- to extend Trade Promotion Authority through June 2007;
- to remain a member of the WTO;
- to replace the WTO-illegal Byrd Amendment, under which US firms that file successful antidumping petitions receive the duties collected as well as the protection they afford; and
- to approve the Central America and Bahrain FTAs.

Extension of TPA is imperative to permit pursuit of any of the new initiatives proposed in this section or indeed continuation of any of those now under way. Continued membership in the WTO is obviously also essential. Both would therefore seem to be routine exercises for Congress and that may indeed turn out to be the case. However, the shaky political support for further globalization in the country and the renewed escalation of the trade deficit, especially if economic growth and job creation were to slow, could jeopardize the ease of passage. It might then become necessary, as well as desirable substantively, to link improvements in the TAA program—as discussed in the next section—to the legislation to win its passage, the same formula that was utilized in Congress in 2002 to obtain TPA in the first place.

Passage of the pending FTAs and rectification of the remaining WTO finding against the United States are less critical but nevertheless quite important in terms of the administration's posture on trade in both international and domestic terms. The specifics of the Central America agreement, in particular, will set the framework for future FTAs for at least the next four years on such key issues as the links between trade and labor or the environment. Likewise, continued failure to bring US laws into compliance with WTO obligations will increasingly erode US credibility in the global trading system and its ability both to use the WTO to contest violations by other countries and to pursue its broader negotiating interests—in addition to the mounting economic costs of foreign retaliation that will undoubtedly start soon in the absence of credible congressional movement on the Byrd Amendment. The administration and Congress thus face a very large and quite urgent trade policy agenda.

Domestic Adjustment

None of these international economic initiatives will proceed very far, or rest on a sustainable basis of internal support, unless the United States substantially improves its domestic support system for those elements of US society that are adversely affected by globalization and may be hurt by further trade liberalization. Globalization and further liberalization carry very large benefits for the United States but, like any dynamic economic change, generate costs as well as benefits for those who experience their impact. There are losers as well as winners.

There are at least three reasons why policy must explicitly address those costs and losers. One is simple equity: When portions of society are harmed by policy choices taken in the general interest, there is a strong case for providing equitable compensation. The second is economic: It is wasteful for national resources to remain unemployed or underemployed when there are good reasons to believe that, with practical assistance, they can contribute more productively to society. The third is political: The domestic backlash against globalization has become so powerful, especially over the past decade, that it has severely limited US foreign economic policy throughout that period. The case for mounting an effective program of domestic assistance to workers, and perhaps entire communities, disadvantaged by globalization, is very strong.

The United States can clearly afford such a program. We have estimated that the benefit to date from internationalization of the US economy over the past half century totals about $1 trillion per year. Current governmental spending for Trade Adjustment Assistance amounts to less than $1 billion per year and would rise only to $1.5 billion to $2 billion annually under the reforms adopted in 2002. Despite the need to bring the federal budget deficit under control, it would be the height of fiscal foolishness to jeopardize the national payoff from globalization through an unwillingness to deal fairly and effectively with the downsides of the phenomenon. Total US government spending for worker assistance programs totals $8 billion to $23 billion, depending on what is counted. Even these numbers are quite small relative to some other advanced industrial countries, as shown in chapter 10. Moreover, these programs bear no direct relationship to dislocation linked to globalization and never seem to have had any mitigating impact on antiglobalization concerns.

Indeed, a case can be made for broadening the traditional program of *trade* adjustment assistance to address the problems of workers who are dislocated from their jobs for *any* reason. There is a strong intellectual argument for such a response: It is very difficult to disentangle globalization from other factors, especially technological change, in assessing the cause of any particular dislocation. Multiple causality is virtually always present, especially in today's economy where technological change and globalization interact in almost every industry and reinforce each other's impact. The worker anxiety that produces backlash against globalization does not of course make neat causality distinctions and, even if globalization plays a minor role in most cases as shown by virtually every study on the topic, will continue to resist further international opening unless the corrective domestic programs are substantially improved. A very practical reason for harmonizing TAA with the rest of the US worker dislocation programs (such as unemployment insurance) is that it is now an "orphan" in the Department of Labor and has never been implemented very vigorously; treating trade-impacted workers like all other dislocated workers in the country would increase the attention as well as benefits they receive.

The attitudes of American workers, and especially of their chief labor union organizations and political supporters, will be critical for the future evolution of these issues (Baldwin 2003). For the past decade or so, the AFL-CIO and its proponents in Congress (and sometimes the administration) have conditioned support for new trade agreements on their incorporating requirements for stronger labor standards in other (especially developing) countries. Such standards would clearly be desirable but, even if they could be widely agreed and implemented, would produce very small benefits for American workers in terms of job security and levels of pay (Elliott and Freeman 2003). Moreover, most of the low-income countries that are the target of such efforts are hostile, viewing labor standards as a thinly disguised cover for traditional protectionism, and the chances of negotiating major commitments in this area are negligible.

Hence it would seem far more sensible for US labor to put its political weight behind substantial improvements in domestic assistance programs for trade-impacted (and perhaps other) dislocated workers. The AFL-CIO endorsed the initial TAA concept in 1962, when President Kennedy launched it as the domestic component of his Trade Expansion Act that produced the Kennedy Round, and indeed maintained its traditional support for trade liberalization through that period. But organized labor subsequently soured on TAA, understandably in view of the parsimonious implementation of the legislation, and indeed came to label it as "burial insurance" for its members. The union movement then turned against almost all further trade liberalization, a stance that it maintains today. The administration should pursue a "grand bargain" with labor that would encompass a shift by the AFL-CIO from emphasizing international labor standards to TAA, along with its support for future trade agreements, in return for governmental adoption and effective implementation of a dramatically improved and broadened TAA program.

Despite the lack of enthusiasm of organized labor, TAA has maintained a surprising degree of political traction. Supporters of trade liberalization have insisted on expanding the program in virtually every important trade bill over the past 40 years since Kennedy instituted the idea. Senate Democrats insisted on a major expansion, which proved decisive when the bill returned to the House for final passage as well, when passing TPA in 2002. The reforms of 2002 in fact set the stage for the next, much more generous and far-reaching expansion of the program that is essential if a firm domestic foundation is to be restored for US trade policy and foreign economic policy more broadly.

When the public, including American workers, are asked whether they "favor free trade" if the US government has "programs to help workers who lose their jobs," the 50-50 split on the simple "yes/no" question becomes a comfortably favorable two-to-one majority (Scheve and Slaughter 2001, 96). The obvious requirement is to beef up the TAA program so that it will become, and be seen as, effective in addressing the needs of disadvantaged workers. Two sets of issues are involved: an adequate safety net that cushions the transitional impact of job dislocation, with income supports and continuation of key benefits such as health insurance and pension rights, and empowerment of workers to find new jobs with decent wages through basic education and training/retraining along with job search and relocation assistance—especially to achieve skill upgrading and better matching of skills to jobs. Both programs need to include all workers directly and indirectly dislocated due to changes in international trade and investment patterns, and to provide benefits that are both generous quantitatively and effective qualitatively in achieving the short-run and longer-run objectives of the policy.

Kletzer and Rosen suggest many of the specific components of such a program in chapter 10. The key additions to current legislation would include

- identifying "import-impacted" industries and automatically qualifying all workers in those industries rather than requiring groups of workers to apply individually;
- eligibility for services workers, especially in light of the growing role of services in total US trade and the present debate over outsourcing in that sector, since only manufacturing workers are now covered;
- restoration of eligibility for affected communities as well as individual groups of workers;
- eligibility for workers displaced by plant relocations to all countries rather than only countries with which the United States has FTAs;
- technical corrections in the new wage insurance and health care tax credit programs to enhance their utilization;
- substantial increases in funding, especially for the training component of the program;
- a human capital investment tax credit, to induce US companies to sharply expand their own training efforts (see chapter 9 and Mann 2003);
- extension of the wage insurance concept to cover other assets that are important to workers, notably their homes (Richardson, forthcoming); and especially

- further reforms in the basic K–12 education system in the United States, which is the fundamental underpinning for all American workers but which continues to underperform both its own potential and its counterparts in many other countries.

Until quite recently, the annual budget costs of TAA were running at only $200 million to $300 million per year. The amount has increased to an estimated $800 million for 2004 and will probably rise to $1.5 billion to $2 billion per year when the reforms of 2002 are fully implemented. Adoption of all the reforms proposed here would take the total to about $3 billion. All of these numbers are obviously very small, and readily affordable, compared with the $1 trillion per year that the US economy already gains from globalization and the potential future benefits of another $500 billion annually from moving to global free trade.

The biggest policy issue in this area, as noted, is whether to extend these programs to cover all dislocated workers whatever the cause of their difficulty. There is a strong case for such reform on moral, economic, and political grounds. The estimated annual budget cost would be $12 billion, only four times the cost of the trade-only program and an even tinier fraction of the benefits from permitting continuation of the dynamic changes that fuel the overall US economy. From the standpoint of foreign economic policy, on the other hand, de-linkage from the international agenda would probably reduce the political benefits of the program in achieving congressional support for future trade bills.

Whether the narrower or broader routes are taken, passage of the proposed reforms should rank very high on the agenda of the US government in the period ahead. One early possibility would be to link at least the more technical parts of the needed legislation to one or more of the trade bills that Congress will be addressing during the first half of 2005, as discussed earlier. More extensive changes could then be included in bills that will be needed to implement a successful Doha Round, in late 2007 or early 2008, especially if that legislation includes (as it should) a renewal of TPA for future negotiations. If a future administration and Congress were inclined to overhaul the totality of worker dislocation benefits, presumably including unemployment insurance, that would be a natural vehicle to incorporate such changes.

Energy Policy

Energy policy is another issue area, like correcting the current account imbalance and reaping further gains from trade liberalization while rebuilding domestic support, that requires a skillful blend of internal and international initiatives. Perhaps even more so than those topics, energy policy will require full integration with the rest of US foreign policy since a number of other countries, both importers and exporters of oil, will need to be intensively engaged at a time when some of them are at odds with the United States on a range of other topics.

The international focus for the US energy policy recommended here is twofold. First, the United States needs to reopen the NAFTA discussion with Canada and Mexico on their roles as producers of energy resources, as described by Schott in chapter 8. Both have large reserves of both crude oil and natural gas, which could substantially increase and diversify world (as well as US) supply if they were willing to permit the needed investments (including by foreign-based companies) to realize that potential. Delicate political sensitivities constrain such policies in both, and the United States may have to offer concessions on other issues, including immigration policy for Mexico (as discussed by Gordon Hanson in chapter 11), to win their agreement. The payoff is so important, however, particularly in terms of boosting output by large amounts in relatively secure locations, that the United States should be willing to do so.

Second, the United States needs to launch a major international effort, conducted in close cooperation with the other key (developed and developing) oil-importing countries, to counter OPEC's (and especially Saudi Arabia's) long-standing manipulation of the world oil market. The payoff from restoring global energy prices to levels that bear at least some resemblance to the underlying economics of the commodity would be enormous: probably on the order of $500 billion a year for the world, of which perhaps $150 billion to $200 billion annually would accrue to the United States. Any US administration or indeed the world as a whole could not envisage a more effective "jobs program."

Such an international effort will only be feasible, however, if the United States implements a series of new domestic energy measures. The chief reason is that the United States remains the dominant global consumer of energy, accounting for about 25 percent of world demand.[16] Serious efforts to put downward pressure on global energy prices for the longer run, and thus to strengthen the negotiating position of the demand side of the market, are thus possible only if the United States takes serious actions to restrain its appetite. In addition, the United States needs to rein in its gas-guzzling sport-utility vehicles (SUVs) and other excessive consumption of energy products if it is to obtain a sufficiently high moral ground to enable it to lead such an international effort.

The domestic component of the new energy policy should also be twofold, primarily addressing the consumption pattern but covering pro-

16. This number is sometimes compared with the US share of world population of about 5 percent, suggesting huge unfairness in the US consumption total. As indicated in the text, US consumption of energy does indeed need to be significantly reduced. But the United States also produces about 25 percent of global economic output, a much more relevant comparator that suggests that US energy demand is not disproportional in the global context.

duction as well. For the longer run, and especially if the United States can succeed in reducing the cartel's pricing power and thus cut world prices toward a market-related level of about $20 per barrel, the key step would be a significant gasoline tax (at about $1 per gallon, legislated promptly and phased in over several years during the next downward phase of the price cycle to both minimize economic disruption and maximize political feasibility). Such a tax could also provide a significant source of revenue to help reduce the budget deficits, or alternatively be rebated through cuts in other taxes to have a neutral effect on the overall economy while achieving the desired cut in energy usage (and environmental damage).

Even more immediate needs relate to the refinery and other infrastructure bottlenecks that have contributed substantially to the recent run-up in prices, as described in detail by Philip Verleger in chapter 7.[17] New environmental rules, with respect to the sulfur content of oil products, have precluded the usual resort to imports of refined products to meet the surge in demand and need to be relaxed at least temporarily. Competition policy decisions by the Federal Trade Commission have required merged oil firms to sell parts of their refining capacity to smaller companies, which have been unable to expand (or even maintain) output levels due to their weaker financial positions, and should not be repeated. The administration should stop buying for the Strategic Petroleum Reserve when the price is high and rising.

On the supply side, there is no risk of "running out of oil" (let alone carbon fuels more broadly, like coal) à la David Malthus or the Club of Rome or their more recent successors. But OPEC has substantially limited its output levels (as have non-OPEC countries, including Canada and Mexico). The needed private investment is deterred by high political risks in many producing areas, restrictive energy policies in many of those countries, the economic risks stemming from periodic price plunges, and the endemic instability of the current energy regime itself. Hence Congress must also break the logjam that has blocked new US production. A serious program to expand renewable energy sources is vital as well.

None of this can have much impact in the short run, however. The only available policy measure to bring prices down quickly would be large sales from the Strategic Petroleum Reserve (and similar governmental stocks in other importing countries). These reserves are now sufficiently large, at almost 700 million barrels in the United States and 1.4 billion barrels worldwide, to have a considerable impact on prices for quite a while.

17. These recent increases, beyond say $40 per barrel, *cannot* be blamed on OPEC except in the sense that the cartel's unwillingness to increase its capacity over time precluded its having the ability to expand output to a level that would have enabled it to moderate the price surge when it wanted to. Part of the latest surge relates to the insecurity of supply in Russia (highlighted by the Yukos case), Nigeria, and Venezuela as well as the Middle East, where it of course relates as well to broader political and security issues.

Verleger estimates in chapter 7 that an administration announcement of its willingness to exchange 100 million barrels of light crude for 100 million barrels of heavy crude over a 90-day period could reduce severe refining constraints and cut the world price by $10 to $20 per barrel. Sales from the reserves would also send a strong signal to producing countries that the oil-importing nations were serious about promoting regime changes in this issue area.[18]

The fundamental policy focus, however, should be on restoring a semblance of market-related pricing to world oil. It is too much to hope that true market forces could replace the current producer control. The "theory of the second best" concludes that a significant market distortion should be countered by an offsetting market distortion whenever feasible, however, and oligopolistic selling should be countered by oligopsonistic buying in this case. The oil-importing countries, rich and poor, need to combine to offset the market power of the oil-exporting countries and push global prices toward levels that would be likely to ensue in the absence of their market manipulation. The first step in any new US effort in this area should thus be to seek support from the other major importing countries, including key developing countries such as China and India as well as the members of the International Energy Agency (IEA) in the Organization for Economic Cooperation and Development (OECD).

The results of such a successful strategy would be dramatic. Even the highest-cost production in present locales is no more than $15 to $20 per barrel. Marginal costs in the Gulf remain below $5 per barrel. Some studies suggest that OPEC's market power has kept world prices at levels that averaged about double their underlying value for much of the last 30 years. An equitable equilibrium price might be on the order of $25 per barrel, averaged over time and fluctuating within a fairly wide range of $22 to $28 per barrel as traditionally espoused by OPEC itself, or even wider, to allow for cyclical, seasonal, and other variations in market conditions.

All countries, producers as well as consumers, would also reap substantial benefits from reducing the enormous instability in world oil prices that derives from the current regime. Just as there is no mechanism to check sharp upward spikes, as occurred in 2004, there is no mechanism to avoid severe downward spikes as in 1986 and 1998. Abrupt price rises in the past have triggered the three largest postwar recessions. But dramatic price declines are also poisonous for the world economy, deterring investment as well as retarding the development of large low-income countries (such as Iraq, Mexico, Nigeria, Russia, and Venezuela) as well as small higher-income countries (including Saudi Arabia, Kuwait, and others in the Gulf).

18. The president of OPEC publicly called for release of crude oil from the US strategic reserve on October 27, 2004, and claimed, "I am always asking them to do that" (*Platts Global Alert*, August 31, 2004).

The mechanics of a new regime, to stabilize prices around a market-related level, are laid out in chapter 7 and are relatively simple. Exporting and importing countries would agree on the limits of the price range, and on the size and decision rules for the buffer stock (which could, for the first time, provide useful guidance for US government use of its strategic reserve rather than the totally ad hoc process that has applied to date). To start the latter, the importing countries would pledge some or all of their current strategic reserves. Those reserves should, over time, be roughly tripled from current levels (through purchases when the price dips toward the floor of the range) to provide an adequate stock to maintain the ceiling price. The existence of such a regime would clearly have precluded the sharp run-up in prices in 2004.[19]

The tactics for pursuing the new producer-consumer agreement are fairly straightforward as well. The United States would probably want to discuss it informally at the outset with Saudi Arabia. It would be essential to multilateralize the formal talks from their beginning, though it would not be a simple IEA-OPEC negotiation because both groups would presumably be joined by nonmembers that are important participants in the market (importers such as China and India and producers such as Mexico, Norway, and Russia).

The presence of mutual gains to producers and consumers, from the resulting stronger world economy and more stable oil market, offer reasonable prospects for a successful negotiation. Some producers might object to the short-term loss of income and market control that they would experience, so the United States and other large importers would have to convince them of their serious intent both to substantially alter the demand side of the market by cutting their own consumption and to reduce the world price by sales from their national reserves. In addition, the importers would have to be flexible in working out the level of the price band. They could also offer trade concessions, particularly on energy-related products, to enable the producers to diversify their economies into downstream industries and thereby achieve more sustainable and beneficial development. The importers would have to exhibit firm resolve in seeking an agreement, however, including the use of broader political leverage to induce cooperation.

19. Most previous efforts to construct and maintain international commodity agreements have failed to sustain their targeted price ranges and ultimately collapsed. Most of them, like the International Coffee Agreement and components of UNCTAD's Integrated Commodity Program of the 1970s, were explicitly adopted to transfer resources from consumer to producer countries and were inherently uneconomic. The principles required to implement such agreements are well understood, however, and some, like the International Tin Agreement, did work for many years. However, no agreement has ever been pursued for a product anywhere near the importance of oil nor for purposes of global economic stabilization. If major consuming and producing countries pursued the idea, a much more serious effort to make it work would clearly have to be undertaken.

Such a two-stage negotiation, initially to achieve agreement on a negotiating stance among the importers and then between them and the exporters, would be complex and take time. Its success, like that of other major foreign economic policy initiatives proposed in this book, would depend heavily on the backing provided by changes in domestic policies. It would inevitably interact with other foreign policy issues, particularly in light of the present delicate situation in the Middle East, and other economic issues such as the Doha trade negotiations. However, the stakes for the United States and other oil-importing countries are extremely high, and a successful negotiation on oil might even help restore effective working relationships among the key countries. The energy issue should rank very high on the agenda of foreign economic policy, indeed overall US policy, in the coming period.

Development Policy

The fifth focus of US foreign economic policy must be the developing nations, particularly the poorest people in those countries. Half the world's population continues to "live" on less than $2 per day and about 1 billion people exist on less than $1 per day. The consequences of this poverty are overwhelming in moral and humanitarian terms. But lack of development also exacts a serious cost on the world economy and fosters major security problems by producing "failed states" (or at least areas) that become breeding grounds for global terrorism as well as regional instability. Hence both the more advanced and the poorest developing countries deserve priority attention by the United States.

The development strategies of the past 25 years have recorded substantial successes, reducing the number of people in poverty by over 1 billion and extending to most parts of the world (Bhalla 2002). Inequality among individuals across the world, which had been increasing for almost two centuries, declined over the last 20 to 30 years. The main exception to these positive results has been sub-Saharan Africa where, despite a few individual success stories, poverty has risen by about 250 million since 1960 and per capita incomes have fallen over recent decades. In addition, large numbers of people remain poor in many countries where overall progress has been good, including such large nations as Bangladesh, Brazil, China, India, Indonesia, Mexico, Nigeria, and Pakistan.

US development policy should continue its two-part focus: promoting growth in all developing countries, without which lasting poverty reduction is impossible, and targeting efforts to curb poverty directly. In light of the enormity of the task, in intellectual as well as resource terms, US efforts in this policy area should be imbedded as extensively as possible in a multilateral context of cooperation with other donors. Official foreign assistance programs should be maintained and increased in some cases.

Private capital investment should be fostered, especially in the more advanced developing countries but in the poorest as well (Commission on Capital Flows to Africa 2003).

Trade policy, however, should become the chief tool of US and global development policy. It has now been convincingly demonstrated that a move to global free trade would represent the most powerful available instrument for spurring growth in the poorer countries and reducing poverty directly. Cline and Williamson show in chapter 13 that each additional percentage point in export growth has been associated with an additional 0.15 percentage point in a country's economic growth. Each 1 percent rise in the ratio of a country's trade to its GDP has been associated with a rise of 0.5 percent in long-term output per capita. Paul Krugman has concluded "that every successful case of economic development this past century . . . has taken place via globalization . . . by producing for the world market rather than trying for self-sufficiency" (Krugman 2003).

Elimination of all trade barriers by both the developing countries themselves and the richer nations, with each accounting for about half the benefits, could add $200 billion per year to incomes in the former. It could lift 500 million people earning less than $2 per day out of poverty, cutting the world poverty level by about 25 percent over 15 years (Cline 2004). Complete trade liberalization by the United States and other advanced countries could transfer about twice as much benefit to the poor countries as all current foreign assistance programs, which total about $50 billion per year.

The best development policy for the United States, and the rich countries as a group, is thus the trade policy already recommended: the maximum possible elimination of barriers to international exchange as quickly as possible. Reduction in barriers toward developing countries in fact maximizes the benefits of trade for the United States itself in light of the greater complementarity than in its trade with other high-income nations. At the same time, larger adjustment problems may be triggered. Hence increased domestic adjustment assistance for US workers dislocated by such trade should be viewed as part of the United States' "foreign aid" contribution, with higher payoff than most other expenditures for that purpose, as well as support for the very large gains that result for the overall US economy.

The second big issue concerning US development policy is whether the amount of financial assistance to the poor countries should be increased substantially. Such increases would be needed to have any hope of reaching the Millennium Development Goals for 2015 that the world's leaders adopted in 2000. The United Kingdom has proposed a new financing facility to double the flow of aid over the next few years for that purpose. For its part, the United States remains simultaneously the largest national donor of aid in absolute terms (about $10 billion) and the least generous of all donor countries as a share of its GDP (about 0.2 percent).

Two misconceptions have undermined US aid policy for many years. One is that "aid does not work" in promoting development and thus is wasted. Recent analysis at the Center for Global Development refutes this view by showing that the type of aid that supports short-run growth, like infrastructure projects and budget support, as opposed to aid for humanitarian purposes and long-term structural reforms (such as education), has very strong positive growth effects (Clemens, Radelet, and Bhavnani 2004). The second misconception is that the United States spends far more on aid than is the case in reality; polls show that the public thinks that 15–20 percent of the budget is allocated for these purposes, rather than the true figure of about 1 percent, and that the US government ought to be spending ten times as much as it does (which would make it the most generous donor by far).

The Bush administration pledged a 50 percent boost in annual US aid in 2002 and has sought to maximize the development benefits from that increase by creating the Millennium Challenge Account, which is to choose recipient countries strictly on the soundness of their policies and institutions as presented by the countries themselves (Radelet 2003). The United States should stick to this course, rigorously assessing the use of its aid but increasing the amounts thereof as substantially as can be justified. It should also steadily expand its contributions to the other demonstrably effective aid institution, the International Development Association of the World Bank Group, which lends (at very generous terms) only to the poorest countries. Several other specific ideas, including additional debt relief for the poorest countries, are presented in chapter 13.

The final element of US policy toward developing countries in the coming years should be institutional: expanding their roles in the multilateral economic organizations, both to enhance the effectiveness of those institutions and to increase their political legitimacy. Most importantly, the existing G-20 of finance ministers and central bank governors—which includes eleven of the most systemically significant emerging-market economies[20]—should gradually but steadily replace the G-7 of rich industrial democracies, including eventually at the level of heads of state and government, as the chief steering committee for the world economy. The failure of three of the G-7's recent major initiatives reveals its inability to fulfill that function by itself in the modern world:

20. The G-20 is made up of the finance ministers and central bank governors of 19 countries: Argentina, Australia, Brazil, Canada, China, France, Germany, India, Indonesia, Italy, Japan, Korea, Mexico, Russia, Saudi Arabia, South Africa, Turkey, the United Kingdom, and the United States. Another member is the European Union, represented by the council presidency and the president of the European Central Bank. The managing director of the IMF and the president of the World Bank, plus the chairpersons of the IMF's International Monetary and Financial Committee and the IMF/World Bank Development Committee, also participate in the talks as ex-officio members.

- realignment of exchange rates to correct the global current account imbalances in an orderly manner, without participation by China or other Asian countries (such as Korea and India) whose currencies must play a central role in any such adjustment;
- resolution of the Argentine debt crisis, with its profound effect on the IMF and global capital markets, without participation by Argentina itself or other debtor countries (such as Brazil and Mexico) with huge stakes in the outcome; and
- reduction of world oil prices without participation by Saudi Arabia, Russia, or any of the other major producing nations.

In addition, the United States needs to accelerate its long-standing effort to realign the "chairs and shares" in the international economic institutions to reflect the major shifts in economic importance of the different countries and groups thereof (as analyzed by Boyer and Truman in chapter 5). The chief need is for a sharp drop in European representation, to reflect their move to a single economy and currency and thus the internalization (à la US states) of much of their former "international" activity, and the consequent freeing up of additional space for China and other rapidly developing countries. In the IMF, for example, the large emerging-market economies (LEMs) should pick up 10 to 15 percent of the total quota and as many as five seats on the executive board.

The legitimacy of the global economic institutions, in particular the role of developing countries in their formal voting arrangements and management systems, has justifiably become a central issue in the contemporary debate over globalization. The United States has a major interest in preserving, indeed strengthening, the role of those institutions. It should use its considerable influence to push the institutions in the proposed directions, both at the formal level of "chairs and shares" and at the informal but powerful level of steering committees like the G-20. Initiatives in this area, conducted with skill and persistence, could turn out to be among the most significant elements of US cooperation with the rapidly emerging countries that will be increasingly central to the global economy (and perhaps global politics) in the coming years and beyond.

US Foreign Economic Diplomacy

The fundamental changes in the structure of global economic power relationships described early in this chapter, and the proposed agenda for US foreign economic policy in the coming years, imply a significant alteration in the conduct of that policy. Major shifts are called for in the allocation of US attention to different countries and groups thereof, and therefore in the institutional underpinnings of US strategy.

For the past 40 years, since the onset of the modern world economy in the early 1960s, the United States has centered its international economic attention on the other large industrialized countries. Europe has been the chief focus throughout that period. Japan forced its way into the core group in the early 1970s. The institutional manifestations were the various "Gs": the G-10, created in the early 1960s to shore up the dollar-based monetary system of the day; the G-5, born in the wake of the first oil shock and onset of global stagflation in the mid-1970s; and its evolution, mainly for political reasons, into the G-7 (for the summits shortly after they were created in 1975 but not among finance ministers for another decade). Since the creation of the Common Market, and its decision to immediately centralize trade policy in the European Commission, the United States and the European Union have maintained a "G-2" relationship in an effort to steer the global trading system.

To be sure, individual developing countries have received considerable attention from time to time. Saudi Arabia and other key OPEC countries became centerpieces during the oil shocks of the 1970s and periodically thereafter. The newly industrialized economies, especially Korea and Taiwan, drew much notice when they burst into competitive prominence in the 1980s. Mexico moved into the spotlight with the creation of NAFTA in the early 1990s. China drew growing notice in the late 1990s and early 21st century, especially as it became a locomotive for the world economy and negotiated entry to the WTO. A number of developing countries played central roles in the succession of debt crises in the 1980s and currency crises in the 1990s.

A central theme of this volume, as developed in detail in chapter 5, is that the United States now needs to systematically shift an important part of its foreign economic policy focus to the large emerging-market economies (LEMs). Their markets offer the most attractive targets in the current and foreseeable rounds of international trade negotiations. Their full cooperation will be essential to reduce the adverse impact of the present energy regime on the world economy. Their buildup of foreign exchange reserves (along with that of Japan) has thwarted much of the needed adjustment of the threatening US current account deficit. Some of them remain potentially important sources of global financial disruption and even renewed crises. Their desires for larger roles in the global economic institutions are thus both justified and constructive, and the United States will need to work with them to fulfill those aspirations.

Overall foreign policy concerns suggest a similar shift in emphasis. World population is becoming more and more concentrated in developing countries. So are the sources of security threats to the United States, whether in the Middle East or in Muslim Asia (or in failed states on all continents). China alone is rapidly becoming the dominant player in East Asia, the most dynamic (and, in some senses, most unstable) part of the world. Russia, another emerging-market economy with particular importance on energy issues, will also remain a top security concern for the indefinite future because of its nuclear capabilities.

The United States should thus work with both its traditional allies and the new powers to amend the international decision-making structure. The G-20 should gradually but steadily supplant the G-7 at the center of the system. The emerging economies should be granted a significant increase in their "chairs and shares" in the key international institutions. The United States should thoroughly revamp its internal decision-making machinery to recognize, and respond to, this new power alignment (as proposed in chapter 5).

This new US strategy would focus on creating and supporting institutions in which industrialized and developing countries can work together on issues of common interest. There will also be opportunities for regional manifestations of this approach. US cooperation with Mexico in NAFTA should be sharply expanded. So should US collaboration with Brazil and other key Latin American countries in an FTAA.

A particular opportunity, and possible imperative, lies in APEC. The accelerating process of regional economic cooperation in East Asia, in both the financial sphere with the Chiang Mai Initiative and active negotiations for a large number of preferential trade arrangements, raises again the specter of "drawing a line down the middle of the Pacific" that sparked US interest in APEC in the early 1990s in the first place (Funabashi 1995). The United States may now find it essential to refocus on building transpacific institutional ties, along the lines of the transatlantic ties that have paid off so handsomely since the Second World War, to channel Asia-only arrangements that could do serious damage to US economic and even security interests in directions that would be supportive, rather than destructive, of US interests and the global system (see C. Fred Bergsten, "East Asian Regionalism," *The Economist*, July 15, 2000; and Bergsten 2001). One approach, which could also play a major role in galvanizing further trade liberalization at the global level, would be pursuit of a Free Trade Area of the Asia Pacific (FTAAP) as proposed by the APEC Business Advisory Council in 2004 (Bergsten 2004b). In this context, the need for new US emphasis on both the LEMs and East Asia comes together in a compelling manner.

In addition, the United States will on occasion need to work much more systematically with groups limited to developing countries themselves. A current case in point is the "G-22" that blocked agreement on the Doha round at Cancún in September 2003—correctly, because of the grossly inadequate offer by the United States and the European Union on liberalization of agricultural trade. Future instances may include an Asian Monetary Fund, evolving from the Chiang Mai Initiative of bilateral swap agreements among the East Asians, and any East Asian Free Trade Area that might evolve. The United States must devote much more time, resources, and priority to understanding and seeking cooperation with such groups—which are likely to expand at a rapid pace over the coming years as more and more developing countries realize both the commonality (albeit not uniformity) of their interests and their potential for successfully pursuing those interests when they mobilize effectively.

At the same time, the United States obviously cannot forget its traditional allies and their continuing major role in the world economy. The expanded European Union, despite its disappointing growth in recent years, remains the only other economic superpower and possible global rival to the United States. Japan, for all its recent travails, is still by far the world's largest surplus and creditor country. The United States would downgrade relations with these historic partners only at its peril.

However, the United States needs to refine its relationships with these countries to pursue its interests more effectively, including to take account of the new global context where the LEMs are becoming so important. In essence, it needs to create and maintain a series of special relationships (or "G-2" arrangements) in which it teams up with the other key player in each issue area to both provide the needed global leadership and to manage the central bilateral relationship in that issue area more systematically and effectively.

At least four such arrangements can be envisaged. The first, and broadest, would be with the European Union (C. Fred Bergsten and Caio Koch-Weser, "Restoring the Transatlantic Alliance," *Financial Times,* October 6, 2003). In addition to the "trade G-2," which has existed for many years, there are several issues on which only these two largest and most sophisticated players can take an effective lead: competition policy, where extensive cooperation already exists but has broken down in a number of high-profile cases; international capital markets (Draghi and Pozen 2004); international currency markets, perhaps to deal with the euro-dollar exchange rate during the coming adjustment period as well as systemic questions when and if the euro does begin to move up alongside the dollar; and possibly development assistance, investment, migration, and several others (Bergsten and Koch-Weser 2004).

Europe's lack of dynamic growth, however, means that it has now ceded its position as the world's second growth locomotive (along with the United States) to China. Indeed, in 2000–03 China accounted for over 20 percent of the expansion in world trade and has become the chief driver of prices in many global commodity markets—which means inter alia that it will be an essential player in any attempt to stabilize the international energy regime. A hard or even prolonged landing in China over the next few years, as a result, could have a major impact on the world economy. Moreover, as noted throughout this volume, China's exchange rate and related policies are playing a central role in the adjustment (or lack thereof) in the world's major international economic imbalances centered on the US current account deficit. China's trade policies, especially implementation of its WTO commitments, and other countries' behavior toward it in the WTO (as the Multi-Fiber Arrangement [MFA] expires, for example), will go far to determine the success of the global trading system. Hence the United States and China need to develop an informal "G-2" relationship to address all these issues together on a systematic and cooperative basis.

A third "special relationship" needs to be maintained with Saudi Arabia to address energy policy. It was stressed earlier that a new multilateral regime, bringing together the main producing and consuming countries, is essential to reduce the enormous instabilities in the global energy market and to bring prices much closer to levels that would be generated by market forces. Within such a broader grouping, however, the leaders of the two camps would have to steer the process. The currently tense state of affairs in the Middle East, and the hostilities toward the United States throughout the Arab world due to Iraq and the Palestinian question, will undoubtedly make it harder to construct such a relationship. At the same time, development of such ties might help ameliorate overall relations and carry some spillover benefits for the broader issues.

The United States will also need to strengthen its existing "G-2" relationship with Japan to protect its economic (and broader strategic) interests in East Asia. In part, the goal here is simply to maintain a counterweight against the rise of China in classic balance-of-power terms. In the context of growing East Asian tendencies toward regional economic cooperation, however, Japan's stance will be particularly critical for the United States. China will increasingly be the leader of these regional initiatives but none will proceed very far, particularly in the crucial areas of finance and trade, without active cooperation by Japan—still by far the region's richest country, source of capital and top companies, and technological leader. Japan thus has considerable leverage to shape the nature of East Asian regionalism in an outward-looking manner that will be compatible with the interests of the United States, defined in terms of both its narrow commercial interests and its broader systemic focus on continued credibility of the IMF, WTO, and other multilateral institutions (Bergsten, Ito, and Noland 2001).

Japan strayed sharply from such a course with its initial proposal for an Asian Monetary Fund in 1997 that carried an overtly anti-Washington orientation. Given the progress of East Asian cooperation since that time, the United States now might not be able to torpedo such an idea nearly so easily. Hence Japan's recent sensitivity to American concerns, in shaping the substance and rhetoric of the Chiang Mai Initiative on finance (Henning 2002) and other pan-Asian steps, has been extremely important to the United States. Japan's cooperation with the United States in both Afghanistan and Iraq has of course added a further security dimension to the ties between the two countries.

The best way to pursue this particular "G-2" would be through negotiation of either an FTAAP, for which Japan–United States agreement would be a crucial pillar, or a bilateral Japan–United States FTA. In addition to the trade policy benefits enumerated earlier, such a major institutional step would provide the framework for broader Japan–United States cooperation on a wide range of international economic topics. It would thus serve a number of important US objectives and should be part of any new agenda for US foreign economic policy.

Whatever the outcome of these efforts to create new steering committees and avenues to pursue US interests, the United States will maintain a strong stake in the effective functioning of the existing multilateral economic institutions—especially the IMF, World Bank, and WTO. Indeed, one of the central goals of the proposed new subgroups, whether the series of new "G-2s" or the encouragement of the G-20 to steadily supplant the ineffective G-7, is to strengthen the performance of these formal organizations by providing them with more effective leadership. Moreover, new multilateral institutions may be needed to manage the proposed stabilization arrangement for world oil prices and to coordinate new global environmental initiatives (Esty 1994). Such organizations will be essential for the successful pursuit of US political and security as well as economic interests around the world.

Conclusions

The agenda for US foreign economic policy over the next few years is very full. A number of issues, especially the exploding current account deficit and energy prices, need to be addressed immediately with decisive new strategies. Trade policy and development policy must be recalibrated modestly and pursued consistently. Expanded domestic policies will be essential to counter the backlash against globalization, consolidating the huge gains that it has brought the United States and enabling it to pursue the very large additional benefits that are available by restoring a firm political foundation on which an outward-oriented international stance can be sustained. All this must be done within a rapidly evolving global economic framework with the expanded European Union moving up alongside the United States as the world's largest economy and China, with the rest of Asia not far behind, becoming an economic superpower as well.

The president and Congress will have to work closely together to initiate key parts of this process soon after taking office in early 2005. They will need to launch a credible and effective program to reduce the budget deficit substantially over the next few years, to begin the process of reducing the current account deficit as well as to avoid higher interest rates and crowding out of private investment. They should adopt a series of new energy policies, some of which (notably a new gasoline tax of perhaps $1 per gallon) could also be part of the budget program while others (especially to increase domestic energy production, including of renewables as well as of traditional carbon fuels) would be added separately. A series of trade bills must be passed in early 2005, particularly to renew TPA so that the president can maintain an active and progressive program of trade negotiations. Special priority must be attached to strengthening the safety nets for workers dislocated by trade flows and other ramifications of globalization, and even more so to expanding and improving education and training programs to enable more Americans to take advantage of the opportunities generated by international trade and investment, hopefully with the full support of organized labor. Full funding for development initiatives must be pursued.

With this domestic foundation in place, the administration should be able to pursue the ambitious international agenda outlined in this chapter and detailed in subsequent chapters. It will need to work closely with its G-7 colleagues, and especially with China and other key Asian countries, to maintain the gradual and orderly downward adjustment of the exchange rate of the dollar, which began in 2002–03 and resumed in late 2004, until it has gone far enough to restore a sustainable US current account position. It will need to promptly approach the other major oil-importing countries, both via the IEA and bilaterally in the case of key developing countries (notably China and India), to initiate any cooperative program of sales from their strategic reserves that is needed to counter high world oil prices in the short run and to prepare for a joint approach to the oil-exporting countries in pursuit of a new international price stabilization agreement for the longer run. The United States will probably want to simultaneously approach Saudi Arabia, and perhaps some of the other main oil exporters, to pave the way for the consumer-producer negotiations that will be needed to effect such a new energy regime.

Another element of the proposed new international energy policy is the development of a North American energy strategy that promotes greater investment in energy production and distribution channels in all three NAFTA countries. To get this, the United States may have to offer "concessions" on migration and other border issues. These initiatives can, however, be structured in ways that will also advance US interests and essentially convert the existing trade pact into a much broader security agreement.

A number of additional trade policy initiatives should be pursued once TPA has been extended to 2007, confirming that date as the target for completing negotiations for both the Doha Round in the WTO and an FTAA. The United States should alter its priorities in the Doha Round to an important degree, placing even greater emphasis on maximum reduction of agricultural subsidies (including to help reduce the US budget deficit) and extensive liberalization of services markets (to help reduce the US current account deficit over time without additional dollar depreciation). The United States should strongly support a new initiative in APEC to pursue an FTAAP, in part to deploy the competitive liberalization strategy aggressively in promoting support for a meaningful Doha Round outcome with the European Union and other non-APEC countries. A series of new bilateral FTAs, with larger countries such as Japan and/or Korea as well as India and Egypt, should be pursued as well. All these trade initiatives should be viewed as an integral part of US development policy, in light of the substantial gains they can generate for poor countries and especially for poor people within them, as well as for their benefits for the United States itself and for the world economy.

The cumulative result of these several initiatives, if successful, would be threefold. First, there would be sizable additional benefits for the US economy: perhaps $250 billion or so per year from reducing and stabilizing energy prices, another $150 billion to $200 billion annually over the longer run from a successful Doha Round once its results were fully phased in, additional modest gains from new FTAs, and sharp reduction of the risk of a hard landing if the current account deficit were permitted to spiral upward and the dollar to crash.

Second, the world economy as a whole would derive substantial benefits. Other countries would gain even more than the United States from overcoming the global imbalances in a noncrisis manner, by avoiding both a hard landing and the continued escalation of US protectionism that would otherwise be spurred by dollar overvaluation. The rest of the world would gain at least twice as much as the United States, perhaps as much as half a trillion dollars per year, from restoration of market-related energy prices. Developing countries would derive particular benefits from continued reductions in (their own and others') trade barriers. More subtly, but perhaps even more importantly, the world as a whole would gain enormously from US adoption of new domestic programs that would decisively roll back the constant threats of protectionism and other internal reactions against globalization.

Third, vigorous pursuit of such a foreign economic policy would go far to restore US global leadership in overall foreign policy as well as purely economic terms. It should thus be extremely welcome around the world at this time. Indeed, it is quite possible that new economic initiatives of this type, encompassing important new negotiations with countries and regions ranging from Europe through the Middle East to East Asia, could play an important catalytic role in strengthening overall relationships that have been frayed in recent years both by the Iraq war and by more widely perceived US deviations from international norms and prior agreements.

There is thus a compelling case for the early adoption of new foreign economic policy initiatives by the United States. Some, as with the dollar and energy, are urgently needed to head off severe risks for both the US and world economies as well as to address longer-term structural problems. Others, as on trade and its domestic ramifications, turn more on potential long-run and systemic benefits. All bear directly on major economic and foreign policy interests of the United States.

Both the proposed currency and energy initiatives would seek in large part to counter market manipulation by other countries. China and others in Asia have been intervening massively in the currency markets to block the needed reduction of the US current account deficit. Saudi Arabia and other oil producers have been restricting output and doing whatever else they can to raise the world oil price, often with considerable success, for over three decades. Some observers will object to proposals for new governmental measures, carried out and led by the United States, to counter-intervene in these same markets. But it is folly to stand by idly when other powerful players actively seek to distort markets, especially in ways that are detrimental to US interests in very substantial ways. The only test should be whether practical methods can be found to effectively counter those distortions and thus to restore outcomes that would conform much more closely to those that would result from market forces.

Partly because of this problem of market manipulation, it may be necessary for the United States to "get tough" to achieve some of the goals set out here. The administration may have to impose new trade barriers against countries that refuse to let their currencies adjust against the dollar, as the Nixon administration did with its import surcharge against developed countries for three months in 1971, or at least threaten to do so. It may have to intervene in the currency markets to counter directly the unwillingness of some countries to let their exchange rates appreciate. It may have to provide preferential treatment for imports from oil-producing countries that agree to participate in constructive price stabilization arrangements and discriminate against those that do not. It would obviously be far preferable to work out all these problems through cooperative means but it is not clear that such methods will succeed on all fronts.

The rest of this book will analyze in depth the key issues facing US foreign economic policy in the early part of the 21st century, assess the impact of each on both the US and world economies (and, in some cases, on broader foreign policy concerns as well), and present proposals for addressing them. We hope they will provide a solid foundation for the adoption of a new international economic strategy for the United States for the next decade.

References

Baily, Martin Neil. 2003. Persistent Dollar Swings and the US Economy. In *Dollar Overvaluation and the World Economy*, eds., C. Fred Bergsten and John Williamson. Washington: Institute for International Economics.

Baily, Martin Neil, and Jacob Kirkegaard. 2004. *Transforming the European Economy*. Washington: Institute for International Economics.

Baily, Martin Neil, and Robert Z. Lawrence. Forthcoming. What Happened to the Great American Job Machine? The Impact of Trade and Electronic Offshoring. *Brookings Papers on Economic Activity 2:2004*. Washington: Brookings Institution.

Baldwin, Robert E. 2003. *The Decline of US Labor Unions and the Role of Trade*. Washington: Institute for International Economics.

Baucus, Max. 2004. Toward a Strong Asia Trade Policy. Speech delivered at the First Annual Asia Forum, September 21, Washington, United States Senate Committee on Finance. http://finance.senate.gov/press/Bpress/2004press/prb092104b.pdf.

Bergsten, C. Fred. 1994. APEC and World Trade: A Force for Worldwide Liberalization. *Foreign Affairs* 73, no. 3 (May/June): 20–26.

Bergsten, C. Fred. 1996a. Globalizing Free Trade. *Foreign Affairs* 75, no. 3 (May/June): 105–20.

Bergsten, C. Fred. 1996b. *Competitive Liberalization and Global Free Trade: A Vision for the Early 21st Century.* Washington: Institute for International Economics.

Bergsten, C. Fred. 2001. America's Two-Front Economic Conflict. *Foreign Affairs* 80, no. 2 (March/April): 16–27.

Bergsten, C. Fred. 2004a. The G-20 and the World Economy. *World Economics* 5, no. 3 (July–September): 27–36.

Bergsten, C. Fred. 2004b. Toward a Free Trade Area of the Pacific. Remarks at the APEC CEO Summit, Santiago, Chile, November 19.

Bergsten, C. Fred, and C. Randall Henning. 1996. *Global Economic Leadership and the Group of Seven.* Washington: Institute for International Economics.

Bergsten, C. Fred, Takatoshi Ito, and Marcus Noland. 2001. *No More Bashing: Building a New Japan–United States Economic Relationship.* Washington: Institute for International Economics.

Bergsten, C. Fred, and Caio Koch-Weser. 2004. The Transatlantic Strategy Group on Economics, Finance and Trade. In *From Alliance to Coalitions—The Future of Transatlantic Relations,* eds., Werner Weidenfeld et al. Gütersloh, Germany: Bertelsmann Foundation Publishers.

Bergsten, C. Fred, and John Williamson. 1983. Exchange Rates and Trade Policy. In *Trade Policy in the 1980s,* ed., William R. Cline. Washington: Institute for International Economics.

Bergsten, C. Fred, and John Williamson. 2003. *Dollar Overvaluation and the World Economy.* Washington: Institute for International Economics.

Bergsten, C. Fred, and John Williamson. 2004. *Dollar Adjustment: How Far? Against What?* Washington: Institute for International Economics.

Bhalla, Surjit S. 2002. *Imagine There's No Country: Poverty, Inequality, and Growth in the Era of Globalization.* Washington: Institute for International Economics.

Brown, Drusilla K., Alan V. Deardorff, and Robert M. Stern. 2003. *Developing Countries' Stake in the Doha Round.* Research Seminar in International Economics Discussion Paper 495. Ann Arbor, MI: University of Michigan School of Public Policy (June).

Clemens, Michael A., Steven Radelet, and Rikhil Bhavnani. 2004. *Counting Chickens When They Hatch: The Short-term Effect of Aid on Growth.* CGD Working Paper 44. Washington: Center for Global Development.

Cline, William R. 1992. *The Economics of Global Warming.* Washington: Institute for International Economics.

Cline, William R. 2004. *Trade Policy and Global Poverty.* Washington: Institute for International Economics.

Commission on Capital Flows to Africa. 2003. *A Ten-Year Strategy for Increasing Capital Flows to Africa.* Commission on Capital Flows to Africa. New York: Corporate Council on Africa.

Draghi, Mario, and Robert Pozen. 2004. US-EU Regulatory Convergence: Capital Markets Issues. In *From Alliance to Coalitions—The Future of Transatlantic Relations,* eds., Werner Weidenfeld et al. Gütersloh, Germany: Bertelsmann Foundation Publishers.

Elliott, Kimberly, and Richard B. Freeman. 2003. *Can Labor Standards Improve under Globalization?* Washington: Institute for International Economics.

Esty, Dan C. 1994. *Greening the GATT: Trade, Environment, and the Future.* Washington: Institute for International Economics.

Fratzscher, Marcel. 2004. Exchange Rate Policy Strategies and Foreign Exchange Interventions in the Group of Three Economies. In *Dollar Adjustment: How Far? Against What?*

eds., C. Fred Bergsten and John Williamson. Washington: Institute for International Economics.

Funabashi, Yoichi. 1988. *Managing the Dollar: From the Plaza to the Louvre*. Washington: Institute for International Economics.

Funabashi, Yoichi. 1995. *Asia Pacific Fusion: Japan's Role in APEC*. Washington: Institute for International Economics.

Galal, Ahmed, and Robert Lawrence. 2005 (forthcoming). *A US-Egypt Free Trade Agreement*. Washington: Institute for International Economics.

Goldman Sachs. 2003. *Dreaming with BRICs: The Path to 2050*. Goldman Sachs Global Economics Paper 99.

Goldstein, Morris. 2003. China's Exchange Rate Regime. Testimony before the Subcommittee on Domestic and International Monetary Policy, Trade, and Technology Committee on Financial Services, US House of Representatives, Washington, October 1.

Goldstein, Morris. 2004. *Adjusting China's Exchange Rate Policies*. Working Paper 04-1 (June). Washington: Institute for International Economics.

Henning, C. Randall. 2002. *East Asian Financial Cooperation*. POLICY ANALYSES IN INTERNATIONAL ECONOMICS 68. Washington: Institute for International Economics.

Hufbauer, Gary C., and Paul Grieco. 2004. *Senator Kerry on Corporate Tax Reform: Right Diagnosis, Wrong Prescription*. International Economics Policy Brief 04-3 (April). Washington: Institute for International Economics.

Hufbauer, Gary C., and Paul Grieco. Forthcoming. *US Taxation of Business in a Global Economy*. Washington: Institute for International Economics.

Hufbauer, Gary C., and Rita M. Rodriguez. 2001. *The Ex-Im Bank in the 21st Century: A New Approach?* Special Report 14. Washington: Institute for International Economics.

Hufbauer, Gary C., Jeffrey J. Schott, and Kimberly Ann Elliott. 1982. *Economic Sanctions Reconsidered*. Washington: Institute for International Economics.

Hufbauer, Gary C., Jeffrey J. Schott, and Kimberly Ann Elliott. 1990. *Economic Sanctions Reconsidered, 2nd Edition*. Washington: Institute for International Economics.

Hufbauer, Gary C., Jeffrey J. Schott, and Kimberly Ann Elliott. 2005 (forthcoming). *Economic Sanctions Reconsidered, 3rd Edition*. Washington: Institute for International Economics.

Hufbauer, Gary C., and Yee Wong. 2004. *China Bashing 2004*. International Economics Policy Brief 04-5 (September). Washington: Institute for International Economics.

Kletzer, Lori G. 2001. *Job Loss from Imports: Measuring the Costs*. Washington: Institute for International Economics.

Krugman, Paul. 2003. *The Great Unraveling: Losing Our Way in the New Century*. New York: W.W. Norton & Company.

Kubelec, Christopher. 2004. Intervention When Exchange Rate Misalignments Are Large. In *Dollar Adjustment: How Far? Against What?* eds., C. Fred Bergsten and John Williamson. Washington: Institute for International Economics.

Lawrence, Robert Z., and Rajesh Chadha. 2004 (forthcoming). Should a US–India FTA Be Part of India's Trade Strategy? In *India Policy Forum 2004*, ed., Suman Bery and Barry Bosworth. New Delhi and Washington: National Council of Applied Economic Research (NCAER) and Brookings Institution.

Mann, Catherine L. 2003. *Globalization of IT Services and White Collar Jobs: The Next Wave of Productivity Growth*. International Economics Policy Brief 03-11. Washington: Institute for International Economics.

Mann, Catherine L. 2004a. Managing Exchange Rates: Achievement of Global Re-balancing or Evidence of Global Co-dependency. In *Journal of National Association for Business Economics* 34, no. 3 (July): 20–29.

Mann, Catherine L. 2004b. The US Current Account, New Economy Services, and Implications for Sustainability. *Review of International Economics*.

Moran, Theodore. 2003. *Reforming OPIC for the 21st Century*. POLICY ANALYSES IN INTERNATIONAL ECONOMICS 69 (May). Washington: Institute for International Economics.

Peterson, Peter G. 2004. *Running on Empty: How the Democratic and Republican Parties are Bankrupting Our Future and What Americans Can Do About It*. New York: Farrar, Straus and Giroux.

Posen, Adam S. 2004. *What Went Right in Japan*. International Economics Policy Brief 04-6. Washington: Institute for International Economics.

Posen, Adam S. 2005 (forthcoming). *The Euro at Five: Ready for a Global Role?* Washington: Institute for International Economics.

Radelet, Steven. 2003. *Challenging Foreign Aid: A Policymaker's Guide to the Millennium Challenge Account*. Washington: Institute for International Economics.

Richardson, J. David. Forthcoming. *Global Forces, American Faces: US Economic Globalization at the Grass Roots*. Washington: Institute for International Economics.

Rubin, Robert, and Jacob Weisburg. 2003. *In an Uncertain World: Tough Choices From Wall Street to Washington*. London: Random House.

Scheve, Kenneth F., and Matthew J. Slaughter. 2001. *Globalization and the Perceptions of American Workers*. Washington: Institute for International Economics.

Schott, Jeffrey J., ed. 2004. *Free Trade Agreements: US Strategies and Priorities*. Washington: Institute for International Economics.

Scollay, Robert. 2001. *New Regional Trading Arrangements in the Asia Pacific?* POLICY ANALYSES IN INTERNATIONAL ECONOMICS 63 (May). Washington: Institute for International Economics.

Srinivasan, T. N., and Suresh D. Tendulkar. 2003. *Reintegrating India with the World Economy*. Washington: Institute for International Economics.

US Chamber of Commerce. 2003. *International Policy Objectives for 2003 and Beyond*. Washington (February).

Williamson, John. 1998. Crawling Bands or Monitoring Bands: How to Manage Exchange Rates in a World of Capital Mobility. *International Finance* (Inaugural Edition).

Williamson, John. 2000. *Exchange Rate Regimes for Emerging Markets: Reviving the Intermediate Option*. POLICY ANALYSES IN INTERNATIONAL ECONOMICS 60. Washington: Institute for International Economics.

Zoellick, Robert B. 2001. American Trade Leadership: What Is at Stake? Speech before the Institute for International Economics, Washington, September 24.

II

THE POLICY CONTEXT

2

The Payoff to America from Global Integration

SCOTT C. BRADFORD, PAUL L. E. GRIECO, and GARY CLYDE HUFBAUER

Since the end of the Second World War, the United States has led the world in negotiating freer international trade and investment. Eight multilateral bargains have been concluded under the auspices of the General Agreement on Tariffs and Trade (GATT) and its institutional successor, the World Trade Organization (WTO). GATT/WTO agreements have been supplemented by regional and bilateral pacts, notably the European Union, the North American Free Trade Agreement (NAFTA), and numerous other regional and bilateral free trade agreements (FTAs).

Postwar commercial negotiations, both in GATT/WTO and in regional accords such as NAFTA, have devoted far greater attention to trade barriers than investment barriers. In fact, most investment liberalization over the past 50 years has resulted from unilateral policies, as one country after another has sought to improve its standing in the global beauty contest. Various international agreements cemented unilateral liberalization: OECD codes, bilateral tax and investment treaties, and chapters in trade agreements (e.g., Chapter 11 in NAFTA). While investment liberalization largely reflects national policy initiatives rather than international accords, the benefits of trade and investment liberalization go hand in hand.

Scott C. Bradford is assistant professor at the department of economics, Brigham Young University. Paul L. E. Grieco is a research assistant at the Institute for International Economics. Gary Clyde Hufbauer is the Reginald Jones Senior Fellow at the Institute for International Economics.

Box 2.1 Channels through which trade increases output[1]

Comparative advantage. David Ricardo's classic analysis, which dates to 1816, holds that free trade between countries with different cost structures enables each nation to specialize in producing goods that it makes most efficiently relative to its trading partners and import goods that it makes less efficiently. Trade thereby allows a country to consume more goods than it could produce on its own with the same resource endowments (capital, land, and labor).

Economies of scale. Firms and industries become more efficient when they increase their output, both during a year and over a period of years. At the firm level, scale economies result from spreading fixed costs—such as plant and research outlays—over a larger quantity of output. Firms also capture scale economies by discovering and applying better techniques as they repeat their production cycles again and again over a period of years. At the industry level, scale economies result from sharing experience as skilled personnel move between more firms and as each firm learns from the best practice of numerous competitors. Freer trade enables both firms and industries to achieve greater economies of scale by enabling them to sell to a larger market and to interact with more firms in the same industry.

Technological spillovers. International trade and investment flows increase the speed at which new production and distribution techniques spread from country to country, increasing the level of productivity in all countries. Innovations created by market leaders—such as Siemens, Sony, Intel, and Wal-Mart—are shared with (or emulated by) less advanced firms and countries through investment and trade. These firms and countries enjoy the potential for closing their productivity gap more quickly than if they had to create the technology themselves. At the same time, a firm with operations

(box continues next page)

Deeper investment ties foster more intense trading relationships and vice versa (Graham 2000, appendix B).

Almost all economists advocate trade liberalization as a proven method of increasing national income (measured by gross domestic product, GDP) and thereby per capita GDP and GDP per household. Contrary to popular wisdom, which celebrates exports and questions imports, economists attribute gains to *both* exports and imports. Indeed, imports are often a more important driver of economic growth than exports.

Before summarizing the gains already realized through postwar trade and investment liberalization, and the gains that remain to be harvested through future liberalization, we briefly identify four basic channels through which exports and imports increase income; these channels are discussed further in box 2.1:

- Comparative advantage allows countries to specialize in those goods they are relatively efficient at producing.
- Economies of scale occur when firms spread fixed cost by producing for a larger market.

Box 2.1 *(continued)*

spread throughout the world is best positioned to acquire new techniques wherever they may be created.

Import competition. While import competition is politically sensitive, rising imports boost the incomes not only of buyers (both households in their daily shopping and firms as they purchase intermediate inputs) but also of domestic competitors as they improve their performance in response to the loss of market share.

- *Consumers benefit directly:* When more firms compete for market share—either through exports or foreign direct investment (FDI)—household consumers and industrial purchasers benefit in two distinct ways. First, market entrants erode the monopolistic power of local suppliers, with the consequence that markup margins are compressed. Second, consumers can choose from a wider variety of products and thus achieve a closer match between their own needs and the available array of goods and services.
- *Domestic productivity increases:* When buyers (whether firms or households) shift from domestic products to imports, less productive domestic firms in import-competing industries lose market share. These firms either shrink or boost their own productivity. Some unproductive firms will be forced to close. The reallocation of resources that results when unproductive firms shed capital and labor may be politically unpopular, but it enables more productive firms to expand, thereby benefiting the economy as a whole.

1. To some extent, the channels overlap and reinforce one another.

- Technological spillovers accelerate the dissemination of technology throughout the world.
- Import competition reduces the monopoly power of domestic firms.

In light of the hugely successful postwar record of trade and investment liberalization, this chapter summarizes the payoff to the United States as a nation and to average individuals and households.[1] We draw on the ex-

1. We do not dwell on the security benefits from freer trade, but in the mind of Cordell Hull (Franklin Roosevelt's secretary of state from 1933 to 1944) Depression-era trade restrictions were a contributing cause of the Second World War. Hull believed that a postwar agenda of freer trade would serve as a bulwark for peace. In Europe, Jean Monnet—sometimes referred to as the architect of the European Union—viewed freer trade as an essential element of a plan to unite Europe and ensure peaceful relations on the continent and avoid a third world war. Another aspect of postwar trade history that we mention and pass over is the enormous drive that US economic policy imparted to the world commercial system. Without US leadership, it would have been difficult or impossible for other nations to slash their barriers and open their markets. In the first decades after the war, Europe, Japan, and the

isting empirical literature to quantify these various gains. To this end, we survey different methodologies and estimates; taken together they suggest very substantial past and future payoffs to the United States from expanded trade and investment ties with the global economy. We express gains in three common metrics: contribution to total GDP, GDP per capita, and GDP per household in 2003 (all measured in 2003 dollars). Since policy liberalization and lower transportation and communication costs permanently raise national income (unless liberalization is rolled back, as in the 1930s), these gains are enjoyed annually.[2]

Table 2.1 previews our results. We use four very different methods to estimate past gains. Each of these methods entails its own set of assumptions. Estimated annual gains are on the order of $1 trillion. The estimated gain in 2003 income is in the range of $2,800 to $5,000 additional income for the average person and between $7,100 and $12,900 for the average household. Future gains are harder to quantify, not surprisingly since the future is always difficult to predict. The estimates range from $450 billion to $1.3 trillion.

Although we express estimated gains in a comparable metric, the methods themselves are not directly comparable. In table 2.2, we summarize the basic differences between the methods and leave further explanation to the remaining sections. Some methods tally gains only on the production side of the economy, while others do so only on the consumption side. More importantly, some of the methods focus solely on liberalization policy (the outcome of multilateral, regional, and bilateral agreements, as well as unilateral policy changes) while others include deeper trade integration resulting from better transportation and communication technologies (e.g., container ships, air freight, and voice and data transmission), and an income elasticity of demand for imported products that exceeds unity.[3] As might be expected, methods that focus solely on policy reforms indicate somewhat smaller gains than methods that combine the effects of policy reforms, technological innovation, and rising income. Since we do not attempt to guess the pace of future innovation, or the

Asian tigers all came to view participation in the world economy as central to their development strategies. Chile, Mexico, China, and even India have followed suit. Widespread adoption of market-oriented policies, including freer trade and investment, contributed to the best half-century of world economic growth since the time of Christ (Maddison 2003, table 8b; Bhalla 2002).

2. For simplicity, our calculations leave aside arguments that liberalization can permanently increase the *rate* of per capita income growth (Romer 1996, Baldwin and Forslid 2000) and instead concentrate on the one-time boost in the *level* of per capita income due to economic integration. This tenet of "endogenous growth theory" implies that our calculations understate the total gains, perhaps by a great deal.

3. When the income elasticity of demand for imported products exceeds unity, the ratio of trade to GDP will rise as income rises. This has been the case within the United States during the postwar era (Marquez 2002, chapter 3).

Table 2.1 Summary of results: Past and future annual payoff from US trade and investment liberalization

Method	Methodology source	Percent of 2003 GDP	2003 billion dollars	2003 dollars per capita	2003 dollars per household
Past gains					
Output elasticity (1950–2003)	OECD (2003)	13.2	1,451	5,000	12,900
Sifting and sorting (1947–2003)[a]	Bernard et al. (2003)	8.6	940	3,200	8,400
Smoot-Hawley CGE (1947–2003)[a]	Bradford and Lawrence (2004b)	7.3	800	2,800	7,100
Intermediate imports (1960–2001)[b]	Richardson (2004)	9.6	1,058	3,635	9,377
Future gains					
Global free trade CGE	Brown, Deardorff, and Stern (2003)	5.5	600	2,000	5,000
Market fragmentation	Bradford and Lawrence (2004a)	4.1	450	1,500	4,000
US-world FTA	Rose (2003) and OECD (2003)	12.0	1,307	4,500	11,600
Memorandum:					
2003 GDP (trillions of 2003 dollars)	11				
2003 population (millions)	291				
2003 GDP per capita (2003 dollars)	37,748				
2003 GDP per household (2003 dollars)	97,390				

CGE = computable general equilibrium model
FTA = free trade agreement

a. Includes estimate of gains due to increased product variety between 1972 and 2001, 2.8 percent of GDP (Broda and Weinstein 2004).
b. Presented in appendix 2A.

Source: Authors' calculations.

Table 2.2 Methodology comparisions

Method	Source of growth	Products counted	Gains realized in
Past gains			
Output elasticity (1950–2003)	Policy and technology	All merchandise and services	Production and consumption
Product variety (1972–2001)	Policy and technology	All merchandise	Consumption
Sifting and sorting (1947–2003)	Policy	All merchandise	Production[a]
Smoot-Hawley CGE (1947–2003)	Policy	All merchandise	Production and consumption[a]
Intermediate imports (1960–2001)[b]	Policy and technology	Manufacturing	Production
Potential future gains			
Global free trade CGE	Policy	All merchandise and services	Production and consumption
Market fragmentation	Policy	All merchandise and services[c]	Production and consumption
US-world FTA	Policy	All merchandise	Production and consumption

a. The estimates shown in table 2.1 for these methods incorporate the estimate for the product variety method.

b. Presented in appendix 2A.

c. The reported calculations are extrapolated from potential benefits from liberalizating merchandise trade in industrial countries.

future rise in GDP, our estimates of potential gains focus strictly on the consequences of policy liberalization.[4]

Finally, some of the methods measure the effect of liberalization only in merchandise trade (leaving aside services) or specifically in manufactures trade (leaving aside agriculture and minerals, as well as services). While trade in manufactured goods has been the focus of postwar liberalization, attention is increasingly drawn to agriculture and services. Our estimates suggest that gains due to liberalization of services trade will be a much higher component of future gains than past gains. This is partly a measurement issue. Some of the methods used to estimate past gains simply neglect services. In addition to measurement issues, a change may be taking place in the relative importance of goods trade versus services trade. With Internet technology, and widespread FDI in services, the international exchange of services could outstrip trade in goods within a few decades.

4. Our estimates of potential future gains should be viewed as the gains from wholesale reforms that would move the current trading system to *complete* liberalization. Ongoing negotiations (WTO Doha Development Round, Free Trade Area of the Americas, among others) are not that ambitious.

The Payoff from Past Liberalization

First, we consider how far the world has come since 1945. The initial round of GATT negotiations (the Geneva Round) was completed in 1947 between 23 countries. The current Doha Development Round, the ninth set of multilateral negotiations, includes 147 countries. Meanwhile, important regional and bilateral agreements have been concluded. In this section, we present three calculations of the payoff from past trade and investment liberalization, accompanied in some of the calculations by the trade-enhancing benefits of lower transportation and communication costs. (Estimates from the product variety method are not presented as standalone estimates of postwar gains. In table 2.1, the consumer benefits of enhanced product variety are grouped with producer benefits from greater efficiency.) A fourth methodology is reported in appendix 2A.

An important qualification applies to the calculations of past gains. Since the Second World War, the US economy has undergone tremendous transformation. Many of the inputs to our calculations (such as population, share of manufacturing value added, and labor productivity) rise or fall dramatically over the full period. For this reason, where possible, we break the full period down into several subperiods and then perform intermediate calculations to arrive at the total postwar gains.[5]

Output Elasticity: Cross-Country Estimates of Trade and Growth

The first approach draws on an OECD study designed to determine the sources of economic growth through cross-national econometric analysis (OECD 2003, chapter 2). The aim of the study was to identify economic attributes and policies that have the strongest effect on per capita income growth.[6] The study used a pooled mean group technique to estimate the effect of identified variables on per capita output. This technique allows a distinction between long-term determinants of growth and short-term fluctuations that are more likely to be country specific. Long-term determinants are expressed as level variables and are assumed to have the same effect in all countries.

5. However, the intermediate results that appear in the tables—gains *due* to liberalization—do *not* reflect gains realized solely during that subperiod. Most of the structural changes set in motion by trade openness take a decade or longer to mature in terms of greater productivity and higher income. Thus, our subperiod figures are an estimation of annual gains that will eventually result from policy liberalization or technology changes that occurred in the subperiod. We then add up subperiods to arrive at a final figure of annual gains due to policy and/or technology liberalization.

6. Among the attributes and policies are physical and human capital accumulation, inflation (both level and volatility), government spending, taxes, research and development spending, financial sophistication, and trade exposure.

Among other results, the OECD study calculates the positive effect on per capita income from a higher long-term level of trade exposure. The technique does not identify the individual channels through which increased trade increases per capita output; instead it imputes a broad relationship between the two based on their statistical correlation.[7] Interpreting the OECD study, we assume that it broadly captures the effect of all channels at play that lead from more trade to higher output.[8] Moreover, the OECD study uses observed trade exposure as its instrument (adjusted as described below), and does not explore the extent to which policy, technology, or other factors influenced the change in trade levels. Cline (1997, 265) makes a rough guess that about half the increase in trade levels reflects policy liberalization (lower tariffs, fewer quotas) and half reflects better transportation and communication technology. If this partition is roughly correct, then about half the estimated gains in the OECD study can be attributed to policy liberalization.

A traditional measure of merchandise trade exposure is the ratio of a country's total trade to GDP, expressed as (X+M)/GDP.[9] However this quantity is strongly influenced by a country's size and geography.[10] For example, Singapore, a small economy with a strategically placed port, has a trade exposure of over 100 percent. Such a figure would be incredible for a large country like the United States or Japan.[11] To control for country

7. Questions of causality (i.e., whether faster output growth increases trade or vice versa) and the possibility that omitted variables explain the statistical connection between trade and growth have bedeviled this line of inquiry (Berg and Krueger 2003, Hallak and Levinsohn 2004). Frankel and Romer (1999) use instrumental variables based on gravity models to make a strong case that trade causes growth rather than vice versa. Berg and Krueger (2003) survey the literature and summarize the cases for and against; they conclude that the literature shows that "openness is fairly robustly a cause of growth," although "there is substantial uncertainty surrounding these estimates."

8. This analysis also captures any effects of trade that would lower per capita output. For example, if a large number of workers were unemployed as a result of expanded trade, output would be depressed and the estimated coefficient would be reduced. As expected, the sign of the trade to output level coefficient is positive and statistically different from zero in all of the reported OECD regressions.

9. The OECD study uses a slightly different measure, (X/GDP) + [M/(GDP – X + M)], which scales imports by domestic consumption rather than GDP. The difference is slight, and we disregard it for clarity. Other studies, most notably Sachs and Warner (1995), have constructed policy-based indices in an attempt to focus directly on a liberal trade policy rather than trade levels. Rodriguez and Rodrik (2001) point out several methodological problems with these studies. However, other authors argue that the Sachs and Warner technique is relatively successful (Berg and Krueger 2003, Cline 2004).

10. Dollar and Kraay (2004) argue that while the level of trade exposure depends on size and geography, *changes* in the level of trade exposure over the medium term (e.g., a decade) do not depend on size or geography, since these factors are invariant in the medium term. We adopt this logic in our analysis of subperiods (table 2.3).

11. However, a large country enjoys the economic stimulus of *intra*national trade and investment, which boosts output according to the same channels as international trade and investment.

size, the OECD calculated a regression equation of trade exposure as determined by population size. The country residuals from the predicted regression equation values were then used to measure whether a country was relatively closed or open, given its population size.[12]

In order to estimate the response of per capita income to trade exposure, the OECD growth regression equation was written in log-log form.[13] The trade variable was lagged by one year. Across several specifications of the model, the long-term coefficient on trade exposure was consistently about 0.2 and statistically significant. On balance, holding everything else equal, a 10 percent rise in a country's long-term trade exposure (imports plus exports) results in a 2 percent increase in the level of annual per capita output (or income, which is the same thing).[14]

Comparing the OECD result with similar studies, Cline (2004, table 5.1) found the coefficient of 0.2 to be relatively low. One possible explanation is that the other studies surveyed by Cline covered a wider range of poorer countries than the comparatively affluent OECD area. Developing countries might well experience greater output gains from openness because they have more scope for adopting beneficial technology. If this explanation is correct, it means that the lower OECD coefficient is more appropriate for measuring the payoff to the United States from freer trade.

Armed with the estimate that a long-term increase in trade exposure boosts per capita output (or income) with an elasticity of 0.2, we can cal-

---

12. The residual is the difference between the actual value and the estimated value from the regression equation. If a country's actual trade exposure is greater than the "adjusted trade exposure" predicted by the model, the residual is positive, and the country is considered relatively open. The OECD study defines the "adjusted trade exposure" as the residual of the simple regression on population plus the constant term. In other words, "adjusted trade exposure" is the predicted trade exposure for the country after removing the effect of population.

13. The dependent variable was the natural logarithm of per capita output (income), while the independent variable of interest for our purposes was the natural logarithm of the trade exposure level adjusted for population (see previous footnote). With this formulation, the estimated coefficient represents an elasticity measure, namely the percentage change in per capita output for each 1 percent change in the adjusted trade exposure. We apply this elasticity to the percent change in actual US trade exposure to arrive at a figure for growth due to increased trade exposure. Assuming that changes in the population of the United States over the estimation periods (decades) are modest, the percent change in the actual trade exposure is a very close approximation to the percent change in adjusted trade exposure.

14. OECD (2003) explains its result by saying that a 10-percentage-*point* increase in trade exposure will typically result in a 4 percent increase in per capita output. The OECD assumes that typical trade exposure level is 50 percent of GDP. Thus, a 10-percentage-*point* increase from 50 to 60 percent of GDP represents a 20 percent increase in exposure, and 20 percent times 0.2 is a 4 percent increase in per capita output. For another example, the current US trade exposure is 24 percent, so a 10-percentage-point rise over the next decade would bring US trade exposure to 34 percent, a 42 percent increase in the exposure ratio. Under these hypothetical conditions, the OECD coefficient would predict an 8 percent increase in US per capita output.

Table 2.3 Output elasticity: Benefits of increased trade exposure

Year	Centered three-year trade exposure[a] (percent)	Period change (percent)	Per capita output growth due to trade[b]		Benefit in 2003[b,c] (billions of 2003 dollars)
			Percent	2003 dollars	
1950	8.8				
1960	9.2	4.5	0.9	112	33
1970	10.9	18.4	3.7	537	156
1980	19.8	81.8	16.4	3,213	935
1990	20.2	2.3	0.5	111	32
2003	23.7	17.0	3.4	1,011	294
Total				**4,986**	**1,451**

a. Calculated as (X+M)/GDP. 2003 figure is 2001–03 average.

b. Subperiod gains are an intermediate calculation, not an estimate of short-term gains from liberalization. Gains due to liberalization may require 10 to 20 years to be fully realized.

c. Benefit in 2003 is calculated by multiplying the benefit per capita measured in 2003 dollars by population in 2003.

Note: In order to better account for changes to the US economy over time, this table presents total gains from liberalization as the sum of subperiods. If instead a single calculation is used to estimate gains between 1950 and 2003, the total gains are estimated to be $1,218 billion. Numbers may not sum evenly due to rounding.

Sources: BEA (2004b), OECD (2003), and authors' calculations.

culate the effect of increased trade on GDP, per capita income, and household income. We apply the 0.2 coefficient to decadal changes in US trade exposure, using a three-year average centered on the decade turning year (1950, 1960, etc.) to dampen the effect of year-to-year fluctuations.

Table 2.3 shows the evolution of US trade exposure (including goods and services), together with the calculated payoff in terms of higher income levels. The fourth column is the eventual increase in per capita income, expressed in 2003 dollars, generated by the increase in trade exposure during each decade. The sum of this column, $5,000, is the total increase in per capita GDP resulting from deeper trade exposure in each of the decades between 1950 and 2003. The payoff of $5,000 per person represents 20 percent of the total per capita GDP gains over this period. It represents an additional $1.45 trillion of GDP, or a $12,900 increase in annual GDP per household.[15]

Product Variety

We now try to quantify a narrow portion of the benefits realized by domestic consumers. While this measure is significant in its own right, we

15. In 2003, the US population was 291.1 million persons, with an average of 2.58 persons per household (US Census Bureau 2003, table 65).

do not present it as a stand-alone estimate of postwar gains. Instead, where appropriate, we add the result to other methods that clearly do not account for variety-based gains in order to estimate the total payoff to the US economy.

Consumers gain when they are able to acquire a larger array of goods and services with the same budget. Import competition thus benefits consumers through lower prices and greater choice. Lower prices translate statistically into a reduced rate of inflation. However, it is far from clear that trade liberalization played a major role in the US disinflation process of the past two decades.[16] Nor is it clear—once inflation falls below the double-digit level—that further reductions contribute significantly to GDP growth. For both reasons, we do not pursue the anti-inflation line of analysis, but we do summarize the research in box 2.2.

Gains due to greater product variety would seem even more difficult to measure. A recent paper by Christian Broda and David E. Weinstein (2004) takes up the challenge. They find that the number of varieties available to US consumers increased by a factor of four between 1972 and 2001.[17] The benefits of new varieties are not taken into account in the conventional import price indexes, which evaluate price changes only for goods that are available in both periods. Broda and Weinstein attempt to remedy this shortcoming. They extend Feenstra's (1994) work on single goods to develop an aggregate "exact" price index.

To abbreviate their method, Broda and Weinstein hypothesize that the benefit of a new variety for a given good is positively related to expenditure on the new variety relative to existing varieties and negatively related to the elasticity of substitution between varieties of the good (if the varieties are perfectly substitutable, consumers will be indifferent to the introduction of a new variety). The Broda-Weinstein exact import price index implies that the conventional import price index overstated import inflation by 28.1 percent from 1972 to 2001 (an average overstatement of 1.2 percent—*not* percentage points—per year). Using product-level data on the fraction of imported goods in total consumption, the authors cal-

16. Clark (2004) reasoned that, while global inflation has fallen precipitously in the last two decades and while goods inflation (which is more susceptible to import competition) has declined relative to services inflation, much of the decline within the United States was due to dollar appreciation. In Clark's view, increased global competition played only a supporting role.

17. Broda and Weinstein (2004) define a variety as an 8-digit or 10-digit (HS or TSUSA system, respectively) good produced in a particular country for export to the United States. For example, if red wine is a product, French red wine is a single variety; Chilean red wine is a second variety. Given the way Broda and Weinstein measure variety, their estimate does not reflect the gains from greater variety introduced by US producers intending to meet an export market or preserve their domestic market share from foreign competition.

Box 2.2 Trade openness, inflation, and per capita output

Arguments can be made in both directions about the connection between trade openness and inflation. On the one hand, greater openness increases a country's exposure to foreign inflation generally and to industry-specific shocks, such as a surge in oil prices. When prices rise worldwide, an open country is more vulnerable, through higher import and export prices. On the other hand, increased trade openness reduces the power of domestic producers to raise prices and may permit a country to "export" its own inflationary policies (easy money and fiscal deficits) by borrowing from foreign capital markets.

Truman (2003) used cross-country data to analyze the connection between trade openness and inflation and found a small but significant and negative correlation. Using Truman's estimates, a 10-percentage-point increase in the trade openness coefficient reduces the annual inflation rate by as much as 0.2 percentage points.

The next question is the effect of a lower inflation rate on per capita output. In a cross-country regression of OECD countries, OECD (2003, table 2.8) found that a 1 percent reduction in the inflation level, acting through increased investment, would result in a 0.4 to 0.5 percent increase in per capita income. In addition, the study found that a 1 percent reduction in the volatility of inflation—measured as the three-year standard deviation—would directly affect economic efficiency and boost per capita income by 2 percent. However, this study covered the years 1971–98, bridging periods of high and low inflation, and the experience of the 1970s may have less salience in today's environment, where inflation rates are well below 10 percent.

It is generally accepted that extremely high rates of inflation have a disastrous effect on economic performance (Fischer, Sahay, and Végh 2002). However, there is little consensus on whether reducing an inflation rate that is already below 5 percent will significantly increase output. Andrés and Hernando (1997) estimate that, at inflation levels of 3 to 4 percent annually, a 1-percentage-point reduction in inflation will result in an average 1 percent increase in steady-state income. However, reviewing the inflation and growth literature, Fischer (1996) reports that "the overall conclusion must be that it is not possible at this stage to draw any firm conclusion on the relationship between inflation and growth at very low inflation rates. . . . The data leave open the possibility that there is a negative relationship between growth and inflation at rates of inflation as low as 1 to 3 percent. Or, there may be no significant relationship."

With the exception of the late 1970s and early 1980s, the United States has subscribed to low inflation policies since the Second World War, and greater openness over the past two decades played at most a supporting role in the disinflation process (Clark 2004). Even under optimistic assumptions, the contribution to GDP from trade-induced disinflation is likely to be modest. Therefore, we do not attempt to quantify the trade-inflation-output linkage.

culate that the increase in consumer purchasing power is the equivalent of a 2.8 percent increase in GDP, or $300 billion annually.[18]

This estimate of product variety benefit is a narrow measure of the total benefits to consumers from import competition—for example, it does *not* reflect the compression in markup margins as a result of import competi-

18. This estimate requires the assumption that an increase in imported variety has no effect on domestic varieties. If new foreign varieties substitute for domestic varieties, this model overstates variety-based income gains (see Rutherford and Tarr 2002). Alternatively, if foreign variety allows increased vertical specialization and complementary domestic varieties are introduced, income gains are understated.

tion. Since consumers realize product variety benefits in addition to the "standard" efficiency gains from greater international trade, we can combine the measured effect with some of the production-based estimates presented below.[19]

Sifting and Sorting: The Microdata

In this section, we consider the effects of liberalization and international integration on productivity.[20] In both traditional and new models of global market integration, "differences" are the foundation. Differences (on both a macro and micro scale) stimulate trade and investment and underpin the payoff from liberalization. The traditional and new models emphasize complementary differences:

- Traditional models emphasize differences across industries and countries in factor input intensities, differences across countries in factor endowments and technologies, and differences in the extent of scale economies between industries.
- New models add an emphasis on differences across *firms* in innovation, product differentiation, production techniques, productivity, and size.
- Traditional models show how a country's comparative advantage—defined in terms of differing degrees of competitive advantage across industries relative to global benchmarks—underlies its trade and investment performance.
- New models add reasons why competitive advantage at the *firm* level—relative to benchmark firms in the same industry at home and abroad—*also* underlie a country's trade and investment performance.

Microdata on individual plants make it possible to measure the differences between the new and old foundations for trade and investment. For almost every sector of the world economy, such measurements show that differences across firms *within* an industry are larger than differences *between* industries in characteristics of the average firm and larger also than most differences *between* countries in endowments, technologies, and other traditional determinants of trade. To quote one group of scholars (Foster, Haltiwanger, and Krizan 2001): "Within-sector differences dwarf between-sector differences in behavior." To quote another scholar: "A

19. Because the output elasticity method is based on a statistical correlation of openness and growth, without asserting how growth is achieved, we do not add the product variety method to that calculation.

20. Large portions of this section are paraphrased from Richardson (2004).

large number of studies have documented a strong correlation between firm exit and low [firm] productivity" (Melitz [2003, 1695], citing Roberts and Tybout [1996] and Davis and Haltiwanger [1999]). Quoting still another (Klein, Schuh, and Triest 2003, 10): "Membership in a particular broad *industry* group explains little of the behavior of job creation and job destruction for *firms* in the most narrowly defined industrial categories" (emphasis added).

The strong inference from such findings is that differences among firms are critical in tracing the payoff from global trade and investment. Some abbreviate this inference by saying that "differences *within* are as important as or more so than differences *between*" industries and countries. Several important messages emerge from the new models:[21]

- Increased global market opportunities—declining tariffs and transportation costs, declining start-up costs of marketing abroad, and opening of new, formerly closed foreign markets—can *all* cause favorable gains in industry-level and aggregate productivity. More productive firms tend to expand when they come into contact with the global market, while less productive firms tend to contract. The result is an increase in *average* productivity of the industry even though there may be *no* effect on any single firm's productivity. This can happen because more productive firms gain market share while less productive firms lose market share.

- The "sifting and sorting" mechanism by which these productivity gains emerge reflects market selection among heterogeneous firms that differ either in their inherent overall productivity or in their access to worker pools of varying skills, creativity, and reliability. As a result, (1) increased global market opportunities enable higher-productivity firms everywhere to begin exporting or to increase exporting; and (2) the ensuing cross-penetration of markets reduces the residual demand facing lower-productivity firms (which generally serve only domestic markets). The least productive firms are forced out of business.

- Models describe how the sifting and sorting mechanisms can affect productivity in *every* industry, whether export oriented or import oriented. However, the quantitative magnitude of the sifting and sorting is greatest in *export*-oriented industries, as is the corresponding job churning (job losses *and* job gains).

- Bernard and Jensen (2004) find that together, intraindustry and interindustry reallocation contribute roughly equally to account for 40

21. Summary points come from Melitz (2003); Yeaple (2003); and Bernard, Redding, and Schott (2004).

percent of all productivity growth in US manufacturing industries.[22] But sifting and sorting also *magnifies* the favorable productivity effects of deeper global integration because average productivity increases most in those industries that already constitute a country's comparative advantage, thereby magnifying the traditional gains from trade.

Drawing on the new view, some scholars have tried to estimate the firm-level payoff from trade and investment liberalization, where sifting and sorting is the main mechanism. Econometric results are still at a preliminary stage.[23] However, a simulation by Bernard et al. (2003) suggests that a 5 percent reduction of global trade barriers (tariffs and other costs expressed on an ad valorem basis) could lead to the closure of 3.3 percent of US firms. At the same time, according to their simulation, the sifting and sorting of resources toward more productive firms could boost overall US manufacturing productivity by 4.7 percent. In a moment, we borrow this simulation coefficient—approximately one-to-one—to calculate US productivity gains from the sifting and sorting process. But it is important to emphasize that the coefficient is derived from a model simulation, not a longitudinal estimate. The actual coefficient could be higher or lower than one-to-one.

US productivity research (without regard to global integration) has underscored the role of the sifting and sorting mechanisms that are emphasized in the new models. For example, almost half of the productivity growth of US manufacturing from 1977 into the late 1990s can be associated with entry, exit, and reallocation of market shares toward high-productivity plants and away from low-productivity plants (Foster, Haltiwanger, and Krizan 2001; and Foster, Haltiwanger, and Syverson 2004). Even stronger results are estimated for retailing and other services industries.[24]

22. Bernard and Jensen provide a wide range for this estimate. As a lower bound, some 8 percent of total factor productivity growth in the US manufacturing sector was due to sifting and sorting caused by export activity; as an upper bound the estimate was 65 percent.

23. Bernard, Jensen, and Schott (2003, table 3) used an econometric model to further examine this relationship. For the 67 US industries (at the SIC 4-digit level) that represent the upper one-third of industries in terms of OECD import penetration (e.g., industrial machinery, electronics, transportation equipment, and instruments), a 1 percent reduction in trade costs over five years led to a 1.6 percent increase in labor productivity. However, for all SIC 4-digit industries, the relationship was not statistically significant.

24. For example, in US retailing, virtually *all* of the 11.4 percent growth in labor productivity between 1987 and 1997 can be associated with new entry of higher-than-average-productivity retailers and exit of lower-than-average-productivity retailers (a little more than half for entry, a little less than half for exit). See Foster, Haltiwanger, and Krizan (2001, 2002). Note that only labor productivity growth is examined in the services industries, whereas both labor productivity and overall (total, or multifactor) productivity are evaluated in manufacturing, with similar findings.

Corroborating worldwide evidence can be found in case studies and panel econometric analysis. For example, Eslava et al. (2004) find that, for Colombian manufacturing, virtually all the productivity growth from 1982 to 1998 can be associated with growing market shares of high-productivity plants and shrinking market shares of low-productivity plants.[25] Other scholars have examined panel data to discern the effects of "competition" on aggregate productivity, both levels and growth. For example, Disney, Haskel, and Heden (2003) find that several indicators of competition correlate with accentuated plant-level productivity gains from sifting and sorting in British manufacturing from 1980 to 1992.[26]

The sifting and sorting methodology estimates production-based gains but from a "bottom-up" rather than "top-down" perspective. Gains are realized through the same channels as other methods that concentrate on production efficiencies: import competition, economies of scale, and comparative advantage; but the gains are examined at the firm level. At the grass roots, these microdata correlations between performance and global integration are impressive. While there is still no definitive method for "adding up" microdata patterns, we draw on the reported simulation coefficient—that a one-percentage-point decrease in trade barriers raises manufacturing productivity by about 1 percent (Bernard et al. 2003)—to make a guess.[27]

Other methods of summarizing gains are possible, but all require some speculation. In appendix 2A (based on Richardson 2004), we present a separate methodology that examines the growing use of intermediate imports in US manufacturing. The intermediate imports method calculates benefits of roughly the same magnitude as those in the text (table 2.1). However, in the paragraphs below, we assume a coefficient—the reported simulation coefficient, one-to-one—running from a decrease in trade barriers to an increase in productivity.

Using this coefficient to estimate the benefits from sifting and sorting, our first task is to calculate the postwar reduction in US trade barriers. To do this, we look at the difference between the simple average column

25. Other studies on the causes of productivity growth in manufacturing include Lewis (2004) and Baily and Gersbach (1995).

26. Trefler (2004) uses Canadian plant-level data to estimate productivity improvements as a result of the Canada-US FTA. Other competition studies include Bayoumi, Laxton, and Pesenti (2004) and Carlin, Schaffer, and Seabright (2004). Corroborating worldwide evidence is found in empirical studies of the effects of regulatory barriers to entry on aggregate productivity levels and growth: Djankov et al. (2002); Hoekman and Kee (2003); Klapper, Laeven, and Rajan (2004); and Nicoletti and Scarpetta (2003).

27. There is support for a relationship of this magnitude in the econometric analysis of Bernard, Jensen, and Schott (2003). We assume that a one-to-one payoff also results when agriculture and mining trade barriers are decreased.

(2) ad valorem rate in the US tariff schedule—essentially the Smoot-Hawley tariffs inherited from the 1930s—and the simple average applied tariff rate in 2001.[28] The column (2) rates—rates imposed on the bulk of US imports immediately after the Second World War and now imposed on only three US diplomatic enemies (North Korea, Cuba, and Laos)—have a simple average of about 40 percent.[29] In 2001, the simple average applied rate for other countries (except FTA partners like Canada and Mexico) was 3.9 percent (WTO 2003, USITC 2004). We take the difference of 36.1 percentage points as a rough estimate of the decline in tariff barriers from the first GATT agreement to the present day.[30]

While early multilateral trade rounds focused almost exclusively on merchandise tariffs, later rounds have turned to other liberalization issues (e.g., regulation of services industries, agricultural subsidies, and other nontariff barriers). These elements of liberalization are not captured by our tariff barrier measure; hence the estimate of induced sifting and sorting may be conservative.[31]

Trade liberalization has typically been negotiated and comes in spurts rather than a smooth decline in barriers. To take this into account, we examined the trend in the ratio of duties collected to dutiable imports between 1947 and 2002 (USITC 2004) and used the figures to construct a rough estimate of the path of the simple average tariff barrier at five-year intervals from 40 percent in 1947 to 3.9 percent in 2002.[32] The constructed percentage point changes for each period are shown in table 2.4. They indicate that the bulk of US tariff reduction occurred in three periods:

28. The simple average applied tariff rate is the simple average of so-called most favored nation (MFN) or normal trade relations (NTR) rates applied in 2001.

29. This figure is the simple average tariff rate of 10,704 tariff lines for which a column (2) specific or ad valorem rate is reported in the 2004 Harmonized Tariff Schedule of the United States, accessed via the USITC (2004). For tariff rate quota lines (e.g., cane and beet sugar), we assume a 100 percent ad valorem tariff equivalent. In cases where a specific rate was assessed (e.g., 25 cents per kilogram) we add 20 percentage points to the reported ad valorem rate (if any).

30. This method ignores nontariff barriers. In the aftermath of earlier GATT rounds, nontariff barriers may have been substituted for tariff reductions, dampening the effect of liberalization. In later trade rounds, reductions to nontariff barriers were negotiated, but these reductions have no effect on the simple average applied tariff.

31. The tariff decline from 40 to 3.9 percent could leave the false impression that little US liberalization is left for future negotiations. In reality, much liberalization remains to be accomplished. For example, Brown, Deardorff, and Stern (2003) attributed over 80 percent of the US benefits of a proposed Doha Round cut in trade barriers to commerce in services. Furthermore, the tariff measure refers only to US merchandise imports; the United States generally faces higher tariff barriers on its merchandise exports.

32. In order to divide the period into 11 five-year intervals, we use the simple average of US applied tariff lines measured in 2001 (3.9 percent) as the figure for 2002.

Table 2.4 Sifting and sorting: Productivity benefit of reduced import tariff barriers

Period	Estimated ad valorem tariff at end of period (percent)	Estimated ad valorem tariff reduction[a] (percentage points)	Average share of traded goods sectors in US value added[b] (percent)	Growth in output per worker in full economy due to tariff change[c]		Benefit in 2003[c,d] (billions of 2003 dollars)
				Percent	2003 dollars	
1947	40.0					
1947–52	22.7	17.3	37.7	6.5	1,905	262
1952–57	18.9	3.8	36.5	1.4	466	64
1957–62	21.5	–2.6	33.9	–0.9	–336	–46
1962–67	21.2	0.2	31.7	0.1	32	4
1967–72	12.7	8.6	29.3	2.5	1,241	171
1972–77	4.9	7.8	27.7	2.2	1,148	158
1977–82	3.9	1.0	27.2	0.3	141	19
1982–87	4.6	–0.7	24.5	–0.2	–96	–13
1987–92	4.6	0.0	21.3	0.0	0	0
1992–97	3.2	1.4	20.1	0.3	188	26
1997–02	3.9	–0.7	17.8	–0.1	–88	–12
Total					**4,601**	**633**

a. Estimated productivity growth in traded goods sector due to tariff reduction.
b. Traded sectors are manufacturing, agriculture, and minerals.
c. Subperiod gains are an intermediate calculation, not an estimate of short-term gains from liberalization. Gains due to liberalization may require 10 to 20 years to be fully realized.
d. Benefit in 2003 is calculated by multiplying the benefit per worker measured in 2003 dollars by total employment in 2003.

Note: In order to better account for changes to the US economy over time, this table presents total gains from liberalization as the sum of subperiods. If instead a single calculation is used to estimate gains between 1947 and 2002, the total gains are estimated to be $404 billion.

Sources: USITC (2004), CEA (2004), BEA (2004a), WTO (2003), and authors' calculations.

1947–52, 1967–72, and 1972–77.[33] However, the economic payoff is spread over much longer periods since structural responses take a decade or two to play out.

Applying the one-to-one coefficient gleaned from the literature—that a 1-percentage-point ad valorem decline in tariff or other barriers will induce a 1 percent improvement in labor productivity in traded goods sectors (i.e., manufacturing, mining, and agriculture)—we use the constructed series in table 2.4 as a measure of induced productivity gains in the traded goods sectors for each period as a result of tariff cuts.[34] To find the productivity improvement to the entire economy due to reduced tariff barriers, we multiply this figure by the average share of traded goods sectors in the total economy.[35] Based on these productivity increases (and in some cases, decreases) for the 11 periods, we estimate an annual GDP benefit of $2,200 per capita and $5,600 per household for all liberalization between 1947 and 2002. This equates to a benefit of $600 billion to the US economy in 2003 (measured in 2003 dollars). Unlike the OECD output elasticity calculation, which reflects both policy and technology liberalization, the sifting and sorting estimates reflect only policy liberalization.

Moreover, since the sifting and sorting estimate measures just productivity gains due to resource reallocation, we can combine this estimate—a gain of approximately 5.8 percent of GDP from lower tariff barriers—with the additional 2.8 percent gain calculated by Broda and Weinstein (2004) for greater product variety.[36] The result is an increase of 8.6 percent of GDP, or roughly $940 billion of annual GDP in 2003 dollars. This equates to an additional $3,200 of GDP per capita due to liberalization annually, or $8,400 per household. The bulk of these gains are a direct result of

33. By this measure, the Uruguay Round and Tokyo Round negotiations reduced tariff barriers by only a small extent. This may be due to the changing composition of trade, partly in response to tariff cuts on products that still had higher-than-average tariffs after the cuts. According to WTO (2004), the first five GATT rounds collectively reduced US industrial product tariffs by 36 percent, and the Kennedy, Tokyo, and Uruguay rounds reduced industrial product tariffs of developed countries by 37, 33, and 38 percent, respectively (weighted by preround imports).

34. In some periods, the ratio of duties collected to dutiable value actually rises (again, most likely due to shifts in the structure of imports; see previous footnote), causing a rise in our tariff barrier estimate. We treat these increases as costs to productivity and account for them when summing the total gains in output per worker.

35. This methodology assumes that workers moving from agriculture, mining, and manufacturing to other industries (such as services) maintain their productivity levels. Given the studies presented above on the positive effects of capital and labor reallocation between industries, this assumption appears to be reasonable.

36. While the production side measures gains between 1947 and 2003, the Broda and Weinstein (2004) estimate applies to the period between 1972 and 2000. By adding these two estimates together, we implicitly assume that product variety gains before 1972 and after 2000 were zero, an obvious underestimate.

changes in public policy and do not encompass additional gains due to improved communication and transportation technology or trade enhancement on account of import demand elasticities greater than unity. Taking these factors into account could reconcile the higher figure from the OECD study ($1,450 billion annually) with the somewhat smaller figure from the sifting and sorting method ($940 billion annually).

Smoot-Hawley CGE: Writing History Backward

The third approach we report imagines a world in which postwar liberalization had never occurred. Using a computable general equilibrium (CGE) model, Bradford and Lawrence (2004b) have attempted to construct this world. The CGE model is first calibrated using base-year data (in this case, 1997) on tariffs, nontariff barriers, trade, production, the extent of monopolistic competition, and a set of embedded parameters. The CGE model used by Bradford and Lawrence includes monopolistic competition, scale economy features, and capital accumulation, as well as the standard efficiency gains from better exploitation of comparative advantage.

Bradford and Lawrence then imposed a hypothetical tariff regime on the model, specifically the highly restrictive Smoot-Hawley Tariff of 1930. Except for countries with which the United States negotiated reciprocal trade agreements in the 1930s and 1940s, this was the generally applicable US tariff schedule after the Second World War.[37] To complement the Smoot-Hawley tariff and mimic the rash of tariff retaliation in the 1930s, Bradford and Lawrence imposed similar restrictive tariffs on US exports to the trading partners identified in the CGE model. The calculated decrease in national income can be interpreted as a lower-bound estimate of the payoff from postwar liberalization.

The results from the simulation, which boil down to the difference in income levels under the current tariff profile and the Smoot-Hawley tariff, appear in table 2.5.[38] We briefly note two lessons from the international calculations. First, as a consequence of retrenchment, world income falls, and losses are suffered in every country or region measured. Second, much of the harm is self-inflicted. While the United States is among the largest losers when the Smoot-Hawley regime is imposed by itself, US

37. The Reciprocal Trade Agreement Act of 1934 authorized bilateral trade agreements for the reciprocal reduction in tariffs. After the Second World War, a successor edition of the act was invoked to permit US participation in the first few rounds of GATT negotiations.

38. In the parlance of CGE models, the figures presented in table 2.5 represent "equivalent variation." Roughly, this is the increase in purchasing power as a result of the new trade regime, measured in the prices of the base year. For our purposes, we treat this figure as an increase in GDP.

Table 2.5 Smoot-Hawley CGE: Effect of reverting to 1930s tariff regimes (percent of GDP)

Impact on	US reverts to Smoot-Hawley	All countries retaliate with equivalent regime
Australia	–0.77	–8.39
Canada	–5.71	–11.95
Germany	–0.64	–10.40
Italy	–0.47	–15.10
Japan	–0.34	–0.84
Netherlands	–0.81	–20.75
United Kingdom	–0.64	–9.37
United States	**–2.40**	**–4.47**
China	–0.99	–4.74
South Korea	–0.83	–1.97
Rest of Asia	–1.62	–13.01
Brazil	–0.67	–3.62
Rest of Latin America	–3.60	–10.95
Rest of Europe	–0.44	–13.91
Middle East	–1.39	–11.53
Rest of the world	–0.35	–7.60
World	**–1.33**	**–7.35**

Source: Bradford and Lawrence (2004b).

losses are modest compared with what other countries suffer once they join the tariff retaliation game.[39]

Turning to the United States, the reintroduction of the Smoot-Hawley tariff regime causes GDP to decline by 2.4 percent. The introduction of reciprocal tariff regimes by US trading partners further contracts the US economy by 2.1 percent. In all, the Bradford and Lawrence simulations indicate that the US economy is 4.5 percent larger due to sharply lower worldwide tariff barriers since 1947. This equates to $500 billion in 2003.

The calculated decrease of $500 billion in US GDP illustrates the impact of a shock back to 1930s-style protectionism rather than a parallel universe without liberalization over the past 50 years. The Bradford and Lawrence calculation does not purport to measure the expansion of trade owing to the dramatic fall in transportation and communication costs. Nor does it capture technological spillovers that resulted from interaction between US firms and foreign markets. Perhaps for these reasons, the Bradford and Lawrence calculation suggests a lower US payoff from global integration than the OECD coefficient.

39. Terms-of-trade effects that would likely favor the United States under the Smoot-Hawley regime are included in this calculation. However, US terms-of-trade gains are overwhelmed by other losses in the simulation.

As with previous methods, we can add the consumption variety gains estimated by Broda and Weinstein (2004) to gains estimated using the Bradford and Lawrence CGE model.[40] The result is a total estimate of 7.3 percent of GDP. This equates to $800 billion of GDP, an increase in annual per capita income of $2,800, and an increase in average annual household income of $7,100.

Using three different methodologies (four, including the methodology reported in appendix 2A) to calculate the payoff from the postwar reduction in trade barriers and transportation/communication costs, we find results that are of the same order of magnitude: roughly $1 trillion of annual US GDP is attributable to global integration.

The Payoff from Future Liberalization

In light of the great progress made in trade and investment liberalization (reflected in the falling US ad valorem tariffs portrayed in table 2.4), it might be questioned whether the United States will realize substantial benefits from eliminating its remaining barriers. Indeed, the classic Ricardian model indicates that the deadweight loss due to a trade barrier is roughly proportional to the height of the barrier squared.[41] Since remaining US tariff barriers are low on average, the prospective benefits of future liberalization in terms of enhancing US productivity and reducing prices would appear to be modest.

Against this view, three points may be made. Many industries remain highly protected—not only abroad but also in the United States. Many countries continue to sharply restrict trade and investment in services, ranging from finance to health care. Indeed, while many estimates of past gains ignore the services sector, the potential gains to the United States from the future liberalization of services trade may exceed the gains that can be derived from the future liberalization of merchandise trade. Even so, substantial gains remain to be achieved in merchandise trade. Agriculture is notorious for its high trade barriers and expensive subsidies. The United States and many other countries severely limit textile and clothing imports. The same is true of leather goods, ceramic dishware, cast iron grates, and a number of other low-technology imports.

40. The Bradford and Lawrence CGE model itself reflects the benefit of lower consumer prices for the goods identified in the model. However, it does not reflect the variety increase measured by Broda and Weinstein (2004).

41. In the classic (though perhaps simplistic) Ricardian framework, deadweight loss is represented as a triangle with the height equal to the size of the trade barrier and base equal to the amount of trade displaced by the barrier. If the amount of trade displaced varies linearly with the height of the barrier, the deadweight loss simplifies to a constant times the height of the barrier squared.

Second, average protection levels in many developing-country markets are much higher than those in the United States. Negotiated tariff reduction with these countries holds the potential for high payoffs from larger US exports.

The third important point is that complete elimination of trade barriers creates an atmosphere of commercial certainty—because it is politically hard to walk away from an FTA or customs union. In a moment, we report on "border effect" research that implies substantial gains could be captured by the final march to free trade in the context of binding agreements.

In several estimates of past gains, the results of policy liberalization, technological innovation, and income elasticities are entangled. By contrast, all estimates of future gains are based on policy liberalization alone. Technological innovations that reduce trade costs (e.g., information technology) will produce gains in addition to those described below. The same is true of trade expansion that results from high income elasticities of import demand. With that preamble, we report on three approaches that scholars have used to estimate the unrealized payoff from future liberalization.

Global Free Trade CGE: Writing History Forward

CGE models were first devised to forecast the outcome of reducing tariff and nontariff barriers—multilaterally, regionally, or bilaterally. Brown, Deardorff, and Stern (2001, 2003), for example, use their Michigan Model of World Production and Trade to envisage (among other outcomes) a world of zero tariff and nontariff barriers. The Michigan Model adds several useful features to the standard CGE model—accounting for economies of scale, less monopolistic competition, and greater product variety.[42] Moreover, and this is quantitatively very important, the Michigan Model calculates gains from liberalizing trade in services as well as goods. Like other CGE models, the Michigan Model is concerned with policy liberalization, not lower transportation and communication costs.

In the Michigan Model, the world is divided into 20 countries or regions, and traded products are classified into 18 sectors. The base year for the model was constructed by projecting 1995 data to 2005 (including liberalization agreed in the Uruguay Round). From this point, the model is used to estimate the GDP payoff from global free trade. The payoff figure is $2.1 trillion for the world as a whole and a 5.5 percent increase in GDP for the United States, equivalent to $600 billion in 2003 (Brown, Deardorff,

42. The Michigan model does not, however, assume capital accumulation or technological improvements as a consequence of freer trade. For a complete formal description of the Michigan Model, see www.fordschool.umich.edu/rsie/model (accessed July 19, 2004).

and Stern 2003, table 1). For the US population in 2003, this equates to an annual payoff of $2,000 per capita or $5,000 per household.[43]

When compared with other CGE results, the Michigan Model predicts a relatively large gain for the United States through multilateral liberalization. One reason may be the use of increasing returns to scale and other elements of new trade theory. Perhaps most importantly, the Michigan Model accounts for liberalization in the services sector; by contrast, many CGE models only account for liberalization in merchandise trade, a shrinking share of the US economy. As much as 4.1 of the total 5.5 percent of GDP increase due to global free trade calculated by the Michigan Model may be due to liberalization in services.[44]

Market Fragmentation: A Price Convergence Approach

In a theoretical world of perfect competition and free trade, arbitrage would enforce the law of one price for most goods and some services: The price of an identical product in two locations would differ only by the cost of transportation from one place to another. In the real world, this rarely happens. Imperfect competition is the rule, and firms discriminate in quoted prices across space and time. However, political barriers to trade are responsible for a large portion of the price gaps between states.[45] As barriers to trade and investment fall, the world moves closer to the law of one price. For example, Rogers, Hufbauer, and Wada (2001) showed that between 1990 and 1999, the EU single market and common currency reduced the dispersion of prices for traded goods between Euroland cities to approximate the dispersion found between US cities.[46]

43. The payoff, of course, would not be instantaneous. A period of five to ten years might be required for complete adjustment. Like all CGE models, this method internalizes terms-of-trade losses and contraction of import-competing industries into its calculation of production gains.

44. In a separate experiment, the Michigan Model indicates that a one-third reduction in world service barriers would boost US GDP by 1.48 percent, more than three times the income benefit (0.48 percent) of a one-third reduction in manufactures barriers (Brown, Deardorff, and Stern 2003, table 1). We assume a proportional distribution of gains in the total liberalization experiment.

45. Using a gravity model with log price differentials as the dependent variable, Anderson and Smith (2004) have shown that the effect of an international border is a significant disruption of the arbitrage process, whereas the effect of distance, while positive, is not statistically significant. Anderson and van Wincoop (2004) show that total international trade costs are roughly 74 percent ad valorem, consisting of a 21 percent cost for transportation and a 44 percent cost due to border-related trade barriers (0.74 = 1.21*1.44-1).

46. Other studies, among them ECB (2002), have reported less significant declines in European dispersion. See Engel and Rogers (2004) for a more current discussion of European integration and price convergence.

When prices converge, benefits are realized from *both* falling and rising prices. This is a direct result of the law of comparative advantage. The price of an item tends to be less than the world price in places and times where it is efficiently produced, so a price rise generates gains for producers that more than offset the losses to consumers. Meanwhile, the price of an item tends to be higher where it is less efficiently produced, so a price fall benefits consumers more than it hurts producers.

In an early application, Hufbauer, Wada, and Warren (2002) estimated that world GDP would increase by 2 to 6 percent (weighted by market exchange rates or purchasing power parity, respectively) if world prices converged to the level of dispersion found between US cities.[47] Subsequently, Bradford and Lawrence (2004a) used OECD price data on consumer and capital goods in eight countries to develop a "fragmentation index" based on the ratio of a good's producer price to a constructed landed price (i.e., including transportation costs) from the most competitive foreign market.[48] This ratio can be considered the average *effective* ad valorem barrier (including tariff and nontariff barriers).[49] Using a CGE model based on Harrison, Rutherford and Tarr (1997), the authors calculate that the removal of fragmentation (i.e., the removal of price differences that are created by tariff and nontariff barriers) in the eight countries would increase US GDP by 1 percent.[50] Scaled to 2003 GDP and population, this would amount to an increase of $110 billion in GDP, an additional $400 per capita or $900 per American household annually.

This result is significantly smaller than that of the Michigan Model (reported earlier). However, the Michigan Model calculates the result of global free trade in both goods and services whereas the Bradford and Lawrence experiment involves the removal of barriers on goods trade alone by only eight industrial countries (these eight countries account for about 86 percent of the GDP of the industrialized world, roughly 65 percent of total world GDP).[51] Ignoring services barriers leaves out a large

47. The authors used data from the Economist Intelligence Unit for their calculations.

48. The countries are Australia, Canada, Germany, Italy, Japan, the Netherlands, the United Kingdom, and the United States.

49. Since the fragmentation index applies only to final goods, the barrier used for each product is a weighted average of the GTAP database tariff and the fragmentation index for that product. The share of final goods imported in the product category weights the fragmentation index. In sectors where a barrier was not estimated, most notably all services sectors, the GTAP barrier is used.

50. Unlike the Michigan Model, the Harrison, Rutherford, and Tarr (1997) model allows for dynamic capital accumulation. The model provides for increasing returns to scale, monopolistic competition, and product differentiation in 25 of 33 sectors. The model is publicly available at http://dmsweb.badm.sc.edu/Glenn/ur_pub.htm (accessed July 27, 2004).

Table 2.6 MFN applied tariffs for all products and estimated tariff equivalents in traded services (percent)

Country/region	Simple average merchandise tariff	Business and financial services	Construction
India	31.4	13.1	61.6
Brazil	14.6	35.7	57.2
China	12.4	18.8	40.9
Russia, central and eastern Europe[a]	10.7	18.4	51.9
Turkey	10.2	20.4	46.3
South Africa	5.8	15.7	42.1
North America[a]	5.4	8.2	9.8
Western Europe[b]	4.4	8.5	18.3
Australia and New Zealand[a]	4.0	6.9	24.4
Japan	3.3	19.7	29.7

MFN = most favored nation

a. Average merchandise tariff weighted by 2002 imports.
b. Merchandise tariff of the European Union.

Note: Tariff reported for latest available year, 2001 or 2002. Services barriers estimated using a gravity model.

Sources: WTO (2003), Francois (1999) cited in Deardorff and Stern (2004, table 9).

portion of potential gains, since barriers within the services sector are relatively high (table 2.6).[52] Another difference worth emphasizing is that the Bradford and Lawrence experiment only covers trade between industrial countries. Developing-country trade barriers tend to be much higher than those in industrial countries (table 2.7). CGE modeling by Anderson et al. (2001) indicates that the potential gains to North American income from liberalized merchandise trade with developing countries are more than twice the potential benefits of liberalized trade with industrialized countries.[53]

51. Bradford and Lawrence (2004a) did not estimate fragmentation in services industries and some goods industries (particularly agriculture and natural resources). In these cases, they instead use the protection level from the GTAP 5 database (also used by Harrison, Rutherford, and Tarr 1997). This database assumes the protection level of its three services sectors to be 0 in the eight countries considered by Bradford and Lawrence, an obvious underestimate (Bradford and Lawrence 2004a, table 4.4). For more on the GTAP 5 database and subsequent improvements, see www.gtap.org (accessed August 3, 2004).

52. As well as being high, barriers to services trade are difficult to measure. The estimates presented in table 2.6 compare predicted services trade using a gravity model with the actual level of services trade. See Deardorff and Stern (2004) for more on this and alternative methods for estimating barriers in services.

53. Anderson et al. (2001, table 4) report that total gains to North America from developing-country merchandise trade liberalization would be $19 billion, while "rich-country" liberalization would provide only a $3 billion benefit. However, the rich-country benefit can be decomposed into a *cost* of $9 billion due to a terms-of-trade loss from rich-country liberalization of manufactures, offset by an $11 billion gain in primary merchandise. Ignoring the terms-of-trade loss, gains from developing-country liberalization still constitute the bulk of potential North American gains.

Table 2.7 Simple average applied MFN tariff, selected countries (percent)

Country/region	Tariff
Bradford-Lawrence study	
European Union	4.4
United States	3.9
Australia	4.1
Canada	4.1
Japan	3.3
Selected other countries	
India	31.4
Pakistan	20.1
Egypt	19.9
Brazil	14.6
Poland	13.9
China	12.4
Korea	12.4
Colombia	12.2
Russia	9.9
Malaysia	7.3
Indonesia	6.9
South Africa	5.8

Note: Tariff in latest available year, 2001 or 2002.

Source: WTO (2003); Bradford and Lawrence (2002).

To better compare the Bradford and Lawrence methodology with other approaches, we made two extrapolations. First, we scaled up US gains to reflect the elimination of fragmentation vis-à-vis the entire world. Together, the seven partners of the Bradford and Lawrence study account for 45 percent of US merchandise exports. As table 2.7 illustrates, these countries have low tariff barriers compared with other US trading partners. However, we have no data on fragmentation (reflecting both tariff and nontariff barriers) for other countries. Separate simulations performed by Bradford (2004) allow us to extrapolate the gains that might be realized from complete liberalization with the rest of the world. Bradford shows that when estimates of barriers from the GTAP database alone are removed from the eight countries in the Bradford-Lawrence study (i.e., tariff barriers only), US income grows by 0.33 percent of GDP. However, full tariff liberalization by all countries provides US gains of 0.85 percent of GDP.[54] Given the large additional gains that accrue to the United States when tariff elimination by the Bradford-Lawrence countries

54. GTAP barriers are typically drawn from tariff measures, so we characterize them roughly as a measure of tariff barriers, while market fragmentation estimates take into account both tariff and nontariff barriers to trade. When Bradford estimates the removal of fragmentation in Bradford-Lawrence countries, simultaneously with the removal of tariff-based barriers elsewhere, US gains are 1.18 percent of GDP.

is extended to the entire world (more than doubling US gains), it seems logical that the removal of market fragmentation worldwide would likewise have an amplified effect. To be conservative, we scale Bradford and Lawrence's estimated gains from eight countries by a factor of 2 to encompass the merchandise trade with the entire world.[55] This calculation yields total gains of roughly 2.04 percent of US GDP due to full merchandise liberalization.[56]

Second, we scale up the potential gains from free trade in goods to estimate the additional gains from free trade in services. Barriers to services trade are much higher, on average, than barriers to merchandise trade (Findlay and Warren 2000; Stephenson, Findlay, and Yi 2002). Studies project that gains due to services liberalization may be extremely large (Bradford 2005, forthcoming). As mentioned earlier, Brown, Deardorff, and Stern (2003) estimate that gains from services liberalization amount to four times those of goods liberalization (despite the fact that US total trade in services was less than one-fourth that of goods in 2003). From this evidence, we conservatively assume that gains in services-sector liberalization will be at least as large as those calculated for the goods sector. Therefore, we estimate potential US income gain of 2.04 percent of GDP due to global liberalization of services.

In combination, these assumptions (built around the fragmentation index) allow us to speculate that elimination of policy barriers would raise US GDP by about 4.1 percent. Scaled to 2003, this amounts to an additional $450 billion in US GDP, $1,500 per capita, or $4,000 income increase per household annually.

US-World FTA: A Gravity Model Estimate

In the past decade, empirical and theoretical research has revived the gravity model, which posits that bilateral trade between two countries is directly proportional to their size and inversely proportional to their distance (Frankel 1997).[57] The gravity model can be extended to quantify the

---

55. We do not scale the 1.02 from Bradford-Lawrence country liberalization by the full 2.5 due to the conventional wisdom that industrial countries tend to rely on nontariff barriers more heavily than developing countries, which typically protect through high tariffs. Against this, we note that the gains from liberalization in Bradford-Lawrence countries expand by a factor of 3 when using Bradford-Lawrence fragmentation estimates versus the GTAP barriers (typically tariff barriers).

56. The findings of Anderson et al. (2001), together with the observation that trade barriers in the developing world are significantly higher than those imposed in the OECD (table 2.7), suggest that freeing $10 billion of representative US trade with developing countries will deliver more gains than freeing $10 billion of representative trade with OECD countries.

57. The gravity model was used as early as 1946 to analyze trade. Linnemann (1966) provided significant refinements to the technique.

Table 2.8 US-world FTA: US merchandise trade with FTA and non-FTA partners, 2003 (billions of dollars)

	Total	FTA[a]	Non-FTA
US imports	1,259	376	884
US exports	724	274	449
Total trade	1,983	650	1,333
Estimated total trade if United States had an FTA with all countries[b]	3,163	650	2,513
Change (percent)	59.5	0.0	88.5
Memorandum:			
Estimated percent gain in GDP			11.9

a. Existing FTA partners in 2003 were Canada, Mexico, Israel, and Jordan.
b. The estimate assumes that a network of bilateral FTAs would boost bilateral trade by 89 percent, based on Rose (2003), adjusted as explained in the text.

Sources: USITC (2004), Rose (2003), and authors' calculations.

effects of common language, shared borders, postcolonial relationships, and other variables that potentially affect the size of bilateral trade flows.

Andrew Rose (2003) extended the gravity model to test the influence of international institutions (the GATT/WTO, IMF, OECD, and regional or bilateral FTAs) on bilateral trade.[58] Using IMF data on bilateral merchandise trade between 178 countries over 1948–99, he reports that participation in a regional FTA is strongly positive.[59] In particular, Rose estimates that a regional FTA can increase bilateral trade by 118 percent.[60] For reasons explained below, we adjust this coefficient downward to 89 percent. We then borrow this adjusted coefficient of 89 percent to estimate the increase in US merchandise trade if FTAs were concluded with all trading partners. This is the same as assuming that all countries eliminated their policy barriers to merchandise trade with the United States and vice versa. In 2003, the United States had FTAs in force with four countries, Canada, Mexico, Israel, and Jordan, which together accounted for roughly one-third of US trade (mostly NAFTA trade).[61] Applying Rose's adjusted coefficient, concluding FTAs with all other trading partners would have increased total US trade by 60 percent (table 2.8).

58. Rose has made his data set publicly available at http://faculty.haas.berkeley.edu/arose/RecRes.htm (accessed July 27, 2004).

59. In the same model, Rose also tried to assess the effect of GATT/WTO, IMF, and OECD membership on bilateral trade. Subramanian and Wei (2003) dispute Rose's result that GATT/WTO membership does not have a strong positive impact on trade linkages. Rose (2004) offers a riposte to their arguments. As we do not employ Rose's result pertaining to GATT/WTO, we do not pursue this debate.

60. The dependent variable was the natural log of bilateral trade, the regional FTA coefficient controlling for fixed country-pair effects is 0.78, 100*(exp(0.78)-1)=118 percent. This is the smallest regional FTA coefficient of the three reported benchmark regressions.

61. US FTAs with Singapore and Chile entered into force in January 2004.

The rationale for the downward adjustment from 118 percent to 89 percent is to reflect trade diversion.[62] Bilateral and regional free trade agreements increase trade among members both through trade creation (increased trade as a result of relative efficiency) and trade diversion (increased trade as a result of privileged access).[63] CGE estimates by DeRosa and Gilbert (2004, table A.6) for 14 prospective US FTAs enacted simultaneously suggest that trade diversion—measured as the dollar decline in nonpartner trade—could account for up to 25 percent of the gross gain in trade with partner countries. In view of this estimate, we reduce the gravity model trade augmentation effect from 118 to 89 percent.

While the gravity model estimate of regional trade agreements nevertheless appears large, research into so-called border effects puts the Rose coefficient into perspective.[64] McCallum (1995) launched this literature by comparing trade between Canadian provinces with their trade with US states and found that interprovince trade tended to be 22 times larger than state-province trade, controlling for size and distance.[65] Anderson and van Wincoop (2003) made several refinements, arguing that theory expects the border effect to be higher from the Canadian perspective—as Canada has fewer options for *intra*national trade—than from the US perspective.[66] Anderson and van Wincoop estimate the border effect of the US-Canada border—expressed as the ratio of trade with a domestic partner to a foreign partner controlling for size and distance—to be 11 from the Canadian perspective and 2 from the US perspective *in the presence of an FTA*.[67] Even so, the Anderson and van Wincoop calculations suggest that US trade with Canada would increase by between 79 and 144 percent if the border effect could be eliminated.[68] Given their interlocking cultures,

62. The 118 percent coefficient may also be exaggerated because of selection bias—the tendency of countries to put priority on FTAs with partners that promise the largest trade gains. However, in the case of the United States, noneconomic factors appear to play a large role in the selection of FTA partners (e.g., Bahrain); see Schott (2004, 365-73).

63. The trade diversion gains to partner countries of course become diluted as more nations enter into FTAs.

64. As it is used in this context, the term "border effect" is somewhat of a misnomer. The term refers to the difference in trade intensity due to separation into distinct political units. The border effect is present regardless of whether the two units share a border.

65. McCallum uses data from 1988, the year before the Canada-US FTA entered into force; Anderson and van Wincoop (discussed below) used 1993 data, the year before NAFTA entered into force.

66. Intuitively, the border effect must *both* decrease international trade *and* increase intranational trade. In Canada, the increase in intranational trade is more noticeable, since the Canadian economy is small relative to that of the United States.

67. The US-Canada FTA had been in force for four years at the time of the Anderson and van Wincoop data, and the border effect was still large.

68. Depending on whether a multicountry model (including Japan, Europe, Australia, and other developed nations) or a two-country model, respectively, is used.

common language, and lengthy trading history, it seems safe to assume that the US-Canada border effect is relatively small compared with other bilateral trading relationships. With this in mind, Rose's adjusted coefficient indicating that a regional FTA could augment trade by 89 percent—reducing, but far from eliminating, the border effect—seems plausible.

Bearing such caveats in mind, we calculate how incomes would be affected by a world where the United States concluded FTAs with all its trading partners, resulting in an increase in US trade of 60 percent. Applying the OECD (2003) per capita income coefficient of 0.2, as outlined above, suggests an increase in per capita income of 12 percent. In 2003 dollars this increase equates to $4,500 per capita, or $11,600 per household.[69] In the aggregate, GDP would increase by $1.3 trillion. Neither the Rose nor the OECD methodologies identify specific channels through which bilateral agreements affect bilateral trade or increased trade affects output per person, so we must assume that all channels play a role in this very large figure.

Conclusion

Past integration, through both policy liberalization—fostered by every postwar president—and technological progress, has been an unambiguous boon to the US economy. We have presented four very different methods of estimation—each of which entails its own set of assumptions—and have estimated gains of roughly $1 trillion. While the estimates are speculative, the important result of this exercise is that gains are consistently estimated to be large and positive.

Our estimates of future gains range from $450 billion to $1.3 trillion. To be conservative, we settle on a range defined by the market fragmentation method and the Michigan Model. These two approaches (which both make use of CGE models) suggest that removing all remaining barriers to trade would increase US production approximately $450 billion to $600 billion annually.[70] Gains in this range would increase US per capita income between $1,500 and $2,000 annually and US household income between $4,000 and $5,300 annually. The "final push" to free trade might

69. Rose's coefficient is a prediction of the increase in trade in merchandise only, while the OECD (2003) trade ratio includes both merchandise and services. When applying the OECD coefficient to the predicted rise in merchandise trade, we assume that the coefficient relating total trade to output per capita is the same for the goods and services sectors.

70. CGE models may understate gains because they ignore technological spillovers and the increased efficiency through the sifting and sorting of firms that usually accompanies increased trade. Furthermore, they do not account for the "certainty" effect of trade agreements—that tariffs are eliminated by international agreement. Some credit the certainty effect for the boom in US imports after NAFTA, since US tariffs on imports from Mexico were low prior to the agreement.

generate gains that are nearly half the size of the gains already realized through the reduction of policy barriers and transportation costs from the formation of the GATT in 1947 to the full implementation of the Uruguay Round and NAFTA in 2003.

Readers might ask why potential future gains are so large, since the United States has *already* dramatically slashed its average tariff barriers—from 40 percent in 1947 to 4 percent today. Clearly, far less room remains to cut US tariff barriers in 2003 than in 1947. On the precept "no pain, no gain," the fact that there is far less room for future pain implies far less room for future gain from US liberalization. We have three answers to this critique.

First, US liberalization still has a long way to go—not only in agriculture, textiles, clothing, and similar politically sensitive merchandise sectors but also in services. As internet technology has opened new vistas for offshore sourcing—both inward and outward—the potential scope for services trade and the importance of services barriers is much larger today than just a decade ago. Moreover, the decline in the simple average tariff rate does not reflect the enduring prevalence of nontariff barriers. Investigations of geographic price convergence and market fragmentation indicate that nontariff barriers continue to impose barriers to trade (Bradford and Lawrence 2004a, Anderson and Smith 2004, Anderson and van Wincoop 2004). Second, barriers abroad, particularly those surrounding developing markets, are very high and have not been reduced nearly to the same extent as barriers surrounding OECD markets. Third, certainty and lock-in effects of eliminating all trade barriers—in the context of a binding agreement (such as NAFTA)—spur trade and investment to a highly disproportionate extent. In other words, eliminating the last 4 percentage points of a tariff barrier probably makes a greater difference than reducing tariffs from 12 to 8 percent.

In this chapter, we have expressed gains in terms of the average person and the average household. We have not tried to express the gains in terms of benefits to wealthy, middle class, and poor individuals and households.[71] Moreover, the gains summarized in this chapter inevitably entail adjustment costs that fall disproportionately on unlucky individuals, industries, and communities. In appendix 2B, we estimate that the lifetime cost of all worker dislocations that were triggered by expanded trade in 2003 could be as high as $54 billion, although probably much less. While the gains from increased trade generate a permanent rise in

71. The distribution of gains from trade—the benefits to poor versus middle-class or wealthy households—is an important issue in the political economy of trade liberalization. This topic is taken up in the chapter by Lori Kletzer and Howard Rosen in this book, as well as in the Globalization Balance Sheet Series—including Kletzer (2001), Lewis and Richardson (2001), and Richardson (forthcoming)—published by the Institute for International Economics.

income, the associated losses are temporary. Nevertheless, they are very real, and are concentrated on a small fraction of Americans. Uncompetitive firms fail, jobs disappear, and some communities wither. While general safety net programs (such as unemployment insurance and urban grants) assist workers and communities that bear the costs of globalization, the US federal government spends less than $2 billion annually on explicit trade adjustment assistance (OMB 2004, 708)—less than 1 percent of prospective annual benefits from complete free trade.

It would take us far afield to explore trade adjustment policies or the distribution of benefits across American households. However, the *permanent* gains from past and potential liberalization are so enormous that the United States can easily afford the modest sums necessary to alleviate the *temporary* pains of adjustment. In the future as in the past, free trade can significantly raise income—and quality of life—in the United States.

References

Anderson, Michael A., and Stephen L.S. Smith. 2004. Borders and Price Dispersion: New Evidence on Persistent Arbitrage Failures. Washington and Lee University and Gordon College. Photocopy (April).

Anderson, James E., and Eric van Wincoop. 2003. Gravity with Gravitas: A Solution to the Border Puzzle. *American Economic Review* 93, no. 1 (March): 170–92.

Anderson, James E., and Eric van Wincoop. 2004. Trade Costs. *Journal of Economic Literature* XLII (September): 691–751.

Anderson, Kym, Betina Dimaranan, Joe Francois, Tom Hertel, Bernard Hoekman, and Will Martin. 2001. *The Cost of Rich (and Poor) Country Protection to Developing Countries.* CIES Discussion Paper 0136. Adelaide, Australia: Adelaide University (September).

Andrés, Javier, and Ignacio Hernando. 1997. *Does Inflation Harm Economic Growth?* NBER Working Paper 6062. Cambridge, MA: National Bureau of Economic Research.

Baily, Martin Neil, and Hans Gersbach. 1995. Efficiency in Manufacturing and the Need for Global Competition. *Brookings Papers on Economic Activity: Microeconomics 1995:* 307–58. Washington: Brookings Institution.

Baily, Martin Neil, and Robert Z. Lawrence. 2004. Trade and US Job Loss. Presentation at the Institute for International Economics conference on dollar adjustment, Washington, May 25.

Baldwin, Richard E., and Rikard Forslid. 2000. Trade Liberalization and Endogenous Growth: A q-Theory Approach. *Journal of International Economics* 50, no. 2 (April): 497–517.

Bayoumi, Tamin, Douglas Laxton, and Paolo Pesenti. 2004. *Benefits and Spillovers of Greater Competition in Europe: A Macroeconomic Assessment.* NBER Working Paper 10416. Cambridge, MA: National Bureau of Economic Research.

BEA (Bureau of Economic Analysis). 2004a. GDP-by-Industry Data. www.bea.gov/bea/dn2/gdpbyind_data.htm (accessed August 31, 2004).

BEA (Bureau of Economic Analysis). 2004b. National Income and Product Account Tables (NIPA). www.bea.gov/bea/dn/nipaweb/index.asp (accessed July 30, 2004).

Berg, Andrew, and Anne Krueger. 2003. *Trade, Growth, and Poverty: A Selective Survey.* IMF Working Paper WP/03/30. Washington: International Monetary Fund.

Bernard, Andrew, Jonathan Eaton, J. Bradford Jensen, and Samuel Kortum. 2003. Plants and Productivity in International Trade. *American Economic Review* 93, no. 4 (September): 1268–90.

Bernard, Andrew B., J. Bradford Jensen, and Peter Schott. 2003. *Falling Trade Costs, Heterogeneous Firms and Industry Dynamics.* IFS Working Paper 03/10. London: Institute for Fiscal Studies.

Bernard, Andrew, and J. Bradford Jensen. 2004. Exporting and Productivity in the US. Tuck School of Business at Dartmouth, National Bureau of Economic Research, and the Institute for International Economics. Photocopy (July).

Bernard, Andrew B., Stephen Redding, and Peter Schott. 2004. *Comparative Advantage and Heterogeneous Firms.* NBER Working Paper 10668. Cambridge, MA: National Bureau of Economic Research.

Bhalla, Surjit S. 2002. *Imagine There's No Country: Poverty, Inequality, and Growth in the Era of Globalization.* Washington: Institute for International Economics.

BLS (Bureau of Labor Statistics). 2004. Current Employment Statistics. www.bls.gov/ces/ (accessed October 6, 2004).Bradford, Scott C. 2005. The Welfare Effects of Distribution Regulations in OECD Countries. *Economic Inquiry* (forthcoming).

Bradford, Scott C. 2005. The Welfare Effects of Distribution Regulations in OECD Countries. *Economic Inquiry* (forthcoming).

Bradford, Scott C. 2004. CGE Simulation Results. Brigham Young University. Photocopy.

Bradford, Scott C., and Robert Z. Lawrence. 2004a. *Has Globalization Gone Far Enough? The Costs of Fragmented Markets.* Washington: Institute for International Economics.

Bradford, Scott C., and Robert Z. Lawrence. 2004b. Non-MFN CGE Simulations. Brigham Young University and Harvard University. Photocopy.

Broda, Christian, and David E. Weinstein. 2004. *Globalization and the Gains from Variety.* NBER Working Paper 10314. Cambridge, MA: National Bureau of Economic Research.

Brown, Drusilla K., Alan V. Deardorff, and Robert M. Stern. 2001. *CGE Modeling and Analysis of Multilateral and Regional Negotiating Options.* Research Seminar in International Economics Discussion Paper 468. Ann Arbor, MI: University of Michigan School of Public Policy. January.

Brown, Drusilla K., Alan V. Deardorff, and Robert M. Stern. 2003. *Developing Countries' Stake in the Doha Round.* Research Seminar in International Economics Discussion Paper 495. Ann Arbor, MI: University of Michigan School of Public Policy. June.

Carlin, W., M. Schaffer, and P. Seabright. 2004. *A Minimum of Rivalry: Evidence from Transition Economies on the Importance of Competition for Innovation and Growth.* CEPR Discussion Paper 4343. London: Centre for Economic Policy Research.

CEA (Council of Economic Advisers). 2004. *Economic Report of the President.* Washington: US Government Printing Office.

Clark, Todd E. 2004. An Evaluation of the Decline in Goods Inflation. *Federal Reserve Bank of Kansas City Economic Review* 89, no. 2 (Second Quarter): 19–52.

Cline, William R. 1997. *Trade and Income Distribution.* Washington: Institute for International Economics.

Cline, William R. 2004. *Trade Policy and Global Poverty.* Washington: Institute for International Economics.

Davis, Steven J., and John Haltiwanger. 1999. Gross Job Flows. In *Handbook of Labor Economics,* volumes 3 and 4, ed., Orley Ashenfelter and David Carr. New York: Elsevier Science/North Holland.

Deardorff, Alan V., and Robert M. Stern. 2004. *Empirical Analysis of Barriers to International Services Transactions and the Consequences of Liberalization.* Research Seminar in International Economics Discussion Paper 505. Ann Arbor, MI: University of Michigan School of Public Policy (January).

DeRosa, Dean A., and John P. Gilbert. 2004. Quantitative Estimates of the Economic Impacts of US Bilateral Free Trade Agreements. In *Free Trade Agreements: US Strategies and Priorities,* ed., Jeffrey J. Schott. Washington: Institute for International Economics.

Disney, Richard, Jonathan Haskel, and Ylva Heden. 2003. Restructuring and Productivity in UK Manufacturing. *Economic Journal* 113, no. 489 (July): 666–94.

Djankov, Simeon, Rafael La Porta, Florencio Lopez-de-Silanes, and Andrei Schleifer. 2002. The Regulation of Entry. *Quarterly Journal of Economics* 117, no. 1 (February): 1–35.

Dollar, David, and Aart Kraay. 2004. Trade, Growth, and Poverty. *Economic Journal* 114, no. 493 (February): 22–49.

ECB (European Central Bank). 2002. Price Level Convergence and Competition in the Euro Area. *Monthly Bulletin* (August): 39-50. Frankfurt: European Central Bank.

Engel, Charles, and John H. Rogers. 2004. European Product Market Integration After the Euro. *Economic Policy* 19, no. 39 (July): 347–84.

Eslava, Marcela, John Haltiwanger, Adriana Kugler, and Maurice Kugler. 2004. *The Effects of Structural Reforms on Productivity and Profitability: Evidence from Colombia.* NBER Working Paper 10367. Cambridge, MA: National Bureau of Economic Research.

Feenstra, Robert C. 1994. New Product Varieties and the Measurement of International Prices. *American Economic Review* 84, no. 1 (March): 157–77.

Findlay, Christopher, and Tony Warren. 2000. *Impediments to Trade in Services.* London and New York: Routledge.

Fischer, Stanley. 1996. Why are Central Banks Pursuing Long-Run Price Stability? In *Achieving Price Stability.* Jackson Hole, WY: Federal Reserve Bank of Kansas City.

Fischer, Stanley, Ratna Sahay, and Carlos A. Végh. 2002. Modern Hyper- and High Inflations. *Journal of Economic Literature* 40, no. 3 (September): 837–80.

Foster, Lucia, John Haltiwanger, and C.J. Krizan. 2001. Aggregate Productivity Growth: Lessons from Microeconomic Evidence. In *New Developments in Productivity Analysis,* ed., Charles R. Hulten, Edwin R. Dean, and Michael J. Harper. Chicago: University of Chicago Press.

Foster, Lucia, John Haltiwanger, and C.J. Krizan. 2002. *The Link Between Aggregate and Micro Productivity Growth: Evidence from Retail Trade.* NBER Working Paper 9120. Cambridge, MA: National Bureau of Economic Research.

Foster, Lucia, John Haltiwanger, and Chad Syverson. 2004. Reallocation, Firm Turnover, and Efficiency: Selection on Productivity or Profitability. US Census Bureau, University of Maryland, and University of Chicago. Photocopy (March).

Francois, Joseph. 1999. Estimates of Barriers to Trade in Services. Erasmus University. Photocopy.

Frankel, Jeffrey A. 1997. *Regional Free Trading Blocs in the World Economic System.* Washington: Institute for International Economics.

Frankel, Jeffrey A., and David Romer. 1999. Trade and Growth: An Empirical Investigation. *American Economic Review* 89, no. 3 (June): 379–99.

Graham, Edward M. 2000. *Fighting the Wrong Enemy: Antiglobal Activists and Multinational Enterprises.* Washington: Institute for International Economics.

Hallak, Juan Carlos, and James Levinsohn. 2004. Fooling Ourselves: Evaluating the Globalization and Growth Debate. Ann Arbor, MI: University of Michigan and NBER. www.econ.lsa.umich.edu/~jamesl/ (accessed August 12, 2004).

Harrison, Glenn W., Thomas F. Rutherford, and David G. Tarr. 1997. Quantifying the Uruguay Round. *Economic Journal* 104 (September): 1405–30.

Hoekman, Bernard, and Hiau Looi Kee. 2003. *Imports, Entry, and Competition Law as Market Disciplines.* World Bank Policy Research Working Paper 3031. Washington: World Bank (April).

Huether, David M., and J. David Richardson. 2001. Imputing and Interpreting Trade in Intermediate Goods and Services: A US Illustration for the 1990s. National Association of Manufacturers and Syracuse University. Photocopy (October).

Hufbauer, Gary C., Erika Wada, and Tony Warren. 2002. *The Benefits of Price Convergence.* POLICY ANALYSES IN INTERNATIONAL ECONOMICS 65. Washington: Institute for International Economics (January).

Hufbauer, Gary C., and Yee Wong. 2004. *China Bashing 2004.* International Economics Policy Brief 04-5. Washington: Institute for International Economics (September).

Klapper, Leora, Luc Laeven, and Raghuram Rajan. 2004. *Business Environment and Firm Entry: Evidence from International Data.* World Bank Policy Research Working Paper 3232. Washington: World Bank (March).

Klein, Michael W., Scott Schuh, and Robert K. Triest. 2003. *Job Creation, Job Destruction, and International Competition.* Kalamazoo, MI: W. E. Upjohn Institute for Employment Research.

Kletzer, Lori G. 2001. *Job Loss from Imports: Measuring the Costs.* Washington: Institute for International Economics.

Lewis, Howard, III, and J. David Richardson. 2001. *Why Global Commitment Really Matters!* Washington: Institute for International Economics.

Lewis, William W. 2004. *The Power of Productivity: Wealth, Poverty, and the Threat to Global Stability.* Chicago: University of Chicago Press.

Linnemann, Hans. 1966. *An Econometric Study of International Trade Flows.* Amsterdam: North-Holland.

Maddison, Angus. 2003. *The World Economy: Historical Statistics.* Paris: Development Center of the Organization for Economic Cooperation and Development.

Marquez, Jaime. 2002. Estimating Trade Elasticities. In *Advanced Studies in Theoretical and Applied Econometrics,* volume 39. Boston, MA: Kluwer Academic Publishers.

McCallum, John. 1995. National Borders Matter: Canada-U.S. Regional Trade Patterns. *American Economic Review* 85, no. 3 (June): 615–23.

Melitz, Marc J. 2003. The Impact of Trade on Intra-Industry Reallocations and Aggregate Industry Productivity. *Econometrica* 71 (November): 1695–725.

Nicoletti, Giuseppi, and Stefano Scarpetta. 2003. *Regulation, Productivity, and Growth.* Economics Department Working Paper 347. Paris: Organization for Economic Cooperation and Development.

OECD (Organization for Economic Cooperation and Development). 2003. *The Sources of Economic Growth in OECD Countries.* Paris: Organization for Economic Cooperation and Development.

OECD (Organization for Economic Cooperation and Development). 2004. International Trade by Commodity Statistics Database. Paris: Organization for Economic Cooperation and Development.

OMB (Office of Management and Budget). 2004. *Budget of the United States Government, Fiscal Year 2005—Appendix.* Washington: US Government Printing Office. www.whitehouse.gov/omb/budget/fy2005/appendix.html (accessed August 18, 2004).

Public Citizen. 2004. Consolidated Trade Adjustment Assistance Database. Washington: Public Citizen. www.citizen.org/trade/forms/taa_search.cfm?dataset=3 (accessed October 7, 2004).

Richardson, J. David. 2004. 'Sizing Up' the Micro-Data Benefits. Institute for International Economics. Photocopy.

Richardson, J. David. Forthcoming. *Global Forces, American Faces: US Economic Globalization at the Grass Roots.* Washington: Institute for International Economics.

Roberts, Mark, and James Tybout, eds. 1996. *Industrial Evolution in Developing Countries.* New York: Oxford University Press.

Rodriguez, Francisco, and Dani Rodrik. 2001. Trade Policy and Economic Growth: A Skeptic's Guide to Cross-National Evidence. In *NBER Macroeconomics Annual 2000,* ed., Ben S. Bernanke and Kenneth Rogoff. Cambridge, MA: MIT Press.

Rogers, John H., Gary Clyde Hufbauer, and Erika Wada. 2001. *Price Level Convergence and Inflation in Europe.* Working Paper 01-1. Washington: Institute for International Economics. www.iie.com/publications/wp/2001/01-1.pdf (accessed July 20, 2004).

Romer, Paul M. 1996. Why, Indeed, America? Theory, History, and the Origins of Modern Economic Growth. *American Economic Review* 86, no. 2 (May): 202–06.

Rose, Andrew K. 2003. Which International Institutions Promote International Trade? http://faculty.haas.berkeley.edu/arose/Comparer.pdf (accessed August 3, 2004).

Rose, Andrew K. 2004. Response to Subramanian and Wei. University of California, Berkeley; NBER; and CEPR (January). http://faculty.haas.berkeley.edu/arose/SWResponse.pdf (accessed August 3, 2004).

Rutherford, Thomas F., and David G. Tarr. 2002. Trade Liberalization, Product Variety, and Growth in a Small Open Economy: A Quantitative Assessment. *Journal of International Economics* 56, no. 2 (March): 247–72.

Sachs, Jeffrey D., and Andrew Warner. 1995. Economic Reform and the Process of Global Integration. *Brookings Papers on Economic Activity* 1: 1–118. Washington: Brookings Institution.

Schott, Jeffrey J. 2004. Assessing US FTA Policy. In *Free Trade Agreements: US Strategies and Priorities*, ed., Jeffrey J. Schott. Washington: Institute for International Economics.

Slaughter, Matthew J. 2004. Globalization and Employment by US Multinationals: A Framework and Facts. *Daily Tax Report* 58 (March 26). Washington: BNA, Inc.

Stephenson, Sherry, Christopher Findlay, and Soonhwa Yi. 2002. *Services Trade Liberalization and Facilitation.* Canberra, Australia: Asia Pacific Press at The Australian National University.

Subramanian, Arvind, and Shang-Jin Wei. 2003. *The WTO Promotes Trade, Strongly but Unevenly.* NBER Working Paper 10024. Cambridge, MA: National Bureau of Economic Research.

Trefler, Daniel. 2004. The Long and Short of the Canada-US Free Trade Agreement. *American Economic Review* 94, no. 4 (September): 870–95.

Truman, Edwin M. 2003. *Inflation Targeting in the World Economy.* Washington: Institute for International Economics.

US Census Bureau. 2003. Statistical Abstract of the United States, 123rd edition. Washington: US Government Printing Office.

USITC (United States International Trade Commission). 2004. Tariff and Trade Dataweb. Washington: USITC. http://dataweb.usitc.gov (accessed August 4, 2004).

WTO (World Trade Organization). 2003. *World Trade Report 2003.* Geneva: World Trade Organization. www.wto.org/english/res_e/booksp_e/anrep_e/world_trade_report_2003_e.pdf (accessed August 30, 2004).

WTO (World Trade Organization). 2004. Doha Ministerial 2001: Briefing Notes. Geneva: World Trade Organization. www.wto.org/english/thewto_e/minist_e/min01_e/brief_e/brief21_e.htm (accessed September 22, 2004).

Yeaple, Stephen R. 2003. Firm Heterogeneity, International Trade, and Wages. University of Pennsylvania. Photocopy (November 21).

Appendix 2A
Intermediate Imports: Gains Through Worker Productivity

The growth accounting technique adapted by J. David Richardson (2004) analyzes the gains to firms through a portion of the import competition channel, namely productivity gains to domestic firms that result from more intense use of *imported* intermediate inputs by US firms.[72] Roughly half of US imports are intermediate goods; the fact that they are purchased by US firms reveals superiority in quality or price to domestic alternatives. The growth accounting technique captures not only output gains from the use of superior or cheaper inputs but also gains that arise from sifting and sorting when less efficient suppliers of intermediate inputs shrink in the face of import competition, and their resources (capital and labor) are used by more efficient firms in the US economy.

To estimate the role of imported intermediates on a macro level, Richardson (2004) extends the basic growth accounting model—which expresses total production (Q, defined as value added, or GDP) as a function of technological knowledge (A), physical and human capital (K), and labor (L) as inputs—to include imported inputs (M).

$$Q = A(L, K, M) \tag{2.1}$$

Richardson then expresses the production function on a per worker basis, by dividing all variables by the number of workers (L). This causes the labor term to drop out of equation (2.1). The per worker production function can be written using lowercase variables.[73]

$$q = A(k, m) \tag{2.2}$$

Equation (2.2) suggests that to increase output per worker (defined as value added per worker), the country has three options:

- Increase A, the level of technological expertise (total factor productivity) so that the same amount of capital and imported inputs can produce more output. The benefits of trade through technology spillovers and more competitive markets would raise A. Since this approach does not estimate technology benefits of global integration, it understates the total payoff from greater trade.
- Increase the amount of physical and human capital each worker has to work with, k. Indirectly, an increase in trade can boost k by increas-

72. This section draws heavily on a draft appendix prepared by Richardson (2004).

73. Therefore, q is output (value added) per worker, k is the capital-labor ratio, and m is imported inputs per worker. We assume that equation (2.1) is homogenous of degree 1 with respect to L, K, and M.

ing the profitability of new investment, both in physical capital and training. Again, this approach does not measure the capital-deepening channel.

- Increase the amount of intermediate imports per worker, m. This is the focus of Richardson's approach. It assumes that firms import intermediate inputs only when such imports lower the overall cost of production. To pay for imports, the country must export goods and services that it produces at a comparative advantage. If there were no cost savings from switching from domestic to imported intermediate imports, and no improved productivity due to rationalization of domestic industry, the shift (accompanied by an increase in exports) would result in an increase in trade but no change in output.

When imports and exports both increase or decrease by the same amount, with no induced change in productivity, measured GDP does not change (recall the accounting identity: $Q = C + I + G + [X - M]$). Richardson's approach assumes that firms would have no reason to switch from domestic to imported intermediate inputs unless the switch yielded higher output per worker (q). He quantifies the gains using the methodology of growth accounting. However, as discussed in a moment, the mechanics of growth accounting may attribute too much or too little importance to imported intermediate inputs.

As a first-order simplification, an increase (or decrease) in q can be decomposed into three changes: a change in A, a change in k, and a change in m. In a standard growth accounting framework, the contribution that changes in k and m make to increase q are calculated by multiplying their respective percentage changes by their shares in total production costs.[74] Using S_k to denote the share of capital (human and physical) in total production costs (measured in percent of GDP), S_m to denote the share of imported inputs in total production costs, and $\%\Delta$ to denote the percentage change in a variable, equation (2.2) can be expressed as:

$$\%\Delta q = \%\Delta A + S_k\%\Delta k + S_m\%\Delta m \qquad (2.3)$$

The key assumption of the growth accounting model is that the share of imported inputs in production costs accurately reflects the contribution of those inputs to higher output. On the one hand, if intermediate inputs are only slightly better than their domestic counterparts, the share coefficient (S_m) will overstate their importance. On the other hand, if imported inputs set off a chain of sifting and sorting among domestic producers (as

74. This calculation assumes a constant-returns-to-scale production function, usually a Cobb-Douglas function. Any economies of scale are then captured in the technology term, A.

described in the text), S_m may understate their importance. We mention these possibilities without attempting to resolve them.

Returning to equation (2.3), economic statistics can be used to estimate five of the six variables, namely $\%\Delta q$, S_k, $\%\Delta k$, S_m, and $\%\Delta m$. Equation (2.3) can then be solved to determine an estimate of the technology variable, $\%\Delta A$, which measures total factor productivity.

On the basis of data gathered by Huether and Richardson (2001, table 1), it can be estimated that imported inputs (M) grew from $383 billion in 1989 to $940.1 billion in 2000 (measured in 2003 dollars).[75] Over the same period, employment (L) grew from 117.3 million to 136.9 million workers (CEA 2004, table B-36); hence intermediate imports per worker ($m = M/L$) increased by 110.4 percent over the period. Since the average share of imported intermediate imports in total production costs was 7.1 percent, the contribution of imported inputs to output per worker between 1989 and 2000 was

$$S_m \%\Delta m = .071 \times 110.4\% = 7.9\% \tag{2.4}$$

The 7.9 percent increase due to increased trade represents *more than one-third* of the total increase in output per worker over this period. Expressed another way, increased imports of intermediate inputs were responsible for an additional $4,900 in income per worker (measured in 2003 dollars).[76] This equates to an additional $681 billion in GDP, or $2,300 income per capita and $6,000 income per household in 2003 due to increased trade between 1989 and 2000.[77]

To apply this analysis over a longer period, we classify US imports by 3-digit commodity into intermediate, capital, and final categories.[78] Between 1961 and 1989, intermediate imports to the United States (M) rose from $41 billion to $329 billion (valued in 2003 dollars), a 702 percent increase. During the same period, since the labor force (L) almost doubled, from 66 million to 117 million, the net result was a 350 percent increase in intermediate input imports per worker (m). The ratio of intermediate imports to total production (measured in percent of GDP) steadily increased from 1.5 to 4.5 percent. As with our analysis above, we divide this long pe-

75. Since the original Huether and Richardson calculation was in constant 1992 dollars, we inflate these figures using the NIPA GDP deflator (BEA 2004b).

76. This calculation assumes that employment growth was not influenced by the increase in trade. Several scholars contend that increased trade and overseas investment tend to increase employment. See Slaughter (2004).

77. Employment growth outpaced population growth over this period, so the payoff in terms of GDP per capita exceeded the payoff in terms of output per worker.

78. We use the OECD International Trade by Commodity Statistics database (ITCS) available through http://new.sourceoecd.com (accessed August 9, 2004) by subscription. The list of 3-digit SITC codes we assign to the intermediate category is available upon request.

Table 2A.1 Productivity benefit of increase in imported intermediate inputs, 1961–2000

Period	Change in intermediate imports per worker (%Δm) (percent)	Share of intermediate imports in production cost (S_m) (percent)	Growth in output per worker due to intermediate import deepening[a] (S_m%Δm)		Benefit in 2003[a,b] (billions of 2003 dollars)
			Percent	2003 dollars	
1961–68	50.1	1.68	0.84	346	48
1968–75	99.9	2.69	2.68	1,364	188
1975–82	33.9	4.04	1.37	727	100
1982–89	11.9	4.51	0.53	295	41
1989–2000[c]	110.4	7.13	7.87	4,946	681
Total					
1961–2000				7,678	1,058

a. Subperiod gains are an intermediate calculation, not an estimate of short-term gains from liberalization. Gains due to liberalization may require 10 to 20 years to be fully realized.

b. Benefit in 2003 is calculated by multiplying the benefit per worker measured in 2003 dollars by total employment in 2003.

c. Changes in intermediate imports are calculated using Huether and Richardson (2001, table 1).

Note: In order to better account for changes within the US economy over time, this table presents total gains from liberalization as the sum of subperiods. Because of a change in sources, we do not present a single period figure.

Sources: OECD (2004), CEA (2004, tables B-22, B-36), Huether and Richardson (2001), and authors' calculations.

riod into four smaller periods to perform the growth calculation. The results are reported in table 2A.1. In summary, increased intermediate imports accounted for an output increase of 6.6 percent or $2,700 per worker (measured in 2003 dollars) between 1961 and 1989, roughly 13 percent of the total growth in output per worker over the period. In 2003, this increase accounted for an additional $380 billion of GDP, $1,300 per capita, and $3,400 per household annually.

We sum Richardson's results and the calculations sketched above to come up with a figure for increased growth due to intermediate import deepening for the full 1961–2000 period. We estimate a gain of $1.1 trillion for the full period, equating to an additional $3,600 per capita and $9,400 per household.

Appendix 2B
An Estimate of Labor Adjustment Costs

This chapter has calculated large gains from liberalization. However, our methods aggregate national benefits over the medium term and do not highlight the short-term, but significant, costs of worker dislocation. In this appendix, we make a back-of-the-envelope calculation to size up the adjustment costs incurred by dislocated workers in the US economy.

Adjustment costs occur when firms contract as a result of increased trade. We measure these costs through lost wages from time spent out of work and lower wages once reemployed.[79] Adjustment gains occur in expanding industries through an employment surge and higher wages in more productive firms. These gains will offset adjustment losses. However, to isolate the downside of globalization, we ignore adjustment gains.

Job Losses

Calculating the number of jobs gained and lost by trade agreements is one of Washington's favorite parlor games. In reality, separating trade-related job losses from other job losses is extremely difficult. Accordingly, we present several estimates.

First, we offer trade adjustment assistance (TAA) certifications as a proxy for job losses: 199,424 persons were certified for TAA in 2003 (Public Citizen 2004).[80] This is the most concrete figure available on trade-impacted job losses, but it contains elements of understatement and overstatement. The figures are understated because not all workers that are displaced by trade apply for TAA benefits. The figures are overstated because TAA certification only requires a showing that the job was adversely affected by imports or that the firm moved to a free trade partner or preference country; no evidence is required that policy liberalization *caused* either the imports or the relocation of the firm.[81]

79. Labor economists might point out that our calculation takes no account of the value of leisure time. For this and other reasons mentioned below, we regard this estimate as an upper bound.

80. The states administer the TAA program, so no official national statistics on certifications are available. Public Citizen collects state data on certifications and compiles it into a national database. While certifications may occur before or after job loss, we assume the rate of certifications is roughly equal to the rate of job loss. In October 2002, the TAA program was combined with the NAFTA-TAA program, which was originally designed to assist workers affected by trade with Canada and Mexico. The 2003 figure, approximately 200,000, is in line with the sum of TAA and NAFTA-TAA certifications in previous years.

81. It is possible to be certified for TAA even without losing a job, if increased imports are shown to be suppressing wages.

Our second estimate is based on an estimate of the relationship between manufacturing employment, domestic output, and imports. Hufbauer and Wong (2004, appendix table 8.1), using data on quarterly US manufacturing output and employment from 1990 to 2003, estimated that $1 billion of additional annual output would increase manufacturing employment by 8,178 workers. We make the exaggerated assumption that every dollar increase in US manufacturing imports displaces a dollar of domestic manufacturing output.[82] Between 1997 and 2003, US manufacturing imports rose from $750 billion to $1.1 trillion, an increase of about $52 billion annually (USITC 2004).[83] Applying the Hufbauer-Wong coefficient of 8,178 jobs per billion dollars suggests job displacement of up to 422,000 workers annually.

Finally, Baily and Lawrence (2004) use the trade deficit and US worker productivity to estimate job declines. To create a range, they measure productivity both in terms of gross manufacturing output per manufacturing worker and manufacturing value added per manufacturing worker. Between 2000 and 2003, they estimate that trade has caused the loss of between 85,000 and 197,000 manufacturing jobs per year.[84] After surveying these methods—none particularly realistic—we average them to produce an annual job displacement figure of approximately 226,000.[85] We consider this figure to be a high estimate.

The Displacement Experience

To get a handle on the private cost of a dislocated job, we define the loss in terms of forgone wages. Kletzer (2001) offers summary statistics based on displaced worker surveys collected by the US government covering worker experience from 1979 to 1999. We assume that all 226,000 jobs displaced each year are in "high import-competing industries," where dislo-

82. Hufbauer and Wong (2004, appendix table 8.2) show that the size of the trade deficit is *positively* correlated with manufacturing output. This is explained by the fact that both manufacturing output and imports tend to rise and fall with the overall US economy. Nevertheless, for purposes of this exercise, we assume that rising manufactured imports in a particular sector displace sales by firms in that sector, even though overall manufacturing output may be rising thanks to a buoyant economy.

83. Manufacturing imports are defined as NAICS 31–33.

84. This range is set by defining productivity in terms of gross output or value added. The gross production number tends to understate job loss because it does not account for increases in imported inputs. The value-added number tends to overstate job losses in manufacturing because it compares a value-added figure (manufacturing output) with a gross value figure (the trade deficit). The authors argue that the true number is likely to be at the low end of this range, since much of the job loss over this period is a result of the decline in exports.

85. We use both the lower and upper numbers of the Baily and Lawrence range in calculating this average.

cated workers fare the worst. In this category, the average age of a dislocated worker was 39. After dislocation, only 63.4 percent of dislocated workers were reemployed at the time they were surveyed, and of those that were employed, average earnings had declined 13.2 percent from their predisplacement earnings.[86] Finally, we assume that displaced workers were making the average weekly earnings of all manufacturing production workers—$646 in 2003 (BLS 2004).

We first consider the 36.6 percent of displaced workers who were still unemployed at the time of the survey. We assume, somewhat pessimistically, that these workers lose 10 years of employment as a consequence of the displacement episode.[87] Calculating in 2003 dollars (assuming wage increases would have kept pace with inflation), these workers lose $27.8 billion in lifetime earnings owing to long stretches of unemployment. To account for the remainder of time these workers are of working age, we assume they are forced to take a 13.2 percent pay cut for 16 years (bringing them to 65 years of age, on average), costing them another $5.9 billion in lifetime wages.[88]

Next, we consider lost wages of the 63.4 percent who were reemployed at the survey date. We assume it takes each reemployed worker one year to find new employment.[89] Lost wages during the job search period are then estimated to be $4.8 billion. Once reemployed, these workers take an average pay cut of 13.2 percent compared with predisplacement earnings. While we have no data beyond initial earnings, the gap likely narrows over time as the worker gains skills in the new job. However, we assume that the gap is maintained, in constant dollar terms, for the remainder of the worker's tenure—25 years.[90] Based on this assumption, displaced workers lose $15.9 billion due to lower reemployment wages over the remainder of their working lives.

---

86. We have no information on the size of fringe benefits, predisplacement versus postdisplacement, so we do not include fringe benefits in this estimate.

87. Obviously, this is one of many possible scenarios, and we do not argue that it is a typical outcome. It seems very unlikely that a worker could spend 10 years unemployed and then get a full-time job. Workers may choose to exit the labor force early; or they may work part-time jobs and spend less time totally unemployed. We offer the 10-year unemployment scenario merely as a way of arriving at a dollar figure for lifetime costs; we believe it is pessimistic.

88. We believe this to be a significant exaggeration. Workers who were not reemployed at the time of the survey tended to be older so they had fewer years left in the labor force. Kletzer (2001, table 4.1) indicates that workers in the 20 to 44 age group are roughly 10 percent more likely to be reemployed than those 45 and older.

89. Again this is a large overestimate. According to Kletzer (2001, 40) 73 percent of reemployed workers found a job within six months.

90. Recalling that the average age of a dislocated worker is 39, we assume they are out of work for one year and then exit the labor force at age 65.

It deserves mention that the 13.2 percent average wage loss represents a *private* cost of worker adjustment, not a *social* cost. Lower wages reflect the "opportunity value" (in the terminology of economics) of work in the new jobs—in other words, what the new work is worth when goods and services are sold in the market. Since workers are paid less in their new jobs than their old jobs, US buyers of goods and services enjoy the benefit of lower prices.

Summing these values, the lifetime losses incurred by workers displaced in 2003 is estimated to be $54.4 billion. If the number of workers displaced each year due to globalization and expanded trade proves to be a constant feature of the economy, this could be viewed as the annual private cost of labor adjustment.[91] Even so, the private costs are significantly lower than the past or potential annual social gains due to policy and technology liberalization. However, the costs are significantly larger than annual federal outlays (about $2 billion in 2003 [OMB 2004, 708]) designed to alleviate worker pains specifically caused by trade expansion.

91. As contrasted with the benefits of liberalization, which are permanent, adjustment costs are temporary. Once the economy has fully adjusted to a new plateau of trade and globalization, there would be no further adjustment costs of the kind we have calculated, but the economy would continue to enjoy a higher level of GDP.

3

Uneven Gains and Unbalanced Burdens? Three Decades of American Globalization

J. DAVID RICHARDSON

America's average gains from 30 years of deepening global integration have been surprisingly large, as documented in the previous chapter.

But their distribution among Americans has been uneven, according to recent research at the Institute for International Economics and elsewhere.[1] And distributional unbalance has characterized the burdens involved in realizing these gains.

American workers, firms, and communities with high skills, mobility, and global engagement have prospered handsomely. Those with average skills, low mobility, and little capability for global engagement have enjoyed disproportionally few net gains.

The same research also shows, however, that these same subpopulations of Americans face uncertain outcomes from changing technology, business ownership, "outsourcing" arrangements among suppliers and distributors, union attractiveness, and urbanization trends.

So recent global integration may have contributed, but only moderately, to their challenges, unless global integration itself has facilitated

J. David Richardson, senior fellow at the Institute for International Economics, is also a professor of economics and international relations and the Gerald B. and Daphna Cramer Professor of Global Affairs at the Maxwell School, Syracuse University.

1. See Richardson (forthcoming) for a synthesis of the Institute research. See Fischer and Hout (2002); Hornstein, Krusell, and Violante (2003); and Krueger and Perri (2003) for other relevant contributions to the American scene, and Milanovic (2003) and Smeeding and Rainwater (2002) for growing global evidence of uneven distribution of the gains.

productive innovation in product quality, production process, and organization; undercut the effectiveness of union representation; and made it possible for cities to grow at the expense of proximate rural areas on which they used to depend.

In brief, many of the drivers of American change over the past few decades seem to be interdependent and cannot be distilled into a "pure essence of globalization," as distinct from pure technological change, and so on.

Uneven Gains?

Modern research using American microdata has revealed important *new* benefits from "engaging" in the global marketplace but also new concerns about their uneven distribution (see the previous chapter).

For Americans as suppliers, the metaphor that best summarizes these new benefits is fitness. Global markets serve as a kind of fitness center for all kinds of firms, in all kinds of industries, not just the large or lucky, and also for their workers and host communities. Unfortunately, however, those who try to avoid growing global competition face grave and growing health *risks*.

For Americans as demanders, the metaphors that best summarize these new benefits are precision parts and consumer sovereignty. Global markets allow firms to shop the world for the precise kind of components, equipment, and input services that maximize their own productivity and that of their workers and allow households to choose goods and services from an enormous global array of qualities and varieties at affordable prices.

Americans as Suppliers. The same new research shows that global "engagement" is not just export success. It is much more diverse and multidimensional. Global engagement includes importing and cross-border investment and technology exchange, in either direction.

Each type of global engagement is associated with fitness rewards. And when this new research is pulled together, it reveals another unappreciated pattern: Exports, imports, investment, outsourcing, and licensing of technology "hang" together. Industries and communities with lots of one also have lots of the others. The various types of global linkages are an integrated family of fitness commitments. And their distinctive benefits cumulate.

What are those distinctive benefits from global linkages?[2]

- American plants that export continuously grow 0.5 to 1.5 percent faster per year and enjoy 8.5 percent lower plant-closure rates than otherwise comparable locally focused plants.

2. See Lewis and Richardson (2001) and Richardson (forthcoming).

- American plants that are equity-linked to either American or foreign multinational corporations (MNCs) have 2 to 4 percent faster overall productivity growth per year than comparable, yet insular and wholly American-owned plants.
- Such MNC-engaged plants also use 27 to 31 percent more technologies from a standard list of 17 advanced technologies than do their non-MNC twins.
- Worker wages are 10 to 11 percent higher at American plants that export, 2.5 to 7 percent higher at American plants with an equity stake from a foreign MNC, and 7 to 15 percent higher at American plants owned by an American MNC than worker wages at comparable plants that are not globally engaged.
- American workers at plants linked to either foreign or US-owned MNCs maintain these higher wages *even though* their MNC employers "offshore" 1.5 to 2 times as many intermediate input purchases as comparable non-MNC plants. More precisely, MNC plants import—outsource offshore—11 to 16 percent of their supplies and components, whereas comparable non-MNC plants import only 6 to 8 percent.
- In a typical American state, service establishments with equity stakes from foreign MNCs pay workers up to 9 percent more than comparable American-owned service establishments, in both heavily unionized and lightly unionized states and industries.[3]

These sizable fitness rewards for the globally engaged seem to persist in bad times as well as good. They characterize small firms as well as large. They appear in low-tech as well as high-tech activities. And they accrue to normally skilled as well as highly skilled workers, to union members, minorities, small towns, and other unlikely communities. There is little to no evidence in this research that global engagement helps capitalists more than workers, nor the strong and ambitious any more than the small and solidarity-minded. Global engagement seems to benefit all who partake. Only insularity seems to penalize.

But insularity is the source of the *unevenness* of these new fitness benefits. Americans who are unwilling or unable to seize these opportunities do *not* maintain their traditional status quo. In the globally integrated, technically dynamic, mobility-rewarding environment, insular Americans are subjected to unwelcome competitive pressures with an intensity that is far stronger than it used to be. Globalization and complementary

3. See Lewis and Richardson (2001, 33–34). There were no discernible state-by-state premiums for manufacturing establishments owned by foreign MNCs.

change widens the dispersion of benefits as well as raises its mean.[4] The gains are larger than ever for the successful engagers, and large on average, but smaller for the most insular fringe. Those that "have" get more opportunity; those that "have not," get less.

In fact, the principal source of overall fitness gains is a form of Darwinian evolutionary succession—sifting and sorting—in which the population of the "fittest" grows and prospers, but the population of those least fit, and least globally engaged, shrinks (and shrinks faster than it used to). In the United States, *that* population of insular Americans is still quite large.

At the level of firms and workers, models of this effect of global engagement[5] show the following:

- Increased global market opportunities—declining tariffs and trade costs, declining start-up costs of marketing abroad, opening of new, formerly closed foreign markets—can *all* cause favorable gains in worker-level, industry-level, and aggregate productivity, even though they have *no* ensuing salutary effect on any single firm's or worker's productivity (i.e., they merely make it possible for the already most productive to prosper).
- Such globalization-induced increases in overall productivity translate one-to-one into increased average welfare (i.e., standards of living).
- The mechanism by which these productivity and welfare effects emerge is "churning" followed by natural selection among heterogeneous firms that differ either in their inherent overall (total factor) productivity or in the access they have to worker pools of varying skill/creativity/reliability.
- Because firms and workers differ within an industry and occupation, they also differ in global and internal "competitive advantage" vis-à-vis rival firms and workers, and therefore country *comparative advantage must be redefined at the level of firms and workforces* as well as industries.
- But the same increased global market opportunity that rewards high-productivity firms and workers squeezes out low-productivity firms and workers. And this increased churning and dispersion of rewards may be seen as an increase in the endemic risk facing the entire Amer-

4. See a number of chapters in the three-volume *Handbook of Labor Economics* for documentation of the increased dispersion of labor rewards.

5. The following summary points come from Melitz (2003); Yeaple (2003); and Bernard, Redding, and Schott (2004). The models so far developed are for export and import engagement only, not for other modes of global integration such as investment or technology transfer.

ican economy and therefore a potential deduction from the welfare losses associated with increased productivity.[6]

Early attempts to measure the average gains from recent American global integration show them to be quite large:

- Recent reductions in cross-border transactions barriers and costs have caused one-to-one improvements in average US manufacturing productivity (1 percent improvement for every 1 percent decline), according to one study. Greater imports cause some low-productivity US plants to close but reduce input costs for higher-productivity plants and expand export market potential for them.[7]
- In differentiated-product US manufacturing,[8] according to a second study, industry productivity growth rates are 1 to 1.6 percent higher for every 1 percent decline in the cross-border costs of trade across industries and over time. Sifting and sorting is the main mechanism.

But there are no attempts so far to measure the degree to which these gains may be diminished from the increased riskiness of being on the "wrong side" of the American distribution of productivity across firms and capability across workers.[9]

What *is* clear from the Darwinian models of these new gains is that they *must* be distributed *more unevenly* across Americans than the traditional gains from trade. Just how much more unevenly remains to be seen, as does the issue of American policy innovation to more widely disseminate these new gains.[10]

Americans as Demanders. There is also some evidence that the benefits to American buyers from global integration have been unevenly distributed. Roughly one-third of American imports are purchased for "final

---

6. See, for example, Krueger and Perri (2003) and Heathcote, Storesletten, and Violante (2003).

7. See Bernard et al. (2003) for a microsimulation based on a model calibrated to actual US data for recent years.

8. Differentiated-product manufacturing is inferred; four-digit SIC industries with high export and import penetration with OECD countries is the inference lens used by Bernard, Jensen, and Schott (2004, 11–13). Three-quarters of the 67 industries so identified come from the usual family of high-technology manufacturing industries at the two-digit level: SIC 28 (chemicals, pharmaceuticals) and SIC 35–38 (machinery, equipment, instruments).

9. The beginnings of an approach to such measurement can be found in the new research on the welfare costs of growing US wage and income inequality. See Heathcote, Storesletten, and Violante (2003) and Krueger and Perri (2003).

10. Richardson (forthcoming, Part IV) discusses various American policy options and innovations.

use" by households. Yet the policy barriers to trade in these household goods have come down especially *slowly* in the food and clothing categories on which the spending of poor American households is concentrated. One revealing study (Gresser 2002, table 1) calculates that American tariffs fall unduly harshly on the budgets of the poor, causing the working-poor household to lose 5 days of annual purchasing power to protection-inflated prices, whereas a high-income household with $110,000 of annual income loses only 1½ days of annual purchasing power.

Unbalanced Burdens?

Recent microdata research has also been able to profile those Americans who bear the burdens of job dislocation and sluggish wage growth due to global integration, technological change, and other complementary pressures.

Workers in import-sensitive manufacturing industries seem recently to be bearing an increasing share of the labor-market adjustment burdens, whereas in the 1980s and 1990s they were only very slightly more pressured than manufacturing workers in general.[11] In 2000–01, workers from broad import-sensitive sectors (roughly 25 percent of manufacturing and 30 percent of nonmanufacturing jobs) began to experience dislocation rates that were more than double those facing other manufacturing workers (6.1 compared with 2.8 percent, relative to 2.1 percent in nonmanufacturing). Reemployment rates (over roughly three years) also began to diverge in the same way as dislocation rates—dropping to 54 percent compared with 57 percent for dislocated peers in other manufacturing jobs (and relative to 65 percent in nonmanufacturing jobs).

Furthermore in *extremely* import-sensitive sectors, accounting for 6 to 10 percent of manufacturing jobs, workers' *personal* characteristics put them at high risk for technological and global dislocation and made it hard to recover their footing in new jobs. These workers were older, less educated, mostly female, and longer tenured (i.e., more immobile) in their current job than typical American workers.

For example, in the extremely import-sensitive textile and apparel sectors (Kletzer, Levinsohn, and Richardson, forthcoming):

- For apparel workers, the disproportional probability of losing their job has been rising steadily from 1979 through 2001. Textile worker dislocation, though historically only slightly greater than for other manu-

11. Kletzer (2001), reconsidered and updated in Kletzer (forthcoming).

facturing, has surged relatively[12] in the past few years, especially for women textile workers.

- Apparel workers have had lower and slower reemployment prospects than other manufacturing workers over the whole period (textile workers again looked more typical of all manufacturing in reemployment).[13]
- In predicting reemployment success, personal worker characteristics mattered far more than the industry from which the worker was displaced. Dislocated workers who were more educated and more skilled (measured by occupation) were more likely to find new jobs, with men more likely than women. But these personal capability and adaptability traits were found among textile and apparel workers less frequently than among workers in other sectors.

American deunionization trends also seem to be interdependently correlated with education and trade. On the one hand, exports and imports seem to have contributed only modestly to American deunionization according to recent research (Baldwin 2003). But on the other hand, trade had larger estimated impacts on basically educated unionists than on those who are better educated. Surges in imports from 1977 to 1987 and in exports from 1987 to 1997 were each correlated with strong reductions in the employment of basically educated unionists (controlling both for shifts in product demand and for technological change). Job declines attributed to rising imports from 1977 to 1987 accounted for a disproportionate share of employment declines borne by basically educated unionists, amounting to 20 to 25 percent of the decade's total decline in basically skilled unionized jobs. The same research attributes almost one-half million fewer unionized blue-collar jobs to rising *exports* from 1987 to 1997—a disproportionate share of employment declines borne by basically educated unionists, amounting to 42 percent of the decade's total decline in basically skilled unionized jobs.

The export side of these findings is striking and seems initially counterintuitive. Yet surges in US export participation and sales shares in the late 1980s and 1990s are highly correlated in the US Census of Manufactures with strong skill-upgrading in employment and with a decline in the average size (downsizing) of both firms and plants. Export surges during this period were also often the result of global outsourcing—vertical rationalization and specialization of production stages—and

12. All workers' dislocation probabilities turned up in the 2001–02 recession, but the upsurge was especially strong for textile workers.

13. The adverse reemployment gap narrowed somewhat for apparel workers in the recent slump.

of hard-fought corporate struggles over whether to invest in additional exports from American plants or whether to invest abroad, both of which can threaten the jobs of less-skilled and unionized workers. Stronger global export competition facing American firms squeezes their ability to earn profits and to share any such profits with their workers.[14]

Finally, if these results do profile the pattern of globalization's adjustment burdens, then it is no surprise that recent research on opinion surveys finds that higher import and immigration barriers are more favored by voters the less education they have and the lower paid their occupations (Scheve and Slaughter 2001). Protection from both imports and immigrants is associated with individual skills and education (industry and location hardly matter). This research also implies that every extra year's education in a cross-section of voters makes an American 5 to 6 percent less likely to support higher import barriers and 2 to 3 percent less likely to resist immigration. (Mean support for higher import barriers was around 60 percent in the surveys sampled, and toward immigration the typical voter's preference lay somewhere between "less" and "fine as is.")

Quo Vadis American Policy?

Taken together, the various studies of American benefits and burden-bearing imply that politicians who want to appeal more successfully to real people and to the working poor need to choose between two important policy directions. They can slow down global integration and/or protect more aggressively at the American border. Or they can help such Americans directly by domestic policy innovation.

Since the research summarized here (and in the previous chapter) also shows that Americans *on average* gain enormously by keeping borders open, our strong preference is for new American policies whose benefits are strongly concentrated on diffusing the gains and easing the burdens on middle America and the American working poor.

References

Baldwin, Robert E. 2003. *The Decline of US Labor Unions and the Role of Trade.* Washington: Institute for International Economics.

Bernard, Andrew, Jonathan Eaton, J. Bradford Jensen, and Samuel Kortum. 2003. Plants and Productivity in International Trade. *American Economic Review* 93: 1268–90.

14. Slaughter (2001) and Khripounova and Richardson (1998), for example, show how increased global competitive pressures that "flatten" a firm's product demand curves also flatten the demand curves for workers, making them more elastic. Union wage premiums fall toward zero as worker demand curves become more elastic, according to most models of workplace bargaining.

Bernard, Andrew, J. Bradford Jensen, and Peter K. Schott. 2004. Falling Trade Costs, Heterogeneous Firms, and Industry Dynamics. Photocopy (March).

Bernard, Andrew B., Stephen Redding, and Peter Schott. 2004. *Comparative Advantage and Heterogeneous Firms.* NBER Working Paper 10668. Cambridge, MA: National Bureau of Economic Research.

Fischer, Claude S., and Michael Hout. 2002. Differences Across Americans in Living Standards Across the Twentieth Century. Photocopy (August 26).

Gresser, Edward. 2002. *Toughest on the Poor: Tariffs, Taxes, and the Single Mom.* Progressive Policy Institute Policy Report, September. www.ppionline.org.

Heathcote, Jonathan, Kjetil Storesletten, and Giovanni L. Violante. 2003. The Macroeconomic Implications of Rising Wage Inequalities in the U.S. Photocopy.

Hornstein, Andreas, Per Krusell, and Giovanni L. Violante. 2003. The Effects of Technical Change on Labor Market Inequalities. Photocopy.

Khripounova, Elena B., and J. David Richardson. 1998. *U.S. Labor Market Power and Linkages to International Trade: Identifying Suspects and Measures.* Final report to the US Department of Labor, Office of International Labor Affairs, Contract P.O. # B9K53131, January.

Kletzer, Lori G. 2001. *Job Loss from Imports: Measuring the Costs.* Washington: Institute for International Economics.

Kletzer, Lori G. Forthcoming. *Workers at Risk: Job Loss from Apparel, Textiles, Footwear, and Services, 1979–2001.* Washington: Institute for International Economics (forthcoming).

Kletzer, Lori G., James Levinsohn, and J. David Richardson. Forthcoming. *Responses to Globalization: US Textiles and Apparel Workers and Firms.* Washington: Institute for International Economics.

Krueger, Dirk, and Fabrizio Perri. 2003. On The Welfare Consequences of the Increase in Inequality in the United States. *Macroeconomics Annual 2003:* 82–120. Cambridge, MA: National Bureau of Economic Research.

Lewis, Howard, and J. David Richardson. 2001. *Why Global Commitment Really Matters!* Washington: Institute for International Economics.

Melitz, Marc J. 2003. The Impact of Trade on Intra-Industry Reallocations and Aggregate Industry Productivity. *Econometrica* 71 (November): 1695–725.

Milanovic, Branko. 2003. Can We Discern the Effect of Globalization on Income Distribution? Evidence from Household Surveys. Photocopy (September 22).

Richardson, J. David. Forthcoming. *Global Forces, American Faces: US Economic Globalization at the Grass Roots.* Washington: Institute for International Economics.

Scheve, Kenneth F., and Matthew J. Slaughter. 2001. *Globalization and the Perceptions of American Workers.* Washington: Institute for International Economics.

Slaughter, Matthew J. 2001. International Trade and Labor-Demand Elasticities. *Journal of International Economics* 54 (June): 27–56.

Smeeding, Timothy M., and Lee Rainwater. 2002. Comparing Living Standards Across Nations: Real Incomes at the Top, the Bottom, and the Middle. Photocopy (February).

Yeaple, Stephen R. 2003. Firm Heterogeneity, International Trade, and Wages. Photocopy (November 21).

4

China: The Great New Economic Challenge?

NICHOLAS R. LARDY

China has been the world's fastest-growing economy since initiating economic reform two and a half decades ago. Its influence on the global economy has expanded dramatically, particularly its role as a global manufacturer and trader. For example, in 2004, China will overtake Japan to become the world's third largest trading economy (measured as the sum of imports and exports). But its participation in the global economy is not limited to trade. It has been the largest developing-country recipient of foreign direct investment (FDI) for more than a decade and also raises significant amounts of funds in international capital markets. China's economic diplomacy has accelerated as well, as it pursues an increasingly visible role both in global trade liberalization in the Doha Round of multilateral trade negotiations and in regional and bilateral agreements. The latter range from free trade agreements (FTAs) with trading partners as diverse as the Association of Southeast Asian Nations (ASEAN), Australia, and Chile to an Asian regional framework agreement on energy cooperation known as the Qingdao Initiative.[1]

Nicholas Lardy is a senior fellow at the Institute for International Economics.

1. ASEAN and China signed an agreement covering goods in October 2004 and expect to conclude negotiations on services and investment by the middle of 2005. Australia and China reached an agreement to study the prospects for a bilateral FTA in late 2003. The study was launched in January 2004 and is scheduled for completion at the end of October 2005. Chile and China began their FTA study in April 2003. In November 2004 the leaders of the two countries announced their decision to start formal negotiations on an FTA.

For reasons discussed below, China is likely to sustain a relatively high rate of growth for at least another decade, during which it will continue to become an ever-larger economic and trading power. The long-term implications of this for the United States, however, are uncertain. China's rapid emergence on the global economic stage, particularly its burgeoning bilateral trade surplus with the United States, suggests to some that China poses a potential threat to US economic and security interests (US-China Economic and Security Review Commission 2004, 1). As a growing portion of this deficit is composed of advanced technology products, rather than just apparel, footwear, and toys, some see China as eroding US leadership in technological innovation and international competitiveness in advanced technology industries (Preeg 2004).

In contrast, this chapter suggests that China's pace of technological progress is frequently overstated and that China is more of an economic opportunity than an economic threat to the United States and other high-income economies. But China's increasing interdependence with the global economy is likely to be accompanied by growing trade frictions as well. The final section of this chapter contains recommendations for ameliorating these frictions.

China's Emergence in the Global Economy

China's real GDP in 2003 was nine times that in 1978, when reform began, a record that places it among the fastest-growing economies in any two-and-a-half-decade period in modern economic history. Measured at current exchange rates, China is now the world's sixth largest economy, after the United States, Germany, Japan, the United Kingdom, and France. On present trends, in the next year or two China will overtake both the United Kingdom and France to rank fourth globally. In terms of GDP measured by purchasing power (a metric that adjusts for the relatively low price of services in developing countries), the World Bank since 1995 has ranked China number two, behind only the United States. Of course, given its immense population of 1.3 billion, China remains very poor in per capita terms. This has important implications, as discussed below.

China's rapidly expanding international trade enhances the global significance of its growing economy. Since reforms began in 1978, China's trade has grown substantially above average: Its share of global trade expanded from 0.6 percent in 1977 to almost 6 percent in 2003. When reforms got under way, about 30 countries were ahead of China in terms of trade value, but in 2003 China ranked fourth and in 2004 will rank third, after only the United States and Germany. Since 2000, China has made a particularly outsized contribution to global trade growth. Indeed, in 2000–03 China accounted for a larger share of global trade expansion than any other country, including the United States. During that period US trade expanded by only $17 billion, while China's grew by $377 billion.[2] In 2003, China alone accounted for fully a fifth of global trade expansion.

Policies welcoming FDI, particularly in manufacturing, have been a major contributor to China's rapid trade expansion. By the end of 2003, foreign firms had invested about $500 billion in China, the world's third largest stock of FDI after only the United States and the United Kingdom. Indeed, in 2003 direct investment inflows into China for the first time exceeded inflows into the United States (OECD 2004, 3).[3] Over half of this investment has gone into manufacturing, where China places few restrictions on foreign ownership. By 2003, foreign firms accounted for over one-quarter of China's output of manufactured goods, a share that is well ahead of that of the United States and about the same as that of the European Union.[4]

Moreover, through its tariff and other policies, China allows foreign firms that produce for the export market to operate at international prices. Imported machinery and equipment that go into foreign joint ventures and wholly foreign-owned firms, for example, are entirely exempt from import duties. And foreign-sourced parts and components, when reexported in the form of finished goods, also are exempt from import duties. Moreover, manufacturers are eligible for a rebate of almost all domestic value-added taxes they have paid on any content in their exports that is sourced from within China. Combined with relatively low-cost labor, these trade and investment policies have made China one of the most competitive global locations for the assembly of manufactured goods for export. As a result, foreign firms now account for more than half of China's exports.

The expansionary effect of China's growing trade is particularly evident in Asia. In 2002 and 2003, when China's global imports rose by a total of $170 billion, it accounted for one-half the growth of exports of a number of other Asian countries, notably Korea and Taiwan (World Bank 2004, 9). Surging exports to China, for example, were a major driver of the recovery in Japan's economic growth starting in the fourth quarter of 2003. Most notable has been the rapid growth of Japanese exports to China of machinery and electrical machinery, metals, and precision instruments. The acceleration of demand for some products has been so strong that it stimulated a revival of investment activity in these sectors in Japan. Taiwan is also increasingly linked to China; indeed the share of its exports going to

2. In both cases, the trade value is measured as the sum of imports and exports of goods and services in 2003 minus the sum of imports and exports of goods and services in 2000.

3. Technically, Luxembourg remains the largest recipient of FDI, due to large matching inflows and outflows through holding companies and other special purpose entities located there. Apart from Luxembourg, China was the world's largest recipient of FDI for the first time in 2003, according to the Organization for Economic Cooperation and Development.

4. The foreign firms' share is measured by value added. Measured by gross value, the foreign firms' share in 2003 was 30.6 percent. See National Bureau of Statistics (2004, 124).

the mainland now exceeds that of any other economy. Exports of ASEAN countries to China grew by more than 50 percent in 2003 alone.

But China's impact on global economic growth extends far beyond Asia. China, for example, is now the number two trading partner of both Canada and Mexico, ahead of each in the other country's market despite the North American Free Trade Agreement. Trade between Brazil and China, for example, quadrupled in 1999–2003. In 2004, Brazil's expanding exports to China, notably of soybeans and iron ore, are on track to account for half of Brazil's global export growth and a quarter of the country's targeted 3.5 percent GDP growth.

The expansion of China's economy and trade is so large that it had a dramatic effect on global prices for some critical raw materials and basic industrial goods in 2003 and the first part of 2004. China is now the world's largest consumer of copper, tin, zinc, platinum, steel, and iron ore; the second largest consumer of aluminum, petroleum, and lead; the third largest consumer of nickel; and the fourth largest user of gold (Asian Development Bank 2004, 43). For many of these products, China's sharply rising demand has been met increasingly by imports, causing global prices for many commodities to increase at record rates. In both 2002 and 2003, China's steel imports soared as it became the world's largest importer, driving global prices up sharply. It is also one of the largest importers of iron ore to feed its domestic steel industry, which has ranked number one globally since 1996. China's soaring iron ore imports in 2003 led to the largest increase in ore prices in 23 years.

Because China's GDP is very strongly concentrated in manufacturing (for reasons discussed below), rapid growth has also led to a substantial growth of consumption and imports of energy, notably petroleum. In 2003, China's crude oil imports rose more than 30 percent to 91.12 million metric tons, accounting for a third of total petroleum consumption in China (National Bureau of Statistics 2004, 127, 162). China overtook Japan in 2003 to become the second largest consumer of oil, after the United States. China alone accounted for 45 percent of the increase in global oil demand in 2002–03, contributing significantly to the growth of global demand relative to supply, thus driving world oil prices to record levels. It remains a major source of growing world demand for crude oil in 2004 (International Energy Agency 2004).

What are the prospects that China will be able to sustain its record-breaking pace of economic growth and continue to make an outsized contribution to global trade expansion and thus to global economic growth? In the short run, of course, China's leaders have recognized the financial risks associated with the record expansion of bank credit and fixed asset investment that occurred in 2003 and the first part of 2004. They are moderating the growth of credit and of fixed asset investment to slow the pace of overall economic expansion to a more sustainable level. If they succeed, China's trade growth likely will slow from its recent (2001–04) pace of more than 25 percent a year to something closer to its long-term (1980–2000) annual growth of about 15 percent, thus likely diminishing the outsized role that China has played in global growth in recent years.

While China seeks to moderate its pace of growth in the short run, in the medium and long run, several factors are likely to interact to generate growth rates that will be quite high by global standards. First, China's national saving rate of roughly 40 percent of GDP is one of the highest in the world. That provides enormous resources for financing the fixed asset investment that is so important for economic growth, especially in a low-income economy. The saving rate likely will decline as China begins to age rapidly and the share of households that maintain their living standards not from current income but by spending their accumulated savings grows. But based on China's demographics, this decline in the saving rate is likely a decade or so away.

A second positive driver for rapid growth is that China is at a relatively early stage of the transformation of its labor force, from one engaged predominantly in agriculture to one engaged primarily in manufacturing and services. Although the share of the labor force employed in farming has shrunk over the past couple of decades, 350 million workers—or one-half of China's labor force—are still employed in agriculture. Given China's extreme shortage of arable land, output per farm worker is relatively low, so transferring labor to other sectors of the economy raises real economic output. Most observers believe that at least 100 million—perhaps as many as 150 million—workers could be moved from agriculture to either services or manufacturing with little or no adverse effect on agricultural output. This shift will be a major source of growth over the next decade or so.

Finally, China's openness to foreign trade and investment (both analyzed below) also are likely to contribute further to rapid economic growth. Both imports and domestic sales of foreign affiliates are likely to continue to rise relative to GDP. That, in turn, will contribute to a more competitive domestic economy, which will likely stimulate further productivity growth in domestic firms, adding to overall economic growth.[5]

US–China Economic Relations

Bilateral trade and investment ties between China and the United States have grown rapidly in recent years. China is now the United States' third largest trading partner and the sixth largest export market for firms located in the United States. The United States is China's second largest trading partner and has long been the single largest export market for firms located in China, taking over 30 percent of total exports produced

5. For a comprehensive review of the literature on the influence of trade on economic growth, see Cline (2004, 228–38).

within China. These firms are now the second largest supplier of imports to the United States, having gone ahead of Japan in 2002 and Mexico in 2003. But firms located in the United States have been only a modest supplier of imports to China, for reasons discussed below. US firms had made about $45 billion in direct investments in China through the end of 2003, far more than in any other emerging market.

Causes of the Bilateral Trade Imbalance

While bilateral economic ties between China and the United States are robust, they have been characterized by a steadily growing bilateral trade imbalance. Initially the balance in China's favor was small, but it now constitutes United States' single largest bilateral trade deficit. The principal cause of this growing imbalance, which reached $124 billion in 2003, is neither an undervalued Chinese currency nor Chinese protectionist measures that keep out US and other foreign goods. China's bilateral surplus with the United States has grown steadily for more than two decades. During most of this time, China's currency was significantly overvalued. Rather, the growing imbalance is because China has become a leading location for the assembly of a broad range of manufactured goods, mostly by foreign firms that have relocated their assembly activities to China from other sites in Asia. The parts and components that constitute these goods are purchased mainly from other Asian countries. On the other hand, the United States and the EU-15 supply only 12 percent of the inputs but purchase about half of the final goods produced under China's export processing scheme.[6] It is no accident that as the US bilateral deficit with China soared from $10 billion in 1985 to $124 billion in 2003, the share of China's exports produced by foreign firms rose from 1 to 55 percent.

As a result of China's emergence as a major base for foreign firms to assemble manufactured goods, China runs trade surpluses with the United States and the European Union and significant deficits with most Asian countries. Thus China's overall current account surplus is substantially smaller than its bilateral surplus with the United States. As reflected in table 4.1, its global current account surplus has averaged about 2 percent of GDP since it pegged its currency to the US dollar in 1994.

China's global pattern of trade—surpluses with the United States and Europe but deficits with most of its Asian neighbors—stems from China's

6. In 1999, 25 percent of the imports for export processing came from Japan; 20 percent from Taiwan; and 20 percent from Hong Kong, Singapore, and Korea. But only 5 percent came from the United States and 7 percent from the European Union. On the other hand, 26 percent of the resulting product was sold directly to the United States, and adjusting for reexports through Hong Kong, the US share was probably slightly in excess of 30 percent. Comparable numbers for the European Union are 14 and 19 percent, respectively. See Lemoine and Ünal-Kesenci (2004, 833).

Table 4.1 China's current account balance, 1994–2003

Year	Billions of dollars	Percent of GDP
1994	7.7	1.4
1995	1.6	0.2
1996	7.2	0.9
1997	29.7	3.3
1998	29.3	3.0
1999	15.7	1.6
2000	20.5	1.9
2001	17.4	1.5
2002	35.4	2.9
2003	45.9	3.3

Sources: National Bureau of Statistics of China, *China Statistical Yearbook* 2000, 2001, 2002, and 2003; State Administration of Foreign Exchange, 2003 National Income and Expense Accounts Report, www.safe.gov.cn (accessed May 3, 2004).

rapidly increasing role in the global production chains of multinational corporations. China's openness to FDI, its trade policies, and its relatively abundant labor supply have made it the premier location for the assembly of manufactured goods for the global market. This burgeoning role as an assembler of manufactured goods is reflected in two indicators.

First, the migration of global manufacturing capacity to China is so great that it has boosted the share of GDP originating in the industrial sector to an almost unprecedented 45 percent (National Bureau of Statistics 2004, 16).[7] As a consequence, China produces 7 percent of the world's manufactured goods, almost twice its share of global GDP.[8]

China's increasingly competitive global position in labor-intensive manufactures is clearly reflected in a second indicator—the pattern of US imports from China. Starting in the late 1980s, China began to displace Korea, Taiwan, and Hong Kong to become by 1991 the single largest source of imported toys and sporting goods in the US market. China at the same time also started to displace Korea and Taiwan to become by 1992 the single largest source of imported footwear in the US market. A decade later in 2002, China displaced Japan, the European Union, and Mexico to become the largest single source of US imports of consumer electronic products and information technology hardware such as computers (American Electronics Association 2003).

But how does China's outsized role in global production of manufactured goods lead to a pattern of trade in which China runs trade surpluses

7. Industry includes manufacturing, mining, and utilities. The share of GDP originating in manufacturing (excluding mining and utilities) in China is more than half again as large as the average of lower-middle-income countries, the category where China falls (World Bank's *World Development Indicators 2004*).

8. See "The New Workshop of the Globe Is Attracting the Biggest Companies on the Planet," *Financial Times*, June 21, 2004, 8.

with the United States and, to a lesser extent, the European Union, while running trade deficits with many of its Asian neighbors? The explanation lies in three characteristics of China's very large FDI inflows. First, Asian firms account for a much larger share of China's inward foreign investment than do European and American firms. Firms based in Hong Kong, Taiwan, Korea, and Japan, for example, account for about two-thirds of China's inward FDI. In contrast, the United States and the European Union combined account for less than a fifth of China's inward FDI.

Second, Asian firms relocate to China primarily to use China as an export platform whereas most American and European firms invest in China primarily to sell into the domestic market. The best example of the latter is Volkswagen, which has had a dominant share of the Chinese car market for over a decade. The output of Volkswagen's two joint ventures, one in Shanghai and the other in Changchun, is sold entirely on the domestic market. The same is true for the joint venture Buick plant in Shanghai.

Third, foreign firms producing for the domestic market tend also to source their inputs largely on the domestic market rather than from their home countries. Virtually the entire content of Volkswagen's top-selling models in China, for example, is sourced from within China. In contrast, as Asian firms have relocated their assembly operations to China, they have continued to source needed high-value-added parts and components from their traditional suppliers, which tend to be located elsewhere in Asia. This is particularly obvious in the case of Taiwan-based manufacturers of electronic products. As a result, China in 2003, for example, ran a trade deficit of more than $24 billion in its trade with Taiwan, an extraordinarily large amount given the small size of Taiwan's economy. Two-thirds of China's imports from Taiwan consist not of finished goods but of parts and components that subsequently are assembled into final goods in factories owned by Taiwanese firms. These goods then are exported, predominantly to the United States and Europe.

In short, American and European direct investment in China is relatively modest and geared primarily to sell into the domestic market. The investment of Asian firms in China is not only much larger but also tends to be directed to sales in the United States and Europe. And these Asian firms source a large share of parts and components they use from firms in their home countries. The combination of these factors creates the pattern of trade sketched earlier. The result is that China has become the source of many goods the United States once imported from Japan, Hong Kong, Korea, and Taiwan. As shown in figure 4.1, the share of the US global trade deficit arising from East Asian countries as a group has actually declined in the two decades since the bilateral deficit with China first emerged in the mid-1980s.

Finally, China's large and growing bilateral trade surplus with the United States does not constitute evidence that China's trade practices are systematically protectionist. China does protect some specific sectors and

Figure 4.1 Share of US trade deficit, by region (percent)

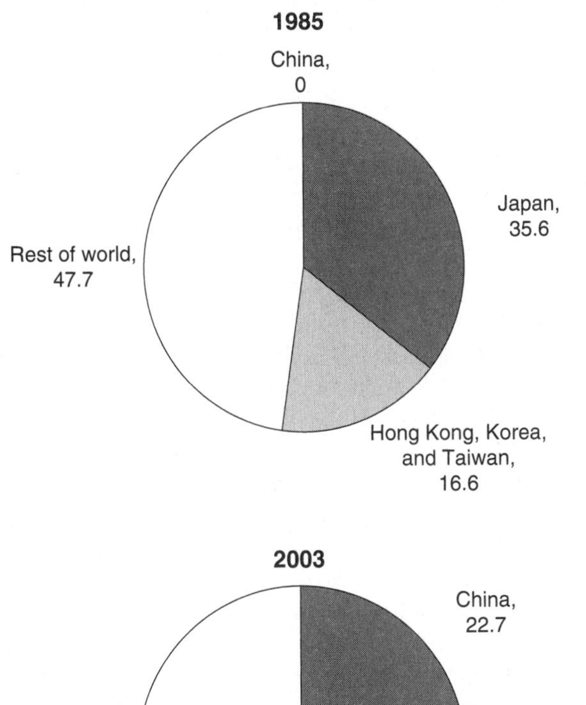

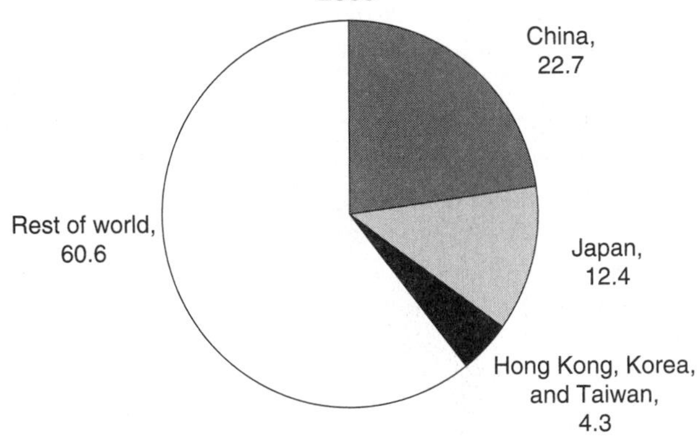

Sources: US Department of Commerce, Bureau of Economic Analysis, International Economic Accounts, US International Transactions Accounts Data, www.bea.gov.

products, to some extent in violation of its commitments to the World Trade Organization (WTO). But by all of the relevant metrics, China is certainly one of the most open—perhaps the most open—of all developing economies.

China's high degree of openness to imports is reflected in several measures beyond its openness to FDI, already analyzed earlier. First, its global imports have been growing at a prodigious rate in recent years: Imports of goods expanded from $53.4 billion in 1990 to $295 billion in 2002, a growth rate of more than 15 percent annually. In 2003, the growth of

China's imports hit an all-time high rate of 40 percent, leading imports to expand by almost $120 billion. In 2003, China's global imports of $413 billion for the first time exceeded those of Japan, making China the third largest importing nation in the world, after only the United States and Germany. In the nine months of 2004, imports grew an additional 38 percent above the level in the same period in 2003. It is a measure of the relative openness of the Chinese economy that as its economic growth accelerated in 2003 and maintained rapid growth in 2004, its import growth accelerated at an even more rapid rate.

China's rapid growth of imports has led to a sharp increase in the ratio of its imports to GDP, a measure referred to as a country's import ratio. China's import ratio increased from under 15 percent in 1990 to 30 percent in 2003. China's import ratio in 2003 was more than three times Japan's import ratio of 9 percent and twice the 14 percent import ratio of the United States.

A second measure of openness is the large volume of sales of foreign affiliates on China's own domestic market. As already noted, foreign affiliates account for one-quarter of all manufactured goods produced in China. There are almost no restrictions on where these goods can be sold, and sales are about evenly divided between exports and China's internal market. Foreign affiliate sales on the domestic market in 2003 reached $285 billion. Goods sold by foreign affiliates in the domestic market in most cases are close substitutes for imports, making China an almost textbook case of how openness to foreign investment can increase competition on the domestic market.

A third measure of China's openness is the modest degree of protection that import tariffs provide for domestically produced goods. Even before China became a member of the WTO, it had reduced its average import tariff rate by about three-quarters, from a peak of 56 percent in 1982 to 15 percent at the beginning of 2001 (Lardy 2002, 34). In 2003, China's average import tariff was 11.5 percent, and the average tariff on manufactured goods was only 10.3 percent. China's tariff rates compare favorably with the rates agreed to by other large emerging markets in the Uruguay Round of trade negotiations that led to the formation of the WTO. China's bound rate across all goods is 10 percent, far lower than the commitments of other large emerging markets. For example, Argentina's bound rate is 31.9 percent, Brazil's is 31.4 percent, India's 49.8 percent, and Indonesia's 37.1 percent.[9]

9. Bound rates are ceilings that cannot be exceeded except under unusual circumstances. All four comparator countries currently have applied tariff rates that are significantly lower than the bound rates cited above. In 2002–03, they ranged from 6.9 percent for Indonesia to 29 percent for India. When China's tariff phase-ins are completed in 2005, its average applied rate will have to fall to the bound rate of 10 percent, which will be somewhat above that of Indonesia, somewhat less than that of Argentina and Brazil, and significantly below that of India.

In short, by all important standards—openness to foreign investment, the large size and rapid expansion of the volume of imports, the high and rising ratio of imports to GDP, the rapid growth of domestic market sales of foreign affiliates, and the sharply declining and relatively low degree of tariff protection—China is a relatively open economy.

China as a Technological Leapfrog

Another concern voiced with regard to China is that government industrial policy is allowing it to move up the technology ladder at an unprecedented rate. China's emergence as a major supplier of information technology, communication, and electronic products is said to be a consequence of policies described as "high-tech mercantilism," which poses a major challenge to US commercial and security interests (Preeg 2004, 9).

China has emerged in recent years as a major producer and exporter of electronic and information technology products, such as consumer electronics, office equipment and computers, and communications equipment. Its global exports of these products soared from only $39 billion in 1999 to $142 billion in 2003.[10] The United States is a major purchaser of such goods, with imports from China more than doubling from $25 billion in 1999 to $59 billion in 2003. In 2000, China ranked behind Japan, Mexico, and the European Union as a supplier of high-tech goods to the United States, but by 2002 it had displaced all three to become the single largest supplier (American Electronics Association 2003).

This critique of Chinese industrial policy falls short on three levels. First, most of the electronic and information technology products, which are classified as high technology or advanced technology in the studies cited above, should not be considered high tech. The single biggest US import products from China in the consumer electronics, office equipment and computers, and communications equipment categories, respectively, are DVD players, notebook computers, and mobile telephones. Each of these is a high-volume commodity sold primarily by mass merchandisers of electronic products. For example, in 2003 the United States imported more than 31 million DVD players from China with an average unit cost of under $80, more than 7.5 million notebook computers with an average unit cost of $550, and more than 20 million mobile telephones with an average unit cost of less than $100.[11] The huge volumes and low unit costs of these products undermine the argument that these are high-tech products.

10. See Ministry of Information Industry's *2003 Electronic and Information Industry Economics Statistical Communiqué,* www.mii.gov.cn/mii/hyzw/tongji/2004-040501.htm (accessed April 20, 2004) and "China IT exports rose 45% year-on-year in 1999," *China Online,* February 8, 2000.

11. Data are from the United States International Trade Commission's Interactive Tariff and Trade DataWeb at http://dataweb.usitc.gov.

Figure 4.2 China's trade in electronics and information technology products, 1995–2003

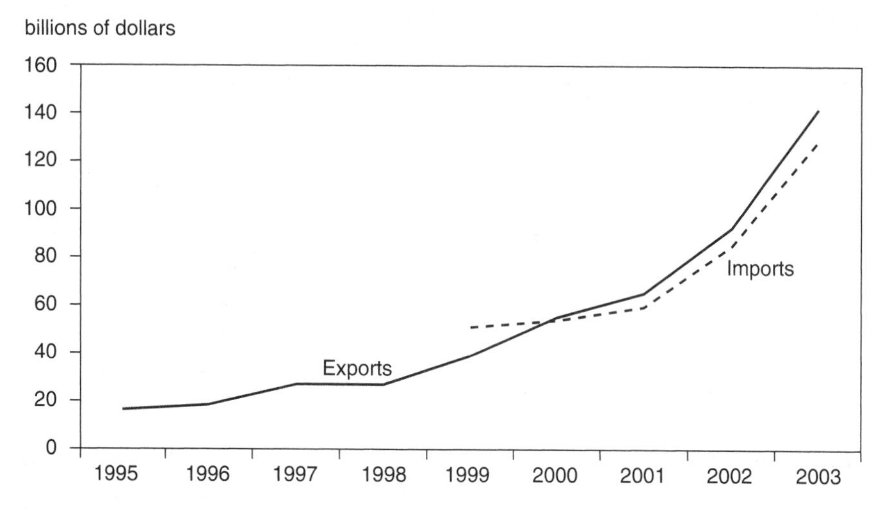

Sources: Ministry of Information Industry, 2003, *Electronic and Information Industry Economics Statistical Communique,* www.mii.gov.cn, (April 20, 2004); "Healthy Forecast for IT Field," *China Daily,* January 17, 2003, 5; Minister on Information Technology Development, Beijing Qiushi, No. 20, October 16, 2002; "PRC Information Minister Wu Jichuan on plans for major IT growth," *China Daily,* February 17, 2001; "China IT exports rose 45% on-year in 1999 *China Online,* February 8, 2000; China Economic Information Service (Xinhua); ISI Securities; and *Zhongguo Jisuanji Bao* (China Info World) No. 12, February 26, 2001.

Second, China is able to export huge quantities of electronic and information technology products only because it imports almost all of the high-value-added parts and components that go into these goods. China, in short, does not in any real sense manufacture these goods. Rather, it assembles them from imported parts and components. Domestic value added accounts for only 15 percent of the value of exported electronic and information technology products; the rest is import content. This dependence on imported parts and components is reflected in figure 4.2, which shows both China's exports and imports of electronic and information technology products. While China exported $142 billion in electronic and information technology products in 2003, China's imports of these products, overwhelmingly parts and components rather than finished goods, were over $128 billion. In short, China's net exports of electronic and information industry products in 2003 were only $14 billion.

A huge share of China's imports of electronic and information technology products is semiconductors and microprocessors, the most sophisticated component of all electronic and information technology products. China's imports of microprocessors and semiconductors quadrupled from $12 billion in 1999 to over $47 billion in 2003. The entire global market for semiconductors in 2003 was $166 billion, meaning that demand from China alone accounted for more than one-quarter of global output. The degree to which China is an assembler of imported parts and components, rather than a true manufacturer of consumer electronic and information technology products, is reflected in the modest volume of China's domestic production of semiconductors and microprocessors compared with the value of its imports of these products. Although domestic semiconductor production is growing rapidly, it is from an extremely small base. In 2003, domestic production was only $4.25 billion, less than one-tenth of the value of imports. Investment in domestic production of semiconductors has increased significantly in recent years, which will provide the capacity for rapidly rising production. However, given the continued expansion of capacity for manufacturing consumer electronics and information technology products in China, it is likely to remain far and away the world's largest importer of semiconductors and microprocessors for years.

Third, most exports of electronic and information technology products are assembled not by Chinese-owned firms but by foreign firms that are using China as an export platform. Taiwanese firms that have relocated to the mainland dominate the production of electronic and information technology products that are exported from China. For example, the importance of foreign firms in China's emergence as the largest supplier of computers to the US market is confirmed by both aggregate data and by the rankings of the top 200 export companies compiled by the Chinese Ministry of Commerce. In 2003, for example, foreign firms accounted for 92 percent of China's $41 billion in exports of computers, components, and peripherals and 74 percent of China's $89 billion in exports of electronics and telecommunications equipment (Gilboy 2004, 39).

The dominance of foreign firms in this sector is confirmed by the firm-level data on the largest exporters from China. In 2003, Hong Fu Jin Precision Industry, a wholly owned subsidiary of Taiwan's Hon Hai Precision Industry Company (better known by its trade name Foxconn), with exports of $6.4 billion, was China's number one–ranked export company for the third successive year. Hon Hai Precision Industry is Taiwan's largest contract electronics manufacturer, churning out videogame consoles, mobile phones, and other electronic products for Sony, Apple, and Nokia, among others. Coming in second was Tech Front (Shanghai), a subsidiary of Taiwan's Quanta Computer, Inc., the world's largest producer of notebook computers. Quanta is the single largest supplier for Dell Computer Company. Tech Front's exports in 2003 were $5.2 billion. Rounding off the top three, with exports of $3.1 billion, was Magnificent Brightness, owned by Taiwan's Asutek Computer, another global heavyweight in the production of notebook computers. In all, there are 28 Taiwan-owned firms on the list of the 200 largest exporting firms in China. All are electronics manufacturers.[12]

12. See "Top Three China Exporters All Taiwan-Invested," Chinese Economic News Service, June 28, 2004, http://news.cens.com.

In short, the rapidly changing commodity composition of China's exports does not constitute evidence that China is leapfrogging ahead technologically. Indeed, there may be a growing technology gap between foreign firms operating in China and domestic Chinese companies. In part this is because foreign firms in the electronics and information technology market in China are almost entirely wholly foreign-owned companies rather than joint ventures. Wholly foreign-owned firms have strong incentives to protect their technology from competitors, both domestic and foreign, limiting the diffusion of technology to indigenous firms. Furthermore, indigenous Chinese firms spend little on research and development to develop new technologies on their own (Gilboy 2004, 40).

China's Exchange Rate

Finally, some charge that China is similar to other Asian countries that have long managed their exchange rates by intervening in foreign exchange markets to limit appreciation of their currencies in order to sustain growth-oriented trade surpluses (Dooley, Folkerts-Landau, and Garber 2003). Is China's currency undervalued? If so what is the appropriate Chinese response? What difference would this response make to bilateral trade between the United States and China?

First, while China's currency is now almost certainly undervalued, it is worth underlining that in contrast with Japan and several other countries in the region, this is a relatively recent phenomenon. Moreover, to some extent the recent very large buildup of foreign exchange reserves in China reflects short-term speculative capital inflows rather than an underlying large capital account surplus.

What is the evidence for the judgment that the currency is undervalued in recent years? Since it pegged its currency to the dollar in 1994, China's current account surplus has averaged 2 percent of its GDP, but this number rose to an average of 3.1 percent in 2002–03. And unlike its Southeast Asian neighbors, in the five years since the Asian financial crisis (1999–2003), China also had a capital account surplus of a little over 2 percent of GDP, and this number also rose to a little over 3 percent in 2002–03. Although China nominally maintains a relatively closed capital account, before 2001 unrecorded capital outflows largely offset these current and capital account surpluses. As a result, China's buildup of foreign exchange reserves was modest by Asian standards. But in 2001 these outflows shrank significantly, and from the beginning of 2002 through 2003 China experienced significant unrecorded capital inflows. To continue to keep the currency pegged at 8.28 renminbi to the dollar, China's authorities since 2001 have had to purchase massive amounts of foreign exchange, and reserves have risen accordingly.

The Chinese authorities, through their own actions, have implicitly admitted that the renminbi is undervalued. To date they have chosen to try to reduce the pressure on the currency through a series of ad hoc measures, rather than making any change to their exchange rate. Beginning on January 1, 2004, the government reduced by an average of 3 percentage points the rate at which it rebates the value-added tax on exports, which tends to make Chinese exports more expensive in international markets. But, unlike a currency revaluation, lowering the rebate rate on the value-added tax on exports does not lower the price of imports in the domestic market. The authorities also have signaled an easing in the approval process for outward FDI, liberalized outbound Chinese tourism, and allowed one domestic financial institution to issue dollar-denominated debt. They are contemplating approving a qualified domestic institutional investor (QDII) program that would allow Chinese financial institutions such as insurance companies to invest, within carefully defined limits, in securities traded on foreign markets. Each of these measures would tend to increase the demand for or reduce the supply of foreign exchange, which would contribute to reducing the buildup in official foreign exchange reserves.

The US policy of encouraging China to liberalize its capital account and adopt a floating exchange rate system, first articulated by Treasury Secretary John Snow in the fall of 2003, is certainly appropriate as a long-term objective. Over the years, the Chinese authorities have repeatedly expressed the goal of moving toward a fully convertible currency and a much more flexible exchange rate regime. There is no debate on the long-term desirability of such a policy. A flexible exchange rate regime would not only help to equilibrate China's international accounts but would also give the authorities considerably more ability to use monetary policy to moderate the cyclical character of fixed asset investment growth.

In the short and medium runs, however, a fully convertible currency with a floating exchange rate is a risky option for China. Chinese households hold more than 12 trillion renminbi (an amount roughly equal to China's GDP) in domestic savings deposits. Very few Chinese savers have had an opportunity to diversify the currency composition of their financial savings. Eliminating capital controls could lead to a substantial move into foreign currency–denominated financial assets, most likely held outside of Chinese banks. Given the well-known weaknesses of China's banks, such a move could precipitate a domestic banking crisis. As a result, the authorities do not anticipate relaxing capital controls on household savings until they have fully addressed the solvency problems of the major state-owned banks. This process is well under way but is likely to take a minimum of three to five years to complete.

If the renminbi continued to be undervalued for three to five years, there would be substantial adverse effects on China's trading partners, and China's central bank would continue to be very constrained in using interest rates as a macroeconomic policy tool. Thus the preferred approach is to revalue the currency in the short term and only much later, after completing the transformation of the domestic banking system, move to eliminate capital controls and, at the same time, float the currency. How large an initial revaluation of the currency is called for? My colleague Morris Goldstein and I tentatively judged in 2003 that the renminbi was undervalued by an amount in the range of 15 to 25 percent. We estimated that a revaluation in this range in 2003 would have led to an overall equilibrium in China's balance of payments, thus ending the buildup of foreign exchange reserves. It would also have assisted the central bank in controlling the expansion of the money supply and credit and thus helped to alleviate inflationary pressure. We also argued that at the same time the authorities revalue the currency, they should take two additional steps. First, they should significantly widen the band within which they permit market forces to determine the value of the currency. Second, at the new parity, the authorities should peg the Chinese currency to a basket of currencies rather than solely to the US dollar.[13]

What difference would a revaluation of the renminbi by 15 to 25 percent in 2003 have made to the bilateral trade balance? Over time, it would have reduced China's current account position by about $55 billion (i.e., imports would increase and exports would contract by an amount summing to $55 billion). Since the United States accounts for somewhat less than one-quarter of China's trade, a crude estimate of the reduction in the US bilateral trade deficit with China would be roughly $15 billion. Given the lags with which price effects of an exchange rate change work through the markets, the reduction would likely be reflected in a slowdown in the rate at which the bilateral trade imbalance grows, rather than a reduction in its absolute size.

As C. Fred Bergsten and Michael Mussa point out in their chapters in this book, the effect of a Chinese revaluation on the overall US current account, however, could be larger than the influence on the bilateral trade balance alone. The reason is that China may be the key to the continued general misalignment of Asian currencies. Given China's increasing competitiveness as a global exporter, Malaysia, Korea, Taiwan, and other Asian economies have been intervening in the market, adding substantially to their foreign exchange reserves to limit the appreciation of their currencies vis-à-vis the renminbi. China's revaluation should be part of the coordinated adjustments of the other Asian currencies. The cumulative effect on the overall US current account deficit of such a general realign-

13. See Morris Goldstein and Nicholas Lardy, "A Modest Proposal for China's Renminbi," *Financial Times*, August 26, 2003, and Goldstein and Lardy, "Two-Stage Currency Reform for China," *Asian Wall Street Journal*, September 12, 2003.

ment of Asian currencies would be several times the $15 billion estimated reduction in the US bilateral trade deficit with China.

Implications for US Policy

China's rise as a global economic power appears to represent primarily an opportunity rather than a challenge for the global economy and the United States. China's openness to FDI and relatively low barriers to imports are unprecedented for a large, low-income economy. The results are apparent in record foreign capital inflows and a doubling of the ratio of imports to GDP between 1990 and 2003. US firms have benefited substantially from this trend. Since the beginning of the 1990s, exports by US firms to China have been growing more rapidly than to any other large market. In 2003, US exports to China, led by soybeans, aircraft, semiconductors, and cotton, grew by almost 30 percent to reach $28.4 billion.[14] In contrast, US exports to the rest of the world grew less than 4 percent. As a result China alone accounted for one-fifth of the growth of US exports in 2003.

China's large and rising surplus in its trade with the United States reflects primarily the relocation to China from elsewhere in Asia of substantial capacity to assemble manufactured goods, rather than Chinese protectionism. Since these goods are assembled with parts and components imported preponderately from elsewhere in Asia, whereas the major markets for the final products are in the United States and Europe, China's trade with Asia is in deficit while that with the United States and Europe is in surplus. This pattern is almost certain to persist and even deepen as the global share of manufactured goods assembled in China continues to rise over the next few years.

While the appearance of a growing share of its exports suggests that China is leapfrogging up the technology ladder at an unprecedented pace, this is not the case. Rather, once China's dependence on imports of high-value-added parts and components is taken into account, its pattern of trade largely conforms to the classic pattern of comparative advantage: It exports products that are produced with relatively large amounts of unskilled labor and little capital or land and imports products produced with large amounts of capital, highly skilled labor, and land. As China's national income rises, it will move up the technology ladder. But given the 100 million or more underemployed workers who are available to move out of agriculture and into the modern sector, real wages for entry-

14. Like all official US data on exports to China, this number excludes goods that are sold to Hong Kong companies and subsequently reexported to China. I estimate the value of these sales in 2003 at $5.5 billion.

level unskilled jobs are likely to increase relatively slowly. Thus China's comparative advantage is likely to remain in labor-intensive products for many years.

Even if China's general pattern of trade continues to conform to its underlying comparative advantage in labor-intensive goods, it is almost certain to be the source of significant, growing trade frictions. The underlying reason is that no other relatively poor country has ever had as large a share of global trade as China now enjoys. Despite more than two decades of rapid economic growth, China's per capita income calculated at the current exchange rate exceeded $1,000 for the first time in 2003. Low per capita income means relatively low wages, which, when combined with foreign technology and international marketing skills of foreign affiliates provides China with a strong comparative advantage in labor-intensive manufacturing. China's ability to ramp up production of labor-intensive goods poses a competitive threat to many industries that are likely to seek protection from rapidly expanding imports from China.

Nowhere is this likely to become more apparent than in apparel. At the end of 2004, the quota system, which has long distorted global trade in textiles and apparel, will be dismantled. China, given its relatively low production costs, will be able to perhaps as much as double its share of the global apparel market, assuming trade is market determined (Lardy 2002, 123–25). This is certain to lead to large domestic adjustment costs in the United States and other apparel-producing countries.

How should the United States mitigate what are likely to be growing bilateral trade frictions? First, because the large and growing US trade deficit with China will become more difficult to sustain politically if it is attributable to lack of access by US firms to China's domestic market, the Office of the United States Trade Representative and other US government agencies should continue to press China to fulfill all of the commitments it made to open its own market at the time of joining the WTO. Significant trade frictions, such as China's plan to adopt its own wireless encryption standard and to provide preferential treatment of domestically produced semiconductors, have already been resolved, suggesting that bilateral negotiations can solve some frictions. For others, notably protection of intellectual property, there has been little or no progress. In this area, the United States should pursue formal cases against China in the WTO if bilateral negotiations do not lead to significant progress. While China's full compliance with its WTO commitments could be quite important for some individual US exporters, it is crucial to bear in mind that it is unlikely that even complete compliance would have a major impact on the US bilateral trade deficit with China. This deficit is primarily a function of the structural factors discussed earlier, not protectionism in China.

Second, revaluation of the renminbi should be a key US policy goal, even though it would be expected to reduce the US bilateral trade deficit with China only modestly, as long as China continues to maintain global surpluses on both its current and capital accounts. The bulk of the US bilateral trade deficit with China is in products such as apparel, footwear, toys, and sporting goods. Production of these goods began to move out of the United States decades ago, primarily to Asia. Beginning in the late 1980s, in response to sharply rising real wages as well as currency appreciation in these Asian countries, production of these goods began to move to China. Revaluation of the renminbi is very unlikely to bring a significant number of these jobs back to the United States. On the other hand, more recently increased competition from imports originating in China has led to job losses in tool and die, plastic moldings, and so forth. Revaluation clearly would slow the decline of employment in the United States in these industries. Equally important, China's revaluation could pave the way for adjustments in other Asian currencies, which cumulatively could contribute significantly to reducing the US global current account deficit.

Third, the United States and other high-income economies should seek to maintain open markets for Chinese goods, particularly labor-intensive manufactures. When it became a member of the WTO, China made unprecedented commitments to open its markets. Under pressure from the United States, it also agreed to allow other members to utilize unique provisions to restrict the flow of Chinese goods into world markets. One of these provisions allows other WTO members to continue to use quotas to restrict imports of Chinese apparel through 2008. In short, while quotas will be suspended for all other suppliers at the beginning of 2005, at their option the United States and other countries can continue to apply restrictive quotas to imports of Chinese apparel for four additional years. If this authority is widely invoked it will deprive China of the opportunity to expand production in a sector in which it clearly has a strong comparative advantage. That, in turn, would deprive China of a significant source of additional export earnings that it could use to further expand its imports of capital- and land-intensive products in which US producers have a strong comparative advantage. Similarly, in antidumping cases the US Department of Commerce should continue when appropriate to use methodologies that take into account the increasingly market-oriented character of the Chinese economy.[15]

Finally, given China's already large and likely continuing expanding role in the global economy, the United States and other industrialized countries should enhance the role of China in international bodies that seek to promote cooperation on international economic policy issues. In their chapter in this book, Jan Boyer and Edwin Truman propose to trans-

15. In the antidumping case against Chinese furniture, the US Department of Commerce in June 2004 found lower-than-expected preliminary antidumping margins because it used market economy prices for a majority of the inputs used to produce the furniture rather than surrogate prices.

form the G-20, established at the level of finance ministers and central bank governors in 1999, from a discussion forum into an action committee. Eventually the G-20 might replace the G-7. Since China and ten other large emerging-market economies are members, enhancing the role of the G-20 would recognize the growing role of large emerging markets in the global economy. If this proposal were adopted, however, there would likely be a substantial transition period during which the G-7 likely would continue to play an important role. Thus, the United States and other G-7 countries should invite China now to participate regularly in the meetings of the G-7 finance ministers. Initially this might be done by inviting China as a guest participant (as was done in the fall of 2004), but because of China's increasing weight in the global economy and the world financial system, China should be invited to become a formal member of the group in the near term.

The case for singling out China for inclusion in the G-7 finance ministers meetings rests on its vastly greater international economic weight than India and the other emerging-market economies that are members of the G-20. For example, on virtually any metric, China is a far larger player than India in the global economy. In 2003, China's foreign trade of $850 billion was almost seven times that of India's $130 billion, a gap only partially explained by the fact that China's economy is about twice as large as India's. The *increase* in China's foreign trade in 2003 ($230 billion) was almost twice the *level* of India's foreign trade in the same year. The huge difference in trade volumes in part reflects India's more protectionist trade and investment policies. For example, India's 29 percent average applied tariff rate in 2002 was more than twice the Chinese level of 12 percent. FDI inflows into China of $55 billion in 2003 were more than a dozen times India's level of $4 billion. Indeed inflows into China in 2003 alone substantially exceeded the *cumulative* FDI inflows into India since independence in 1947. China is also a much more substantial industrial power than India. For example, in 2003, China *increased* its steel production by 40 million metric tons, an amount substantially greater than the *level* of Indian output that year of only 38 million metric tons.

China's role in the global economy is likely to continue to expand at a rapid pace. While an ever-growing bilateral trade deficit composed increasingly of high-technology goods might suggest that China poses an unprecedented economic challenge to the United States, the analysis in this chapter suggests that China should be regarded largely as a huge economic opportunity. The United States should continue to press China to fulfill all of its WTO market-opening commitments and at the same time keep its market as open as possible to goods from China. That combination of policies is most likely to generate increased exports of sophisticated US capital goods as well as agricultural products in which the United States enjoys a comparative advantage.

References

American Electronics Association. 2003. *Tech Trade Update 2003*. Washington.

Asian Development Bank. 2004. *Asian Development Outlook 2004*. Manila.

Cline, William R. 2004. *Trade Policy and Global Poverty*. Washington: Institute for International Economics.

Dooley, Michael P., David Folkerts-Landau, and Peter Garber. 2003. *An Essay on the Revived Bretton Woods System*. NBER Working Paper 9971. Cambridge, MA: National Bureau of Economic Research.

Gilboy, George J. 2004. The Myth Behind China's Miracle. *Foreign Affairs* 83, no. 4 (July/August): 33–48.

International Energy Agency. 2004. *Oil Market Report*, May 12. www.oilmarketreport.org (accessed May 12, 2004).

Lardy, Nicholas R. 2002. *Integrating China into the Global Economy*. Washington: Brookings Institution Press.

Lemoine, Françoise, and Deniz Ünal-Kesenci. 2004. Assembly Trade and Technology Transfer: The Case of China. *World Development* 32, no. 5: 829–50.

National Bureau of Statistics. 2004. *China Statistical Abstract 2004*. Beijing: China Statistics Press.

OECD (Organization for Economic Cooperation and Development). 2004. *Trends and Recent Developments in Foreign Direct Investment*. Paris.

Preeg, Ernest H. 2004. *The Threatened U.S. Competitive Lead in Advanced Technology Products (ATP)*. Washington: Manufacturers Alliance/MAPI.

US-China Economic and Security Review Commission. 2004. *2004 Report to Congress*. Washington: US Government Printing Office.

World Bank. 2004. *East Asia Update*. Washington.

5

The United States and the Large Emerging-Market Economies: Competitors or Partners?

JAN E. BOYER and EDWIN M. TRUMAN

The world has seen over the past 30 years a substantial expansion in the number of sovereign actors whose decisions can have important positive and negative implications for the global economy. Essentially all of the new actors are large emerging-market economies (LEMs)—the top tier of developing economies. Over the same period, the relative economic importance of the industrial economies, large and small, has waned.

The LEMs are important to the United States because collectively they are now a major source of growth for the world economy and of stimulus and economic and financial opportunity for the US economy, businesses, and investors. The 11 LEMs that we focus upon in this chapter represent over 31 percent of world GDP (on a PPP basis) and grew at about a percentage point faster than the world or G-8 economies in the 1992–2002 period.[1] Two of these countries (China and India) rank first and second (respectively) in terms of their trade growth over this period. Finally, the 11 countries currently control over 30 percent of total international reserves.

Jan E. Boyer is a visiting fellow at the Institute for International Economics. Edwin M. Truman is a senior fellow at the Institute for International Economics. *The authors are grateful to Anna Wong for her high-quality research assistance.*

1. The eleven countries are Argentina, Brazil, China, India, Indonesia, Korea, Mexico, Russia, Saudi Arabia, South Africa, and Turkey. They account for about 14 percent of world income and production at current exchange rates (World Bank atlas method).

As has been seen over the past 10 years, starting with the Mexican external financial crisis of 1994–95, the LEMs individually also can be the source of disturbances that disrupt the international financial system, with adverse effects on the United States. In addition, choices by countries such as China to limit the adjustment of their currencies can impair the working of mechanisms for adjusting international payments imbalances and negatively impact many sectors of the US economy.

Increasingly, many observers see the LEMs as serious competitors to the United States. However, our view is that the interests of the United States and the LEMs can be aligned sufficiently so that they can and should be partners.[2] As consequential players on the world economic stage, and in their own interests, the LEMs will want to share responsibility for global prosperity.

In this chapter, we address why being partners with the United States, as well as with the European Union and Japan, is in the best interest of the LEMs as well as the United States and other major industrial countries and what the specific areas of most immediate and profitable partnership are. The potential impacts of the LEMs' decisions on the global system as well as on the United States are substantial at the same time that their aspirations are sizable. Their aspirations include a desire for sustained growth along with global economic and financial stability. The LEMs also desire increased recognition of their importance and to share responsibility for global decisions, in particular decisions that affect their needs and priorities.

We also argue that the LEMs should receive higher priority in US international economic policy. In the past three decades, US policy toward emerging-market economies, to the extent that there was one, has oscillated between preaching the virtues of market-determined foundations for growth and designing cooperative interventions to address particular problems on a case-by-case basis, such as a debt crisis in Brazil, legal uncertainty in Russia, or openness to investment in India. On the political/diplomatic front, the United States has for the most part dealt with the individual LEMs in isolation, with one issue dominating the agenda (for instance, nuclear proliferation with India, trade openness with Brazil, and human rights with China). This "one-note" approach has not contributed to building stronger, more diversified relationships with the LEMs—individually or as a group. In plain terms, there has not been a comprehensive US policy or one that takes into account the challenges the United States has in common with these countries or that the LEMs consider important in dealing with and integrating into the world economic system.

In the cases of Brazil, China, and India, for example, severe energy deficiency is a common economic problem whereas technology sharing with

2. In his chapter in this book, Nicholas Lardy argues that China should be seen as a US partner rather than as a competitor, and we make the same argument for the broader set of LEMs.

the rest of the world and scientific development within each country are common aspirations. Regional economic leadership and integration are challenges for South Africa, India, Brazil, and Russia. On the strategic economic front, protection of the Sea Lanes of Communication (SLOC) is as vital to India and South Africa as it is to Japan and the United States. The solution to military conflicts within and along their borders is of crucial importance to India, Russia, and, potentially in the future, Brazil. It is worth remembering that many of the LEMs border several of the so-called failed states, which implies future risks and the need for resources and knowledge to deal with the security and human dimensions of problems that ultimately have economic consequences.

The above examples illustrate how the United States is not weighing appropriately the aspirations of LEMs in formulating its policies. Let us be clear: We expect US policymakers to pursue vigorously the economic interests of the United States. But we also believe that this can be best accomplished by gradually bringing the LEMs individually and collectively into US counsel on the major matters affecting the world economy and their strategic objectives. It is only by doing so that the United States can reduce the influence of reactionary (i.e., "anti–global integration") forces within these countries—for instance, parts of the foreign policy establishments in Brazil and India or parts of the military hierarchies in China and Russia.

Summary of Recommendations

We have two sets of recommendations on US policy toward the LEMs. The first set of three recommendations requires initiatives and changes by the G-7 countries and, therefore, strong US leadership to bring them about. The second set of five recommendations requires the agreement and active involvement of the LEMs if it is to be implemented. We believe these two sets of recommendations taken together are uniquely relevant to the largest of the emerging-market economies and as such offer a crucial opportunity to engage these countries and improve the governance of the world economy.

Our central recommendation is that US policy toward the LEMs should be reorganized and refocused. The LEMs should receive a substantially greater share of the intellectual and other resources of the US government. As we describe, the LEMs have certain characteristics related to their economic prowess as well as aspirations for participation in the global economic system that justify this differentiation of treatment from other industrialized and developing countries. Under our proposed approach, the United States would have a more coherent and effective posture toward these countries, whose problems, interests, and aspirations are often very similar.

Governance and Institutions

Our three principal recommendations regarding the governance and institutions of economic policy with respect to the LEMS are:

1. replace the finance G-7 with a refocused G-20
2. redistribute chairs and shares in the international financial institutions (IFIs)
3. reorganize US policymaking toward the LEMs

Active Collaboration

Our five proposals for areas of active collaboration between the United States and the LEMs are grouped under two headings: (1) poverty-reducing economic growth and (2) crisis resolution and global financial stability. Our objective in making these recommendations is both to suggest action areas that are in the US interest and to identify relevant issues that would respond to LEMs' aspirations.

Poverty-Reducing Economic Growth

4. undertake initiatives in private-sector development
5. increase cooperation on development issues
6. increase cooperation on tax evasion

Crisis Resolution and Global Financial Stability

7. create a proactive framework for crisis resolution
8. resume regular annual special drawing rights (SDR) allocations

In the following sections, as a preamble to our specific proposals, we address the following questions: Who are the LEMs? Why should the United States be interested in these countries? Why should LEMs care about taking a more responsible role in the existing governance structure of the world economy? We explore the aspirations and objectives of LEMs and what, in particular, distinguishes the largest countries from the smaller emerging-market economies. We then briefly describe our three recommendations on how US foreign economic policymakers should deal with the growing importance of LEMs in global economics and politics, followed by our five recommendations for active collaboration between the United States and the LEMs. A budgetary reality check on our recommendations concludes that they are fiscally responsible.

Who Are the LEMs?

The LEMs are a subset of the continuum of economies that extends from the wealthiest industrial country to the poorest developing country. The LEMs have not yet attained the level of per capita income nor have they generally established the public and private institutions that are characteristic of an industrial country such as Canada, Australia, or most members of the European Union. At the same time, they are no longer poor or very poor because they have either experienced or are experiencing a period of rapid economic expansion. Economic, financial, and political institutions have been developed in parallel with their economic maturation, although they are generally not as robust as institutions found in industrial countries.

We are primarily interested in the *large* emerging-market economies—for example, India rather than Singapore. The LEMs' size means that their policies and subsequent development successes or failures have potential measurable impacts on the US and other global economies. They also can mobilize real and financial resources on a sufficient scale to contribute significantly to the achievement of global objectives.

Of the 11 LEMs we focus on, 5 stand out prominently as an inner circle of countries with which US economic policymakers need to upgrade and intensify their level of interaction: Brazil, China, India, Russia, and South Africa. One might argue that China deserves to be in a category of its own, that South Africa is too small in economic terms to be in the same company of the other countries, that Russia is being included for historic and military reasons, or that Mexico ought to be included in the inner circle.

On these points, our view, first, is that China, despite its progress and dynamism, is still an underdeveloped economy with only a rudimentary financial system compared with the rest of the world and therefore not yet in a position to be a full participant of the world economy (see Nicholas Lardy's chapter in this book). Second, Africa as a continent cannot be excluded from global economic decision making, and South Africa seems to us a better representative politically and economically of that necessity than any other African country or grouping. In addition, South Africa ranks slightly ahead of India and Russia but just behind China in terms of the financial stake in the country by US investors and lenders—foreign direct investment (FDI), bank claims, and portfolio investments (table 5.1). Third, although Russia was included in the G-8 primarily for political motivations, it currently ranks above India, Brazil, and Australia in terms of its share of world trade. Fourth, Mexico is politically important to the United States, though its posture vis-à-vis the Iraq war also clearly demonstrated its independence. However, as an economic actor on the world stage, Mexico is not that different from the state of California in terms of its linkages to, and dependence upon, the US economy.

Table 5.1 Economic and financial importance of the five principal large emerging-market economies (LEMs) (annual percent change 1992–2002, except as noted)

Country	Real GDP growth	Real trade growth[a]	Growth in reserves[b]	United States: Growth in trade[c]	United States: Investment[d] (billions of dollars)
Brazil	2.6	7.4	5.3	7.7	91.8
China	9.8	15.4	30.3	16.1	28.0
India	5.8	12.3	27.9	10.7	27.6
Russia	–2.0	5.3	22.4[f]	13.8	26.2
South Africa	2.2	5.2	19.5	4.7	24.4
Average (5)[e]	5.1	9.1	20.8	10.6	197.9
World	2.5	6.4	11.0	6.6	5,572.8

a. Merchandise exports plus imports.
b. Excluding gold.
c. Exports plus imports in nominal terms.
d. Foreign direct investment plus bank claims plus portfolio investment.
e. Total US dollar amount of US investment.
f. Base year 1993; 1992 data unavailable in source.

Sources: Real GDP growth and real growth in merchandise trade: World Bank's *World Development Indicators 2004.* Growth in reserves: IMF's *International Financial Statistics* (June 2004). US trade growth: *Direction of Trade Statistics* (June 2004). US investment: FDI—Bureau of Economic Analysis (2003); bank claims—Federal Financial Institutions Examination Council (2003). Portfolio investment (equity securities and long-term and short-term debt securities): *IMF Coordinated Portfolio Investment Survey* 2003, based on US Treasury international capital system surveys.

Table 5.1 presents data on the five principal LEMs. These five countries have been and will continue to be a major source of stimulus and economic and financial opportunity not only for the US economy but also for the global economy. On average over the 1992–2002 decade, their economies grew more than a percentage point faster per year than the world as a whole, their real trade grew almost three percentage points faster, and their international reserves grew almost 10 percentage points faster. Despite differences in their respective performances, as a group these countries have been a source of dynamism for the world economy.

From the standpoint of the United States (the last two columns in table 5.1), merchandise trade with these five countries grew, in nominal terms, four percentage points faster per year from 1992 to 2002 than US trade with the world as a whole. Moreover, by 2003 the stock of US investment in these countries (FDI, bank claims, and portfolio investment, including investments in both equity securities and long-term and short-term debt securities) was 3.6 percent of total US investment in the world.[3]

3. In his chapter in this book, Lardy cites, from Chinese sources, a figure for US FDI that is about twice as large as the one embedded in table 5.1. We are forced to use US data to be consistent. Available data do not provide adequate time series for US overall or direct investment in individual countries. However, from 1992 to 2002, FDI from all countries in these

The six other LEMs, which make up the outer circle, share most of the potential and interests of the inner circle of five, but the additional countries are smaller and likely to remain so. This second concentric circle of economically significant LEMs includes countries that may take leadership roles on a certain issue—for example, Saudi Arabia on energy issues. It is convenient to identify this larger group of LEMs with the 11 large emerging-market economies that are members of the Group of Twenty (G-20) finance ministers and central bank governors—the finance G-20: Argentina, Brazil, China, India, Indonesia, Korea, Mexico, Russia, Saudi Arabia, South Africa, and Turkey.[4] Membership in the G-20, which was established in 1999, was based in part on considerations of political balance. One can certainly quibble with where the lines were drawn, but our judgment is that the balance is about right.[5]

Table 5.2 presents data on the six other LEMs. The growth rates of their economies, trade, and international reserves were also higher, on average, than for the world as whole. Of course each of these countries, with the exception of Saudi Arabia, experienced a major financial crisis during 1992–2002, which influenced the data presented in the table. Nevertheless, their share of global international reserves (excluding gold) increased from 6.5 percent in 1990 to 10.3 percent in 2003. During the same period, the share of total reserves held by all 11 LEMs rose from 11.2 to 30.8 percent, led by the increase in China's share from 3.5 to 13.1 percent.

US trade with the six additional LEMs did not expand particularly rapidly from 1992 to 2002, in part because of their economic and financial difficulties. However, US investors have a larger stake in these countries, on average, than in the five principal LEMs.[6] The US investment stake in the 11 LEMs is 8.3 percent of its stake in the world. The 11 countries as a group accounted for 30.2 percent of total US merchandise trade (exports plus imports) in 2003. The share of the five principal LEMs, led by China

five countries increased by 724 percent compared with an increase in total world FDI of 229 percent. The increase in FDI in the EU-15 was 220 percent and in the United States was 219 percent. Of the five principal LEMs, the smallest increase in FDI was for South Africa at 347 percent.

4. The other members of the G-20 are the G-7 countries, Australia, and the country holding the EU presidency, when not a G-7 country. The G-7 countries are Canada, France, Germany, Italy, Japan, the United Kingdom, and the United States.

5. In terms of 2002 GDP on a PPP basis, the G-20 includes most of the largest countries. Iran and Thailand rank ahead of Argentina. Argentina is followed by the Philippines and Colombia. These latter two countries rank ahead of Saudi Arabia—the smallest of the emerging-market economies, on this criterion, that is a member of the G-20.

6. FDI in these six countries from all countries increased 175 percent from 1992 to 2002, slightly below the figure for the world as whole (229 percent). However, Korea (535 percent), Argentina (372 percent), and Mexico (332 percent) were significantly above that figure, while Turkey (44 percent), Indonesia (32 percent), and Saudi Arabia (14 percent) were below it.

Table 5.2 Economic and financial importance of six other LEMs (annual percent change 1992–2002 except as noted)

Country	Real GDP growth	Real trade growth[a]	Growth in reserves[b]	United States: Growth in trade[c]	United States: Investment[d] (billions of dollars)
Argentina	1.7	3.2	0.5	0.9	18.0
Indonesia	3.9	2.7	11.5	5.7	16.1
Korea	5.7	12.5	21.6	6.4	75.4
Mexico	2.9	10.8	10.3	11.8	137.3
Saudi Arabia	1.9	3.2[e]	13.3	0.1	5.9
Turkey	3.3	9.5	16.0	5.8	9.7
Average (6)[f]	3.2	7.7	12.2	5.1	262.4
Average 5 principal LEMs[f]	3.7	9.1	20.8	10.6	197.4
Average 11 LEMs[f]	3.4	8.4	15.6	7.6	460.4
Industrial-country average[f, g]	2.2	5.3[h]	8.6	5.0	2,886.6
World	2.5	6.4	11.0	6.6	5,572.8

a. Merchandise exports plus imports.
b. Excluding gold.
c. Exports plus imports in nominal terms.
d. Foreign direct investment plus bank claims plus portfolio investment. Portfolio investment data for Saudi Arabia are not available.
e. 1992–2002 data on nominal trade from IMF's *Direction of Trade Statistics.*
f. Total US dollar amount of US investment.
g. G-7 plus Australia less United States.
h. 2002 *World Development Indicators* trade data unavailable for Canada, deflated 1992–2002 data from IMF's *International Financial Statistics* used.

Sources: Real GDP growth and real growth in merchandise trade: World Bank's *World Development Indicators 2004.* Growth in reserves: IMF's *International Financial Statistics* (June 2004). US trade growth: *Direction of Trade Statistics* (June 2004). US investment: FDI—Bureau of Economic Analysis (2003); bank claims—Federal Financial Institutions Examination Council (2003). Portfolio investment (equity securities and long-term and short-term debt securities): *IMF Coordinated Portfolio Investment Survey* 2003, based on US Treasury international capital system surveys.

at 9.4 percent, was 13 percent, and the share of the other six LEMs was 17.2 percent, led by Mexico with 11.7 percent.

The economic circumstances of the individual LEMs, of course, are not identical. Latin American economies tend to have lower growth rates, in part attributable to chronic low saving rates and associated fiscal pressures, large internal and external debts, and current account deficits, which have contributed to multiple external financial crises over the past couple of decades. The East Asian economies tend to have high saving rates and, more recently, chronic current account surpluses and rapid rates of accumulation of international reserves. Nevertheless, they have not avoided external financial pressures and crises.

Why Are the LEMs Important to the United States and the World?

The LEMs have common aspirations for rapid and sustained economic growth and development, for recognition of their interests in shaping the policies and institutions that guide and regulate the global economy, and for inclusion in global decision-making processes. It is in the US interest to evaluate and incorporate, if appropriate, these aspirations—and not solely to minimize the inevitable political and economic competition and confrontation. The challenge for the United States is to build relationships with the LEMs in the absence of substantial economic leverage.

The absence of such leverage over most of the 11 LEMs could reflect the relative decline in the US direct economic and financial stake in these countries over the past decade.[7] Although the dollar value of the US direct investment in them rose by almost 150 percent between 1994 and 2002, the US share of total FDI in these countries declined from 19 to 12 percent. US bank claims on these countries rose slightly, about 5 percent, between 1993 and 2003, but the US share of total international bank claims on them declined from 19 to 14 percent. US bank claims declined in absolute terms by 26 percent from 1997 to 2003. Over the same period, US portfolio investment (equity and longer-term debt securities only) rose by 14 percent, substantially less than the 70 percent increase for the world. Partly as a result, the historical absence of a focus on the LEMs as a group on the part of US policymakers and the financial community may be explained by the small share of US FDI, bank claims, and holdings of securities in the total portfolio of US foreign investments that are accounted for by the LEMs—only 8.3 percent in 2003. It is also relevant that in 2003, trade with the United States represented only 21.2 percent of the external trade of these 11 countries on average.[8]

Brazil, China, India, and South Africa are leaders of the so-called G-20 caucus of countries actively involved in the Doha Round of World Trade Organization (WTO) trade negotiations. These four countries have begun to establish leadership roles within their respective geographic regions that are commensurate with their size as well as their consequent broader interests in the smooth functioning of the global economy and financial system. As with most countries, external economic and financial conditions affect them, but a major difference is that their own policy decisions and performances also affect other countries.

Russia is not yet a WTO member, though its negotiations are well advanced, and it is an active participant in the global trading system. This

7. The data we present in this paragraph come from a number of different sources and may not be strictly comparable, but we believe that they support this broad conclusion.

8. Trade with the United States was only 13.9 percent of total trade of the inner circle of five countries.

observation underlines a further point: these five countries are large and important but not identical in their political and institutional development. China is not a democracy; doubts exist about the commitment of Russia's current leadership to democratic principles. What is interesting is the extent to which these very important political factors have not to date hindered for the most part their economic growth performance.

The LEMs, in particular those in the inner circle, have important differences that deserve the special attention of US policymakers, but they also have a number of common interests, as illustrated by the several areas in which we propose that the United States, the European Union, and Japan work together with the LEMs. Moreover, if these countries can maintain a generally stable macroeconomic environment and establish increasingly transparent regulations and robust institutions, they can expect rapid growth on a sustained basis for an extended period. This should translate into dynamic markets for US exports and profitable opportunities for US investors. The LEMs also are a source of competition for individual US firms and at the sector level. Many do not welcome competition, but it is the principal source of technical innovation and growth of US productivity (see the chapters in this book by David Richardson and Catherine Mann). At the same time, the LEMs look to the mature industrial countries, in general, and the United States, in particular, for open markets, capital, and technology.

Regardless of their policies or the international environment, the economic success of the LEMs will not be uniform or free from at least occasional financial crises. How well the emerging-market economies prepare their defenses against such crises and how well the inevitable crises are managed will strongly influence the US and global economies as well as the individual countries. Recall the reaction of global financial markets to the Russian default in 1998 in the wake of the Asian financial crisis and in the context of a slowly developing financial crisis in Brazil. The Federal Reserve lowered interest rates defensively, and the US economy rode out the global disturbance. However, deeper and more sudden crises like Mexico's in 1994–95 potentially can have quite severe implications for US economic activity and jobs. The bigger the emerging-market economy and the deeper its links with the US and global economies, the more disruptive any crisis will be.

As has been seen over the past several years with respect to China especially and a number of other emerging-market economies in Asia as well, their economic size and influence relative to the US and global economies have increased. They have the potential to contribute to global economic imbalances should they fail to adjust their monetary, fiscal, and exchange rate policies to sustain their economic and financial stability as well as their own growth rates. Increasingly, the United States must persuade these countries to exercise global economic and financial leadership by adjusting their policies in their own interests and the global interest. As noted, the United States lacks substantial economic leverage with these countries. Leverage available in the future is likely not to be derived primarily from military or even economic strength but from a track record of two-way cooperation—in other words, helping the LEMs meet their economic, financial, and political objectives. Thus, the principal challenge in dealing with these countries, which are so important to the United States' own prosperity, is to recognize and incorporate their important economic—but also strategic—aspirations to the extent that they are compatible with US objectives. This will not be easy, as the realities of an interdependent and interlinked US economy will require the United States to do so as a partner rather than as a coopting economic hegemon.

What is an alternative scenario? The absence of substantive cooperation with the LEMs will, at best, lead to impasses and an increasing number of inefficient confrontations as happened, for example, in the wake of the WTO ministerial in Cancún. Each LEM is an economic competitor for the United States, and the United States must insist that the competition be fair, and that these countries play by the existing or, if necessary, mutually agreed upon revised global rules of the game. However, a formal grouping among the LEMs to the exclusion of the United States could become formidable competition for the G-7. On many economic as well as other key global issues (energy, technology and science, and security affairs), the LEMs could very well work among themselves to achieve similar, albeit not equal or as speedy, outcomes.

The worst possible strategic scenario would be the emergence of two economic blocs confronting and competing with each other: the G-7 countries and a substantial coalition among the LEMs. This would be reminiscent of the Cold War; only this time the stakes would be principally economic rather than ideological. From a realpolitik point of view, this path along with whatever outcomes it produces might even be in the long-term strategic interests of China, India, Russia, and/or Brazil. In that light, what now appear to be skirmishes in the international economic arena, in fact may be the "prewar" maneuvers of accumulating resources, getting organized, and testing strengths for an upcoming world economic clash. For instance, can the tenfold increase in the international reserves of the 11 LEMs since 1990 be explained by macroeconomic policy considerations alone? Do those 11 countries wield special influence over the global economy by virtue of the fact that they held 30 percent of total international reserves at the end of 2003—more than the combined holdings of the G-7 industrial countries, of which Japan's share was 70 percent? A scenario of a world economic clash, however remote, is the most compelling rationale for why the United States should care about the LEMs and for why the United States should undertake the substantive initiatives we suggest.

How Should the United States Deal with the LEMs?

We have established why the LEMs are important to the United States and vice versa. We now address how to reorganize some of the institutions of the international financial governance system and US policymaking to recognize the importance of the LEMs to the United States.

The US government should support institutional changes globally and in its internal organization so as to better position itself to interact with the LEMs. Globally, it should support the replacement of the finance G-7 with the G-20 as the principal international body to promote cooperation on international economic policy issues. The United States should also make common cause with the LEMs to redistribute chairs and shares in the IFIs. Internally, the United States should recognize the common interests and aspirations of the LEMs and reorganize its internal policymaking on an intra-agency and an interagency basis to reflect this reality.

Recommendation 1: Replace the Finance G-7 with the G-20

Meetings of G-7 finance ministers started in 1973 as meetings of the G-5.[9] Central bank governors soon joined most of the meetings. The countries also began meeting at the level of heads of state or government in 1975. At the initiative of the United States, the G-20 was established at the level of finance ministers and central bank governors by the G-7 industrial countries in 1999 in the wake of the Asian financial crisis "to broaden the dialogue on key economic and financial policy issues among systemically significant economies and promote cooperation to achieve stable and sustainable world economic growth that benefits all" (G-7 1999). Over the past five years, the G-20 has been a discussion forum; we recommend that it become an action committee and that the finance G-7 be gradually disbanded.[10]

In contrast with the mid-1970s, when the performance of the G-7 countries almost exclusively controlled the destiny of the global economic and financial system, today the finance G-7 finds itself addressing issues over which it has little control (for example, Asian exchange rate policies) and has left unaddressed issues closer to home (for example, US fiscal policy and the US external deficit). The G-7 grouping for many reasons, including the complex representation of the European Union, is less relevant and less effective than in the 1970s and 1980s (Bergsten and Henning 1996). Reducing the prominence of the G-7 in economic and financial affairs and raising the prominence of the G-20 would recognize the reality of the changing shape of the world and the increasing interdependence among a larger number of important countries. This step also would respond to the aspi-

9. The G-5 is the G-7 minus Canada and Italy.

10. Earlier versions of this proposal were made in Bergsten (2004) and Truman (forthcoming 2005); subsequently Bradford and Linn (2004) made a similar proposal.

rations of the LEMs for a seat at the global economic policy table. It would also contribute to an important efficiency gain if the present G-7/G-8 structure of meetings were to atrophy.[11] On the other hand, informal caucuses would persist. The G-7 is likely to play an informal coordinating role for a period.[12] However, the United States should also use the G-20 to encourage the five principal LEMs to take on greater responsibility for the health of the global system in return for having their own concerns addressed more fully.

As was the case in the early days of the G-10, which included countries in deficit as well as those in surplus, the economic and financial circumstances of the G-20 countries are not identical.[13] The G-20 brings together the representatives of the right group of countries to address issues of macroeconomic stabilization, including the policies of the individual G-7 countries—which have tended to receive a free pass in most G-7 discussions in recent years—and the macroeconomic policies of the LEMs themselves. The coverage of G-20 activities would include not only issues directly affecting economic prosperity and financial stability but also other issues with indirect effects such as private-sector development, multilateral finance, health, education, poverty reduction, environment, energy, and some aspects of trade issues.[14]

If the G-20 is to be transformed from a discussion forum into an action committee, the United States will have to take the lead to convince other G-7 countries that this is the way to go. Although the G-20 would continue to be a forum for information exchange, dialogue, and mutual education, in its enhanced form it should endeavor to reach concrete agreements on common objectives and to make joint commitments to take coordinated actions. Today those objectives and actions would be expected to cover modifications of exchange rate policies, smooth adjustment of global external imbalances, and a focus on major debt cases, such as Argentina and Turkey. The representatives of the relevant countries would be taking part in the discussions. In some cases—for example, exchange rate policies—actual decisions might involve a smaller group of countries but, as in the case of the Plaza Agreement in 1985 with respect to the G-5, the G-20 could in advance promote and later support those decisions.

11. The G-8 includes Russia and is a political group, not an economic and financial group, that meets at the summit level.

12. As Lardy suggests in his chapter, during a transition period, the G-7 may want to invite China to participate in some of its deliberations, as occurred on an ad hoc basis on October 1, 2004.

13. The G-10 includes the G-7 plus four small European countries: Belgium, the Netherlands, Sweden, and Switzerland.

14. The G-20 should not take over trade issues from the WTO, but it could lead by exhortation. For example, the communiqué issued following the G-20 meeting in October 2003 in Morelia, Mexico—a month after the inconclusive Cancún meeting of WTO ministers—endeavored to give a boost to the Doha Round.

Most importantly, the G-20 also needs to focus its energy on the aspirations and objectives of the LEMs. These include dealing with four key issues: first, infrastructure financing and rural development so that these economies can better integrate their marginal economic areas into their own economies and world markets by having access to resources beyond those afforded by the market, IFIs, corporations, NGOs, and foreign aid. An approach similar to the European Regional Development Program comes to mind. Second, sustained poverty-reducing growth that involves an evolution of the orthodoxy of the Washington Consensus to include flexibility in the area of structural adjustments and a focus on poverty programs, as currently advocated, albeit not fully and successfully implemented, by the International Monetary Fund (IMF) and World Bank. Thus, it would be an appropriate outlet for elaborating the development assistance strategy as it applies to these countries, outlined by William Cline and John Williamson in their chapter in this book. Third, technical and possibly financial resources aimed at correcting institutional and fiscal weakness at all levels of government within individual LEMs. Fourth, political support for regional economic groupings led by individual LEMs such as Mercosur, the Southern African Development Community, and the Association of South East Asian Nations (ASEAN) free trade area. The United States should support regionalism and regional groups as long as they do not impede future cooperation with existing groups or the nondiscriminatory participation of third parties in the economic opportunities in those regions.

The new G-20 should evolve in several dimensions. It should meet more often than the current once a year. Greater use should be made of working groups to study specific problems of common interest. The G-20 deputies should become more involved in monitoring the implementation of decisions than in talking about alternatives. The new G-20 might establish a permanent secretariat, replacing the rotating national secretariat of today. An efficiency gain would be achieved by consolidating EU representation into one seat, but this would be difficult to accomplish. In due course, starting perhaps with ad hoc meetings, the G-20 could become the new framework for summit meetings, replacing the G-7/G-8 summits, but we favor starting at the level of finance ministers and central bank governors to increase the probability that the group will deal with substantive economic and financial issues.[15]

More generally, an enhanced G-20 would provide impetus to the trend to include important emerging-market economies on international standard-

15. Canadian Prime Minister Paul Martin proposed on May 10, 2004, the establishment of a G-20 at the level of heads of state while retaining the G-8. His proposal built on work of the Canadian Centre for International Governance Innovation and Centre for Global Studies (2004). They have looked at the case for a G-20 at the level of leaders, but neither Martin nor the Canadian research institutions specify which 20 countries they would include in their G-20.

setting bodies such as the Financial Action Task Force (FATF), which sets standards for dealing with money laundering and the financing of terrorism, and the Basel Committee on Banking Supervision, which sets international banking and capital standards.[16] We recommend providing LEMs with a rotating seat on the Financial Stability Forum, which consists of finance ministry, central bank, and regulator representatives from the G-7 countries; representatives from the standard-setting bodies; representatives from a few key markets (for example, Singapore, the Netherlands, Hong Kong); and representatives from the IFIs, including the Bank for International Settlements (BIS) and a couple of its committees.

Some might favor the International Monetary and Financial Committee (IMFC) of the IMF replacing the G-7 in these roles. Three arguments against such an approach can be made: (1) The IMFC has had a dismal record in economic policy coordination, in contrast with guiding the policies of the IMF itself; (2) most members of the IMFC are constrained to represent the views of their multicountry constituencies rather than their own; and (3) the G-20 would be better placed to address broader economic policy and related issues than the IMFC, which is dominated by the IMF bureaucracy and focuses primarily on issues where the IMF plays a major role.

Partly for this last reason, a need to address a broader range of issues, Kenen et al. (2004) have recommended the establishment of a Council for International Financial and Economic Cooperation (CIFEC) with standing and term members. They argue it would have greater legitimacy, accountability, and representativeness than the existing G-20. They also propose that the CIFEC have a broader mandate to cover economic issues. However, Kenen et al. are vague about where that mandate would come from in order to provide more legitimacy than the G-20 now has. It is unclear how much more representative their CIFEC would be than the G-20. Moreover, the G-20 exists today, and it would be better to enhance it than to add another body, as the world does not need yet another supercommittee![17]

Recommendation 2: Redistribute IFI Chairs and Shares

The LEMs have major interests in the structure and functioning of the IFIs: the IMF, the World Bank (International Bank for Reconstruction and De-

16. The FATF has targeted China and India for membership once their anti–money laundering regimes are judged to be sufficiently robust in design and implementation.

17. We considered the alternative of streamlining the membership of the G-8, by reducing European representation and adding China and perhaps one or two other LEMs from the inner circle to a newly created "super G." This idea has some merit but would be very challenging to implement. Unfortunately, on issues of world economic governance, one does not have the luxury of starting with a blank sheet of paper. We see a more immediate payoff in working with what is already available in the form of the existing finance G-20.

velopment), and the regional development banks (RDBs). For the LEMs, these institutions are sources of financial resources, policy advice, professional expertise (including the training of their own officials), and influence. The LEMs long have clamored for more voices and votes in them.

The United States should use its considerable influence to support these aspirations.[18] The principal means to do so is to reduce the representation of old and new EU members on the IMF executive board; see Truman (2004). These 25 EU countries now appoint, or play a major role in the election of, 10 of the 24 members of the IMF executive board. Seven of the 24 executive directors and 8 of the 24 alternate executive directors are nationals from these countries. EU members directly control 32 percent of IMF votes.[19] They potentially control an additional 12.5 percent of the votes of EU nonmembers. The decision-making process in the IMF executive board is primarily one of consensus, in which the number of speakers in the room is important. Currently, European voices are heard disproportionately, and that excess tends to bias IMF decisions, for example, in the direction of limiting the scale of financial assistance to countries in Latin America and East Asia.

The United States should seek agreement from the EU countries, first, to drop from their IMF executive board constituencies all EU nonmembers, reducing the number of EU first-row or second-row chairs below 10 to at most five or six.[20] Second, the EU countries should consolidate their chairs into one appointed chair.[21] As a consequence, the size of the executive board could be shrunk to its original 20 seats by reducing the EU seats by a further five or four, freeing up five new seats for LEMs and thus achieving broader representation on the board.

As part of this overall agreement, the United States should support a reduction of the combined EU share in IMF quotas, which is justified based on traditional quota formulas, because about half of their trade is now internal to the European Union. If the EU quota share were reduced from its current 32 percent to the US 17.5 percent, or perhaps a bit higher at 20 percent, the LEMs, many of which have ample reserves, could be granted substantial quota increases out of the combined 10 to 15 percent share of

18. The precise details of this recommendation apply to the IMF, but a parallel argument can be made for the World Bank and, to a lesser extent, the RDBs.

19. The 10 members that joined the European Unions in May 2004 have 2.1 percent of the votes.

20. EU members now have the majority of votes in five IMF constituencies, including three appointed directors and alternates. In one other constituency, the Netherlands has the largest number of votes and the European Union almost a majority adding Cyprus. We are assuming that the European Union would consolidate into these five or six chairs and not seek to displace any other chairs.

21. Representation of the European Central Bank (ECB) on the IMF executive board could be achieved by having the alternate executive director come from the ECB.

quotas that would be released. Thus, both the voice and the vote of the emerging-market economies would be enhanced.[22]

The United States has considerable leverage in this area, which it should use judiciously in support principally of the aspirations of the LEMs. As long as the IMF executive board is larger than the 20 seats mandated in the IMF Articles of Agreement, a vote is required every two years to maintain its size. That vote requires an 85 percent majority, which means US support is required to maintain the current 24 seats. Thus, the United States should make it clear to the Europeans that progress is expected on this issue in the IFIs. If progress is not made, the United States should hold the Europeans responsible for the actions the United States would be forced to take with respect to contracting the size of the IMF executive board. The United States also could consider offering to support a move of the headquarters of either or both the IMF and/or World Bank to a European capital, which would be consistent with the provision in their charters that their headquarters are in the country with the largest quota, to entice the Europeans to embrace this recommendation. Of course, a relocation would be potentially costly and highly disruptive to the organizations and the lives of their staffs.

Recommendation 3: Reorganize US Policymaking Toward the LEMs

At present, US policy toward the LEMs is not developed and implemented in recognition of the extensive common interests among these countries in their relations with the United States. US policy toward each of these countries flows either from a regional orientation—Brazil is part of Latin America—or on an ad hoc basis—Brazil faces a major crisis and a mechanism needs to be developed to deal with that crisis. We recommend a restructuring of the US intra-agency and interagency policy apparatus in recognition of the need to develop and implement a set of consistent and unique policies toward the LEMs.[23] We outline below the procedural steps to implement our recommendation, some of the challenges, and one payoff in the area of US policy toward regionalism.

The initial step in this restructuring process would be to issue a presidential executive order instructing the relevant parts of the government to propose the actions each will take to reorganize itself in a manner that will address the challenge of a coordinated policy toward the LEMs. This executive order would include the appointment of a "coordinator for large emerging-market economies," with the rank of senior director, dual-

22. A similar allocation of seats could occur at the same time in the World Bank and the RDBs, but the reallocation of capital subscriptions would have to be spread over a longer time period so as not to endanger the banks' credit standing.

23. Garten (1997) points out the extent of compartmentalization that exists within the US government and its adverse effects on the formulation and implementation of a comprehensive strategy toward LEMs.

hatted from the National Security Council (NSC) and National Economic Council (NEC) and reporting directly to the national security adviser and the head of the NEC.

Initially, the coordinator would be charged with the task of determining, in consultation with Congress and the Office of Management and Budget, the responsibilities of each part of the government, including the identification of synergies and elimination of any overlaps. A three-month deadline should be set for the completion of this analysis, and the threat of presidential action without consultation would help to limit interagency or executive-legislative branch squabbling. When completed, this blueprint would describe the formal interagency consultative and decision-making process that would generate, on an ongoing basis, a focused and coordinated policy toward the LEMs. The final step would be to propose its approval by the principals of the NSC/NEC in the form of a national security directive.

Turning to some implementation challenges, a decision-making process focused on policy toward the LEMs would be catalytic in the larger departments, for example, State, Treasury, and Commerce, which tend to look at issues in regional or intraregional terms but not global terms. In the case of the quasi-independent agencies such as the Export-Import Bank and the Overseas Private Investment Corporation, countries and regions end up reporting to functional or product areas, creating a further challenge to a LEM-focused strategy. In addition, the reorganization might help to rationalize resources now devoted to the panoply of institutionalizations of bilateral US relations, for example, the US-(country) forum, commission, committee, or dialogue.[24] These entities are usually launched as a "deliverable" in the context of a presidential visit to or from the country and later fall into substantive disuse as they use up resources.

However, even in smaller units, such as the NSC/NEC and the Council of Economic Advisers (CEA), it would be desirable to think of organizing staff responsibilities for the LEMs as a group. At the CEA, for example, a priority might be placed on choosing a member who has extensive experience in the policies and problems of emerging-market economies.[25] As Destler (1996) has analyzed, another dimension of the implementation challenge will have to do with the NSC's historic inability to give economic issues adequate weight and with the removal of control of LEM-related international economic issues from the NEC, thus severing the link between domestic and international economic policy. At the NSC currently, each of the LEMs is looked after by a separate senior director, who, in turn, has one person responsible for economic issues and one responsi-

24. Of the 11 LEMs that are the focus of our attention, at least six, in principle, have some form of annual, high-level bilateral forum, dialogue, or partnership on economic and financial issues with the US government: Brazil, China, India, Mexico, Russia, and Turkey.

25. Kristen Forbes, a member of the CEA in 2004, fits this profile.

ble for several countries within a region (e.g., the southern cone of Latin America, which includes Brazil). As situations arise, teams are assembled and tasked with interacting with different parts of the executive branch and with formulating recommendations for the principals of the NSC. Today, there is no dedicated, senior-level group or effort focused on the LEMs, in particular one able to be proactive and with access to decision makers. Our approach would imply a reallocation of personnel and reorganization of the NSC so that continuity and focus on the LEMs is ensured.

In the interagency process, it would be desirable to establish a staff-level working group on the LEMs that would help to develop and coordinate common policies to deal with their problems and meet their needs, presumably under the leadership of the NSC/NEC senior director for large emerging-market economies mentioned above. This approach would have several advantages. It would tend to promote common solutions to common problems, rather than ad hoc country-specific solutions, thereby providing greater consistency to US policy.[26]

Not only would policy be more consistent but also proactive policies might be developed and presented for this set of important countries as a group. Moreover, reduced reliance on ad hoc policies would tend to depoliticize at least their presentation, recognizing that political and strategic interests would always come into play. In implementing this approach, care needs to be taken not to usurp the traditional policy leadership of a given department or agency (for example, policies on debt rescheduling at Treasury and foreign assistance policies at State) so as not to create a low-level but paralyzing bureaucratic territorial war (Juster and Lazarus 1997).

This reorganization of intra-agency and interagency work with the LEMs would tend to reinforce the enhanced role of the G-20 recommended above and vice versa, just as the establishment of the finance G-5, later G-7, was helpful in guiding the federal bureaucracy in developing common policies toward the G-5/G-7 countries. These changes will encounter resistance, yet the rationale for them is clear: to identify and realize the knowledge synergies within the White House and the executive branch and to have a consistent policy relating to the LEMs.

An important benefit of the refocusing of US foreign economic policy toward LEMs involves the US government's position—or lack thereof—on regionalism. The United States historically has been a promoter of regional economic and financial arrangements, for example the European Common Market in the 1950s and the North American Free Trade Agreement.

26. To cite an example from the past, the approach taken toward a current financial crisis in Brazil would be developed in the context of the approach taken in a prior crisis in Korea. That this is not occurring systematically is illustrated by Korean complaints that greater demands were placed on their country in 1997–98 than were placed on Brazil in 1998–99 in connection with their respective IMF-supported programs.

More recently, the United States has been somewhat ambivalent about regional groups in which it is not included. For example, it has been a skeptic about, if not in open opposition to, former Malaysian Prime Minister Mahathir's proposed East Asian Economic Group and later the Japanese-proposed Asian Monetary Fund (Henning 2002).

In particular instances, US positions have been influenced by strategic or political considerations as well as economic considerations—for example, damage to US exports. The US attitude also has been affected by the potential adverse impact of new regional institutions on existing global institutions. For example, the Asian Monetary Fund was seen as a rival to the IMF with its near-universal membership. It had and still has the potential to undermine the IMF's influence and at the same time to complicate the implicit rules and understandings guiding the functioning of the international financial system as a whole with respect to flexibility of exchange rates and capital movements.

In the future, it would be useful for the United States to articulate the standards it intends to apply in evaluating regional arrangements in which it does not participate. Subsequently, the United States should support those regional arrangements that meet its standards. Less controversial examples might be India's desire to build bridges to the Association of Southeast Asian Nations (ASEAN) and Turkey's efforts to become part of the European Union. On the other hand, an example of a regional arrangement that would require hard, unbiased analysis on the part of the US government would be China's interest in creating an East Asia Community similar to the European Union.

This approach would be analogous to establishing, at the level of national policy, self-disciplines such as those found in GATT Article XXIV and GATS Article V with respect to free trade areas (Schott 2004). Unfortunately, those multilateral disciplines have not worked very well, and similarly the task of articulating criteria for self-discipline may be too difficult because of the actual or perceived sui generis nature of each regional proposal. However, the effort, in particular if it were conducted in a relatively open and transparent manner, might earn the United States points with the LEMs that tend at times to be mystified by why the United States takes the positions it does on these matters. It might also help to provoke a healthy debate within the United States about the place of regionalism in the world of the 21st century.

Active Collaboration Between the United States and LEMs

We now address the opportunities US policymakers have to work in collaboration with the LEMs. We organize our recommendations under two headings: (1) poverty-reducing economic growth and (2) crisis resolution and global financial stability.

Poverty-Reducing Economic Growth

The dominant interest of the LEMs is sustained economic growth to raise their standards of living on average and to reduce the incidence of poverty. The United States, along with the European Union and Japan, should respond more effectively to this overriding interest. We suggest below three areas where the United States could work with the LEMs to achieve their objectives via the promotion of initiatives in private-sector development and increased cooperation on development issues and on tax evasion.

Recommendation 4: Undertake Initiatives in Private-Sector Development

It is fashionable to emphasize microeconomic objectives in the context of US foreign economic policy. Yet the ability of government policy to promote private-sector contributions to economic development in the world remains limited.

In the financial sector, the crisis-prevention pillar of the improved international financial architecture developed over the past decade or so has placed substantial emphasis on the development of international standards and codes, surveillance of compliance with those codes, improved data provision, and increased transparency. On the other hand, in the sectors producing goods and services (sometimes referred to as the "real economy"), US government policy has been, at best, a passive, reactive participant and, at worst, a verbose but not particularly useful enabler. This is particularly true for small and medium-sized enterprises (SMEs), which are particularly relevant to development given that small firms and entrepreneurs are the main source of innovation and employment creation in both industrialized and emerging-market economies.

Promotion of private-sector development in the LEMs requires US policymakers to focus on the issues that most stand in the way of growth and development both within LEMs and between them and the United States. Among these issues are competition policy, governance, regulation, corruption, legal streamlining and cost reduction, and removal of other impediments to private-sector growth or threats to the integrity of the financial system. Competition policy includes antitrust issues within countries and barriers that prevent the efficient allocation of resources across borders. Regulatory capacity building needs to be provided to the LEMs so that major inputs into the productive sector are priced in the interests of consumers as well as investors. Finally, differences in legal standards, degree of litigiousness, and arbitration and enforcement capabilities within and between industrialized countries and emerging markets remain a monumental barrier to private-sector development.

The private sectors in LEMs require partnership opportunities (for example, marketing and distribution), local financing alternatives, and access to technology broadly defined. Their SME sectors finance themselves primarily with internally generated funds and desperately need access to local, long-term financing that is competitive with larger players. The G-8 has identified remittances and microfinance as very important sources and uses, respectively, of capital for the SME sector in developing countries. The challenge for the G-8 and the multilateral institutions, as their implementation agents, is how to achieve meaningful and measurable results. This area might represent a nice opportunity for partnership between the government and the private financial sector. What can financial-sector institutions in both industrialized and emerging economies do to promote widespread lending to entrepreneurs in LEMs on terms comparable to their peers in developed economies? What can the G-20 financial policymakers do to promote access and openness within each other's financial markets?

From the vantage point of industrialized countries, access to the LEMs for their small business sector is of high interest. US policy needs to foster concrete enabling factors (for example, tax incentives and financing) to make this a compelling and more accessible opportunity.

The issues identified by the emerging-market economies do not always coincide with the views of the United States or other industrial countries—for example, not placing sufficient emphasis on anti–money laundering or on combating the financing of terrorism. In these areas, it would be appropriate for the United States to support or supply technical assistance, including the financing of institutional changes, in support of the achievement of objectives that involve important global public goods but whose availability is limited in emerging-market economies.

Recommendation 5: Increase Cooperation on Development Issues

Many LEMs continue to rely heavily on borrowing from the World Bank, the RDBs, and on a less sustained basis from the IMF. At the end of 2003, these institutions had $231.9 billion outstanding to 10 of the 11 LEMs that are members of the G-20.[27] This group of countries includes ones that are making net repayments or are no longer borrowing from the banks, such as Korea, as well as countries that have recently graduated from International Development Association (IDA) eligibility, such as China, and countries that are currently blend borrowers from IDA and the World Bank, such as India and Indonesia. The United States has a shared interest in increasing its cooperation with the LEMs in development lending. Three steps should be considered.

First, as sketched out earlier, the United States should support a more meaningful voice for the LEMs in the direction of the development banks.

27. Saudi Arabia has no obligations to the multilateral development financial institutions.

Also in the common interest is promoting a gradual transition from the status of borrowers from those institutions to the status of financial supporters of them, via progressively increasing their costs of borrowing from them and other means.

Second, the more advanced LEMs should retain the scope to borrow from development banks in certain circumstances. Those circumstances should include periods of external financial crisis, as was the case for Korea in 1997–98, in particular to provide fiscal support for the continuation of social programs. They should also include limited support for public and private infrastructure investment in periods where the countries are operating under tight fiscal constraints. On the other hand, a delicate balance has to be struck between the buildup of government debt, especially to preferred creditors such as the IFIs even when the interest cost is lower, and the restoration of debt sustainability.

Third, the United States should explore foreign assistance partnerships with the LEMs. These partnerships should have the objective of increasing the efficiency of existing delivery mechanisms and the encouragement of contributions or increased contributions to the soft-loan or grant windows of the development banks, such as IDA in the World Bank Group or the Fund for Special Operations in the Inter-American Development Bank (IDB) or the Multilateral Investment Fund of the IDB, which supports private-sector development with an emphasis on the small and microenterprise sector.

These partnerships should also involve joint bilateral assistance programs for individual countries or regional groups in which a substantial share of the funding would come from the United States or other industrial countries, but the LEM partner countries could provide expertise and delivery systems based on their own experiences. In addition, greater effort should be made to consult and coordinate aid disbursements among major donors to avoid duplication and competition.[28] The G-20 should establish a one-stop shopping and clearinghouse for recipients of bilateral aid. This initiative could be blended with the process of graduating the LEMs from borrowing from the development banks by actively encouraging them to take on greater global leadership responsibilities.

Recommendation 6: Increase Cooperation on Tax Evasion

Dependence on foreign investment, borrowing, and aid is to some degree due to the inability of many LEMs to collect taxes from their citizens and corporations. The United States has played a global leadership role in

28. The issue of aid project proliferation has been a focus of considerable criticism (Roodman 2004). Birdsall and Deese (2004) point out that this phenomenon diverts the time and attention of officials in recipient countries from broader and more persistent problems of governance.

combating financial crimes. One area of substantial attention has been the global anti–money laundering regime, and most recently the use of that regime to reduce and disrupt the financing of terrorism (Reuter and Truman 2004). The LEMs do not all attach the same high priority to these objectives though many of them are increasingly concerned about the integrity of their financial systems. For the United States, the achievement of these goals is a necessity; for many other countries they are luxuries. A quid pro quo for help in achieving US objectives in this area would be to pursue with the LEMs the "shared" objective of reducing tax evasion.

Many LEMs are very concerned about tax evasion. In Latin America, in particular, saving rates are low and fiscal resources are scarce. Historical patterns of capital flight are engrained, which deprives countries of tax revenues on income from investments abroad. These weaknesses contribute to excessive foreign borrowing by the private and public sectors and to external financial crises. The United States has an interest in helping these countries deal with tax evasion analogous to the US interest in facilitating the flow of remittances at lower costs to the private sector.

Today US international cooperation on tax evasion with most countries, including the LEMs, is limited. Tax evasion in the United States or abroad is not a basis for US anti–money laundering prosecutions. Bilateral tax treaties generally provide for the exchange of information, but the procedures are cumbersome and the scope of the provisions does not extend to operations of US institutions outside the United States—for example, islands in the Caribbean—with which the home country has to have an additional layer of legal arrangements.

On the other hand, the United States has put into place mutual assistance arrangements with other industrial-country jurisdictions, such as Australia, Canada, and the United Kingdom, to combat abusive tax avoidance transactions. Similar arrangements should be put in place with interested LEMs. In addition, the United States should make common cause with them to establish an international tax organization, as suggested by former Mexican President Ernesto Zedillo's panel on the mobilization of resources for development (United Nations 2001). This organization could start with the collection and sharing of statistics and information on problems and also provide technical assistance. The ultimate goal might be to achieve international agreement on the comprehensive sharing of tax information and better convergence in the tax treatment of multinationals.

One should not be too sanguine about achieving rapid progress in this area. The experiences of the Organization for Economic Cooperation and Development (OECD) on reducing harmful tax competition and of the European Union in endeavoring to agree on its savings directive have involved years of negotiation and, in the EU case, may still fail to establish an admittedly second-best accord if Swiss voters block the new Swiss-European treaty that covers this area, among others. Nevertheless, the United States as well as Europe and Japan could create valuable bonds with emerging-market economies if they upgraded cooperation on tax evasion with the LEMs.

Crisis Resolution and Global Financial Stability

Most of the LEMs have experienced one or more external financial crises over the past 15 years, some of which have not yet passed.[29] Even with the widespread adoption of more flexible exchange rate regimes, improved macroeconomic and structural policies, and greater transparency, only a fool would wager that over the next decade none of the LEMs will experience new crises requiring substantial ex post international financial support. The United States should adopt policies that recognize this reality. In addition to continuing to support economic reform and macroeconomic stability in these countries, the United States should endeavor through the refocused G-20 as well as other channels to establish consensus on a proactive framework for crisis resolution, including actively exploring alternative means of providing financing for countries in crisis, and support a resumption of regular annual SDR allocations.

Recommendation 7: Create a Proactive Framework for Crisis Resolution

The most severe economic and financial effects of financial crises can be ameliorated somewhat by better prevention policies, but they will not be eliminated. The recent policy of the United States combines the rhetoric of limited access to IMF financing with actions that result in the provision of increasingly large access to IMF financing without a clear rationale for doing so (see Morris Goldstein's chapter in this book). It is unrealistic to take the firefighter out of the game; meanwhile the gap between what the United States says and what it supports is widening, sowing uncertainty among the LEMS about US policy intentions. The LEMs, the United States, and the global economy need a realistic, constructive, proactive strategy for crisis resolution.

Roubini and Setser (2004) provide a comprehensive review of experience over the past dozen years with the resolution of external financial crises and a framework for dealing with future crises. The key elements of the Roubini-Setser framework are (1) distinguishing promptly between liquidity and solvency crises, (2) adopting appropriate adjustment measures to match external financing with the nature of the crisis, (3) using large-scale IMF financing for a variety of purposes, including in conjunction with coercive debt restructuring as necessary, (4) avoiding the trap of

29. Of the 11 emerging-market economies in the G-20, only Saudi Arabia has not received IMF financial support for its economic policies over the past two decades, although the possible need was considered in the mid-1990s. China borrowed from the IMF in 1986 and made its last repayment in 1992.

countries that are too strategic to fail, and (5) recognizing that the IMF has a central coordinating role in the management of crises.

Taken as a package, this set of recommendations, with the proper support, political and financial, would substantially rationalize the process of resolving external financial crises. This framework for crisis resolution should be adopted by the US government, explained to and examined with representatives of the emerging-market economies, and promoted in bodies such as the G-20, IMFC, and IMF executive board.

The need for external financing in the resolution of crises is likely to increase in the future because of nominal growth and the fact, documented in Roubini and Setser (2004), that the financing provided in some cases in the past has been too skimpy, while in other cases international financial support has been too generous for too long.

One approach to meeting the reasonable financing needs of countries in crisis is through the more aggressive use of a coercive bail-in process. A second approach is to augment the IMF's traditional quota resources for use to support adjustment programs, which will almost certainly be desirable at some point over the next three to five years. A third, largely complementary, approach is to augment emergency funds available to the IMF via the New Arrangements to Borrow (NAB) from a subset of IMF members, including importantly the United States and six emerging-market economies (Chile, Hong Kong, Korea, Malaysia, Saudi Arabia, and Thailand). These six economies were included in the NAB in 1996 because at that time they were perceived as having the financial capacity to provide resources to the IMF in addition to their quota subscriptions. It would be appropriate for the other 9 of the 11 LEMs that are members of the G-20 to join the NAB as well.

It is possible that these approaches will prove not to generate sufficient resources, or they may founder on political opposition to them. Therefore, consideration should be given to alternative sources of financing to and through the IMF. For example, Truman (2001) proposed the establishment of an International Financial Stability Fund (IFSF) that would be financed by annual fees on stocks of cross-border investments and could be tapped under certain circumstances to finance in whole or in part large programs of IMF financial support. While this may not be the most attractive or saleable alternative financing mechanism, it has the advantage of prepositioning financing from the private sector that can be disbursed, in part, for the benefit of the private sector.

Recommendation 8: Resume Regular Annual SDR Allocations

SDRs are reserve assets issued by the IMF. There have been two issues of SDR, in 1970–72 and 1979–81, for a total of SDR 21.4 billion ($33 billion), and under the pending fourth amendment of the IMF Articles of Agreement an additional SDR 21.9 billion ($34 billion) would be issued. The amendment was approved by the IMF's Board of Governors in 1997 and has been ratified by enough members that it will go into force as soon as the US Congress ratifies it.

The original rationale for the SDR mechanism, as a supplementary reserve asset to stabilize the international monetary system, and a briefly acquired rationale, as the principal reserve asset in place of gold in an international monetary system of fixed exchange rates, are no longer relevant to the smooth functioning of the international monetary system that features the widespread adoption of more flexible exchange rate regimes, the de facto phasing out of gold, and the ready access of major countries in most circumstances to borrowed liquidity. However, a case can be made that the resumption of SDR allocations on a regular, annual basis would benefit the functioning of the international monetary system (Clark and Polak 2004). Moreover, the resumption of SDR allocations at the rate of, say, 10 percent of IMF quotas per year would be welcome by most LEMs.

The case against resuming SDR allocations rests on several arguments. First, SDR allocations, it is argued, would add to global inflation; this argument is no longer, if it was ever, relevant to current economic conditions. Second, the allocations would go to the wrong countries, encouraging them to delay necessary adjustment measures; this would not be the case if annual allocations were small. Third, the allocation of SDRs is inconsistent with an international monetary system based on floating exchange rates in which it is unnecessary to hold reserves.

The facts fly in the face of the third argument in particular. The 11 LEMs that are members of the G-20 have increased the ratio of their international reserves (excluding gold) to GDP from 4.2 percent in 1990 to 13.7 percent in 2003.[30] Over the same period, the average ratio of reserves to imports rose by 30 percentage points. The present form of reserve increases is inefficient and costly; the cost of borrowing reserves is larger than the return on holding them, whether the reserves are accumulated through sovereign borrowing or private capital inflows. In addition, reserve accumulation via larger current account surpluses or smaller current account deficits requires the use of real resources that can be better applied to domestic investment and consumption. Moreover, those larger surpluses or smaller deficits distort the adjustment of international payments imbalances.[31] Exhibit A for the last proposition is the huge defensive accumulation of reserves by China and other Asian economies in the wake of the Asian financial crisis and the reluctance of China and other

30. Because we lack comparable data for Russia in 1990, we have excluded that country from these calculations.

31. Clark and Polak (2004) argue that in addition to global efficiency gains from greater reliance on SDR as reserve assets, the stability of the international financial system would be enhanced because of reduced reliance on borrowed reserves, which need to be refinanced; the availability of such financing is subject to sudden stops if market conditions change.

emerging-market economies to allow their exchange rates to adjust lest they slip back into current account deficit. By recognizing the reality of the LEMs' desire to increase their reserves and by supporting a resumption of SDR allocations, which the LEMs also favor, the United States would buy some influence over these countries' decisions with respect to their exchange-rate and reserve-accumulation policies, which would improve the functioning of the international adjustment process.

Thus, the United States as well as emerging-market economies should welcome the resumption of SDR allocations on a regular annual basis. The United States would also demonstrate to the emerging-market economies and the rest of the world that it takes its international financial agreements seriously by ratifying the fourth amendment of the IMF Articles of Agreement. Both steps would lay the groundwork for the possibility of special large SDR allocations, largely as a symbolic action, if concerns about global deflation again emerged, or the cancellation of SDR if global inflation threatened to get out of hand.

Budgetary Reality Check

Because of the large US budget deficit, the US government over the next four years and beyond most likely will be operating under a severe budgetary constraint. The risk is that pressures to cut the budget deficit will lead to a disproportionate cutback in official US external financial operations, which some would argue have been shortchanged in the past. This could adversely affect US external interests at the same time that the small absolute size of the cutback has little effect on the overall US budgetary position. Even if such a near-sighted posture is avoided, the reality will be tight budget resources. Therefore, in the spirit of responsible policymaking, we provide a reality check on our eight recommendations by summarizing them from the standpoint of their impacts on the US federal budget. The basic budgetary impacts fall into two categories: negligible and small.

Five of the recommendations would have negligible impacts on the budget.

- Recommendation 1, replacing the finance G-7 with a refocused G-20, would involve only a reallocation of existing US personnel resources from G-7 activities to G-20 activities.[32]
- Recommendation 2, redistributing IFI chairs and shares, would have no cost to the United States and might provide financial benefits over time if the LEMs were encouraged to graduate more rapidly from bor-

32. If the refocused G-20 took up our suggestion for consideration of a program of regional development assistance on the EU model, this might involve substantial amounts of budget resources unless current expenditures were reprogrammed.

rowing from the development banks and become net providers of support for these institutions.[33]

- Recommendation 3, reorganizing US policymaking toward the LEMs, also would involve only a reallocation of existing resources along with the promise of some efficiency gains.
- Recommendation 6, increasing cooperation on tax evasion, should pay for itself if the United States can bring itself to embrace such an initiative.
- Recommendation 7, creating a proactive framework for crisis resolution, should not involve an additional US financial commitment to the IMF compared with the realistic alternative, which is that an increase in IMF quotas is likely to be required at some point over the next three to five years. By involving some of the LEMs in the NAB and exploring alternative devices to finance the IMF, the US financial contribution—which technically does not now involve budgetary outlays, but is a budgetary issue—might be smaller than otherwise. Moreover, existing and potential resources might be more efficiently spent to resolve external financial crises than has been the case in recent years.

We now turn to recommendations where the implications for the US federal budget would be nonnegligible but small.

- Recommendation 4, promoting initiatives in private-sector development, would involve legislative and regulatory initiatives to accompany actions taken by the private sector itself. It might require some modest additional expenditure for technical assistance if resources could not be reprogrammed from existing less effective programs. Any cofinancing or colending to private-sector institutions would be done above the US government's cost of funds and would take into account appropriate risk premiums.
- Recommendation 5, increasing cooperation on development issues, could require an increased US financial commitment in this area over the near term (three to five years), but that commitment might be compensated down the road as the LEMs graduated more rapidly from the status of borrowers, to making net repayments, and finally to the status of important financial contributors. In addition, increased funding is already contemplated as part of the new Millennium Challenge Account initiative that, if anything, is suffering from disbursement not funding challenges.
- Recommendation 8, resuming regular annual SDR allocation, would involve a small net budgetary expense to the extent that the interest

33. In the unlikely event that the headquarters of the IMF or the World Bank were relocated from Washington, there would be substantial expense for those institutions, and the United States might condition its support on not participating in covering them.

rate on US net holdings of SDR (in excess of our allocation) exceeded the average cost of US borrowing. However, the projected amounts would be small.

Our conclusion is that our recommendations not only provide the framework for constructive US policy toward the LEMs but also are fiscally responsible.

References

Bergsten, C. Fred. 2004. The G-20 and the World Economy: Speech to the Deputies of the G-20, Leipzig, Germany. Photocopy (March 4).

Bergsten, C. Fred, and C. Randall Henning. 1996. *Global Economic Leadership and the Group of Seven*. Washington: Institute for International Economics.

Birdsall, Nancy, and Brian Deese. 2004. Hard Currency: Unilateralism Doesn't Work for Foreign Aid Either. *Washington Monthly* (March).

Bradford, Colin I., and Johannes F. Linn. 2004. *Global Governance at a Crossroads: Replacing the G-7 with the G-20*. Brookings Institution Policy Brief 131. Washington: Brookings Institution (April).

Clark, Peter B., and Jacques J. Polak. 2004. *International Liquidity and the Role of the SDR in the International Monetary* System. International Monetary Fund Staff Papers 51, no. 1: 49–71.

Centre for Global Studies. 2004. CFGS/CIGI Report: The G-20 at Leaders' Level. February 29. The University of Victoria, Victoria, British Columbia, Canada.

Destler, I. M. 1996. *The National Economic Council: A Work in Progress*. POLICY ANALYSES IN INTERNATIONAL ECONOMICS 46. Washington: Institute for International Economics.

G-7 (Group of Seven). 1999. Statement of G-7 Finance Ministers and Central Bank Governors, September 25. Washington.

Garten, Jeffrey E. 1997. *The Big Ten: The Big Emerging Markets and How They Will Change our Lives*. New York: Basic Books.

Henning, C. Randall. 2002. *East Asian Financial Cooperation*. POLICY ANALYSES IN INTERNATIONAL ECONOMICS 68. Washington: Institute for International Economics.

Juster, Kenneth I., and Simon Lazarus. 1997. *Making Economic Policy Work: An Assessment of the National Economic Council*. Washington: Brookings Institution.

Kenen, Peter B., Jeffrey R. Shafer, Nigel L. Wicks, and Charles Wyplosz. 2004. *International Economic and Financial Cooperation: New Issues, New Actors, New Responses*. Geneva: International Center for Monetary and Banking Studies.

Reuter, Peter, and Edwin M. Truman. 2004. *Chasing Dirty Money: The Fight Against Money Laundering*. Washington: Institute for International Economics.

Roodman, David. 2004. *An Index of Donor Performance*. Center for Global Development Working Paper 42. Washington: Center for Global Development.

Roubini, Nouriel, and Brad Setser. 2004. *Bailouts or Bail-ins? Responding to Financial Crises in Emerging Markets*. Washington: Institute for International Economics.

Schott, Jeffrey J., ed. 2004. *Free Trade Agreements: US Strategies and Priorities*. Washington: Institute for International Economics.

Truman, Edwin M. 2001. Perspectives on External Financial Crises. Speech to the Money Marketeers of New York University. Photocopy (December 10).

Truman, Edwin M. Forthcoming 2005. The Euro and Prospects for Policy Coordination. In *The Euro at Five: Ready for a Global Role?* ed., Adam Posen. Washington: Institute for International Economics (draft February, forthcoming).

United Nations. 2001. *High-Level International Intergovernmental Consideration of Financing for Development* (Zedillo Report, A/55/1000). New York: United Nations.

III

THE KEY ISSUES

6

Sustaining Global Growth while Reducing External Imbalances

MICHAEL MUSSA

With renewed deterioration of the external balance in recent months, it now appears that the US current account deficit will exceed $600 billion in 2004—or over 5½ percent of US GDP. Plausible estimates suggest that, at present exchange rates and with US economic growth continuing to exceed that of most other industrial countries, the US external deficit could reach $1 trillion or more by the end of this decade. The cumulative effect of the persistent external deficits of the past 30 years (which have averaged about 3 percent of US GDP) is already reflected in the transformation of the United States from the world's largest net creditor to the world's largest net debtor. Specifically, the United States has shifted from a position in the mid-1970s when US net external assets exceeded 25 percent of US GDP to a position where US net external liabilities now exceed 25 percent of annual GDP. If current account deficits persist at a level of more than 5 percent of GDP (and rising), the US external liability position is on track to reach 50 percent of GDP within a decade and to exceed 100 percent of GDP within the next 25 years.

It is possible that US current account deficits of 5 percent or somewhat more of US GDP could persist for a while longer. And there is no indication yet that the prospect that US net external liabilities might reach 50 percent of US GDP is a cause for fright and likely instability in global financial markets. However, there is good reason to doubt that US current account deficits of 5 percent or more of GDP can be sustained indefinitely

Michael Mussa is a senior fellow at the Institute for International Economics.

or that US external liabilities can expand up to and beyond 100 percent of GDP—a record never achieved by any significant country. Almost surely, adjustments will occur—in the United States and the rest of the world—that will forestall long-run deterioration of the US external position of this extreme magnitude.

Sooner or later, one way or another, a substantial downward correction of these imbalances will come. Whenever and however it comes, the correction will necessarily involve three broad and interrelated macroeconomic developments: (1) The US dollar will need to depreciate substantially in real terms against the currencies of most other countries in order to shift the distribution of total world demand for goods and services toward those of the United States and away from those of the rest of the world. (2) In the United States, domestic demand will need to grow more slowly than domestic output in order to make room for an expansion of US net exports; and as logically necessary counterparts of this downward adjustment of US demand relative to output, there must be a corresponding improvement in the US national savings/investment balance and an equivalent reduction in the net use of foreign savings by the United States. (3) In the rest of the world, domestic demand will need to grow more rapidly than domestic output in order to allow for the reduction of net exports that corresponds to the improvement of US net exports; and as logically necessary counterparts of this upward adjustment of demand relative to output, there must be a corresponding deterioration in the savings/investment balance and an equivalent reduction in the net outflow of capital to the United States from the rest of the world.

The key concern is that these adjustments need not occur in an entirely salutary manner. Economic activity in some countries (particularly in the rest of the world) could be persistently depressed to levels meaningfully below potential, while excessive demand pressures in other countries (notably the United States) could push up inflation and necessitate monetary policy tightening that would depress investment and impair longer-term growth. Indeed, some experienced observers, including Paul Volcker, fear that if the problem of the large US external deficit is not vigorously addressed, there is substantial risk of a major global financial crisis.

Thus, the crucial issue for policymakers—in the United States and the rest of the world—is what responses would be appropriate to facilitate the gradual and orderly reduction of the US external deficit in a manner that is consistent with achieving the most fundamental objectives of economic policy. Specifically, the challenge is to ensure that the timing and method of this inevitable correction in the US external imbalance (and its counterpart for the rest of the world) is such as to support, as best as possible, continued noninflationary growth at the maximum sustainable rate throughout the world economy. Most importantly, the challenge is to avoid an abrupt and disorderly correction of external imbalances, which would disrupt world financial markets and depress global economic activity—

a danger that becomes more acute as external imbalances continue to accumulate at an accelerating rate.

After reviewing the causes behind the deterioration of the US external balance and the reasons why the present (and probably growing) imbalance is not likely to be sustainable in the longer term, this chapter looks specifically at policy adjustments, first in the industrial countries and then in the developing countries, that would facilitate a constructive and orderly reduction of international payments imbalances. To conclude this introduction it is useful to anticipate briefly the content of that discussion.

Among the industrial countries, the United States faces the task of slowing the growth rate of domestic demand below the growth rate of output, particularly in circumstances where the dollar has depreciated sufficiently to make net exports a positive contributor to GDP growth. Fiscal consolidation, which is needed for its own sake to restore longer-term fiscal sustainability, can aid in restraining the growth of domestic demand and can reduce the need for restrictive monetary policy to play this role as US output rises to its potential level. An easier monetary policy (than would otherwise prevail) should, in turn, contribute to a necessary downward correction in the foreign exchange value of the dollar, which will assist in improving the US external balance.

For other industrial countries, the principal policy challenge will probably be to achieve and sustain adequate growth of domestic demand. In these countries, domestic demand growth over the past decade has generally needed a boost from improving net exports but will now need to compensate for a deterioration of net exports that is a necessary (partial) counterpart to improvement in the US current account. Moreover, unlike the United States where fiscal consolidation, which is needed for its own sake, can help to curb domestic demand growth and thereby contribute to the reduction of external imbalances, in other industrial countries expansionary fiscal policies are generally not a desirable means of boosting domestic demand growth. More vigorous efforts at structural reform in most of western Europe and Japan are highly desirable because they will aid growth in the longer term, thereby also contributing to somewhat stronger growth of demand for US exports. But in the medium term of the next few years, structural reforms are unlikely to do much to support adequate growth of domestic demand. That policy task will fall largely to the monetary authorities, who will have to pay careful attention to the need for adequate demand growth, as well as to any dangers of a resurgence of inflation.

Aside from Japan, industrial countries generally allow market forces to determine exchange rates. This approach has permitted a significant downward correction of the US dollar since early 2002. Further (hopefully gradual) market-determined adjustments in this direction are likely to be needed in the medium term and should not be resisted. For Japan, the policy of vigorously resisting appreciation of the yen through occasionally massive official intervention was desirable when the Japanese economy was very weak. But as the Japanese economy has gathered strength, this policy is no longer defensible. The Japanese authorities should allow the yen to appreciate—especially in the context of a broader necessary appreciation of the currencies of most Asian developing countries.

For developing countries, the issue of exchange rate adjustments is generally a more pressing policy issue than for industrial countries. This is so both because many developing countries actively manage their exchange rates (in contrast to the laissez-faire policies of most industrial countries) and because the exchange rates of most developing countries (including those with strong balance-of-payments positions) have not adjusted upward against the US dollar—as will clearly be needed as part of the process of reducing the US external deficit. At present, this issue is most pressing for emerging Asia—certainly including, but not limited to, China.

Because the situations of individual developing countries differ considerably, little can be said in general about policies that may be needed to support demand growth in the face of some deterioration of net exports (as a partial counterpart to the necessary improvement in US net exports). Probably this should be less of a problem for most developing countries than for most industrial countries because underlying forces of economic growth are generally stronger in developing countries.

One general concern that bridges the interests of developing and industrial countries is the need for more reliable—less crisis-prone—mechanisms to facilitate international capital flows from industrial to developing countries. Here, the bedrock requirement is for developing countries to pursue economic policies that support sustainable growth and avoid excessive risks from either poorly run domestic financial systems or imprudent foreign borrowing. But, as revealed in the series of disastrous emerging-market financial crises of the past decade, the international mechanisms for helping to avoid or resolve such crises can use some work. With more reliable mechanisms to facilitate capital flows to developing countries, these countries should be able to grow more rapidly and (as a secondary benefit) be able to contribute more constructively to sustainable reduction of global payments imbalances.

Forces Behind the Recent Rise of the US External Deficit

As a prelude to the discussion of policies that might facilitate an orderly reduction of present international imbalances, it is useful to review briefly the causes and consequences of the US external deficit—and the corresponding surplus of the rest of the world—as they have evolved over the past quarter century. These developments involve complex interactions among the broad macroeconomic forces that have shaped the course of the world economy. In light of these developments in the global economy, it is important to recognize that the generally growing and fluctuating US external imbalance has, in several important respects, been beneficial both to the United States and the rest of the world.

From the end of World War I through the 1960s, the US current account was in persistent surplus. As a consequence, the United States accumulated net financial claims on the rest of the world and ultimately became the world's largest net creditor nation. By the late 1960s, however, the US external payments surplus began to erode, and a substantial depreciation of the US dollar (associated with the collapse of the Bretton Woods system of pegged exchange rates) was needed to restore a US external payments surplus.

Emergence of the "Twin Deficits" During the 1980s

During the 1980s, the US current account fell into substantial and persistent deficit. The relatively strong recovery of the US economy following the worldwide recession of the early 1980s (especially as measured by growth of domestic demand) was one important force behind this deterioration in the US current account. But the most important proximate cause of the current account deterioration was the spectacular appreciation of the US dollar between 1980 and early 1985—the lagged effects of which induced further deterioration in the US current account through 1987.

Several factors lay behind the exceptional strength of the dollar in the early to mid-1980s and may be regarded as underlying causes of the deterioration in the US current account that operated through the mechanism of dollar appreciation. In particular, the strength of the US economic recovery and the restoration of confidence in prospects for the US economy encouraged a sharp rise in investment spending in the United States. When domestic savings proved inadequate to finance this surge of investment, foreign savings was called upon to fill the gap. And foreign investors enthusiastically poured funds into the United States, thereby contributing to upward pressure on the dollar.

In this connection, the US macroeconomic policy mix of the early 1980s—featuring tight monetary and loose fiscal policies—undoubtedly contributed to dollar appreciation and to the deterioration of the US current account. This policy mix raised directly the demand for the use of foreign savings to finance increased government deficits, and it tended to raise US real interest rates, which made it more attractive for foreigners to move funds into the United States. Probably more importantly, the success of the policy mix both in bringing a rapid and sustained victory over inflation and in promoting a vigorous economic recovery helped to stimulate both demand for the use of foreign savings to finance US investment and the appetite of foreign investors to supply the requisite funds.

More simplistically, the apparent coincidence of the rise in the US current account deficit and the rise in the structural (or cyclically adjusted) fiscal deficit in the early 1980s encouraged some analysts to proclaim that these were really "twin deficits." The clear implications of this simplistic view were first that the rise of the structural fiscal deficit was the primary cause of the deterioration in the current account and second that reducing the fiscal deficit was the surefire way to reduce, probably about one-for-one, the current account deficit. Subsequent developments, however, would dispel these simplistic notions.

The depreciation of the US dollar from early 1985 through 1987 effectively reversed the massive appreciation of the early 1980s. With the usual lag of about two years, the US current account deficit peaked and began to turn downward by 1988. The current account deficit generally continued on a downward course over the next three years and briefly shifted into surplus in early 1991 (thanks partly to transfer payments received by the US government in connection with the Gulf War). The continued relatively low value of the US dollar and the relative weakness of demand growth in the US economy after 1988 in comparison with growth in key trading partners clearly contributed to this improvement in the current account. Notably, the actual fiscal deficit worsened considerably between 1987 and 1991, and the structural fiscal deficit showed no meaningful improvement—pointing to the fallacy in the simplistic notion of the "twin deficits."

As the US economy recovered from the recession of 1990–91, the US current account again fell into significant deficit, but this deficit remained below 2 percent of US GDP through 1997—well below the peak of nearly 4 percent of GDP in 1987. Recovery in the growth of US domestic demand after the recession was certainly one factor contributing to the deterioration in the US current account. So too was the weak performance of other industrial countries. In particular, boosted by the bubble economy, Japan continued with over 4 percent real GDP growth through 1991; but growth then fell off sharply and generally remained very sluggish under the impact of the collapse of the bubble. In western Europe, growth received a strong boost in 1990–92 from the effects of German policies pursued in connection with reunification. As a consequence, the recession that hit the United States in 1990–91 did not start until two years later in continental Europe—by which time the tightening of monetary policy by the Bundesbank to combat rising inflation helped to induce a general economic slowdown in Europe.

Notably, the foreign exchange value of the US dollar remained weak through the first half of the 1990s, reaching all-time lows against the yen and the deutsche mark in early April 1995. This weakness of the dollar (which is partly attributable to the relative ease of US monetary policy in comparison with Bundesbank policy) contrasts dramatically with the spectacular strength of the dollar in the initial period of recovery from the recession of the early 1980s. And this difference in the behavior of the dollar in the recovery from the 1990–91 recession helps to explain why the deterioration in the US current account was smaller on this occasion.

In this connection, it is also relevant that US fiscal policy was pursuing a course of gradual consolidation during the 1990s, in comparison with the fiscal expansion of the early 1980s. Also, while the Federal Reserve tightened US monetary policy sharply in 1994 as a preemptive move against risks of rising inflation, this monetary tightening was nothing compared with the massive tightening that the Federal Reserve had to pursue to bring down rapid inflation at the start of the 1980s. Thus, the stances of US monetary and fiscal policies in the early 1990s were, for good reasons, very different from the policy mix of a decade earlier. Not surprisingly, this difference in macroeconomic policies was reflected in the more moderate behavior of the dollar and of the US current account in the first half of the 1990s in comparison with what happened a decade earlier.

From its trough in early 1995, the dollar generally appreciated throughout the remainder of the 1990s (for a cumulative rise of about 40 percent), reaching a broad and flat peak (measured in real effective terms) from roughly mid-2000 through early 2002. With the usual two-year lag, the proximate effects of this dollar appreciation are apparent in the substantial and continuing deterioration of the US current account from 1997 onward to 2004.

Factors Behind the Strong Dollar of the Late 1990s

As is always the case, a complex of interacting forces lies behind the strength of the dollar and the deterioration of the US current account since the mid-1990s. The effect of any particular factor on these developments is difficult to measure with precision. But the main forces that have been at work can be identified.

First and foremost, an unexpected but sustained acceleration of productivity growth in the United States boosted both the recorded growth of the US economy and assessments of prospects for its future growth; and these productivity developments were particular to the United States and not widespread across other countries. As usual, stronger output growth supported stronger growth of domestic demand in the United States, and this boosted US imports. The absence of similar developments abroad, however, meant that there was no comparable boost to demand for US exports—with the result that the US trade balance deteriorated.

The strengthening of US productivity growth, along with other developments, also affected the difference between output and demand and, correspondingly, the national savings/investment balance. Absent structural changes in fiscal policy, stronger growth and rising asset values (which tend to be induced by stronger growth prospects) raise government revenues and improve the fiscal balance—ultimately with the effect of pushing the US budget into significant surplus in 1999–2000. By itself, such an improvement in the government fiscal balance implies a corresponding improvement in the national savings/investment balance.

But stronger growth and stronger growth prospects also tend to boost investment spending. And rising incomes and rising asset values (associated with stronger growth prospects) tend to boost household consumption and diminish household saving (as measured in the national income accounts). The result is that the private savings/investment balance tends to deteriorate. Indeed, this happened on such a massive scale in the late 1990s that it swamped improvements in the government's fiscal balance and induced a substantial deterioration in the national savings/investment balance. This, in turn, was reflected in US demand to make use of foreign savings and, correspondingly, in a deterioration in the US current account.

Stronger growth prospects and higher expected returns to investment also made the United States more attractive to foreigners as a place to allocate their savings. This meant a stimulus to voluntary net capital flows to the United States that put upward pressure on the foreign exchange value of the dollar. The stronger dollar, in turn, provided a key part of the mechanism for a deterioration in the US trade balance, which was the means through which the US economy made use of increased net inflows of foreign savings.

Another general factor that has contributed to the deterioration of the US current account and the strengthening of the dollar since the mid-1990s was the economic difficulties suffered by other countries (beyond their failure to achieve accelerations in productivity growth similar to that in the United States). Among the industrial countries, Japan's economic performance was particularly weak, with outright declines in real and nominal GDP realized between 1997 and 2002. In the face of this persistent economic weakness, Japanese imports fell, and the Japanese current account thereby tended to improve. The Japanese yen also tended to be weak; and the Japanese authorities actively encouraged this weakness as one of the few available means to help stimulate recovery in the Japanese economy.

In the euro area, economic performance since the mid-1990s has been more satisfactory than in Japan. But the recovery from the recession of 1992–93 was not particularly robust, and recovery from the worldwide recession of 2001 has so far been quite disappointing. Moreover, it appears that pessimism about investment returns in Europe (possibly linked to inadequate progress on key structural reforms) may have played some role in the unexpected and substantial weakening of the foreign exchange value of the euro in 1999–2000—a development that has been reversed in the past two years.

For developing countries, a key development that has influenced the evolution of payments imbalances at the global level during the past decade is the series of catastrophic financial crises that afflicted many emerging-market countries. Faced with a sudden loss of external financing, country after country was forced into a large devaluation of its exchange rate, a sudden and massive improvement in its current account, and a sharp reduction in output and even larger reduction in domestic demand. Individually, these developments did not matter much at the global level. But taken together the crisis-induced improvements in the current accounts of emerging-market countries required a similar offsetting deterioration in the current account balance of (mainly) the industrial countries—and this was absorbed primarily by the United States. Similarly, taken together, the crisis-induced real depreciations of the currencies of a number of important emerging-market countries had a meaningful effect on the real effective foreign exchange value of the US dollar.

Recent Developments and Future Prospects

Looking to more recent developments, it is noteworthy that from its high average value between mid-2000 and early 2002, the US dollar has depreciated substantially against the currencies of most other industrial countries since early 2002: by more than 30 percent against the euro (and closely linked currencies) and by roughly 20 percent against the Canadian and Australian dollars and the British pound. Against the Japanese yen, the dollar has depreciated in nominal terms by more than 10 percent, but adjusted for differentials in inflation there has been no real depreciation of the dollar against the yen.

Normally, it should be expected that with about a two-year lag, the recent depreciation of the dollar against other industrial-country currencies would be reflected in at least a leveling off of the US current account deficit—if not a modest improvement. During the second half of 2003 and early 2004, such a leveling off appeared to be in progress. More recently, however, the US current account has deteriorated further and now appears to be headed for a deficit of about $600 billion (or about 5½ percent of GDP) for 2004. This renewed deterioration probably reflects two phenomena: (1) The growth of domestic demand in the United States since mid-2003 has been particularly rapid (exceeding 5 percent), while growth of domestic demand in the major industrial-country markets for US exports has remained tepid; and (2) there has been no downward correction of the dollar against the currencies of countries with rapidly expanding demand—most notably emerging Asia and especially China.

Another key development that has not yet exerted, but may eventually exert, an important influence on the US current account (and possibly on the dollar) is the massive shift in US fiscal policy since 2000. Measured by the actual fiscal position, the shift from budget surplus to budget deficit between 2000 and 2004 amounts to a massive 6 percent of US GDP. Measured by the structural fiscal position, the shift is somewhat smaller; I would put it at about 4 percent of GDP. Notably, with the US current account deficit up only moderately from the 4¼ percent of GDP registered in 2000, the massive shift in US fiscal policy appears, so far, to have had only a modest effect on the US current account.

This result suggests further caution in proclaiming a tight link between the fiscal and current account deficits—particularly the simplistic notion of the "twin deficits." It is also partly an illusion. As the US economy fell into recession in 2001, with a particularly sharp decline in business investment, the private savings/investment balance improved dramatically. This offset substantial deterioration in the government net savings and left the national savings/investment balance (and hence the current account) little changed. More recently, business investment has begun a vigorous recovery, but increased investment spending has been financed primarily by a spectacular recovery in corporate profits (which is reflected in business savings). Going forward, however, it remains to be seen whether the United States can sustain the combination of continued strong growth of private investment and large structural budget deficits without further deterioration in the current account.

Sustainable Scale of External Imbalances

For nearly a quarter of a century, the United States has persistently run significant current account deficits. The cumulative consequence of these deficits is that the United States has been transformed from the world's largest net creditor to the world's largest net debtor—with a total shift in the US net asset position relative to GDP of nearly 50 percentage points since 1980. So far, the United States does not appear to have suffered significant ill effects from these developments, despite widely expressed fears of a "hard landing" in the 1980s and other dire warnings of imminent catastrophe. Nevertheless, this massive shift in the US net asset position and the persistent deficits that underlie it naturally give rise to the question: Is there any limit?

Plausible Limits to US Net External Liabilities

In an analysis prepared for the Institute for International Economics five years ago, Catherine Mann (1999) answers this question—firmly and in the affirmative. Like many others, I share her basic conclusion and agree with much of the analysis on which it is based. There must be some upper limit on the amount of net claims that foreigners will wish to hold against the United States (and its resident businesses and households) on terms that will be attractive both to the foreigners who hold these assets and to the US residents who have the obligations to service them. There is, however, little indication yet that we may be approaching that upper limit, nor is there any way to estimate with precision and confidence where that limit might be.

To gain some perspective on this issue, we can easily calculate what would happen in the long run to the ratio of US net foreign liabilities to GDP under various assumptions about the persistent level of the current account deficit. Let N denote the nominal value of US net foreign liabilities, let C denote the nominal US current account deficit, let Y denote nominal GNP, and let g denote the percentage growth rate of nominal GNP. The relevant mathematical formula states that $n = N/Y$ stabilizes when n times g is equal to C/Y. When n times g is less than C/Y, n is rising; and when n times g is greater than C/Y, n is falling.[1]

For example, suppose that nominal GNP continues on its recent trend and registers a long-term growth rate of 5 percent per year (comprising about 3 percent real growth and about 2 percent annual rise in the GNP deflator). If the US current account deficit continued to run, on average, at 5 percent of GNP, then the mathematics say that the US net foreign liability ratio, $n = N/Y$, would continue to rise from its present level of about 25 percent of GNP reaching 50 percent of GNP within about eight years and would ultimately level out at 100 percent of GNP. If the current account deficit ran, on average, at 6 percent of GNP, then the net foreign liability ratio would rise faster, reaching 50 percent within about five years, and would ultimately rise to 120 percent of GNP.

To put these figures in context, it is noteworthy that only a few present-day industrial countries have ever recorded net foreign liability ratios above 50 percent of GNP, and no significant-sized country has ever reached a net foreign liability ratio of 100 percent of GNP. Moreover, there is reason to fear that if the United States proceeds on its present course in terms of its current account deficit, it would be headed for a net foreign liability ratio well in excess of 100 percent of GNP.

In particular, recent estimates by Mann suggest that, at present exchange rates, three important factors are likely to dictate continued significant expansion of the US current account deficit—expansion of about 1 percent of GNP each year for the foreseeable future: higher growth of the US economy than other industrial countries, a higher income elastic-

1. This formula assumes that the US net foreign liability position changes only as a consequence of net purchases and sales of assets and liabilities by US and foreign residents and not as a consequence of capital gains and losses on already existing asset and liability positions. Allowing for capital gains and losses makes the analysis more complex but does not fundamentally alter the basic conclusions.

ity of demand for imports in the United States than the foreign income elasticity of demand for US exports, and the effect on net factor payments to the rest of the world of rising US net foreign liabilities. These estimates for the current account deficit imply a very steeply rising path of US net foreign liabilities toward ratios well in excess of 100 percent of GDP within the next two decades.[2] This prospect—which is clearly plausible even if not the most likely—serves to heighten concerns that the cumulative consequences of a large and persistent US current account deficit will, within a few years, reach the point where such deficits are no longer consistent with the willingness of foreigners to continue to accumulate net claims against the United States or with the willingness of US residents to accumulate ever-increasing net liabilities to the rest of the world.

On the other hand, there are good reasons to believe that the United States is a particularly attractive place for foreigners to invest substantial fractions of their wealth, and there is little indication yet that foreigners are becoming concerned about the growing volume of these investments. Along with the downward correction of equity prices since early 2000, private flows of foreign capital to the United States have diminished from the torrid pace of the late 1990s. But the diminished pace of private capital inflows does not suggest serious worries about the longer-term security of massive (and still growing) foreign private investments in US-based assets. Increases in foreign official purchases of US assets, especially by Asian governments and central banks, have recently more than made up for the slowdown in private capital inflows. Hopefully, the pace of these foreign official acquisitions of US assets will abate somewhat, along with policy changes to allow significant appreciation of (especially Asian) currencies against the dollar. As discussed below, this needs to be a key element of the strategy to achieve a gradual and nondisruptive reduction of the US external deficit. However, foreign official entities will almost surely have a strong interest in avoiding sudden large changes in their acquisitions of foreign assets (or in their existing portfolios of such assets) that might have costly and disruptive effects on their own exchange rates, financial systems, and economies.

Moreover, the United States has an exceptional record of economic and political stability—unrivaled by any other large country over the past century. Property rights are respected and protected. There is a wide diversity of assets available to foreign investors, including vast quantities of equities, real estate, and other real assets, and privately issued bonds and mortgages, as well as highly secure government debt. Investors are generally well treated, and there is no record of any significant discrimination

2. Another senior fellow at the Institute, William R. Cline, has alternative projections for the US current account that rise less rapidly than indicated by Catherine Mann's estimates. According to Cline's projections, the US current account deficit will rise to just over 6 percent of GDP by 2010. Even with this projection, however, US net foreign liabilities would appear to be headed above 100 percent of GNP.

against foreign as compared with domestic investors. These attractions to foreigners of investment in the United States are probably an important part of the explanation of why, with a net debtor position of already about 25 percent of GDP, the United States stills seems able to secure inward foreign investment on terms (e.g., interest rates on bonds) that are below the returns that US residents earn on their investments abroad.

Nevertheless, as the US net debtor position rises higher, the United States will need to offer more attractive terms in order to continue to attract large additional inflows of foreign investment. This, in turn, should make US residents less enthusiastic about increasing their net foreign liabilities. When we reach the point where US residents are unwilling to offer the improved returns necessary to attract further increases in net foreign investment, the game will end. No one knows where this point is, although it appears to be well beyond the present ratio of US net foreign liabilities to GDP. My guess is that for the United States, a net liability ratio of 50 percent of GDP is still not a critical problem; but I would worry a great deal about ratios rising toward 100 percent of GDP.

This guess suggests that the United States could continue to run current account deficits in the range of 5 to 6 percent of GNP for another few years without serious risk of reaching the effective limit for US net external liabilities. However, going on at this rate for another decade, or for a shorter time if current account deficits expand as suggested by some forecasts, should raise serious concerns about the potential for a crisis that would bring an abrupt end to the continued rapid rise of US net external liabilities. How serious is the risk that such a crisis might do important damage to the United States and to the world economy?

In assessing this risk, it is prudent to be cautious—in both directions. The large US current account deficits that accumulated in the 1980s were brought down to manageable proportions with the aid of the massive depreciation of the dollar (from extraordinarily high levels) that occurred between early 1985 and late 1987. The US economy felt no immediate ill effects from this dollar correction, and the short-term negative impact on growth in the rest of the world was relatively mild. Thus, in contradiction of widely expressed fears of a "hard landing," the large and rapid correction of the US external imbalance in the late 1980s cannot reasonably be characterized as a damaging crisis. Moreover, it should be emphasized that the United States is not similar to a number of emerging-market countries that experienced very damaging foreign financing crises during the past decade. In particular, the United States is not a net debtor to the rest of the world in foreign currency, and it does not have a fragile financial system that would be devastated by sudden depreciation of the dollar.

In the direction of greater concern, it should be noted that (leaving aside the threat to economic growth from the recent escalation in world oil prices), the US economy could be approaching its potential level of output in the next year or two. At that point, a sharp depreciation of the dollar (brought on by unwillingness of foreigners to continue to accumulate US assets on such a massive scale) could add to inflationary pressures in the United States. This could induce the Federal Reserve to accelerate monetary tightening, with significant adverse consequences for the United States and the world economy. It can be argued that this is at least a part of the story of what happened in the early 1970s—a sharp downward correction of the dollar contributed first to a global acceleration of inflation, then to monetary tightening, and finally to global recession. It should also be noted that in 1979–80, when sharp depreciation of the dollar was associated with a more general collapse in confidence concerning US economic policy, the consequences for the United States and for the world economy were quite serious.

This experience embodies the vital lesson that the risk of a serious crisis arising from correction of the US external imbalance is critically dependent on the circumstances that underlie this imbalance and its prospective evolution. In particular, the growth of the US current account deficit during the 1990s appears to have been benign—even beneficial—in light of what was going on that helped to induce this deficit. Surely the acceleration of productivity growth in the United States was a good thing, even if it did not spread in equal measure to the rest of the world. The difficulties in other industrial countries and the catastrophic crises that afflicted emerging-market economies were not good things. But, given that these bad things happened, the widening of the US current account deficit and the appreciation of the US dollar were favorable developments from the perspective of the performance of the world economy. Moreover, the widening of the US external deficit in the 1990s was clearly not the result of an irresponsible and unsustainable US fiscal policy; the US government budget moved into significant surplus for the first time in three decades.

Looking forward, if the next decade looks like a repeat of the 1990s—with the US economy driven by rapid productivity growth and the US budget moving to surplus while much of the rest of the world economy is mired in difficulty—then continuing large US current account deficits, financed by large voluntary foreign capital inflows, would probably also be a good thing. (This would be more likely the case if the US external deficit were on a modestly declining or at least level path, rather than on a sharply escalating one.) In contrast, if US economic performance is modest while the rest of the world booms, and if large US current account deficits persist because of a failure to address US fiscal problems, then this will not be a good thing. Moreover, in this latter situation, foreign wealth holders would have good reason to become less enthusiastic investors in the US economy, with the result that the United States may experience significant difficulties in financing continued large external deficits.

Indeed, the greatest worry about a disruptive correction of the US external deficit probably derives from the potentially reinforcing character of the developments that might drive such a crisis—for example, weak economic performance that impairs efforts to reduce the budget deficit, upward pressures on US interest rates because of growing worries about the longer-term fiscal situation that feeds back to restrain growth, further upward pressure on US interest rates because of increased concerns of foreign investors about the returns on and value of US-based assets, depreciation of the dollar that heightens these concerns but brings little (initial) apparent reduction of the US external deficit because of long lags (J-curve effects), and other adverse developments (such as very high world energy prices). Policy efforts to encourage an orderly reduction of the US external deficit—and thereby minimize the risk of a disruptive correction—should be particularly attuned to avoiding such a combination of mutually reinforcing adverse developments through actions that will begin to put the US external liability position on a more clearly sustainable path as soon as possible.

General Need for Exchange Rate Adjustment

Assuming that the relevant economic scenario for the next five years or so is between the extremes just described—and without endeavoring to be unduly precise—what would be a reasonable objective for adjustment of the US current account balance, and what would need to happen to bring this about?

As a starting point, it should be emphasized that achieving a zero current account deficit is not necessary in order to stabilize the US ratio of net external liabilities to GDP at a reasonable and sustainable level. With an annual nominal GNP growth rate of about 5 percent, the analysis described before indicates that reducing the current account deficit by 3 percent of GNP to a level of about 2.5 percent of GNP would stabilize the net foreign liability ratio at 50 percent of GNP. As just discussed, a net foreign liability ratio of 50 percent would appear to be sustainable for the United States. Moreover, because of a variety of technical problems that probably lead to some overstatement of the measured US current account deficit relative to its true value, it is likely that a true reduction of that deficit by somewhat less than 3 percent of GDP would be sufficient to stabilize the net external liability ratio at 50 percent.

As is clear from the description of the factors involved in the rise of the US current account deficit in the 1990s (and the earlier episode of the 1980s), achieving a reduction of about 3 percent of GNP in the US current account deficit will depend on complex interactions among the key macroeconomic forces shaping the evolution of the world economy. There is no unique combination of these forces that produces that prescribed result for the US current account; and, as noted earlier, there is no good reason to believe that this particular result is necessarily desirable independent of the forces that might produce it.

Nevertheless, there is a reasonably stable proximate relationship between the real exchange rate of the dollar and (with a lag of about two years) the US current account deficit. This relationship suggests that a substantial depreciation of the dollar will be an essential part of virtually any process that leads to a substantial improvement in the US current account (Bergsten and Williamson 2004, Wren-Lewis and Driver 1998). A variety of estimates of the sensitivity of the US current account to the dollar exchange rate are available. I assume that a 10 percent real effective depreciation of the dollar will be associated with an improvement of about 1 percent in the ratio of the current account to GDP. This is a somewhat larger response than suggested by many estimates, but it is not out of the ballpark and is consistent with both the precision of our knowledge and the spirit of this exercise. Using this estimate, it follows that a 30 percent real depreciation of the dollar would be needed in connection with an improvement in the US current account of about 3 percent of GDP.

It should be emphasized that this estimate of a 30 percent required real effective depreciation of the dollar is no more than an educated guess—as is the assumption that a reduction of about 3 percent of GDP in the current account deficit is needed to stabilize the net foreign liability ratio at a sustainable level. If the current account deficit is more responsive to exchange rate changes than I have assumed, if an important part of the effect of recent depreciation of the dollar against most industrial-country currencies is yet to materialize, or if other factors (such as stronger growth of foreign demand for US exports or weaker world oil prices) help to reduce the current account deficit, then the extent of required dollar depreciation would be meaningfully less than 30 percent (but still significant). On the other hand, if the current account deficit is less responsive to exchange rate changes or if at present exchange rates that deficit is slated to grow significantly (as suggested by some plausible forecasts), then the magnitude of the needed dollar depreciation would likely be significantly larger than 30 percent.

To achieve a substantial downward adjustment in the real effective foreign exchange value of the dollar of about 30 percent, by how much should the dollar adjust against individual foreign currencies? There is really no clear way to answer this question. The simple baseline assumption is that all currencies would move against the US dollar in the same proportion—i.e., appreciation by a common 30 percent. However, there is some reason to believe that the responsiveness to exchange rate changes is larger for countries—notably Canada and Mexico—that have particularly close linkages to the US economy. This might suggest somewhat smaller exchange rate adjustments for these countries. Complexities arising from third-party effects might also be considered. However, because the appropriate evolution of various bilateral exchange rates will undoubtedly be influenced by a complex of economic factors that are not tightly related to a general improvement in the US current account balance, there is good reason not to try to be too precise about adjustments of individual exchange rates. Suffice it to say two things: On average, exchange rates of foreign currencies against the dollar will probably need to appreciate by about 30 percent; and virtually all significant US trading partners will need to participate significantly in this general appreciation against the US dollar.

Because of the general need for foreign currencies to appreciate against the dollar, it is tempting to suggest that this should be a subject for international policy cooperation. In my view, some international cooperation on this subject would be useful, especially in establishing better understanding of the likely need for substantial exchange rate adjustments as a critical element in the process of reducing external payments imbalances. As discussed below, international attention might also usefully be focused on the specific issue of exchange rate adjustments by Asian emerging-market economies (and Japan), where official policies have sought to resist aggressively strong market pressures in favor of appreciation against the US dollar.

However, considerable skepticism is warranted about any grand design to coordinate global exchange rate adjustments.[3] At this stage, no one can be highly confident about the general extent of dollar depreciation that will be needed to help reduce the US external deficit to a sustainable level or, even more so, about the magnitudes of the appreciations of individual foreign currencies that would be appropriate in this regard. Moreover, even if economic analysts could establish reasonably precise estimates for these magnitudes, it is exceedingly doubtful that policymakers could or would agree on concerted efforts to attempt to enforce the estimated exchange rate adjustments. For a considerable time, there has been broad agreement among policymakers in most industrial countries (including the United States and most of Europe) that market forces should be allowed wide latitude in setting exchange rates and that official efforts to influence exchange rates should be limited to relatively extreme situations where market forces appear to be pushing exchange rates well beyond the ranges consistent with underlying fundamentals. The consensus on this approach has been sufficiently strong that substantial appreciation of most industrial-country currencies against the US dollar has been accepted since early 2002, despite concerns about the negative short-term impact of these appreciations on economic growth. Presumably, if driven by market forces and provided it does not occur too rapidly, further significant dollar depreciation against most other industrial-country currencies would be similarly acceptable; and there might be some advantage in international policy cooperation that confirms this general approach. However,

3. I share these sentiments with a number of my colleagues at the Institute for International Economics, in particular Morris Goldstein and Edwin Truman. Others are more enthusiastic in their support for policy cooperation directed at influencing significantly the behavior of exchange rates, in particular C. Fred Bergsten and John Williamson.

efforts to agree that the official sector should promote specific exchange rate adjustments (for example, a 20 percent further appreciation of the euro against the dollar) would almost surely be rejected—and rightly so.

Three exceptions to this general rule should be noted. First, many important emerging-market economies, especially in Asia (and including Japan), do not allow market forces to determine exchange rates and have recently engaged in massive one-sided official intervention to resist currency appreciation against the US dollar. As discussed below (and in Morris Goldstein's chapter in this book), these policies need to be changed substantially to accord with the general principle that even pegged or heavily managed exchange rates need to adjust to reflect economic fundamentals. Second, for most industrial countries that generally allow market forces wide latitude to determine exchange rates, it should be recognized that if the dollar were to appreciate significantly from the present level and/or remain so strong that there was a clear international consensus that the dollar needed to come down (as there was at the time of the Plaza Agreement in September 1985), then it would be appropriate for the official sector to send a strong message to private markets about the need for and desirable direction of exchange rate adjustments. It does not make sense, however, to attempt to build such an international consensus when, like now, it clearly does not exist. Third, if the dollar fell precipitously and to an extent that appeared to be a significant threat to economic performance and/or financial market stability, then the official sector should act forcefully, in a clearly coordinated manner, to resist unduly rapid dollar depreciation. Channels of communication and the mechanisms of international cooperation that would support such an emergency operation should be kept in working order. However, more specific contingency planning about what to do in a possible crisis—the nature and circumstances of which are difficult to foresee—impress me as unlikely to be fruitful.

Finally, on the general issue of exchange rate adjustments necessary to contribute to a reduction of the US external deficit to sustainable levels, it is essential to recognize the fallacy that a substantially weaker dollar is generally good for the US economy and bad for the rest of the world. This may be true for the short run. Specifically, when there is significant excess capacity in the US economy, a weaker dollar will usually help to accelerate the return of output to potential by adding to the growth of demand for US output (or, at least, by reducing the demand drag from continuing deterioration in US net exports). Similarly, in the short run, when there is excess capacity in the rest of the world, currency appreciation tends to slow the return to potential output by weakening net exports.

In the longer-term, however, the US economy does not consistently operate below potential; indeed, during the past 30 years, high inflation, which is symptomatic of lack of excess capacity, has been more of a policy problem for the US economy than sustained high levels of unemployment. In the long run, on average, a weaker dollar will not generally imply higher levels of output and employment in the United States. Instead, the long-run effect of a weaker dollar will be felt in the adverse real income effects of a lower relative price of US exports and a higher relative price of US imports. For a given path of potential and actual real output, residents of the United States will have to contract their real consumption and investment in order to supply increased real exports to the rest of the world in exchange for (a possibly reduced quantity of) more expensive imports. The rest of the world stands on the other side of these developments—enjoys gains in real consumption and investment from the increased relative value of their exports when exchanged for imports of goods and services from the United States. Thus, it is fundamentally wrong for the United States to believe that a weaker dollar directly improves its long-run economic welfare. The correct view is that a weaker dollar is needed in the long run—despite its adverse effects on US real consumption and investment—because the United States cannot continue to run very large current account deficits that will ultimately raise its net foreign liabilities to unsustainable levels.

Industrial-Country Policies to Contribute to Orderly Reduction of External Imbalances

In the usual targets and instruments approach to the analysis of economic policy, the standard procedure is first to identify the desirable objectives of policy and then to enumerate the policy adjustments that should be made to meet these objectives. In examining the role that economic policies should play in addressing present global concerns about payments imbalances, however, a simple version of this targets and instruments approach is not very useful. As the preceding discussion has made clear, the US external deficit and the corresponding external surplus of the rest of the world are not developments that can be viewed in isolation from broad macroeconomic forces shaping the course of the world economy. Nor are there policies (with the exception of some narrow elements of exchange rate policy) that can be directed specifically at the objective of reducing external imbalances. Rather, the objective of securing an orderly reduction in external imbalances needs to be a consideration—but generally not the dominant consideration—in the design and implementation of key economic policies whose principal objectives relate to other purposes.

Fiscal Consolidation in the United States

In particular, for the United States, a gradual and cumulatively substantial tightening of fiscal policy is clearly necessary to achieve longer-term fiscal sustainability, especially in view of the fiscal strains arising from an aging population. In particular, recent analysis by the Congressional Budget Office suggests that under plausible assumptions about the evolution of government policies (including preservation of most of the Bush tax cuts, scaling back of the alternative minimum tax, substantial winding down of the present level of expenditures related to Iraq and Afghanistan, and growth of other federal discretionary spending in line with the growth of nominal GDP), the federal fiscal deficit in 2010 would run in the range of $450 billion to $500 billion. In nominal terms, this would be up modestly from the $412 billion deficit recorded in fiscal 2004; as a share of GDP it would be down by about one-half percent, from 3.6 to 3.1 percent. With federal deficits running roughly 3½ percent of GDP, the public debt to GDP ratio would rise moderately from 37.5 to about 44 percent by 2010.

Beyond 2010, the federal deficit and debt situation begin to look much more bleak.[4] With the retirement of the baby boom generation and the general escalation of health care costs, federal outlays on Social Security and Medicare benefits will rise from 6 percent of GDP in 2004 and nearly 8 percent of GDP in 2010 to something in the range of at least 15 percent to more than 25 percent of GDP by 2050. The extremely wide range of uncertainty about the costs of these key entitlement programs in the long term reflects primarily great uncertainty about the expense of government-supported health care, under the impact of continually improving medical practice, as an increasingly large share of the population is retired and lives longer. Clearly, important decisions will need to be made about how to balance the advancing benefits and rising costs of medical care for the elderly and about how to share those costs. These decisions will need to be made over time, as the relevant options become clearer, by the people (both beneficiaries and taxpayers) whom they will primarily affect. What is clear at present is that this is not a time when the US government should normally be running substantial fiscal deficits outside of the operation of the Social Security and Medicare entitlement programs (which still show "off-budget" cash surpluses). In particular, while continuing federal deficits of around 3½ percent of GDP and a rise in the ratio of visible public debt to GDP from 37.5 percent today to about 44 percent by 2010 do not, by themselves, seem very threatening, they are not a sound or sensible fiscal policy in light of the enormous longer-term challenges facing the federal budget.

Moreover, reduction of the federal deficit to below 1 percent of GDP by 2010—on a cyclically adjusted or "structural" basis—is an economically feasible as well as a desirable goal. There is still some slack in the US econ-

4. Peter G. Peterson provides a passionate exposition of the grave long-term dangers facing the US government budget is his new book, *Running on Empty: How the Democratic and Republican Parties Are Bankrupting Our Future and What Americans Can Do About It* (New York: Farrar, Straus and Giroux, 2004).

omy that probably added at least one-half percent of GDP to the federal deficit in fiscal 2004. As the US economy recovers more fully, this cyclical component of the federal deficit should disappear. Beyond this, structural fiscal consolidation of one-half of 1 percent of GDP each year, on average, for the next six years would cut the federal deficit cumulatively by another 3 percent of GDP, with the implication that overall fiscal balance would be achieved in fiscal 2010 assuming that the US economy was operating at potential. And structural fiscal consolidation at that pace of one-half of 1 percent of GDP per year should not unduly burden the US economy in achieving its potential output. Between 1992 and 2000, the actual federal deficit was transformed from a deficit of 4.7 percent of GDP to a surplus of 2.4 percent, with the structural fiscal improvement amounting to about 5 percent of GDP. The US economy boomed in this period, notwithstanding both the substantial fiscal consolidation and the drag from a significant deterioration in US net exports.

In sum, even without any reference to the objective of reducing the US external deficit, a strong case can be made that cumulatively significant fiscal consolidation is desirable for the United States over the next few years as an essential contribution to placing US fiscal policy on a sound and sustainable path for the longer term. The need to reduce a large external deficit means that fiscal consolidation (which is desirable for more basic reasons) can also play a useful role in constraining the growth of domestic demand relative to domestic output. Part of the reduction of growth of domestic demand falls directly on imports and thereby tends directly to improve the trade and current account balances. A larger part of the reduction of domestic demand growth falls on US products and services, but the impact of this is offset by the shift of foreign demand toward US output occasioned by downward correction of the dollar and other forces. The entire reduction in growth of domestic demand relative to output is a reduction in national spending relative to national income and, therefore, an improvement in the US net savings/investment balance—an essential counterpart to an improvement in the US current account balance. The improvement in the US national savings/investment balance associated with fiscal consolidation also corresponds to a reduction in the foreign capital inflow necessary to finance this imbalance. This smaller foreign capital inflow, in turn, is associated with diminished enthusiasm of foreign investors to acquire US-based assets and, accordingly, with downward adjustment in the foreign exchange value of the US dollar.

This prescription that US fiscal consolidation should make an important contribution to the orderly reduction of external imbalances does not rely on the simplistic notion that the US fiscal deficit and the US current account deficit are closely related "twins" and that reduction in the fiscal deficit will automatically result in an essentially simultaneous, one-for-one reduction in the current account deficit. As in the 1990s, it is possible that despite determined fiscal consolidation (or perhaps partly because of it), investment in the US economy may be particularly buoyant, contributing to continued strong growth of domestic demand. At the same time, foreign wealth holders might remain especially enthusiastic about shifting capital into the United States, thus helping to keep the dollar unduly strong. The result could then be little or no improvement in the US current account, despite significant US fiscal consolidation. And this could go on for some time until foreign wealth owners ultimately become persuaded that further rapid accumulation of US-based assets is no longer desirable—or even safe.

With this possibility in mind, it is relevant to emphasize that US fiscal consolidation is not a surefire cure-all for the US external deficit. Nevertheless, fiscal consolidation is clearly needed for its own sake, and it should normally be expected to aid in the reduction of the US external deficit over the medium to longer term.

For US monetary policy, the fundamental objectives are to keep inflation low while supporting sustainable growth of output and employment. Fiscal consolidation implies that monetary policy should be able to achieve these fundamental objectives by pursuing a course for policy interest rates that is lower than it would be in the absence of such fiscal action. Other things being equal, an easier course for monetary policy should normally mean a lower path for the foreign exchange value of the US dollar. A cheaper dollar, in turn, should help to bring both an improvement in the US external balance and a positive (or less negative) contribution from net exports to output and employment growth in the United States. The latter effect will help to offset the short-run negative impact of fiscal consolidation on output and employment.

Enhancing Growth in Japan and Europe

In the rest of the world, the main macroeconomic adjustments necessary to achieve a smaller external surplus are essentially the reverse of the adjustments needed in the United States—i.e., an increase in domestic demand growth relative to output growth (and a corresponding deterioration in the savings/investment balance and a reduction in net capital outflows) and real currency appreciation to help shift demand away from domestic output to US output. Unfortunately, the macroeconomic situation in much of the rest of the world is not the reverse of that in the United States; and the policies that would contribute to reducing the rest of the world's external surplus, while maintaining sustainable noninflationary growth, are somewhat difficult to prescribe.

In particular, in Japan and most of western Europe, margins of slack are generally wider than in the United States, while the medium- and longer-term need for fiscal consolidation is generally no less pressing. This implies that fiscal expansion cannot generally be prescribed in these countries as a means for stimulating domestic demand growth in order to offset the loss of effective demand inevitably associated with declining external surpluses. As a consequence, monetary policy faces an increased responsibility for sustaining adequate growth of domestic demand—especially if fiscal policies are oriented toward consolidation rather than mere neutrality.

After more than a decade of disappointing growth and five years of outright deflation, facing a large fiscal deficit and a massive buildup of government debt, and with policy interest rates effectively at zero, Japan confronts particularly difficult challenges in designing policies to achieve sustainable growth while contributing appropriately to the reduction of global payments imbalances. Indeed, this particularly difficult situation of Japan in recent years provides a relevant rationale for their highly aggressive policy of resisting rapid appreciation of the yen through massive foreign exchange market intervention. From a global as well as a purely Japanese perspective, the key priority has been to get the Japanese economy back onto a sustainable growth path, and to rebuild the business and consumer confidence that is essential to that result. Resistance to rapid yen appreciation that could have undermined the present Japanese recovery has contributed to the success so far achieved—even if it has retarded exchange rate adjustments that are needed in the longer term to contribute to the reduction of global payments imbalances.

However, now that the Japanese economy appears to have regained substantial forward momentum, massive intervention to resist further orderly appreciation of the yen is not a desirable or defensible policy. The decision of the Japanese authorities to refrain from massive intervention since March of 2004 appears to recognize this point; and this decision has appropriately been given international endorsement. Nevertheless, it is relevant to recognize that sudden and substantial appreciation of the yen (say below 95 to 100 yen to the US dollar) could be destabilizing, and official resistance to such a development could be warranted in the near term. Over the next five years or so, it is reasonable to expect that the Japanese yen (along with the currencies of most other Asian economies) should appreciate substantially against the US dollar. Persistent and determined resistance to such appreciation, in the context of a generally improving Japanese economy, would not be appropriate.

With significant margins of slack remaining in the Japanese economy (despite some official estimates to the contrary) and with no signs of a resurgence of inflation, Japanese monetary policy should continue to pursue a course of unusual ease for a considerable period. This, in turn, will tend to imply a somewhat weaker course for the foreign exchange value of the yen than would likely prevail with a more robust Japanese economy. If driven by the market, such yen weakness—unlike weakness artificially induced by official intervention—is appropriate in light of Japan's economic situation and should not be subject to international criticism. In the longer term, as the Japanese economy recovers its traditional strength, substantial further real appreciation of the yen against the US dollar should reasonably be expected as part of the process of gradually reducing global payments imbalances. This prospective real appreciation of the yen against the dollar, however, does not apply equally to the real effective foreign exchange value of the yen against all of Japan's trading partners.

For industrial countries other than Japan, exchange rate adjustments since the peak of the US dollar in 2000–02 are already quite substantial. In general, these adjustments should be enough to achieve some part (although not the entire amount) of what is needed to restore a sustainable pattern of international payments. In three key US trading partners—Canada, the United Kingdom, and Australia—demand growth in recent years has also been sufficient to achieve reasonable output growth. For these countries, further fiscal expansion cannot generally be recommended as a responsible means to augment demand growth (especially not in the United Kingdom). But longer-term fiscal prospects appear to be sound without the need for substantial consolidation—implying that fiscal contraction will not add to problems of sustaining output growth in the face of some deterioration of net exports. In addition, monetary policies in Australia, Canada, and the United Kingdom have all been tightened somewhat since the end of the global recession of 2001, and this leaves significant room for monetary easing, should that seem needed to ward off excessive weakness in output growth.

In the euro area, economic performance since the mid-1990s has been better than in Japan but somewhat worse (especially in terms of domestic demand growth) than in Australia, Canada, and the United Kingdom (as well as the United States). Fiscal deficits and government debt burdens are generally not as large in Japan but are more of a concern than in Australia, Canada, and the United Kingdom. Monetary easing by the European Central Bank (ECB) to combat recent sluggishness has cut policy interest rates down to only 2 percent, compared with zero in Japan (and 1 percent in the United States). But, for good reason, there has not yet been any move by the ECB to begin the cycle of monetary tightening already under way in Australia, Canada, and the United Kingdom (and more recently in the United States). Thus, it is fair to say that economic policy in the euro area retains greater room for maneuver to address issues arising from the correction of external imbalances than in Japan, but less so than in Australia, Canada, and the United Kingdom. Moreover, it is relevant that, unlike Japan, authorities in the euro area have not intervened at all to resist the substantial appreciation of the euro against the US dollar that has occurred since early 2002. Indeed, significant euro appreciation (at least to parity with the dollar) has been welcome as a reversal of the earlier excessive weakness of the euro and as a factor tending to reduce inflationary pressures in the euro area.

Looking forward, however, economic policy in the euro area faces critical challenges that will not be made easier to meet by the need to contribute to the reduction in global payments imbalances. Substantial fiscal deficits and government debt burdens and the fiscal demands of aging populations do not allow much room for expansionary fiscal policies to prop up domestic demand growth in order to offset declining net exports. Indeed, unlike the United States, desirable medium-term adjustments of fiscal policies to meet their primary objectives are not the adjustments that would likely have the side benefit of contributing to the orderly reduction of international payments imbalances.

Moreover, monetary policy for the euro area does not provide a reliable escape from of this conundrum (even if the ECB were willing to recognize this possibility). Facing prospective weakness in domestic demand growth (especially if fiscal consolidation is pursued), as well as weakness in output growth from deterioration of net exports, monetary policy would normally be expected to follow a somewhat easier course in order to properly serve its basic objectives. But an easier course for monetary policy should normally be expected to work against the exchange rate adjustments (i.e., further appreciation of the euro against the US dollar) that are needed to facilitate the reduction of external imbalances.

From the perspective of reducing external payments imbalances, it may be regarded as fortunate that euro area fiscal authorities show little inclination toward significant fiscal consolidation and that the ECB is fixated on the objective of price stability and is generally unwilling to acknowledge virtually any responsibility for output growth. However, like the attitudes of some key US policymakers who effectively deny the need for specific expenditure and revenue measures to bring about actual fiscal consolidation, the cherished illusions of too many European policymakers threaten to generate outcomes that are below the best that their economies are capable of achieving.

With respect to the issue of reducing global payments imbalances, these illusions bite primarily in the absence of a reasonable strategy to achieve sustainable demand and output growth. Structural reform is rightly seen as the most important element in the strategy to strengthen growth over the longer term; and progress is being made in this area even if it is less rapid than desirable.[5] But structural reform is clearly not the whole answer to the issue of maintaining adequate and appropriate demand growth. Exhortations about the need for more rapid structural re-

5. An extensive and insightful discussion of these issues is provided in Baily and Kirkegaard (2004). As they emphasize, after many years of controversy, a broad consensus has been reached among analysts and most policy leaders that deep structural reforms are needed to enhance longer-term growth in most of western Europe and to help to address the challenges posed by aging populations. Significant progress in some key areas of structural reform has been made in a number of these countries; but much remains to be done.

form should not be the excuse for the fiscal and monetary authorities to ignore their responsibilities in demand management.

Clearly, western Europe and Japan have the most to gain themselves from policies that will promote stronger economic growth, both in the near term and in the longer run. But success in this endeavor also has important likely benefits for the rest of the world. Stronger growth in other industrial countries means stronger growth of their demand for exports from the United States and from developing countries. This, in turn, should mean less need for dollar depreciation to help bring improvement to the US current account (and accordingly smaller real terms of trade losses for US residents), as well as somewhat less adjustment by developing countries as the counterpart of improvement in the US current account.

The main impetus for policies to promote more rapid growth in other industrial countries must inevitably come from within these societies. It is they that must face up to the sometimes difficult trade-offs and special interest pressures that often oppose growth-promoting reforms—just as the United States must face up to the critical choices in tax and expenditure policies needed to achieve fiscal consolidation. However, experience suggests that cogently argued external advice can play a positive role in supporting policies that have global benefits while also serving the fundamental national interests of the countries that are advised to adopt them.

More specifically, going back to the Carter and Reagan administrations, US officials have pressed both Europe and Japan to adopt more growth-oriented policies. Arguably, the record regarding demand management policies is somewhat mixed. Some praise while others condemn the effort from the Bonn Summit of 1978 to get western Europe (especially Germany) and Japan to pursue more expansionary demand policies in exchange for a rationalization of US energy policy. During the second Reagan administration, initial US advice favoring demand stimulus to offset the short-term contractionary impetus from dollar depreciation on western Europe and Japan was probably correctly timed. But persistent advice to Japan to maintain easy fiscal and monetary policies extending into the administration of President George H. W. Bush probably contributed to the rise of the "bubble economy" in Japan and to the difficulties stemming from its subsequent collapse.

On international advice concerning structural reform policies, the record is clearly not one of immense and immediate success. Over time, however, a consensus has built up in western Europe and, more recently, in Japan about the important benefits to be derived from key structural reforms. International advice has played a constructive role in helping to build this consensus. In my view, this is primarily because the advice, by and large, has been substantively correct and because that advice has been reinforced by careful and steady work at key international institutions, including the OECD and the IMF. Western Europe really did have (and still has) important structural impediments to more rapid economic growth, especially in its labor-market and related policies. Following the collapse of the bubble, the Japanese financial system and the financial situation of many Japanese businesses really was a horrendous mess—a mess that Japanese officials and political leaders appeared more intent on ignoring than on addressing. Careful analysis and persistent advice on these problems from (relatively) unbiased international institutions has helped to make an increasingly persuasive case that these problems need to be seriously and vigorously addressed—not because of American pressure, but because this is very much in the national interests of the countries themselves.

Key Issues for Developing Countries in the Orderly Reduction of International Imbalances

For developing countries, the nature and timing of the macroeconomic and policy adjustments necessary to contribute to an orderly and successful reduction of external imbalances differs considerably across regions and specific countries. Indeed, the contrast between most of emerging Asia and much of Latin America is particularly striking. Aside from the brief setbacks associated with the global recession of 2001 and the SARS scare of the spring of 2003, economic growth in virtually all of emerging Asia has been very strong since recovery from the Asian crisis began in late 1998. In contrast, several key Latin American countries have experienced considerable economic weakness in recent years. In particular, Argentina and Venezuela have had catastrophic recessions, Brazil has experienced significant difficulty in achieving robust growth following the moderate recession of 2003, and even Mexico has not avoided recent economic sluggishness despite robust recovery in the United States.

Another important difference between Asia and Latin America is that Asian emerging-market economies have recently generated large current account surpluses and, in many cases, substantial capital inflows that have put upward pressure on exchange rates and led to massive accumulation of official foreign exchange reserves. In contrast, in Latin America, recent current account surpluses, where they have occurred, have mainly been the consequence of large market-induced exchange rate depreciations and (in some cases) sharp declines in domestic demand arising from economic and financial crises.

Clearly, in considering the roles that developing countries should play in the general reduction of international imbalances, it is important to keep in mind the differing circumstances of different countries. Nevertheless, taking account of these differences, three general points should be made about the necessary role of developing countries.

Need for Aggregate Current Account Adjustment

First, it is important to recognize that nearly 40 percent of US trade now takes place with developing countries and that a significant fraction of the deterioration of the US external payments position since the mid-1990s corresponds with the improvement in the aggregate current account position of developing counties. From these facts, it is apparent that substantial reduction of the US external deficit must correspond with a significant movement in the other direction of the external balance of developing countries as a group, as well as with a significant movement toward deficit for the aggregate of all (other) industrial countries.

This does not mean that on a bilateral, country-by-country basis the US trade balance should be expected to improve against all individual developing countries. Indeed, it would be a serious error of economic logic and of economic policy to attempt to target specific reductions in bilateral imbalances as the means for allocating responsibility for the counterpart of an improvement is the US external balance. Leaving aside the nettlesome issue of the changes in the global current account discrepancy, the aggregate improvement in the US external balance must correspond to the aggregate deterioration in the external balance of the aggregate of all other countries. But the allocation of this aggregate deterioration among individual countries depends on complex and shifting economic forces and cannot be prescribed on an a priori basis.

Nevertheless, developing countries as a group are far too large a fraction of "the rest of the world" for anyone to reasonably believe that a substantial reduction in the US external deficit could occur without a significant movement in the other direction in the aggregate external payments position of developing countries. For the mooted improvement in the US external balance of about 3 percent of US GDP, no one can confidently say whether the counterpart for developing countries would be more or less than about one-third. But the need for developing countries as a group to participate significantly as the counterpart of a substantial improvement in the US external balance is undeniable.

Exchange Rate Policies of Developing Countries

Second, as with (other) industrial countries, the decline in the net external payments balance of developing countries that is the necessary counterpart of the improvement in the US external balance requires—as one essential ingredient—real depreciation of the US dollar against the currencies of developing countries. For developing countries, however, this required exchange rate adjustment poses policy difficulties that do not generally arise in industrial countries. With the notable exception of Japan, industrial countries generally allow the exchange rates of their currencies to fluctuate freely against the US dollar in response to market forces—without resorting to massive official intervention or other policies to influence the exchange rate against the dollar. Over the past two years, these floating exchange rate policies have allowed substantial real appreciations of most industrial-country currencies against the US dollar—real appreciations that will help to achieve a more sustainable pattern of international payments positions.

In contrast, for most developing countries, there has been very little real currency appreciation against the US dollar during the past two years. Indeed, on a real effective basis (i.e., for exchange rates against the weighted average of trading partners), many developing countries have experienced at least modest real depreciations. This is not generally the result of market forces operating on market-determined exchange rate (although it may be so in some cases, such as Mexico). Instead, it is primarily the result of exchange rate policies of many developing countries that either peg the exchange rate against the US dollar (de jure or de facto) or aggressively limit fluctuations in the exchange rate against the US dollar.

One important manifestation of these exchange rate policies is the massive buildup during the past three years of official foreign exchange reserves by several key Asian emerging-market economies (and the similar buildup of official reserves by Japan). In this regard, China is the country whose exchange rate policy and reserve accumulation are most often cited as issues of concern; and this book appropriately has a chapter (by Nicholas Lardy) devoted to these specific concerns. But, important as the Chinese case is, the issues about exchange rate policies and reserve accumulation apply much more broadly than just to China. Indeed, combined official reserve accumulation since 2001 by the main Asian surplus economies other than China has been more than double the reserve accumulation of China, and the combined current account surpluses of these countries are much larger than China's surplus both in absolute terms (measured in US dollars) and relative to GDP (table 6.1).

Because exchange rates are—by definition—exchange values between different national currencies, no country can logically claim exclusive property rights in "its" exchange rate. And, especially because present concerns about external imbalances are fundamentally global concerns, exchange rate adjustments necessary to reduce these imbalances need to be assessed and addressed from a multilateral and global perspective.

The importance of a multilateral and global perspective on exchange rate issues is well illustrated by the case of China. As convincingly advocated by Goldstein and Lardy (see Lardy's chapter in this book), an appreciation of the Chinese renminbi by 15 to 25 percent against the US dollar, together with repegging to a basket of the dollar, the euro, and the yen and allowance for a wider band of market-determined exchange rate fluc-

Table 6.1 Key comparative data on external payments: Japan, China, and other emerging Asia

Country/region	GDP, 2003 (billions of dollars)	Current account balance, 2003 (billions of dollars)	Current account as percent of GDP, 2003	International reserves at mid-2004 (billions of dollars)	Change in reserves since 2001 (billions of dollars)	Change in real exchange rate versus dollar from average, 2000–01 (percent)
Japan	4,750	150	3.2	808	420	–7
China	1,400	45	3.2	480	260	–5
Other emerging Asia	1,870	120	6.4	860	350	–6

Notes: Other emerging Asia (with estimated 2003 GDP in round figures) consists of Hong Kong ($160 billion), India ($500 billion), Indonesia ($180 billion), Malaysia ($100 billion), Singapore ($90 billion), South Korea ($500 billion), Taiwan ($300 billion), and Thailand ($140 billion). Changes in real exchange rates are calculated by adjusting nominal exchange rate changes for changes in consumer prices indices (CPIs) (minus the change in the US CPI). GDP weights are used to aggregate real exchange rate changes for other emerging Asia.

tuation, is a reasonable response to the clear need for a significant modification of Chinese exchange rate policy. However, the Goldstein-Lardy proposal makes much more sense if (as they intend), it is part of a broader modification of exchange rate policies of most Asian emerging-market economies (and Japan). Appreciation of the renminbi against the US dollar means much less in terms of effective appreciation against all Chinese trading partners if it is accompanied by significant appreciations of other Asian emerging-market currencies (and the Japanese yen). Similarly, for other Asian emerging-market economies, upward adjustments in the foreign exchange values of their currencies will appear much more digestible if they are not pursued in isolation but rather as a part of a general upward adjustment in the value of Asian currencies against the dollar. And this general upward adjustment in the values of Asian currencies against the US dollar—rather than isolated exchange rate adjustments by individual Asian economies—is really what is needed as an essential contribution to the gradual process of reducing global payments imbalances.

Moreover, much experience indicates that, even when the case for a policy change is quite apparent, it is often difficult to persuade national authorities to alter their exchange rate policies—especially when adjustment involves changing a well-established exchange rate peg in either a downward or an upward direction. This generally difficult task, however, cannot be made easier by suggesting that national authorities should act in isolation, when the true need is for coordinated adjustments by several countries that reduce the risks for individual countries and that properly share the responsibility for necessary exchange rate policy adjustments with the international financial community.

Dealing with Potential Financial Crises

Third, while a number of developing countries (especially those with large current account surpluses and favorable access to global capital markets) have considerable policy flexibility to meet the challenge of sustaining adequate demand growth in the face of deteriorating external payments positions, others are not so fortunate. This is particularly so for developing countries that are potentially vulnerable to external financing crises, such as those that afflicted many emerging-market economies during the 1990s.

At present, with global economic recovery under way, with policy interest rates in industrial countries still quite low, and with global financial markets still taking a relatively benign view of the risks in emerging markets, these vulnerabilities appear less worrying than they did a few years ago. Nevertheless, some countries (notably those with relatively high government and external debt ratios and histories of financial turbulence) are viewed with some concern. And, as suggested by the increase in spreads for several emerging-market borrowers since early 2004, these concerns appear to be on the rise.

Over the next couple of years, as interest rates in industrial countries probably rise and as the global expansion probably loses some of its recent robustness, it is not unlikely that one or more emerging-market country will have to face a potential external financing crisis. As occurred in the 1990s (and in earlier episodes of emerging-market financial crises), it is also not unlikely that a financial crisis afflicting one emerging-market economy will spread through a variety of mechanisms to affect others. In contrast with the 1990s, however, a rapidly expanding US current account deficit (supported by particularly rapid growth of domestic demand in the United States) is unlikely to provide the necessary counterpart for emerging-market countries seeking rapid improvements in their current account positions under the pressure of external financing crises.

This concern also applies in reverse. Emerging-market financial crises that generate the need for rapid improvements in the external payments positions of these countries will tend to interfere with the orderly reduction of the US external payments deficit. And the effects of this problem will not be limited to emerging-market countries and the United States. If expansion of the US external deficit is to be less of a counterpart to crisis-induced improvements in the external payments positions of emerging-market countries, then adjustments in the external positions of other industrial countries will need to shoulder more of the load—and this will be in addition to, not as a substitute for, adjustments that are needed as the counterpart of improvements in the US external position.

Thus, it is fair to say that all countries have a self-interest in avoiding or ameliorating possible future emerging-market financial crises—as one element in the broader strategy to secure orderly reductions in international payments imbalances. Of course, the primary responsibility for reducing vulnerabilities to a crisis inevitably rests with an emerging-market country itself—and there is much that countries can do in this regard. But the international community also has an important role to play in reducing the risk of crises and in ameliorating the consequences when crises occur (see the chapter by Morris Goldstein).

Conclusion: Virtues of Some International Policy Cooperation

The preceding discussion has emphasized that large persistent US external payments deficits—on the order of 5 percent or more of US GDP—are not sustainable in the longer term and that important macroeconomic adjustments will be needed, in the United States and in the rest of the world, in order to bring these external imbalances down to sustainable levels. Achieving these necessary adjustments, while also securing maximum sustainable economic growth and minimizing the risk of a disruptive foreign exchange or financial crisis, poses important challenges for the conduct of economic policies around the world. The interconnectedness of these policy challenges implies that the strategies for meeting them ought to be a key subject for international economic policy cooperation.

Indeed, the importance of such cooperation has been emphasized especially with regard to exchange rate adjustments by Asian emerging-market economies (and Japan) and reform of the international financial system to deal more effectively with the potential problem of emerging-market financial crises. International cooperation among the industrial countries on exchange rate issues is also important, and it should confirm that for most industrial countries with generally market-determined exchange rates, official policies should not aggressively and persistently resist further market-driven depreciation of the US dollar. International cooperation should also insist that for countries that more actively manage their exchange rates (in particular, Japan and most Asian emerging-market economies), a similar principle should apply. Efforts beyond this to establish particular levels or ranges for exchange rates to be actively pursued by the official sector strike me as unwise, unwarranted, and unlikely to be adopted. Rather, attention on international cooperation regarding industrial-country exchange rates should be limited to two contingencies: (1) recognizing the possibility that, if the dollar were to appreciate significantly and/or remain excessively strong, there might be at some future time broad international consensus to encourage dollar depreciation; and (2) recognizing that there is some risk of a crisis involving large and excessively rapid depreciation of the dollar and being prepared to deal forcefully with such a crisis when and if it threatens.

In other areas of economic policy, there is surely no harm in the rest of the world's pressing the United States on the importance of moderate-paced and cumulatively substantial fiscal consolidation. Similarly, there is no harm in the United States' pressing other countries to maintain adequate growth of domestic demand and to vigorously pursue structural reforms that will strengthen growth in the longer term. There should be no illusion that in both cases, domestic considerations and political pressures will largely determine the outcomes. But, as in the past, cogent external advice and encouragement can play a useful role when the direction of policies is right from both national and global perspectives.

Finally, on issues of international economic policy cooperation at the global level, the participation and leadership of the United States are essential; and the effectiveness of the United States in this area of international cooperation spills over to affect other important areas. This means that key US officials need to devote attention to improving international economic policy cooperation both as regards key substantive issues and with respect to the mechanisms and modalities of cooperation. Other chapters in this volume, particularly those by Jan Boyer and Edwin Truman, William Cline and John Williamson, and Morris Goldstein, provide further food for thought on these subjects.

References

Baily, Martin Neil, and Jacob Funk Kirkegaard. 2004. *Transforming the European Economy.* Washington: Institute for International Economics.

Bergsten, Fred C., and John Williamson. 2004. Designing a Dollar Policy. In *Dollar Adjustment: How Far? Against What?* ed., C. Fred Bergsten and John Williamson. Washington: Institute for International Economics.

Mann, Catherine L. 1999. *Is the U.S. Trade Deficit Sustainable?* Washington: Institute for International Economics.

Wren-Lewis, Simon, and Rebecca Driver. 1998. *Real Exchange Rates for the Year 2000.* Policy Analyses in International Economics 54. Washington: Institute for International Economics.

7

Energy: A Gathering Storm?

PHILIP K. VERLEGER JR.

The rise in energy prices after the successful invasion of Iraq focused attention again on energy markets. Crude oil prices were 56 percent higher 15 months after hostilities "ended," while three weeks before the November 2004 presidential election prices were 109 percent higher. The market's response in 2004 contrasted starkly with the events that followed the end of the first Gulf War (table 7.1).

The steady and unexpected rise in crude prices led to many meetings between global energy officials and numerous appeals to representatives of the Organization of Petroleum Exporting Countries (OPEC), especially Saudi Arabia, to boost production. OPEC members responded but to no avail.

Overlooked in the intense focus on immediate day-to-day price changes was a more troubling shift in prices quoted for oil to be delivered toward the end of the decade. These prices, which historically had fluctuated in a very narrow range around $22 per barrel, began a steady, inexorable increase following the conclusion of formal hostilities in Iraq. Between May 19, 2003—the day President George W. Bush declared "mission accomplished" from the deck of the *USS Abraham Lincoln*—and early October 2004, the price quoted for oil to be delivered in December 2009 rose from $23.92 per barrel to $39, a 70 percent increase. During this 17-month period, the increase was unrelenting (figure 7.1).

This increase in forward prices was matched by increases in prices bid for high-quality equity units, offering investors a return directly linked to

Philip K. Verleger Jr. is a senior fellow at the Institute for International Economics.

Table 7.1 Changes in world crude prices following the end of the Gulf War and the Iraq War

	Gulf War	Iraq War
Price at beginning of hostilities (dollars per barrel)	30.17	24.49
Price at end of hostilities (dollars per barrel)	20.11	26.27
Percent change following end of hostilities:		
3 months after	–7.2	11.4
6 months after	2.9	7.9
9 months after	–5.8	28.3
12 months after	–13.2	36.1
15 months after	3.8	56.0

Note: Prices are for Dated Brent Crude.

Source: Platts.

oil prices. Share prices offered for the BP Prudhoe Bay Royalty Trust, a trust issued by British Petroleum for production from Prudhoe Bay in Alaska, rose from $14 per share in May 2004 to almost $55 per share. The increase in the BP share price corresponds to a change in investor expectations regarding the rate of increase in future oil prices. In May 2003, investors thought prices would rise at a modest 2 percent, reaching $33 per barrel by 2010. Fifteen months later, the expected rate of increase had risen to 5.5 percent, and investors now expect that prices will reach $55 per barrel by 2010 (table 7.2).[1]

This shift in expectations warns of a gathering energy storm, an economic event that threatens greater damage than the worst hurricane. This summer's price increases were but the first tropical squalls from the approaching system. Increasingly severe harm will be inflicted on the global economy in the absence of action. In the worst case, limited energy supplies could result in a bidding war that thrusts the world economy into a serious and possibly prolonged recession.

In this chapter, I examine seven factors that have thrust energy to the forefront of global economic concerns. I then investigate several possible policy alternatives. I conclude by suggesting that the world situation can only be resolved by adopting a global cooperative agreement or imposing draconian and politically unpalatable taxes on petroleum use.

Sources of Strain in Global Energy Markets

In this section I offer seven explanations for the coming crisis. First, China and India have emerged on the global energy scene as major market par-

1. The derivation of table 7.2 from the BP Prudhoe Bay Royalty Trust is explained in appendix 7A.

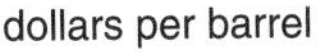

Figure 7.1 Settlement price of spot, 12-month forward, and 24-month forward WTI futures, 1999–2004

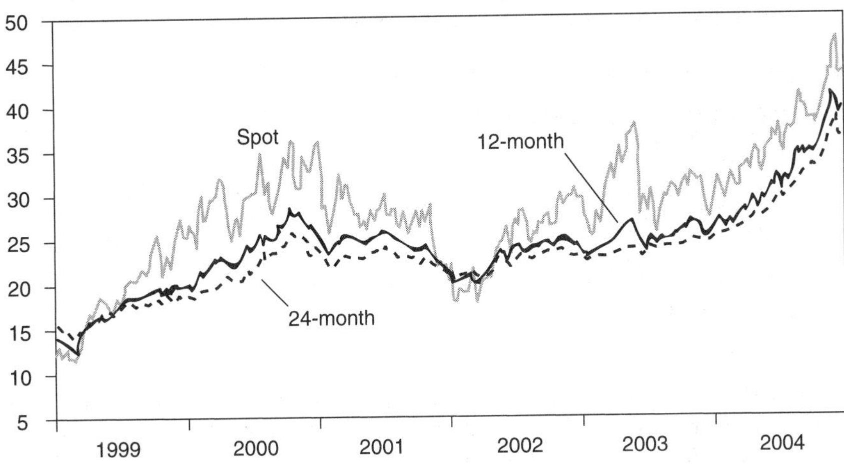

WTI = West Texas intermediate crude oil prices

Sources: Platts; NYMEX.

ticipants. Increased industrial output in these countries and a more affluent citizenry have boosted energy demand, particularly for petroleum, at record rates in both. Second, the key players in the global energy industry—OPEC nationals and the large multinational companies—failed to anticipate the demand growth and did not expand capacity to meet it. Investment slowed or stopped following the price collapse at the end of the 1990s, and companies have been reluctant to accelerate programs since. Third, precarious political circumstances in key oil-exporting countries make supplies from these nations uncertain. Internally or externally caused disruptions in Iran, Venezuela, Saudi Arabia, or Iraq could result in a significant loss of world oil supplies, sending prices even higher. Fourth, energy processing and transportation capacity—particularly at refineries—has lagged growth in demand. World refiners today cannot produce the types of products demanded by consumers in the required volumes. Fifth, environmental regulations adopted in the United States and Europe have adversely affected refiner capacity to manufacture key transportation fuels such as gasoline, diesel fuel, and jet fuel. Supply limitations have led to large product price increases, which have pulled up crude prices. Sixth, consumers have heard a mixed and confusing message from governments and industry. Energy companies warned of shortages, while the auto industry signaled no supply problems. These conflicting signs have discouraged conservation, laid the foundation for large

Table 7.2 Expected future oil prices derived from BP Royalty Trust (dollars per barrel)

Year	May 2003	August 2004
2005	27.17	41.92
2006	28.26	44.23
2007	29.39	46.66
2008	30.57	49.23
2009	31.79	51.94
2010	33.06	54.79
2011	34.38	57.81
2012	35.76	60.98
2013	37.19	64.34
2014	38.68	67.88
2015	40.22	71.61
2016	41.83	75.55
2017	43.51	79.70
2018	45.25	84.09
2019	47.06	88.71
2020	48.94	93.59

Source: Author's calculations.

increases in use, and created conditions that could cause very large price increases. Finally, Saudi Arabia and the other OPEC members engaged in a coercive effort to squeeze global supplies. This effort, which would be illegal in any developed nation, denied consuming nations the opportunity to prepare for the impending storm.

The new presidential administration must begin a program to address the tightening situation in world energy markets. The effort will require cooperation with other nations to achieve three goals: reducing uncontrolled growth in consumption, stimulating increased production, and stabilizing markets. However, the attempt will fail without large and painful measures at home. The cost of failure will be high. Inaction will no doubt lead to sharply lower rates of global growth and possibly a severe recession.

Influence of China and India

The emergence of China and India as principal players on the global energy scene represents the most important change in the global energy economy in 30 years. In 1990, consumption in these two countries amounted to no more than 3.5 million barrels per day, approximately 5 percent of global petroleum use. In 2003, 13 years later, use in the two countries has more than doubled and now accounts for more than 10 percent of global oil consumption.

Table 7.3 Sources of growth in world oil consumption, 1990–2003 (millions of barrels per day)

Source	1990	2003	Annual growth rate (percent)
China and India	3.6	8.7	7.0
Total world	66.2	78.1	1.3
World, less China and India	62.6	69.4	0.8

Source: BP *Statistical Review of World Energy Markets,* 2004.

The impact of the two countries on world markets can be seen in table 7.3. The top row of this table shows total use by these two countries in 1990 and 2003, as well as the annual rate of growth, which is 7 percent. The second row shows total global use, which grew at the far more sedate rate of 1.3 percent per year. Row three of table 7.3 shows the growth rate for global consumption excluding India and China. Global consumption exclusive of India and China increased at a rate of only 0.8 percent per year.

The slower growth in use in the non-China/India world is explained by lower rates of economic growth in these areas and lower intensities of oil use. China and India, without question, recorded more rapid rates of economic expansion from 1990 to 2003 than the rest of the world. Furthermore, the income elasticities of oil demand growth in India and China appear to be roughly 50 percent greater than those estimated for the rest of the world.[2]

This finding should not come as a surprise. A number of studies of petroleum and energy demand have found that elasticities are very high for developing countries emerging as newly industrialized nations (see, for example, Dunkerley 1990).

Inadequate Investment in Developing Oil Reserves

The rapidly changing global oil environment can also be traced to underinvestment. Between 1990 and 2003, the productive capacity of the global oil industry increased at a rate of 1.1 percent annually (compared with growth in global consumption of 1.3 percent per year). For a number of years, the slower expansion of productive capacity was not important be-

2. Very rough econometric estimates suggest the elasticity of demand for petroleum for the world as a whole is around 0.5, while the elasticities of demand for China and India are closer to 0.75.

cause OPEC nations collectively held substantial surplus capacity. However, this surplus was exhausted in 2004.[3]

Caution on the part of producers as well as political disruptions explain the lack of investment. The 1998 oil price collapse profoundly affected private firms and government companies in OPEC nations. In addition, private investors—particularly major oil companies—have not put large sums into significant projects outside major industrialized countries because they fear their investments would never be recovered.

The absence of investment has been noted by international energy officials, who have repeatedly called on oil-exporting nations and major oil companies to boost expansion. These pleas have largely been rejected. *The Wall Street Journal* reported in August that officials from OPEC countries and multinational companies rebuffed a direct appeal to heighten investment from Claude Mandil, executive director of the International Energy Agency (IEA).

> After a heated debate over the outlook for demand, the oil officials—including officials from the Organization of Petroleum Exporting Countries and major international oil companies—stood firm, according to four participants. Fearful that prices would collapse again as they did in 1998, no one was willing to raise spending sharply. "The OPEC countries said they would wait and see if there was a structural shift up in demand," said one participant. "But that could take years."[4]

In September 2004, Thierry Desmarest, chief executive of Total, the world's fifth largest multinational oil company, told *Financial Times* that private companies could not meet the world's increasing demand by investing outside of OPEC. Instead, he warned that the world's rising need for oil could be satisfied only if OPEC countries allow the multinationals to invest and develop added production within their borders.[5]

Missing from Desmarest's remarks was a caution that both private and national companies in OPEC nations were once concerned that increased production from Iraq could quickly drive prices down. Prior to the war in March 2003, there was widespread speculation that a swift Iraqi victory would lead to a flood of oil on world markets. Just as the invasion was about to start, a *Washington Post* reporter wrote,

---

3. Measuring capacity in the petroleum industry is very subjective. In the case of non-OPEC countries today, capacity is almost always fully utilized. What surplus capacity exists is found in OPEC. The calculations of OPEC's surplus capacity have always been biased. For years *Petroleum Intelligence Weekly* (*PIW*) has published estimates of OPEC productive capacity and production. The *PIW* figures are usually cited in press and expert reports. They indicate that OPEC had a surplus of 8 million barrels per day in late 1989 (12 to 14 percent of global capacity) before Iraq invaded Kuwait. This surplus dwindled to 0.5 million barrels per day (less than 1 percent of global capacity) by September 2004.

4. Bhushan Bahree and Patrick Bartak, "Awash in a Gusher of Cash, Oil Firms are Reluctant Investors," *The Wall Street Journal*, August 26, 2004, 1.

5. Interview with Thierry Desmarest, *Financial Times*, September 13, 2004.

Would a postwar Iraq, an original member of the Organization of Petroleum Exporting Countries that has been on OPEC's sidelines since its defeat in the 1991 Gulf War, support Saudi goals of keeping world oil prices within a stable range, about $25 a barrel? Or would Iraq rush to refill its treasury by boosting production, and driving down oil prices, at the expense of the Saudis, Iran, Kuwait, and other producers? In that scenario, could OPEC survive?[6]

The concern of world investors regarding Iraq's intentions seemed warranted. The country is acknowledged to possess reserves in excess of 100 billion barrels and might be able to more than double production. Another prewar *Post* article explained,

Iraq, which has the world's second-largest oil reserves after Saudi Arabia, has produced at most 2.5 million barrels a day in recent years and is exporting nothing now. It is likely to raise production to 3.5 million barrels a day within two years, when, by opening fields that have gone untapped because of the sanctions, it could increase production to as much as 6 million barrels a day in five to seven years.[7]

With this background, the conservative approach to investing by oil companies and oil-exporting countries seems reasonable. Unfortunately, the inability to boost production from Iraq immediately contributes to the problem where world supply is likely to increase at a rate slower than global demand would rise if the oil were available.

Political Instability in Oil-Exporting Countries

Market expectations have also been altered by anxiety associated with the future tenure of governments in a number of oil-exporting countries, as well as worries that internal conditions may adversely affect oil production. Iraq is clearly the most prominent concern. Oil exports have been repeatedly upset by attacks on production and transportation facilities.

However, Iraq is not unique. Many other producing nations have problems. Exports from Nigeria have been threatened repeatedly by a low-level civil war between those living in oil-producing areas and those ruling the country. Venezuelan output was disrupted in early 2003 and continues to be vulnerable to a dispute between radical president Cesar Chavez and the large middle class that ran the oil industry for decades. Prospects for output increases from Russia, the world's largest non-OPEC producer, are now at risk because of the dispute between Yukos, the country's largest oil company, and President Vladimir Putin.

---

6. Peter Behr, "Iraq May Regain Status as an Oil Industry Power," *The Washington Post*, March 23, 2003, A08.

7. Robert J. McCartney, "OPEC May Feel Pressure with Return of Iraqi Oil," *The Washington Post*, April 27, 2003, A26.

Another concern is Iran. The country is under pressure not from internal disputes but from the United States and the European Union demanding dismantlement of its nuclear enrichment program. Foreign policy scholars have warned that Iran's acquisition of nuclear weapons would quickly destabilize the Middle East.[8] Others warn that Israel may take preemptive military action against Iranian nuclear facilities just as it did years earlier against Iraq.[9] An Israeli attack or UN sanctions on Iran could destabilize production from the Middle East. Iranian output could be disrupted. More likely, though, Iran will attempt to influence exports from other countries. World oil supplies were affected periodically during the 10-year Iran-Iraq war in the 1980s. Battles then had only modest impacts on world oil prices because the capacity of producing countries drastically exceeded the needs of consuming nations. Today, as already noted, no such surplus exists. Conflict with Iran would likely lead to a large price increase.

Finally, the political situation in Saudi Arabia, the world's largest oil-exporting country, must concern the new US administration. Terrorists have increased their attacks on the most visible targets in the kingdom following the US invasion of Iraq, and foreign workers (particularly British and American citizens) have become targets. There is a small but nontrivial probability that exports from the country will be disrupted by some political or terrorist act in the next four years. Such an incident would cause serious global economic dislocations.

In short, a variety of threats to oil production exist in countries that supply much of the world's oil needs. Some of these risks have been listed in this chapter. Over the next four years, one must expect to see supplies interrupted to an extent that averages at least 1 percent of world capacity each year.

Inadequate Investment in Refining Capacity

The lack of investment in the refining capacity required to produce—from the crude oils being pumped today—the quantity of fuels demanded by consumers in Europe, Japan, and the United States, fuels that must comply with increasingly stringent environmental standards, is complicating the developing energy crisis. In particular, world refiners will apparently not be able to manufacture sufficient gasoline, diesel fuel, and jet fuel that meet current environmental standards at price levels close to those that prevailed in 2003.

8. See Fareed Zakaria, "Iran: the Next Crisis," *The Washington Post*, August 10, 2004, A19, and Walter Russell Mead, "Iran: A Darker Shadow than Iraq," *The Los Angeles Times*, July 25, 2004.

9. Tyler Marshall, "Iran Threat Grows among Rising US Divisions," *The Los Angeles Times*, September 12, 2004.

Figure 7.2 Refining margin on unleaded gasoline, US Gulf Coast, 1997–2004

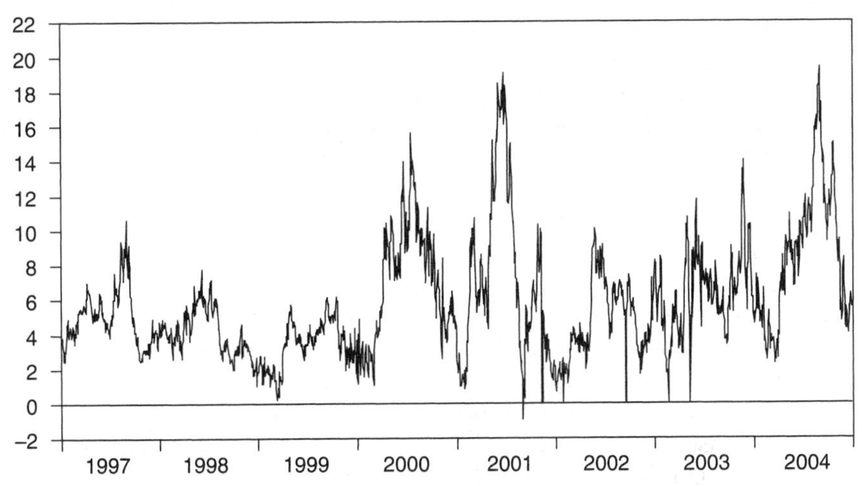

Source: Author's calculations.

The shortage of refining capacity has developed for three reasons. First, the world's largest oil companies refrained from expanding refining during the last decade because returns on investment were low.[10] Second, China did not forecast the growth in its demand for products and build sufficient capacity. Third, competition regulators in Europe and the United States demanded that the large companies divest themselves of refining assets. In the United States, the Federal Trade Commission (FTC 2004) is proud of its actions, believing the divestitures enhanced competition. Unfortunately, the smaller firms that acquired refineries cannot raise capital as easily as the multinationals. Capacity expansion has slowed. The costs of the shortsighted FTC policy became all too visible in the spring of 2004 when the industry could not boost production to meet surging demand. Spot gasoline prices rose by 50 percent from March to June, refining margins surged to record levels (as can be seen in figure 7.2), and the higher gasoline prices pulled up spot crude prices.

(There is a widespread belief that petroleum product prices follow crude oil prices. Federal Reserve Board Chairman Alan Greenspan often expresses this view.[11] This economic theory is sometimes correct. How-

10. See the forthcoming National Petroleum Council study on refining (draft on file with author).

11. See remarks by Chairman Alan Greenspan, "Central Bank Panel Discussion: Economic Developments," at the International Monetary Conference, London, England, June 8, 2004, www.federalreserve.gov.

ever, when refining capacity constrains supply, product prices will lead crude prices; see box 7.1.)

The 50 percent rise in gasoline prices recorded in the spring of 2004 might have been partially avoided had competition regulators adopted a different strategy toward mergers. At the time, the rule makers reviewed existing refining capacity without regard to potential increases in global product demand or the synergies achievable if merging companies had been able to link refineries together. In one case, the opportunity to boost US refining capacity by as much as 300,000 barrels per day (1.7 percent of US capacity) was lost.[12] The potential supply of products in the United States and Europe today would be as much as 10 percent greater had the FTC and its counterpart in Europe conditioned merger approvals on commitments by refiners to expand capacity.

China's failure to invest in refining capacity also contributed to (and will continue to contribute to) the rise in crude prices, particularly in the fall of 2004. China did not construct adequate refining capacity to meet its growing demand. China also did not build the type of capacity required to process high-sulfur Middle Eastern crudes. Thus to meet growing distillate demands in the fall of 2004, China was forced to bid for the world's limited supplies of light, low-sulfur crude. China's action may have added as much as $10 per barrel to crude prices.[13]

New, More Stringent Environmental Requirements

New environmental rules that require sulfur removal from gasoline and diesel fuel make the situation more precarious. These regulations began to take effect for US gasoline in 2004 and will apply to European diesel in 2005. When US regulations were finalized in 1999, the US Environmental Protection Agency (EPA) predicted that refiners would have no difficulty meeting the requirements because they would invest in the capacity needed to reduce sulfur (EPA 1999a).

The EPA predictions were proven wrong. The agency failed to account for the separate FTC policy that ordered major integrated oil companies to divest refining capacity. The acquiring firms lacked the financial resources to proceed with investments at the rate predicted by the EPA. In theory, imports might have offset the absence of US supply. However, many foreign refiners that had previously provided gasoline to the United

12. The opportunity occurred when Shell and Texaco merged refining operations. The two companies owned adjacent refineries in the state of Washington with combined capacity of less than 200,000 barrels per day. The merger produced a chance to create one giant refinery of 500,000 barrels per day or more, which might have met much of the West Coast's demands.

13. See "Refiners at the Limit on Sulfur," *Argus Global Markets*, September 27, 2004, 3, and "China Leads Race to Secure Sweet Supply," *Argus Global Markets*, September 13, 2004, 2.

Box 7.1 Arbitrage between crude and product

There is a widespread view that prices of petroleum products follow world crude prices. Federal Reserve Chairman Alan Greenspan often cites this thinking in his testimony before Congress.

The empirical evidence refutes the position that product prices always follow crude, as does economic theory. Traders at oil companies have understood the role of arbitrage for decades. Every day they calculate the gross product worth (GPW)[1] of a number of different crudes and then compare them with crude spot prices. After deducting transportation and processing costs, they rank the crudes according to profitability and bid for the most profitable. The bidding process drives the crude spot price toward the GPW. Financial economists describe this process as arbitrage.

Arbitrage has been explained regularly by all major petroleum market publications. The most complete presentation dates back to 1979 in *Petroleum Intelligence Weekly (PIW)*. The 1982 version of the explanation begins with this advice: "Oil price developments are now attracting the attention of many non-specialists without a background in the understanding of the marketplace and the analytical tools used in assessing trends."[2] EIG, the publisher of *PIW*, has reissued the explanation periodically, most recently in the organization's *International Crude Oil Market Handbook*.

The financial importance of netbacks to the oil industry is evidenced by how frequently they are estimated and published. These numbers provide traders and managers with stylized rankings of various crude values. *Argus Global Markets* prints weekly netback estimates for a variety of crudes at three markets: northern Europe, US Gulf Coast, and Singapore. The netbacks are based on Argus' valuation of markets. *Platts Global Alert* publishes daily estimates of netbacks in a number of markets based on Platts' estimates of spot prices in markets.

The arbitrage theory can be demonstrated analytically by statistically comparing the GPW of a crude with the crude's reported spot price. The results of such a test, shown in figure 7B.1, demonstrate the relationship between crude prices and spot product

Figure 7B.1 Brent spot price versus gross product worth at Houston, 1997–2004

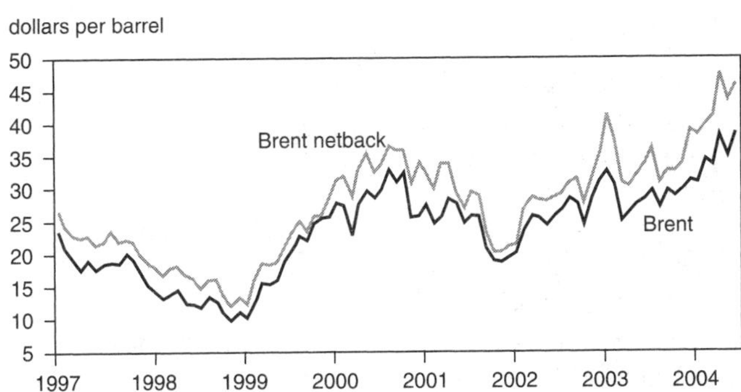

Source: Author's calculations, from *Weekly Petroleum Argus* data.

1. The gross product worth of a crude is nothing more than the weighted average value of all the refined product components of a barrel of crude at the refinery gate. The value is determined by multiplying the spot price of the products produced from the crude by the percentage volume of product yielded from a barrel.

2. "The ABCs of Measuring Oil Market Price Trends," *Petroleum Intelligence Weekly*, March 8, 1982, special supplement, 2.

(box continues next page)

Box 7.1 Arbitrage between crude and product *(continued)*

Figure 7B.2 Brent spot price versus spot price predicted from gross product worth at Houston, 1997–2004

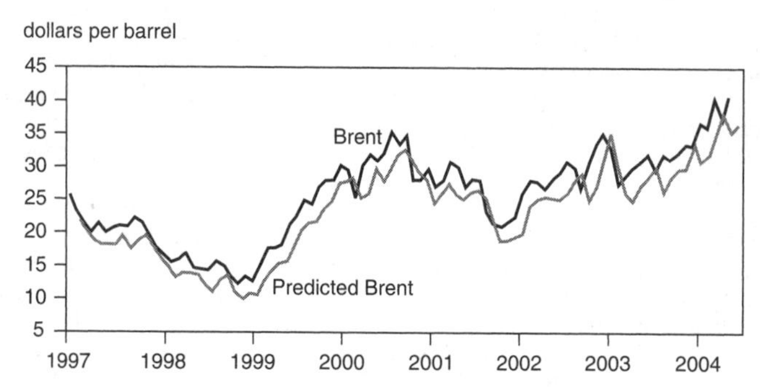

Source: Author's calculations.

prices. Figure 7B.1 shows the spot price of Brent crude (Dated Brent) as reported by *Weekly Petroleum Argus*. Also shown is the GPW of Brent computed at the US Gulf Coast (Houston).[3] One can note that the spot price of Brent closely follows the GPW.

There is a strong linkage between the spot price of Brent and the GPW. A regression of the change in the Brent spot price on the change in the GPW yields an R-squared of 0.71 and a highly significant coefficient on the change in GPW (the *t*-statistic is 12.6).[4] Figure 7B.2 compares the actual spot price with the predicted spot price. The arbitrage during periods of high crude inventories (1998–99) and low crude inventories (late 2000, 2003–04) is obvious.

3. The GPW of Brent was computed using refining yields published in *The International Crude Oil Market Handbook 1999–2000* published by EIG.

4. The regression is estimated in first difference form to correct for the covariance with time in the data. A test of the relationship estimated in level form (regression of spot prices on GPW) reveals the presence of a unit root.

States found they could not comply with the new regulations. The EPA, in effect, had erected a nontariff trade barrier.

Absence of Conservation by Key Consumers

The absence of conservation has increased the intensity of the looming crisis. The American motorists' love of sport-utility vehicles (SUVs) and trucks provides the most obvious manifestation of the problem. The Department of Energy (*DOE Monthly Energy Review*, May 2004, 17) reports that average fuel economy of all vehicles increased from 11.9 miles per gallon in 1973 to 17 miles per gallon in 2002. This trend has now been reversed. Increased demand from less efficient SUVs probably imposes an additional 200,000 to 500,000 barrels per day of incremental demand on a refinery industry that is, as noted earlier, short of capacity. The incremental demand causes an unnecessary rise in gasoline prices—and the higher gasoline prices translate into higher crude prices.

OPEC's Aggressive Effort to Keep Inventories Tight

Oil-exporting countries have clearly contributed to the precarious balance in global energy markets by pursuing a production strategy aimed at keeping inventories extremely lean. Saudi Arabia introduced this tactic in 1999 when crude prices hovered around $10 per barrel. The policy's proponents asserted that oil exporters would enjoy much higher revenues if they actively discouraged private parties and governments of consuming nations from holding excess stocks. Their plan succeeded.

The higher price levels have been achieved by collusion and intimidation. OPEC members have met regularly to set and adjust production quotas. At the same time, they have coerced other countries—principally Mexico and Norway—into joining agreements to cut output. In March 1999, when crude prices hovered briefly around $10 per barrel, Saudi Arabia pressured OPEC countries and three other nations into pumping less. At the time, the kingdom threatened to boost production and drive prices below $5 per barrel unless the others cut back (*Petroleum Intelligence Weekly*, March 22, 1999, 1).

Oil-exporting countries announced two production cutbacks during late 2003 and early 2004. While not fully implemented, these reductions removed any incentive for refiners or traders to hold inventories, leaving the global economy vulnerable to large price increases when unexpected consumption growth occurred in China and India.

OPEC's continued pursuit of these anticompetitive policies will only make crude oil prices more volatile and much higher over the rest of the decade. The impacts will be particularly pernicious if oil-exporting nations act aggressively to thwart efforts to protect consuming economies against OPEC's domination of the world oil market.

Strains on the Oil Market: Repeating History

The situation regarding energy markets in January 2005 will be very similar to the one that confronted Richard Nixon on the eve of his inauguration in 1973. At that time, James Akins, former US ambassador to Saudi Arabia, published a seminal article in *Foreign Affairs* entitled "The Oil Crisis: This Time the Wolf Is Here" (Akins 1973). Akins focused on efforts by oil-exporting countries to wrest control of their resources from multinational Western oil companies and the attempts by producers to stand together within OPEC to "manage" the oil market. He noted but then disparaged the prevailing view that producer attempts to restrain output would fail. He also ridiculed forecasts that oil prices would remain below $2 per barrel until at least 1980.

Akins cautioned that then-prevalent competitive bidding by consuming countries for oil sold by an increasingly united cartel could result in an uncontrolled upward rise in oil prices.

> With OPEC production limitations in the future, or even with normal slow growth, with only Saudi Arabia and perhaps Iraq capable of substantial expansions, bidding for supplies could soon get out of hand, and the projected price of $5.00 per barrel in 1980, or even a price of $7.00, could seem conservative. (Akins 1973, 487)

Akins' contribution was to foresee the need for cooperation among consuming countries to avoid bidding against one another for oil supplies. He advocated developing alternative energy sources, a relatively new idea in 1973; cooperation among consuming countries, particularly in developing oil resources outside OPEC; and finally, conservation, noting that such measures "could do much to limit our present profligate use of energy for a host of marginal purposes" (Akins 1973, 489).

Scenarios for World Oil Markets and the World Economy

The situation in the world oil market today bears a remarkable similarity to the one Akins observed. The foundations of the earlier crisis were laid between 1960 and 1970, just as the foundation of the current crisis was formed between 1990 and 2002. In the earlier episode, economic growth in Europe and Japan stimulated increased oil consumption, while the world's multinational companies simultaneously limited investment. In Europe, small automobiles replaced bicycles and motor scooters, and then larger cars replaced smaller cars. In Japan, economic growth stimulated increased oil use across the economy. Simultaneously, a surplus developed in world oil markets. The United States responded by imposing quotas on oil imports, creating significant downward pressure on oil prices. Multinational oil companies, then the stewards of OPEC oil, forced producers to accept price cuts. Investment lagged.

The similarity between the first decade of the 21st century and the 1970s can be seen by comparing table 7.3 with table 7.4. Table 7.3 shows the "but-for" growth rate for global oil consumption excluding the rapid development of India and China between 1990 and 2004. Table 7.4 shows similar statistics for the period 1965 to 1971. However, in the case of table 7.4, the sources of higher-than-average growth are Europe and Japan. The data for the earlier time reveal that global consumption grew

Table 7.4 Sources of growth in world oil consumption, 1965–71 (millions of barrels per day)

	1965	1971	Annual growth rate (percent)
World, less USSR	23.2	36.1	7.6
Europe	7.4	12.5	9.1
Japan	1.7	4.6	17.9
World, less Europe and Japan	14.1	18.9	5.0

Source: BP *Statistical Yearbook.*

at a rate of 7.6 percent per year over the six-year period. However, growth in the more developed areas (primarily the United States and Canada) was a more "sedate" 5 percent.[14] Free-world consumption in 1971 would have been 14 percent, or 5 million barrels per day, lower in 1971 than actually recorded, had use in all countries expanded at 5 percent rather than the recorded 7.6 percent rate. The difference of 5 million barrels per day was enough to set the stage for the 1973–74 energy crisis.

A few experts writing in the late 1960s and early 1970s recognized that the rapid growth in global demand combined with the lack of investment in exploration in OPEC countries, as well as other energy policies such as price controls imposed on natural gas, created the potential for a future energy crisis. A task force convened by President Nixon under the direction of George Schultz considered the issue in detail. Their study of the effect of US limitations on crude oil imports noted the need for new investment but expressed little concern. Instead, the members concluded that Saudi production would have to double by 1980, filling the gap (US Cabinet Task Force on Oil Import Control 1970). This did not happen. Rather, prices increased by 450 percent in two years and remained high, while oil production remained essentially unchanged over the decade (figure 7.3).

The situation today is no different from the one in 1973. An oil price rise of unpredictable magnitudes will occur if there are further unexpected increases in demand that cannot be met by boosting output—or if global production is disrupted. "Shortage conditions" (defined as periods when global demand cannot be satisfied at current prices) will likely emerge at times of stronger economic growth or at those times of year when global use crests (peak summer months and winter).

14. Energy consumption statistics for the period before 1990 generally exclude use in the former USSR. That convention is followed here.

Figure 7.3 Spot price of Arab light and Dubai crude oil, 1972–2002

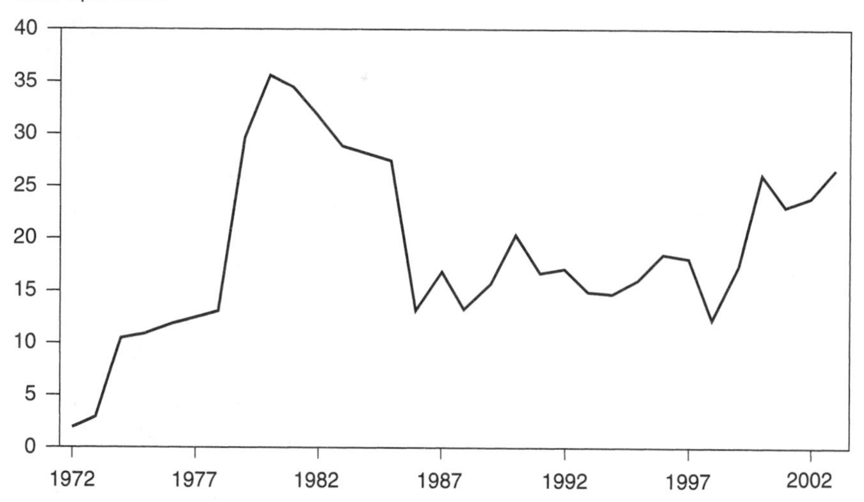

Source: BP *Statistical Review of World Energy Markets*, 2004.

Crude prices could climb from the present average in the $40s to perhaps $55 by mid-2005 and as high as $70 in 2006 should "shortage conditions" occur in those years. Even higher prices might be seen later in the decade. In theory, crude prices might reach $160 per barrel if history follows the 1973 script precisely. As already noted, conditions today are propitious for such an increase. This does not imply, though, that prices will go up in 2005 or 2006. Circumstances are favorable, but that is all that can be said.

Such extraordinary price increases could be moderated today by using the strategic stocks created following the 1973 crisis. Today, governments of the major industrialized nations own or control more than 1.4 billion barrels of oil that might be deployed to address supply disruptions and steady prices. However, current policies preclude such action. Campaigning in 2004, Vice President Dick Cheney explained to voters that the United States would not use public stocks to stabilize prices.

> The reason we set up the [Strategic Petroleum Reserve, SPR] back in the '70s, and maintain it since, is to deal with the emergency that would arise if . . . something were to suddenly happen to one of the major nations supplying petroleum to the US . . . [and] we were dealing with a situation [in which] we lost 5- or 6-mil b/d . . . out of the 20-mil b/d that we currently consume. That would be the kind of national crisis that would drive prices so high and probably bring large parts of our economy to a halt. . . . We keep the [SPR] to deal with exactly that kind of contingency.[15]

15. *Platts Global Alert*, August 24, 2004. Secretary of Energy Spencer Abraham affirmed that this was the US policy a week later (*Platts Global Alert*, August 31, 2004).

Figure 7.4 OPEC crude output versus OPEC estimated productive capacity, 1971–2006

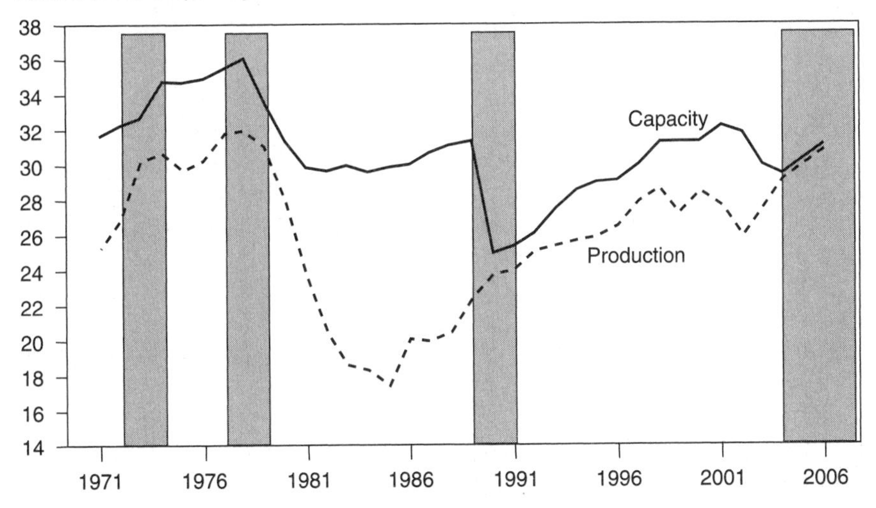

Note: Shaded bars denote periods of price increases.
Source: Author's calculations.

This statement implies that the US government would allow prices to rise to $70, $80, or even $100 per barrel without acting.[16]

The situation's tenuous nature is captured in figure 7.4, which shows OPEC productive capacity and OPEC output from 1971 through 2006. Note that periods of price increases (shaded on the graph) correspond to periods of sharp production boosts.

Economic Impacts of the Next Price Shock

Market events that took crude to $60 or $70 per barrel or higher would affect global and US growth rates. Macroeconomic Advisers (*Economic Outlook*, August 24, 2004, 11) calculates that each $10-per-barrel rise would reduce GDP growth relative to its baseline forecast by 0.3 percentage points in the current and next years. Federal Reserve Governor Edward Gramlich's estimates are approximately the same when the calculations are

16. The vice president's statement implies that strategic reserves are to be used only if the global supply unexpectedly falls 25 percent short of demand. Most models of global oil supply and demand would predict that such a shortfall would cause prices to rise by as much as 2,000 percent in the short run, although increases of such magnitude are unlikely to occur—or persist for long. Today, $100 crude would represent a 200 percent increase from early 2000 price levels.

made using large-scale econometric models, but larger if one uses reduced-form models such as those put forward by Hamilton (1983, 2003b).[17] The estimates offered by Gramlich and Macroeconomic Advisers suggest that a price increase of $40 per barrel that took crude to $70 would cut GDP growth by less than 2 percent, although nonlinearities in their model might cause the impact to be larger.

Today, though, most economists are talking not of $70-per-barrel oil but of $40-per-barrel oil. Furthermore, they begin by contrasting the $40 per barrel with a price level of $30 and conclude that the economic impacts are relatively modest. Such analyses tend to obscure the aggregate effect of oil price impacts on the global economy because the "consensus" is that oil prices would stay in the mid-$30s absent any market disorder. The impacts become significantly larger if one assumes that crude oil prices would be in the mid-$20s in a more stable world.[18] The losses associated with the shift between a $20-per-barrel world and a $40-per-barrel world are roughly double. One could argue that the macroeconomic calculations should start from this lower-price base because most studies show that crude oil prices would fluctuate around $20 per barrel if oil markets were not controlled by a cartel that aggressively cuts production to keep prices higher (Verleger 2004).

I have attempted to calculate the economic impacts of shifting from a low-price environment to a high-price one by employing results published by the IEA and the European Central Bank (ECB). Both organizations recently issued reports evaluating the macroeconomic impacts of higher oil prices (IEA 2004, Jiménez-Rodríguez and Sánchez 2004). The IEA published estimates of the impacts of a $10-per-barrel increase in oil prices on every region of the world.

I first examine the impacts on the US economy and then present summary results for the rest of the world. I created three macroeconomic scenarios for the United States using the multipliers published in these studies and quarterly consensus forecasts of GDP. I started with a base-case projection of GDP through 2006 founded on an assumed oil price in the low $30s. I then recalculated economic growth under two alternative assumptions. In the first, I assumed the West Texas intermediate (WTI) crude oil prices dropped to $23 per barrel on January 1, 2004, and stayed at that level through 2006.[19] In the second, I assumed WTI rose from $38 per barrel in 2004 to $48 in 2005 and $55 in 2006.

17. Speech by Edward M. Gramlich, "Oil Shocks and Monetary Policy," September 16, 2004, www.federal-reserve.gov/boarddocs/speeches/2004/20040916/default.htm.

18. I selected a price of $20 as the one that would prevail in a stable world because most oil firms today use that price to evaluate investment opportunities. Projects that can be profitable with prices in the low $20s are approved. Projects that cannot meet this test are not.

19. I use $23 per barrel for WTI because WTI tends to trade at a $3-per-barrel premium to globally traded crude.

Table 7.5 Impact on US economic growth under three alternative oil price scenarios, 2004–06

Scenario	2004	2005	2006
Annual rates of change in GDP (percent)			
Base case	4.7	4.1	3.7
Low prices	5.6	4.7	4.3
High prices	4.7	3.2	2.0
Q4-to-Q4 growth in GDP (percent)			
Base case	4.4	3.9	3.6
Low prices	5.3	4.5	4.3
High prices	4.4	3.0	1.9
WTI assumptions (dollars per barrel)			
Base case	36.9	33.2	31.0
Low prices	23.0	23.0	23.0
High prices	38.8	45.3	55.0

Q4 = fourth quarter
WTI = West Texas intermediate crude oil prices

Source: Author's calculations.

I derived the high crude prices assumed in the third case from an analysis of US gasoline price levels that will be required in 2005 and 2006 to cap the growth in use of that fuel. As already noted, a lack of new refining capacity combined with stricter regulations regarding gasoline sulfur content will limit the product's available supply. Annual retail price increases of between 30 and 50 cents per gallon will be required to arrest the expected demand growth. The higher gasoline prices will *pull up* crude oil prices during the spring and summer, leading to the crude price levels used here.

Table 7.5 shows the results of these scenarios for the United States. The findings of these simulations suggest that US GDP growth would be twice as high under the low-price scenario as the high-price one.

The IEA study also provided estimates of the economic impact of higher oil prices on other world regions. Table 7.6 shows these estimates for four price scenarios.

The impacts of higher oil prices calculated here reveal the obvious fact that the world would be better off with lower oil prices. Suggestions that higher oil prices are not as damaging to the world economy today as in the past may be correct. Nevertheless, lower oil prices are still better for the economy than high prices. As Governor Gramlich stated, "All things considered, although the present oil shock may not be as significant as the shocks we remember from the 1970s and 1980s, it will definitely register."[20]

20. Speech by Edward M. Gramlich, "Oil Shocks and Monetary Policy," September 16, 2004, www.federal-reserve.gov/boarddocs/speeches/2004/20040916/default.htm.

Table 7.6 Impact on global economic growth under four oil price scenarios, 2005 and 2006 (percent)

	2005		2006	
Region	**Mid price**	**High price**	**Mid price**	**High price**
Organization for Economic Cooperation and Development	–0.4	–0.9	–0.3	–1.3
United States	–0.3	–0.7	–0.2	–1.0
Eurozone	–0.5	–1.1	–0.4	–1.6
Japan	–0.4	–0.9	–0.3	–1.3
Oil-importing developing nations				
Asia	–0.8	–1.8	–0.6	–2.6
China	–0.8	–1.8	–0.6	–2.6
India	–1.0	–2.2	–0.8	–3.2
Malaysia	–0.4	–0.9	–0.3	–1.3
Philippines	–1.6	–3.6	–1.3	–5.1
Thailand	–1.8	–4.0	–1.4	–5.8
Latin America[a]	–0.2	–0.4	–0.2	–0.6
Argentina	–0.4	–0.9	–0.3	–1.3
Brazil	–0.4	–0.9	–0.3	–1.3
Chile	–0.4	–0.9	–0.3	–1.3
Highly indebted poor countries	–1.6	–3.6	–1.3	–5.1

a. Includes Mexico.

Source: Author's calculations.

Moreover, these three scenarios by no means offer a best-case/worst-case comparison. One can imagine a far worse case if the situation in the Middle East degenerated into a true crisis. The Middle East today faces the risk of continued chaos in Iraq as well as a potential confrontation with Iran. One can imagine a scenario where supplies from Iran were disrupted for a long time due to an attack on the country's nuclear facilities, while Iraq's efforts to boost production continue to be hampered by internal fighting. In such circumstances, prices could easily rise to levels above $100 per barrel even if the IEA authorized a release from strategic reserves.

Moderating or Avoiding the Impending Energy Crisis

The approaching energy crisis will cause serious economic dislocations despite the optimistic predictions of economists and central bankers.[21]

21. See Chris Giles and Andrew Balls, "Why This Time the World Economy Can Cope with an Oil Price Shock," *Financial Times*, October 20, 2004, 6. A number of central bankers and senior monetary officials quoted in the report commented that rising oil prices did not pose risks to the global economy similar to those created in 1973. The authors quote Federal Re-

The higher oil prices associated with limited available supplies will cause global growth rates to fall short of projected and achievable levels. However, many and perhaps all of these losses can be avoided if the United States and other nations adopt different energy strategies.

The United States must lead this effort because as the largest global economy it is also the world's largest petroleum consumer. In the eyes of many, the United States is also the most profligate oil consumer. Thus, the current course of energy markets, which seem to be taking the world toward economic catastrophe, will not change unless the United States acts.

Upon taking office, the new presidential administration will want to put forward policies to address the domestic and international dimensions of the crisis. These actions must attend to the short- and long-term situations. A number of measures are described in this chapter. Some of these focus solely on domestic energy policies. Such suggestions may seem out of place in a chapter centering on international issues. However, it can be argued that little will be achieved in the global policy arena until the United States institutes policies that correct the most obvious deficiencies of its domestic energy program.

Ultimately, the new administration will want to push other nations to accept an agreement to stabilize global oil prices. Such a program would require converting current strategic stocks to buffer stocks, doubling current storage capacity, and using buffer stock purchases and sales to stabilize prices within an agreed range. Adopting this program in January 2003 likely would have kept crude prices below $40 per barrel in 2004, effectively avoiding the loss of as much as 1 percent of global GDP. Adopting the program in January 2005 could raise global growth rates in 2005 and 2006 by as much as a full percentage point each year.

Creating a global agreement to stabilize prices will not, however, resolve current difficulties. Other polices must be pursued as well, if for no other reason than to convince oil-exporting countries that it is in their best interest to agree to a stabilization agreement.

In the petroleum sector, changes in short-term regulations, promotion of seasonal inventory management practices, development of measures that ensure better inventory management practices, aggressive advocacy of conservation, promotion of greater flexibility in environmental standards, adoption of policies that encourage refinery expansion, and expansion of global inventories can probably moderate most, if not all, of the short-term threat.

---

serve Board Governor Ben Bernanke, who explained that the world is more resilient today than in 1973 because investors have greater faith in central banks. This faith will reduce the necessity of raising interest rates in response to further oil price increases. Economic losses associated with the 1973 increase were doubled when central banks raised interest rates in response to the oil price rise (see Schultze and Fried 1975).

The long-run crisis can be avoided by adopting aggressive measures to conserve energy and by working with producing countries to manage the global market. This management requires the expansion and frequent use of public stocks.

Short-Term Measures to Address the Current Problem

The current crisis results from the unexpectedly rapid growth in global consumption. This imbalance is exacerbated by the inability of many refineries to process available crude oils. The disparity can be rectified by adopting measures to limit consumption growth, promoting inventory accumulation whenever consumption declines, and relaxing environmental regulations temporarily.

Releasing Strategic Reserves Through a Swap

Conservative economist Stephen Hanke has asserted that George W. Bush's first administration's management of the US Strategic Petroleum Reserve (SPR) added $10 per barrel to crude prices. In a *Wall Street Journal* op-ed, Hanke argued that adopting a policy to lend reserves to the oil industry[22] as proposed in legislation authored by Senators Carl Levin and Susan Collins would lower oil prices by more than $10 per barrel.[23]

Hanke's proposal, which is similar to arguments other economists and I have made for years, adds conservative support to a discussion that has been very partisan to date. Unfortunately, his support is unlikely to lead to action because many politicians see strategic reserves as strategic, not economic tools. As noted earlier, Vice President Cheney emphasized that strategic stocks were being held solely to protect against very large oil supply disruptions. His view is widely held.

Nevertheless, the new administration, confronted with record high oil prices, will have to reconsider this position. In assessing the issue, it must be recognized that the high prices recorded at the end of 2004 were caused by a shortage of light, low-sulfur crude oil, not a crude oil dearth in general. This fact will provide the new administration with an opportunity to (1) quickly affect global oil prices while (2) actually adding oil to the reserve. This outcome can be achieved by selling inventories of light, low-sulfur crude oil held in the reserve while acquiring more than equal volumes of higher-sulfur, heavy crude. For example, if the market conditions

22. A proposal to "lend" oil from the SPR would involve selling crude to buyers under the condition that they return oil to the government in a specified time. The Clinton administration used such a strategy in October 2000.

23. Stephen Hanke, "Over a Barrel," *The Wall Street Journal*, October 21, 2004, A18.

prevailing at the end of October persist, the new administration could sell 100 million barrels of light, low-sulfur crude while purchasing 120 million barrels of heavier crude.

This swap can be achieved because the US SPR contains both types of crudes. At the end of October 2004, 270 million of the 690 million barrels in the SPR were described as light crude oil.[24]

The swap policy would not increase the exposure of the United States or any other country to the impacts of a severe energy supply disruption because the world refining industry has sufficient capacity to process the limited global crude supply available during such a disruption. As noted earlier, Vice President Cheney has stated that US policy envisions using the SPR only if the United States loses 5 to 6 million barrels per day of current supplies (25 to 30 percent). Under such circumstances, the world refining industry could process the available supply without difficulty. During the disruption, up to 25 percent of the world's refineries could be idled. If a light crude shortage occurred, those refineries requiring light crude could be shut down without causing any additional economic harm.

The immediate economic benefits of this swap strategy in 2005 would be tremendous. Hanke suggests that it could reduce crude oil prices by $10 per barrel. This estimate is probably conservative. A decision to put 100 million barrels of light crude oil on the market to be sold over 90 days could easily bring light crude oil prices down by $20 per barrel. WTI and Brent could trade for $35 per barrel by January 2005 if the strategy were implemented on November 1, 2004.[25]

Raising the Gasoline Tax

A gasoline tax matched by a reduction in other taxes should be the critical component in a policy adopted to deal with the current imbalance in global markets. Today, taxes in the United States are well below those imposed in other countries, as can be seen in figure 7.5. Putting in place a tax of $1 per gallon would go a long way toward relieving the current pressure on world oil prices. A $1 tax would cut US gasoline consumption by roughly 8 percent (or 800,000 barrels per day) within a year. The reduced demand would ease pressure on world refineries and significantly moderate global crude prices.

24. See Strategic Petroleum Reserve Inventory for October 26, 2004, www2.spr.doe.gov/DIR/SilverStream/Pages/pgDailyInventoryReportViewDOE_new.html.

25. The prediction of a $20-per-barrel decline is calculated as follows. First, at the end of October the normal differential between light and heavy crude oils had increased by as much as $10 per barrel. Release of 100 million barrels of light crude oil would easily eliminate this premium. Second, the decline in the WTI cash price would start a liquidation of contracts for delivery in two to seven years if past trends hold. This liquidation could lower the entire forward price curve by as much as $20 per barrel but is more likely to cause a decrease of around $10.

Figure 7.5 Gasoline taxes by country, second quarter 2004

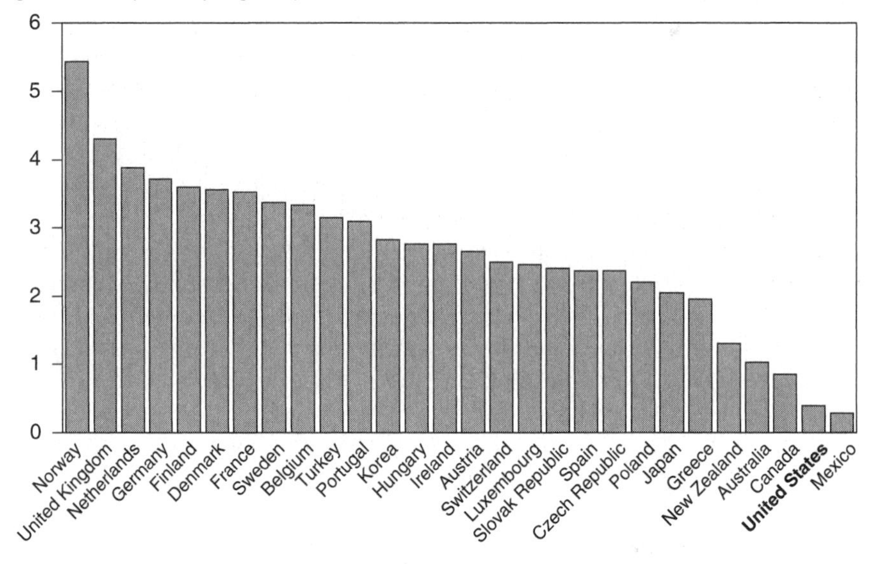

Source: IEA Energy Prices and Taxes, second quarter 2004.

A gasoline tax would also impose a serious fiscal drag on the US economy. At $1 per gallon, the tax would raise approximately $140 billion in revenues. This burden would need to be offset by lowering other taxes. A standard proposal offered by many economists involves compensating for the higher tax by eliminating or reducing the employee portion of the Social Security tax. Such an act would ameliorate the macro effects of the gasoline tax while preserving the conservation impact. Economic simulations repeatedly reveal that a revenue-neutral tax will not cause serious macro losses, although the effect on specific regions could be serious.

Unfortunately, a gasoline tax is always seen as politically impractical and regressive, even if coupled with a rebate such as waiving the worker portion of OASDI tax payments. Proposals such as a prospective gasoline tax joined with an SUV buyback program are also considered totally impractical.[26]

There are, though, two very strong arguments for adopting a gasoline tax. First, the low level of US gasoline taxes represents a serious imped-

26. This proposal would involve enacting a tax to take effect in two years. The time delay would allow consumers to readjust lifestyles, including moving closer to work. It would also allow cities and towns time to expand and improve mass transit. Associated with it would be a government commitment to buy back fuel-inefficient SUVs at market prices so owners would not suffer large financial losses. The SUVs would be scrapped.

iment to economic relations between the United States, the European Union, and Japan. Second, a large gasoline tax could frustrate efforts by oil-exporting nations to artificially elevate world oil prices.

A gas tax would contribute to improved global economic relations, possibly making it easier to achieve other important economic goals. Officials of many US allies confront enormous difficulties when they ask their citizens to accept further energy policy measures to cut usage. If the United States enacted a higher tax, it would make it easier for officials from these countries to cooperate on energy policy and other economic policy issues.

Instituting a large gasoline tax would also directly confront efforts by oil-exporting countries to raise prices artificially. Econometric studies show each $0.25-per-gallon increase in gasoline taxes would cut US motor fuels consumption by 200,000 barrels per day in the short run (defined as six months) and 700,000 barrels per day in the long run (two to three years).[27] Within two years, a $1 tax would reduce global demand by more than 2 percent, easing pressures on global oil markets. The reduced demand could ease upward pressure on oil prices, shifting as much as two-thirds of the tax burden from consumers to world oil producers.[28]

Revising the EPA Program for Reducing Sulfur in Gasoline

Recently implemented rules requiring gasoline sulfur reduction may also need to be rolled back. The plan was promulgated in 1999 and mandated a lowering of the refinery average of gasoline sulfur content to 30 parts per million (ppm) with a maximum per-gallon cap of 80 ppm by 2006 (EPA 1999b, 2004).

The program imposes a nontariff barrier to trade because refiners that export gasoline to the United States face tighter regulations than domestic refiners. As such, it has reduced the volume of exports that can be shipped to the United States in 2004 and may further lower the amount that qualifies for sale in the United States in 2005 and 2006 (Energy Information Agency 2004).

These rules contributed to the 50 percent increase in spot gasoline prices in the spring of 2004, which led to the crude price rise from the low $30s to $40. The EPA requirements will contribute to further large jumps in gasoline prices in the spring of 2005 absent regulatory relief.

---

27. Short-run price elasticities of demand range from –.2 to –4, while long-run elasticities are twice as large. See Dahl and Sterner (1991) or Houthakker, Verleger, and Sheehan (1976).

28. Imposing a tax on US motor fuels would raise the average price of all petroleum consumed in the United States by approximately $0.55 per gallon or $23 per barrel. The price increase would lower consumption by more than 1 million barrels per day. A decline of this magnitude under current market conditions could easily drop oil prices from the mid-$50s back to the mid-$30s, effectively shifting the burden of the tax to oil producers.

Figure 7.6 Incentive to hold stocks: Crude oil price spreads, 1999–2004

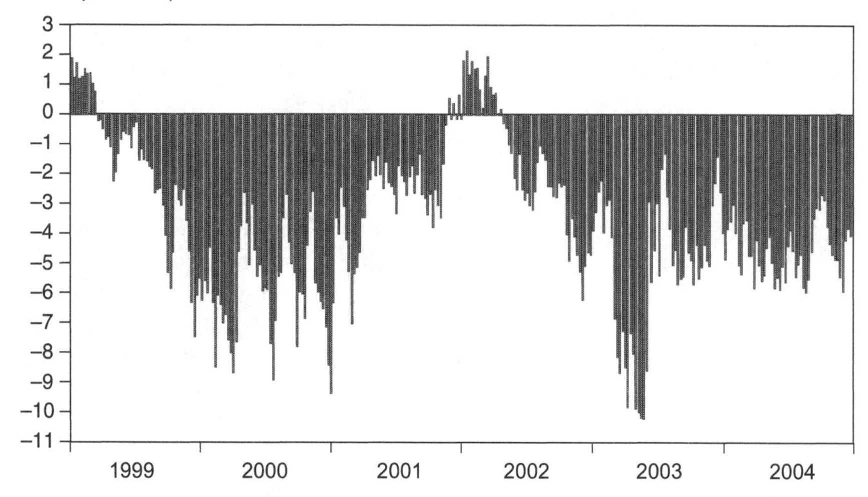

Source: Author's calculations.

The current upward pressure on prices can be relieved by modifying the program. However, relief should be granted in a form that preserves returns on investments made in desulfurization equipment. Specifically, imported or domestic gasoline that does not meet the standards should be subject to a fee of $2.50 to $5 per barrel (5 to 10 cents per gallon). Such a fee would guarantee the returns of refiners but would potentially cap the increase in crude costs.

Adopting Policies to Promote Inventory Accumulation

Oil markets have been in "backwardation"[29] for more than five years, with the exception of a brief period following 9/11. In this situation, the price for crude oil or product to be delivered in a few months' time or a year is *less* than the product's cash price. For example, at the end of September 2004 the WTI spot price was $49.58 per barrel. On the same day, crude for delivery in a year settled for $43.73, a discount of $5.85 per barrel. Over the last year, backwardation has ranged from minus $2.70 to

29. Governor Gramlich defines the term as follows: "A stock exchange term for a percentage paid by a seller of stock for the privilege of delaying its delivery until some agreed on future date. In effect, the futures price is less than the spot price."

Figure 7.7 Usable commercial stocks in OECD countries, 1987–2004

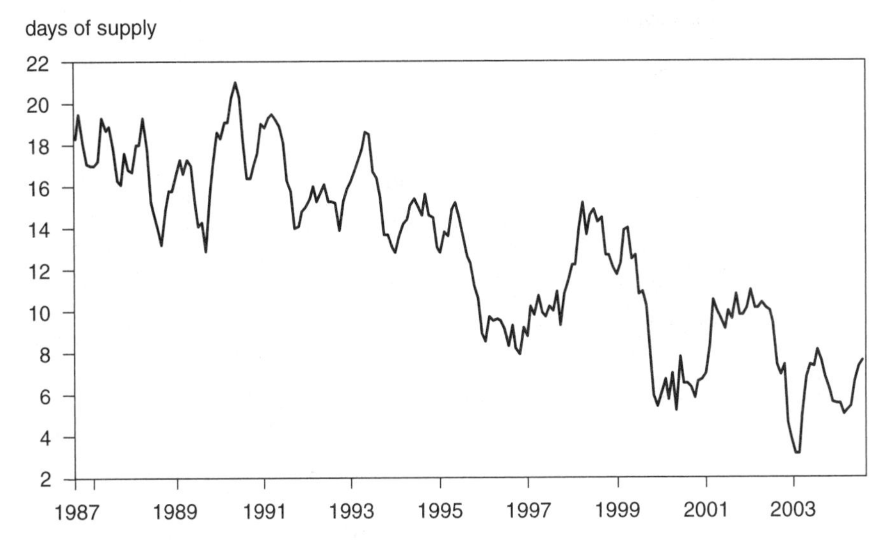

Source: Energy Intelligence Group.

minus $6 per barrel (figure 7.6). This market condition discourages refiners and traders from holding inventories (Williams and Wright 1982).

The incentive to hold stocks is further reduced by the very high cost of crude oil and limited financial resources of several of the independent refiners created by FTC divestiture actions. These firms often cannot obtain credit to add stocks. As a result, privately held crude volumes have continually declined. One indication of this is the downward trend in commercially available inventories as reported by the Energy Intelligence Group as shown in figure 7.7. These stocks are measured in days of supply held in OECD countries that companies can draw to meet unexpected demand. One can observe that inventories have dropped from 17 days in 1990 to seven days in 2004.

The situation has become so extreme that three refineries—all owned by an independent firm—were forced to shut down following Hurricane Ivan because they exhausted their crude inventories. These plants were not affected by the storm, and the logistical facilities that supplied crude were disrupted for less than a week. The refineries ceased operations because they held less than a week's supply of crude. Such events did not occur in the past because refiners had larger inventories.

At the same time, peak global demand for key economic products such as gasoline, distillate fuel oil, and jet fuel has increased relative to refiner capacity. In other industries—and historically in the oil industry—such a situation has been addressed in the short term by building inventories during periods of low seasonal demand. This has not occurred in 2004, though, because access to short-term capital has been limited and markets have been in backwardation.

Creating market conditions (contango) that encourage stock building would promote inventory accumulation. Contango could be promoted by releasing strategic stocks to private buyers. Converting strategic stocks to a buffer stock system designed to stabilize prices could achieve this goal. The stabilization program is discussed in more detail later.

Long-Term Strategies for Addressing the Energy Problem

President Bush proposed a detailed energy program in May 2001. His plan contained measures that would have boosted oil and gas production, expanded coal use, streamlined US regulation of the electricity industry, and removed many regulatory barriers that impeded energy investment projects. Missing from the Bush program were any serious steps to reduce energy consumption. Several versions of the Bush energy program were passed by the House of Representatives, and one version passed the Senate, but none ever passed both legislative bodies. The new administration will need to revisit the issue, putting forward legislation that can muster support from both houses.

Among other elements, long-term legislation must contain programs to reduce petroleum use, promote refinery capacity upgrades, and create a multinational system to stabilize oil price fluctuations. Some elements of a program are outlined here.

Adopting Programs to Reduce Oil Conservation

The new administration must take steps to limit growth in oil use. Historically, the primary tool for reducing use has been the corporate average fuel economy (CAFE) standards. CAFE rules require automakers to achieve certain specific fuel efficiency standards for each model year. These requirements, originally imposed in 1976, were effective until the mid-1990s. However, in recent years the auto industry has circumvented them by convincing consumers to substitute trucks (which were not subject to CAFE standards) for automobiles or to purchase SUVs, which under the law are treated as trucks. Going forward, this regulatory loophole needs to be closed and steps taken to improve vehicle fleet efficiency substantially by 2010.

A study by the National Academy of Sciences (NAS) published in 2002 concluded that a further increase in CAFE standards would reduce gasoline consumption by 2015 from levels that otherwise would be expected to occur. However, the committee also noted that a number of alternative policies would be superior to mandated standards, including tradable credits for fuel economy standards, "feebates" (a combination of taxes on vehicles with low gas mileage and rebates for very efficient vehicles), higher fuel taxes, or standards based on vehicle attributes (NAS 2002). The NAS committee recommended that any changes in CAFE standards should include a broad program that allowed trading of fuel economy credits.

The NAS study forms the basis by which the new administration can frame a policy to reduce gasoline and diesel consumption substantially over the next 10 years. The opportunity should not be missed.

Implementing tighter fuel economy standards, particularly through market incentives, could save substantial volumes of petroleum by 2015 and 2020. Today, US consumers burn 10 million barrels per day of petroleum on US roads and highways, one out of every eight barrels of crude produced in the world. If current trends continue, US motor fuel consumption could rise to 12.3 million barrels per day by 2020 and account for one of every nine barrels consumed in the world. This projected figure might be reduced by as much as a third if fuel economy standards were tightened. As the NAS panel suggested, progress could probably be achieved most rapidly if these standards were imposed using market-based incentives. For example, a program of "feebates" could provide the necessary financial incentives for automakers to substitute lighter materials, composites, and more efficient drive trains for existing technologies.[30]

Adopting domestic policies that focus on reducing petroleum consumption will pay large dividends in international negotiations in the energy area by reversing present perceptions of US energy policy. A more favorable view of US policies will also facilitate talks in other economic policy areas.

Accelerating Introduction of Alternative Fuels such as Cellulosic Ethanol

The United States should also speed up programs to find environmentally acceptable fuel feed stocks that can be substituted for petroleum. Introducing significant volumes of such fuels would serve at least two purposes. First, OPEC's control over the oil market would be reduced. Second, total emissions of global warming gases would be cut. Such fuels exist. One of these fuels is cellulosic ethanol. Lugar and Woolsey (1999) list the advantages of the fuel:

30. A recent report by the Rocky Mountain Institute (2004) highlights the potential savings achievable through automobile redesign.

- "Cellulosic ethanol is a first-class transportation fuel, able to power cars of today as well as tomorrow, use the vast infrastructure already built for gasoline, and enter quickly and easily into the transportation system."
- "It can be shipped in standard rail cars and tank trucks and is easily mixed with gasoline."
- "Although somewhat lower in energy content, it has a substantially higher octane rating than gasoline, allowing for more efficient combustion."
- "It can radically reduce the emission of global warming gases, help reduce the choking smog of our cities, and improve air quality."
- "It is far less toxic than petroleum, far less likely to explode and burn accidentally, and far simpler physically and chemically, making possible simpler refining procedures."

The impediment to the use of cellulosic ethanol has always been cost. A study published by DOE in 2000 (Dipardo 2000) put the price of producing ethanol in this manner at between $1.15 and $1.43 per gallon (in 1998 prices). At the time, spot gasoline was trading at much lower prices. However, at the end of April 2004, spot gasoline prices were at a level that would make the ethanol process competitive.

Revising US and EU Merger Rules Regarding the Oil Industry

For the last decade, the US FTC has aggressively enforced US antitrust law to preserve competition in refining. The agency trumpets the fact that it has accomplished this goal (FTC 2004). Preserving competition has meant that consumer prices are lower than they would otherwise be, given the level of refining capacity.

The agency neglects to note, though, that its policies have effectively destroyed refining capacity. Investments that might have been made to expand facilities have not been made. For example, in the 1997 merger of Shell and Texaco refining assets, the companies could have converted two adjacent facilities into one giant refinery. That one very large, extremely sophisticated unit might have had 400,000 to 500,000 barrels per day of capacity (3 percent of total US capacity). However, the opportunity was lost because the FTC forced Shell to sell one of the units to an independent.

The rise of independent refiners is analogous to the rise of low-cost airlines. These firms receive assistance from the government in the form of waivers from environmental rules and other actions, just as the low-cost airlines have received special benefits from the Department of Transportation.[31] However, the multinational companies have adopted a different strategy than the network airlines. Whereas network carriers such as United Airlines have sought to compete with the low-cost carriers, the major oil companies have gradually withdrawn from the market, selling other refineries and cutting investment.

The FTC policy to preserve competition, then, has slowed growth in refining capacity. Consumers are paying much higher, but competitive, prices for these actions. A new policy that promotes investment and quite possibly acquisition of independent refiners by multinational companies is urgently required to encourage the creation of more capacity.

Negotiating an Agreement Between Consuming and Producing Countries to Stabilize Prices

The last element of the new administration's energy program must be negotiating an agreement between oil-consuming and producing countries to stabilize oil prices. The program should be based on stabilization programs implemented with varying success for other commodities. In such programs, inventories are managed to moderate the price movements of a storable commodity by selling the commodity when its price threatens to exceed a target price and buying the commodity when the price falls below the target level.

Bosworth and Lawrence (1982, 152) note that such programs are a tool that can rapidly reach its goal. However, they also caution that buffer stock programs are difficult to establish. First, they require sufficient investment capital. Second, they require the participation of most if not all countries to avoid free riding. Third, buffer stock programs can discourage private stockpiling. Finally, buffer stock programs require producers and consumers to agree on a price stabilization range.[32]

The first three conditions have already been satisfied for oil. Government stockpiles have been created. The United States, Japan, and EU members today hold 1.4 billion barrels of strategic stocks. These could form the basis of the buffer stock program. The countries holding these inventories need only agree to permit their use for price stabilization pur-

31. For example, Frontier Airlines has been allowed to fly nonstop from Denver to Washington National while United Airlines has not, despite the fact that United Airlines has its major hub in Denver.

32. Bosworth and Lawrence also explain that it is not possible to create buffer stocks for all commodities. To be a candidate for stabilization, a commodity must be relatively homogeneous, an organized international market must exist for the commodity, and the market must be global so that commodity stabilization in one geographic location will affect prices across the globe. Petroleum clearly qualifies. See Verleger (1994).

Table 7.7 Estimates of OECD petroleum inventories and world petroleum consumption for selected years

Year	Public stocks (billions of barrels)	Private stocks (billions of barrels)	Total stocks (billions of barrels)	Worldwide consumption (millions of barrels per day)	OECD days of coverage from private stocks
1982	.6	2.8	3.4	61.7	72.4
1990	1.1	2.6	3.7	66.0	61.3
2000	1.2	2.5	3.7	76.2	51.8
2003	1.4	2.5	3.9	79.7	50.0

Sources: BP *Statistical Yearbook* and International Energy Agency.

poses. In addition, India and China, the two countries accounting for the current growth in oil use, are both planning to create their own stockpiles. These nations account for 80 to 90 percent of global consumption by oil-importing countries. Thus, there is little danger that other consuming countries will free ride.[33]

The development of strategic stocks has also already resolved the issue of substituting public stocks for private ones. Bosworth and Lawrence note that public stabilization programs can discourage firms from holding private stocks. Williams and Wright (1982, 341–53) predicted that private oil companies would reduce oil inventories if strategic stocks were created. Their hypothesis has been confirmed. At the end of 2003, public stocks totaled 1.4 billion barrels of oil (table 7.7). These inventories represent 30 percent of world stocks. Public stocks increased from 600 million barrels in 1982. During the same period, private stocks held in the OECD declined by 200 million barrels, despite a 30 percent increase in consumption. As a result, the days of coverage of private stocks fell from 72 days in 1982 to 50 days in 2003 (table 7.7).

Following practices established for buffer stocks, G-7 governments could use their inventories to moderate high oil prices by selling stocks when prices are above the target range and buying when prices fall below a lower level. Alternatively, governments could lend or swap stocks to buyers when prices are high, calling in the loans when prices fall.[34]

33. Free riding is a clear problem with buffer stock programs. Ideally, one wants all consumers to participate in the program. In the case of oil, one wants all oil-importing countries to join in a buffer arrangement. Between 80 and 90 percent of oil-importing countries have or are planning to build strategic stocks.

34. Central banks often lend their gold reserves to private firms to earn a return on otherwise stale assets. A jeweler, for example, will borrow 100 ounces of gold today for a cash payment, agreeing to return a like amount of gold in a year.

Figure 7.8 US private oil stocks versus weekly forward price spread, 1992–2004

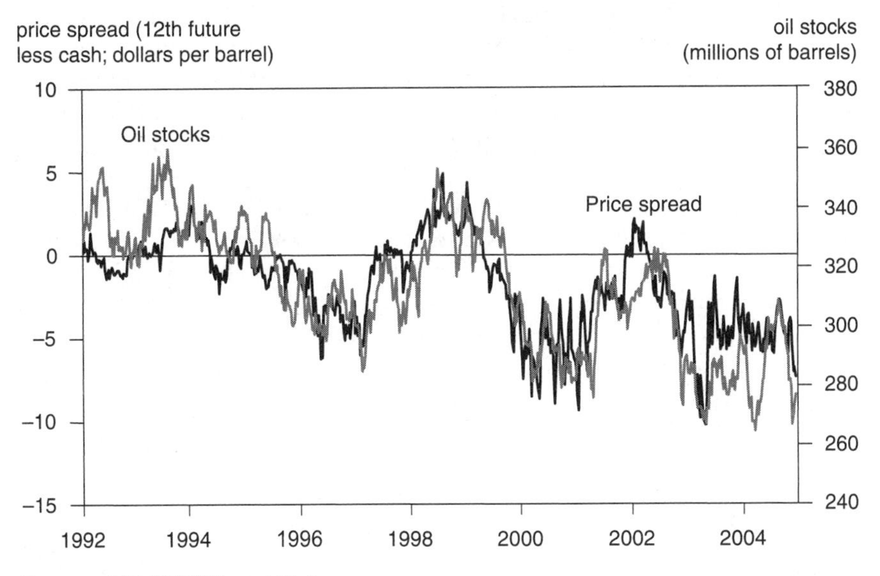

Sources: API, NYMEX, and Platts.

A swap transaction would promote contango in the market, thereby boosting the incentive of private firms to hold inventories. Buyers would enter such transactions when oil for forward delivery sold for less than oil offered for delivery today. For example, on October 21, 2004, the price quoted for immediate delivery of Brent crude oil was $50.46 per barrel. However, on that date a buyer could acquire Brent for delivery in December 2006 for $44.36, a $6-per-barrel discount compared with prompt supplies. Under an exchange program, buyers could have taken oil from government stocks on October 21, while purchasing oil to be returned to the government in December 2006. Such sales of oil for delivery in 2006 would increase inventories and lower spot prices, while simultaneously raising prices of oil to be delivered a year later.

The use of swap transactions as a means of encouraging private stock building would address the difficulty described by Bosworth and Lawrence. Policymakers would promote forward buying. Swaps of strategic stocks would reduce backwardation or might even convert backwardation to contango. The shift toward contango would cause private inventories to increase.

The potential effectiveness of the strategy can be seen from figure 7.8. This graph compares levels of private crude oil inventories in the United

States, measured in millions of barrels, with the spread between the 12th future and cash WTI. The spread is graphed against the left vertical axis. Inventories are graphed against the right vertical axis. The period of coverage is 1992 to 2004. A very clear relationship can be observed from figure 7.8. The graph confirms the conclusion that a buffer stock policy relying on swaps would promote private inventory accumulation. Had such a policy been in effect in 2004, it is very probable that oil prices never would have surpassed $40 per barrel.

To be fully successful, the next administration should negotiate a program to expand governmentally controlled stocks that would form the base of the buffer stock. The additional storage capacity would be filled whenever world oil production exceeded world demand. Governments would acquire inventories at times when prices fell below an agreed purchase threshold. For example, stocks would have been augmented in 1998 when crude prices dipped below $20 per barrel.

The creation of a guaranteed market for crude reduces the risk of investing in high-cost projects that promise to deliver large volumes of oil in three, four, or five years. Most forecasts of world energy supply-and-demand balances indicate that these supplies will be required within five to ten years. Yet, as already noted, many firms refuse to invest because they fear a repetition of the 1998 oil price collapse. Price stabilization at a level that brought out such investment would remove the destructive economic cycle of underinvestment that is inevitably followed by a period of very high prices and macroeconomic losses.

The negotiators of a stabilization agreement will confront two strong objections. First, authorities in oil-consuming countries have argued repeatedly that strategic stocks have been built to meet a disruption in global oil supplies. Second, representatives of oil-exporting countries will complain that the imposition of a price stabilization authority deprives them of control over the market.

The first objection can be met by expanding the scope of the stocks allocated to the stabilization of oil markets and meeting future disruptions. Public support for such stocks—and willingness to support them—will no doubt increase if consumers observe that these stocks mitigate oil price increases such as occurred in 2004. Ultimately, a swap policy that promoted private stock building may result in a higher level of global inventories than the current policy based on the creation of large, "sterilized" public stocks combined with essentially no private stocks.

The second objection must be met by a declaratory statement from oil consumers that oil producers will no longer be allowed to artificially raise the price of oil above competitive levels as they have from 2000 to 2004. In the end, oil-consuming nations have the capacity—through taxation of petroleum—to frustrate the cartel's effort to raise oil prices above the marginal costs of production. Further, oil-consuming nations can neutralize the coercive actions of some cartel members through the use of sanctions and fees on the imports of these countries.[35]

However, there should be no need for confrontation. One would hope that exporting and importing countries could quickly agree if consuming countries approach oil-exporting nations with a constructive proposal to stabilize prices in the price band advocated by OPEC for the last four years of $22 to $28 per barrel for a representative average of OPEC crudes. (The equivalent range for WTI would be $19 to $25 per barrel.) Agreement by the nations sponsoring the buffer stock to buy when world prices fall below $22 for the mix of OPEC crudes (the "OPEC basket") ought to convince exporting countries to cooperate with the effort.

Conclusion: Time Is Short and Action Is Required

Crude oil prices rose to record levels in 2004. In the next three years, they will climb even higher if action is not taken. Economic recession or worse will surely follow. It is not an exaggeration to say an economic storm of immense proportions lies just over the horizon.

In May 2001, President Bush called on Congress to pass a new energy policy. His request for action was correct; however the policies he put forward, even if adopted immediately, would do little to avoid the coming tumult. Today, the United States, the European Union, Japan, Russia, China, and OPEC members, particularly Saudi Arabia, must act as one to address this problem. Each country can take many steps by itself. However, the crisis can be avoided only if they all work together.

References

Akins, James E. 1973. The Oil Crisis: This Time the Wolf Is Here. *Foreign Affairs* 51, no. 3.

Bosworth, Barry P., and Robert Z. Lawrence. 1982. *Commodity Prices and the New Inflation.* Washington: Brookings Institution.

Dahl, Carol, and Thomas Sterner. 1991. Analyzing Gasoline Demand Elasticities: A Survey. *Energy Economics* 13, no. 3: 203–10.

Dipardo, Joseph. 2000. *Outlook for Biomass Ethanol Production and Demand.* Washington: Energy Information Agency, US Department of Energy. www.eia.doe.gov/oiaf/analysispaper/pdf/biomass.pdf.

35. In 1999 some OPEC members threatened non-OPEC oil-producing countries with dire economic consequences if they did not cut production. Several countries complied. Such coercion, if practiced by a private company, would be illegal in every OECD country. Any company caught engaging in such practices would be the subject of serious sanctions. Oil-consuming nations can impose similar sanctions on oil-exporting countries through the WTO if the exporter is a member, or through direct action if the country is not a member.

Dunkerley, Joy. 1990. *Patterns of Energy Use in Developing Nations*. New Delhi: Wiley Eastern Limited.

Energy Information Agency. 1990. *An Analysis of Increasing the Size of the Strategic Petroleum Reserve to One Billion Barrels*. SR/ICID/90-01. Washington: US Department of Energy.

Energy Information Agency. 2004. Summer Gasoline Update. *Short-Term Energy Outlook*. Washington: US Department of Energy. www.eia.doe.gov.

EPA (Environmental Protection Agency). 1999a. *Regulatory Impact Analysis—Control of Air Pollution from New Motor Vehicles: Tier 2 Motor Vehicle Emissions Standards and Gasoline Sulfur Control Requirements*. EPA420-R-99-023. Washington: US Government Printing Office.

EPA (Environmental Protection Agency). 1999b. *EPA's Program for Cleaner Vehicles and Cleaner Gasoline*. EPA420-F-99-051. Washington: US GPO. www.epa.gov/otaq/regs/ld-hwy/tier-2/pubs.htm.

EPA (Environmental Protection Agency). 2004. *Rollout of the Tier 2 Vehicle & Gasoline Sulfur Program*. EPA420-F-04-002. Washington: US Government Printing Office. www.epa.gov/otaq/regs/ld-hwy/tier-2/pubs.htm.

FTC (Federal Trade Commission, Bureau of Economics). 2004. *The Petroleum Industry: Mergers, Structural Change, and Antitrust Enforcement*. www.ftc.gov/os/2004/08/040813mergersinpetrolberpt.pdf.

Hamilton, James D. 1983. Oil and the Macroeconomy since World War II. *Journal of Political Economy* 91, no. 2: 228–48.

Hamilton, James D. 2003a. Historical Effects of Oil Shocks. University of California at San Diego. Photocopy.

Hamilton, James D. 2003b. What is an Oil Shock? *Journal of Econometrics* 113, no. 2: 363–98.

Houthakker, Hendrik, Philip K. Verleger Jr., and Dennis P. Sheehan. 1976. A Study of the Quarterly Demand for Gasoline and the Impacts of Alternative Gasoline Taxes. In *Econometric Studies of US Energy Policy*, ed., Dale Jorgenson. Amsterdam: North Holland Publishing Co.

IEA (International Energy Agency). 2004. *Analysis of the Impact of High Oil Prices on the Global Economy*. www.iea.org/Textbase/Papers/2004/High_Oil_Prices.pdf.

Jiménez-Rodríguez, R., and M. Sánchez. 2004. *Oil Price Shocks and Real GDP Growth, Empirical Evidence for Some OECD Countries*. European Central Bank Working Paper Series 362. Frankfurt: European Central Bank.

Lugar, Richard G., and R. James Woolsey. 1999. The New Petroleum. *Foreign Affairs* 78, no. 1 (January/February). www.lugar.senate.gov/new_petroleum.html.

NAS (National Academy of Sciences). 2002. *Effectiveness and Impact of Corporate Average Fuel Economy (CAFE) Standards*. Washington: National Academies Press.

Rocky Mountain Institute. 2004. *Winning the Oil Game*. Snowmass, CO: Rocky Mountain Institute.

Schultze, Charles L., and Edward R. Fried. 1975. *Higher Oil Prices and the World Economy: The Adjustment Problem*. Washington: Brookings Institution.

US Cabinet Task Force on Oil Import Control. 1970. *The Oil Import Question*. Washington: US Government Printing Office.

Verleger, Philip K., Jr. 1994. *Adjusting to Volatile Energy Prices*. Washington: Institute for International Economics.

Verleger, Philip K., Jr. 2004. Energy Policy Issues for EU-US Consideration. In *From Alliance to Coalitions—The Future of Transatlantic Relations*, ed., Werner Weidenfeld et al. Gûtersloh, Germany: Bertelsmann Foundation.

Williams, Jeffrey C. 1986. *The Economic Function of Futures Markets*. Cambridge, England: Cambridge University Press.

Williams, Jeffrey C., and Brian D. Wright. 1982. The Roles of Public and Private Storage in Managing Oil Import Disruptions. *The Bell Journal of Economics* 13: 341–53.

Appendix 7A
The BP Prudhoe Bay Trust's Link to WTI

The BP Prudhoe Bay Royalty Trust is a financial instrument created by BP in 1989. BP sold the trust approximately 16 percent of the first 90,000 barrels per day of production from the Prudhoe Bay unit. BP undertook to buy the production back from the trust as the oil was produced at a price that was tied to the spot price of West Texas intermediate (WTI) at Cushing as reported by *Platts*. More than 21 million shares were sold to the public, and the units trade on the New York Stock Exchange under the symbol BPT.

The trust is passive. BP manages the Prudhoe Bay unit, produces the oil, and credits the trust with revenue less certain costs specified at the time the shares were issued. The trustee cannot spend the trust's revenue on further development of the field. Instead, all revenue must be passed back to shareholders.

The amount of revenue received by the trust is equal to the WTI price less certain deductions that were specified in 1989. These costs include production, taxes, and fixed costs. The prospectus for the shares indicated that costs of $4.50 per barrel would be deducted from the revenues received when the unit was first issued. The prospectus also stated that the cost charge would be adjusted upward over time to reflect the rising cost of operation and inflation. The most recent 10Q filed by the trust indicates that charges of $15.71 per barrel were deducted in the fourth quarter of 2002. These charges will rise gradually over the next 10 years.

The trust will end after 2010 if shareholders vote to terminate it or if revenues after cost deductions are negative for two consecutive years after 2010. There will be no residual payment for shareholders when the unit terminates.

The absence of a residual payment combined with the structure of the quarterly dividend mean that investors buying shares in BPT buy one and only one thing: a stream of payments tied to the price of oil. The payments will rise if crude oil prices increase and fall if crude oil prices decrease.

The linkage of payments to the price of oil means that the discounted value of expected payments ought to be linked to the expected trend of future oil prices. Indeed, if the share price of BPT is uncorrelated with the overall stock market (i.e., the beta is zero), then the stream of expected dividends discounted by the risk-free interest rate should equal the share price.

The beta of BPT happens to be statistically insignificant, i.e., zero. This means that the projected revenues discounted by the risk-free interest rate can be used to determine investor expectations of oil prices. Expectations of price increases are calculated by trial and error as follows:

- A rate of price increase of WTI is assumed (say, 2 percent per year).
- The rate is translated into quarterly estimates of WTI prices.

- The dividend flow from today to 2020 is calculated given the projected WTI trajectory.
- Dividends are discounted by the price of zero-coupon US Treasury instruments of identical maturity. (For example, the price of treasuries expiring in 2006 is used to discount 2006 projected revenues.)
- Discounted dividends are summed and compared with the quoted share price of the BPT. If the sum exceeds the share price, the process is repeated with a lower rate of price increase. If the sum is less than the share price, a higher rate of increase is tried.

The calculation stops when the sum of discounted revenues equals the quoted share price. As noted in the January 2003 *Petroleum Economics Monthly*, share prices of BPT have been a good predictor of the trend in oil prices over a long period.

8

Confronting Current Challenges to US Trade Policy

JEFFREY J. SCHOTT

Trade policy is usually not at the top of the "to do" list of a new administration, but in early 2005 US officials will have to make several important decisions regarding both trade legislation and trade negotiations. Failure to do so could foreclose negotiating options and limit prospects for advancing US trade initiatives throughout the administration's term in office. Some of these choices will require the investment of political capital to ensure support for trade bills before Congress; others will require commitment of negotiating resources to bolster ongoing trade talks so that US objectives can be achieved in agreements concluded later in the term.

How times have changed! The United States has long been the world's leading trading nation, but US trade policy never used to be a central concern of US economic policy. In part, this is a remnant of bygone times when trade played only a small role in the US economy. In the 1960s, US merchandise exports and imports of goods together averaged about 6.7 percent of US GDP; by 2003, however, the trade/GDP ratio had almost tripled to 18 percent. Add services to the equation and the US ratio now reaches 23 percent (figure 8.1). In short, the US economy is now much more open to international trade than a generation ago.

Greater openness to trade confers substantial advantages for the US economy as a whole, though the aggregate benefits mask difficult adjust-

Jeffrey J. Schott is a senior fellow at the Institute for International Economics. *The author benefited from valuable comments from C. Fred Bergsten, Mac Destler, Kimberly Elliott, and other IIE colleagues on earlier drafts of this chapter.*

Figure 8.1 Ratio of US trade to GDP, 1960–2004

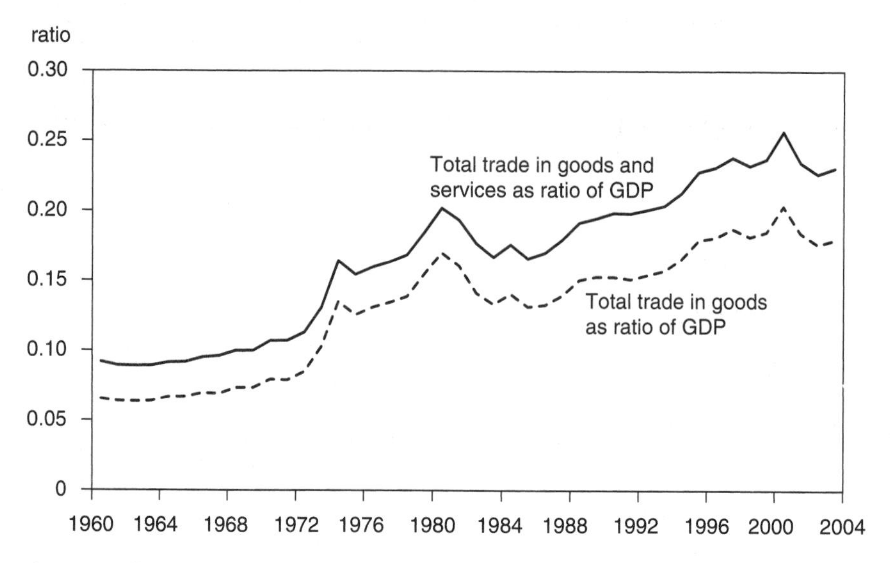

Sources: US Census Bureau (2004); Council of Economic Advisers, *Economic Report of the President* (2004).

ment burdens for some US firms and workers and their communities.[1] Consumers benefit from more choices and lower prices, as import competition dampens inflationary pressures. US companies that "consume" imports gain as well from access to better and/or cheaper inputs to their production of finished goods like autos or computers. Overall, openness has helped propel dramatic increases in US productivity by prompting companies to retool and restructure, and workers to retrain, to keep pace with global competition.

At the same time, however, greater openness means that US companies face stiffer competition at home and abroad, and US workers face greater uncertainty regarding job security and the maintenance of wages and benefits even though US unemployment levels remain relatively low. Record job creation in the 1990s occurred amid substantial churning in US labor markets in which millions of workers lost their jobs. Some workers found equal or better opportunities in the expanding US economy, while others suffered significant losses through prolonged unemployment or large wage cuts. Many more felt vulnerable to future job shocks (see the chapter by Lori Kletzer and Howard Rosen in this book).

1. Cumulatively, postwar trade reforms have raised US GDP by almost 6 percent, worth $600 billion in 2003 dollars. Eliminating all barriers to trade in goods and services—a task likely to progress incrementally and incompletely over the next decade—would increase US production by an additional $450 billion to $600 billion annually (see the chapter by Scott Bradford, Paul Grieco, and Gary C. Hufbauer in this book).

Table 8.1 US merchandise and services trade, 2002–04 (billions of dollars)

Year	Goods			Services			Goods and services balance
	Exports	Imports	Balance	Exports	Imports	Balance	
2002	681.8	1,165	–482.9	294.1	232.9	61.2	–421.7
2003	713.1	1,261	–547.6	307.4	256.3	51.1	–496.5
2004[a]	789.8	1,422	–632.4	335.1	284.1	51.0	–581.4

a. Data are for January-July 2004 at an annualized rate.

Source: US Department of Commerce, Bureau of Economic Analysis.

For the past two decades, succeeding US administrations have extolled the virtues of trade as an engine of job creation. At best, these promises have been misleading, since trade creates both winners and losers in the US economy.[2] By shifting resources from less productive to more productive sectors in the economy, trade affects the composition of jobs in the economy; in the aggregate, trade improves the "quality" of jobs, since exports generally support higher-paying and more secure jobs. But trade does not significantly influence the total level of employment, which is primarily determined by macroeconomic policies.

Nonetheless, the fear of job loss has been a powerful motivation for critics of trade and globalization more broadly. Concerns about globalization now color public attitudes and influence congressional deliberations on US trade policy and negotiations. As a result, the task of formulating and implementing US trade policy has become more complicated, just when US policymakers face two urgent tasks:

- to keep protectionist pressures at bay and to help reduce the massive US trade deficit; and
- to open new opportunities for US firms, workers, and farmers by reducing trade and investment barriers around the globe.

To date, calls for new protectionist measures have been limited (apart from the steel safeguards of 2002–03) despite the deterioration in the US trade accounts. The US merchandise trade deficit will exceed $600 billion in 2004 and has averaged more than 5 percent of GDP annually for the past three years. The traditional US surplus in services trade has been shrinking to less than $55 billion annually (table 8.1). As the US deficit in-

2. Consumers and investors generally benefit, while less-skilled laborers and factory workers often end up worse off. It is thus not surprising that support for freer trade among American workers broadly turns on their level of education; those with high school degrees or less are much more opposed to further increases in globalization than those with college and graduate degrees (Scheve and Slaughter 2001).

creases, however, pressures are mounting to do more—through both border controls (e.g., against Chinese goods) and new subsidies for US industries (which already have gotten a big financial fillip under the 2004 tax "reform"). To blunt these protectionist impulses, US policymakers will need to pursue domestic programs and international negotiations that promote US exports by competitive producers of goods and services while at the same time addressing the adjustment needs of import-competing industries and their workers.

This chapter details what the next administration needs to do to confront the challenges facing US trade policy in the coming years. Trade promotion authority (TPA) and other legislative initiatives require immediate attention to ensure that US officials have the requisite congressional mandate and guidance to conduct trade negotiations. At the same time, new efforts are needed to ensure that ongoing trade talks—particularly the Doha Round of multilateral trade negotiations—produce comprehensive results. In addition, US officials need to upgrade the United States' most important trade partnership, the North American Free Trade Agreement (NAFTA), to better meet the economic and security demands of the post-9/11 world. Finally, the next administration needs to reassess US policy regarding other free trade agreements (FTAs) and refocus efforts in areas with the biggest trade and foreign policy payoffs.

Domestic Trade Policy Agenda

By coincidence or design, the domestic trade policy agenda is congested right from the start of the next administration with contentious and politically sensitive issues. Several require legislative action *in the first half of 2005*; others involve crafting detailed negotiating proposals for ongoing multilateral, regional, and bilateral trade talks. In addition, trade officials are likely to be faced with petitions for import relief from the textile and apparel industries in the wake of the elimination of quotas under the Multi-Fiber Arrangement (MFA) at the end of 2004 and concerns about unfair foreign trade practices (especially by China).

Legislative Agenda

Trade issues will be prominent on the legislative agenda in 2005–06. By June 2005, Congress will likely hold two key trade votes. Both are mandated under existing statutory provisions. One involves the extension of TPA; the other concerns the continuation of US participation in the World Trade Organization (WTO). Congress may also be asked to consider several FTAs, which the president signed in 2004 but for which he had not previously submitted implementing legislation to Congress under the

TPA procedures. Trade officials undoubtedly will spend much of their time on Capitol Hill during the first half of 2005.

Trade Promotion Authority

Securing the extension of TPA is the highest priority. The Trade Act of 2002, as amended, provided for a two-year extension of the negotiating authority beyond its expiry on June 30, 2005—if the president requests it by April 1, 2005, and neither house of Congress disapproves before July 1, 2005 (Section 2103). Any member can request a vote to deny the extension of TPA, which could lead to a floor vote if reported out by one of the designated committees.[3]

The last time Congress was confronted with a vote to extend "fast-track" authority was in 1991. That debate focused on the use of fast-track procedures for the prospective negotiation of the NAFTA. Before the vote, congressional leaders demanded and received assurances from the administration that labor and environmental interests would be safeguarded in the NAFTA negotiations. The disapproval resolution was then defeated by 231 to 192 in the House and by 59 to 36 in the Senate (Destler 1995, 98–103). A similar debate could evolve in 2005 with TPA critics demanding either changes in existing provisions of the Central American Free Trade Agreement (CAFTA) or supplementary obligations added to the body of the agreement on labor and the environment, as a condition for extending TPA.

While it would be extremely disruptive for Congress to revoke the administration's negotiating mandate in the midst of ongoing trade talks, it is entirely possible that Congress could add—through separate legislation—new conditions on the use of fast-track implementing procedures.[4] Calls for product-specific exceptions from trade reforms, earmarked spending programs, and stricter trade enforcement provisions will likely flood the congressional debate on TPA extension.

Could US trade policy operate effectively if TPA is not extended? Without TPA, trade initiatives would be implemented through regular legislative procedures. Several sectoral trade pacts plus China's protocol of accession to the WTO passed Congress in the second Clinton administration despite the fact that fast-track authority (renamed TPA in 2002) lapsed in 1994. The rub is that none of those deals required significant change in existing US laws, regulations, or levels of trade protection. Without TPA, other countries probably would be unwilling to commit to reforming their own politically sensitive trade restrictions. Why risk inflaming one's own

3. In the House of Representatives, such resolutions are referred to the Committees on Ways and Means and on Rules, which must report them out before the resolutions can be considered on the floor.

4. The Trade Act of 2002 includes the exact wording of the extension resolution, which does not allow consideration of amendments to TPA provisions.

political constituencies if there is a good chance that Congress will balk at reciprocal liberalization of US barriers, or demand that the negotiations be reopened? At best, US officials would be offered second-best deals; at worst, trade talks would collapse (or never engage), subjecting US negotiators to involuntary retirement.[5]

WTO Participation

About the same time that Congress considers TPA extension, it will likely be required to take another trade vote on a resolution to withdraw from the WTO. Section 125 of the Uruguay Round Agreements Act of 1994 requires the president to report to Congress every five years on the costs and benefits of US participation in the WTO. After receipt of the president's report, both houses of Congress have 90 days to vote on a joint resolution calling for the withdrawal of US membership in the world trade body.[6] If adopted, the withdrawal resolution is subject to presidential veto, in which case Congress has an additional 15 days to override the veto. The first WTO withdrawal vote took place in June 2000; the withdrawal resolution was rejected by a vote of 35 to 0 by the House Ways and Means Committee, and by 363 to 56 by the full House.

The WTO vote in 2005 could be more contested, in part due to a number of controversial WTO rulings against the United States in dispute settlement cases. Overall, the United States has a strong winning record in disputes that it has brought to the WTO but has lost many of the cases brought by others against US trade practices. In particular, WTO dispute panels have found that the US foreign sales corporation (FSC), US cotton subsidies, the Byrd amendment, and other specific provisions of antidumping law violate WTO obligations.[7] When US policies have not been brought into conformity with WTO norms, WTO members have received multilateral authorization to retaliate against US exports to their markets (as the European Union has done in the FSC case). The "scorecard" for WTO rulings involving the United States is summarized in table 8.2.

Recent WTO rulings against the United States have prompted criticism from members of Congress. Ironically, the new authorities vested in WTO panels derived from US demands at the start of the Uruguay Round in the

5. Arguments for and against fast-track procedures were actively debated in the late 1990s and reported in Schott (1998).

6. This period is actually longer than three months because it excludes most days when either the House or the Senate is not in session (see section 154 (b) of the Trade Act of 1974).

7. Unlike many other countries, the language of the agreements is not directly included into US statutes; rather, implementing legislation revises US law to conform to the new trade obligations. Some WTO violations have resulted from how Congress interpreted US obligations when crafting that legislation. In other cases, Congress passed and the president signed laws—like the Byrd amendment—that many experts thought would not pass WTO challenge.

Table 8.2 US record in WTO dispute resolution cases, 1995–2004 (number of cases and percent)

	Total	Won	Mixed result	Lost	Pending or inactive	Won and/or mixed (percent)
United States as complainant	71	22	22[a]	4	23	62
United States as respondent	72	10	14[b]	25	23	33

a. USTR defines as won on core issues.
b. USTR defines as resolved without completing litigation.

Source: US Trade Representative, WTO Dispute Settlement Proceedings, www.ustr.gov/Trade_Agreements/Monitoring_Enforcement/Dispute_Settlement/WTO/Section_ Index.html (accessed October 2004).

late 1980s. In the Trade Act of 1988, Congress made the establishment of a strong system of dispute resolution one of the highest US priorities in those talks to ensure that the new rule-making obligations under negotiation in areas like services and intellectual property would be enforceable. By the end of the Uruguay Round, however, Congress had second thoughts about giving up US power to block dispute rulings as in the past. Senator Robert Dole (R-KS) proposed a "three strikes and out" procedure in which the Congress could vote to quit the WTO if a panel of former federal judges found that three dispute rulings wrongly went against the United States. The Dole amendment failed. However, Congressman Newt Gingrich (R-GA) won approval of a simpler proposal requiring that the administration report every five years on US participation in the WTO, at which time Congress could vote by joint resolution to withdraw from the organization.

Because the effect of WTO withdrawal would be so disruptive to US production, trade, and employment, it is extremely unlikely that such a resolution would pass and override a certain presidential veto, but defeating the resolution also could be costly if it requires acceptance of new negotiating constraints or other types of political side payments. The timing of the vote will depend on when the president issues his report on US participation in the WTO. Since the second five-year period ends on December 31, 2004, the report presumably should be presented in early 2005 after the new Congress convenes, with the prospective vote on the withdrawal resolution in late spring.[8] Members of Congress thus could face two trade votes during May–June 2005.

8. President Clinton's report on the WTO was issued on March 2, 2000, as part of the annual report to Congress on the US trade policy agenda and on the operation of the US trade agreements program. The House of Representatives rejected the resolution on June 21, 2000.

Ratification of FTAs

In July 2004, the House and the Senate approved by wide margins legislation implementing FTAs concluded with Australia and Morocco.[9] However, several FTAs signed in 2004 still await congressional ratification. The most politically contentious of these pacts is the CAFTA, where some Democrats have demanded that the pact be renegotiated prior to congressional action. FTAs with Bahrain and the Dominican Republic (which has been integrated in the CAFTA) are also part of this legislative backlog. The longer the delay in implementing these pacts, the less US firms and workers (and US trading partners) will benefit from the trade reforms—and thus the harder it will be to maintain political support for the pacts. For the CAFTA countries in particular, a key benefit of the pact is the head start that they get over other Latin American and Asian countries in securing open access to the US market and in attracting foreign investment to their economies.

The TPA and CAFTA debates may become intertwined politically, thus perhaps forcing a delay in submission of CAFTA legislation until after Congress acts on the extension of TPA implementing procedures. Rejection of CAFTA, or even prolonged deferment of congressional action, would have negative consequences both for US relations with Central America and for the pursuit of other FTAs with developing countries.

Opposition to CAFTA comes primarily from US sugar producers, labor unions, and some textile firms. The unions criticize the pact's limited labor obligations and enforcement procedures (even though—unlike NAFTA—those provisions are included in the core agreement).[10] Textile and sugar producers oppose CAFTA because it subjects them to more competition in the US market.

Neither critique justifies scrapping the trade deal. The protectionist demands of the sugar and textile industries are straightforward; the problems with labor (and the environment) are more complex and require additional explanation.

In a nutshell, the labor critique about CAFTA is that the pact (1) only requires the Central American countries to enforce their own national laws, which are deemed too weak to ensure conformity with international core labor standards codified by the International Labor Organization (ILO);[11] (2) omits some CAFTA obligations on labor from the pact's dispute settlement regime; and (3) is inadequate to deter abuses (which have been com-

9. The Australia FTA passed the House by 314 to 109 and the Senate by 80 to 16. The Morocco FTA passed by 323 to 99 in the House and 85 to 13 in the Senate.

10. The same critique has been applied by environmental lobbies to CAFTA's environmental provisions.

11. The ILO standards cover freedom of association, abolition of forced and child labor, and nondiscrimination. See Elliott (2004).

monplace in much of the region) because the enforcement provisions provide minimal penalties for violations of CAFTA's labor obligations. These concerns are echoed by many members of Congress as the reason why implementing legislation for the CAFTA was put on hold in 2004.

Labor abuses persist in Central America; the question is how to reduce their frequency and improve working conditions in the region. Given severe budgetary constraints in Central America, and limited financial assistance from the United States, CAFTA critics favor strengthening both CAFTA's labor obligations and noncompliance penalties to pressure those countries to crack down on abusive labor practices. They argue that the CAFTA should have provided the same recourse to trade sanctions, as in the US-Jordan FTA. But the sanctions issue is a red herring. For such provisions to be acceptable to US trading partners, recourse to retaliation has to be so severely constrained as to make the use of those provisions extremely unlikely. That is true as well for the US-Jordan precedent. As a practical matter, there is no difference between the Jordan and CAFTA enforcement standards.

The labor provisions included in the FTAs attempt to balance concerns of: (1) US partner countries that easy-to-use trade sanctions would be abused; (2) US business lobbies that FTA obligations could force changes in US labor laws; and (3) labor unions that the threat of retaliation would deter labor abuses. The compromise reached in these FTAs has been to include new obligations on labor practices, cooperative projects to promote labor reforms, and dispute settlement via monetary fines or trade sanctions in cases where cooperation among the partner countries breaks down.

As a practical matter, CAFTA's shortcoming is inadequate commitment to labor and training programs as well as administration of existing laws and monitoring of compliance. The CAFTA contains annexes that establish cooperative programs to deal with labor and environmental problems in Central America. Putting these good intentions into action, however, has been constrained by inadequate funding. The next administration should provide greater support for these initiatives. With financial incentives from the United States, on top of funds provided by the Inter-American Development Bank, these countries also might be more willing to augment their national laws to expand protections of core labor standards.

Farm Bill

Last, but not least, the next Congress will need to begin work on legislation that will have a profound effect on US trade policy for the rest of the decade—the new farm bill. The US Farm Security and Rural Investment Act of 2002 runs for six years through the end of the 2007 crop year. Some US farm programs have been found to contravene WTO obligations; reforms of some others have been promised in the Doha Round of WTO negotiations in return for reciprocal cuts in subsidies provided to foreign farmers and market access reforms.[12] As the WTO negotiations advance, US trade officials will have to work closely with the agriculture committees to ensure that what is on offer in the Doha Round is compatible with what is under consideration in the legislative process.

US farm programs can be revised through a new farm bill or Doha Round implementing legislation, or both. Given the likely timetable for the WTO talks, the next farm bill will probably set the parameters, and provide more specific negotiating guidelines, for the final Doha Round deal.

All the major US farm lobbies supported the initial US farm proposals in the Doha Round, tabled just two months after President Bush signed the 2002 farm bill, which called for radical reductions in farm subsidies and border protection as part of a comprehensive package of agreements in the Doha Round. Their rationale was clear, since other countries support their farmers more generously than the United States. For example, on average OECD farmers received 31 percent of their gross farm receipts through transfers from consumers and taxpayers (measured by the producer support estimate, or PSE) during 2001–03, while the average PSE was 20 percent for the United States, 35 percent for the European Union, 58 percent for Japan, and 64 percent for Korea. For specific products, the differences among countries can be much greater (OECD 2004). A big WTO deal on agriculture is feasible, involving substantial cuts in farm subsidies and border protection, if it substantially narrows the gap between the permissible amount of farm support provided to European and other farmers compared with US farmers and includes reforms by middle-income developing countries.

In short, the success of the Doha Round depends importantly on reaching agreement on substantial agricultural reforms—and thus directly as well on what Congress includes in the next farm bill. The need to reduce the large US budget deficit adds urgency to the task of scaling back expensive farm programs. Making a virtue of necessity, Congress should reduce or eliminate some of the generous programs added to the 2002 farm bill to help both reduce the budget deficit and spur reciprocal reforms in other WTO member countries.

Fallout from MFA Reform

On January 1, 2005, the United States and other industrial countries will eliminate their quotas on imports of textiles and apparel from developing countries, which have been in effect for the past three decades under the

12. Deliberations on the farm bill may also have to address how to handle US cotton subsidies, which have been found by a dispute panel to contravene WTO obligations. If the US appeal of that ruling fails, then the WTO will likely require that US programs be brought into conformity with WTO rules within the normal compliance period of 15 months.

Multi-Fiber Arrangement (MFA). Other forms of protection for those industries will remain in force. Imported goods will still face US tariffs that average 6.6 percent for textile mill products (mainly yarns and fabrics) and 11.3 percent for clothing;[13] in addition, those goods will continue to be vulnerable to antidumping and countervailing duty actions as well as safeguard measures. Imports from China are subject to special and more stringent controls under those US statutes. Efforts to delay the elimination of the MFA quotas are designed in part to stiffen resistance to reducing these remaining protections in the Doha Round.

Even with quotas in place, and other trade barriers in effect or in reserve, US industries have faced increasingly sharp import competition, particularly from East Asian suppliers. Total US apparel imports have increased in value by more than 70 percent since the WTO entered into force in 1995 and in 2003 exceeded $70 billion. China accounted for 17 percent of the total, increasing its lead over Mexico substantially over the past three years as the main source of imports to the US market (Nordås 2004).[14]

In large measure, Chinese shipments have been growing at the expense of other foreign suppliers; for some products, the growth has been so rapid that it already provoked the imposition of special and discriminatory textile and clothing safeguards against China that are allowed under China's protocol of accession to the WTO.[15] Some econometric forecasts suggest that, after removal of the MFA quotas, China could capture in short order about half of the US import market. However, a survey of these forecasts conducted by WTO economists argues that the increase will be tempered, inter alia because (1) existing tariffs and preferential arrangements will continue to benefit suppliers in FTA partner countries, especially those closer to the importing country than the distant Asian suppliers;[16] and (2) Chinese competitiveness is greater in low-value-added products compared with the higher-end fashion segment of the market shipped by higher-wage countries.

Nonetheless, imports from China probably will grow substantially, and demands for import relief by US industry will become more strident. The specter of a broader surge of Chinese imports triggered new petitions for import relief in the fall of 2004 and is likely to be supplemented with additional demands in 2005 after the quotas are lifted. The next administration will be required to consider these petitions at the same time that it

13. The data are trade-weighted average tariffs in 2002 for these product sectors. See USITC (2004).

14. The Chinese total does not include clothing imports from Hong Kong, valued at $4 billion in 2003.

15. See Hufbauer and Wong (2004, appendix A) for a description of the safeguard and antidumping remedies available to blunt import surges from China.

16. Nordås (2004, 33) cites studies that argue "that distance matters because of its correlation with time to market, not primarily because of transport costs."

will be working with Congress to pass important trade legislation—and the issues will almost inevitably be joined in congressional deliberations and bargaining over the extension of TPA.

Rebuilding the Trade Coalition

Rebuilding the bipartisan support for US trade policies—which progressively weakened in the postwar period and substantially unraveled since the fractious NAFTA debates of a decade ago—is critical to the achievement of US objectives. It won't be an easy task.

Over the past decade, US trade politics has become more salient but more contentious. Congress (and particularly the House) often has been sharply divided on trade. Major trade bills have provoked fractious debates and close votes in the House: NAFTA passed in 1993 by a vote of 234 to 200, fast-track legislation was withdrawn before a negative vote in 1997 and then rejected in 1998, and the Trade Act of 2002 (including TPA and trade adjustment assistance [TAA]) cleared by 215 to 212. Only the Uruguay Round Agreements Act of 1994 passed with relative ease by a vote of 288 to 146.

In part, fractious congressional debates on trade reflect increasing partisanship on a broad range of issues dividing Democrats and Republicans. In addition, trade politics has become more complicated because of the success of past trade negotiations in reducing border trade barriers. Trade talks no longer are limited to the arcane world of tariffs and quotas. Instead, they target farm subsidies, regulatory policies on food safety, telecommunications and financial services, and protection of intellectual property rights as well as border barriers to trade. As a consequence, politicians now worry about how trade agreements will affect domestic programs of concern to their constituents.

The broader trade agenda also means that more members of Congress want to be involved in trade policymaking. The Senate Finance and House Ways and Means Committees no longer hold sole jurisdiction on trade matters, which are now also vetted by the Agriculture, Banking, and Judiciary Committees among others. Such diversity helps inform the congressional debate but complicates the process of building support for big trade initiatives.

Rebuilding the traditional majority in Congress in favor of more open US trade policies will likely require a mix of major domestic policy reforms and substantial liberalization of foreign trade barriers of interest to US farmers, workers, and companies. Strengthening US worker assistance programs to better meet the needs of those who suffer job dislocations is important; so, too, are trade initiatives that address labor and environmental problems of interest to Democratic members. However, such policies risk weakening support among business and other groups that have been the core supporters of US trade policy. Balancing these competing interests will be a challenge for both parties and test executive branch–congressional relations in the new administration.

International Trade Agenda

While priority attention must be focused on the "domestic" negotiations just discussed, the next administration also will have to confront a large, unfinished agenda of trade negotiations. The Doha Round has been revived but is far from complete. The negotiation of the Free Trade Area of the Americas (FTAA), involving the 34 democratic countries of the Western Hemisphere, has lagged as well. The NAFTA has entered its second decade with notable achievements; however, important new challenges to regional trade and investment have arisen since 9/11, which need to be addressed by the three partners in the context of their North American compact. In addition, FTA talks with the Southern African Customs Union (SACU), plus those started in 2004 with Colombia, Ecuador, Panama, Peru, and Thailand, will likely spill over into 2005 with the hardest issues left for last, and negotiations will begin with Oman and the United Arab Emirates in early 2005. The new administration will also need to decide to accept or defer requests from other countries to join in new FTA negotiations.[17]

Before turning to these trade initiatives, it is worth examining who the United States actually trades with and why it negotiates with them in bilateral, regional, and multilateral fora.

US Trading Partners and Trade Negotiating Objectives

The United States has global trading interests, but about $1.4 trillion or 70 percent of US merchandise trade takes place in a few key markets. In 2003, NAFTA partners Canada and Mexico accounted for 32 percent of total US exports and imports, the European Union (EU-15) took another 20 percent, and China and Japan each about 9 percent. These countries also host two-thirds of US foreign direct investment (FDI) abroad and account for 82 percent of FDI in the United States (table 8.3). Adding the other countries that have concluded or are negotiating FTAs with the United States brings the cumulative total to $1.6 trillion or more than 80 percent of total US merchandise trade (see tables 8.3 and 8.4).

This pattern of trade explains a lot about US trade negotiating objectives and priorities. For the major US trading partners, trade barriers are generally low due to GATT reforms and/or bilateral FTAs that give US exporters preferential access to that market. However, some intractable prob-

17. For example, Pakistan, Sri Lanka, and Taiwan have actively lobbied for FTAs with the United States, and others seek to negotiate FTAs in the context of the Middle East and East Asian trade initiatives (Schott 2004).

Table 8.3 Main US trading partners, 2003 (billions of dollars)

Partner	Exports[a]	Imports[b]	Trade balance	FDI in United States[c]	US FDI abroad[c]
NAFTA	267	362	–95	112	254
EU-15	151	245	–94	856	845
China	28	152	–124	n.a.	12
Japan	52	118	–66	159	73
World total	724	1,259	–536	1,378	1,789

n.a. = not available
FDI = foreign direct investment
NAFTA = North American Free Trade Agreement

a. "Free alongside ship" value of total exports.
b. Customs value of general imports.
c. Historical-cost basis, year-end 2003.

Sources: USITC Dataweb (2004); US Department of Commerce, Bureau of Economic Analysis (2004).

lems remain, particularly in agriculture (e.g., European farm subsidies and Japanese rice and Canadian dairy restrictions) and services, but also involving compliance with WTO norms (e.g., Chinese protection of intellectual property, restrictions on genetically modified crops, and operations of state-trading enterprises). In these areas, bilateral initiatives by the United States have not been sufficient to overcome strong political resistance to reform of those foreign practices. Progress on these matters will require a bigger deal that can only be crafted in multilateral negotiations. Most of them are under discussion in the Doha Round.

While the major industrial countries will continue to be the most important US trading partners, US trade officials also need to work more closely with partners in the developing world, for two reasons. First, agreement among the industrial countries is still necessary but no longer sufficient to conclude global trade talks. As the WTO ministerial in Cancún in September 2003 plainly demonstrated, the interests of developing countries have to be addressed if talks are to succeed in a forum where decisions are taken by consensus of the large membership. Second, the best prospects for US export growth probably lie in expanding trade with developing countries like Brazil, China, India, Indonesia, and Malaysia, among others. Liberalization of the generally much higher barriers to those markets could open substantial new opportunities for US trading interests.

Compared with its trading partners, average US tariffs on farm and industrial products are low, and nontariff barriers are scattered and relatively benign. Table 8.5 compares the US most favored nation (MFN) tariffs with those applied by the major US trading partners. Simple tariff averages can mask substantial variations in protection among products, but the differences are noteworthy. In agriculture, only Hong Kong and Malaysia maintain lower average tariffs, while tariff barriers in Nigeria,

Table 8.4 Current and prospective US FTA partners

Partner	2003 GDP[a] (billions of dollars)	2003 GDP per capita (dollars)	US merchandise trade, 2003			
			Exports to[b] (billions of dollars)	Imports from[c] (billions of dollars)	Trade balance (billions of dollars)	Total two-way trade (billions of dollars)
Current FTA partners						
Canada	867	27,408	169.5	224.2	–54.7	393.6
Mexico	626	6,121	97.5	138.1	–40.6	235.5
Chile	72	4,568	2.7	3.7	–1.0	6.4
Singapore	91	21,492	16.6	15.2	1.4	31.7
Jordan	10	1,858	0.5	0.7	–0.2	1.2
Israel	109	16,228	13.1	12.8	0.3	25.9
Australia	508	25,553	6.9	6.4	0.5	13.3
Morocco	45	1,481	0.5	0.4	0.1	0.9
Subtotal			**307.3**	**401.5**	**–94.2**	**708.5**
FTAs subject to ratification						
Bahrain	9	13,028	0.5	0.4	0.1	0.9
CAFTA-5	60	1,690	10.9	12.4	–1.5	23.3
Dominican Republic	16	1,827	4.2	4.5	–0.2	8.7
Subtotal			**15.6**	**17.2**	**–1.7**	**32.8**
FTAs under negotiation						
Colombia	81	1,835	3.8	6.4	–2.6	10.1
Ecuador	27	2,082	1.4	2.7	–1.3	4.2
Peru	61	2,233	1.7	2.4	–0.7	4.1
Panama	13	4,339	1.8	0.3	1.5	2.1
Thailand	143	2,309	5.8	15.2	–9.3	21.0
SACU-5	177	3,412	2.9	5.3	–2.4	8.2
Subtotal			**17.4**	**32.3**	**–14.8**	**49.7**
Other FTAA[d]	776	2,835	23.0	44.8	–21.8	67.8
United States	10,985	37,745	723.7	1,259.4	–535.7	1,983.1

CAFTA-5 = Costa Rica, El Salvador, Guatemala, Honduras, and Nicaragua
SACU-5 = Botswana, Lesotho, Namibia, South Africa, and Swaziland

a. GDP is in current US dollars.
b. "Free alongside ship" value of total exports.
c. Customs value of general imports.
d. Includes the following countries: Belize, Bolivia, Caribbean islands (Bahamas, Antigua and Barbuda, Barbados, Jamaica, Netherlands Antilles, St. Kitts and Nevis, St. Lucia, St. Vincent and Grenadines, Dominica, Grenada, Haiti, and Trinidad and Tobago) Suriname, Guyana, Mercosur-4, and Venezuela.

Sources: For GDP: IMF *World Economic Outlook* (2004); for trade: USITC Dataweb, http://dataweb.usitc.gov.

Table 8.5 Tariffs of US trading partners

Country	Total trade with United States, 2003 (billions of dollars)	MFN applied tariffs, 2002 (simple average, percent)				
				All products		
		Agriculture	Nonagriculture	Applied	Bound	Tariff gap[a]
United States[b]		4.7	3.8	3.9	3.6	–0.3
EU-15	396	5.9	4.2	4.4	4.1	–0.3
Canada	394	3.0	4.3	4.1	5.1	1.0
Mexico	236	23.4	17.1	17.9	34.9	17.0
China	181	19.2	11.3	12.4	10.0	–2.4
Japan[b]	170	7.1	2.7	3.3	2.9	–0.4
Korea[b]	61	45.5	7.5	12.4	16.1	3.7
Taiwan[b]	49	17.3	6.3	7.8	6.1	–1.7
Malaysia[b]	36	2.1	8.1	7.3	14.5	7.2
Brazil[b]	29	12.5	14.9	14.6	31.4	16.8
Hong Kong	22	0.0	0.0	0.0	0.0	0.0
India[b]	18	37.0	30.5	31.4	49.8	18.4
Philippines	18	9.2	5.2	5.7	25.6	19.9
Indonesia	12	8.2	6.7	6.9	37.1	30.2
Nigeria	11	53.9	26.3	30.0	118.4	88.4
Turkey[b]	7	42.2	5.5	10.2	29.4	19.2
Egypt	4	22.8	19.4	19.9	37.2	17.3
Pakistan[b]	3	22.0	19.9	20.1	52.4	32.3

MFN = most favored nation

a. Tariff gap = bound minus applied rates

b. Refers to countries with 2001 tariff data.

Sources: WTO *World Trade Report* 2003; USITC Dataweb, US Trade by Geographic Regions.

Korea, Turkey, and India are about 10 times higher than the US average. In nonagricultural sectors, the tariffs protecting the developed-country markets average about 3 to 4 percent; in comparison, some developing countries have lowered their average tariffs to less than 10 percent (Philippines, Taiwan, Indonesia, Korea, and Malaysia), while others maintain tariff walls of 15 percent (Brazil) to 30 percent (India). While many developing countries have reduced their tariffs over the past decade, they have not necessarily "bound" that liberalization in their WTO schedules and can thus raise them at any time without violating WTO obligations. The "tariff gap" between the bound and applied tariffs (averaged across all products) is most pronounced for Nigeria (88 percentage points), Pakistan, and Indonesia (more than 30), but also is substantial for the Philippines, Turkey, India, Brazil, and Egypt (17 to 20).

To be sure, there are a few notable exceptions in agriculture and apparel where US restrictions remain high. The US International Trade Commission (2004) reported that the combined effect of tariffs and quotas in 2002 conferred effective protection of 109 percent for sugar, 38 percent for dairy, and 20 percent for tobacco and apparel. Clearly, protection that has survived the past eight rounds of multilateral trade reforms benefits politically powerful interests.

Therein lies the challenge for US trade officials: The remaining US trade negotiating chips are politically sensitive items and will require large concessions from US trading partners to convince Congress to change existing practices. To get congressional support for changes in long-standing US trade barriers, US negotiators need to bring home agreements that offer substantial new trading opportunities for US farmers, manufacturers, and services industries.

What does Congress want US trade officials to bring home from the negotiating table? US negotiating objectives are as broad ranging as the countries with which the United States trades. The Trade Act of 2002 lists 16 key US objectives in bilateral, regional, and multilateral trade negotiations, encompassing "traditional" issues like tariffs and quotas as well as trade-related policies on intellectual property, labor, and the environment. Not all of the objectives need be achieved in each trade pact. In some areas, progress is more feasible in FTAs than in the WTO (e.g., intellectual property rights); in others, results are possible only through agreement on multilateral disciplines (e.g., domestic farm subsidies). Some issues have been excluded from the WTO agenda (e.g., labor practices, investment, and competition policy) and currently can be vetted only in bilateral or regional talks. In those cases, FTA provisions could establish precedents for possible future WTO accords. Note, however, that adding those issues to WTO talks would likely require a "rebalancing" of the negotiating agenda to include issues of priority to developing countries—such as fundamental antidumping reform and new exceptions to obligations on intellectual property rights.

Each type of negotiation presents different opportunities to advance US trade objectives. The bilateral initiatives can help catalyze broader regional reforms and build alliances in support of multilateral initiatives in the WTO. Success in the WTO in turn can help minimize the adverse effects of trade diversion generated by FTA trade preferences and help ensure that the bilateral and regional initiatives complement the objectives of the multilateral trading system. US officials should take advantage of them all, and thus follow the precedents of the past two decades, in both Republican and Democratic administrations, by pursuing a multitrack trade negotiating strategy that links bilateral, regional, and multilateral trade initiatives.

Completing the Doha Round

As the world's leading trading nation, the United States has substantial interests in the successful conclusion of the Doha Round of multilateral trade negotiations. Global trade reforms provide the biggest bang for the US negotiating buck, even though the outcomes may not eliminate border barriers to trade as FTAs seek to do.[18] Even partial liberalization of existing trade barriers could yield global welfare gains of almost $700 billion, of which about one-quarter would accrue to the United States (Brown, Deardorff, and Stern 2003). A new round is also needed to fix the problems that have arisen in the WTO's first decade of operation (e.g., dispute settlement reforms) and to augment the trading rules to keep pace with the rapidly changing developments in world commerce in goods and services (e.g., electronic commerce).

As in previous GATT rounds, the United States was the key *demandeur* of the Doha Round for both economic and foreign policy reasons. From the US perspective, the launch of new WTO negotiations in November 2001 served three critical purposes: first, it sent a signal that the United States and others would resist growing protectionist demands despite deepening economic slumps in the United States, Europe, and Japan; second, it promoted development and growth in member countries; and third, the new WTO initiative helped solidify the international alliance of nations working together to confront global terrorism just two months after the tragic events of September 11, 2001. Indeed, some of the countries that previously had been reluctant to engage in new WTO talks became key allies in the war on terrorism and supported the launch of new negotiations.

After an early flush of activity, spurred by the passage of TPA and marked by radical US proposals to slash agricultural protection and to eliminate industrial tariffs by 2015, the negotiating momentum soon

18. WTO negotiations elicit incremental reforms from the now 148 member countries, although the least developed countries generally are required to make only token contributions.

ebbed. Many WTO members were skeptical that the United States would abandon the generous new subsidies promised in its 2002 farm bill, or that the European Union would recast its Common Agricultural Policy. In addition, the Doha Round was burdened by sharp differences on access to medicines and WTO obligations on patents and strident demands from developing countries for special and differential treatment.

Talks languished until the summer of 2003, when EU negotiators finally received a new negotiating mandate on agriculture. By that point, Geneva negotiators had failed to meet their assigned deadline to agree on "modalities" for farm trade talks. Indeed, Geneva officials missed *every* negotiating deadline set in the Doha Declaration, leading ministers to inaugurate a series of ad hoc meetings, called "mini-ministerials," to try to circumvent the roadblocks erected in the WTO talks in Geneva. While these meetings achieved at least an interim solution to the dispute on patent rights and access to medicines, they failed to narrow differences on agriculture—especially regarding cutbacks in subsidies disbursed by the United States and the European Union—which was a high priority for many developing countries.

Fearing failure at the upcoming WTO ministerial in Cancún, Mexico, in September 2003, participants at the July 2003 mini-ministerial held in Montreal asked US and EU trade officials to put forward a new proposal on farm trade reform before the Cancún meeting. The subsequent US-EU proposal closely followed the recently minted EU negotiating mandate and called for few changes in existing US and EU farm policies. The reaction was immediate and harsh; Brazil, China, India, and South Africa organized a new coalition of prominent developing countries (the G-20) to oppose the transatlantic proposal.[19] The backlash against the US-EU compromise contributed importantly to the breakdown in negotiations at Cancún.

The G-20 was founded—and still exists in large measure—to push the United States, Europe, and Japan to liberalize their barriers to agricultural trade. That position is not antithetical to US interests and objectives in the Doha Round, provided that the large and middle-income developing countries in the group also reduce barriers to trade in their markets. Indeed, the United States and Brazil share key objectives regarding agriculture in the WTO and should be working together to advance their common interests.

WTO members finally did agree in July 2004 on new guidelines for the negotiation of global trade reforms in agriculture, industrial products, and services. Members also agreed to launch new negotiations on customs reform and other so-called trade facilitation measures and to delete

19. While united on their demands for reform by industrial countries, the G-20 members could not agree on a common position for their own contributions, provoking the ire of US and other officials.

the other "Singapore issues" (investment, competition policy, and transparency in government procurement) from the negotiating agenda.

However, the progress achieved at that meeting simply revived talks that had been stalled since the failed Cancún ministerial in September 2003. Priority was given to clarifying negotiating options on agriculture. In the area of nonagricultural market access (NAMA), officials merely accepted as a basis for further negotiation the disputed text that had been tabled in Cancún. On services, the WTO Council offered only a charge to try harder to table requests and offers. In all areas, decisions on the most contentious issues were deferred.

Clearly, extensive work remains on all issues on the Doha Round agenda before hard decisions can be taken to reduce trade barriers and trade-distorting subsidies protecting agriculture, manufacturing, and services industries. Substantial results will be needed in all three areas. To get the United States, Europe, and Japan to commit to significant reforms in long-standing protection in agriculture and some manufacturing sectors, other WTO members—including middle-income developing countries—need to offer concrete reductions in their protection as well. To date, developing countries have objected to lowering their own generally much higher trade barriers without increased and more secure access to industrial markets. Now that the United States, European Union, and Japan have signed onto the new WTO framework for farm negotiations, signaling their willingness to change their current policies *in the context of an overall WTO deal*, substantive talks can be reengaged in all areas of the Doha Round agenda.

The next big test of the Doha Round takes place in December 2005 at the WTO ministerial in Hong Kong. That meeting will surely not conclude the negotiations but needs to produce an agreement on specific numbers or ranges for the depth of cuts in agriculture and NAMA and on specific areas in which countries will commit to augment existing GATS obligations.[20] Only then can negotiators develop a final package of agreements—hopefully limiting exceptions and special treatment for sensitive products—a task that will take at least another year. Thus, a more realistic deadline for the Doha Round may now be the expiration of TPA in June 2007 (if extended by Congress in 2005).

Agriculture, of course, holds the key—though not because of its importance in international trade (less than 10 percent of global merchandise trade). Farm trade barriers remain high in both developed and developing countries, and many developing countries could reap large dividends from policy reform. Without agricultural reforms, developing countries probably will balk at liberalizing their own trade barriers in services and

20. Including in the area of labor services, where reforms could yield new export opportunities for developing countries. But commitments will need to be carefully tailored to safeguard security interests and to avoid conflict with immigration policies.

industrial products—which are generally much higher than those in the OECD area. Without contributions in those areas by at least the middle-income developing countries—including market access reforms—it is hard to see how the OECD countries could agree on a deal to sharply reduce farm subsidies and border protection. In short, a big package of farm reforms may be the sine qua non of the overall Doha Round accords.

Based on the WTO Council decision in July 2004, WTO negotiators agreed to eliminate export subsidies, substantially reduce domestic farm support that distorts prices and production decisions, and implement tariff cuts/quota increases that expand trade opportunities for foreign suppliers. Concrete results are needed in all three areas of the agricultural negotiations for the Doha Round to succeed.

Eliminating export subsidies is the easiest of the three tasks. European farm reforms and higher world prices have reduced the size of total European export subsidies from about $10 billion a decade ago to $3 billion in 2003, slightly more than US payments. The Europeans agreed to eliminate these subsidies by a fixed date, provided that the export subsidy component of US export credits and food aid programs is also removed. Such "parallelism" will require revisions in both programs to prohibit credit maturities of more than six months and to avoid food aid shipments that displace commercial sales. The most difficult issue in this area is whether the operation of state trading enterprises (such as the Australian and Canadian Wheat Boards) confers benefits akin to export subsidies.

Domestic subsidies account for the bulk of the payments provided by governments to their farmers for production and income support, research and development, and conservation and other environmental purposes. WTO members agreed in the Uruguay Round to cut these subsidies by 20 percent from a level calculated as their Aggregate Measure of Support (AMS). But WTO negotiators adopted an intricate set of "accounting principles" to determine which farm programs should be included in the cuts and which should be exempted. Simply put, the AMS is adjusted to exclude certain de minimis payments, plus specific programs sheltered from cuts by placement in the blue box (minimally trade distorting) or green box (nondistorting). As a result, actual subsidy disbursements have been generally well below the maximum permissible amounts under the Uruguay Round Agreement on Agriculture.[21]

In the Doha Round, the conventional wisdom is that cuts in the AMS will average about 60 percent, but whether this will require a change in existing policies will depend on how much the de minimis thresholds are reduced, whether and how the blue and green boxes are redefined, and

21. For a detailed analysis of the WTO negotiations on agriculture, see Josling and Hathaway (2004).

whether value caps are placed on either of those types of exceptions. The WTO Council decision of July 2004 is vague on all of these issues—leaving to further negotiation, for example, whether US countercyclical payments (reconstituted under the 2002 farm bill) qualify for the blue box.

Market access reforms are the most contentious area of the farm trade talks. For many products, cuts in subsidies may not improve trading opportunities unless those reforms are implemented in conjunction with the liberalization of tariffs, the expansion and more flexible administration of tariff-rate quotas (TRQs), and reductions in other nontariff barriers (including sanitary and phytosanitary restrictions that are inconsistent with the letter or spirit of WTO obligations). The WTO Council decision left unresolved decisions on the type of formula to cut tariffs, how to impose lesser requirements on developing countries (plus whether to give the least developed countries a "free pass"), how to structure safeguard measures that could "temporarily" reverse agreed reforms, and—most importantly—exceptions for "sensitive" products.

What is a "sensitive" product? As a practical matter, a product is "sensitive" if it is subject to high trade barriers—usually a sure sign that the protection benefits influential political constituencies. "Sensitive products" will be spared the full thrust of reforms but will not be excluded from liberalization initiatives as they effectively were in the Uruguay Round. For the United States and European Union, this means that protection of livestock, dairy, and sugar must be scaled back from current levels. Japan and Korea will also need to open new trading opportunities for foreign suppliers of rice and beef. Much of the time spent on negotiations in these sensitive areas will involve how to minimize reforms without so diluting the farm package as to render the entire negotiation unacceptable. Without concessions in these sensitive areas, however, it will be difficult to obtain concrete results in other areas of the Doha Round of interest to manufacturing and services industries.

In sum, for the agricultural negotiations to succeed, developed countries will need to demonstrate their willingness to reduce both the absolute value of subsidies provided to their farmers and the tariffs, quotas, and other nontariff barriers that protect agriculture. Middle-income developing countries also will have to liberalize their restrictions (though to a somewhat lesser extent) to provide benefits for other poorer countries and OECD exporters. Concrete commitments can't be expected soon but could be forthcoming once the United States, European Union, and Japan proceed with their own domestic reviews of farm policy in 2006.

In industrial products, the best result would be to accept the US proposal to eliminate tariffs by 2015 (with some exceptions or longer implementation periods for developing countries). This is extremely unlikely: US apparel firms strongly oppose further trade reforms on top of the removal of MFA quotas; and many developing countries fear the impact of deep tariff cuts both on their trade preferences in industrial markets and on their fiscal balances.[22] In any event, developing countries will not be asked to cut as deeply or quickly as developed countries. WTO members seem to agree, however, that the tariff-cutting formula should require deeper reductions for higher tariffs (i.e., "nonlinear" cuts). Such an approach would have the added advantage of mitigating problems with tariff escalation. In addition, WTO members may agree to remove tariffs and liberalize key nontariff barriers on a sector-by-sector basis (following the precedent of the Information Technology Agreement).

In services, the Doha Round negotiations provide a great opportunity to put flesh on the skeletal commitments to trade reform that WTO members undertook a decade ago in the Uruguay Round. Negotiations on services offer substantial promise on a sector-by-sector basis. Industrial countries seek reforms in infrastructure services where their industries are competitive (e.g., banking, insurance, telecom, energy, and air transport), while developing countries want new opportunities to provide labor-oriented services (e.g., health care, construction, and low-value-added information technology services). These talks are particularly important for the United States, which runs a substantial surplus in services trade. More than half the surplus is in business, financial, and other private services that are the focus of most reciprocal bargaining in the GATS negotiations. Catherine L. Mann (in her chapter in this book) calculates that a large portion of the prospective US gains from the Doha Round derive from liberalization of traded services.

The original framework of WTO rules on services, embodied in the General Agreement on Trade in Services (GATS), did not require significant liberalization of services trade barriers. Instead, WTO members committed to continue negotiations on basic telecommunications and financial services (concluded in 1995 and 1996, respectively) and movement of natural persons (i.e., "mode 4" labor services), and to restart broader negotiations by 2000 "with a view to achieving a progressively higher level of liberalization" (GATS Article XIX:1). The new accords required almost no changes in US and European laws and regulations and mostly codified existing policies of developing-country signatories that had been revamped in response to financial crises of the 1990s. Sectoral talks on labor services were abandoned until the new services talks began in 2000.

Despite starting before the launch of the Doha Round, services trade negotiations have lagged; most countries have not even tabled offers. The WTO Council decision of July 31, 2004, simply asks members to submit new offers by May 2005.

The challenge in the Doha Round is twofold: broaden the scope of services reforms under existing GATS obligations and augment the GATS rules to take account of important technological changes (e.g., electronic

22. Some Caribbean countries, for example, derive 25 to 40 percent of total government revenues from trade taxes. See Schott (2001, table 2.10).

commerce) that increasingly affect international transactions of goods and services. The task will not be easy. Most GATS disciplines apply only to services that are listed in national schedules, and getting countries to top up their offers requires sector-by-sector and country-by-country efforts. Moreover, creating new trading opportunities often requires reform of domestic regulatory policies—a contentious process when the regulations also reflect national security and other noncommercial objectives.

For US providers of financial, telecom, air transport, and other services, this is an area where developing countries in particular can make valuable contributions to global trade reform. Some of those countries are now working constructively on a big package of services reforms—but they want in turn access to US and other industrial markets for their labor-intensive services. A big deal on services is possible, but only if the United States and others negotiate seriously on all areas of the GATS agenda, including labor services. To date, however, Congress has tied the hands of US negotiators by forbidding coverage of visa and immigration issues in trade pacts—thus complicating efforts to negotiate the cross-border provision of temporary labor services (known as "mode 4" in GATS parlance).

In sum, the Doha Round will succeed only if WTO members agree to a big package of reforms in all the major areas under negotiation. Major trading nations, both developed and developing, will have to undertake reforms in long-standing trade barriers. Poorer countries should be given more flexibility in liberalizing their border restrictions but should be encouraged to do so over time through a combination of trade concessions and development assistance from the industrial countries.

Reviving the Free Trade Area of the Americas

A decade ago, leaders of the 34 democratic nations in the Western Hemisphere agreed at the Summit of the Americas in Miami to negotiate a Free Trade Area of the Americas (FTAA) by January 2005. Trade ministers formally launched negotiations in 1998. The United States and Brazil assumed the cochairmanship of the FTAA negotiations in November 2002 and are supposed to remain in that leadership position for the duration of the talks. The decision to share this task between the dominant economies of North and South America makes sense, since the ultimate success of the hemispheric accord depends importantly on bridging the gap between the positions of the two countries.

Like the Doha Round, the FTAA negotiations stalled due to differences over agriculture and the inclusion of issues like investment and intellectual property in the overall package of agreements. As a result, the trade talks will extend well past the original deadline and probably will proceed in parallel with the Doha Round for another two years or so—here again, the timetable probably is linked to TPA.

The recent progress in the Doha Round has reopened prospects for reviving the FTAA talks, which have not advanced since the last FTAA ministerial meeting in Miami in November 2003. Under pressure "not to fail" so soon after the WTO fiasco in Cancún, trade ministers issued a declaration at the Miami meeting that simply papered over major substantive disputes. The FTAA process did not break down, but Miami's muddled mandate raised additional stumbling blocks.

At the Miami meeting, ministers "affirmed their commitment to a comprehensive and balanced FTAA" (paragraph 5), which includes "provisions in each of the [FTAA] negotiating areas" (paragraph 10). However, countries were permitted to take specific issues or products off the table, and some "countries may assume different levels of commitments" (paragraph 7). If other countries want to do more, say on investment, they could enter into so-called plurilateral agreements that obligate only those countries that sign the specific pact.

In essence, the Miami Declaration presaged a "hollow core" agreement in which individual countries could avoid committing to reforms in politically sensitive areas (hence "FTAA-lite"). Thus, if Brazil and others did not want to negotiate on investment and intellectual property issues, they could opt out of a hemispheric accord in those areas while the United States and others could adopt a more comprehensive accord among a subset of FTAA participants (probably the same countries that already have signed FTAs with the United States). The value of this plurilateral approach is unclear, since there is little "additionality" if the plurilateral pacts only involve existing US FTA partners. At best, plurilateral pacts would harmonize the terms of existing FTAs by, inter alia, augmenting Canadian obligations in NAFTA and unraveling politically sensitive compromises on FTA origin rules for textiles, clothing, and agricultural products. Such a result is highly unlikely. A more limited outcome would not seem sufficient to justify the political cost/risk of going back to Congress for another vote on these pacts.

By suggesting the possibility of an "FTAA-lite"—i.e., allowing countries to exclude trade reforms in sensitive areas like agriculture, intellectual property, and services—the Miami Declaration opened loopholes that substantially reduce the prospect of achieving a "balanced" package of agreements.[23] Not surprisingly, the talks have drifted since then while US and Brazilian negotiators switched their focus to both the WTO and other FTA initiatives. For Congress to approve changes in existing US trade barriers of interest to Brazil and other Latin American countries, US negotiators need to receive concrete commitments that open access to those markets for US exporters and investors. In short, the FTAA has to be a big deal, or the deal won't fly.

23. Furthermore, a so-called FTAA-lite agreement probably would run afoul of the requirements of US TPA and also could trigger a WTO challenge based on GATT Article XXIV provisions due to extensive exceptions from the free trade obligations.

Crafting a free trade pact among 34 countries that span the world's richest and poorest, and largest and smallest, was never going to be easy. The task has been further complicated by the financial crises and political turmoil that beset many Latin American participants since the FTAA talks began, the US economic downturn in 2001–02, and the new security imperatives of the post-9/11 world.

However, the United States has important economic and foreign policy interests in the region that can be advanced by a successful FTAA (Schott 2001). The trade pact is the economic engine that drives hemispheric cooperation on a number of political, socioeconomic, and cultural issues (e.g., promoting education, strengthening the rule of law, and protecting the rights of indigenous peoples) that have been put forward in the Summit of the Americas process. Progress on the FTAA is critical to sustain efforts in these other areas.

To get the FTAA process back on track, ministers must recognize that the negotiations need to aim higher than the Miami 2003 mandate and thus will take longer to produce results. The next ministerial is slated for Brazil—now probably in 2005. At that meeting, ministers should reassess the state of play and redirect negotiators to fulfill the original Summit of the Americas mandate for a growth-enhancing FTAA.

What could be achieved? Eliminating all industrial tariffs is likely to be the basis of the deal, with some balance struck between US farm trade reforms and enhanced access to Latin American procurement and services markets. Smaller and poorer economies should be afforded longer transition periods to implement the free trade obligations, but not exemptions from the FTAA disciplines (see IGE 1997).

On agriculture, tariffs should be phased out over a 10-year period with only limited exceptions, and reforms of nontariff barriers should yield concrete market access benefits for other sensitive products (even if some protection is left intact). Trade problems related to domestic subsidies cannot be resolved in the context of a regional agreement but could be substantially reduced in reforms likely to be accepted in the Doha Round. Regarding procurement, FTAA negotiators should be able to agree on principles that provide transparency for public tenders and guidelines for open tendering. In addition, such rules should be complemented by a commitment to negotiate within five years or so a list of entities whose purchases would be covered by these new obligations. Regarding services, the preferred outcome would be agreement on a "negative list" that covers all services subject to FTAA obligations except those explicitly listed, but the more likely outcome will simply augment WTO commitments on a sector-by-sector basis, with particular emphasis on infrastructure services and e-commerce.

In sum, the key to success in the FTAA is agreement on a big package of market access reforms, including agriculture and other goods and services. That means both liberalization of existing tariffs and quotas plus reform of regulatory and administrative practices that effectively impede the ability to sell in foreign markets (including discriminatory standards and customs procedures, sector-specific investment reforms, and import relief policies—particularly safeguards). Opening new opportunities for trade and investment in the hemisphere is a prerequisite to closing the FTAA deal and ensuring its ratification by national legislatures.

Upgrading NAFTA

By most standards, NAFTA has been a great success for all three countries, contributing to unprecedented growth in regional trade and investment. During its first decade, trade among the NAFTA partners doubled to more than $600 billion. Integration of the three economies has advanced—though the gains have been distributed unevenly within each country and mask adjustment problems besetting some workers and firms.

Since 9/11, however, the NAFTA partners have had to face a new and overriding challenge: addressing the added security measures needed to deal with recurring terrorist threats. Heightened security measures have made it more costly and cumbersome to move goods and people across borders and pose a particular challenge to businesses that have integrated their operations on a regional basis—one of NAFTA's great virtues. The "Smart Border" initiative concluded with Canada and the "Border Partnership Action Plan" with Mexico have been a good start. These initiatives are designed to both improve security and minimize delays. However, the basic structure of border inspections remains in place—and it was designed to collect tariffs and detect smuggling, not combat terrorism.

After a decade of progress, the three NAFTA partners still have important unfinished business. Trade and investment continue to be clouded by security concerns and residual restrictions; the region remains vulnerable to volatile energy prices and supply shortfalls; illegal immigration still confronts political leaders on both sides of the Rio Grande; and longstanding labor and environmental problems need to be redressed, particularly in the US-Mexico border region. For better or worse, many of these issues are linked politically.

For the United States, improving prospects for sustained economic growth in Mexico is critical to strengthening security on its southern border, while deeper cooperation with Canada on border-security initiatives is essential to ensure the efficient flow of goods and people across our long northern border. Mexico's economic prospects depend importantly on reforms of Mexican tax and energy policies and extensive new foreign investment in the energy sector, which has been barred for the past seven decades. This should be a stand-alone priority for Mexico, though political realities may require attention to the plight of Mexican migrants in the United States as an unstated quid pro quo. Plans for needed energy infrastructure investments will have to balance economic considerations, sovereignty concerns, and environmental effects.

Updating and deepening North American economic integration merits priority attention for both economic and security reasons. New initiatives in the areas of trade, energy, and migration could help deal with pressing problems in each country, while promoting closer security ties to better handle aftershocks of future terrorist attacks. The key is to find the right combination of economic and security initiatives that will spur political leaders of all three countries into action.

First, the NAFTA countries should deepen the trade bargain. While creating a customs union may not be feasible, the three partners could move toward a common external tariff (CET) by lowering and gradually harmonizing MFN tariffs on industrial goods. Though desirable, extending a CET to agriculture probably would overload the political circuits. Even so, a CET would have several advantages: it would reduce the cost of imported goods, mitigate concerns about the protectionist impact of NAFTA rules of origin (since cutting MFN tariffs dilutes the value of the regional tariff preferences that are conditioned on meeting the origin rules), and promote liberalization that would also contribute to the success of the Doha Round. However, a CET would not resolve vexing problems long immune to negotiated fixes, most notably regarding softwood lumber, wheat, and sugar, and countervailing and antidumping duties.

Second, the NAFTA countries need to jointly develop a North American energy security policy that promotes regional production and trade, as well as the buildup of strategic reserves and production capacity in the event of overseas supply disruptions. Since 9/11 and especially since the Iraq war, concerns have resurfaced about the adequacy of North American production of oil and gas in light of problems in the Persian Gulf region and soaring oil prices. Development of oil and gas fields, as well as construction of new energy distribution channels,[24] is a high priority—though for somewhat different reasons—in both Canada and Mexico as well.

The United States, Canada, and Mexico share a common interest in expanding regional energy production, especially oil and natural gas. The US-Canada energy infrastructure is already fairly well integrated, but distribution of energy supplies continues to face obstacles arising from different regulatory policies both within and between countries. In contrast, US-Mexico energy relations continue to be sharply constrained by Mexico's constitutional prohibition against foreign participation in the exploitation of oil and gas. Amending the Mexican constitution will be a difficult task; even incremental energy reforms are problematic. Recognizing the political roadblocks, Mexico will nonetheless have to rethink its oil policies in

24. The blackout that deprived 50 million Americans and Canadians of electricity in August 2003 underscored the problems of aging electrical transmission lines.

the near future to avoid major power shortages and to ensure the success of its development strategies. Necessity may be the mother of intervention. If so, reforms in US immigration policies could provide added incentives for binational cooperation in both areas.

Third, the three countries should coordinate more closely regarding their immigration regulations, starting with common visa standards for most non-NAFTA visitors and immigrants. This goal is highly significant from a security standpoint. For people arriving from outside the NAFTA region, the North American countries need a shared system for excluding non-NAFTA nationals who pose a security threat. In addition, NAFTA partners should develop common document and biometric identification standards for all non-NAFTA visitors. In short, homeland security requires a regional perspective as well.

Refocusing US Strategy on Free Trade Agreements

In the United States, FTAs surfaced as a policy option in the early 1980s and have become a staple of US trade policy in recent years. The FTA with Israel served as the pilot project for this new policy; the Canada-US FTA followed soon after, reinforcing the extensive economic integration already occurring in the North American market and offering negotiating options if new multilateral trade talks stalled (Schott and Smith 1988). This message was echoed at the start of the NAFTA negotiations, which began in 1991, a few months after the GATT ministerial in Brussels in December 1990 failed to conclude the Uruguay Round (Hufbauer and Schott 1992, 42–43). In the aftermath of the failed Seattle WTO ministerial in December 1999, the Clinton administration pursued bilateral FTAs with Jordan, Chile, and Singapore.

As of November 2004, the United States has ratified FTAs with Israel, Canada, Mexico, Jordan, Singapore, Chile, Australia, and Morocco. In addition, FTAs have been signed with the five Central American countries, the Dominican Republic, and Bahrain, and await congressional approval. FTA talks are currently in progress with the five members of SACU, Thailand, Colombia, Ecuador, Peru, and Panama, as well as the other countries in the Western Hemisphere negotiating the FTAA.

Current FTA partners account for more than one-third of total US merchandise trade. Upon completion and ratification of the other bilateral FTA negotiations and the FTAA, more than 43 percent of total US trade, and half of US exports, will be covered by free trade pacts (table 8.4).

To date, most US free trade initiatives have involved Western Hemisphere countries with which the United States is also negotiating the FTAA. Those current and prospective FTAs can be seen as way stations to the larger hemispheric agreement. However, this incremental approach to building the FTAA does not cover Brazil and other countries that account for almost 50 percent of Latin America's GDP.

Other US FTA initiatives involve countries that also are engaged in regional integration arrangements in their own neighborhood. In both southern Africa and southeast Asia, and to a lesser extent in North Africa and the Middle East, US initiatives seek to create new bilateral trade and investment opportunities with and to deepen the integration among the partner countries. Except for southeast Asia, where US merchandise trade and investment with the Association of Southeast Asian Nations (ASEAN) is substantial (about $127 billion in 2003), US economic ties with these other FTA partners are small.

Assuming TPA is extended, the next administration will need to decide whether to continue the ambitious program of bilateral FTAs, and if so, which negotiations to give priority. At the same time, US officials will need to finish ongoing bilateral FTA negotiations. In addition, there is a possibility that the CAFTA will need to be embellished to mitigate opposition from labor and environmental groups that threaten to block congressional approval of the pact.

Based on extensive analysis of and recommendations for US FTA policy reported in Schott (2004), and cognizant of the significant negotiating resources that will have to be devoted to completing the Doha Round, US trade officials should focus on fewer but bigger FTAs, with three distinct objectives:

- complete the FTAA;
- preempt/offset discrimination against US exporters/investors generated by current and prospective FTAs among other countries; and
- consolidate regional negotiations in southeast Asia and the Middle East and North Africa when the largest countries in those regions (i.e., Indonesia and Egypt, respectively) are ready to engage in FTA talks.

The FTAA is the biggest US free trade initiative and merits priority attention. Election year politics have constrained US and Brazilian offers to reduce their main trade barriers, but new efforts should be made at the next FTAA ministerial in Brazil—as noted above—to reengage negotiations on liberalization of goods and services in the hemisphere. A deal will not get done unless the leading economies of North and South America bridge their differences and offer concrete new opportunities for their exporters and investors in each other's markets.

Second, US officials should prepare for new talks with Korea and Japan in the next few years. The current line-up of FTA initiatives is notable for its length as well as for its exclusion of countries in one important region, northeast Asia. That omission is explained by the fact that Japan and Korea have been unwilling to talk about key US demands in areas like agriculture. But trade policies are changing rapidly in East Asia, and events there may lead to new initiatives in the near future.

Why? Part of the impetus for US officials to pursue FTAs is to redress discrimination generated by pacts to which a country is not a party. This factor will gain prominence if Japan and Korea conclude a bilateral trade pact as well as FTAs with other countries in East Asia. Japanese-Korean trade covers many of the same products that US firms export to both countries; US firms could suffer trade diversion of key US exports such as semiconductors and telecommunications equipment (Schott and Goodrich 2004). US industries and farmers will demand that trade officials "level the playing field" by negotiating similar trade preferences with Japan and Korea.[25] So by later this decade, one may well see a new burst of US FTAs with Asia-Pacific countries or a rash of new trade friction between the United States and its northeast Asian trading partners.

Third, new initiatives should target big countries that drive regional integration efforts in southeast Asia and the Middle East and North Africa region. The prospect of concluding FTAs with the United States could energize domestic economic and political reforms in countries like Indonesia and Egypt that are needed to meet the requirements of a comprehensive free trade pact. At the same time, such reforms could spur integration initiatives among countries in those regions and thus help advance the broader goals of the US Enterprise for ASEAN Initiative and the Greater Middle East FTA.

Conclusions

The United States can achieve important economic and foreign policy objectives if it continues to pursue a broad set of trade pacts and if it underpins those efforts with domestic programs that bolster competitiveness and facilitate adjustment of US firms. To do so, the new administration needs to set its trade policy priorities right from the start.

First, US officials need to ask Congress to extend TPA so they can complete ongoing WTO and FTA negotiations. Without TPA, US trade policy will be severely constrained for the duration of the administration's term in office. Note, however, that TPA is necessary, but not sufficient, to ensure that the United States maximizes its benefits from trade agreements. New farm legislation also is needed to induce trade reforms abroad and to reduce the domestic budget deficit. In addition, TPA needs to be complemented by domestic policies that enhance the competitiveness of US firms and workers so that they can better take advantage of the new opportunities created by foreign trade liberalization, plus new or expanded programs that help manage the adjustment burdens of those adversely affected by the resulting restructuring in the US market.

25. New US FTA initiatives could prompt agricultural and services-sector reforms in those countries that will have to be pursued in any event to fulfill the likely demands of the WTO talks.

Second, the administration should give priority to concluding the Doha Round of WTO negotiations. The WTO talks provide the biggest bang for the US negotiating buck, the only practical venue for confronting farm subsidy problems and the only channel for improving rules and fixing flaws (particularly in the dispute settlement system) in the multilateral trading system. Concerns about FTA trade preferences and discrimination would be more pronounced in the absence of such efforts.

Third, the administration should give priority to upgrading NAFTA and to "big stakes" FTAs—particularly the FTAA—that also yield substantial payoffs for US firms, workers, and farmers. It is important to emphasize, however, that the substantial US gains from these efforts result from both the liberalization of trade and investment by US trading partners and the *reductions in US trade barriers and subsidies*. Big FTAs can yield larger benefits than those generated by many recent US FTAs but will also require significant US adjustment.

In sum, the United States should continue to pursue a multitrack approach to trade negotiations but devote more resources and effort to address the significant challenges facing US workers, farmers, and firms as they compete in markets at home and abroad.

Lowering foreign trade barriers and reducing home-grown impediments to the competitiveness of US firms and workers can open up substantial new trading and investment opportunities and promote better relations with more prosperous and stable trading partners.

References

Brown, Drusilla K., Alan V. Deardorff, and Robert M. Stern. 2003. Developing Countries' Stake in the Doha Round. Research Seminar in International Economics, Discussion Paper 495. Gerald R. Ford School of Public Policy, University of Michigan, June 11. www.spp.umich.edu/rsie/workingpapers/wp.html.

Destler, I. M. 1995. *American Trade Politics*, 3rd ed. Washington: Institute for International Economics.

Elliott, Kimberly. 2004. *Labor Standards, Development, and CAFTA*. Policy Brief PB04-2. Washington: Institute for International Economics, March.

Hufbauer, Gary Clyde, and Jeffrey J. Schott. 1992. *North American Free Trade: Issues and Recommendations*. Washington: Institute for International Economics.

Hufbauer, Gary Clyde, and Yee Wong. 2004. *China Bashing 2004*. Policy Brief PB04-5. Washington: Institute for International Economics.

IGE (Independent Group of Experts). 1997. Overcoming Obstacles and Maximizing Opportunities: Smaller Economies and Western Hemispheric Integration. Report of the IGE on Smaller Economies and Western Hemispheric Integration. Photocopy. Washington: Organization of American States.

Josling, Tim, and Dale Hathaway. 2004. *This Far and No Farther? Nudging Agricultural Reform Forward*. Policy Brief PB04-1. Washington: Institute for International Economics.

Nordås, Hildegunn Kyvik. 2004. *The Global Textile and Clothing Industry post the Agreement on Textiles and Clothing*. WTO Discussion Paper. Geneva: World Trade Organization.

OECD (Organization for Economic Cooperation and Development). 2004. *OECD Agricultural Policies 2004: At a Glance*. Paris: OECD.

Schott, Jeffrey J., ed. 1998. *Restarting Fast Track.* Washington: Institute for International Economics.

Schott, Jeffrey J. 2001. *Prospects for Free Trade in the Americas.* Washington: Institute for International Economics.

Schott, Jeffrey J., ed. 2004. *Free Trade Agreements: US Strategies and Priorities.* Washington: Institute for International Economics.

Schott, Jeffrey J., and Ben Goodrich. 2004. Reflections on Economic Integration in Northeast Asia. In *Strengthening Economic Cooperation in Northeast Asia,* Yoon Hyung Kim and Chang Jae Lee, eds. Seoul: Korea Institute for International Economic Policy.

Schott, Jeffrey J., and Murray G. Smith, eds. 1988. *The Canada-United States Free Trade Agreement: The Global Impact.* Washington: Institute for International Economics.

Scheve, Kenneth F., and Matthew J. Slaughter. 2001. *Globalization and the Perceptions of American Workers.* Washington: Institute for International Economics.

USITC (United States International Trade Commission). 2004. *The Economic Effects of Significant US Import Restraints: Fourth Update 2004.* Publication 3701. Washington.

WTO (World Trade Organization). 2003. *World Trade Report.* Geneva.

9

Offshore Outsourcing and the Globalization of US Services: Why Now, How Important, and What Policy Implications

CATHERINE L. MANN

US services are globalizing at a rapid rate, are increasingly in trade surplus, and, through foreign investment and affiliate sales abroad, are deepening the global integration of the US economy. There is even a new term for the phenomenon—"offshoring"—that is, the offshore outsourcing of service activities. While outsourcing is not new—the breakdown of the process of goods production to local and global locations is well advanced—the rapid pace of globalization of services has given new life to the outsourcing term and to the debate about the gains and costs of global engagement of the US economy. What changed to speed up this pace and expand the set of services that can be traded across borders? To what extent is this globalization of services different from or similar to the globalization of goods? How important is globalization of services for US productivity and growth? Do workers, firms, and the US economy face new challenges from this kind of offshore outsourcing? Is there any natural stopping point for globalization of services? Does the globalization of services yield new policy recommendations?

Since global integration of services is just beginning, assessment of its impact on US economic performance necessarily relies on existing research on globalization, which focuses primarily on international trade in

Catherine L. Mann is a senior fellow at the Institute for International Economics.

goods. However, the information technology (IT) sector offers an explicit example of the real and potential gains to the US economy from globalization of both goods and services. This sector is one where the synergies and dynamic interaction between technological and global forces are particularly pronounced and where firms are rapidly changing products and activities, with both positive and negative effects on the US economy.

IT also offers a specific example of the channels through which technological change and globalization affect the US economy. Dramatic price declines for IT hardware come mostly from domestic innovation that supports technological change. But globalization has furthered these price declines. Overall, capital investment in IT responds more than one-for-one with price declines. The resulting widespread (although incomplete) diffusion of IT investment throughout the US economy has transformed business processes, altered workplace practices, and created new products (goods and services). While disruptive, these changes spurred by technological as well as global forces have led to significant macroeconomic gains in terms of productivity, output growth, and employment.

IT hardware was at the root of the first wave of productivity growth and employment gains. Going forward, a second wave of technology-based investment and economywide transformation is possible as technology allows the breaking down of the production process of software and IT services and enables their globalized production, just as the production of IT hardware was so globalized in the 1980s and 1990s. Breaking down the production process and global sourcing will lower prices of software and services, which can help diffuse technology into the sectors that lagged in productivity performance during the 1990s, such as health services. As before, innovation at home to meet the needs of US customers will be the most important factor in driving productivity and job creation, but global sourcing will play an important supporting role.

Because services account for a larger and growing share of the US economy, both productivity gains and adjustment challenges from the technological changes that advance the globalization of services are likely to be greater than has been the case for globalization so far. Policymakers need to more effectively leverage these greater productivity gains that accrue to the US economy as a whole to ameliorate the potentially more widespread job dislocations and skill mismatches that result from the interaction of trade and technological change. Initiatives on international economic policy and domestic labor policies need to be more tightly integrated.

On the international front, empirical research indicates that US exports of services are even more dependent on foreign growth than are US exports of goods. In addition, the share of US exports of services in total exports rises with the level of economic development. Yet the markets for services abroad have been liberalized far less than those for goods. Hence promoting robust growth in markets abroad and focusing trade negotiations on opening those markets are particularly important to ensure that growth in global services markets translates into exports and sales for US producers and gains to the US economy.

Trade and technological change affect the type of skills being demanded by firms in the United States. On the domestic front, a commitment to and funding of new ideas that promote labor-market adjustment are crucial. Otherwise the US economy will not maximize the potential gains of this new globalization of services. Such policies include wage insurance, portability of social insurances, and importantly education and training tax credits built around partnerships between workers and employers along with local educators and governments.

Gaining from globalization of services requires that businesses and workers change what they do. These changes in activities and resource reallocations are a prerequisite for fully enjoying the productivity gains from technological change and globalization. A combined outward-looking and domestic policy effort is needed to maximize the gains and best adapt to the pace of change.

Globalization of Services: How New? How Different?

International trade in services has always existed. Transportation and communications services bridge the physical distance between a buyer and seller of a good. Tourists travel to experience new cultures, students go to school abroad, and temporary immigrant workers send money home. However, in most economic models of international trade, services have been called "nontradable" because, as a matter of fact, high international *transactions costs* (measured in time, distance, or otherwise) prevented the close proximity between a buyer and seller deemed necessary for the service activity to take place. For archetypal services—e.g., the haircut—it is still not cost-effective to make an international trip. But beyond transportation, culture, custom, and regulation also often required proximity between a buyer and seller and limited international trade in services: Financial, legal, or administrative services have required handshakes, physical presence to sign papers, or licensure examinations that are unique to a jurisdiction (such as accounting or law).

In addition to transactions costs, the "production" of certain services has been *functionally integral* to an organization's business activity or product and therefore not easy to separate from the main activity of the firm: for example, reading a radiological image at the hospital as part of the diagnosis; iterating through blueprints as part of designing a building; and reviewing of mortgage applications by the local bank manager before processing a loan.

How New?

Technological change, as well as policy change and changes in customer and business attitudes over time, has eroded these attributes of services—transactions costs and functional integration—that heretofore made them "nontradable." However, for *offshore* outsourcing to take place, it is not just the response of firms in the United States that matters. Globalization of services through trade and direct investment requires that firms in other countries also can react to reduced transactions costs and functional disintegration. That is, globalization of services is limited unless both sides of the transaction can participate.

What are the key technological changes? First, the raw technology of the internet in conjunction with international telecommunications networks and IT hardware (such as personal computers) create the potential for linkages between countries and businesses that simply did not exist before. For example, the average price of an international call between the United States and India dropped in half between 1996 and 2001, making offshore call centers much more attractive in terms of telecommunications cost. The penetration of personal computers into the Chinese marketplace increased nearly sevenfold over the same period, making this marketplace more accessible to fast-paced technology-based businesses (World Bank data).

Second, digitization of services activities further reduces transactions costs of trade. With digitization, information, software, or advice need not be put on paper, or transported by a person, or be embedded on a hard disk to be traded. All these activities can be digitized—consultants can provide advice via video, and software can be downloaded—in order to trade internationally. In fact, international trade around the world in such business and professional services grew nearly 40 percent between 1996 and 2002 (IMF data).

Third, codification of information puts information into an ordered format, which reduces the need for specific knowledge to perform skill- and information-intensive tasks. For example, computer-based so-called expert systems in customer-service centers replicate some aspects of the process by which an expert reaches a decision on a question. This expert system allows people with less expertise to, step by step, follow the on-screen menu to work through complex problems. Or, for example, the ability to download data into spreadsheet software that has embedded equations allows people with only modest financial training to prepare financial reports and presentations. And computer programming increasingly is modularized so that the design of a program can be separated from the implementation in computer code, which is itself globally standardized in computer languages such as C++ or Java.

Networked information technology, digitization, and codification can also create new products and activities inside firms, which add to domestic output and job creation, and can be internationally traded if markets are open abroad. For example, using IT to monitor quality of products on the factory line may be a task that a firm initially does for its own reasons but then sells it as an information services product to other firms. Or, a comprehensive database of financial relationships can yield new financial instruments (such as derivatives) or new sources of revenue (for example, collecting small-value past-due accounts-receivables). Using IT to integrate health information about a patient can reduce life-threatening drug interactions, and a database that includes information about many patients and their therapies can help determine which procedures yield the best outcomes. Creating these new products demands workers not only skilled in technology but also knowledgeable of the specific business or sector.

All told, cheaper internet and information technology, digitization, and codification of information allow many tasks to be separated from the main activity of a business and also creates the potential for many new products and activities within a business. While some of these activities and products can be separated from a firm's core activities, others become core products. What becomes "outsourced" or "offshored" depends in part on the activities of the US firm, and the characteristics of US labor, and in part on whether the foreign location has the needed technological infrastructures and worker and firm characteristics.

How Different?

To a great degree, the forces promoting tradability and hence globalization of services—reduced transactions costs and fragmentation of production and separability of business functions—are the same forces that underpin globalization of goods. So, in what ways is the globalization of services different from the globalization of goods?

First, the pace of change in the globalization of services is more rapid than globalization of goods and has greater potential to accelerate. Global international trade in services doubled over the last 12 years compared with growth of goods trade (WTO data). Global foreign direct investment (FDI) in services accelerated over 1990–2002, increasing fourfold to account for about 60 percent of the global stock of FDI in 2002, up from 50 percent in 1990 (UNCTAD data). Going forward, trade and investment in services worldwide will increase because the share of services in consumption tends to rise with the level of income and development.

Second, with both trade and direct investment in services increasing, the share of labor exposed to international market forces is rising. In industrial countries, where services account for the majority of output and employment, rapid globalization of services means that a large and increasing share of the labor force and the economy face international competition. At the same time, in developing countries, more workers are being drawn into the services sector. Consequently, an increasing share of the global labor force is engaged in activities that are exposed to technological change and will need to respond to global competition and the resulting international division of labor. In contrast, the shares of agricultural and manufacturing employment have been declining in both industrial and developing worlds as technological change increases productivity in these sectors and labor's share falls.

Third, synergies between the skill profile demanded by globalized services and the policy changes in key developing countries may enhance globalization of services. The educational demands for internationally traded services range from low (e.g., call-center and transcription services) to high (engineering design and computer programming), but underlying both is a generalized set of skills that are not industry- or firm-specific (Autor, Levy, and Murnane 2003). In contrast, workers in goods production are often characterized by industry- and firm-specific skills gained through on-the-job training that are less applicable to a different factory or product.

Although educational attainment overall remains higher in industrial countries, research suggests that they have been spending less on education than the developing countries (Siqueira 2003). As a result, educational attainment in broad-based skills in developing countries has increased relatively faster. In the United States, for example, the share of the labor force with the level of educational attainment that pits them against workers in developing countries (e.g., a high school degree or less) is expected to *increase* over the next 15 years (Ellwood 2001). So the skills gap is narrowing. At the same time, wage differentials between the industrial and developing worlds remain large. Together, the narrowed education gap, the wide wage differential, and the technology drivers of digitization and codification enhance the incentives for international trade in services. Moreover, targeted policies in some countries (for example, Ireland and India) that offer attractive combinations of infrastructure, human skills, and tax arrangements have been important factors driving the pattern of international trade in services.

Fourth, globalization of services and globalization of goods may differ in how easily firms can change the location of their activities to take advantage of better capabilities in another country. Digitized and codified knowledge of a service activity requires little complementary capital compared with producing goods in a factory. Firms that focus on an intermediate segment of the international value chain in services production (and do not serve the domestic market) may be more footloose than factories because their links to the local economy are fewer and physical investment is low.

In sum, a broad range of services increasingly can be separated from a firm's central activity. These activities are coming to be known as information technology–enabled services (ITES). This name acknowledges first that the information and communications technologies (both data transmission—the hardware—as well as data manipulation and classification—the software) are what enables these services to be digitized and codified and therefore fragmented and separated, and therefore undertaken at any distance from the core business and final customer. Second, it acknowledges that the services activities are not just narrowly IT-related (e.g., computer programming or database administration) but range broadly to include accounting, financial analysis, call-center services, architectural drafting, and health-record transcription, among other services activities. Technology drives the potential globalization of these activities. The extent of globalization is limited by the characteristics of the trading countries and the degree of potential digitization and codification of the activity.

How Important Is Globalization of Services for the United States?

There are several approaches to measuring the importance of services in the US economy and in international engagement: production, job occupations, international trade, and foreign investment. Taken together, without a doubt, services are increasingly important in the US economy and in international engagement. Yet, despite the numerous measures, there is not a crystal clear picture of the path and implications of globalization of US services. Nevertheless, because of the pace of change, and even as additional data are collected, policy initiatives must rely on the imperfect picture of the implications of technology and globalization of services on the US economy and jobs.

Services in the Domestic Economy

The importance of services for the domestic economy can be viewed from three perspectives: national accounts decomposition into major spending groups (consumption, investment, government spending, and net exports); production groups, as measured by GDP decomposed by industry of origin; and characteristics of the labor force, as measured by sector or occupation.

First, consider the spending groups. Services account for about 60 percent of real personal consumption expenditure. In real gross domestic investment, there is no breakdown for services, but if treated as a service, software accounts for about 16 percent of real nonresidential gross private domestic investment.[1] In international trade, net exports of services con-

1. Treating software as a service in the national accounts is not standard practice. However, international trade data sometimes classify software as a service and sometimes embed it with a good, which points out the challenges and difficulties to be observed in the national and international accounts.

tribute in a positive accounting fashion to GDP; services account for about 30 percent of exports and about 15 percent of imports. When one adds up these spending categories on services and divides by real private GDP (real GDP less government spending[2]), one finds that around 50 percent of real private GDP comes from services that can be relatively straightforwardly identified in the national accounts.

On the production side, services (including transportation; wholesale and retail trade; finance, insurance, and real estate; and other services) add up to 84 percent of private industry product, much larger than on the spending side. The difference between the spending percentage and the production percentage suggests that measurements on spending bundle together spending on services and goods (which are easier to track and measure), which tends to underestimate the share of spending on services.

In terms of private employment, a sectoral breakdown shows 80 percent of labor is employed in the services sector and 13 percent in the manufacturing sector (the remainder is in mining, farming, etc.). However, many people employed in the manufacturing sector are not production employees but have service-type jobs. Analyzing the US private labor force from the standpoint of occupations, only 8 percent are in "production" occupations, leaving 92 percent in services occupations.

Taking all these measures together, services account for a majority of spending, are larger in terms of output measures, and account for almost all the employed. No wonder globalization of services has generated concern.

US Services in Global Engagement

Table 9.1 displays data on global engagement of the US economy comparing goods and services. Global engagement comes through three channels: cross-border international trade, direct investment by US firms abroad and by foreign firms into the United States, and sales by affiliates of those firms. US global engagement in services through cross-border trade, direct investment, and affiliate sales is large, positive, and growing faster than almost all the channels of global engagement in goods.

With respect to the first channel of global engagement, data on cross-border services trade includes three distinct types of transactions: transactions related to moving people, products, and government activities; transactions in so-called other private services, which include education, insurance, finance, business and professional services, and so on; and cross-border accounting for trade in intellectual property.

The first category of services trade—transportation-related and military services—has moved significantly into deficit in recent years, due to gov-

2. The rationale for using private GDP is that it is even more difficult to determine the nature of spending or production for the government sector.

Table 9.1 Measures of global engagement (billions of dollars)

	1992	Latest data	Change
Cross-border net trade[a]	–39.1	–593.4	–554.2
Goods	–96.9	–641.4	–544.5
Services:	57.8	48.1	–9.7
Of which:			
Other private services	25.0	48.0	23.0
Intellectual property	15.7	27.8	12.2
Foreign direct investment, net position[b]	78.9	410.9	332.0
Of which:			
Financial services	90.4	90.3	–0.2
Professional services	–50.4	–80.4	–30.0
Affiliate sales (net)[c]	69.0	505.1	436.1
Affiliate services sales (net)	12.6	14.4	1.8
			Growth (percent)
Cross-border exports	616.8	1,133.0	84
Goods	439.6	797.1	81
Services:	177.3	335.9	89
Of which			
Other private services	50.3	141.7	182
Intellectual property	20.8	50.6	143
US foreign direct investment	502.1	1,789.0	256
Of which:			
Financial services	161.8	363.5	125
Professional services	17.2	115.0	568
US affiliate sales abroad	1,291.6	2,548.6	97
Affiliate services sales abroad	140.6	401.1	185
Cross-border imports	656.0	1,726.4	163
Goods	536.5	1,438.6	168
Services:	119.4	287.8	141
Of which			
Other private services	25.3	93.6	271
Intellectual property	5.2	22.8	342
Foreign direct investment in the United States	423.1	1,378.0	226
Of which:			
Financial services	71.4	273.2	283
Professional services	67.6	195.5	189
Foreign affiliate sales in the United States	1,222.7	2,043.5	67
Foreign affiliate services sales in the United States	128.0	386.7	202

a. Latest data are annualized from data from 2004 Q1, Q2, and Q3. Data are from the BEA International Transactions table 1.

b. Latest available data are for 2003(p). Data are from BEA detailed annual balance of payments and position estimates.

c. Latest available data are for 2002. Data are from "Majority Owned Affiliate Sales From BEA" detailed estimates at www.bea.doc.gov/bea/di/1001serv/intlserv.htm and www.bea.doc.gov/bea/ai/ iidguide.htm#SRVS.

ernment spending on services abroad and to increasing costs of transporting the large volume of imported goods. Technology as discussed in this chapter is not the main driver of these trends.

The second category of services trade—other private services—is growing faster than cross-border trade in goods and increasingly is in surplus. Exports of other private services are growing more than twice as fast as goods exports, and imports of other private services are growing about 50 percent faster than goods imports. These services account for about 10 percent of total exports and about 7 percent of total imports. The net positive trade balance in other private services has increased over the last 12 years and stands in contrast to the large and increasingly negative balance of trade in goods. Because cross-border trade in goods often bundles in other private services (such as maintenance and repair services embedded in merchandise exports), the positive services trade balance could be underestimated.

Technology may well be increasing two-way trade in these services, but these data do not corroborate the concern that technology-enabled cross-border trade will disproportionately favor services imports over exports. In fact, the robustness of these exports even in the face of slow growth in major industrial markets abroad suggests global competitiveness of US providers of these private services (Mann 2004a).

The third category of cross-border trade, intellectual property receipts and payments, also shows a doubling of the trade surplus, as well as rapid growth.

The next main channel of global engagement is direct investment. As was observed in the global data, the services sector accounts for an increasing share of US direct investment abroad and direct investment into the United States.

Direct investment abroad in the activities where technology is enabling trade (such as finance and insurance, business and professional services, and information services) accounted for about one-third of the stock of US investment abroad in the 1992, but a smaller share in 2003. Foreign investment in these activities into the United States stayed stable at about one-third. Consistent with these stock data, in terms of the flows of investment, the foreign inflow is trending much more toward these private services, such as finance and business services with 60 percent of the foreign investment inflow into the United States in these services activities. US direct investment outflows in these activities were only about a third of total outflows of direct investment. Looking at the whole picture, direct investment in private service activities is growing more important on the inbound side, rather than US service-sector multinationals investing more and more abroad.

Finally, the third channel—affiliate sales. Even with information technology, digitization, and codification, many aspects of the production and delivery of services require local proximity (knowledge of local regulations and tastes, for example). US direct investment abroad (and foreign investment in the United States) is the platform to tailor and deliver services to the local marketplace. This channel of global engagement has been growing much more quickly than the channel of international trade transactions, and the growth of affiliate sales of services swamps affiliate sales of all goods and services. But, just as for direct investment, affiliate sales of services in the US by foreign multinationals is a higher share of their total affiliate sales than is the comparable share of services sales for US affiliates abroad.

Trade and Investment Links: US Versus Foreign Multinationals

Examining the linkages between the three channels of global engagement—trade, direct investment, and affiliate sales—is important for a number of reasons. First, to what extent is direct investment a complement or substitute for trade? To what extent is direct investment a prerequisite for foreign sales? How do these relationships play out for macroeconomic measures of the United States in global trade? These questions have been researched in the context of trade and investment in goods but are only now beginning to be examined in the context of services (Helpman, Melitz, and Yeaple 2003; Van Welsum 2004).

Do the linkages between direct investment and trade differ between manufacturing and private services? At first blush, no. But looking deeper the answer is yes, perhaps with consequences for the US going forward. Consider the large categories: For manufacturing, intrafirm trade—that is, cross-border trade between the parent company and its affiliates in the other country—accounts for about 30 percent of imports and about 40 percent of exports. For private services as a whole, intrafirm trade is about the same—40 percent for both imports and exports. However, this apparent similarity masks very different intrafirm trade shares for individual categories of private services.

Drilling down further into the data on other private services to sectors where information technology may be playing a leading role in driving international trade reveals the following: In finance, the intrafirm share of imports rose from 46 to 60 percent (1997–2002) whereas the intrafirm share of exports was substantially lower and held nearly constant at 20 percent. In business and professional services, the intrafirm share of imports held steady at 70 percent whereas the intrafirm share of exports rose from 50 to 58 percent (BEA data). From 1997 to 2002, the increase in direct investment in these services activities was about the same amount for US firms abroad and foreign firms in the United States. Collecting the data on cross-border trade and direct investment in these services sectors most affected by information technology suggests a complementarity between direct investment and trade that is stronger for US imports than for exports. US direct investment abroad in private services may be limited by restrictions in foreign marketplaces, so that US firms satisfy market demand via arm's-length exports to these markets. In contrast, foreign firms apparently are less restricted in investing in the US marketplace and thus satisfy local demand relatively less through arm's-length imports.

Pulling together the data on the private services share of direct investment, affiliate sales, and cross-border trade, and comparing the behavior of US and foreign multinationals in these activities, it appears that foreign firms in private services use the direct investment platform for a higher percent of their sales in the US market. But, since they have a higher percentage of *intrafirm* trade in these sectors, they, in some sense, are less effective at turning their investment platform into value-added in the United States. That is, although foreign firms have a high share of affiliate sales, they also have a high share of intermediate imports to produce those affiliate sales. Hence, foreign multinationals generate relatively lower value-added in the US marketplace.

In contrast, US firms export more services directly, have looser ties between direct investment abroad and trade (reflected in a lower share of intrafirm trade), and generate an equally high share of affiliate sales in the destination market for private services. Thus US firms generate relatively more value from their investment platforms abroad.

What economic value accrues to the United States through direct investment and increased affiliate sales in marketplaces abroad? US multinational profits on the overall relationship of trade, direct investment, and affiliate sales will be greater. And to the extent that US affiliates abroad sell products (such as software) that are protected by intellectual property rights, such sales contribute positively to the balance of payments through net receipts on intellectual property.

Figure 9.1 shows one way to assess, in the macro context, the benefits of global engagement beyond cross-border trade. The goods and services trade balance is the traditional presentation. The ownership-based balance sums the trade balance with net receipts—that is, value-added—from sales by affiliates (US affiliates abroad less foreign affiliates in the United States).

The ownership-based balance mimics the traditional account, but with a positive difference. The positive difference reflects, apparently, the ability of the US firms to effectively and efficiently combine US management and other assets with foreign inputs to create greater value in markets abroad than that created by the reverse combination of foreign management and US resources in the United States for foreign affiliates (Kravis and Lipsey 1988, the first in a long line of research).

The positive difference identified between the standard measures of cross-border trade and the ownership-based measure of the current ac-

Figure 9.1 Measures of US external balance and global engagement

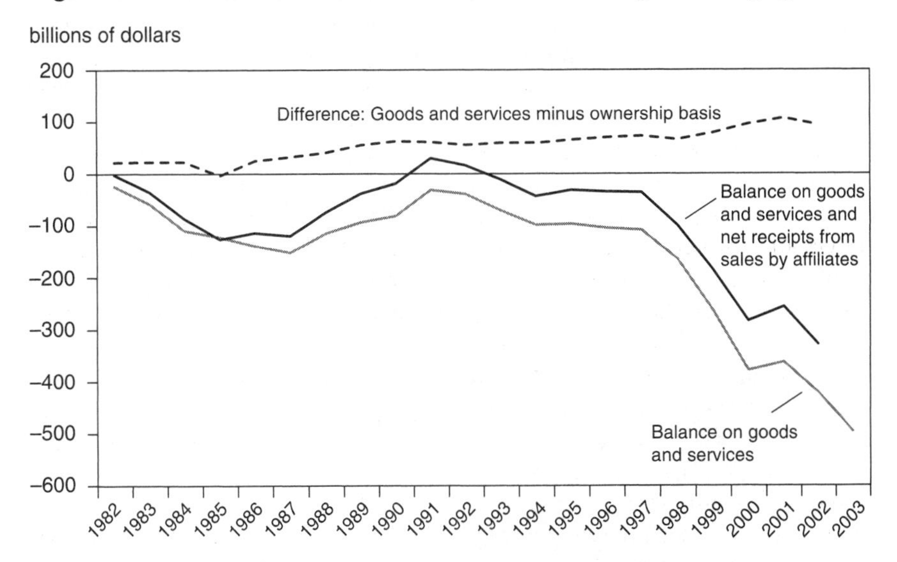

Source: Bureau of Economic Analysis, International Transactions table 1, Survey of Current Business October 1995, January 2003, and January 2004.

count is about $100 billion and has increased modestly over the last 20 years, with a widening since about 1998. This widening in recent years could suggest an increasingly important competitive edge enjoyed by US firms in their global relationships, which may be related to the increased role of private services in trade, direct investment, and affiliate sales. Although these net receipts do not represent a cross-border flow of goods or capital, they do suggest the importance of international integration of production and distribution for US corporate fitness and dynamism, which is part of the underpinnings of continued productivity growth and US economic performance.

Globalization of Services and Jobs: The Numbers for the United States

By themselves, the offshore activities of firms and development of cross-border trade in services might not have garnered much attention. But domestic jobs, particularly white-collar jobs, have become the focus of much concern against a backdrop of a modest technology turnaround, a business cycle that has not yet yielded sustained robust job creation, a trend decline in manufacturing employment that has spread to white-collar manufacturing employees, and an international environment of tepid growth in key markets abroad and, until several years ago, an appreciated dollar that has limited exports and hence exacerbated the domestic situation. Workers, both blue- and white-collar, see substantial threats to their jobs coming not only from goods produced abroad but also from the technology that allows white-collar jobs, ranging from back-office to research and development, to be done abroad rather than in the United States.

Data on the dynamics of the US labor market from the Bureau of Labor Statistics (BLS) are quite comprehensive but do not disentangle the many factors (domestic, international, and technological) that affect job creation and job loss. The ability of the data to specifically address how many jobs have been lost to increased global activity of US firms in general or to offshore outsourcing of ITES in particular is quite limited (GAO 2004).

It is even more challenging to project forward in time the implications for US labor of changes in technology, trade, or global business strategies. Theory helps outline the long-run effect of increased international trade and global engagement in services on income distribution, but the short-run dynamic effect on jobs may be more germane for immediate policy purposes.

Overview of the Current Employment Situation

Official data are difficult to wade through and interpret, so there has been a tendency to answer questions about offshore outsourcing of jobs using anecdotes and proprietary surveys. With respect to jobs lost, several consultancies estimate that around 500,000 to 1 million jobs may have been lost to trade roughly since the technology boom peaked and recession started around the end of 2000 and early 2001. Using a methodological decomposition and input-output matrices, Martin Baily and Robert Lawrence suggest that 314,000 jobs were lost on account of trade (2000–03)—with the drop in exports more than accounting for all the job losses. By either estimation survey or anecdote, these job losses are not large for an economy where 130 million are employed and where "job churn" is quite high in both good and bad economic times.

One problem with many analyses is that they take the peak of the business cycle and technology cycle as the benchmark performance of the US economy. While 3.9 percent unemployment without inflation is enviable, using a generational low as benchmark economic performance will exacerbate any estimate of job loss. Moreover, manufacturing job loss, white-collar job loss, and the causes of job loss are often conflated. Finally, classification changes in the official data in 1999 and 2000 correspond with the exact timing of economic fluctuations, making it even more difficult to discern a clear picture of US labor market dynamics.

Despite the difficulty in interpretation, it is important to return to the BLS data. First, offshore activities cut across industries so that it is important to look at employment data categorized by occupation (software programmer) rather than sector (information publishing). Second, it is important to cut through the boom and bust period and start the assessment before the end of 2000. (For a detailed discussion of alternative BLS data, see Kirkegaard 2004.) What do these data say about the evolution of US employment, particularly in those services occupations thought to be most affected by information technology, digitization, and codification and therefore most at risk for offshoring? (See table 9.2.)

The employment situation has not recovered to its prerecession peak, but the mix of jobs has moved relatively more *toward* those services activities thought to be most affected by globalization and technological change, rather than away from them. (A detailed discussion of the IT sector and occupations is in the next section.) Over the whole economy, the main decline in jobs has been in the manufacturing sector, although a substantial share of the jobs lost (20 percent) are services occupations within manufacturing. Jobs in the private services–providing sector have more than fully recovered to the prerecession level. Among three categories of jobs thought to be most at risk for technology to drive the jobs offshore, occupations in business and financial occupations never declined even through the recession, architecture and engineering (mostly engineering occupations) and computer and math occupations (mostly computer occupations) are recovering and are very near or have exceeded their technology-boom peaks.

Another perspective is to examine recent job performance in the context of ongoing creation and destruction of jobs in the US economy. In the US economy, there is remarkable *job churn*—that is, the constant creation and destruction of jobs, where "destruction" measures job losers and job *leavers* (figure 9.2). Between 7 and 8 percent of all private jobs in the United States are created and destroyed every quarter. During the boom years of the late 1990s, an increasing number of jobs were created and lost every quarter in the United States. Of course, in those boom years more jobs were created than lost, so the unemployment rate fell.

One of the notable features of the difficult job situation since the recession has been the dramatic drop in job churn. Even now, well after the official end of the recession, the job churn rate has barely turned up. An increased rate of job creation is key for lowering the unemployment rate. But an increased rate of job destruction may also be a measure of a healthy economy to the extent that it indicates that individuals leave jobs by choice to get new ones.

Several researchers have investigated the nature of job churn and job change in recent years (Figura 2003, Groshen and Potter 2003). The research suggests that structural changes in the distribution of jobs and firms in the economy help to explain recent job market behavior. Permanent job destruction—for example, associated with structural increases in the demand for more skilled workers throughout the economy, a

Table 9.2 The current employment situation (millions at end of period)

	1999	2000	2001	2002	May 2003	November 2003	November 2004
Total nonfarm private employment	110.0	111.6	109.3	108.5	108.3	108.5	110.4(p)
Manufacturing	17.3	17.2	15.7	14.9	14.6	14.3	14.4(p)
Of which:							
Production workers	12.5	12.3	11.1	10.5	10.2	10.1	10.1(p)
Nonproduction workers	4.8	4.9	4.6	4.4	4.3	4.3	4.2(p)
Private service providing	85.4	87.1	68.2	86.3	86.5	86.8	88.4(p)
Business and financial occupations	4.4	4.6	4.7	4.7	4.9	5.0	5.4[a]
Computer and mathematical occupations	2.6	2.9	2.9	2.7	2.9	2.8	2.9[a]
Architecture and engineering occupations	2.5	2.6	2.5	2.4	2.4	2.4	2.5[a]

a. The November 2004 number has been generated using the rate of change from November 2003 to November 2004 in the unseasonally adjusted data from the BLS Current Population Survey (CPS), series LNU02032454 (Business and Financial Occupations), LNU02032455 (Computer and mathematical Occupations), and LNU02032456 (Architecture and Engineering Occupations).

Note: All data seasonally adjusted from BLS Current Employment Statistics (CES) 1999–2002 end of period, 2003, and 2004 monthly data. Occupational data are from BLS Occupational Employment Statistics (OES) National Occupational Survey.

Source: BLS CES, OES, and CPS surveys.

Figure 9.2 US job turnover, 1992–2004 (millions)

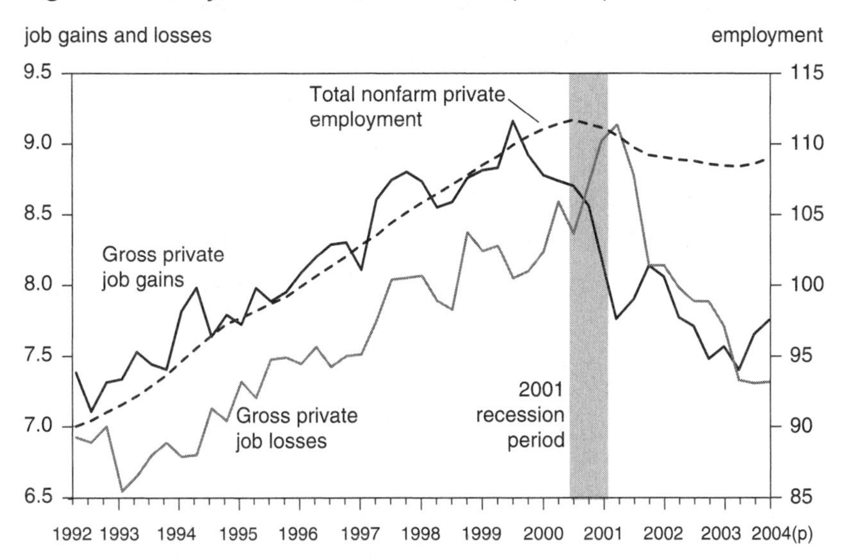

Note: Data are for March, June, September, and December of the years indicated.

Source: US Department of Commerce, Bureau of Labor Statistics, Current Establishment Survey data and business dynamics data.

structural shift away from manufacturing toward services, and a structural reduction in unionization—has a larger and more extended effect of raising unemployment than permanent job creation has to reduce unemployment. This is because job loss is permanent and job gains are delayed. These same structural factors also contribute to slow job creation. Hence, the pace of technological change and its impact on globalization of services may be part of the reason behind lower job churn.

Technology Driver and Potential for Job Creation

How might technology and globalization of services affect job creation and destruction going forward? Numerous consultancy reports detail how companies are outsourcing services activities to domestic or foreign locations, what the growth of the markets here and abroad might be, and the implications for job growth and loss. Some offer a more generalized framework for how information technologies that lower transactions costs, allow production fragmentation, and promote separability of services activities might have different effects on the types of jobs to be created in the United States and abroad (Bardhan and Kroll 2003).

A key consideration when evaluating these projections is not just the potential for increased international trade in services but also the corresponding growth in demand for services in the US market. Many analyses assume a fixed demand for services and a one-for-one replacement of jobs in the United States with jobs abroad. But in a world where the demand for services is both income and price elastic, the future for services output (and the jobs that go with that) is very bright. The fragmentation of production and the local specialization of services activities enabled by IT yields rising demand for internationally traded services production as well as rising demand for domestically sourced services activities. What is at issue is not the number of jobs but the kind of jobs in the services sectors where technology is enabling international trade.

The BLS offers projections for growth in occupations. In February 2004, the BLS issued a new *Occupational Outlook Handbook* for 2002–12. In this recent outlook, three of the top 10 and seven of the top 30 fastest-growing occupations are IT-related occupations—the same type of jobs as those considered to be at risk for being done abroad. In the November 2001 handbook, 8 of the top 10 and 10 of the top 30 fastest-growing occupations were IT-related. Does the difference in projections warrant concern about job creation in IT-related occupations and point to the pressures on US job creation from technology-enabled international trade in services and offshore job creation? Not really.

The main difference between the two projections is a reduction of the projected growth rate of what were the top growing IT occupations from 100 percent projected growth to 45 percent projected growth. That drops the IT occupations from the top 10 to the next 20. It appears that the BLS employment outlook in November 2001 suffered from a technology bubble of its own! On the other hand, projected growth of 45 percent for IT occupations is still three times the projected growth of jobs overall in the economy. Hence, even with increased tradability of services, the demand for workers with skills to match jobs in IT-enabled services in the domestic marketplace is huge. Moreover, based on average wages now, these IT jobs pay more than twice the average wage. Indeed, some have wondered whether there are sufficiently skilled workers to match the demand in the United States.

Economic theories of the effect of international trade offer another look at the future. International trade theories assume full employment, so the impact of global engagement comes through wages of certain workers, not the overall number of jobs. The simplest models of international trade (Ricardo and Heckscher-Ohlin) show that the wages of the scarce factor (US manufacturing workers in the context of a US–China comparison, for example) decline when trade opens up. This story, albeit about wages, is consistent with the observed decline in manufacturing employment already experienced. Rybczynski's model of international trade with expanding resources shows that a new supply of white-collar workers made available in the world economy (well-trained Indian English speakers, for example) should reduce the wages of that type of factor—workers in the sectors where technology enables international trade. But jobs have increased since the recession for the three main occupational categories thought most at risk and wages are rising.

These simple theories ignore key realities that are particularly important when modeling globalization of private services: how *demand* for activities and workers changes with the price of services and the income level of the consumer, and how technology of digitization and codification allows the *fragmentation of production* and international division of labor. Specifically, these simple international trade models assume a price and income elasticity of one (rather than the estimated income- and price-elastic nature of services discussed earlier) and assume unchanging technology of production (which misses the whole point). These assumptions do not match the reality of technology and trade in private services.

In contrast to the other theories, for Bhagwati, Panagariya, and Srinivasan's model the ability to trade skilled services internationally is an innovation. Trade increases economic well-being in both countries because the newly tradable product acts as a productivity-enhancing intermediate to the overall production process. In the context of the United States, the increased tradability of private services is a concrete example of this model. Empirical evidence in support of this model will be discussed in the next section, which focuses explicitly on international trade in IT products.

Globalization of IT and US Performance

The benefit achieved through globalization of IT hardware is a model for the potential benefits of globalization of private services.

Gains from Global Sourcing: The First Wave Based on IT Hardware

Hard evidence on the gains from global sourcing comes from looking at patterns of production, investment, and use of IT. In the United States in the 1990s, globalization of IT hardware resulted in IT prices some 10 to 30 percent lower than they would have been based on domestic production and domestic technological advances alone (Mann 2003). Lower prices increased investment and use of IT hardware. Because the price elasticity of demand of IT is greater than one (Bayoumi and Haacker 2002), price declines spurred a greater than one-for-one increase in investment throughout the economy. Also, lower prices freed up resources for other activities within firms, including the important reorienting and transforming of business activities within the firm and changing workplace practices to use IT more effectively (Black and Lynch 2004; Bresnahan, Brynjolfsson, and Hitt 2002).

The increased IT investment and transformation of business activities and workplace practices raised productivity and real GDP growth in the United States. Altogether, IT accounted for well over half of the acceleration of structural productivity growth of the 1990s, which supported both the higher GDP growth (4 percent) and lower unemployment (3.9 percent) enjoyed by the US economy in the second half of the decade.

The diffusion of IT capital through the US economy was uneven, with some sectors leading in IT investment and productivity growth and others lagging the average. These different experiences offer important contrasts that help to understand the future role of global sourcing of IT services and software. Some sectors, such as wholesale trade, electronic products, and financial institutions, invested relatively more in IT, whereas other sectors such as health services, business services, and construction invested relatively less. Productivity performance at the sector level is similarly uneven, with the sectors with the highest investment having the highest productivity growth (figure 9.3).

IT investment throughout the economy prompted an increase in demand for IT workers throughout the economy. The diffusion of IT investment throughout the economy is reflected in a similar diffusion of workers in IT occupations. As of mid-2003 (latest available data), more than two-thirds of the people employed in IT jobs did not work in the IT sector, but rather designed, modified, and integrated IT for companies outside the IT sector. Not surprisingly, there is a positive correlation between the leading sectors in terms of IT hardware investment and the sectors that hired the most IT professionals: IT investment and IT jobs go hand in hand (Mann 2004a).

As is well known, the structural change in the US economy toward IT has not been without bumps. Figure 9.4 shows that the technology boom and crash have been felt in both investment and occupations. The complementarity between IT capital and IT workers, described above with the detailed sectoral data, worked to increase IT occupations during the technology boom, but has been a drag on IT job creation recently. Nevertheless, as shown here, and noted in the job performance data in table 9.2, as IT investment has rebounded, so too has the demand for IT workers.

Software and IT Services: The Next Wave of Global Sourcing

Going forward, the United States is poised for (indeed, perhaps is in the midst of) a second wave of IT investment, growth in IT jobs, and faster overall productivity growth, as components of software and IT services are produced more cheaply abroad as part of a digitized, codified, and therefore fragmented international production of private services. A key source of the gains to investment, jobs, and productivity will be the diffusion of IT into the sectors that did not take up IT during the 1990s, as well as a deepening of investment in the leading sectors.

How does globalization of services meet the challenges of lagging sectors? Despite the technology boom of the 1990s, large sectors in the US

Figure 9.3 IT intensity and contribution to GDP per FTE growth, 1989–2000 (size of bubbles indicate shares of GDP by individual sector)

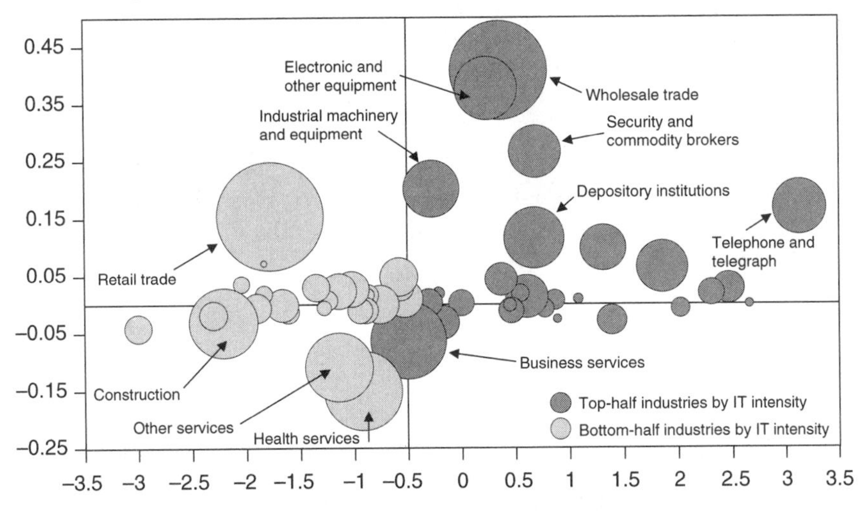

ITEQ/FTE = information technology equipment/full-time equivalent (worker).

Source: US Department of Commerce, Economic and Statistics Administration, *Digital Economy 2002*, table A4.4.

economy—such as health services (5 percent of GDP) and education (2 percent of GDP)—and many small and medium-sized enterprises (SMEs) do not use IT very intensively. Reasons range from cost to culture to regulatory constraints. For example, SMEs are very cost-conscious, often need tailored (rather than cheaper off-the-shelf) software, and demand proximity for customer care and other IT services. In health services, regulatory issues are quite important for software and services design as is the complexity of the relationships in health services delivery (between doctors, hospitals, and pharmacies).

These issues have interacted with the higher relative cost of software and services to put IT further out of reach of these firms. That is, as hardware prices fell in the 1990s, the importance of software and IT services rose in overall spending on the IT package of hardware, software, and services. In 1993, for each $1 spent on hardware, firms in the United States spent $1.40 on software and services. But by 2000, the ratio was $2.20 on software and services per $1 on hardware (World Information Technology and Software Alliance [WITSA] data).

Figure 9.4 IT investment and IT services employment (annual growth)

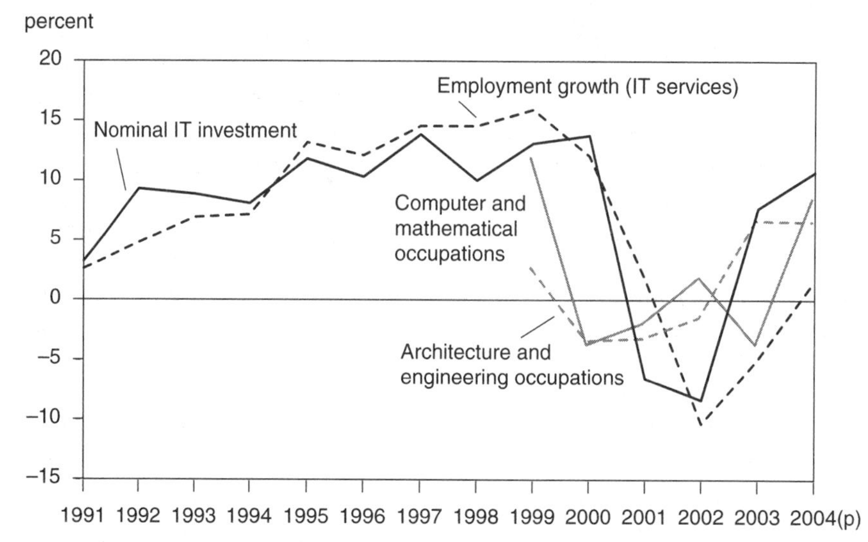

Note: IT services consists of software publishing (NAICS category 5512), internet service providers, search portals and data processing (NAICS 518), and computer systems design and related services (NAICS 5415). Does not include IT employment outside these sectors. 2004 data for IT investment are the average of Q1, Q2, and Q3 final data. 2004 IT services employment data are last available data for September 2004(p). Computer and Mathematical Occupations and Architecture and Engineering Occupations are annual OES data benchmarked to the last quarter of 1999, 2000, 2001, and 2002. 2003 data refers to May 2003, whereas 2004 data have been created by growing the May 2003 OES data point by the rate of change from the CPS monthly data from May 2003 to September 2004.

Source: Bureau of Labor Statistics and author's calculations.

The United States gains from cheaper globally sourced components in software and IT services production because doing so will reduce the price of customized software and tailored services. Econometric estimates show that the demand for software and services increases more than one for one with reductions in price to an even greater degree than IT hardware (Bayoumi and Haacker 2002). Therefore, as prices fall, demand for services and software will rise more than one for one, helping to diffuse IT into the lagging sectors, deepening the use of IT in the leading sectors, raising productivity growth throughout the US economy, and increasing the demand for workers with integrative IT skills in all sectors.

What are "integrative skills"? Demand will increase for workers with the IT skills necessary to design, customize, and integrate IT applications and services, particularly for the lagging sectors and SMEs. These workers, although they may be classified in the occupational category of "IT occupations," will have a wealth of sector-specific knowledge that is absolutely crucial. Although the technology skills may be importable, the local knowledge specific to a customer need is unique to the United States. Jobs that mesh the technical and the locality-specific knowledge will be the ones that stay in the United States.

In fact, data point in this direction to how technology and globalization are affecting the mix of skills being demanded in the United States (table 9.3). Between 1999 and November 2003 (time period for which data are available), the number of "programming" jobs, earning on average $64,000, fell by about 125,000. But, jobs held by applications and systems software engineers, database analysts, and network engineers earning on average $74,000 increased by some 425,000. Overall jobs for high-wage IT occupations increased some 10 percent against the increase in jobs of just 1 percent in the US economy overall. Thus global sourcing of software and services, even as it increases the number of IT jobs, changes the mix of IT jobs—with a greater emphasis on creating products that use IT to meet the needs of US businesses.

On the other hand, the combined effect of technology and international trade can also be seen in occupations that use IT but are less highly skilled and pay lower wages—around $25,000. These occupations—telemarketers, switchboard operators, telephone operators, computer operators, data entry keyers, word processors and typists, and office machine operators—experienced very large job losses (545,000) over the entire period of available data (from 1999 to November 2003)—a decline of 30 percent employment. These jobs are not likely to return to the United States or indeed anywhere, to the extent that they have been replaced by technology itself.

Broader Implications

Examining the IT sector alone is a useful model for considering the broader implications for the United States of technology and globalization of services. First, IT investment is price elastic. Lower prices obtained in part through the fragmentation and global sourcing of IT raised the demand for these products in the United States and increased jobs and wages for workers with complementary IT skills. IT investment alone, and through the way it transformed business activities and promoted new workplace practices, raised productivity and growth in the United States. The process of technological change and globalization of software and services is just beginning but has the same characteristics as IT hardware where the process and implications are well in train.

Private services such as finance and professional services are a broader set of activities where technology is lowering transactions costs of trade as well as allowing the fragmentation of production and separation to locations remote from both core business and final customer. But, the demand for these services is price elastic, just as for IT hardware and IT services and software. Hence globalization and technological change reduce prices

Table 9.3 Selected US technology occupations, 1999–November 2003

	1999–November 2003		November 2003	
	Absolute change in employment	Percent change	Employment (number of workers)	Wages (dollars)
Call-center type occupations[a]	–126,110	–22	444,500	~25,000
Low-wage technology workers[b]	–419,140	–33	856,720	~24,000
Total call-center and low-wage technology workers	–545,250	–30	1,301,220	25,191
Comparable: Production workers in the manufacturing sector		–20		
High-wage technology workers				
Computer programmers, SOC 15-1021	–125,380	–31	403,220	65,170
Computer software engineers, applications, systems software analysts, SOC 15-1031, 1032, 1051	263,980	22	1,188,820	~73,000
Database administrators, SOC 15-1061	–3,920	–4	97,540	62,100
Network and systems administrators and data communications engineers and analysts, SOC 15-1071, 1081	137,800	21	645,490	~65,000
Computer hardware and electrical engineers, SOC 17-2061, 2071, 2072	34,430		350,890	~77,000
Total high-wage technology workers	264,470	11	2,465,120	69,992
Comparable: Total CES employment		1		

a. Call-center type occupations: Telemarketers and telephone operators: SOC 41-9041;43-2021

b. Low-wage technology workers: Switchboard, answering services, computer operator, data entry, and word processors: SOC 43-2011,9011, 9021,9022

Source: Bureau of Labor Statistics CES data, 1999, 2000, 2001, 2002, May 2003, and November 2003, National Occupational Employment and Wage Estimates.

and augment demand. In addition, private services are income elastic. Thus, income growth at home and abroad, as well as the process of market opening and development abroad, will increase the local and global demand for these services. Globalization of services is different from globalization of manufactured goods because of these two key elasticities.

Globalization of Services: Is There No End to It?

If the main motivator propelling international trade in private services is technology, along with lower wages in developing countries and a narrower education gap, is there nothing to stop all such services and jobs from going to lower-wage countries?

Several factors point to retained jobs in industrial countries (in addition to the market-expansion effect noted earlier). First and foremost, not all jobs can be codified and digitized. Face-to-face interaction is still required at many points in product development, marketing, delivery, and maintenance. Local knowledge is critical, for example, to understand the thicket of health care regulations or legal codes. Businesses of a certain size need more customer care and demand proximity of the service provider. At rock bottom, there are differences in tastes and preferences, such that some transactions and their jobs will remain local.

Another factor that may limit globalization of private services is the interface between the global marketplace and the local jurisdiction of policy. For example, there are no global rules specifying how cross-border transactions of data should be treated with respect to privacy rules or treatment of intellectual property (the Agreement on Trade-Related Aspects of Intellectual Property Rights [TRIPS] notwithstanding). Consumer and business attitudes toward the balance between market-oriented and government-legislated solutions in these issue areas are not homogeneous across countries (nor even within a country) (Mann 2001, 2002). The best that is likely to be achieved in the long run is mutual recognition agreements, but in general these agreements do not yet exist. With differing rules across countries, globalization of transactions in some fragmented private services could founder.

Responding to Global Sourcing: Maximizing Gains and Moderating the Backlash

The advent of the internet, along with codification, and digitization of knowledge, has separated services into components so that they do not need to be done contiguously and can instead be done globally. While this may contribute positively to job creation and productivity growth, as detailed earlier, the specter of immediate job loss, particularly in high-skill, white-collar occupations, looms large. Although the market-expanding aspects of the globalization of private services points to more jobs overall, the skills demanded to do those jobs will change during this technologically volatile time, and some jobs will be lost. A framework for describing in general terms the kinds of jobs lost helps to structure policies to address the issue.

One type of job loss comes, as it has in manufacturing, from technology itself. Automated teller machines, voice-answering technologies, and word-processing software are replacing bank tellers, answering services, and secretaries. A second type of job loss is at the low-wage, low-skill end of the services-job spectrum—jobs that are being replaced by cheaper workers abroad. A third kind of job loss comes as some higher-skill jobs are now codified and digitized and therefore can be separated from the core business activity (for example, computer programming and financial analysis) and may be done abroad. A fourth type of job loss is projected job loss: Although higher-paid jobs demanding IT skills are, by BLS projections, expected to grow very quickly, if workers in the United States do not have the requisite skills, then workers in foreign countries may get these jobs. Policy initiatives on the international and domestic fronts are needed to respond to these four types of real and potential job loss. On the international side, the potential for markets abroad should be maximized through macroeconomic stimulus and a focus on trade and investment negotiations. On the domestic side, domestic sourcing should be maximized through labor policies that promote skill upgrading and skill matching for the jobs being created in the United States by technological change and globalization.

International Dimension of Policy

As discussed earlier, data on international trade in services show that US providers dominate global trade. Econometric analysis shows that exports of these services rise disproportionately with increases in income abroad. The data also show the relatively lower US foreign direct investment in private services in markets abroad, which inhibits the growth of affiliate sales. Promoting foreign macroeconomic growth as well as engaging in trade negotiations to open the markets abroad for US services are key to growth in output, trade, and services-sector jobs at home.

Research on potential gains from trade negotiations makes clear that the United States (as well as developing countries) has much to gain from a Doha Round that moves beyond agriculture and market access for manufactures. Table 9.4 details just how dramatic these gains might be. For the world, the gain from liberalization of services alone is greater than liberalization of manufactures and agriculture put together—$390 billion versus $223 billion. For the United States, the gain from liberalization of all

Table 9.4 Estimated gains from trade and investment liberalization

	All sectors		Manufacturing only		Services only	
Region/country	Percent of GDP	Billions of dollars	Percent of GDP	Billions of dollars	Percent of GDP	Billions of dollars
World		613.0		211.0		390.0
United States	2.0	177.3	0.34	31.3	1.65	150.0
European Union & EFTA	1.5	168.9	0.58	63.3	0.94	103.4
Japan	1.9	123.7	0.89	57.8	0.85	61.7
China	1.5	13.6	0.54	4.9	0.79	7.1
Korea	2.8	14.1	1.40	8.0	0.91	5.2
Malaysia	2.8	3.4	1.99	2.4	0.54	0.6
Chile	2.4	1.9	1.29	1.0	1.17	0.9
Mexico	1.8	6.5	0.32	1.1	1.49	5.2

EFTA = European Free Trade Association

Note: Services coverage includes construction, trade and transport, other private services, and government services. Protection is measured by excess operating profits of firms listed on stock markets. Scenario shows liberalization of implied protection of 33 percent for all three sectors (agriculture, manufacturing, and services).

Sources: Brown, Deardorff, and Stern (2003, table 2, 25); see also Dee and Hanslow (2001).

services is five times greater than might be obtained from increased market access for manufactures.

Industrial-country exporters of services gain in these scenarios that liberalize trade in services. But the gains to GDP in the developing countries of allowing trade in services are nearly as large as the gains they would get if their trading partners reduced tariffs on the manufactured goods that these economies sell into global markets. How so?

Given the generally small size of the services sector in most developing countries, the empirical results mean that the multiplier effect to raise GDP must be larger for services liberalization than for increased exports of manufactured goods. This makes sense given that improved services-sector performance increases the competitiveness and efficiency of all other sectors in the economy. All told, the welfare gains throughout an economy from improving domestic services-sector performance are dramatic.

Domestic Dimension of Policy

On the domestic side, complementary strategies are needed to address labor market dislocation and change. Overall, technological change and globalization put an even higher premium on more education and higher skills (measured by formal schooling or trade apprenticeships, or other means). Policies are particularly needed to address two types of job losses in the technologically volatile marketplace. First, workers whose jobs have been permanently dislocated by technology or trade need to get back to work quickly to avoid loss of job skills and labor-force attachment. Second, for some skilled workers, particularly in science and technology, technology does not eliminate the whole job category, but it might alter the career path by speeding up skill depreciation and by removing certain 'rungs' of the career ladder. In this case, market imperfections argue for a human-capital investment tax credit to promote skill upgrading within an organization and career path.

For the first set of workers, extended unemployment benefits (which provide more time for adjustment), training assistance, wage insurance, and portable social insurance (such as health and pensions) are all strategies to ease the transition to a new job and new career. In particular, policies that promote a move to a new job increase the likelihood that the worker will gain new skills, which will move the worker toward a permanent career path. For example, wage insurance replaces part of the earnings lost between a previous job and the new one but is available only after the person leaves unemployment to get a new job (Kletzer and Litan 2001; also see the chapter by Lori Kletzer and Howard Rosen in this book).

A human-capital investment tax credit is a policy designed to achieve a better-functioning pipeline of skilled technology workers. Two places in the pipeline are particularly exposed to technological change and globalization: the incumbent worker, whose skills depreciate with the rate of technological progress and openness to foreign labor competition, and the entry-level job, which may no longer be done in the United States because foreign workers have those skills and do the job at lower wages. This notion of a skill pipeline is applicable not only to IT-specific skills but also to other technical workers whose skills are depreciating quickly in the face of international trade enabled by technology.

An investment tax credit recognizes three realities of the marketplace for skills: free riders, incomplete information, and spillovers. First, firms that engage in substantial training of their own workers to move their skills up the ladder beyond the threat of outsourcing face the disincentive of "free riding" by other firms that do not train. "Incomplete information" about the whole career ladder could keep students from entering into high-skills training and mid-career workers from knowing which new skills they should train for. An internship credit and incumbent training credits recognize that the first job of the technical career ladder for a worker entering from school may be a job no longer done in the United States and that even highly skilled mid-career workers face technological skill depreciation. Finally, an investment tax credit recognizes the "spillover" benefits to the economy as a whole of having a technologically trained workforce that diffuses to all sectors of the economy. Investment tax credits to address these types of imperfections in the marketplace are routinely used for physical capital investment and for research and development—amounting to some $50 billion in tax expenditures, according to the Congressional Budget Office. In today's "knowledge economy," the most important asset is people, so an investment tax credit explicitly focussed on people makes sense.

In the end, globalization of services specifically and transformation in economic activities generally mean volatility in business, job churn, and differential returns to skills. To the extent that the government's social policy prevents these changes from taking place, the gains from transformation may not occur and the cost of smoothing them out could be quite high in terms of income support. Therefore, labor market policies to deal with this technologically driven globalization of services should focus on approaches that encourage and enable workers and firms to fill opportunities coming from change, rather than focusing on moderating outcomes and avoiding change.

Final Words

The positive effects of global sourcing are undeniably real and large but depend on an environment where public, business, and worker relationships are fostered. Breaking the links, by restricting technological change, by tempering global sourcing, or by failing to upgrade the skills of US workers, puts the prospects for higher US economic growth and job creation at risk.

Analysis of information technology shows that critical ingredients for the nation as a whole to benefit from outsourcing include business transformation, new workplace practices, and technically trained workers. Workers with technical skills combined with integrative skills need to be diffused even more widely through the economy, particularly into health care services and small and medium-sized enterprises. Lower prices of software and services will promote IT investment in these sectors and raise the demand for workers with both technical and integrative skills.

More generally, labor market policies to promote adjustment and to finance skill upgrading give workers and firms the ability to gain from the technological driver and global trade and investment. At the same time, opening markets abroad to two-way trade in private services is crucial to ensure that US firms and workers can tap into foreign markets to export as well as to invest in and develop products for sale in the marketplace abroad.

References

Autor, David, Frank Levy, and Richard Murnane. 2003. The Skill Content of Recent Technological Change: An Empirical Exploration. *Quarterly Journal of Economics* 118, no. 4 (November).

Baily, Martin N., and Robert Z. Lawrence. Forthcoming. What Happened to the Great American Job Machine? The Impact of Trade and Electronic Offshoring. *Brookings Papers on Economic Activity 2: 2004*. Washington: Brookings Institution.

Bardhan, Ashok, and Cynthia Kroll. 2003. *The New Wave of Outsourcing*. Fisher Center for Real Estate & Urban Economics Research Report 1025. University of California Berkeley (November).

Bayoumi, Tamim, and Markus Haacker. 2002. *It's Not What You Make, It's How You Use IT: Measuring the Welfare Benefits of the IT Revolution Across Countries*. IMF Working Paper WP/02/117. Washington: International Monetary Fund.

Bhagwati, Jagdish, Arvind Panagariya, and T.N. Srinivasan. Forthcoming. The Muddles over Outsourcing. *The Journal of Economic Perspectives*.

Black, Sandra, and Lisa Lynch. 2004. *Workplace Practices and the New Economy*. FRBSF Economic Letter 2004-10 (April 16). Federal Reserve Bank of San Francisco.

BLS (US Bureau of Labor Statistics). 2004. *Occupational Outlook Handbook*, 2004-05 edition. Washington: Bureau of Labor Statistics.

Bresnahan, Timothy, Erik Brynjolfsson, and Lorin Hitt. 2002. Information Technology, Workplace Organization, and the Demand for Skilled Labor: Firm-Level Evidence. *The Quarterly Journal of Economics* (February): 339–76.

Brown, Drusilla K., Alan V. Deardorff, and Robert M. Stern. 2003. Impacts on NAFTA Members of Multilateral and Regional Trading Arrangements and Initiatives and Harmonization of NAFTA's External Tariffs. In *North-American Linkages*, ed., Richard G. Harris. Ottawa: Industry Canada.

Dee, Philippa, and Kevin Hanslow. 2001. Multilateral Liberalization of Services Trade. In *Services in the International Economy*, ed., Robert M. Stern. Ann Arbor, MI: University of Michigan Press.

Ellwood, David. 2001. The Sputtering Labor Force of the 21st Century: Can Social Policy Help? In *The Roaring Nineties: Can Full Employment Be Sustained?* ed., Alan Krueger and Robert Solow. New York: Russell Sage Foundation.

Figura, Andrew. 2003. The Effect of Restructuring on Unemployment. Federal Reserve Board of Governors. Photocopy (October 27).

GAO (US Government Accountability Office). 2004. *Current Government Data Provide Limited Insight into Offshoring of Services*. GAO-04-932 (September). Washington.

Groshen, Erica L., and Simon Potter. 2003. Has Structural Change Contributed to a Jobless Recovery? *Current Issues in Economics and Finance* 9, no. 8 (August). Federal Reserve Bank of New York.

Helpman, Elhanan, Marc J. Melitz, and Stephen R. Yeaple. 2003. *Export vs. FDI*. NBER Working Paper 9439. Cambridge MA: National Bureau of Economic Research.

Kirkegaard, Jacob. 2004. Outsourcing: Stains on the White Collar? Washington: Institute for International Economics. www.iie.com/publications/papers/kirkegaard0204.pdf.

Kletzer, Lori, and Robert Litan. 2001. *A Prescription to Relieve Worker Anxiety*. Policy Brief 01-2 (February). Washington: Institute for International Economics and Brookings Institution.

Kravis, Irving B., and Robert E. Lipsey. 1988. *The Competitiveness and Comparative Advantage of US Multinationals, 1957–1984*. NBER Working Paper 2051. Cambridge, MA: National Bureau of Economic Research.

Mann, Catherine L. 2004a. Global Sourcing and High-tech Jobs: Economic Gains and Policy Challenges. Presentation, March. www.iie.com/publications/papers/mann0304.pdf

Mann, Catherine L. 2004b. The US Current Account, New Economy Services, and Implications for Sustainability. *Review of International Economics* 12, no. 2 (May).

Mann, Catherine L. 2003. *Globalization of IT Services and White-Collar Jobs: The Next Wave of Productivity Growth*. International Economics Policy Brief 03-11 (November). Washington: Institute for International Economics.

Mann, Catherine L., assisted by Jacob F. Kirkegaard. 2003. Globalization and Information Technology Firms and the Impact on Economic Performance. Institute for International Economics, Washington. Photocopy (May).

Mann, Catherine L. 2002. Balance and Overlap in the Global Electronic Marketplace: The UCITA Example. *Washington University Journal of Law & Policy* (summer).

Mann, Catherine L. 2001. International Internet Governance: Oh, What a Tangled Web We Could Weave! *Georgetown Journal of International Affairs* (summer/fall).

Siqueira, Tiago Neves. 2003. High-Tech Human Capital: Do the Richest Countries Invest the Most? *The BE Journals in Macroeconomics, Topics in Macroeconomics* 1, no. 3.

UNCTAD (UN Conference on Trade and Development). 2004. *World Investment Report.* Geneva: United Nations.

US Department of Commerce. 2003. *Digital Economy 2002.* Washington: Department of Commerce.

US Department of Commerce. 2004. *Digital Economy 2003* (January). Washington: Department of Commerce.

Van Welsum, Desiree. 2004. In Search of "Outsourcing": Evidence from US Imports of Services. Birbeck College, London. Photocopy (May).

WITSA (World Information Technology and Software Alliance). 2002. *Digital Planet.* Arlington, VA: WITSA.

10

Easing the Adjustment Burden on US Workers

LORI G. KLETZER
and HOWARD ROSEN

US employment growth has been slow in recovering from the last recession. Two and a half years after the recession ended, total employment remains close to 1 million less than it was at the start of the recession in March 2001.[1] By comparison, total employment had grown by close to 5 million and 10 million, at the same point in the business cycle, after the recessions in the 1990s and the 1980s, respectively (table 10.1). A similar pattern is evident in manufacturing employment, although the numbers for net employment decline following the 1990 and current recessions are far greater than for total employment.

The cyclical nature of employment fluctuations gets headline attention, but monthly data on employment levels released by the Bureau of Labor Statistics (BLS) hide a much deeper and more interesting story about the US labor market. Data on total employment tend to understate the flexibility of the US labor market. Figure 10.1 presents recent BLS data for total

Lori Kletzer is a senior fellow at the Institute for International Economics and professor of economics at the University of California, Santa Cruz. Howard Rosen is executive director of the Trade Adjustment Assistance Coalition. *The authors are grateful to Shara Aranoff, C. Fred Bergsten, Mac Destler, Kimberly Elliott, Catherine Mann, Greg Mastel, Bill Reinsch, Randy Soderquist, and Ted Truman for their useful comments.*

1. Based on recession start date as determined by the National Bureau of Economic Research, with employment levels to July 2004.

Table 10.1 Change in employment 39 months into recovery (in millions)

Period	Total	Manufacturing
1980s	9.9	1.0
1990s	5.3	–0.2
2000s	–0.9	–2.4

Source: Authors' calculations based on BLS data.

job gains and losses. These data, rather than the more popular monthly or annual change in *net* employment, provide a more accurate picture of job turnover and dynamism in the US labor market.

Between 1992 and 2004, on average, 32.5 million jobs were created each year. Over the same period, on average, 30.8 million jobs were lost each year. Taking both job creation and destruction into account, total employment grew by approximately 1.6 million each year.[2]

A flexible labor market can benefit an economy, especially when workers have the opportunity to move from low- to high-productivity jobs. Young workers in particular benefit from turnover, when they gain skills and experience and find productive matches with employers. At the same time, labor-market flexibility can impose significant costs on workers and their families. Workers can experience prolonged unemployment, and once reemployed, they may experience large and persistent earnings losses.[3]

The United States has a well-developed and broad set of labor-market adjustment policies and programs, with Unemployment Insurance (UI) at their center. Other programs include advance notice for major layoffs, mandated by the Worker Adjustment and Retraining Notification (WARN) Act, and training and job search assistance, provided under the Workforce Investment Act (WIA). In addition, the United States is the only country that provides special assistance to workers who lose their jobs due to increased imports and international shifts in production.

Despite the breadth of labor-market policies and programs, there is considerable evidence that these interventions are inadequate. By many standards, US assistance to unemployed workers is modest. Only a minority of workers are eligible for and receive UI when they lose their jobs. Over the last five years, only one-third of unemployed workers received assis-

2. The BLS reports that the average annual change in total employment over the same period was approximately 1.8 million. These employment data are derived from the payroll survey as reported in the Current Employment Statistics and differ from the job losses and job gains discussed above in the text.

3. See Jacobson, LaLonde, and Sullivan (1993) and Kletzer (2001) for estimates of earnings losses associated with job displacement.

Figure 10.1 Quarterly job gains and losses, 1992–2002

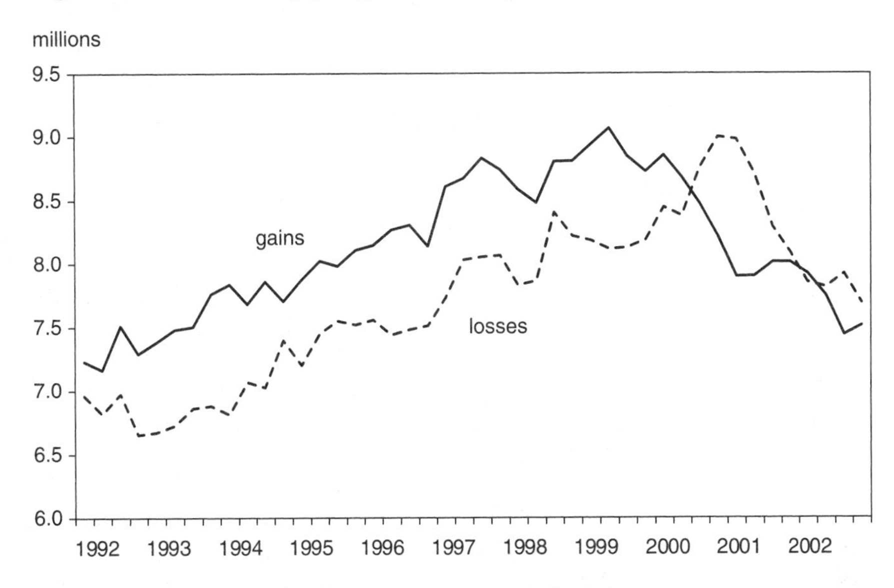

Source: Business Dynamics Database, Bureau of Labor Statistics.

tance under the UI program. The level of UI assistance is also low. Eligible workers receive up to 26 weeks of assistance, at an average of $250 per week, which is below the poverty rate for a family of four (US Bureau of the Census 2004). Training and job search assistance are available only on a first-come, first-served basis, and funding caps limit availability. States often exhaust their federal allocation of funds well before the end of the fiscal year. As a result, very few workers receive meaningful training (GAO 2002).

US spending on active labor-market adjustment programs, such as training, job search assistance, and wage subsidies, is also modest compared with other countries (table 10.2). Relative to five other major industrialized countries, the United States spends the least on active labor-market adjustment programs, even after taking into account each country's unemployment rate. France and Germany each devote about five times more to their active labor-market programs than does the United States.

The technical and methodological issues involved in properly evaluating the effectiveness of US (or any country's) labor-market adjustment programs are considerable. These issues aside, evidence on program effectiveness is mixed at best. Past evaluations find that unemployment insurance and training programs do not appear to make any significant difference in shortening the duration of unemployment or raising incomes once workers are reemployed (see, for example, Betcherman, Olivas, and Dar 2004 and Dar and Tzannatos 1999).

Table 10.2 Spending on active labor-market adjustment programs, 2000–01

Country	As a percent of GDP	Ratio of spending as a percent of GDP to the unemployment rate	As a percent of total spending on all labor-market programs
Canada	0.41	0.06	36.4
France	1.32	0.14	44.4
Germany	1.21	0.16	38.6
Japan	0.28	0.06	34.2
United Kingdom	0.37	0.07	40.0
United States	0.15	0.03	32.9

Source: OECD, *Employment Outlook 2003.*

Weak evidence of program effectiveness has not stopped the United States, or other countries for that matter, from continuing to introduce and administer labor-market adjustment programs. This suggests that governments are motivated by other factors in assisting displaced workers, such as social and political factors.

Modest US labor-market adjustment programs heighten anxiety over job loss. Because workers bear most of the burden of labor-market flexibility, there is understandably great concern over government policies that might place more pressure on them. These concerns have intensified calls to compensate workers adversely affected by government policies and have resulted in targeted assistance to select groups of workers.

Trade Adjustment Assistance

President John F. Kennedy and Congress established the Trade Adjustment Assistance (TAA) program in 1962 to provide assistance to workers who lose jobs due to increased import competition. A combination of weak labor-market adjustment programs for all workers and the unique manner in which trade policy is made in the United States contributed to TAA's establishment. In the United States, in contrast to other countries, Congress must temporarily transfer authority to the president in order for the government to participate in trade negotiations. This provides Congress an opportunity to influence the negotiating agenda. Congress has also used this opportunity to compensate US workers potentially adversely affected by any resulting changes in foreign competition.

Between 1974 and 2002, approximately 25 million workers were eligible, and 2.5 million workers received assistance under TAA. More than half of these workers were employed in the auto, textiles, apparel, and steel industries. Assistance included up to 52 weeks of income maintenance (beyond the standard 26 weeks of UI), training, and job search and relocation assistance.[4] The average weekly payment for income maintenance in fiscal 2000 was a little above $200 per week, less than half the total average weekly earnings, which was $474, and considerably less than the average weekly earnings in manufacturing, which was $598 (data from the US Department of Labor).

With the approval of the North American Free Trade Agreement (NAFTA) in 1993, Congress established a separate program for workers who lost their jobs due to increased imports from and/or shifts in production to Canada and Mexico. The NAFTA–Transitional Adjustment Assistance (NAFTA-TAA) program provided almost identical assistance to that provided under the general TAA program, with the exception of some differences in the scope of coverage. In addition to covering workers who lost their jobs from import-competing industries, NAFTA-TAA provided assistance to workers who lost their jobs due to shifts in production. The US Department of Labor (DOL) also provided assistance to some "secondary workers"—for example, people who worked for suppliers or downstream producers for firms that faced increased import competition from Canada or Mexico.[5] NAFTA-TAA created considerable overlap, confusion, and arbitrary discrimination between workers.

Political Support for TAA

TAA has never received strong or enthusiastic support. Although labor unions ensure that their members receive the assistance provided under the program, they have always feared that supporting TAA could be seen as weakening their position against trade liberalization. TAA's link to job

4. Income maintenance under TAA is an entitlement—Congress must appropriate sufficient funds to provide payments to any worker who is eligible and participates in the program. There is a cap on funds appropriated for training under TAA. By contrast, the Workforce Investment Act (WIA), the program that provides assistance to all dislocated workers regardless of cause, is not an entitlement. Workers receive training only if there are adequate funds available. Most states exhaust training funds under WIA well before the end of the year, denying workers the opportunity to enroll in training. In addition, states can deny training if it is determined that a worker can find a job that pays a subsistence wage without training.

5. Under NAFTA-TAA, a downstream producer was defined as "a firm that performs additional, value-added production processes, including a firm that performs final assembly, finishing, or packaging of articles produced by another firm."

loss and the modest amount of assistance have led unions to characterize TAA as "burial insurance." Union support for TAA further weakened in the 1990s, as unions began placing a higher priority on raising labor standards in low-wage countries.[6]

Support from both Democratic and Republican administrations has also been mixed, divided along agency lines. The US Trade Representative (USTR) has long supported TAA as a means for winning congressional support for trade negotiating authority. This support, however, is essentially political, since USTR has no legislative authority over TAA. By contrast, the DOL, which does have legislative authority over TAA, has only reluctantly administered the program and has never promoted expansion or reform. TAA requires higher levels of energy and resources to administer than other dislocated-worker programs (primarily WIA), due to its petition and eligibility process and its wider range of assistance services. From a purely administrative perspective, the DOL would prefer to administer a single program for all workers regardless of cause of dislocation.

The lack of clear political support for TAA is not unique to the executive branch. Although most congressional Republicans tend to aggressively support trade liberalization, they tend to view labor-market adjustment programs as welfare. For most congressional Republicans, TAA is a "side payment," and they are willing to accept only the least amount of TAA necessary to win support for trade liberalization. By contrast, support for TAA from congressional Democrats is mixed. Like unions, some Democrats are concerned that their support for TAA might be misconstrued as weakening their resolve against trade liberalization. A smaller group of Democrats favors trade liberalization and thinks that TAA is necessary if the government wants to pursue trade liberalization.

All of this adds up to weak support for TAA, despite the fact that the program has made a significant difference for over 2.5 million US workers since it was established. In fact, until the Trade Adjustment Assistance Coalition was established in 2004, no group advocated primarily on behalf of TAA and the workers served by the program.[7]

Until recently, calls for reform were few, and the only changes to TAA since 1974 were made in 1981, when assistance was reduced—e.g., income support was reduced from the average manufacturing wage to the prevailing UI rate and made conditional on enrollment in training—and in 1993, when Congress created the separate NAFTA-TAA program.

---

6. Although raising international core labor standards in developing countries would improve the welfare of workers in those countries, there is little evidence that it would help American workers. Elliott and Freeman (2003) find no systematic evidence showing a relationship between core labor standards, as identified by the International Labor Organization, and labor costs. They find that even if higher standards raised labor costs a bit in the short run, it would not be enough to endanger the comparative advantage of poor countries in labor-intensive exports.

7. For more information, see www.TAACoalition.com.

Since its inception in 1962, changes in TAA have been highly correlated with congressional consideration of trade-liberalizing legislation. Some have considered TAA as a quid pro quo for support on trade-liberalizing legislation. In recent years, significant weaknesses in the program depreciated its value in "buying" that support (Rosen 2003).

With the lapse in fast-track trade negotiating authority during the 1990s, TAA lost its logical legislative "hook" for program reauthorization and expansion. Over this period, the already fragile support for TAA further weakened, especially as the organized labor community made international labor standards one of its major trade policy priorities.

A number of events in 2000 and early 2001, however, improved the prospects for action on TAA.

- In 1997, Levi Strauss Company announced its intention to close 13 factories around the United States, laying off approximately one-third of its US workforce. Three of those plants were in New Mexico. In response to the layoffs, Senator Jeff Bingaman (D-NM) undertook an aggressive set of measures to streamline assistance to the dislocated workers in his state (Rosen 2001). Senator Bingaman's efforts revitalized calls for reform and expansion of TAA.
- One of the Bush administration's early priorities was passage of Trade Promotion Authority (TPA). In June 2001, as Congress began considering TPA legislation, the Democrats took control of the Senate. The most important consequence for passage of TPA was that Senator Max Baucus (D-MT) became chairman of the Finance Committee. Almost immediately after assuming the chairmanship of the committee, Senator Baucus enthusiastically embraced the idea of making a major expansion and reform of TAA a centerpiece of the TPA legislation.
- One of the proposals under consideration in the package of TAA reforms was the inclusion of a tax credit, for eligible displaced workers, to lower the costs of maintaining health insurance. This proposal caught the attention of Senator Thomas Daschle (D-SD), who became senate majority leader when the Democrats took control of Congress in March 2001. Inclusion of assistance for health insurance quickly became the centerpiece of the TAA reform effort. In some sense, the critical support of two senators—Daschle and Baucus—for TAA reform and expansion significantly improved the chances for final Senate passage of TPA.

The Trade Act of 2002, which Congress passed in July and which President Bush signed into law in August 2002, provided TPA to the president and included provisions that substantially expanded and reformed TAA. The bill passed the House of Representatives by a vote of 215 to 212 and the Senate by a vote of 64 to 34. Although it is difficult to prove empirically, it is widely believed that the inclusion of the TAA reform provisions helped secure the votes necessary to pass the Trade Act (Destler forthcoming). These provisions included:

- **merge TAA and NAFTA-TAA**. Eligibility criteria and the assistance package under both programs were harmonized and unified into one program.
- **secondary workers**. TAA eligibility was expanded to include workers who lose their jobs from plants producing inputs into goods that face significant import competition. Some of these workers were already covered under NAFTA-TAA. The General Accounting Office (GAO 2001) estimated that this provision could add between 40,000 and 50,000 new participants each year.
- **shift in production**. TAA eligibility criteria were expanded to include workers who lose their jobs due to shifts in production to countries with bilateral free trade agreements with the United States and "where there has been or is likely to be an increase in imports. . . ."[8]
- **refundable tax credit for health insurance**. Workers are eligible to receive a 65 percent advanceable, refundable tax credit to offset the cost of maintaining health insurance for up to two years.
- **wage insurance**. Workers over 50 years old and earning less than $50,000 a year may be eligible to receive half the difference between their old and new wages, subject to a cap of $10,000, for up to two years. Workers must find a new full-time job and enroll in the Alternative Trade Adjustment Assistance (ATAA) program within 26 weeks of job loss and cannot receive other assistance from the TAA program.[9]
- **training appropriation**. Congress doubled the legislative cap on the training appropriation, from $110 million to $220 million. Final funding is still subject to the regular congressional appropriations process.
- **extension of income maintenance by 26 weeks**. Workers can be enrolled in training and receive income maintenance for up to two years.
- **increase in job search assistance and relocation assistance**. The amount of assistance was increased to keep up with inflation.

Implementation of 2002 Reforms

The 2002 provisions resulted in the most extensive expansion and reform of TAA since its establishment in 1962. In particular, the health care tax

8. Section 231 of the Trade Act of 2002.

9. The Trade Act of 2002 refers to wage insurance as Alternative Trade Adjustment Assistance.

Table 10.3 Worker petitions for TAA, 2000–03

	2000	2001	2002	2003
Petitions filed	1,382	2,353	2,404	3,562
Petitions certified	845	1,029	1,594	1,880
Petitions denied	534	606	980	1210
Percent of petitions denied	39	26	41	34
Number of workers covered by certified petitions	98,007	139,587	235,071	197,117
New income support recipients	32,808	34,698	42,362	47,992
Take-up rate (percent)	33	25	18	24

TAA = Trade Adjustment Assistance program

Source: US Department of Labor.

credit (HCTC) and wage insurance (ATAA) were significant innovations in assistance to unemployed workers.[10] Despite the considerable technical challenges involved in implementing these reforms, the DOL and the Internal Revenue Service (IRS) met the deadlines set out in the legislation.

In addition to implementing the reforms, the DOL made significant progress in reducing the amount of time it takes to process worker petitions for TAA eligibility. This is an important first step in ensuring that workers receive the assistance they need in a timely fashion.

Although it is too early for a formal evaluation, preliminary evidence suggests that program participation has not met expectations of the bill's initial sponsors. Table 10.3 presents data on worker petitions for TAA. For fiscal 2000 to 2002, data are for TAA only and exclude petitions for NAFTA-TAA. For fiscal 2003, petitions are for the combined TAA.[11]

There are several possible explanations for the 48 percent increase in petitions filed from 2002 to 2003, as reported in table 10.3. Importantly, data for fiscal 2003 include petitions that would have been filed under NAFTA-TAA. Based on data for both TAA and NAFTA-TAA over 1995–99, approximately 30 percent of filed petitions for the two programs were filed for NAFTA-TAA.[12] Even after allowing for the increase due to program consolidation, there remains a sizable increase in petitions from 2002 to 2003.

It is interesting to note that despite the increase in the number of TAA petitions, the number of workers covered by those petitions declined between fiscal years 2002 and 2003. In fiscal years 2001 and 2002 the average number of workers per certified petition was 142, and the average num-

10. In the early 1990s, Canada ran a wage insurance demonstration program (Bloom et al. 1999), and in 2003, Germany instituted a wage insurance program similar to the US program.

11. Unfortunately, the DOL has not provided a complete set of data in order to make the appropriate comparisons.

12. For 1995–99, 12,205 petitions were submitted to both programs. Of those, 3,651 petitions, or 30 percent, were filed for NAFTA-TAA.

Table 10.4 Participation in various TAA programs, 2000–03

	2000	2001	2002	2003
New income support recipients	32,808	34,698	42,362	47,992
New training recipients	22,665	29,941	45,771	47,239
New on-the-job training recipients	304	194	292	386
New ATAA recipients	n.a.	n.a.	n.a.	42
Number of training waivers	19,858	19,169	20,947	30,138

n.a. = not applicable
ATAA = Alternative Trade Adjustment Assistance program
NAFTA-TAA = North American Free Trade Agreement–Transitional Adjustment Assistance program
TAA = Trade Adjustment Assistance program

Note: Income support and training data for fiscal years 2001, 2002, and 2003 include TAA and NAFTA-TAA.

Source: US Department of Labor.

ber of workers per denied petition was 97. These numbers fell to 105 and 68, respectively, in fiscal 2003. There is no immediate explanation for this decline in the number of workers covered by petitions.

It is particularly noteworthy that TAA participation over the last several years has been so low despite

- the overall weak performance of the US labor market;
- the continued growth of imports, leading to potential eligibility for the program;
- the important expansion in eligibility criteria, including shifts in production and secondary workers; and
- no major change in petition denial rates.

Table 10.4 presents data on the number of workers participating in the various TAA programs. The increase in the number of TAA petitions filed may explain the 18 percent increase in the number of workers receiving income support between fiscal 2002 and fiscal 2003. It is interesting to note that there was a 44 percent increase in the number of training waivers provided between fiscal 2002 and fiscal 2003, especially since rules concerning the provision of waivers were tightened in the 2002 law.[13]

One of the ongoing mysteries of TAA is the low percentage of certified workers who receive assistance. In fiscal 2003, only 24 percent of workers covered by certified petitions received income support, otherwise known as the "take-up" rate (see table 10.3). This was a significant increase from the previous fiscal year, when the take-up rate was only 18 percent. Take-

13. Workers need to obtain training waivers to be exempt from the requirement to be enrolled in training in order to receive income maintenance payments.

up rates in fiscal 2000 and fiscal 2001 were 33 and 25 percent, respectively. One potential explanation for the low take-up rates is that workers find employment without needing assistance. Although finding a new job is a desirable outcome, studies reveal a need for reemployment assistance and large earnings losses even with reemployment.[14] Another possible explanation is that workers are not willing to enroll in training in order to receive income support.

The DOL reported that only 42 workers were enrolled in the new wage insurance program in fiscal 2003. This low number of participants is probably due to the fact that the program did not officially begin until August 2003, thus these data reflect only eight weeks of activity. In addition, workers have up to 26 weeks from the date of their job loss to enroll in wage insurance. Some evidence indicates that the number of workers enrolled in the wage insurance program has increased, but the number remains relatively small.[15]

In the eight months between August 2003 and March 2004, approximately 10,250 workers enrolled in the HCTC program. This is an impressive achievement, since the HCTC was formally instituted around the same time as the ATAA program. Approximately 4,500 workers received the HCTC due to their participation in TAA. Almost 6,000 additional workers received the HCTC by participating in the Pension Benefit Guaranty Corporation (PBGC) program.[16] The average cost over the initial eight-month period was approximately $200 a month per participant.

Discussions with workers and state and local service providers repeatedly confirm that insufficient knowledge about TAA helps explain low take-up rates. At less than 50,000 workers per year, the percentage of eligible workers who participate in TAA is significantly less than the percentage of eligible workers who receive UI.[17] In addition, trade-related worker displacement is less frequent than unemployment due to other

14. Kletzer (2001) reports reemployment rates in the range of 60 to 65 percent for trade-displaced workers, with the average reemployed trade-displaced worker experiencing an earnings loss of 13 percent. For a sample of Pennsylvania displaced workers, Jacobson, LaLonde, and Sullivan (1993) report average earnings losses on the order of 25 percent, five to eight years following job loss.

15. Apparently one of the major handicaps for enrollment in ATAA results from a provision inserted in the legislation by congressional Republicans. Under this provision, applicants must signify on their initial petition if they want their workers to be eligible for ATAA. Since most petitioners are not aware of the various forms of assistance provided under TAA, potentially thousands of eligible workers have been denied access to the most cost-effective aspect of TAA.

16. Under the Trade Act of 2002, HCTC eligibility was extended to workers who retired from steel firms that subsequently declared bankruptcy and stopped providing health insurance. In 2003, 5,738 workers qualified for HCTC via this route.

17. Information from the Employment and Training Administration of the US Department of Labor shows that approximately 21 million workers made an initial claim for Unemployment Insurance in 2003. See www.doleta.gov.

Table 10.5 Federal budget outlays for TAA (millions of dollars)

	2002 actual	2003 actual	2004 estimate	2005 estimate
TAA income maintenance	254	348	513	750
TAA training	94	222	258	259
NAFTA income maintenance	32	51	10	n.a.
NAFTA training	37	37	1	n.a.
Wage insurance	n.a.	n.a.	14	48
Total	**417**	**658**	**796**	**1,057**

n.a. = not available
NAFTA = North American Free Trade Agreement
TAA = Trade Adjustment Assistance program

Source: OMB (2004).

factors. Over the last 40 years, the DOL has performed very limited public outreach to inform employers, workers, and communities of the existence of TAA.

TAA Budget

TAA's total budget has more than doubled over the last three years and is expected to increase further over the next few years, as a direct result of the reforms passed by Congress in 2002. The reforms expanded the potential number of workers eligible for TAA, by adding shifts in production and secondary workers to the eligibility criteria, as well as expanded the amount of assistance available to workers—i.e., HCTC, ATAA, and extended income maintenance.[18] In fiscal 2002, prior to the reforms, TAA's total annual budget was $417 million. It is estimated to reach above $1 billion in fiscal 2005 (see table 10.5). Expenditures on TAA are projected to rise to between $1.5 billion and $2 billion once the 2002 reforms are fully implemented.[19]

Effectiveness

The conventional wisdom in the broader policy community is that government-financed labor-market adjustment programs do not work. Although this view is not founded on any empirical basis, policymakers

18. The GAO estimated that expanding the eligibility criteria to include secondary workers could add 40,000 to 50,000 potential program participants, costing approximately $400 million to $500 million each year. See GAO (2000).

19. There is no budget outlay for the HCTC. Its cost is measured by the resulting decline in tax receipts.

cite difficulties in finding reemployment and the size of permanent wage losses to support their claims. It is beyond the scope of this chapter to adequately address this misperception. There is a considerable literature on the effectiveness of displaced-worker adjustment programs (e.g., Kletzer and Koch 2004). Our discussion is based on the premise that every effort should be made to design and implement effective programs that deliver meaningful assistance. From a political perspective, the question is: What would be the alternative to TAA? Political pressures suggest that doing nothing is highly unlikely (Rosen 2003). So the challenge is designing the most effective interventions, not whether to intervene or not.

Unfinished Business

Despite significant changes made to the TAA program enacted in 2002, several issues remain outstanding. Some of the issues are technical and have been discovered while implementing the 2002 reforms. Other issues are proposals that were removed during congressional consideration of the initial 2001 TAA legislation and continue to be desirable. In addition, there are some new proposals, which were not considered in the 2001 TAA legislation. Although the following list of issues is long, it is by no means exhaustive.

Technical Changes

Training Budget

Many states exhaust the funds available for training before the end of the fiscal year. In fiscal 2003, it quickly became clear that the increase in the training cap included in the Trade Act of 2002 was insufficient to cover the potentially significant expansion in participation due to expanded eligibility criteria. The original Senate bill called for the training cap to be increased to $300 million, based on estimates of the expected increase in participation due to the proposed changes in eligibility also included in the bill. House and Senate conferees agreed to increase the funding limit to only $220 million, disregarding the projected increase in eligibility. The resulting shortfall in training appropriation deserves immediate action. At a minimum, the funding cap should be raised to at least $300 million. Eventually the funding cap should be linked to an estimate of how much money would be necessary to provide adequate training to all TAA participants.

In addition to inadequate training funds, their allocation among the states also has problems. Until recently, TAA training funds were allocated to the states on a first-come, first-served basis. The result was that large states with high program participation tended to place heavy demands on available training dollars, leaving few funds for small states and workers who lost their jobs late in the fiscal year. The tightening of training waivers in 2002 exacerbated this problem. The DOL recently introduced a more orderly procedure for allocating training funds to states, taking into account size and experience. Although this procedure may be an improvement, it does little to address the fact that the total training appropriation is too small to enable all TAA participants to receive adequate training.

Shifts in Production

Recent experience suggests that shifts in production are increasingly contributing to job dislocation in the United States. In fiscal 2003, shifts in production accounted for one-third of certified TAA petitions.

As part of the effort to harmonize TAA and NAFTA-TAA, the 2002 bill proposed adding shifts in production to the TAA eligibility criteria. Apparently in an effort to restrict the reform efforts, Republican conferees proposed limiting the criteria to shifts in production to countries with which the United States has a bilateral or preferential trade agreement. Democratic conferees, in an effort to cover US workers who lose their jobs due to shifts in production to China, countered by adding the language "there has been or is likely to be an increase in imports. . . ." Initially, there was some evidence that the DOL was following a restrictive (and some would argue erroneous) interpretation of this language, holding that it applies only when workers lose their jobs due to shifts in production to countries with which the United States has a preferential trade agreement *and* there is an increase in imports.[20] This interpretation not only contradicts the initial legislative intent but also results in denying assistance to workers who lose their jobs due to shifts in production to China and India—likely destinations of a considerable amount of production shifting. A DOL representative recently suggested that the department had changed its interpretation of the law.[21] In any event, this language needs to be clarified to prevent any further confusion.

Health Care Tax Credit

Under the new law, workers must be receiving income maintenance, which means that they must be enrolled in training, in order to be eligible to receive the HCTC. This restriction severely limits the number of displaced workers who can receive the HCTC. A recent GAO report (GAO 2004a) found that this requirement has forced workers to enroll in training and request income maintenance payments. Some argue that this requirement promotes "real adjustment," by requiring training participa-

20. See www.doleta.gov/tradeact/2002act_freetradeagreements.cfm for the list of eligible countries.

21. Private communication with the authors.

tion. Others argue that it results in workers getting expensive assistance that they might not need. One proposal would be to provide the HCTC to TAA-certified workers for up to two years or until the worker finds a new job, regardless of enrollment in training.

The GAO report also found that workers are experiencing difficulties getting the HCTC, because as part of the package of assistance provided under TAA, UI benefits must be exhausted prior to receiving TAA program assistance. Beyond exhausting UI benefits, there is an additional waiting period before workers are enrolled in TAA. As a result, many workers either have lost their health insurance or can no longer afford to maintain it, by the time the HCTC becomes effective. These timing requirements defeat the purpose—of helping workers maintain their health insurance during their period of unemployment. This problem requires prompt attention.[22]

Wage Insurance (Alternative TAA)

In another attempt to confine the program, Republican conferees added a provision requiring firms or groups of workers to indicate that their workers might be interested in participating in ATAA in their initial TAA petition submission to the DOL. This caused two immediate problems. First, the petition being used by the DOL did not include a place for petitioners to identify their interest in ATAA.[23] Second, how could petitioners know if they were potentially interested in a program that never existed before and about which they knew nothing?

Anecdotal evidence confirms that this arbitrary requirement has denied potentially thousands of workers access to ATAA and may help explain why participation in the program has been so low.[24]

ATAA is the only aspect of TAA for which workers must identify their interest during the petition process. It appears that the only motivation for this requirement is to restrict the number of participants in the program. This is particularly ironic, since ATAA is potentially more cost-effective than other forms of assistance under TAA and is the only form of assistance that is directly linked to finding a new job, which should be the ultimate goal of any labor-market adjustment program. All workers eligible for TAA should be eligible for ATAA.

---

22. The DOL issued TEGL 11-2, Change 1, encouraging states to waive the training enrollment deadline so that workers can be eligible to receive the HCTC while receiving UI.

23. Until a new petition was designed, the DOL claims that its staff members called all petitioners to ask if they were interested in ATAA.

24. One glaring example of the problems associated with this arbitrary requirement is the case of the Pillowtex workers in North Carolina. Since some petitioners did not know about the requirement to identify interest in ATAA, Pillowtex workers from some sites are eligible, while those from other sites are not.

Outreach

Another recent GAO report (GAO 2004b) found that many workers are unaware of TAA and that they are eligible to receive assistance under the program. This may help explain why program take-up rates are so low. The DOL has not to date performed any major outreach—for example, using television and radio—to publicize the program. The initial 2001 TAA legislation called on the DOL to ensure that state agencies notify all workers included on a certified petition of all the possible assistance available to them. This provision was also dropped from the final bill.

One possibility would be to expand the organizations that administer TAA within a state to include private community-based organizations. On the one hand, some union representatives are likely to oppose this proposal, for fear that it might risk the jobs of unionized government workers. On the other hand, this proposal might enable unions to get more directly involved in administering TAA and delivering assistance to workers. In any event, more resources need to be devoted to informing workers about TAA and other forms of assistance for dislocated workers.

Issues That Haven't Gone Away

Service Workers

Currently, the DOL follows a narrow interpretation of TAA eligibility, thereby denying TAA to thousands of workers laid off from the services sector. According to the law, workers must prove that they lost their job from a firm that makes a product that is "similar to or like an imported good." Although the law does not specifically restrict TAA eligibility only to workers employed in manufacturing industries per se, over the years the DOL's interpretation of the law has de facto resulted in such a restriction. Many workers have appealed the DOL's decision to the Court of International Trade, the court with judicial responsibility over TAA.

Recently, the court's rulings have taken on a rather angry tone, as the court has strongly criticized the DOL for its narrow interpretation on this and other issues. The following excerpts from recent court decisions provide examples of the court's frustration with the administration of TAA.

In the opinion in the case of the *Former Employees of Ameriphone, Inc. vs. the US Secretary of Labor*, the court commented,

> There is something fundamentally wrong with the administration of the nation's trade adjustment assistance programs if, as a practical matter, workers often must appeal their cases to the courts to secure the thorough investigation that the Labor Department is obligated to conduct by law.
>
> It would be wholly inconsistent with Congress' intent if the trade adjustment assistance programs were to become little more than "claims mills," where all but the most well-documented and patently meritorious claims were denied at the

agency level, and thorough investigations were largely reserved for those few cases, which were appealed to the courts.

It can hardly be said that "all's well that ends well," when the workers here have been for over a year deprived of the job training and other benefits to which they are entitled.[25]

The court's opinion in the case of the *Former Employees of Chevron Products Company vs. the US Secretary of Labor* further states,

> In a word, this case stands as a monument to the flaws and dysfunctions in the Labor Department's administration of the nation's trade adjustment assistance laws—for, while it may be an extreme case, it is regrettably not an isolated one. The relatively high number of requests for voluntary remands in trade adjustment assistance cases appealed to this Court speaks volumes about the calibre of the Labor Department's investigations in general, and the Government's ability to defend them . . . Similarly telling is the growing line of precedent involving court-ordered certifications of workers, evidencing the bench's mounting frustration with the Labor Department's handling of these cases. Clearly, there is a message here. Only time will tell whether the Labor Department, and Congress, are listening.[26]

It appears that recently the DOL has "heard the message," as it has begun exploring ways to provide assistance to workers who might have been denied assistance in the past.

Community Adjustment

One of the lessons learned from the experience of the Levi Strauss plant closings in New Mexico is that local economic and social conditions can exacerbate the adjustment process. For example, Levi Strauss was the single largest private employer in Roswell, New Mexico, before closing in 1998. The plant closing dealt a terrible blow to the community and the surrounding region. Providing temporary financial assistance and training alone to workers was not enough to restore economic stability to the region.

Building on the Defense Department's experience in addressing and enhancing economic adjustment in response to military plant closings in the 1990s, Senator Jeff Bingaman reached out to various community leaders and representatives and developed a strategy for responding to the hardships resulting from the Levi Strauss plants closing. Senator Bingaman requested technical assistance from the Department of Defense. In

25. Former Employees of Ameriphone, Inc., Plaintiffs, v. United States, Court No. 03-00243, US Court of International Trade, 288 F. Supp. 2d 1353, October 24, 2003.

26. Former Employees of Chevron Products Company, Plaintiffs, v. United States Secretary of Labor, Defendant, Court No. 00-08-00409, US Court of International Trade, December 30, 2003.

addition, the community applied for and received grants from the Department of Commerce's Economic Development Administration, to develop a strategy for revitalizing the local economy, and from the North American Development Bank (NADBANK), to expand training resources to accommodate the large number of dislocated workers.

Labor-market adjustment is exacerbated when job creation is weak. This linkage is even more important at the local or regional level. The initial 2001 TAA legislation called for the establishment of a TAA for communities program, in order to formalize some of the efforts tried in Roswell, New Mexico. This initiative was an attempt to acknowledge that income support and training alone may be insufficient for assisting dislocated workers find new jobs. House-Senate conferees removed this provision from the final bill.

The weak performance of the US labor market over the last few years has renewed support for some targeted assistance tailored to communities facing severe economic dislocation. The Defense Department's experience in addressing economic adjustment in light of the base closings in the 1990s may provide a good start, with some lessons on community-targeted economic adjustment. In any event, the linkage between labor-market adjustment and community economic development needs greater consideration. One way to begin would be to introduce some limited demonstration projects.[27]

Data Reporting

Over the last decade, the DOL, under both Democratic and Republican leadership, has been extremely reluctant to release data related to TAA, despite the fact that these data, which were widely available in prior years, do not appear to include any sensitive information. Accordingly, the initial 2001 TAA legislation included language requiring the DOL to issue regular reports on program participation and performance. Senate Republicans complained that this requirement was onerous and insisted on removing it from the final legislation. The DOL has taken only small steps in making public data available.[28] Participation data are crucial to determining how well TAA is working and which aspects of the program need to be improved, eliminated, or expanded. Throughout TAA's history, all reform efforts have originated outside the DOL. Providing public access to TAA program data is therefore critical to monitoring and evaluating the program.

27. A limited Adjustment Assistance for Communities program was initiated as part of the Trade Act of 1974 (Public Law 19 USC 2371) but was later repealed.

28. The DOL recently began providing some TAA participation data on its website. This is a welcomed development, but the department's efforts in this regard should be expanded.

A More Ambitious Agenda

As mentioned at the outset of this chapter, the US labor market is remarkably flexible. In fact, on average, close to one of every five working-age people is expected to lose and/or gain a job in any given year. The extent of this flexibility recently highlighted a number of shortcomings in the country's existing labor-market adjustment programs.

Despite all the calls for customizing labor-market programs to the needs of individual workers, the US unemployment insurance system continues to operate based on the "one-size-fits-all" model. States determine the amount of assistance, disregarding the reason for dislocation or a worker's difficulty in finding a new job. The triggers for extended unemployment insurance also appear to be ineffective, as evidenced during the last recession. Receiving government-financed training is similar to playing the lottery since funds allocated to states have little connection to current need, and the demand for training funds is always greater than the total amount budgeted.

Pressures on the US labor market due to technological change, productivity improvements, and international competition call for significant reform and expansion of all US labor-market adjustment programs. Unfortunately, both Democratic and Republican policymakers have not shown any political will in pursuing such needed reform. The only area in which Congress and the president have been willing to even consider reform is TAA, and those reforms have been accepted only to get Congress to approve trade negotiating authority. Given the lack of political will to reform, redesign, and expand programs that would better meet the needs of US workers and their families, the second-best strategy appears to be to continue incrementally expanding TAA. Recent attention paid to services outsourcing further underscores the need for comprehensive expansion and reform. Concern over job loss is clearly broadening. Currently, services outsourcing is receiving more attention than traditional trade-related job loss. It is difficult to determine the extent of this phenomenon, since existing data do not accurately capture this activity (see Catherine Mann's chapter in this book).

What is clear is that the impact of outsourcing on US employment once again reveals the limits of targeted labor-market adjustment programs. For the most part, US services-sector workers adversely affected by outsourcing are not currently eligible for TAA. This has further fueled calls to expand TAA eligibility to cover services-sector workers. This change alone will not be sufficient to fully address the problem, due to difficulties associated with clearly identifying the various causes of job loss—an issue that is central to TAA.

Another group of workers left out of TAA's reach are those employed in export-related industries. Between 2000 and 2002, US exports fell by 11 percent, most likely contributing to job loss in related industries.[29] Al-

29. See Kletzer (2002) for an analysis of the link between changes in exports and job loss.

though export-related job loss does not occur as frequently as job loss from import competition and/or shifts in production, it is no less painful or disruptive to workers and their families. Despite this fact, workers who lose their jobs due to a fall in exports are not eligible for assistance under TAA.

These holes in coverage give rise to questions about America's fundamental commitment to assisting all workers adversely affected by changes in international trade and investment, as enunciated by President Kennedy in 1962 as well as by all subsequent presidents.

One way to address these administrative difficulties would be to remove the requirement to identify the causes of job loss from TAA eligibility criteria. One proposal would be to preidentify industries and provide TAA to *any* worker displaced from them. Another proposal would be to provide more assistance to *all* displaced workers, regardless of industry or cause of dislocation. An immediate problem with this proposal is that it would break the link between TAA and trade policy. Although in reality the relationship has been evident only in periodic legislation, some policymakers may be opposed to weakening that link.

Providing TAA-type assistance to all dislocated workers would also require a major reform in the country's unemployment insurance system, including the UI trust fund. Similar to the issues raised by health care and social security, building a coalition to reform the country's unemployment insurance system would be difficult to do. In the meantime, incremental changes may be easier to achieve.

An immediate area to begin reform efforts is to provide the HCTC to all displaced workers. Providing the HCTC to all unemployed workers would reduce the discrimination between those workers who lost their jobs due to "trade" and all other displaced workers. It could also have the added benefit of reducing the growing number of uninsured.

Another option would be to provide wage insurance (ATAA) to a larger set of, and perhaps all, displaced workers. Wage insurance encourages workers to accept a new job more rapidly, thus addressing one of the criticisms of unemployment insurance. It also offers targeted assistance for an important aspect of involuntary job loss—i.e., potentially lower earnings on the new job.

The following section provides cost estimates for these proposals. Estimates of the number of potential recipients are derived from the Displaced Worker Survey, a biennial supplement to the Current Population Survey.[30] Program costs are based on current average program costs per participant.[31]

30. Data for 1998, 1999, 2000, and 2001 were initially analyzed. Impact and cost estimates for 2001 were significantly different from those for the earlier three years due to the recession's influence. Table 10.6 reports averages for 1998 to 2000 for estimating projected costs.

31. The average cost for income maintenance and training under TAA is approximately $10,000 per worker per year. Because current training funds continue to be inadequate, an average of $100 per worker per month was used in these estimates. The average cost for the HCTC is approximately $200 per month per worker. Workers can receive the credit for up to 24 months.

Table 10.6 Estimated budget costs for TAA expansion

	Number of potentially eligible participants	Spending estimates (millions of dollars)				
		Income maintenance	Training	ATAA (50–$50–50%)	HCTC	Total
Fiscal 2003 (actual)	48,000	399	259	n.a.	n.a.	658
Fiscal 2004 (projected)	57,000	523	259	14	n.a.	796
Preidentified trade displaced	165,000	1,900	750	100	375	3,125
All workers	575,000	7,000	2,800	900	1,400	12,100

n.a. = not available
ATAA = Alternative Trade Adjustment Assistance program
HCTC = Health Care Tax Credit

Source: Authors' calculations from the 2000 and 2002 Displaced Worker Surveys.

Cost Estimates for Reform Proposals

Table 10.6 presents cost estimates for several proposals to expand coverage of the existing TAA program.

All dislocated workers from preidentified trade-impacted industries. Under the current program, groups of three or more workers must submit a petition to the DOL to determine eligibility for TAA. By contrast, this proposal would end the certification process and automatically provide assistance to any worker displaced from industries preidentified as facing competition from imports or shifts in production. To receive assistance, workers would only have to prove that they worked in one of these industries.

Approximately 83,000 workers are estimated to be displaced annually from the 27 industries determined to be "high-import" industries.[32] In addition, GAO (2000) estimates that one secondary worker may lose his/her job for every worker displaced from an import-competing industry. Thus, approximately 165,000 workers per year could be expected to receive assistance under this reform proposal. It is estimated that covering all of these workers would cost approximately $3 billion per year.

All dislocated workers. Enrolling all dislocated workers in TAA would not only remove any remaining discrimination between workers but also significantly reduce the burden of administering a targeted program with

32. See Kletzer (2001) for the "highly import-competing" classification scheme. See appendix table 10A for a list of industries.

specific eligibility criteria. Under this proposal, all dislocated workers, regardless of cause of dislocation or industry, would be eligible to receive the entire package of assistance currently provided under TAA.[33] There would be no petition process. Similar to current TAA participants, all dislocated workers enrolled in training would be eligible for up to 104 weeks of income support, the HCTC, and wage insurance (ATAA), as well as job search and relocation assistance.

Using data from the Displaced Worker Survey, we estimate that approximately 575,000 workers could potentially receive assistance under this proposal. Program costs for enrolling these workers in TAA, with the complete set of benefits, would be approximately $12 billion per year.[34]

HCTC for all dislocated workers. Short of providing the entire package of TAA assistance to all dislocated workers, another option would be to extend only the HCTC component of TAA to all dislocated workers. This larger set of dislocated workers would continue to be eligible for standard UI, as in the current "dual system" of UI and TAA. We estimate that this would cost approximately $1.4 billion per year.

ATAA for all dislocated workers (50–$50–50%). Similar to the above proposal, another option would be to expand the current ATAA program to include all displaced workers. Under the current program, workers 50 years of age or older, earning less than $50,000 a year (on a new full-time job) can receive 50 percent of the difference between their new and old wage, up to a maximum of $10,000, for up to two years. It is estimated that 70,000 workers could potentially participate in this program at an approximate cost of $900 million per year. Removing the minimum age requirement would raise the number of potential participants to approximately 450,000, at an estimated cost of $4 billion per year.[35]

Financing Reform Proposals

Currently, UI is primarily financed through a complicated web of federal and state payroll taxes.[36] TAA is financed through general revenues, with-

33. Dislocation (displacement) is commonly understood to be the involuntary loss of a job, without regard to an individual worker's performance. Dislocation does not include quits or firings.

34. Based on these estimates, trade-related displaced workers account for 14 percent of all dislocated workers.

35. In order to be eligible to participate in ATAA, workers must find a job within 26 weeks of the job loss. Thus ATAA participants are *not* included in the number of workers potentially eligible for income maintenance, training, and the HCTC.

36. The federal payroll tax accounts for approximately one-quarter of the UI trust fund.

out any dedicated revenue offset.[37] One proposal would be to dedicate customs duties to finance a further expansion of TAA. In fiscal 2003, total customs duties equaled approximately $20 billion, and they are expected to rise to $25 billion over the next few years (OMB 2004). Since funds collected from customs duties are currently considered general revenue, diverting them to finance these proposals would contribute to the federal budget deficit. A more limited proposal would be to dedicate only the *increase* in customs duties over the next few years to offset the costs associated with expanding adjustment programs. This would also exacerbate the fiscal deficit and might not be sufficient to cover the total costs of the more ambitious proposals outlined above. Nonetheless, it might be a good way to jump-start the reform process.[38]

Congress is currently discussing whether and how to respond to recent World Trade Organization (WTO) rulings against the Byrd Amendment, which provides for the US government to repatriate to the domestic industry revenue generated from antidumping and countervailing duty cases. Another option would be to dedicate the Byrd Amendment revenues to finance the *expansion* of US labor-market adjustment programs. Although many in the trade policy community oppose the idea of dedicating revenues generated from safeguard measures, doing so for adjustment purposes may be more compatible with the WTO. The amount of money currently collected under this provision is significantly less than the current TAA budget, but like the other options, these funds could be used to finance an expansion of the program.[39]

Another option would be to increase the UI payroll tax. Currently, the federal UI payroll tax is extremely modest—0.8 percent on the first $7,000 of taxable income. For the vast majority of workers, this amounts to only $56 per year. The ratio of taxable wages to total wages has fallen from 98 percent in 1938, when the UI trust fund was established, to 33 percent in 1997.[40] A simplistic, straight-line calculation suggests that raising the tax base by $1,000—i.e., from $7,000 to $8,000—would generate an additional $80 million in revenue. Raising the tax rate by one-fifth of 1 percent—i.e., from 0.8 to 0.85 percent—would generate an additional $35 million in revenue.[41]

37. The Trade Act of 1974 called on the Department of Treasury to establish a trust fund, financed by all customs duties, from which to finance TAA. This trust fund has never been established.

38. It should be noted that there is long-standing opposition among economists to dedicated funding schemes.

39. The US Customs and Border Protection Agency reports that more than $200 million was available under the program in fiscal 2004.

40. The DOL has not published more recent data due to technical problems.

41. Both of these estimates do not consider any income or substitution effects. They are advanced only to suggest the magnitudes involved.

Obviously, a third option would be to finance these reforms the same way TAA is currently financed—i.e., through general revenues with no direct revenue offset.

The bottom line is that none of these proposals would "break the bank." For example, as mentioned above, providing the HCTC to all dislocated workers would cost approximately $1.4 billion per year. This figure amounts to less than a rounding error in the federal budget. Also, according to our estimates, all dislocated workers could be eligible for wage insurance at two-thirds that price.

Recent Congressional Activity

In March 2004, Senators Max Baucus and Norman Coleman (R-MN) introduced legislation (S2157) that addressed many of the issues raised above. In May, Senators Coleman and Ron Wyden (D-OR) proposed amending the JOBS Act with the following provisions in the Baucus bill:[42]

- expand TAA to cover services workers by adding the term "goods and services";
- increase the training appropriation cap;
- clarify the shift in production eligibility criteria to include all countries;
- increase the HCTC from 65 to 75 percent;
- make technical changes to the HCTC, including reducing the waiting period;
- require the DOL to periodically report program data; and
- establish a community adjustment program.

The amendment received a majority of votes in the Senate but not enough to overcome the 60-vote rule under the budget act.

MFA Removal

US employment in textiles and apparel has declined from 2.3 million in 1974 to 1.1 million currently. Some of that job loss has been associated with technological change and increased pressure from imports and overseas

42. S1367 presents an alternative to the Foreign Sales Corporation, which the WTO has ruled is illegal.

production. As a result, since its inception, textile and apparel workers have constituted the second largest single group of TAA participants.[43]

The Multi-Fiber Arrangement (MFA), the international regime of textile and apparel quotas, is scheduled to be phased out by January 1, 2005. There has been very little preparation for the upcoming phaseout, despite the expectation that the phaseout is likely to place additional pressure on an already battered sector. In the event that shifts in international production result in a significant increase in imports, it is likely that the textile and/or apparel industries may petition the government for temporary relief, either through the imposition of safeguard measures or antidumping and countervailing duties. Petitions for TAA might also significantly increase.

The second-term Bush administration should consider providing "blanket" eligibility to any worker displaced from the textile and apparel industries, regardless of cause.[44] This would relieve some of the administrative burden and would provide workers with assistance in a more timely fashion.[45]

Legislative Opportunities

As argued above, congressional support for TAA is not strong enough to enable both houses of Congress to pass stand-alone legislation implementing the changes outlined in this chapter. All previous changes in the program have been part of broader trade legislation—primarily legislation granting the president trade negotiating authority and implementing multilateral trade negotiations. This will probably remain the case, at least into the near future.

The president's trade negotiating authority, granted under the 2002 TPA bill, must be renewed in 2005. Under a "fast-track"–like process set out in the 2002 bill, Congress must pass a nonamendable resolution to renew that authority. This denies the traditional opportunity to link trade

43. Between 1974 and 2000, textile and apparel workers constituted 21 percent of TAA recipients. Automobile workers made up 29 percent of TAA recipients. Together, workers from these three industries represented half of all TAA recipients. In 2000, textiles and apparel together accounted for 32 percent of workers certified for TAA, with motor vehicles accounting for 21 percent.

44. The precedent for this proposal was set in 1975 for the footwear industry. In response to its request for safeguard protection from an import surcharge, the Ford administration offered expedited TAA for all workers who lost their jobs from the footwear industry.

45. A modification of this proposal would be to provide a blanket certification to any industry found by the International Trade Commission to have experienced injury due to international competition.

negotiating authority to TAA reform. On the other hand, TAA reform could be included in other trade legislation scheduled to be considered by Congress, such as the Dominican Republic–Central America Free Trade Agreement (CAFTA) implementation legislation.

We urge Congress and the president to consider implementing the following proposals as a first step toward reforming the nation's labor-market adjustment programs:

- increase the TAA training budget cap;
- clarify the TAA eligibility criteria to include shifts in production to any country;
- correct the HCTC waiting period;
- provide the HCTC to all TAA-certified workers by removing the link to receiving income maintenance;
- provide ATAA to all TAA-certified workers by removing the requirement to prerequest ATAA on the initial TAA petition;
- expand resources available for outreach;
- require the DOL to provide periodic data and performance reports; and
- grant blanket TAA certification to all workers displaced from the textile and apparel industries.

Under the 2002 Act, the president's trade negotiating authority expires in mid-2007. If the Doha Round of the WTO negotiations is successful, Congress will be asked to pass implementation legislation. If not, the president will most likely ask Congress to pass new legislation, granting him new authority to pursue multilateral trade negotiations. Either one of these scenarios would provide an opportunity for Congress to consider the more ambitious TAA reform agenda set out in this chapter. These provisions would include:

- expand TAA eligibility criteria to include services workers;
- provide TAA package of assistance to all dislocated workers, regardless of cause of dislocation;
- provide the HCTC to services workers, if not all dislocated workers, regardless of cause of dislocation;
- provide ATAA to services workers, if not all dislocated workers, regardless of cause of dislocation; and
- establish TAA for communities.

Summary and Conclusion

The US labor market is remarkably flexible. Most of the burden of this flexibility is borne by US workers and their families. Worker anxiety is therefore heightened whenever there is discussion of changes in economic policy that might affect the labor market. Trade liberalization is one example of such a policy change. Other developments also heighten worker anxiety, such as the potential growth of services outsourcing.

Given recent labor-market trends and given continued and intensified pressures on the labor market from technological change and international competition, the entire system of US labor-market adjustment programs is in dire need of reform, redesign, and expansion. The current dual system of assistance to unemployed workers—a general yet modest UI program and some training for all workers (WIA), and a targeted program providing more extensive assistance to workers whose job loss is associated with an increase in imports or a shift in production (TAA)—is no longer adequate. Unfortunately, neither Democratic nor Republican policymakers have displayed any leadership in undertaking the necessary steps to begin this reform process.

TAA appears to be the only area in which policymakers have been willing to reform and expand assistance to dislocated workers. In 2002, Congress enacted the most extensive reform of TAA since its creation in 1962. The eligibility criteria were extended to include shifts in production and secondary workers. Assistance was expanded to include a health care tax credit and wage insurance. Most of the reforms have been implemented, but there remain significant problems with ensuring that all eligible workers receive the assistance they so gravely need.

Short of reforming and expanding the system of labor-market programs designed to assist all displaced workers, regardless of cause of dislocation, the next option would be to continue expanding TAA. Technical corrections to the 2002 reforms and modest expansion require immediate attention. Policymakers should also begin the process of implementing a more ambitious reform agenda.

References

Betcherman, Gordon, Karina Olivas, and Amit Dar. 2004. *Impacts of Active Labor Market Programs: New Evidence from Evaluations with Particular Attention to Developing and Transition Countries*. Social Protection Discussion Paper Series 0402. Washington: World Bank.

Bloom, Howard, Saul Schwartz, Susanna Lui-Gurr, with Jason Peng and Wendy Bancroft. 1999. *Testing a Re-employment Incentive for Displaced Workers: The Earnings Supplement Project*. Social Research and Demonstration Corporation, Canada (May).

Dar, Amit, and Zafiris Tzannatos. 1999. *Active Labor Market Programs: A Review of the Evidence from Evaluations*. Social Protection Discussion Paper Series 9901. Washington: World Bank.

Destler, I. M. Forthcoming. *The Politics of Trade Policy.* Washington: Institute for International Economics.

Elliott, Kimberly Ann, and Richard B. Freeman. 2003. *Can Labor Standards Improve under Globalization?* Washington: Institute for International Economics.

GAO (US General Accounting Office). 2001. *Trade Adjustment Assistance: Trends, Outcomes, and Management Issues in Dislocated Worker Programs.* GAO-01-59. Washington: General Accounting Office.

GAO (US General Accounting Office). 2002. *Workforce Investment Act: Better Guidance and Revised Funding Formula Would Enhance Dislocated Worker Program.* GAO 02-274. Washington: General Accounting Office.

GAO (US Government Accountability Office). 2004a. *Health Coverage Tax Credit: Simplified and More Timely Enrollment Process Could Increase Participation.* GAO-04-1029. Washington: Government Accountability Office.

GAO (US Government Accountability Office). 2004b. *Reforms Have Accelerated Training Enrollment, but Implementation Challenges Remain.* GAO-04-1012. Washington: Government Accountability Office.

Jacobson, Louis, Robert LaLonde, and Daniel Sullivan. 1993. *The Costs of Worker Dislocation.* Kalamazoo, MI: W. E. Upjohn Institute for Employment Research.

Kletzer, Lori G. 2001. *Job Loss from Imports: Measuring the Costs.* Washington: Institute for International Economics.

Kletzer, Lori G. 2002. *Imports, Exports, and Jobs: What Does Trade Mean for Employment and Job Loss?* Kalamazoo, MI: W. E. Upjohn Institute for Employment Research.

Kletzer, Lori G., and William L. Koch. 2004. International Experience with Job Training: Lessons for the U.S. In *Job Training Policy in the United States*, eds., C. O'Leary, R. Straits, and S. Wandner. Kalamazoo, MI: W. E. Upjohn Institute for Employment Research.

Kletzer, Lori G., and Robert E. Litan. 2001. *A Prescription to Relieve Worker Anxiety.* International Economics Policy Brief PB01-2. Washington: Institute for International Economics and Brookings Institution.

Leigh, Duane E. 1989. *Assisting Displaced Workers: Do the States Have a Better Idea?* Kalamazoo, MI: W. E. Upjohn Institute for Employment Research.

OMB (US Office of Management and Budget). 2004. *FY Budget of the United States.* Washington: Government Printing Office.

Rosen, Howard. 2001. A New Approach to Assist Trade-Affected Workers and Their Communities: The Roswell Experiment. *Journal of Law and Border Studies* 1, no. 1.

Rosen, Howard. 2003. *Congress and Trade: End of an Era.* Washington: Center for National Policy.

US Bureau of the Census. 2004. *Income, Poverty, and Health Insurance in the United States: 2003.* Washington: Government Printing Office.

Appendix 10A
Highly Import-Competing Industries, 1979–2001

Electrical machinery, I
Electrical machinery
Radio, TV

Apparel
Apparel
Miscellaneous fabricated textiles

Transportation equipment, I
Motor vehicles
Cycles and miscellaneous transport

Machinery, except electrical, I
Electronic computing equipment
Construction and material-moving machines
Office and accounting machines

Metal industries, I
Blast furnaces
Other primary metals

Miscellaneous manufacturing industries

Leather and leather products
Footwear
Leather products
Leather tanning and finish

Professional and photographic equipment
Scientific and controlling equipment
Photographic equipment
Watches, clocks

Rubber and miscellaneous plastics
Other rubber products
Tires and inner tubes

Textiles
Knitting mills
Dyeing textiles
Floor coverings
Yarn, thread
Miscellaneous textiles

Toys and sporting goods

Pottery and related products

Source: Classification scheme for highly import-competing industries in Kletzer (2001).

11

Challenges for US Immigration Policy

GORDON H. HANSON

Immigration is a source of contention in American life. The issue divides the public, as it divides both major political parties. When asked about the contributions of immigrants to US society, 70 percent of survey respondents recognize these as being positive. But when asked about the level of immigration, 45 percent prefer to see the number of immigrants entering the country reduced (Scheve and Slaughter 2001a). The American public is roughly divided between those that prefer scaling down immigration and those that prefer maintaining it at current levels. Americans appear to believe that immigration offers a range of potential benefits to the country but are also concerned about the costs associated with admitting foreigners.

In this setting, reforming immigration policy might seem like a political minefield better left unexplored. However, ignoring immigration would be a mistake. US immigration policy is broken and in need of repair. Perhaps the most glaring examples of policy failure are that one-third of immigration is illegal and the population of illegal immigrants in the United States is now 10 million. Rampant illegality undermines US economic, legal, and political institutions and threatens US national security. Left alone, the problem will not solve itself. Each year, 400,000 new illegal immigrants enter the country. While the US Border Patrol attempts to control illegal immigration by policing US borders, its efforts have been ineffective.

One reason immigration creates political tension is that immigrant inflows to the United States are growing steadily. Between 1970 and 2003, the share of the foreign-born in the US population increased from 5 to 12

Gordon H. Hanson is a professor of economics at the Graduate School of International Relations and Pacific Studies and the Department of Economics, University of California, San Diego.

percent. Whereas previous generations of immigrants came mainly from Europe, today's immigrants come primarily from Asia and Latin America. In contrast to their predecessors, many of today's immigrants enter with skill levels far below those of the typical US worker.

The economic rationale for immigration is that it increases national income for existing residents. By expanding the labor pool, immigration helps utilize US capital, technology, and natural resources more efficiently. However, the gains from immigration are not evenly distributed. Labor inflows tend to reduce incomes for workers who can be substituted with immigrant labor and to raise incomes for factors that complement immigrant labor. Since many new immigrants are unskilled, immigration tends to depress wages for low-skilled resident workers.

A second way in which immigration redistributes income is through its impact on public finances. Given their relatively low skill levels, immigrants are much more likely than the native-born to use public assistance and other entitlement programs. This has remained true even after welfare reform in 1996, which restricted the access of immigrants to many public benefits. Low immigrant skill levels mean low earning potential and low contributions to tax revenues. The end result is that immigration appears to create a net fiscal burden on US native-born taxpayers.

The new administration will have to make choices on four dimensions of immigration policy: level of immigration, composition of immigrants, rights to grant new immigrants, and enforcement against illegal immigration. On each dimension, there is scope for reforming policy in a manner that increases the net benefits of immigration to the United States and moderates immigration's impact on the distribution of income.

Past and Current US Immigration Policy

Before the 1920s, there were few numerical limits on US immigration.[1] Over the second half of the 19th century, immigration grew in fits and starts (figure 11.1). By 1910, new immigrant arrivals totaled over 1 million individuals a year, and the foreign-born share of the US population reached 15 percent. Opposition to high levels of immigration resulted in the passage of the Immigration Act of 1924, which imposed entry quotas based on national origin, which sharply restricted immigration overall and from countries outside western and northern Europe in particular.[2] After 1924, immigration declined dramatically and did not reach significant levels until the 1960s (figure 11.2).

1. One exception was the Chinese Exclusion Act of 1892, which banned immigration from China.

2. For histories of US immigration policy, see Tichenor (2002) and Daniels (2003).

Figure 11.1 Permanent legal immigration in the United States, 1820–2000 (millions of people)

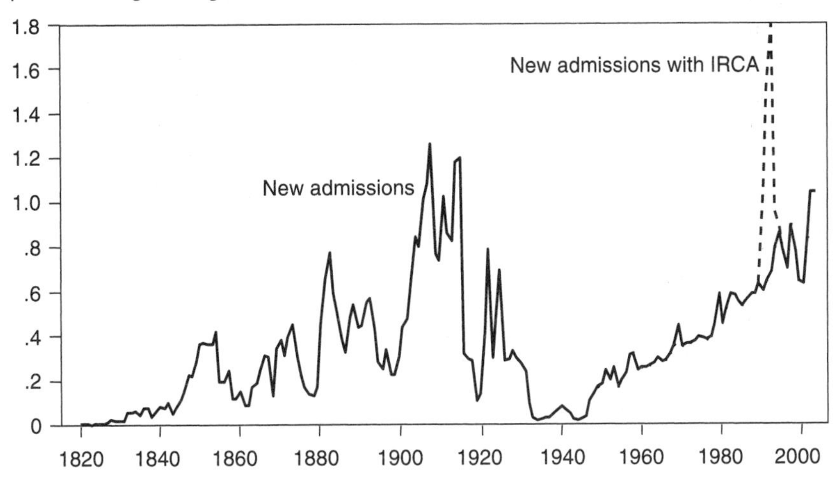

IRCA = Immigration Reform and Control Act of 1986

Source: US Department of Homeland Security, Office of Immigration Statistics *2003 Yearbook of Immigration Statistics.*

Current US immigration policy is based on a quota system established by the Hart-Celler Immigration Bill of 1965. Hart-Celler revised quotas based on national origin and made family reunification a central feature of US admission decisions.[3] Under the present system, US Citizenship and Immigration Services (USCIS) assigns applicants for permanent legal residence to one of seven categories, each subject to its own quota level.[4] The law guarantees admission to immediate family members of US citizens, who are exempt from entry quotas. Specific quotas are assigned to other family members of US citizens, immediate family members of legal US residents, individuals in special skill categories, and refugees and asylum

3. The 1965 law amended the Immigration and Nationality Act of 1952, which had created skill-based categories for immigration, without changing the 1924 restrictions on national origin (Smith and Edmonston 1997).

4. In 2003, the Immigration and Naturalization Service (INS) was moved from the Department of Justice to the Department of Homeland Security (DHS). INS functions were divided among three DHS agencies: immigration-related services moved to US Citizenship and Immigration Services (USCIS), enforcement of immigration laws in the interior United States moved to US Immigration and Customs Enforcement (ICE), and enforcement of US borders, including the US Border Patrol, moved to the Bureau of Customs and Border Protection (CBP).

Figure 11.2 Share of the foreign-born in the US population, 1900–2000

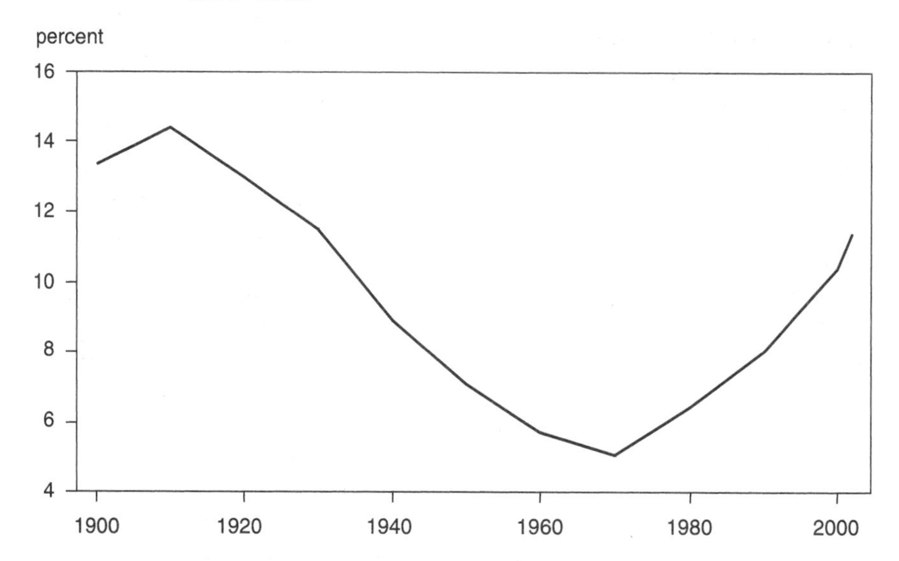

Source: US Census of Population and Housing, various years.

seekers facing persecution in their home countries.[5] Of the 705,827 permanent legal immigrants admitted in 2003, 70 percent gained entry as family members of US citizens or legal residents, 12 percent gained entry on the basis of employment preferences, 7 percent were admitted under the diversity program, 6 percent were refugees, and 5 percent were in other categories. Additional admissions occur through temporary visas, the largest classes of which are for high-skilled workers (H-1B) or short-term manual laborers (H-2A, H-2B), who tend to be low-skilled.[6] In 2003,

5. The Immigration Act of 1990 set a flexible cap for legal admissions at 675,000, of which 480,000 would be family-based, 140,000 would be employment-based, and 55,000 would be "diversity immigrants." The law also set temporary immigration at 65,000 for the H-1B program and 66,000 under the H-2 program and created new categories for temporary admission of workers (O, P, Q, and R). Subsequent legislation created categories for temporary immigration of professional workers from Canada and Mexico as part of the North American Free Trade Agreement (DHS 2004).

6. To obtain a temporary work visa, a worker must be sponsored by a US employer. The H-1B visa applies mainly to workers in high-tech industries. It was created in 1990 to permit foreigners with a college degree to work in the United States for a renewable three-year term for employers who petition on their behalf. In 1998, Congress raised the annual number of H-1B visas from 65,000 to 115,000; in 2000, it raised the limit further to 195,000 visas; and in 2003, it allowed the number of visas to fall back to 65,000. The H-2B visa, created by the Immigration Reform and Control Act of 1986 (IRCA), applies to seasonal laborers in agriculture. The bureaucratic steps to obtain H-2 visas are onerous, which appears to limit their use. In a typical year, no more than 70,000 H-2A or H-2B visas are awarded.

the United States admitted 590,680 temporary workers and 135,933 immediate family members accompanying these individuals (DHS 2004).

After five years as permanent legal residents, immigrants are eligible to apply for US citizenship. Citizenship confers the right to vote and the right to draw on all government benefit programs for which an individual is eligible. In 1996, as part of welfare reform, Congress excluded noncitizen immigrants from access to many entitlement programs (Zimmerman and Tumlin 1999). Since then, some US states have restored immigrant access to some benefits. The Supreme Court has ruled that the government may not deny public education or emergency medical services to foreign-born US residents, even those in the country illegally.

Though the United States does not set the level of illegal immigration explicitly, existing policy in effect allows substantial numbers of illegal aliens to enter the country. The foreign-born share of the US population, shown in figure 11.2, includes substantial numbers of illegal immigrants.[7] In 2004, the illegal immigrant population was 10 million (Passel, Capps, and Fix 2004). Most illegal immigrants enter the United States by crossing the US-Mexico border or by overstaying temporary entry visas. The US Border Patrol checks illegal immigration by policing the US-Mexico border and other points of entry from abroad and by seeking to prevent the smuggling or employment of illegal aliens. While the US Border Patrol has enforced the border against illegal immigration since 1924, the modern experience of high levels of illegal immigration dates back to the 1960s and the end of the *Bracero* program (1942–64), which allowed large numbers of seasonal farm laborers from Mexico and the Caribbean to work in US agriculture on a temporary basis.

Current US policy on illegal immigration is based largely on the Immigration Reform and Control Act (IRCA) of 1986, which made it illegal to employ illegal aliens, mandated monitoring of employers, and expanded border enforcement.[8] IRCA also offered amnesty to illegal aliens who had resided in the United States since before 1982. As a result of IRCA, in the late 1980s and early 1990s the United States granted permanent legal residence to 2.7 million individuals, 2 million of whom were Mexican nationals (Bureau of International Labor Affairs 1996) (figure 11.1). In 2003, the US Border Patrol apprehended 931,557 illegal aliens in the United States, which accounted for 89 percent of total apprehensions of illegal aliens by US immigration authorities (figure 11.3).[9] Of these, 95 percent were Mexican nationals (DHS 2004). Over time, the Border Patrol has dra-

7. These figures are based on the US population census. The Census Bureau estimates that its population figures undercount illegal immigrants residing in the United States by 15 percent.

8. Before this act, it was illegal to "harbor" illegal aliens but not to employ them (Calavita 1992).

9. Apprehensions of illegal aliens overstate attempted illegal immigration, because the Border Patrol may capture a single individual multiple times in a given year

Figure 11.3 Apprehensions of illegal aliens in the United States, 1930–2000

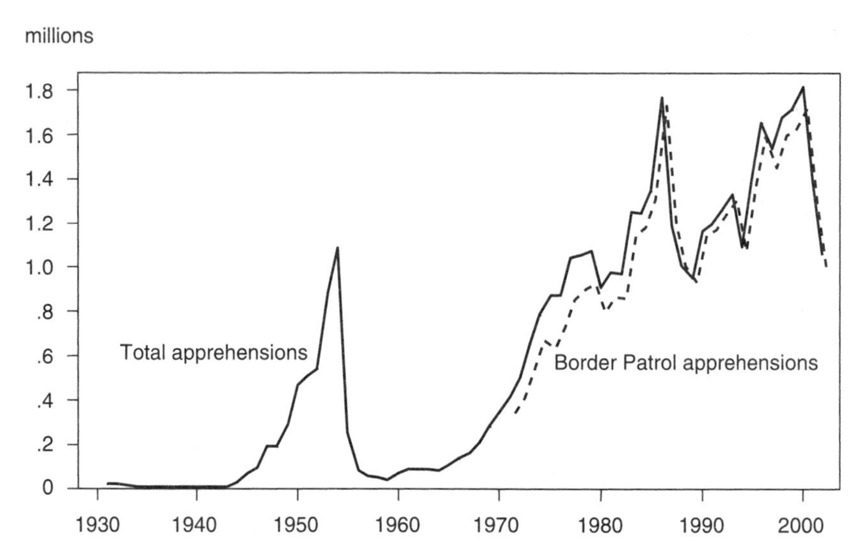

Source: US Department of Homeland Security, Office of Immigration Statistics, *2003 Yearbook of Immigration Statistics.*

matically stepped up enforcement. Between 1980 and 2000, expenditure on border enforcement increased by 5.6 times in real terms (figure 11.4). Most of the Border Patrol's activities are concentrated in US cities that border Mexico, which has encouraged those attempting illegal entry through less populated—and more treacherous—desert and mountain regions of Arizona, California, and Texas. The end result has been an increase in deaths among illegal border crossers from 50 individuals a year in the early 1990s to 300 to 500 per year in the early 2000s (Cornelius 2001).

Profile of US Immigration

Immigration is changing the United States by making the population more ethnically diverse, by increasing the number of low-skilled workers in the labor force, and by expanding the population of individuals residing in the country illegally. In this section, I use data from the US Current Population Survey and US Census of Population and Housing to examine the characteristics of the US immigrant population. These data include both legal and illegal immigrants.

Recent immigrants come primarily from Asia and Latin America. Of immigrants entering the United States between 1990 and 2003, 58 percent came from Latin America and 26 percent from Asia (table 11.1). Mexico is

Figure 11.4 US government expenditure on immigration enforcement, 1960–2000

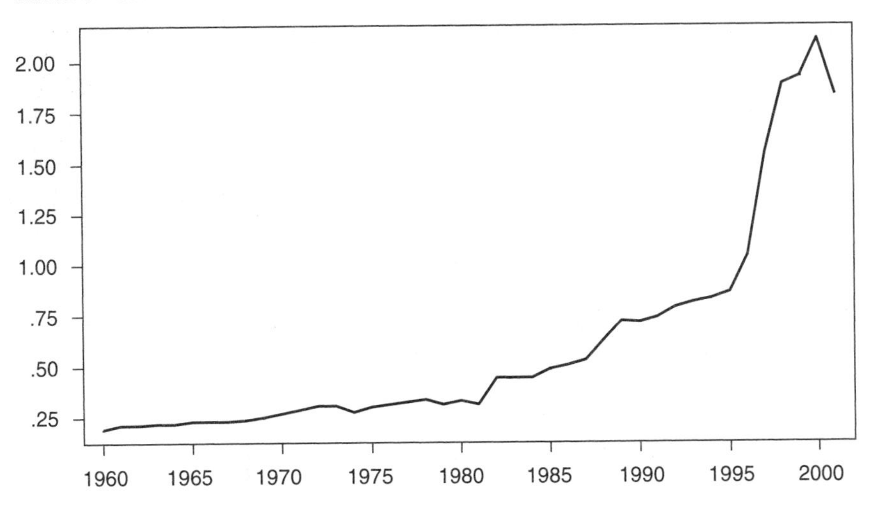

Source: US Department of Justice, Budget Summary, various years, www.usdoj.gov/jmd/.

the most important source country for immigration, accounting for 34 percent of all immigrants arriving since 1990 and about 30 percent of the total US foreign-born population. In Mexico, this labor outflow has had a major effect on the country's population. In 2000, 8 percent of individuals born in Mexico resided in the United States (Chiquiar and Hanson 2004). The shift in US immigration toward Asia and Latin America has diminished Europe's role. Of the total number of immigrants who arrived before 1970, 41 percent were from Europe, but in 2003, only 12 percent of immigrants entering the country since 1990 came from the region.

For illegal immigration, the importance of Asia and Latin America as source regions is even greater. Between 1990 and 2000, the illegal population in the United States increased from 3.8 million to 8.9 million individuals.[10] In 2000, Asia and Latin America accounted for 75 percent of the US illegal immigrant population, up from 69 percent in 1990. Mexico is by far the largest source country for illegal immigrants, accounting for 45 percent of the illegal population in 2000. In 2000, the share of the foreign-born population in the country illegally was (at least) 31 percent for all immigrants, 19 percent for immigrants from Asia, 36 percent for immigrants from Latin America, and 45 percent for immigrants from Mexico (Costanzo et al. 2001).

10. These figures are without adjusting for the undercount of illegal immigrants mentioned in footnote 8. Assuming a 15 percent undercount, the population of illegal immigrants would be 4.4 million in 1990 and 10.2 million in 2000.

Table 11.1 Source countries for US immigration, 2003

	Foreign-born population		Cohorts by arrival year			
	Level (millions)	Distribution (percent)	Pre-1970	1970 to 1979	1980 to 1989	1990 or later
			Millions			
All countries	34.6	100.0	4.8	5.0	8.2	16.7
			Percent of cohort			
Region of birth						
Latin America	18.3	52.8	35.3	47.6	56.4	57.6
Asia	9.0	26.0	14.0	33.3	29.3	25.6
Europe	5.4	15.6	40.6	14.6	9.7	11.7
Other	1.9	5.5	10.1	4.5	4.6	5.0
Country of birth						
Mexico	10.2	29.6	16.0	26.4	30.1	34.1
Philippines	1.5	4.2	2.9	5.9	4.9	3.7
India	1.2	3.4	0.8	3.5	2.5	4.6
China	1.2	3.4	2.6	3.0	3.1	3.8
Germany	1.1	3.2	12.5	2.6	1.8	1.3
El Salvador	1.0	3.0	0.6	2.0	4.3	3.3
Cuba	1.0	2.9	7.9	2.9	2.2	1.9
Vietnam	.9	2.7	0.5	4.5	3.4	2.5
South Korea	.9	2.6	1.3	4.1	3.8	2.0
Canada	.9	2.5	8.2	2.2	1.4	1.4
Dominican Republic	.7	2.1	1.3	2.3	2.3	2.2

Source: Current Population Survey, March 2003.

Immigrants tend to settle in specific US regions. Upon arriving in the United States, immigrants tend to settle in the "gateway" states of California, Florida, Illinois, New Jersey, New York, and Texas.[11] In 2002, these six states were home to 67 percent of immigrants but only 40 percent of natives. California, on its own, is home to 28 percent of all immigrants (but only 12 percent of natives). Within the gateway states, most immigrants live in a few large cities. In 2003, 46 percent of immigrants, but only 17 percent of natives, lived in just five metropolitan areas: Los Angeles, New York, San Francisco, Miami, and Chicago. Illegal immigrants are also regionally concentrated. In 2000, 68 percent of illegal immigrants lived in gateway states, with 32 percent living in California alone (INS 2001).

Breaking with historical patterns, the states with the fastest growth in their immigrant populations during the 1990s were not gateway states but states located in the southeast (Georgia and North Carolina), Mountain West (Arizona, Colorado, and Nevada), and Great Plains (Nebraska and Kansas). These states also had high growth in native employment, suggesting that immigrants tend to move to regions where job growth is

11. In the 1960s and 1970s, Massachusetts and Pennsylvania were also gateway states for immigration.

Figure 11.5 Educational attainment of immigrants and natives, March 2003

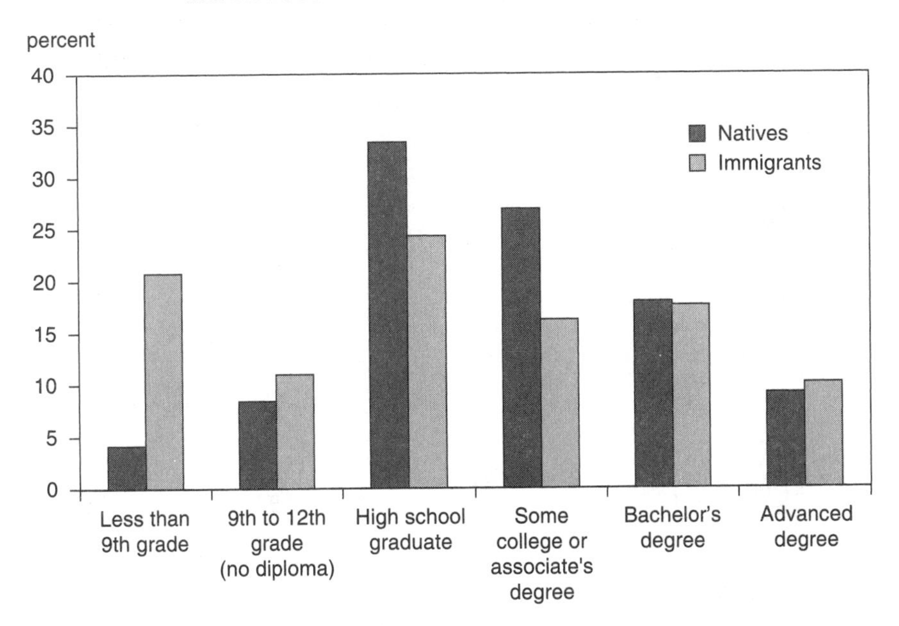

Source: Current Population Survey, March 2003.

strong.[12] The shift in population out of gateway states is even more notable among the illegal foreign-born population. Between 1990 and 2000, the share of illegal immigrants residing outside the six gateway states increased from 20 percent to 32 percent.

Immigrants are concentrated at the extremes of the skill distribution. They are much more likely than natives to have low levels of schooling. In 2003, 33 percent of immigrants 25 years and older had not completed the equivalent of a high-school education, compared with only 13 percent of US natives (figure 11.5). At the same time, immigrants are as likely as natives to be highly educated, with 27 percent of each group having completed a bachelor's degree (and a slightly higher fraction of immigrants having completed an advanced degree). Immigrants are underrepresented in the middle of the skill distribution, among workers with a high-school education or some college. This group accounts for 60 percent of natives but only 41 percent of immigrants. Borjas (1999a) shows that in the 1960s and 1970s, the educational attainment of immigrants was more sim-

12. The correlation between the log change in the share of the state population that is foreign-born and the log change in state native employment from 1990 to 2000 is highly statistically significant at 0.53.

Figure 11.6 Occupational distribution of immigrants and natives, March 2003

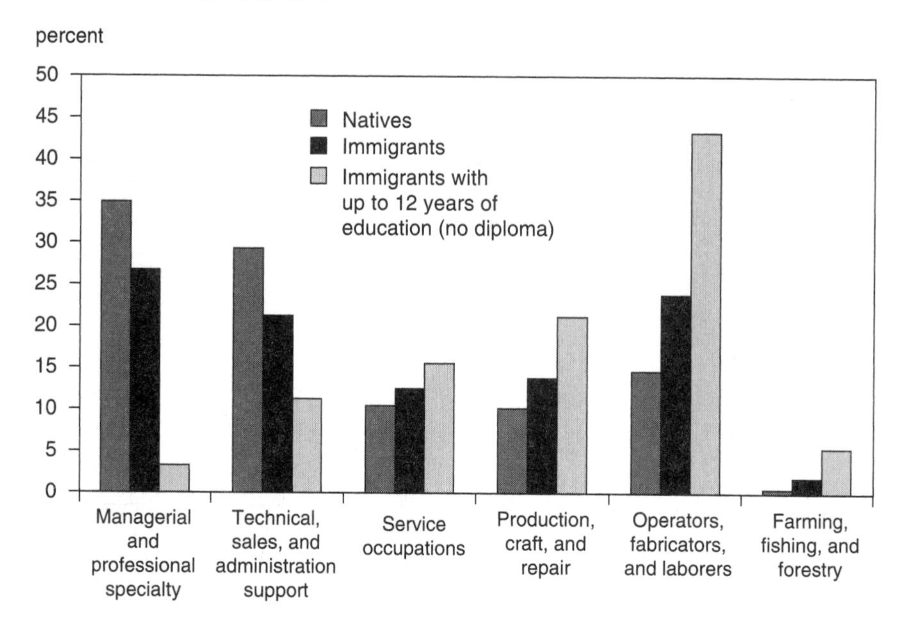

Source: Current Population Survey, March 2003.

ilar to that of US natives. The increasing skill gap between natives and immigrants appears to be a consequence of the shift in immigration from Europe—where schooling levels are similar to those in the United States—to Asia and Latin America, where schooling levels are well below those in the United States.

Immigrants earn less than US natives and tend to be employed in low-wage occupations. A low level of schooling and a lack of legal status confine many immigrants to low-wage jobs. In 2003, while 62 percent of natives were managers, professionals, or technical or administrative staff, only about 48 percent of immigrants were in one of these occupations (figure 11.6). And while only 25 percent of natives worked in low-paying manual labor or agricultural occupations, 43 percent of immigrants held one of these jobs. These occupational differences contribute to earnings differences between natives and immigrants. Among full-time, year-round workers in 2003, 45 percent of immigrants, but only 25 percent of natives, earned less than $25,000 a year (figure 11.7). As is the case with the distribution of skills, immigrants are underrepresented in the middle of the earnings distribution. While 40 percent of native workers earned between $35,000 and $75,000 a year, only about 28 percent of immigrants fell into this category. Overall, median earnings for native workers were 30 percent

Figure 11.7 Yearly earnings distribution of immigrants and natives, March 2002

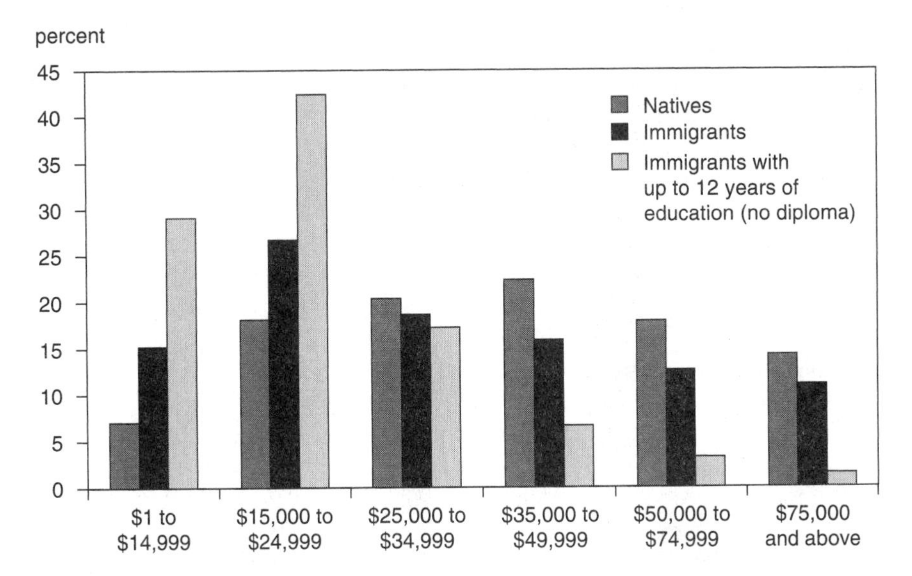

Source: Current Population Survey, March 2003.

higher than for immigrants.[13] Borjas (1999b) shows that, as with the skills gap, the gap between native and immigrant earnings has grown over time.

Low skill levels and limited English-language ability contribute to immigrants' low labor market earnings. Borjas (1999b) finds that in 1990, lower levels of education and US labor market experience accounted for 38 percent of the wage differential between natives and immigrants. Bleakley and Chin (2004) estimate that lack of English-language proficiency substantially lowers an individual's earnings. Illegality also contributes to low wages, by confining immigrants to low-skill occupations or by giving US employers greater bargaining power in setting wages. Kossoudji and Cobb-Clark (2002) examine illegal immigrants who attained legal status as a result of the IRCA amnesty in the late 1980s and early 1990s. They find that the penalty for being an illegal immigrant in the 1980s was a wage that was 14 to 24 percent lower than for legal workers. Lower wages for illegal

13. These differences in earnings do not control for differences in annual hours worked or for differences in age, education, and other characteristics between immigrants and natives. Using data from 1990, Borjas (1999b) finds that controlling for differences in hours worked, natives earned 16 percent more than immigrants; and controlling also for age, education, and other observable characteristics, natives earned 10 percent more than immigrants. This pattern has changed markedly over time. In 1960, natives earned 4 percent *less* than immigrants (controlling for hours worked) and 1 percent *less* than immigrants (controlling for hours worked and other observable characteristics).

immigrants may be one reason that US employers oppose efforts to increase enforcement against illegal immigration (Calavita 1992).

Immigrants are more likely than natives to receive welfare benefits. As a consequence of lower earning power, immigrants are more likely than natives to live in poverty and to be eligible for means-tested entitlement programs. Further enhancing their eligibility is their tendency to have larger families, spreading their smaller incomes across more household members, and to have more children, giving them access to programs targeted to the young. Some entitlement programs—such as TANF (Temporary Assistance for Needy Families), SSI (supplemental security income), and general assistance—provide cash benefits, and other programs—such as Medicaid, food stamps, housing and energy subsidies, and school meal programs—provide in-kind benefits. In 1994, 25 percent of immigrant households and 15 percent of native households received some type of government assistance (table 11.2).[14]

In 1996, Congress undertook a major reform of federal welfare programs (Fix and Passel 2002). The reform mandated work requirements as a precondition to receive benefits, limited the life-time use of certain benefits, gave states more discretion over program design, and excluded noncitizens from access to many benefits. Congress substituted state entitlements to open-ended federal funds with block grants, leaving states with considerable autonomy over individual eligibility criteria. For immigrants who arrived before 1996, states have the option of whether to use their federal block grants to provide this group with TANF, Medicaid, and other benefits (table 11.3). For immigrants arriving after 1996, states may not use federal block grants to provide noncitizens with these benefits, but they are free to use other state funds to create substitute programs. After five years, immigrants may apply for citizenship, which guarantees their access to public benefits for which they meet standard eligibility criteria. For new immigrants, this in effect mandates a five-year waiting period for access to most benefits. States now vary considerably in the programs they offer to immigrants (Zimmerman and Tumlin 1999). Despite major changes in welfare policy, immigrants remain more likely than natives to receive benefits. In 2003, 24 percent of immigrants and 15 percent of natives received some type of government assistance. Continuing high immigrant usage of entitlement programs is primarily due to Medicaid. While immigrant usage of Medicaid remained stable between 1994 and 2003, there were sharp declines (overall and relative to natives) in immigrant usage of cash benefits and food stamps, suggesting welfare reform has had an impact on the type of government benefits that immigrants receive.

---

14. There is abundant academic literature that documents this pattern. See Borjas (1999a). Table 11.2 shows the fraction of households headed by an immigrant or headed by a native, in which at least one household member receives a specified government benefit. US-born children of immigrants who live with their parents are included in calculating the fraction of immigrant households using entitlement programs.

Table 11.2 Use of means-tested programs in 1994 and 2002 by householder's nativity and year of entry (percent)

	Nativity of householder		Immigrants by year of arrival			
Welfare program	**Native**	**Immigrant**	**Pre-1970**	**1970–79**	**1980–89**	**Since 1990**
1994						
Public assistance[a]	4.5	8.1	3.6	8.3	11.1	12.7
SSI	3.9	6.2	7.5	6.0	5.4	5.3
Food stamps	8.4	13.7	8.5	14.4	17.9	17.4
Medicaid	13.3	22.4	16.0	22.4	27.9	27.7
Any of the above	15.3	24.6	17.8	24.9	30.4	29.7
2002						
Public assistance[a]	1.6	2.3	1.2	1.9	2.9	2.6
SSI	3.6	5.0	7.7	6.3	5.0	2.8
Food stamps	5.5	6.5	5.8	5.7	8.0	6.3
Medicaid	13.6	23.2	18.5	21.6	27.3	23.7
Any of the above	14.9	24.2	19.4	22.5	28.3	24.7

SSI = supplemental security income

a. Includes Aid to Families with Dependent Children (for 1994), Temporary Assistance for Needy Families (for 2002), and general assistance programs.

Note: Immigrants and native households defined by nativity of household head. Year of entry based on household head.

Source: Current Population Survey, March 1995 and March 2003.

While welfare reform excludes illegal immigrants from receiving government benefits, US courts have ruled that it is against the law to deny illegal immigrants emergency medical services. This ruling puts states with large illegal immigrant populations in a quandary. Without access to public health care, many illegal immigrants use emergency medical services for routine health problems or delay seeking medical care until their health problems become acute. The expense of providing emergency medical care to the illegal population has led some states, including California and Texas, to provide illegal immigrants with state-funded preventive health care, as a means of holding down costs.[15] It appears some states have found that the prevalence of illegal immigration makes certain aspects of welfare reform inefficient.

Benefits and Costs of Immigration

Immigration increases the incomes of US residents by helping utilize domestic resources more efficiently. These benefits, however, are not shared equally. Immigration redistributes income away from factors that compete with immigrants in the labor market. This redistribution creates

15. See Clay Robison, "Senate approves care for illegal immigrants," *Houston Chronicle*, May 5, 2003, A19.

Table 11.3 Eligibility of immigrants for public benefits

	SSI	Food stamps	Medicaid	TANF	Other federal means-tested benefits	State/local public benefits
Qualified immigrants arriving *before* August 23, 1996						
Legal permanent residents	Yes	No	State option	State option	State option	State option
Asylees, refugees[a]	Eligible for first 7 years	Eligible for first 5 years	Eligible for first 7 years	Eligible for first 5 years	Eligible for first 5 years	Eligible for first 5 years
Qualified immigrants arriving *after* August 23, 1996						
Legal permanent residents	No	No	Barred for first 5 years; state option afterward	Barred for first 5 years; state option afterward	Barred for first 5 years; state option afterward	State option
Asylees, refugees	Eligible for first 7 years	Eligible for first 5 years	Eligible for first 7 years	Eligible for first 5 years	Eligible for first 5 years	Eligible for first 5 years
Unqualified immigrants						
Illegal immigrants	No	No	Emergency services only	No	No[b]	No[c]
PRUCOL immigrants	No[d]	No	Emergency services only	No	No	No[c]

PRUCOL = persons residing under cover of law
SSI = supplemental security income
TANF = Temporary Assistance for Needy Families program

a. Cuban and Haitian entrants, Amerasians, and aliens granted withholding of deportation are also included in this group.
b. States have the option to provide WIC (special supplemental nutrition program for women, infants, and children) to unqualified immigrants.
c. Selected programs are exempted, including short-term noncash relief, immunizations, testing and treatment for communicable diseases, and selected assistance from community programs.
d. PRUCOL immigrants receiving SSI as of August 22, 1996, continued to be eligible until September 30, 1998.

Source: Boeri, Hanson, and McCormick (2002).

political opposition to immigration. A second source of opposition to immigration comes from the costs that immigration imposes on resident taxpayers. If immigrants receive more in government benefits than they pay in taxes, then immigration imposes a net fiscal burden on US natives.

Immigration, much like international trade and international capital flows, tends to raise global welfare. Wage differences between countries reflect economic inefficiencies associated with an oversupply of labor in low-wage countries and an undersupply of labor in high-wage countries. By moving labor from low-wage to high-wage countries, immigration helps raise global productivity. These global efficiency gains are shared by immigrants and by some US factor owners.

Benefits

Immigration generates a surplus in the form of extra income to domestic factors of production. By increasing the supply of labor, immigration raises the productivity of factors that are complementary to labor. More workers allow US capital, land, and natural resources to be exploited more efficiently. These gains in productivity result in income gains to owners of these factors. It is no surprise, then, that US business interests support immigration.[16] But increasing the supply of labor also drives down wages for US workers. Borjas (2003) estimates that over 1980–2000, immigration contributed to a decrease in average US wages of 3 percent. This estimate accounts for the total change in the US labor force due to immigration, including both legal and illegal sources. Since immigration is concentrated among the low skilled, the workers most likely to be adversely affected are low-skilled natives. Over the 1980–2000 period, wages of native workers without a high school degree fell by 9 percent as a result of immigration.[17] Consistent with these effects, Scheve and Slaughter (2001b) find that opposition to immigration in the United States is most intense among native workers with low schooling levels (less than a high school education).

To calculate the net change in national income associated with immigration, I sum up the income changes associated with immigration for all domestic factors of production. Using a simple model of the US economy,[18] the immigration surplus takes a very tractable form:

16. The National Association of Manufacturers, www.nam.org, states, "Foreign nationals have made enormous contributions to US companies, our economy and society as a whole. To continue our economic and technological preeminence we need to ensure that we have access to the talent we need to lead and compete."

17. Borjas (2003) also estimates that over the 1980–2000 period, immigration reduced wages for college graduates by 5 percent, wages for high school graduates by 3 percent, and wages for those with some college by a negligible amount.

18. This model assumes there is one good and two factors of production. It is straightforward to extend this model to allow for a more complicated environment.

> Immigration surplus as a percent of GDP = –0.5 × (percent change in wages due to immigration) × (percent change in labor force due to immigration) × (labor share of national income)

Applying this formula to results in Borjas (2003) for 1980–2000, a crude calculation of the immigration surplus for the US economy in 2000 would be

$$-0.5 \times (-3.2 \text{ percent}) \times (11 \text{ percent}) \times (0.70) = 0.12 \text{ percent}$$

A rough estimate, then, is that immigration raises US GDP by slightly more than one-tenth of a percent. Borjas (1999b) produces more sophisticated estimates of the immigration surplus by allowing for labor of different skill types and by allowing for varying effects of immigration on wages. However, no reasonable alternative estimate would differ from my crude estimate by more than a factor of two. The gain in US income from immigration simply isn't very large.

Since the immigration surplus is larger when the wage effects are larger, the gains to immigration are greater when immigration has a larger impact on the distribution of income. A country gains most from immigration when it admits labor whose skills are scarcest. In this case, immigration has a larger negative impact on the wages of the affected labor group but also yields a larger gain in national income. Holding constant the level of immigration, the United States could increase the immigration surplus by concentrating immigration among skill groups that are in relatively short supply. For the United States, this would mean concentrating immigration even more at the extremes of the skill distribution. Very highly skilled workers are in relatively short supply in the United States, as they are everywhere. It is perhaps less apparent that very low-skilled workers are in increasingly short supply. The share of employed native-born US workers with less than a high school education fell from 50 percent in 1960 to 8 percent in 2000 and is expected to continue to decline (Borjas 1999a). Adding workers in the middle of the skill distribution, which for the United States includes high school through college graduates, would produce a relatively small immigration surplus.

Two factors mitigate the impact of immigration on wages and reduce the potential immigration surplus. One is that the supply of capital in the US economy is not fixed. Immigration raises the productivity of capital, creating incentives for further investment (either by domestic residents or by foreigners). More investment increases the capital stock, raising the productivity of labor and thereby offsetting some of the wage losses associated with immigration. An elastic supply of capital (but one that is less than perfectly elastic) means that immigration has only a modest impact on wages. A second factor that helps mitigate the wage impact of immigration is international trade. Immigration of low-skilled labor reduces US demand for imports from low-wage countries. Reduced imports from low-wage countries increase US domestic demand for low-wage labor, partially absorbing the influx of foreign labor.

Our estimate of the immigration surplus ignores many factors and so should be treated with caution. For instance, during World War II, the immigration of scientists from Europe helped spur US advancements in physics, chemistry, and other fields (Fermi 1971). After the war, these advancements appeared to help raise the pace of innovation in US industry. Such dynamic effects of immigration are plausible but are very hard to gauge. If these effects are important, static estimates of the immigration surplus will tend to understate immigration's true economic impact.

An additional potential benefit from immigration is that it may help the government manage unfunded pension liabilities. Since Social Security operates on a pay-as-you-go basis, the program generates a surplus in years when the population of working Americans is large relative to the population of retired Americans and a deficit in years when the population of retirees is relatively large. Currently, contributions to Social Security exceed payments out of the system, generating a surplus that helps finance US federal budget deficits. With the aging of the US population, this surplus will turn into a small deficit around 2020 and a larger deficit some years later. By increasing the population of younger workers, immigration has the potential to help maintain the solvency of the US Social Security system (Auerbach and Oreopoulos 1999; Fehr, Jokisch, and Kotlikoff 2004).[19] Of course, this benefit applies only if immigrants pay more in taxes than they absorb in public services. If immigrants are a net drain on government revenues, further immigration worsens the US fiscal situation.

Another group that benefits from international migration is the immigrants themselves. Chiquiar and Hanson (2004) estimate that in 1990 the gain in wages for Mexican immigrants from moving to the United States was $2.50 to $4.00 an hour, adjusted for cost-of-living differences. This amounts to an approximate annual gain in real income of $5,000 to $8,000 a year, or 1.5 to 2 times per capita GDP in Mexico. For the migrant, this income gain is larger than the effect of any conceivable development policy. Even the most optimistic estimates of the impact of the North American Free Trade Agreement (NAFTA) on an individual worker in Mexico would be a small fraction of the gain associated with moving to the United States.[20]

The counterpart to an immigration surplus in host countries is an emigration loss in countries that send migrants abroad. By exporting labor, sending countries suffer a loss in GDP associated with less efficient utilization of their resources.[21] As with the immigration surplus, the emigra-

19. Clearly, this benefit is conceptually distinct from the immigration surplus, since it arises only due to existing tax distortions in the US economy.

20. The upper end of the estimated income gain to Mexico from NAFTA was 5 percent of GDP (Brown, Deardorff, and Stern 1992).

21. In theory, the sum of the immigration surplus in receiving countries and the income gain to migrants exceeds the emigration loss in sending countries.

tion loss is proportional to the emigration-induced change in wages. For Mexico, Mishra (2003) estimates that over 1970–2000, emigration increased average wages in Mexico by 8 percent. By 2000, the number of Mexican emigrants in the United States was equal to 16 percent of the labor force in Mexico. Based on these figures, the emigration loss for Mexico in 2000 would be 0.5 percent of GDP. However, in Mexico's case, the loss is more than offset by income that emigrants remit to family members in Mexico, which in 2000 was 1.1 percent of GDP and in 2002 was 1.5 percent of GDP. On net, residents of Mexico—those who do not migrate abroad—appear to gain from emigration, with much of the gain presumably going to the family members of migrants, who are the primary recipients of remittances.

In other countries, remittances are an even larger share of economic activity, exceeding 10 percent of GDP in 2003 in the Dominican Republic, El Salvador, Haiti, Honduras, Jamaica, and Nicaragua (IDB 2004). The Inter-American Development Bank finds that in 2003 in El Salvador, Guatemala, Honduras, and Mexico over 14 percent of adults received remittances from the United States. In that year, Latin American immigrants in the United States sent a total of $31 billion to their home countries, amounting to 1.4 percent of the region's GDP.

For the United States, the impact of immigration policy on Mexico and Latin America should not be ignored. Due to shared geography and history, the United States and Mexico have a special relationship. The opportunity to emigrate to the United States gives Mexico a safety valve, which may have helped the country avert domestic turmoil during the severe macroeconomic instability the country experienced in the 1980s and 1990s. Attempted illegal entry at the US-Mexico border increases sharply following declines in Mexico's real wage (Hanson and Spilimbergo 1999). After Mexico's currency crises in 1982, 1987, and 1995, each of which involved major economic contractions, there was a surge in illegal immigration from Mexico. In the absence of the opportunity to migrate to the United States, these periods of economic crisis would likely have involved even higher levels of unemployment and larger declines in real wages. A richer and more stable Mexico is surely in the US interest.

Beyond the economic consequences of immigration, there have long been complaints that immigration dilutes American cultural identify and weakens the country's social fabric (Daniels 2003, Tichenor 2002). In his 1996 and 2000 presidential bids, Patrick Buchanan attempted to tap into public discontent over bilingual education and increasing ethnic diversity in the United States. His arguments are mirrored in Samuel Huntington's (2004) influential critique of immigration from Latin America. Huntington claims that the values of Latino immigrants conflict with those of mainstream America, putting US culture at risk. What is unconvincing about this argument is that when one examines the behavior of Latino immigrants and their descendents in terms of language, religion, education, and employment they display genuinely American attributes. The large majority of children of Latino immigrants, including those who arrived in the United States at a young age, speak English very well (Bleakley and Chin 2004). Second-generation Mexican-Americans complete 42 percent more schooling than their immigrant parents (Grogger and Trejo 2002). Rates of labor-force participation and of self-employment are higher for Mexican immigrants than for the US population as a whole. And the commitment of the Latino population to church, family, and community appears to be very strong. While the contribution of immigration to ethnic diversity in the United States is undeniable, it is hard to see why greater diversity, on its own, is harmful.

Costs

In a world without distortions, no costs would be associated with immigration. Clearly, we are far from such a world. US tax and spending policies distort individual decisions about how much to work, how much to save, and how much to invest. Immigration, by admitting large numbers of low-skilled individuals, exacerbates inefficiencies associated with the country's welfare system. Also, population growth—whether due to immigration or to other sources—worsens distortions associated with poorly defined property rights over air, water, highways, and common areas. More people mean more pollution and more congestion.

If immigrants pay more in taxes than they receive in government benefits, then immigration generates a net fiscal transfer to native taxpayers.[22] The total impact of immigration on US residents—the sum of the immigration surplus and the net fiscal transfer from immigrants—would be unambiguously positive. On the other hand, if immigrants pay less in taxes than they receive in government benefits, then immigration generates a net fiscal burden on native taxpayers—natives would in effect be making an income transfer to immigrants. Paying for this fiscal transfer would require some combination of tax increases on natives, reductions in government benefits to natives, and increased borrowing from future

22. It is a common misperception that illegal immigrants do not contribute to tax revenues. Illegal immigrants pay sales taxes on their consumption purchases and property taxes on dwellings they own or rent. In addition, many illegal immigrants contribute to Social Security and to federal income taxes. Evidence of this includes the recent large increase in Social Security contributions with invalid numbers. As of 1986, US law requires employers to record the Social Security number and visa information of each immigrant employee. In response, many illegal immigrants present employers with fake Social Security cards, which tend to have invalid numbers. Between 1986 and 2000, annual Social Security contributions with invalid numbers soared from $7 billion to $49 billion (Social Security Administration 2003). While the Social Security Administration does not immediately release these funds, they are eventually rolled into administration general funds (and in the meantime represent a zero-interest-rate loan).

generations (by issuing government debt). In this case, the total impact of immigration on US residents would be positive only if the immigration surplus exceeded the fiscal transfer made to immigrants.

The National Research Council (NRC) recently conducted two detailed case studies of the fiscal impacts of immigration, one on New Jersey and another on California (Smith and Edmonston 1997). Both states have relatively large immigrant populations. In 2000, the share of the adult population that is foreign-born was 34 percent in California and 24 percent in New Jersey, compared with 15 percent in the nation as a whole. However, the two states have immigrant populations with quite different skill profiles and patterns of welfare usage. In 2000, the share of immigrant households headed by someone with less than a high school education was 34 percent in California and 29 percent in the nation as a whole, but only 23 percent in New Jersey. Similarly, the share of immigrant households receiving cash benefits from welfare programs was 13 percent in California and 10 percent in the nation as a whole, but only 8 percent in New Jersey. These differences in welfare uptake are only partly due to immigrants in California being less skilled. California also appears to be more generous in the benefits it offers. While the less-skilled native population is larger in New Jersey (high school dropouts are 11 percent of New Jersey's native adult population and 8 percent of California's), native welfare usage is still greater in California. The share of native households receiving cash benefits is 8 percent in California and 7 percent in the nation as a whole, but only 5 percent in New Jersey.

Based on federal, state, and local government expenditures and tax receipts, the NRC estimates that the short-run fiscal impact of immigration is negative in both New Jersey and California.[23] In New Jersey, using data for 1989–90, immigrant households received an average net fiscal transfer from natives of $1,484, or 2.5 percent of average state immigrant household income.[24] Spread among the more numerous state native population, this transfer amounted to an average net fiscal burden of $232 per native household, or 0.4 percent of average state native household income. In California, using data for 1994–95, immigrant households received an average net fiscal transfer of $3,463, or 9.1 percent of average immigrant household income, which resulted in an average fiscal burden on native households of $1,178, or 2.3 percent of average native household income.

Two factors explain why natives make net fiscal transfers to immigrants: (1) immigrant households are larger with more children, leading

23. The study included as many federal, state, and local government services and sources of tax revenue on which it was feasible to collect data. See Smith and Edmonston (1997).

24. All figures based on the NRC study are in 1996 dollars.

them to make greater use of public education, and (2) immigrant households earn lower incomes, leading them to make greater use of welfare programs and lower contributions to taxes.

It is apparent from the NRC study that variations in welfare policies and immigrant characteristics yield fiscal consequences that vary widely across US states. Native taxpayers in California, with its less-skilled immigrant population and high immigrant uptake of welfare, make relatively large fiscal transfers to immigrant households. Within the United States, it appears the fiscal costs of immigration are borne quite unevenly. States with poorer immigrant populations and more generous policies are likely to shoulder a much larger share of the fiscal burden associated with immigration. Further concentrating the distributional consequences of immigration, California and some other high-immigration states have progressive tax systems, in which high-income taxpayers account for a disproportionate share of tax revenues. Thus, higher-income taxpayers in high-immigration states are likely to pay much of the fiscal cost of immigration.

Public opinion is consistent with this reasoning. High-income individuals in states that provide generous benefits to immigrants appear to be acutely aware of the fiscal costs they bear. Nationally, more-educated individuals tend to be more favorable toward immigration. However, their support varies markedly across US states. The highly educated (college education or advanced degree) are most opposed to immigration in states that have both large immigrant populations and high immigrant uptake of welfare (Hanson, Scheve, and Slaughter 2004). In California, for instance, the anti-immigration sentiments of high-income voters were important in the passage of Proposition 187 in 1994, a ballot measure that denied state benefits to illegal immigrants (which the courts later overturned).

Estimated fiscal transfers associated with immigration are due entirely to transfers at the state and local levels. Immigration has a decidedly negative impact on state and local public finances. But at the federal level, immigrants make a positive net fiscal contribution. This is because national defense accounts for a large fraction of the federal benefits immigrants receive. As a public good, the cost of national defense is unaffected by immigration. Adding taxpayers through immigration lowers the effective amount the federal government must charge native taxpayers to cover defense outlays.

For the nation as a whole, the NRC estimates that immigration imposes a short-run burden on the average native household of $166 to $226, or 0.20 percent to 0.25 percent of US GDP in 1995. Comparing the average of these two estimates with the immigration surplus of 0.12 percent of GDP, a back-of-the-envelope calculation suggests that in the short run, immigration reduces the income of US residents by about 0.1 percent of GDP.

This estimate is only meant to be suggestive. Going from a short-run to a long-run estimate of the fiscal cost of immigration can change the results dramatically. Immigrants are relatively young and far from their peak earning and taxpaying years. As immigrants age, their net fiscal contribution increases. Also, they have children who are likely to obtain more education and to pay more in taxes than their parents. The NRC estimates that the average immigrant admitted in 1990 would produce a net fiscal contribution of $80,000 over the next 300 years (in present discounted value terms). This contribution depends crucially on the immigrant's skill level. The long-run fiscal contribution is negative for low-skilled immigrants (less than a high school education) and positive for higher-skilled immigrants (more than a high school education).

Going 300 years forward obviously requires very strong assumptions about the future economic environment. Even for the average immigrant, the annual net fiscal contribution is negative for the first 25 years after arriving in the United States. The long-run estimate rests on the assumption that the federal government will later raise taxes to bring the federal budget into balance. If this doesn't happen, the long-run fiscal contribution of the average immigrant would be negative.[25] Under any scenario, the long-run fiscal impact of immigration on state and local governments is negative. Thus, in both the short run and the long run state and local governments (and the taxpayers that support them) pick up much of the fiscal tab associated with immigration.

This discussion leaves two perspectives on the fiscal costs of immigration. In the short run, the fiscal impact of immigration appears to be negative. In the long run, the fiscal impact may be positive or negative, depending on how federal taxes and spending change in the future. This leaves uncertainty about whether the total benefits of immigration exceed the total costs. However, it is clear that these benefits and costs are distributed quite unevenly. Capital owners, land owners, and other employers appear to capture many of the benefits associated with immigration (and also benefit from the lower wages they end up paying native workers). Taxpayers in high-immigration states are likely to shoulder immigration's fiscal costs.

When it comes to the politics of immigration, the short-run impacts may matter more than those in the long run. It is probably reasonable to expect many voters to put more weight on the negative fiscal contribution immigrants make during their first 25 years in the country and less weight on the positive fiscal contribution they make 100 years in the future. Those who place more weight on the short-run consequences of immigration are likely to conclude that immigration makes the United States worse off.

25. See Borjas (1999a) for a discussion of this issue.

Reforming US Immigration Policy

The short-run impact of immigration on the United States appears to be on the order of 0.1 percent of US GDP. Whether negative (if one takes a shorter-run view) or positive (if one takes a longer-run view), the effect of immigration is far less significant than the political debate surrounding the issue would suggest.

While the gains or losses associated with changing the level of immigration appear to be small, there are clear gains associated with *changing how the United States manages immigration*. First, those that benefit most from immigration bear few of its costs. Employers capture the immigration surplus, but taxpayers in high-immigration states bear the fiscal burden. The United States could shift the fiscal cost of immigration from taxpayers to employers and to immigrants by restructuring immigrant access to public benefits. Second, current policy in effect allows one-third of immigration to be illegal. Being illegal prevents immigrants from moving freely between jobs, which keeps them poor and lowers the potential immigration surplus. Illegality also creates an underclass of residents with little prospect of participating in US political life. The United States could diminish its reliance on illegal immigrants by expanding temporary immigration and by requiring employers to verify the eligibility of workers they hire. Third, current US policy, by setting the level of immigration without regard to US economic conditions, yields a small immigration surplus. The United States could raise the surplus by concentrating immigration among workers whose skills are in scarce supply and by adjusting admission levels in response to US business cycle conditions. Achieving these objectives would require changing the rights granted to immigrants, enforcement against illegal immigration, and the level and composition of immigration.

Immigrant Rights

Currently, legal immigrants gain permanent legal residence upon entering the country.[26] This gives them access to some public benefits on arrival and to others after five years (when they become eligible to naturalize). One way to lower the fiscal cost of immigration would be to phase in more slowly an immigrant's access to public benefits. This could be done by having all adult immigrants enter on a temporary work visa (of, say, three years), which would give them rights to certain benefits (public education, participation in the social security system) but not to others (pub-

26. Obviously, this doesn't apply to those on short-term entry visas.

lic assistance, food stamps, public housing, and Medicaid). Satisfying the terms of the temporary work visa would lead to automatic renewal and, after a specified number of renewals, to permanent residence. After five years as a permanent resident, an individual could apply for citizenship, as is the case currently. Violating the terms of the temporary work visa—by remaining unemployed for a prolonged period, by using prohibited forms of public assistance, or by committing a serious crime—would be cause for denying renewal of the visa and would require the immigrant to return home. Such a plan would tie admission to the United States to work, and, relative to the current policy, would reduce the short- and medium-run fiscal burden associated with immigration.

This proposal would take welfare reform one step further. By requiring new immigrants to complete several terms as temporary immigrants, it would increase the amount of time during which immigrants lack access to full benefits. It would also make permanent residence conditional on behavior during a probationary phase. Immigrant advocates often criticize guest worker programs for relegating immigrants to second-class status. As distinct from current guest worker programs, the proposed approach would guarantee immigrants a green card, conditional on their complying with the terms of their temporary visas. Labor unions also complain about guest worker programs, citing their lack of labor rights. It would be entirely feasible to grant temporary immigrants full labor protections, including collective bargaining, a federally mandated minimum wage, unemployment insurance, and mandated health and safety standards. The only difference between temporary immigrants and other workers is that the former would not have access to the same entitlement programs.

Temporary work visas would offer a solution for how to deal with the 10 million illegal immigrants currently living in the country. A special pool of visas could be created for illegal immigrants residing in the United States. The granting of these visas would amount to a limited amnesty for these immigrants.[27] There is likely to be vehement opposition to an amnesty to illegal immigrants. However, it is inconceivable that the United States could reduce the illegal population without an amnesty of some sort. An alternative policy, mass deportations of illegal immigrants, would require a police effort on a scale never before seen in this country. Whatever the opposition to an amnesty, opposition to mass deportations would be more intense. One aspect of a limited amnesty that might make it politically palatable is that it would not lead immediately to a green card but to a probationary period on a temporary visa. Former illegal immigrants would have to earn permanent residence by demonstrating their commitment to being legally employed. Another objection to an amnesty is that it would raise the incentive for future illegal immigration. To avoid

27. This approach parallels President Bush's recent plan, although the Bush proposal does not specify how temporary legal immigrants would progress to permanent residence.

perverse incentive effects, the United States would also have to change the way it enforces measures against illegal entry.

Enforcement

Current US enforcement policy, which has been in place since the early 1990s, involves heavy patrols in large cities along the US-Mexico border, light patrols in unpopulated zones along the US-Mexico border, and minimal presence in the US interior (Boeri, Hanson, and McCormick 2002). Immigration authorities devote few resources to investigating or monitoring employers that hire illegal immigrants (GAO 2002). Of the 955,000 apprehensions the Border Patrol made in 2002, fewer than 5,000 occurred at US farms or other worksites (the rest occurred at or near the US-Mexico border). Few employers face penalties for breaking the law. The number of employers fined for hiring illegal immigrants declined from 799 in 1993 to 14 in 2000, with the number of fines above $50,000 falling from 30 in 1993 to 7 in 1997 and to 0 in 2000. The result of this policy is that once in the United States, illegal immigrants face little risk of apprehension or deportation. Overall, US enforcement policy is ineffective. After the United States dramatically increased enforcement expenditures in the early 1990s (figure 11.4), illegal immigration actually *increased*.

What makes current efforts at enforcement difficult is that employers have plausible deniability. They are required to ask employees only for legal documents (e.g., a social security card and a green card). As long as these appear genuine, employers are largely free from legal responsibility. Since employers do not have to verify the authenticity of the documents, this check serves only to weed out obvious forgeries.

An alternative approach would be to create the capacity for automatic verification of an employee's legal status. Suppose employers were required to verify the authenticity of social security numbers with the Social Security Administration (SSA). If the SSA were to create an electronic database to which employers could submit electronic requests, the verification process would be immediate. Suppose also that each immigrant was required to have a social security number and to record this number with the Department of Homeland Security (DHS). If the SSA and the DHS were to cross-list information with one another, the DHS could easily verify that all legal immigrants had valid social security numbers. With these verification processes in place, employers would no longer have plausible deniability regarding the employment of illegal immigrants. The only way they could hire illegal immigrants would be by keeping them off their official payrolls, in which case they would be overtly breaking the law.

These procedures would make audits of employers by immigration authorities more transparent. Any employer failing to verify the social security status of an employee (on which there would be an electronic record) would be guilty of an infraction. A modest increase in interior enforcement could perhaps greatly increase its effectiveness. In addition, the DHS would have a record of employment for each temporary legal immigrant, which would be useful for evaluating applications for renewal of work visas. Any immigrant failing to be employed for a sufficient fraction of the visa period (again, on which there would be an electronic record) would be ineligible for renewal of a temporary visa or for gaining a green card.[28]

Level of Immigration

Congress sets the level of immigration without regard to US economic conditions. The potential immigration surplus is greater when the United States is in a period of economic expansion than when the country is in a period of contraction. A simple alternative would be to create a flexible cap that would *on average* achieve the mandated admission level but that would be higher in years when US GDP growth was high and lower in years when US GDP growth was low. A flexible cap would complement converting legal immigration to renewable temporary work visas. Each year, there would be flows out of temporary immigrant status, as individuals either completed the required number of terms on their visas and obtained permanent residence or violated the terms of their visas and had them revoked. Outflows would create openings for new temporary immigrants, with net total admissions determined by the flexible cap.

Admission quotas for legal immigrants obviously don't apply to illegal immigrants. The United States implicitly sets the level of illegal immigration by choosing how many legal immigrants to admit and how intensively to enforce US borders and workplaces. Given current US policy, about 400,000 new illegal immigrants enter the country each year. Illegal immigration happens in part because US employers value the services illegal workers provide. US immigration authorities appear to accommodate the needs of employers by lowering enforcement against illegal immigration during periods in which labor demand in labor-intensive industries is strong (Hanson and Spilimbergo 2001). Reducing the level of illegal immigration would reduce the immigration surplus US employers capture. An alternative is simply to legalize the illegal inflow. Holding constant the level of immigration, the immigration surplus would be larger for a workforce of legal immigrants than for a workforce of illegal immigrants. The wage penalty associated with being an illegal immigrant appears to be due largely to illegal workers being unable to take advan-

28. Immediate verification of an employee's legal status would not increase information burdens on either employees or employers. Currently, employers must complete and retain I-9 identification verification forms on all employees. This proposal would only make this process electronic.

tage of new job opportunities (Kossoudji and Cobb-Clark 2002). The relative immobility of illegal workers makes them less productive, reducing the surplus they generate.

One way to legalize the inflow of illegal workers would be to offer a number of temporary work visas equal to the current level of legal plus illegal immigration. This would expand *legal immigration* to about 1.1 million admissions a year, but would leave *total immigration* unchanged. Again, for this policy to make any sense it must be combined with enforcement against illegal immigration. One issue in implementing this program would be whether to admit the immediate family members of temporary visa holders. Currently, the United States allows immediate family members to join temporary visa holders on longer-term visas (such as the H-1B) but not on shorter-term visas (such as the H-2A or H-2B). These family members are not allowed to work in the United States and are ineligible to receive most types of social assistance. To keep with this precedent, one would admit immediate family members along with temporary visa holders but place strict limits on their ability to work or to draw public benefits.

Current temporary immigration programs are far too small to address illegal immigration. In a typical year, fewer than 70,000 temporary visas are granted to seasonal laborers in agricultural occupations (H-2A program) and nonagricultural occupations (H-2B program). These visas are nonrenewable and amount to a one-time increase in the stock of immigrants that occurred when the visa program was created. Each year, the stock turns over, as entering temporary immigrants replace exiting ones.[29]

Composition of Immigration

Current immigration policy allocates 480,000 entry slots to family members of US citizens and US legal residents, 140,000 entry slots to employer-sponsored immigration, and 55,000 slots to other categories. Converting these slots to renewable temporary work visas[30] and expanding the number of visas to accommodate illegal immigrants would change the composition of US legal immigration. New legal admissions would rise to about 1.1 million individuals, about 45 percent of whom would be sponsored by family members and about 50 percent of whom would be sponsored by employers. This would move the US system closer to that of Canada, which reserves half of its entry slots for employment-based immigration. As dis-

29. President Bush's proposal to create 250,000 new temporary work visas, which would be renewable once, would also amount to a small one-time increase in the immigrant stock (which is far less than the annual inflow of new immigrants). Presumably, to be effective, the Bush policy would require greater enforcement against illegal entry.

30. Work visas would apply to adult immigrants. Some visas could be reserved for minors and senior citizens.

tinct from Canada, all adult immigrants would have to comply with the terms of the temporary work visa in order to graduate to permanent legal residence.

To increase the immigration surplus, the United States should admit workers who are in relatively scarce supply. One way to achieve this would be for US employers to post electronically jobs that they desire to fill with temporary immigrants. These postings would reflect the excess demand for labor in the United States. Occupations with the largest number of postings would indicate where excess demand for labor was the greatest. Foreigners could apply electronically for job openings (either to employers or to brokers who would match immigrants to employers). The number of foreign applicants per job listing would indicate the excess supply of foreign labor. Occupations in which the number of applicants exceeds the number of job postings (which could be most occupations) would indicate the existence of queues for jobs in the United States. The length of these electronic job queues by occupation would indicate to immigration authorities where the gains to immigration would be the greatest and so where to concentrate the allocation of temporary work visas.

This approach would be likely to maintain immigration of low-skilled workers. These workers are in short supply in the United States and in abundant supply abroad. In particular, they are in abundant supply in Mexico, where workers can migrate to the United States at relatively low cost. Low-skilled immigration creates an immigration surplus. The key to avoid having low-skilled immigration create a net fiscal burden, as current research suggests it does now, is to delay immigrants' access to public benefits.

An alternative way to reduce the fiscal cost of immigration, as Borjas (1999a) and others have suggested, is to curtail low-skilled immigration altogether. Concentrating immigration among the high-skilled would, relative to current US policy, raise the immigration surplus and lower the fiscal cost associated with immigration. There are three disadvantages to purely skills-based immigration. First, it would require a substantial increase in enforcement against illegal immigration. The plan proposed here, which legalizes the illegal inflow, has a much lower enforcement burden. Second, raising high-skilled immigration would likely lower global economic welfare. For poor countries, losing high-skilled labor could have very negative effects on their GDPs and on the performance of their political, legal, and educational institutions. Brain drain removes not just scarce factors of production from a country but also government leaders, judges, and teachers. Third, lowering low-skilled immigration would lower immigration from Mexico, causing considerable hardship for the country. Emigration raises wages in Mexico, serves as a safety valve during times of economic crisis, and through remittances increases national income. Presumably, it also substantially increases the standard of living of migrants. In the end, trying to reduce low-skilled legal immigration would likely only perpetuate low-skilled illegal immigration.

References

Auerbach, Alan J., and Philip Oreopoulos. 1999. Analyzing the Fiscal Impact of U.S. Immigration. *American Economic Review: Papers and Proceedings* 89, no. 2: 176–80.

Bleakley, Hoyt, and Aimee Chin. 2004: Language, Skills, and Earnings: Evidence from Childhood Immigrants. *Review of Economics and Statistics*, forthcoming.

Boeri, Tito, Gordon Hanson, and Barry McCormick. 2002. *Immigration Policy and the Welfare System*. Oxford: Oxford University Press.

Borjas, George J. 1999a. *Heaven's Door: Immigration Policy and the American Economy*. Princeton, NJ: Princeton University Press.

Borjas, George J. 1999b. The Economic Analysis of Immigration. In *Handbook of Labor Economics*, eds., Orley C. Ashenfelter and David Card. Amsterdam: North-Holland.

Borjas, George. 2003. The Labor Demand Curve is Downward Sloping: Reexamining the Impact of Immigration on the Labor Market. *Quarterly Journal of Economics* 118, no. 4: 1335–74.

Brown, Drusilla, Alan Deardorff, and Robert Stern. 1992. North American Integration. *Economic Journal* 102: 1507–18.

Bureau of International Labor Affairs. 1996. *Effects of the Immigration Reform and Control Act: Characteristics and Labor Market Behavior of the Legalized Population Five Years Following Legalization*. Washington: US Department of Labor.

Calavita, Kitty. 1992. *Inside the State: The Bracero Program, Immigration, and the I.N.S.* New York: Routledge.

Chiquiar, Daniel, and Gordon Hanson. 2004. International Migration, Self-Selection, and the Distribution of Wages: Evidence from Mexico and the United States. *Journal of Political Economy*, forthcoming.

Cornelius, Wayne. 2001. Death at the Border: Efficacy and Unintended Consequences of U.S. Immigration Policy. *Population and Development Review*, December.

Costanzo, Joe, Cynthia Davis, Caribert Irazi, Daniel Goodkind, and Roberto Ramirez. 2001. *Evaluating Components of International Migration: The Residual Foreign Born Population*. US Bureau of the Census, Division Working Paper 61. Washington: US Bureau of the Census.

Daniels, Roger. 2003. *Guarding the Door: American Immigrants and Immigration Policy since 1882*. New York: Hill and Wang.

DHS (US Department of Homeland Security). 2004. *2003 Yearbook of Immigration Statistics*. Washington: Office of Immigration Statistics, US DHS.

Fehr, Hans, Sabine Jokisch, and Lawrence Kotlikoff. 2004. *The Role of Immigration in Dealing with the Developed World's Demographic Transition*. NBER Working Paper 10512. Cambridge, MA: National Bureau of Economic Research.

Fermi, Laura. 1971. *Illustrious Immigrants: The Intellectual Migration from Europe 1930–1941*. Chicago: University of Chicago Press.

Fix, Michael, and Jeffrey Passel. 2002. *The Scope and Impact of Welfare Reform's Immigrant Provisions*. Urban Institute Discussion Paper 02-03. Washington: Urban Institute.

General Accounting Office. 2002. Immigration Enforcement: Challenges to Implementing the INS Interior Enforcement Strategy. Testimony before the Subcommittee on Immigration and Claims, Committee on the Judiciary, House of Representatives.

Grogger, Jeffrey, and Stephen J. Trejo. 2002. *Moving Behind or Moving Up? The Intergenerational Progress of Mexican Americans*. San Francisco, CA: Public Policy Institute of California.

Hanson, Gordon, Kenneth Scheve, and Matthew Slaughter. 2004. Local Public Finance and Individual Preferences over Globalization Strategies. University of California, San Diego. Photocopy.

Hanson, Gordon H., and Antonio Spilimbergo. 1999. Illegal Immigration, Border Enforcement and Relative Wages: Evidence from Apprehensions at the U.S.-Mexico Border. *American Economic Review* 89: 1337–57.

Hanson, Gordon H., and Antonio Spilimbergo. 2001. Political Economy, Sectoral Shocks, and Border Enforcement. *Canadian Journal of Economics* 34: 612–38.

Huntington, Samuel. 2004. The Hispanic Challenge. *Foreign Policy* (March/April): 30–45.

IDB (Inter-American Development Bank). 2004. *Sending Money Home: Remittances to Latin America and the Caribbean*. IDB Report (May).

INS (US Immigration and Naturalization Service). 2001. *Estimates of the Unauthorized Immigrant Population Residing in the United States: 1990 to 2000*. Office of Policy and Planning, US INS.

Kossoudji, Sherrie A., and Deborah A. Cobb-Clark. 2002. Coming out of the Shadows: Learning about Legal Status and Wages from the Legalized Population. *Journal of Labor Economics* 20, no. 3: 598–628.

Mishra, Prachi. 2003. Emigration and Wages in Source Countries: Evidence from Mexico. Columbia University. Photocopy.

Passel, Jeffrey S., Randy Capps, and Michael Fix. 2004. *Undocumented Immigrants: Facts and Figures*. Washington: Urban Institute.

Scheve, Kenneth F., and Matthew J. Slaughter. 2001a. *Globalization and the Perceptions of American Workers*. Washington: Institute for International Economics.

Scheve, Kenneth F., and Matthew J. Slaughter. 2001b. Labor-Market Competition and Individual Preferences over Immigration Policy. *Review of Economics and Statistics* 83, no. 1 (February): 133–45.

Smith, James P., and Barry Edmonston, eds. 1997. *The New Americans: Economic, Demographic, and Fiscal Effects of Immigration*. Washington: National Academy Press.

Social Security Administration. 2003. Utility of Older Reinstated Wages from the Earnings Suspense File; Audit Report. Office of the Inspector General, Social Security Administration, A-03-02-22076.

Tichenor, Daniel. 2002. *Dividing Lines: The Politics of Immigration Control in America*. Princeton, NJ: Princeton University Press.

Zimmerman, Wendy, and Karen C. Tumlin. 1999. *Patchwork Policies: State Assistance for Immigrants under Welfare Reform*. Urban Institute Occasional Paper No. 21. Washington: Urban Institute.

12

The International Financial Architecture

MORRIS GOLDSTEIN

For the roughly three decades following the creation of the International Monetary Fund (IMF) in 1944, concerns about the "international monetary system" focused on the exchange rates, international reserves, and balance-of-payments positions of the major industrial countries. The oil-exporting developing countries took center stage during the oil price shocks of 1973–74 and 1979–80 but not beyond that. With the advent of the Mexican debt crisis of 1982 and the subsequent discussions and negotiations between creditors and debtors leading up to the Brady Plan, debt problems in developing countries took on systemic interest—but only temporarily.

The last 10 years have been different in at least four respects. First, the motivating force in the debate about if and how the "system" needs to be reformed has not been the economic situation in the major industrial countries but rather a series of prominent currency, banking, and debt crises (and near misses) in a group of larger emerging economies—namely, Mexico (1994–95), the Asian financial crisis economies (1997–98), Russia (1998), Brazil (1998–2002), Turkey (1999–2002), and Argentina (2000–01).

Second and echoing the renaming of the international monetary system as the "international financial architecture" (hereafter, IFA for short), the scope of reforms has moved beyond exchange rates, international liquidity, and new lending windows at the IMF to encompass broader aspects

Morris Goldstein is the Dennis Weatherstone senior fellow at the Institute for International Economics.

of crisis prevention and crisis management in developing countries—including international standards and codes (covering everything from data transparency to banking supervision to corporate governance), currency and maturity mismatches, early warning systems, and the design of debt contracts (including promotion of collective action clauses).[1] Most of these reforms are aimed either at increasing the role of market forces in emerging economies or at establishing the conditions under which markets would function better in those countries.

Third, when the need for exchange rate realignment and for balance-of-payments correction in the world's largest economy has come to the fore, the proposed remedies now involve policy actions not only in Europe and Japan but also on the part of several of the larger emerging economies, including China.[2] In contrast, the developing countries were at best on the periphery in the earlier discussions of the "dollar overhang."

And fourth, the fora in which architecture issues are now discussed have increasingly included at least the larger emerging economies. Putting aside the IMF, where developing countries have long had a presence, recent years have witnessed the establishment of both the G-20 and the Financial Stability Forum, the increasing involvement of emerging economies in the Bank for International Settlements (BIS), the growth of "regional" monetary, financing, and surveillance arrangements (Association of Southeast Asian Nations [ASEAN] plus 3, the Asia Pacific Economic Cooperation [APEC] forum, among others), and the participation of Russia and China in at least some meetings of the G-7.

The fact that architecture reform has become so emerging market–centric over the past decade does not imply of course that all is well in the major industrial countries. As analyzed in other chapters, the United States is currently facing large actual and prospective fiscal and external deficits, the European Union is grappling with slow economic growth and a host of still-serious structural impediments, and Japan has just in the last year or so begun to break free from a decade of weak economic performance and financial-sector fragility. In addition, there have been cases—the current overvaluation of the dollar being a leading example—when one or more G-3 exchange rates have arguably gotten seriously out of line with fundamentals. But the reality has been that the major industrial countries have not been persuaded that ambitious policy coordination proposals—be they centered around publicly announced exchange rate targets or other proposed reforms—would be preferable to the current system of

1. One can think of the IFA as the institutions, policies, and practices associated with the prevention and resolution of banking, currency, and debt crises, primarily (but not exclusively) in emerging-market economies.

2. See Goldstein (2004) for an explanation of how inaction on revaluing the renminbi inhibits currency appreciation in Asia more widely and how this, in turn, adversely affects adjustment of the excessively large and growing US current account deficit.

monetary policy directed primarily at domestic objectives and of loose and episodic policy cooperation within the G-7.[3] Put in other words, even though it is widely acknowledged there is still much unfinished business to do on policy reform in the major industrial countries, it has proved easier over the past decade to forge international agreement on how emerging markets can reduce their crisis vulnerability than on how greater discipline can be brought to bear to correct policy weaknesses in the G-3.

As Jan Boyer and Edwin Truman argue in their chapter in this book, it is in the strong interest of the new US administration to recognize the increasing importance of the larger emerging economies in the global economic system and to make efforts to see that the closer integration of these economies into the global economy is successful. By a "successful" integration, I mean one where the emerging economies are able to sustain a healthy rate of economic growth, maintain good access to the large markets in the industrial world, and reduce the frequency and severity of currency, banking, and debt crises. Toward that end, I argue in this chapter that the new US administration should concentrate on *six priorities* in reforming the IFA:[4]

- agreeing on and enforcing *stronger injunctions against exchange rate manipulation;*
- *controlling currency mismatches in emerging economies*—a vulnerability that has been present in every prominent emerging-market financial crisis of the past decade;
- giving assessments of, and policy prescriptions for, *debt sustainability a larger role* in IMF surveillance, policy lending, and policy advice;
- improving the quality of compliance evaluations for *international standards and codes* so as to increase their impact on the market cost of borrowing for emerging economies;
- shifting human resources within the IMF to give greater weight to the *early warning of currency, banking, and debt crises* in emerging economies; and
- limiting the extension of very large IMF loans—known as *exceptional access*—to country cases that are truly "exceptional."

3. See the discussions of G-7 policy coordination in the chapters by C. Fred Bergsten and Michael Mussa.

4. I have excluded policies to alleviate poverty in the low-income countries since these are taken up—along with reforms at the World Bank—in William Cline and John Williamson's chapter in this book. Some other issues related to reform of the IMF (e.g., chairs and shares at the Fund and the Bank, SDR allocations, and crisis resolution strategies) and to global governance (e.g., whether the G-7 should be replaced by a G-4 composed of the United States, the European Union, Japan, and China) are discussed in Boyer and Truman's chapter in this book and in Kenen et al. (2004).

Of these six proposed reforms, the first three are the most important; the second three would also be useful but are likely to pay smaller dividends. Also, while several of the proposed reforms can be pursued simultaneously in a number of international organizations and groups, it is implicitly assumed in what follows that the IMF is the institution best placed to take the lead on this set of issues. In the first six sections of this chapter, I lay out the case for each of these policy recommendations. The last section offers some concluding remarks.

Discouraging "Beggar Thy Neighbor" Exchange Rate Policies

One of the main reasons for establishing the IMF was to put in place a set of international rules or guidelines that would discourage "beggar thy neighbor" exchange rate policies. After all, the world had just gone through a troublesome experience with the competitive depreciations of the 1920s and 1930s, and there was widespread agreement that the new "rules of the road" should outlaw such policies for the future.

In addressing the general obligations of members (countries) regarding exchange rate arrangements, the IMF's charter (i.e., its Articles of Agreement) stipulates (in Article IV, Section 1, paragraph iii) that each member shall:

> avoid manipulating exchange rates or the international monetary system in order to prevent effective balance-of-payments adjustment or to gain unfair competitive advantage over other member countries.

The Fund's charter (Article IV, Section 3) likewise delineates important obligations for the IMF in overseeing the operation of the exchange rate system, including the injunction that the Fund shall "oversee the compliance of each member with its obligations . . ." and "exercise firm surveillance over the exchange rate policies of members, and shall adopt specific principles for the guidance of members with respect to these policies."

In 1977, the Fund laid out principles and procedures for its surveillance over countries' exchange rate policies. In that document, a number of developments are identified that might indicate the need for discussion with the country. The first such development is "protracted, large-scale intervention in one direction in the exchange markets." Other developments cover official or quasi-official borrowing, restrictions on trade and capital flows, monetary and domestic financial policies, and behavior of the exchange rate that appears unrelated to underlying economic and financial conditions.

A reasonable reading is that the Fund intended these developments to be a set of presumptive indicators or "pointers" of (inappropriate) efforts to "manipulate" the exchange rate or to maintain the "wrong" exchange rate.[5] The interpretation of these pointers was not intended to be mechanistic but rather judgmental within the framework of a comprehensive analysis of the general economic situation and economic policy strategy of the country.[6]

Unfortunately, very little has been done over the past 25 years either to identify serious episodes of exchange rate manipulation or to enforce/encourage remedial action when such episodes have occurred.

Indeed, several fallacious arguments have often been put forward to rebut charges of currency manipulation. One such argument is that since the IMF rules allow countries to adopt the currency regime of their choice and since maintenance of a fixed exchange rate may involve exchange market intervention, there can be no manipulation for countries that opt for a fixed rate regime.

True enough, countries are free to pick fixed rates, floating rates, or practically any currency regime in between. Countries are also permitted to intervene in exchange markets, and indeed are expected to do so to counter disorderly market conditions. But what countries should *not* do is seek to maintain the wrong exchange rate by relying, inter alia, on large-scale, prolonged, exchange market intervention in one direction. Moreover, this injunction applies to attempts to maintain via intervention both an overvalued and undervalued fixed rate. In short, not all intervention is ruled out: only one particular kind of intervention (large-scale, prolonged, and in one direction) that is likely to be symptomatic of trying to maintain the "wrong" exchange rate.[7]

A second defense is that a country can't be manipulating if it has maintained the same fixed parity over an extended period. This claim fails to recognize that what counts for countries' competitiveness is the real effective exchange rate (that is, the average trade-weighted, nominal exchange rate corrected for inflation differentials among countries). And the

5. By the "wrong" exchange rate, I mean a real exchange rate that differs from the equilibrium rate implied by economic fundamentals; see Goldstein (2004) for an explanation of alternative methodologies for estimating the equilibrium real exchange rate.

6. For example, in assessing a country's exchange rate and the development of its international reserves, one would want to take into account, inter alia, the size of the country's external debt burden, the adequacy of the level of its international reserves, and its ability to shift demand (after an exchange rate change) between external and domestic sources.

7. By the same token, the intention of the IMF guidelines is not to prohibit countries from building up reserves over time if the level of those reserves (say, after a crisis) is undesirably low. In the September 2003 IMF *World Economic Outlook*, the Fund examined reserve holdings in emerging economies. The main finding was that reserves in many emerging economies had increased more quickly since 2001 than warranted by fundamentals. In addition, that study concluded that from both the domestic and international standpoints, there would be advantages for growth in emerging economies of Asia to become more reliant on domestic demand accompanied by a steady reduction in current account imbalances over the medium term.

appropriateness of the real effective exchange rate has to be evaluated against the backdrop of the country's overall balance-of-payments position. Seen from this perspective, misalignment of the real exchange rate can come about just as easily from "nonmovement" of the nominal exchange rate as it can from excessive movement. In addition, a real exchange rate that is appropriate when the balance of payments is in deficit may no longer be appropriate once the balance of payments goes into substantial surplus.

Yet a third fallacious argument is that a country should be permitted to use whatever kind of exchange market intervention is necessary to hold down the real exchange rate if an undervalued exchange rate is needed to generate sufficient employment in the traded goods industries to ensure social stability. The rub here is that since practically all countries have full employment objectives, wholesale application of this line of argument would not provide the right incentives for discouraging currency manipulation in the international system as a whole; in fact, employment concerns were one of the motivating forces behind the competitive depreciations in the interwar period. If many countries believe they can manipulate their way to both an undervalued exchange rate and higher employment in their traded goods industries, the result is likely to be exchange rate instability, continued conflict, and greater resort to protectionist trade measures.

Even if international guidelines about exchange rate policy were better understood, they could not be expected to have much impact if both the IMF and its largest shareholder (the United States) were not prepared to *enforce* those codes of conduct. And the reality has been that neither of them has been very active or consistent in this area over the past 25 years—and not because there were plausibly no serious infractions (that is, instances of countries seeking to maintain wrong exchange rates via inappropriate policies).

The IMF's surveillance guidelines permit the Fund's managing director to initiate and to conduct a so-called ad hoc consultation with a country if there is concern about its exchange rate policies. Yet the Fund has conducted such special consultations only twice (Sweden in 1982 and Korea in 1987) since the surveillance guidelines were drawn up in 1979 and none during the past 17 years! The United States has been somewhat more activist over the past 15 years but without much consistency of approach; in addition, it has applied pressure almost exclusively on a bilateral basis. Since 1988, the Omnibus Trade and Competitiveness Act requires the US Treasury to report to the US Congress any countries engaging in "exchange rate manipulation." The Treasury named several Asian economies as "manipulators" in the 1988–94 period (China, 1992–94; Korea, 1988–90; and Taiwan, 1988–89), but no country has been cited since 1994—including in 2003 when there was perhaps the strongest evidence to date of manipulation by China and several other economies.

If efforts to date in enforcing guidelines against antisocial exchange rate policies have yielded little fruit, why should a push by the new US administration be any more effective? I see grounds for optimism on four counts.

The need to deal with the excessively large US current account deficit has made the US government more sensitive to the exchange rate and reserve policies of other countries, especially those in Asia. In brief, the story here is that a sustainable US current account deficit is at most half as large as the 5½ percent of GDP deficit forecast for this year, that the dollar has to depreciate at least another 15 to 20 percent in real trade-weighted terms to facilitate that adjustment, and that it will be difficult to obtain the needed further depreciation of the dollar unless Asian emerging economies and Japan—which together have a combined weight of 40 percent in the trade-weighted dollar—participate in this appreciation of nondollar currencies. In the first round of dollar depreciation (from February 2002 to 2004), the larger Asian currencies either depreciated in real terms or appreciated only slightly.[8] Yes, if Asian economies reduced their exchange market intervention and acquisition of US Treasury securities, US interest rates—particularly at the short end of the yield curve—would be somewhat higher than otherwise. But with the US recovery now better established and with the Federal Reserve having recently begun a process of tightening US monetary policy, this is not as serious an impediment as in some earlier periods (say, in 2002) when the US economy was weaker and when the Fed was vigorously easing monetary policy.

Exchange rate manipulation in Asia—on the part of both emerging and industrial economies—has also become more obvious over the past two years. As shown in figure 12.1, China has been engaging in large-scale, prolonged, one-way exchange market intervention during this period—and this at a time when China's overall balance of payments was in considerable surplus (particularly in 2003) and when China's economy was overheating.[9] Japan too intervened heavily—to the tune of $200 billion in 2003 and $150 billion more in the first quarter of 2004—before suspending that intervention in the second quarter of 2004. There has also been large-scale exchange market intervention in Taiwan, Korea, India, Singapore,

8. See Bergsten and Williamson (2004) and Goldstein (2004). From February 2002 to November 2004, the real effective exchange rates of China, Hong Kong, India, Malaysia, Taiwan, and Thailand depreciated. There were small (less than 5 percent) appreciations for Indonesia, Japan, and Singapore. Korea was the only one with a significant (9 percent) appreciation.

9. China's current account surplus (adjusted for cyclical developments and for lagged trade effects still in the pipeline) is unlikely to be much smaller in 2004 than in 2003; there were, however, some preliminary signs of slowing in the Chinese economy in the second and third quarters of 2004. China's international reserves probably increased by over $200 billion in 2004, and China's currency is still significantly undervalued (on the order of 15 to 20 percent); see Morris Goldstein and Nicholas Lardy, "Don't Hail China's Soft Landing Too Soon," *Financial Times*, October 6, 2004, for an interpretation of recent and prospective developments in the Chinese economy.

Figure 12.1 China's foreign exchange reserves, 2001–04Q2

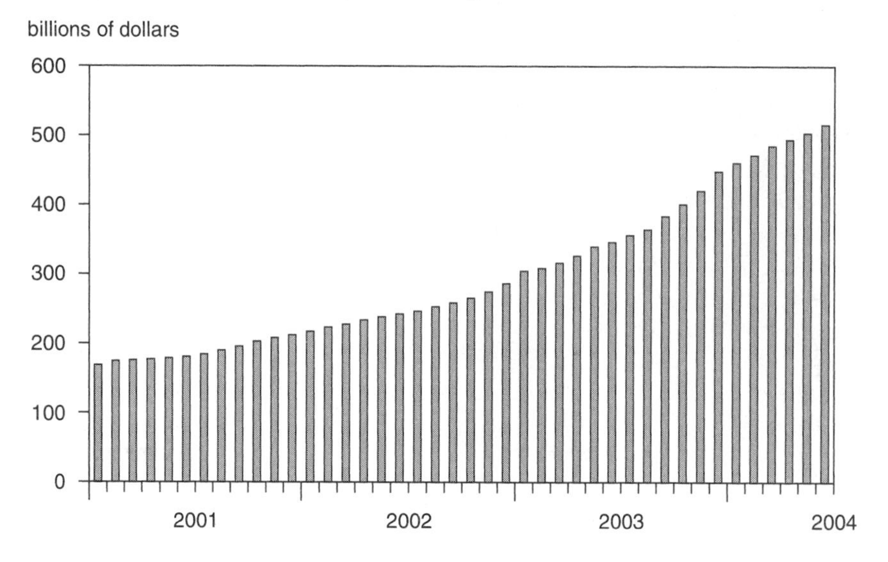

Source: China's State Administration of Foreign Exchange.

and Malaysia.[10] When economies with undervalued exchange rates are intervening heavily to prevent or severely limit exchange rate appreciation, the weakness of the present system (in promoting external adjustment) becomes apparent.

Recent experience has also shown that the alternative to lax enforcement of international guidelines on exchange rate policy is ill-designed policies on exchange rate manipulation applied at the *bilateral* level. For example, a group of bills are now before the US Congress that would impose a unilateral surcharge on China's exports to the United States if bilateral negotiations to end China's currency manipulation are not successful. But the definition of exchange rate manipulation in these bills is poorly framed—relying, for example, on bilateral current account imbalances rather than on the overall balance of payments. More generally, the treatment of alleged currency manipulation at the bilateral level is likely to be more politically motivated and less analytically sound than if it were done in a multilateral context at the IMF.

And fourth, there is now the helpful example of the World Trade Organization (WTO) to lean on. Through the rulings of its adjudication panels

10. Taken as a group, those five Asian emerging economies added about $125 billion to their reserves in 2003—almost as much (77 percent) as China's reserve accumulation in that year. Note that (in contrast to China) economic growth and domestic demand were quite weak in 2003 in Taiwan, Korea, and Singapore; this was not so in India and was less so in Malaysia.

and in contrast to what has happened on exchange rate issues, a body of international case law is unfolding, which is making it clearer what is and what is not acceptable trade policy, on everything from bananas to steel to domestic tax systems.[11] International rules of conduct for exchange rate policy are no less necessary than those for trade policy.

To sum up, with a new managing director of the Fund just having assumed office, now is the time to agree on an operational set of guidelines on exchange rate manipulation and to bring cases of alleged manipulation within the purview of the IMF's executive board. With 40 percent of global international reserves now held by Asian emerging economies, with more larger emerging economies becoming international creditors rather than debtors, and with the United States seeking international financing on a large scale to fund its current account deficit, exchange rate and reserve policies of emerging economies now "matter" for even the largest industrial countries. By the same token, the emerging economies depend heavily for their future prosperity on good access to markets in the larger industrial countries—an access that could well be put in jeopardy if there were a growing perception that there was no one minding the store internationally on what constitutes a level playing field for exchange rate policy.

Controlling Currency Mismatches in Emerging Economies

Given the frequency and severity of financial crises in emerging economies over the past decade, it is natural to ask whether the crisis countries shared any vulnerabilities. Research indicates that perhaps the most important such common vulnerability was "currency mismatch"—that is, a situation where there is a difference in the currency composition of assets and liabilities so that an economy/sector's net worth and/or net income is sensitive to changes in the exchange rate (Goldstein and Turner 2004).

Suppose an individual raises a mortgage to buy a vacation home in Acapulco, Mexico, and then rents it out. Suppose also that he borrows in dollars instead of Mexican pesos. He then is faced with a currency mismatch. The "stock" aspect of the mismatch is that his asset (the villa) is denominated in pesos but his liability (the mortgage) is denominated in dollars. The "flow" aspect is that the rental income from the villa is denominated in pesos, but the mortgage payments are denominated in dollars. The consequence of this currency mismatch is that the owner of the villa gains or loses as the dollar falls or rises against the peso even if the key parameters of his investment (the villa price and rent) do not change.

11. See the discussion of WTO decisions in the chapter by Jeffrey J. Schott. Hufbauer and Wong (2004) analyze recent trade disputes between the United States and China.

In short, the net present value of his investment project has become sensitive to changes in the dollar-peso exchange rate.

Borrowers in emerging economies have at times faced currency mismatches on a massive scale.[12] These mismatches raise a number of concerns.

As hinted at already, there is strong empirical evidence that currency mismatches increase not only the probability of getting into a financial crisis but also the cost of getting out of one. Large currency mismatches have marked all the prominent financial crises of the past decade (Mexico in 1994–95, the Asian financial crisis of 1997–98, Russia in 1998, Turkey in 2000–02, Argentina in 2001–02, and Brazil in 1998–2002). Currency mismatch variables have proven to be one of the better-performing leading indicators of currency and banking crises in emerging economies, and output contractions in the 1990s have been deeper in emerging economies with large currency mismatches and large exchange rate depreciations.

Sizable currency mismatches also undermine the effectiveness of monetary policy during a crisis. Specifically, these mismatches make it harder to reduce interest rates after a deflationary shock because the authorities worry that an interest rate decline could set off a sharp fall in the currency that in turn could initiate a wave of bankruptcies. In contrast, when currency mismatches are small, interest rate cuts can be used to stimulate the economy.

Last but not least, currency mismatches can also severely constrain the operation of floating exchange rates in emerging economies. When currency mismatches are large, the authorities are apt to engage in heavy exchange market intervention and in interest rate management to keep the exchange rate from depreciating sharply. But such a "fear of floating" sacrifices the benefits of greater exchange rate flexibility for monetary policy independence and for better cushioning against external shocks.

The three key questions regarding currency mismatch are how to measure it, what causes it, and how best to control it.

A good measure of aggregate currency mismatch should consider the asset as well as the liability side of balance sheets; it should take account of the potential response of noninterest flows (like exports) to an exchange rate change; and it should reflect the ability to borrow domestically in the local currency—not just the ability to borrow abroad in that currency. The latter factor is particularly relevant since domestic bond markets in developing countries (denominated mainly in domestic currency) are now the largest single source of financing—larger (in flow terms) than domestic bank loans and far larger than international bonds. In many situations, it is also helpful to have a gauge of liquidity/maturity

12. On the whole, industrial countries have found it easier than developing countries to borrow abroad in their own currencies.

mismatches as well as currency mismatches since the two often go together in emerging economies.

While there is no single measure that combines all these desirable attributes, several indicators can be used in tandem to measure currency mismatch. The ratio of short-term external debt to international reserves has proven itself to be a good leading indicator of the probability of getting into a currency crisis. Sectoral balance sheets (where available) are useful for determining how currency mismatches are distributed within an economy. And most recently, Goldstein and Turner (2004) have constructed (for 22 emerging economies) a new measure of "aggregate effective currency mismatch" (AECM), which should serve as a useful, shorthand "stress test" for an indebted emerging economy of the (negative) output effects of a large depreciation of the exchange rate.[13] While AECMs have shrunk significantly in most of the former Asian crisis countries since 1997–98, they are sizable in some other emerging economies.

Although some controversy still exists on the origins of currency mismatch in emerging economies, the most persuasive explanation is that these mismatches derive primarily from past and present weaknesses in macroeconomic, exchange rate, and institutional policies in emerging economies themselves.[14]

An action plan to reduce currency mismatches and keep them under control in emerging economies should encompass the following policy recommendations: Those emerging economies that are substantially involved with private international capital markets should opt for a currency regime of (de facto) managed floating. The de facto movement of the nominal exchange rate will produce an awareness of currency risk as well as an incentive to keep currency mismatches under control. Special care should also be taken to avoid overvalued exchange rates, since experience suggests that crisis vulnerability is highest when large currency mismatches persist against the backdrop of a significantly overvalued exchange rate.

A monetary policy framework of inflation targeting should be employed to provide a good nominal anchor against inflation (Truman 2003). Good inflation performance is crucial for developing a healthy local currency–denominated domestic bond market.

Banks in emerging economies should apply tighter credit limits on foreign currency–denominated loans to customers that do not generate enough foreign-currency revenues, and banking supervisors should

13. The Goldstein-Turner AECM measure is now available for 9 Asian emerging economies; the web site www.asianbondsonline.adb.org/asiabondindicators/default2.php is monitored by the Asian Development Bank.

14. Network externalities and imperfections in global capital markets also play a role in the currency composition of external liabilities (that is, cross-border bank loans and international bonds).

strengthen regulations and capital requirements on banks' net open positions in foreign exchange.

To help harness the forces of market discipline, the IMF should regularly publish data on currency mismatches at the economywide and sector levels and should comment on those mismatches regarded as excessive; the IMF should also make reduction of currency mismatches a condition for IMF loans in cases where the actual or prospective mismatch is deemed to be too large. Although the IMF has put more emphasis within the past two years on "balance sheet" vulnerabilities in its surveillance work, the treatment of currency mismatches in data dissemination, early warning, and loan conditionality is still considerably short of where it needs to be.

Emerging economies that have a high share of public debt denominated in, or indexed to, foreign currency should adopt a medium-run objective of reducing that share; for countries with a poor track record on inflation, inflation-indexed bonds can serve as a useful transition device to fixed-rate, domestic currency–denominated debt.

Higher priority in emerging economies should be accorded to enlarging domestic bond markets, to encouraging the use of hedging instruments, and to reducing barriers to the entry of foreign-owned banks.

To sum up, crisis prevention in emerging economies covers a wide field. But no single source of vulnerability has been as consistently linked with past financial crises as currency mismatches. It is possible to make substantial progress in reducing and controlling currency mismatches in less than a decade but only if the right policies are followed in emerging economies themselves (Mexico's experience since its 1994–95 crisis represents a case in point).[15] The IMF and the US government should therefore take the lead in promoting a comprehensive policy agenda to address currency mismatches.

Debt Sustainability

The last decade has witnessed not just a host of currency and banking crises but a spate of debt crises as well: Argentina, Ecuador, Pakistan, Russia, Ukraine, and Uruguay—to say nothing of the close calls in Brazil and Turkey.

One cannot presume that severe debt problems in emerging economies are now a thing of the past. Indeed, if one asks whether public debt in emerging economies taken as a group is too high, the answer would have to be an emphatic "yes."

15. See Goldstein and Turner (2004) on Mexico's longer-term strategy for reducing currency mismatches.

According to the IMF's figures, the ratio of public debt to GDP now averages about 70 percent in developing economies, reversing the progress made (in reducing that ratio) during the first half of the 1990s and bringing the developing-economy average to a level higher than that in industrial countries (figure 12.2).

Equally if not more troubling, the IMF documents that over half of public debt defaults have occurred at public debt ratios below 60 percent, that the typical emerging economy now has a public debt ratio about 2½ times as high as its track record on fiscal policy suggests is prudent, and that governments usually fail to take corrective fiscal policy actions when the public debt ratio climbs above 50 percent.

To be sure, these averages conceal considerable cross-country variation. For example, because of their relatively high growth rates and high trade openness and their relatively low share of foreign currency–denominated debt, Asian emerging economies have overborrowed less than their counterparts in Latin America, the Middle East, and Africa. Still, the fiscal costs of bank restructuring have pushed public debt ratios up considerably in Asia since the mid-1990s, and that region's relatively high ratio of public debt to government revenues provides little ground for comfort.

Policymakers have in the past been too optimistic about the prudent level of public (and external) debt in emerging economies. Not enough attention has been paid to the foreign exchange constraint facing governments; to contingent liabilities that start out in the private sector but don't stay there; to spillovers among currency, banking, and debt problems; to the high volatility in many emerging economies; to the all-too-frequent resort to exchange rate–linked domestic debt; and to rising pension liabilities as populations age.[16]

A crucial question is what can be done to reduce vulnerability to debt crises? At the individual-country level, much can be done to broaden tax bases, to shoot for fiscal surpluses during cyclical upswings, to limit the generosity of official safety nets directed toward banks and other financial institutions, and to reduce, over time, the now excessive dependence on foreign currency–denominated and on foreign currency–linked debt.

For its part, the IMF should be much tougher than in the past on making debt sustainability a key condition for IMF lending. To its credit, the IMF in June 2002 began implementing a common framework for more rigorous assessments of public and external debt sustainability. This debt sustainability assessment provides a historical decomposition of the country's debt dynamics and a five-year baseline scenario; in addition, sensitivity tests are conducted for the key parameters, including the interest

16. Although industrial countries will be the first to encounter the problems that an aging population poses for fiscal policy, IMF First Deputy Managing Director Krueger (2004) has recently argued that the challenges facing industrial countries on this front—particularly from pension liabilities—pale beside those that emerging-market economies will encounter.

Figure 12.2a Public debt as percent of GDP, 1992–2002

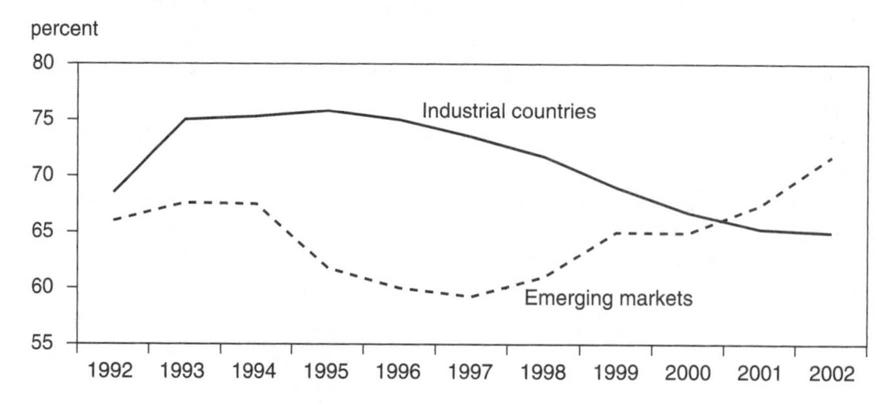

Figure 12.2b Ratio of public debt to revenue (average, 1992–2002)

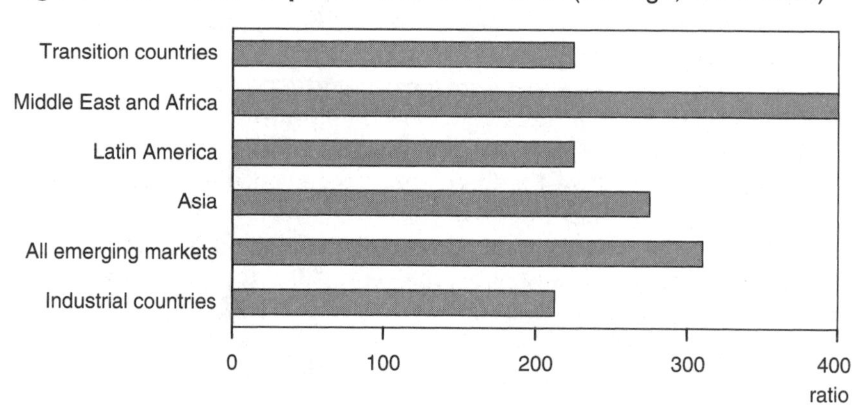

Figure 12.2c External public debt as percent of total debt (average, 1992–2002)

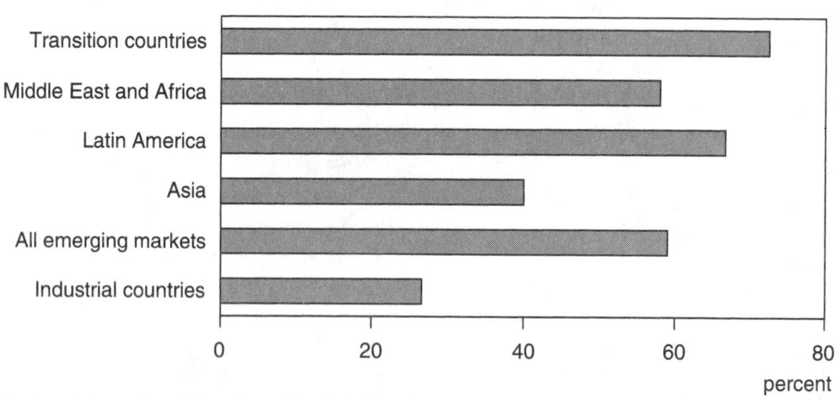

Source: International Monetary Fund staff estimates.

rate, the growth rate of the economy, the GDP deflator, the exchange rate, and the primary (noninterest current account) balance in the budget. This is a step forward. Nevertheless, as the IMF staff's first review of such debt sustainability assessments (IMF 2003b) indicates, problems remain. Baseline projections for public and external debt have shown a bias toward overoptimism; for example, it is notable that, at a five-year horizon, the external debt ratio is underpredicted by an average of more than 7 percent of GDP for countries with Fund programs. Also, the staff concludes (IMF 2003b, 12) that

> in many, if not most, cases . . . the debt sustainability assessments have *not* yet become an integral part of the staff's analysis in the staff report. . . . With one or two exceptions, it is apparent that the sustainability analysis did not form a major part of the discussions between the staff and the [country] authorities.

While technical improvements in the framework (e.g., considering a less extreme set of shocks) may help to some degree, it looks like debt analysis is sometimes driven by the basic Fund lending decision rather than (as it should be) the other way around. As the case of Argentina—especially the decision to provide Fund financing in August 2001 in the face of both an unsustainable debt situation and an overvalued real exchange rate—amply demonstrated, this evaluation problem is sometimes compounded by a reluctance to withhold Fund financing even when the unfavorable debt dynamics are relatively clear.

Realistically, the best that can be done here is to continue to work toward making the Fund's debt sustainability analysis as objective and as competent as possible, to make publication of the Fund's debt sustainability analysis mandatory, and to require stringent approval and accountability requirements for exceeding normal access limits on Fund loans (discussed later in the chapter).

There is also scope for improving the cushioning of emerging-market borrowers against adverse shocks by making debt payments more contingent on the borrowers' ability to pay. Perhaps the most straightforward way to do this would be to experiment with the use of *GDP-indexed bonds*.[17] Although such bonds would encounter the obstacles that most new instruments face along with problems particular to the verification and revision of GDP figures, GDP-indexed bonds offer some significant advantages that should not be dismissed: they restrict the range of variation of the debt/GDP ratio and hence reduce the likelihood of debt crises; they reduce the likelihood of procyclical fiscal policy responses to adverse shocks; they should carry a low insurance premium; they would cover a much higher share of output fluctuations for a typical emerging economy

17. GDP-indexed bonds are ones in which coupon payments on the bond would vary in part with the growth rate of the debtor's economy, being higher in years in which growth of real GDP is higher than trend and lower in years of below-trend growth.

than bonds indexed to commodity prices; and they contain certain protections against manipulation and cheating aimed at lowering debt obligations (e.g., it is high, not low, growth that is considered a success and that gets politicians reelected).[18]

To sum up, it has been said critically (albeit tongue in cheek) that IMF stands for "It's Mostly Fiscal." Yet an objective review of emerging-market debt developments over the past decade suggests that, if anything, the Fund hasn't been fiscal enough. In contrast to monetary policy and inflation developments where progress in developing countries has been widespread, sizable, and (at least so far) persistent, public debt ratios have been rising not falling (since 1995) and now stand out as a clear source of crisis vulnerability. It is time to do something about it before crisis prevention turns into crisis management.[19]

International Standards and Codes

One of the major growth industries in reform of the IFA has been the *promulgation and monitoring of international standards and codes of best practice.* Poor public information on Mexico's international reserves in the run-up to the Mexican peso crisis provided the initial impetus for a data dissemination standard. Widespread financial-sector and disclosure problems in the Asian financial crisis—coming on top of increased recognition of the frequency and costs of systemic banking crises in both developing and industrial countries—motivated the extension of this approach to an international banking standard. Additional standards have since followed to deal with other institutional gaps in emerging economies that are thought to increase vulnerability to financial crises—ranging from poor corporate governance, to weak insolvency and creditors' rights regimes, to inadequate safeguards against money laundering.

The Financial Stability Forum (FSF) has decided that 12 international standards and codes are crucial for sound financial systems and merit priority implementation. As shown in table 12.1, these 12 key standards cover three broad areas: macroeconomic policy and data transparency, institutional market infrastructure, and financial regulation and supervision. Each standard is issued by the appropriate standard-setting body; for example, the Basel Committee on Banking Supervision issued the core principles for effective banking supervision; the International Organization of Securities Commissions issued the objectives and principles of

18. See Borensztein and Mauro (2002) and Williamson (forthcoming) on the properties of GDP-indexed bonds.

19. In 1994, the average rate of consumer price inflation in developing countries was 55 percent; after a decade of trend improvement, that average had fallen to less than 6 percent in 2004.

Table 12.1 Key standards for a sound financial system

Subject area	Key standard	Issuing body
Macroeconomic policy and data transparency		
Monetary and financial policy transparency	Code of good practices on transparency in monetary and financial policies	International Monetary Fund
Fiscal policy transparency	Code of good practices on fiscal transparency	International Monetary Fund
Data dissemination	Special Data Dissemination Standard (SDDS) and General Data Dissemination System (GDDS)	International Monetary Fund
Institutional market infrastructure		
Insolvency	Principles and guidelines on effective insolvency and creditor rights systems	World Bank
Corporate governance	Principles of corporate governance	Organization for Economic Cooperation and Development
Accounting	International accounting standards (IAS)	International Accounting Standards Board
Auditing	International standards on auditing (ISA)	International Federation of Accountants
Payment and settlement	Core principles for systemically important payment systems	Committee on Payment and Settlement Systems
Market integrity	The forty recommendations of the Financial Action Task Force on money laundering	Financial Action Task Force
Financial regulation and supervision		
Banking supervision	Core principles for effective banking supervision	Basel Committee on Banking Supervision
Securities regulation	Objectives and principles of securities regulation	International Organization of Securities Commissions
Insurance supervision	Insurance core principle	International Association of Insurance Supervisors

Source: Financial Stability Forum.

securities regulation; the IMF issued the two data dissemination standards and the codes of good practices on transparency of monetary, fiscal, and financial policies; and so on.

The IMF and the World Bank have been assigned the key task of monitoring and evaluating countries' compliance with many of these standards. Since 1999, the main vehicle for conducting financial-sector surveillance has been the Financial Sector Assessment Program (FSAP), based on country missions conducted jointly by the Fund and the Bank. The main focus of FSAPs has been to analyze the strengths and vulnerabilities of the country's financial system, to assess the country's compliance with financial-sector standards, and to evaluate the governance of the country's regulatory agencies. Through August 2004, 70 FSAPs had been completed and another 42 were under way or agreed (IMF 2004b). FSAPs are not published. The Fund and the Bank also prepare Reports on the Observance of Standards and Codes (ROSCs); more than 560 of those covering over 110 countries have been issued (as of June 2004), and almost three-quarters of those reports have been published (IMF 2004b).

Countries' compliance with international standards and codes could be enhanced by three incentive channels: complying countries could obtain preferred access to IMF resources; they could receive more favorable risk weightings in the Basel II international capital standards; and because implementation of standards is assumed to improve creditworthiness, complying countries could be expected to benefit from a lower cost of borrowing in private international capital markets. The first two incentive channels never really made it on the official agenda, leaving only—albeit potentially—the most powerful channel of lower market borrowing costs.

Given the dismal longer-term track record of financial-sector crises in emerging economies, the standards initiative clearly does not lack for motivation. That said, empirical analysis on the impact to date of these international standards and codes is still in its early stages. The results of most studies are suspect because the authors failed to control for macroeconomic fundamentals and/or other standards in assessing the effect of a given standard either on the costs of borrowing (measured by interest rate spreads or credit ratings) or on financial-sector soundness (measured by capital adequacy ratios and nonperforming loan ratios in the banking system).[20] A recent IMF study by Christofides, Mulder, and Tiffin (2003) does

20. For example, an IIF (2002) study reported that subscription to the IMF's Special Data Dissemination Standard was associated with a 300-basis-point reduction in an emerging economy's interest rate spread, but no allowance was made for the impact of other standards or of macroeconomic fundamentals on such spreads. The studies by Sundararajan, Marston, and Basu (2001) and Das, Quintyn, and Chenard (2004) look at only one subset of standards. Another set of cross-country studies done at the World Bank (e.g., Barth, Caprio, and Levine 2001) does not look at the impact of international standards and codes but rather seeks to assess the effect of the quality of financial supervisory regime on bank efficiency and on vulnerability to crises; they find little effect of the supervisory regime on these outcome variables.

not suffer from these pitfalls. Using a sample of 24 emerging economies, controlling for other determinants of borrowing costs, and employing a wide set of standards-related indicators, Christofides, Mulder, and Tiffin (2003) find that property rights and accounting standards matter (in the expected direction) for interest rate spreads and that accounting standards and measures of corruption affect credit ratings. This work can and should be extended—in particular, by using the results from ROSCs and FSAPs to get a better fix on the impact of the Basel Core Principles of Effective Banking Supervision and of other financial-sector standards.[21]

The way ahead on standards should be to concentrate on the core group of standards (rather than taking on new ones), to seek to raise the quality of FSAPs and ROSCs (by limiting the number done each year and by retaining the best financial-sector specialists), and to increase their influence in the marketplace by publishing more of the compliance results.[22] The Fund should also work harder to ensure that the objectivity of the FSAP process is even-handed across regional and country groups. In this connection, differences between industrial and developing-country groups and across developing-country regions seem to be smaller for FSAP compliance measures (on banking supervision) than for other indicators of bank quality.[23] To sum up, another prominent, shared characteristic of earlier financial crises in emerging economies has been fragile financial sectors. In addition, international capital flows cannot be expected to seek out the highest risk-adjusted rate of return and to discipline errant policies if the information base for those flows is seriously flawed.

As such, technical assistance to improve institutional capacity and international codes and standards to outline international good practice on policy and data disclosure, financial-sector regulation, and market infrastructure go in the right direction. The Fund and the Bank can make a valuable contribution to this process by providing timely, high-quality assessments of compliance with these standards. This is an area where less can be more—at least until such time as the ROSCs gain enough credibility to become part of the standard information kit of international and domestic investors. In contrast, if too many reports are done on too many

21. Christofides, Mulder, and Tiffin (2003) use survey data from the World Economic Forum and an index of economic freedom developed by the Heritage Foundation to measure financial-sector regulation.

22. The Fund has started to move in this direction: The number of FSAPs has been reduced by about a quarter, and their scope has been streamlined.

23. Also, some of the reported differences in compliance results across regions are not in line with a priori expectations. Why, for example, should compliance with the Basel Core Principles of Effective Banking Supervision be higher (on average) in African developing countries than in East Asia, or South Asia, or Latin America—as the FSAP results seem to indicate. Such differences need to be explained if the compliance findings are to be credible in the marketplace.

standards without adding value to what already exists in the marketplace, the whole exercise may lose momentum and may be regarded by emerging economies as not worth the nontrivial compliance costs. The IMF can also improve the incentives for complying with standards by reactivating the proposal that countries with good compliance records receive an interest rate "discount" when borrowing from the Fund.[24]

Early Warning Systems

Another official-sector response to the high incidence and severity of emerging-market financial crises has been to try to build better *early warning systems.* Investing in an early warning system is attractive on at least two grounds. First, banking, currency, and debt crises are extremely costly to the countries in which they originate, as well as to other countries that are affected by the spillover of the original crisis. For example, the IMF (1998) has estimated that the cumulative output losses for emerging-market banking crises and for (severe) currency crises averaged 12 and 8 percent, respectively. Another study found that a currency crisis somewhere in the world increased the probability of a second speculative attack elsewhere by about 7 percent—even after controlling for economic and political fundamentals of the country concerned. Second, empirical research strongly suggests that traditional market indicators of currency and default risks (such as interest rate spreads and credit ratings) frequently do not provide much advance warning of an impending crisis. This is not entirely surprising: If market participants expect an official bailout of a troubled borrower, then the market interest rate is going to reflect the creditworthiness of the guarantor—not that of the troubled borrower. There were almost no credit rating downgrades for the most severely affected countries in the 18-month run-up to the Asian financial crisis. In contrast, early warning indicators like the ratio of short-term external debt to reserves, the appreciation of the real exchange rate (relative to trend), a fall in exports, and a decline in equity prices have shown themselves to be good performers, including in the Asian financial crisis. Berg, Borensztein, and Pattillo (2004) have tracked the performance of alternative predictors of currency crises in emerging economies for the period running from 1996 to 2000. They found that the early warning model outlined in Kaminsky, Lizondo, and Reinhart (1998) and Goldstein, Kaminsky, and Reinhart (2000) did a considerably better job (out of sample) in forecasting emerging-market currency crises than credit ratings, or interest rate spreads, or overall currency risk scores published by analysts.[25]

24. Another option would be to make compliance with international standards an additional factor in determining the size of access to IMF loans.

25. Berg, Borensztein, and Pattillo (2004) also found that the model outlined in Kaminsky, Lizondo, and Reinhart (1998) and Goldstein, Kaminsky, and Reinhart (2000) outperformed the shorter-horizon models published by Goldman Sachs and Credit Suisse First Boston.

The Fund introduced its own high-frequency "vulnerability exercise" in 2001. According to the Fund, the inputs to its early warning system are the multilateral surveillance findings from the *World Economic Outlook* and the *Global Financial Stability Report*, individual-country surveillance feedback from Article IV and program missions, cross-country surveillance in specialist areas (e.g., financial-sector soundness), results from early warning models, and market intelligence. These inputs are then analyzed and presented to management at least once per quarter; some of these vulnerability findings are also shared (in summary form) with the Fund's executive board.

A relevant question is whether the vulnerability exercise is currently receiving the resources and priority it deserves relative to the Fund's other surveillance activities.

The IMF employs about 1,000 economists. I am told that the full-time equivalent of approximately a dozen economists works on the high-frequency vulnerability exercise. Given the much larger resources now devoted to Article IV consultations in the Fund, it would make sense to shift some resources from say, Article IV consultations for smaller industrial countries (e.g., Austria, Belgium, Denmark, Finland, the Netherlands, Norway, Portugal, Spain, Sweden, and New Zealand, among others) to the vulnerability exercise. Consultations for these countries could be put on a lower-frequency cycle. The issue here is one of where Fund resources can make the greatest contribution and produce value added relative to what is available from research supplied by private financial firms. I would submit that the payoff to additional resources is apt to be largest when applied to gauging crisis vulnerability across countries and over time for the 25 or so largest emerging economies. Of course, no amount of additional staff preparation on crisis vulnerability will be effective unless the Fund management is also fully committed to upgrading the early warning exercise and to giving it high priority in terms of their own time and attention.

To sum up, trying to gauge crisis vulnerability in emerging economies is an admittedly difficult task. Although empirical work shows that the better-performing leading indicators anticipate the lion's share of currency and banking crises that subsequently occur, that research also finds that even the best indicators send a nontrivial number of false alarms (Goldstein et al. 2000).[26] This means that any vulnerability exercise will inevitably make some mistakes. But the cost of not doing it—that is, of missing the opportunity to spot impending crises early enough to take corrective action—is apt to be much larger. Also, as experience with the vulnerability exercise accumulates, the official sector should get better at predicting crises and at gauging vulnerability. Evaluating whether coun-

26. See Abiad (2003) for a survey of early warning models and of the operational issues that have to be dealt with in constructing such models.

try A is more vulnerable today to a crisis than countries B and C, and whether country A is more vulnerable today than it was one or two years ago, carries in addition the advantage of forcing the IMF staff to ask the right analytical questions about member countries. Given the stakes involved, the high-frequency vulnerability exercise in the Fund should get more resources and higher priority among surveillance activities than it currently commands.

IMF Lending Policies

Discussions over *IMF lending policies* have been a recurrent theme over the past five years in the debate on IFA reform. There have been both positive and negative developments.

On the plus side of the ledger, the Fund has streamlined its conditionality on structural policies while rejecting proposals for wholesale change that would make Fund lending decisions highly dependent on a small set of preconditions.[27] On the negative side, the Fund has not yet come up with a framework that can effectively discipline decisions about financing in amounts that exceed the Fund's normal lending limits (what the Fund calls "exceptional access").

There was a pronounced upward trend in Fund structural policy conditionality over 1985–2000, and this trend became steeper in the 1990s. In the late 1990s, it became typical for a one-year IMF stand-by program to have on the order of a dozen structural conditions and for a three-year (Extended Fund Financing) program to have on the order of 50 of them (Goldstein 2001). At the same time, obtaining compliance with these structural policy conditions was becoming progressively more difficult. After the experience of the Asian crisis countries, where the number and detail of structural policy conditions were very extensive, it became apparent to most observers as well as to the Fund itself, that IMF structural policy conditionality had become excessive in both scope and detail. As a result, the Fund's executive board in September 2002 agreed to new guidelines on conditionality. These new guidelines make it clear that all Fund policy conditions must be "critical" to achievement of the program's

27. By "structural policies," I mean policies aimed not at the management of aggregate demand but rather at improving the efficiency of resource use and/or at increasing the economy's productive capacity. Structural policies are typically aimed at reducing or dismantling government-imposed distortions or putting in place the institutional features of a modern market economy. Such structural policies include, among others, privatization of public enterprises; liberalization of trade, capital markets, and the exchange rate system; tax and expenditure policies (apart from the overall fiscal stance); financial-sector policies; labor market policies; pricing and marketing policies; transparency and disclosure policies; poverty-reduction and social safety net policies; pension policies; corporate governance policies (including anticorruption measures); and environmental policies.

goals or to monitoring of the program's implementation. The new guidelines also emphasize "parsimony" in the number of policy conditions, and they underline that such conditions should normally stay within the Fund's "core" areas of responsibility and expertise, namely, monetary and fiscal policies, exchange rate policies, and financial-sector policies.

Fortunately, the Fund did not run all the way to the other side of the boat by jettisoning the essence of its "ex post" approach to policy conditionality in favor of an approach centered on "prequalification" for Fund loans. By "ex post" conditionality, I mean disbursing loans in stages or "tranches," after the borrowing country has satisfied the key macroeconomic and structural policy conditions laid out in the program. In contrast, prequalification means selecting a set of well-performing countries that had met a small set of preconditions and making them eligible immediately for large Fund loans; countries that did not meet these preconditions would not be eligible for any assistance. Recall that the majority in the Meltzer Commission (IFIAC 2000) favored just such a prequalification approach; they argued that freedom of entry and operation for foreign financial institutions, regular and timely publication of debt and off-balance sheet liabilities, adequate capitalization of commercial banks, and some (undefined) fiscal policy requirement would be sufficient to differentiate worthy borrowers from unworthy ones. Recall too that the Fund experimented briefly with prequalification when it established the Contingent Credit Line (CCL) in 1999. This was a special Fund lending window for countries that had demonstrated strong policies and that wanted a precautionary line of defense against a loss of market confidence linked to international financial contagion. But the CCL was allowed to expire at end-2003, after not a single country came forward to sign up for it (and this despite efforts to make the CCL more attractive by sweetening its terms).

There are fundamental conceptual and practical problems with prequalifying countries for large-scale Fund loans. To begin with, it is difficult to find a small, common set of macroeconomic and structural policy conditions that, agreed at the time of qualification, would provide a good test of creditworthiness at the time of activation. Not only do policies and external conditions change over time, but there is also a broad range of potential causes of crises. For example, the four preconditions set out in the Meltzer Commission Report (IFIAC 2000) say nothing about profligate monetary policies, and they leave undefined the proper fiscal policy requirement;[28] likewise, problems that surface in the financial sector often have their roots in deeper economic and structural weaknesses. It is instructive that although the CCL was often described as a prequalified line of credit, creditor countries were not prepared to agree to its creation without including the stipulation that a separate "activation" review take place just prior to disbursement. Another problem is that there are apt to

28. See the minority report in the Meltzer Report (IFIAC 2000).

be strong political pressures against declaring countries ineligible if they originally met the preconditions—even where there is strong evidence of subsequent backtracking on performance.

It is also far from clear that prequalification would deter speculative attacks. In this connection, there are examples of economies with large reserves and with large pledges of support that nevertheless faced strong attacks (Hong Kong in 1997–98). Countries may worry additionally that signing up for such a line of credit might be interpreted by the private capital markets as a signal of impending "need" for external assistance; indeed, this adverse selection effect was one of the factors frequently cited in the unwillingness of emerging economies to apply for CCL eligibility.

In the end, warts and all, there is no practical alternative to evaluating program compliance on a regular, phased basis as a quid pro quo for continued financing under a Fund program. Recent calls for creation within the Fund of new large-scale, precautionary lending windows against adverse capital market developments are thus misplaced.

The bad news on the evolution of the Fund's financing facilities is that "exceptional access" in Fund lending arrangements has been activated repeatedly over the past decade, without much agreement on what should determine eligibility for such exceptional treatment and with too little regard for the risks to the Fund's financial position—to say nothing of any moral hazard effects (be they direct or indirect) on private creditors or on official borrowers. The normal access limits for loans under Fund programs are 100 percent of a country's quota annually and 300 percent of quota cumulatively. Despite statements by both incoming US Treasury officials and new managing directors of the IMF about the desirability of limiting the scale of Fund financing, the normal access limits have been surpassed, often by large amounts, in the cases of Mexico (1995), Thailand (1997), Indonesia (1997), Korea (1998), Brazil (1998–2001), Turkey (1999–2002), Uruguay (1999–2001), and Argentina (2000–01); see table 12.2. One result of this de facto access policy has been a concentration of Fund credit among a small number of borrowing countries. Indeed in January 2004, credit outstanding to the Fund's three largest borrowers (Argentina, Brazil, and Turkey) hit an unprecedented 70 percent of total credit—higher than even at the height of the Asian financial crisis; in 1980, by way of comparison, 16 debtors accounted for 70 percent of Fund credit outstanding.

Deciding when access to IMF loans should be exceptionally large is a judgment call (Roubini and Setser 2004). If IMF financial assistance is too small, the adjustment burden placed on the borrowing country in crisis could be too heavy. Likewise, if the borrower is solvent and if the private capital markets are unduly pessimistic about a country's economic prospects, an IMF rescue package that is small relative to the country's short-term external debt obligations might impede a return of market confidence. On the other hand, an IMF loan that is very large could discourage the borrower from taking adequate adjustment measures, could

Table 12.2 IMF exceptional access arrangements

Country and year	Amount agreed: As percent of quota	Amount agreed: In billions of dollars	Amount agreed: As percent of GDP	Total disbursed: As percent of quota	Total disbursed: In billions of dollars	Total disbursed: As percent of GDP
Mexico, 1995	688	18.0	4.4	500	13.1	3.2
Thailand, 1997	505	3.9	2.2	470	3.7	2.0
Indonesia, 1997	557	11.3	5.0	555	11.3	5.0
Korea, 1998[a]	1,938	20.8	4.0	1,802	19.4	3.7
Brazil, 1998	600	18.4	2.3	436	13.4	1.7
Uruguay, 1999–2001	694	2.7	14.5	560	2.2	11.7
Argentina, 2000–01	800	22.1	7.8	461	12.7	4.5
Brazil, 2001	400	15.6	3.1	375	14.6	2.9
Brazil, 2002	752	29.3	5.7	567	22.1	4.3
Brazil, combined	900	35.1	6.9	770	30.1	5.9
Turkey, 1999–2001	1,560	20.7	10.4	1,218	16.2	8.1
Turkey, 2002	1,330	17.6	8.9	1,154	14.8	7.7
Turkey, combined	2,548	33.8	17.0	1,709	23.1	11.4

a. Korea's quota was unusually small in relation to its GDP.

Note: Combined programs = outstanding disbursement plus new commitment; however, some of the new commitment was intended to refinance the IMF's existing exposure. Special drawing rights (SDR) are converted into dollars at the SDR/dollar exchange rate at the time of the initial program.

Sources: Financial data from International Monetary Fund, www.imf.org/external/fin.htm; GDP data from Moody's Investor Service.

bail out private creditors from living with the consequences of poor investment decisions, and could put the Fund's financial position at risk if the borrower is unable or unwilling to meet its financial obligations to the Fund. If the Fund were to get into financial difficulties as a result of concentration of credit to a few large borrowers, access to Fund credit could be constrained for other potential borrowers, the Fund would have to increase its precautionary balances, and creditor countries could either be discouraged from providing additional resources to the Fund in the future or might be willing to finance increased quotas only under different conditions/safeguards than in the past. To date, the empirical evidence has not been decisive either on the influence that loan size has on the effectiveness of IMF programs or on the direct and indirect effects of IMF lending on borrower or lender moral hazard.[29]

29. See Roubini and Setser (2004). On the whole, they interpret the available evidence as suggesting that large IMF loans are more effective when the borrowing country has a low debt burden and is committed to corrective policy actions, and that IMF loans did not produce serious lender moral hazard, except in the cases of Russia (1998–99) and Turkey (2000–03). Benelli (2003) finds that large IMF loans did not improve the likelihood of success for IMF programs, where "success" is defined as meeting or exceeding the program's initial projections for private net capital flows; in contrast, policy adjustment did improve the likelihood of success. Mussa (1999) refers to "indirect" moral hazard as a situation in which international financial support facilitates moral hazard by national governments. Both Mussa (1999) and Jeanne and Zettlemeyer (2001) argue that the direct subsidy effect of IMF lending is not large enough to generate significant lender moral hazard. Dell'Ariccia, Godde, and Zettel-

In an effort to enhance the clarity and predictability of the Fund's response in crisis resolution and to strengthen safeguards on the Fund's resources, the Fund's executive board approved a new framework on exceptional access in February 2003. The new framework set out four criteria that would need to be met to justify exceptional access during a capital account crisis: (1) the country was experiencing capital account pressures that could not be met within normal access limits; (2) there was a high probability that the country's debt would remain sustainable; (3) there were good prospects that the country could regain access to private capital markets during the time when Fund loans would be outstanding; and (4) the country's policy program offered a reasonably strong prospect of success. On top of this, the new framework established tougher procedures for decision making on exceptional access, including a higher burden of proof in program documentation, ex post evaluation of programs with one year of the end of the agreement, and systematic board consultations on program negotiations through confidential informal briefings. In March 2003, the executive board strengthened the presumption that when exceptional access was granted in capital account crises, the funds would be provided under the IMF's Supplementary Reserve Facility (SRF), which carries higher interest rates (300 to 500 basis points higher) and shorter repayment maturities than the Fund's normal lending window. More recently, it was agreed that a country utilizing exceptional access would be required to publish the IMF staff report accompanying the request.

Designing a sensible framework for exceptional access is one thing. Implementing that framework is another. Even if one puts aside exceptional access decisions taken prior to agreement on the new framework that would have violated the new criteria (e.g., Argentina in 2001, Turkey in 2000, and Uruguay in 2002), it is troubling that access decisions taken for Argentina and Brazil in the *aftermath* of the new framework did not comply with it. As the IMF staff acknowledge in a recent paper, Argentina's public and external debt was not sustainable pending a debt restructuring. It is debatable whether there was a "high probability" that Brazil's public debt was sustainable. Brazil's balance-of-payments need was potential rather than actual; indeed, the Brazilians treated their recent Fund arrangement as a precautionary one. Argentina was not likely to reenter international capital markets during the time Fund resources would be outstanding.

meyer (2000) show that the conditions are demanding for obtaining a good empirical test of moral hazard in international crisis lending. Goldstein (2000) maintains that the indirect moral hazard effects of IMF lending can be significant. Dooley and Verma (2003) argue that the timing of emerging-market financial crises and the scale of capital inflows leading up to a crisis are the anticipated outcome of private investors' incentive to exploit a pool of government insurance (including loans from the IMF).

Nor has the presumption been fulfilled in practice that countries obtaining exceptional access would finance all of it under the SRF. While the first large Fund programs that used the SRF (i.e., Korea in 1997, Russia in 1998, and Brazil in 1998) financed all the "exceptional" part of access using the SRF, the more recent (from 2000 on) exceptional access cases typically did not. After all, when emerging economies are under market stress, they want to minimize interest costs and to stretch out repayment schedules—especially if they are not confident about how long it will take to deliver a turnaround in private capital flows and a rebound in market confidence. These financing terms are the opposite of what the SRF offers. As such, there is a strong temptation to invoke arguments for why the SRF should not apply to a particular situation (e.g., it was never a capital account crisis, or it was at one time a capital account crisis but it no longer is, or the country is facing a potential not an actual crisis, or the country's debt repayments or budget financing requirements present a special situation).

If there is no capital account crisis and the SRF is thereby judged not to apply, then exceptional access can still be approved under an undefined "exceptional circumstance" clause contained in earlier (1983) Fund access decisions, and it can be financed by recourse to the Fund's regular lending windows; while here too there is an interest surcharge for large loans, it is lower than the surcharge for the SRF and, more significantly, the repayment periods are considerably longer than with the SRF. Even when exceptional access is funded under the SRF, the country can lengthen its repayment schedule (by switching from an expected payment date to an obligation payment date). And in early 2003, the Fund amended the repayment terms in the SRF window itself to make them more lenient on borrowers. All of this of course blunts the original purpose of limiting exceptional access. Also, as I have argued elsewhere, probably the best one can expect from higher interest charges related to exceptional access is that they would induce faster repayment to the Fund; countries that are badly in need of external funds and that can't obtain those funds from private creditors are not going to be much deterred by higher interest rate charges from seeking exceptional access from the IMF.[30]

What might be done differently in the future to limit exceptional access cases and to give teeth to the new (exceptional access) framework? I would recommend two amendments.[31] First, as proposed earlier in a CFR

30. Under the SRF, the interest rate increases with the length of the repayment period. In contrast, under the Fund's normal lending windows, the interest rate increases (up to a cap) with the size of the loan.

31. Roubini and Setser (2004) propose that the Fund's normal access limits should be increased to 300 percent (annual) and 500 percent (cumulative) to reflect the reality of the size of IMF loans during recent exceptional access cases. The rub, however, is that actual average access has been much below the access limits in nonexceptional access cases, and the actual average access might well increase by an unwarranted amount if the access limits were increased so substantially. Suffice to say that the Roubini-Setser proposal merits further study.

(1999) report, decisions to grant exceptional access should be subject to a supermajority—say 75 to 80 percent of voting strength. This would make it more likely that exceptional access decisions were truly viewed as meriting exceptional treatment by a wide swath of the IMF membership—and not merely regarded as "systemic crises" by the borrowing country, several of its neighbors, and one or two G-7 countries in that neighborhood. In this connection, it should be recalled that there have been a few exceptional access cases where a group of executive directors abstained from the voting—perhaps suggesting that a supermajority voting requirement could have an impact. One hurdle for a supermajority provision is that formal changes in Fund voting majorities would require an amendment of the IMF's charter—a process that can be time-consuming.[32] An informal procedure might therefore be better. Specifically, the exceptional access framework could be amended to say that the managing director would not bring a request for exceptional access to the Fund's executive board unless earlier consultations with the board indicated that at least 75 percent of the voting power was in favor of it.

A second useful amendment would require the Fund's managing director to sign off explicitly that the decision to grant exceptional access met *all* the requirements of the new exceptional access framework.[33] In the spirit of the provision in the Sarbanes-Oxley law that requires CEOs to vouch personally for the accuracy of their firm's financial statements, the purpose here is both to motivate more rigorous due diligence by the (Fund) staff and to give greater negotiating leverage to the Fund's managing director to stand up against even the Fund's major shareholders if he/she regards pressure to grant exceptional access as unwarranted.[34] The aim is not to make exceptional access impossible; it is rather to ensure that when exceptional access is granted, it meets a higher threshold of proof than in the past.

Concluding Remarks

This year marks the 60th anniversary of the IMF. There should be little question about the overall contribution that the IMF has made to the international economic landscape: without the Fund and its conditional fi-

32. The IMF's charter sets out required voting majorities for various kinds of decisions.

33. There is already a strong presumption—laid out in the original conditionality guidelines—that the managing director will only take to the Fund's executive board requests for loans that he/she believes can be implemented successfully; the proposed amendment would go farther for exceptional access cases.

34. Unlike Sarbanes-Oxley, the sign-off procedure would not subject the CEO (the managing director) to personal legal liability; the motivation instead is to increase the burden of proof for recommending exceptional access.

nancing, there would undoubtedly have been deeper recessions, more chaotic debt defaults, and greater resort to trade protectionism. But arguing that the world economy continues to need an IMF should not preclude a new US administration from pressing hard for further reform of the IMF and the IFA. Considerable progress in strengthening the IFA has already been made in moving most emerging economies toward currency regimes of managed flexibility, in increasing the use of collective action clauses in international sovereign bonds, and in making IMF operations and decisions more transparent.[35] That progress can and should be extended.

Three of the reforms proposed in this chapter come under the heading of getting the Fund to return to its roots.

A well-functioning exchange rate system cannot be concerned only with balance-of-payments deficits and with overvalued exchange rates. Balance-of-payments surpluses and exchange rate undervaluations have to be of concern as well—especially when they are being influenced significantly by large-scale, prolonged, one-way exchange market intervention. The IMF should not be ceding its responsibility to speak out against exchange rate manipulation to national governments, lest it risk the very kinds of conflicts on exchange rate policy that its founders sought to avoid. There have been cases when IMF advice to emerging economies on exchange rate policy has been influential, and it could be again.[36] Emerging economies now have a large enough weight in the global economic system that they too have to be part of the international adjustment process, including the appropriate adjustment of their exchange rates. In short, it is past time for the Fund to give substance to its obligation to exercise "firm surveillance" over the exchange rate policies of all its member countries—developing and industrial.

35. See Goldstein (2002a) on the advantages of marrying a managed floating currency regime with a monetary framework of inflation targeting and with measures to reduce currency mismatching. Mexico's embrace of collective action clauses in 2003 seems to have prompted other emerging economies to follow suit: 18 countries now include collective action clauses in their international sovereign bonds issued under New York law, and there has been no sign of higher issuance costs for debt issues with collective action clauses. The IMF now publishes three-quarters of its country reports, along with almost all Fund policy papers; it also releases the weekly calendar of executive board meetings. Less progress has been made in developing a voluntary code of conduct—laying out standards and responsibilities for debtors and private creditors during debt negotiations. The sovereign debt restructuring mechanism (SDRM), initially proposed by Anne Krueger (2001), the IMF's first deputy managing director, seems to be on the back burner, at least until such time as the lessons are identified from Argentina's ongoing debt restructuring saga.

36. To take one notable example, Lardy (1999)—drawing on Chinese sources—documents that the IMF had considerable influence both on China's decision in January 1984 to abandon the internal settlement rate for the renminbi and on the decision in July 1986 to undertake a large (15.8 percent) one-time devaluation of the renminbi—rather than continue with a series of minidevaluations.

With the average public debt ratio (to GDP) in emerging economies now hovering at about 70 percent—nearly three times as high as the IMF (2003b) calculates would be sustainable for the typical emerging economy—debt sustainability and fiscal policy discipline are clearly a second area where the IMF should get back to basics. This means, among other things, trying to persuade emerging economies of the need to increase government revenues and control public expenditures (the latter especially during boom periods) and to reduce over time dependence on interest and exchange rate–linked debt.[37] It also means subjecting all IMF loans to more rigorous and more objective analysis of debt sustainability. Efforts should be made to eliminate the (optimistic) biases that have been evident in the Fund's earlier medium-run projections of public debt for emerging economies (especially those with IMF programs) and to make the analysis of debt sustainability a central element in Fund surveillance and program discussions with member countries. The introduction of GDP-indexed bonds should be explored seriously since they offer the potential to provide greater cushioning for emerging economies against unusually adverse outturns. No one wants to relive the emerging-market debt crisis of the 1980s.

The IMF has been providing loans to countries with a balance-of-payments need for more than 50 years. But the practice of extending loans way beyond the normal access limits has become less exceptional over the past decade than used to be the case. Yes, there have been some very good bottom-line results (that is, V-shaped recoveries, relatively quick return to private capital markets, and repayment to the Fund ahead of schedule) from several of these large loans, most notably Mexico (1994–95) and Korea (1997–98). And yes, no recipient of an enlarged access loan has so far defaulted on its obligations to the Fund. But there is a growing consensus that the use of exceptional access loans has not been discriminating enough. The Fund's recent experience with Argentina has demonstrated dramatically what happens when very large Fund loans are provided to a country with an unsustainable debt situation and an overvalued real exchange rate; when additional Fund loans have to be extended to coax repayment of earlier ones; and when the normal interpretations of Fund conditionality, "good faith" bargaining with private creditors, and "equal treatment" of countries are twisted beyond recognition to avoid a default to the Fund. There have also been other exceptional access cases (Brazil, Turkey, and Uruguay) where Fund repayment might have become problematic, had not earlier loans been topped up after the original programs failed or came under heavy strain. The fact that excep-

37. Again, fiscal policy and public debt problems are by no means confined to emerging economies: witness, for example, recent criticism of the US fiscal outlook over the coming decade and the controversy about noncompliance by several EU countries with the fiscal policy guidelines laid out in the Stability and Growth Pact. See the analysis of fiscal policies in the chapter by Michael Mussa in this book.

tional access loans to three emerging economies (Argentina, Brazil, and Turkey) have brought the concentration of Fund credit to a historic high also rightly worries many observers.

Rodrigo de Rato, the Fund's new managing director, has argued (de Rato 2004, 4–5) that the international community clearly needs a Fund that "can say 'No' selectively, perhaps more assertively, and above all, more predictably than has been the case in the past." He has also maintained that the prospect of the Fund declining to provide financial support would help strengthen the incentives to implement sound policies. The criteria set out in the Fund's new (February 2003) framework for exceptional access (especially the one stressing debt sustainability) provide in principle a way to make more sensible access decisions, but the initial experience with it already indicates that it is being honored in the breach. Something additional is therefore needed to stiffen the backbone of the Fund to say "no" when it is warranted and to return exceptional access policy to its earlier (pre-1994) norm. The supermajority and managing director sign-off amendments suggested above are intended to aid in that objective.

The other three reforms proposed in this chapter involve areas where the IFA needs to evolve—either to meet the changing characteristics of recent financial crises or to strengthen earlier official efforts to improve crisis prevention and crisis resolution.

Taking a "balance sheet" approach to the analysis of crisis vulnerability is warranted by the presence of serious currency mismatches in virtually all the prominent emerging-market financial crises of the past decade. A vital first step here is to obtain better measures of currency mismatch and to monitor those measures more carefully than in the past—including publication of mismatch indicators so that the private capital markets can bring disciplinary pressure to bear when these mismatches become too large. The other key recommendations in this sphere are to encourage more emerging economies to adopt the macroeconomic, exchange rate, and prudential policies that cross-country experience shows tend to reduce currency mismatches. While currency mismatch may sound like a narrow, arcane technical matter, it is at the heart of what makes large currency depreciations in many emerging economies so troublesome. The better emerging markets become at getting and keeping currency mismatches under control, the sooner will the benefits of exchange rate flexibility be more widely seen as outweighing the costs.

Another common characteristic of most emerging-market currency, banking, and debt crises of the past decade has been fragile financial sectors—hence, the global initiative on international standards and codes of good practice that seek to improve financial regulation and supervision, strengthen the financial infrastructure, and upgrade data and macroeconomic policy transparency. The initial skepticism about the feasibility of obtaining agreement on such standards has now been laid to rest. The bigger challenge is creating sufficiently strong incentives to promote effective "implementation." To this end, the Fund and the Bank have to convince private financial markets that their published reports on compliance with standards (ROSCs) are important for assessing countries' creditworthiness and thus should be reflected more strongly in market borrowing costs.

I have argued that prospects for meeting the market test of credibility will be advanced by focusing the standards effort on the existing core group of standards, by limiting the number of assessments done each year, and by seeking greater consistency across countries and regional groups. Giving countries with good compliance records on standards an interest rate discount when they borrow from the Fund would further increase the incentives for compliance.

Finally, it seems like every new managing director of the Fund and every new US Treasury secretary indicates that better early warning systems need to be developed so that the international community is not left with a menu of unpalatable choices after emerging-market financial crises have already occurred. The problem is that, in practice as opposed to rhetoric, early warning systems do not typically get the resources and priority within surveillance work that they need to become more effective. Part of this reflects a reluctance to be seen as precipitating a crisis by blowing the whistle on the most vulnerable cases; part of it is a reflection of the false alarms that will probably accompany the accurate signals; and part of it is the heavy call on staff resources to deal with crises that have already broken out. But the official sector will not get better at early warning until it invests more heavily in it and until it is prepared to accept the "price" of an occasional wrong call in exchange for the larger benefits of a higher number of well-founded early warnings.

It is neither necessary nor desirable to go to extremes in trying to strengthen the IFA. While some have proposed abolishing the IMF altogether (Shultz 1995), or restricting the Fund's activities to surveillance with no lending (Rogoff 1999), or turning the IMF into a lender of first resort that provides (precautionary) loans on a massive scale to countries that meet a few prequalification criteria (IFIAC 2000), better results will be obtained within the existing institutional structure by returning the Fund to its roots and by having it focus on a small number of promising initiatives.

References

Abiad, Abdul. 2003. *Early-Warning Systems: A Survey and Regime-Switching Approach.* IMF Working Paper 03/32. Washington: International Monetary Fund.

Barth, James, Gerard Caprio, and Ross Levine. 2001. *Bank Regulation and Supervision: What Works Best?* NBER Working Paper 9323. Cambridge, MA: National Bureau of Economic Research.

Barth, James, Daniel Nolle, Triphon Phumiwasana, and Glenn Yago. 2002. *A Cross-Country Analysis of the Bank Supervisory Framework and Bank Performance.* Economic and Policy Analysis Working Paper 2002-2. Washington: Office of the Comptroller of the Currency.

Benelli, Roberto. 2003. *Do IMF-Supported Programs Boost Private Capital Inflows: The Role of Program Size and Policy Adjustment.* IMF Working Paper 03/231. Washington: International Monetary Fund.

Berg, Andrew, Eduardo Borensztein, and Catherine Pattillo. 2004. *Assessing Early Warning Systems: How Have They Worked in Practice?* IMF Working Paper 04/52. Washington: International Monetary Fund.

Bergsten, C. Fred. 2004. The IMF and Exchange Rates. Testimony before the Committee on Banking, Housing, and Urban Affairs, US Senate, Washington (May).

Bergsten, C. Fred, and John Williamson. 2004. Designing a Dollar Policy. In *Dollar Adjustment: How Far? Against What?*, ed., C. Fred Bergsten and John Williamson. Washington: Institute for International Economics.

Borensztein, Eduardo, and Paolo Mauro. 2002. *Reviving the Case for GDP-Indexed Bonds.* IMF Policy Discussion Paper 02/10. Washington: International Monetary Fund.

Christofides, Charis, Christian Mulder, and Andrew Tiffin. 2003. *The Link Between International Standards of Good Practice, Foreign Exchange Spreads, and Ratings.* IMF Working Paper 03/74. Washington: International Monetary Fund.

CFR (Council on Foreign Relations). 1999. *Safeguarding Prosperity in a Global Financial System: The Future International Financial Architecture,* Carla Hills and Peter Peterson, co-chairs, Morris Goldstein, project director. Institute for International Economics, Washington.

Das, Udaiabir, Marc Quintyn, and Kina Chenard. 2004. *Does Regulatory Governance Matter for Financial System Stability: An Empirical Analysis.* IMF Working Paper 04/89. Washington: International Monetary Fund.

Dell'Ariccia, Giovanni, Isabel Godde, and Jeromin Zettelmeyer. 2000. Moral Hazard and International Crisis Lending: A Test. International Monetary Fund, Washington. Photocopy.

Dooley, Michael, and Sujata Verma. 2003. Rescue Packages and Output Losses During Crises. In *Managing Currency Crises in Emerging Markets,* ed., Michael Dooley and Jeffrey Frankel. Chicago, IL, and Cambridge, MA: National Bureau of Economic Research and University of Chicago Press.

Goldstein, Morris. 1997. *The Case for an International Banking Standard.* POLICY ANALYSES IN INTERNATIONAL ECONOMICS 47. Washington: Institute for International Economics.

Goldstein, Morris. 1998. *The Asian Financial Crisis.* POLICY ANALYSES IN INTERNATIONAL ECONOMICS 55. Washington: Institute for International Economics.

Goldstein, Morris. 2000. *Strengthening the International Financial Architecture.* Institute for International Economics Working Paper 00-8. Washington: Institute for International Economics. Revised version in *Managing Currency Crises in Emerging Markets,* ed., Michael Dooley and Jeffrey Frankel. 2003. Chicago, IL, and Cambridge, MA: National Bureau of Economic Research and University of Chicago Press.

Goldstein, Morris. 2001. *IMF Structural Conditionality.* Institute for International Economics Working Paper 01-4. Washington: Institute for International Economics. Revised version in *Economic and Financial Crises in Emerging Market Economies,* ed., Martin Feldstein. 2003. Chicago, IL, and Cambridge, MA: National Bureau of Economic Research and University of Chicago Press.

Goldstein, Morris. 2002a. *Managed Floating Plus.* POLICY ANALYSES IN INTERNATIONAL ECONOMICS 66. Washington: Institute for International Economics.

Goldstein, Morris. 2002b. Lessons of Recent Currency Crises. *Brookings Trade Forum 2002.* Washington: Brookings Institution.

Goldstein, Morris. 2003. *Brazil, Debt Sustainability, and the IMF.* Institute for International Economics Working Paper 03-1. Washington: Institute for International Economics.

Goldstein, Morris. 2004. *Adjusting China's Exchange Rate Policies.* Institute for International Economics Working Paper 04-1. Washington: Institute for International Economics.

Goldstein, Morris, Graciela Kaminsky, and Carmen Reinhart. 2000. *Assessing Financial Vulnerability: An Early Warning System for Emerging Markets*. Washington: Institute for International Economics.

Goldstein, Morris, and Philip Turner. 2004. *Controlling Currency Mismatches in Emerging Economies*. Washington: Institute for International Economics.

Hufbauer, Gary, and Yee Wong. 2004. *China Bashing 2004*. International Economics Policy Brief 04-5. Washington: Institute for International Economics.

IIF (Institute for International Finance). 2002. Action Plan Proposals and Dialogue with the Private Sector. Appendix D to *Does Subscription to the IMF's Special Data Dissemination Standard Lower a Country's Credit Spread?* Washington: Institute for International Finance.

IFIAC (International Financial Institutions Advisory Commission). 2000. *Meltzer Commission Report*. Washington: US Congress.

IMF (International Monetary Fund). 2003a. *Access Policy in Capital-Account Crises: Modifications to the Supplemental Reserve Facility and Follow-up Issues Related to Exceptional Access Policy*. Washington: International Monetary Fund.

IMF (International Monetary Fund). 2003b. *Sustainability Assessments: Review of Application and Methodological Refinements*. Washington: International Monetary Fund.

IMF (International Monetary Fund). 2004a. *Review of Exceptional Access Policy*. Washington: International Monetary Fund.

IMF (International Monetary Fund). 2004b. *Report of the Acting Managing Director to the International Monetary and Financial Committee on the IMF's Policy Agenda*. Washington: International Monetary Fund (September).

IMF (International Monetary Fund). 2004c. IMF Executive Board Concludes Review of Policy on Exceptional Access to Fund Resources. Public Information Notice 04/54. Washington: International Monetary Fund.

Jeanne, Olivier, and Jeromin Zettelmeyer. 2001. International Bail-Outs, Moral Hazard, and Conditionality. *Economic Policy* 33 (October). Washington: International Monetary Fund.

Kaminsky, Graciela, Saul Lizondo, and Carmen Reinhart. 1998. *Leading Indicators of Currency Crises*. IMF Staff Papers 45, no. 1 (March). Washington: International Monetary Fund.

Kenen, Peter, Jeffrey Shafer, Nigel Wicks, and Charles Wyplosz. 2004. *International Economic and Financial Cooperation: New Issues, New Actors, New Responses*. Geneva and London: International Centre for Monetary and Banking Studies and Centre for Economic Policy Research.

Krueger, Anne. 2001. International Financial Architecture for 2002: A New Approach To Sovereign Debt Restructuring. Speech at the National Economists' Club Annual Members' Dinner, American Enterprise Institute, Washington, November 26.

Krueger, Anne. 2004. Virtuous in Old Age: How the IFIs Can Help Prepare for Demographic Change. Speech delivered at Federal Reserve Bank of Kansas City Symposium, Jackson Hole, Wyoming, August.

Lardy, Nicholas. 1999. China in the International Financial System. In *China Joins the World: Progress and Prospects*, ed., Elizabeth Economy and Michael Oksenberg. New York: Council on Foreign Relations.

Manase, Paolo, Nouriel Roubini, and Axel Schimmelpfennig. 2003. Predicting Sovereign Debt Crises. International Monetary Fund, Washington. Photocopy.

Mussa, Michael. 1999. Reforming the International Financial Architecture: Limiting Moral Hazard and Containing Real Hazard. In *Capital Flows and the International Financial System*. Sydney: Reserve Bank of Australia.

de Rato, Rodrigo. 2004. The IMF at 60: Evolving Challenges, Evolving Role. Opening remarks at conference on Dollars, Debts, and Deficits—60 Years after Bretton Woods, Madrid, June.

Reinhart, Carmen, Kenneth Rogoff, and Miguel Savastano. 2003. Debt Intolerance. Brookings Papers on Economic Activity I. Washington: Brookings Institution.

Rogoff, Kenneth. 1999. Institutions for Reducing Global Financial Instability. *Journal of Economic Perspectives* (Fall).

Roubini, Nouriel, and Brad Setser. 2004. *Bailouts or Bail-ins? Responding to Financial Crises in Emerging Markets*. Washington: Institute for International Economics.

Shultz, George. 1995. Economics in Action: Ideas, Institutions, and Policies. *American Economic Review* 85.

Sundararajan, V., David Marston, and Ritu Basu. 2001. *Financial Systems Standards and Financial Stability: The Case of the Basel Core Principles*. IMF Working Paper 01/62. Washington: International Monetary Fund.

Truman, Edwin. 2003. *Inflation Targeting in the World Economy*. Washington: Institute for International Economics.

Williamson, John. Forthcoming. *Curbing the Boom-Bust Cycle: Stabilizing Short-Term Capital Flows to Emerging Markets*. Washington: Institute for International Economics.

13

Fostering Development

WILLIAM R. CLINE
and JOHN WILLIAMSON

Throughout the postwar period, a combination of humanitarian concern and enlightened self-interest has made global economic development a persistent goal in US foreign policy, even if at times this goal has seemed to command only a low priority. The Cold War spurred US assistance to South Korea in the 1950s and Latin America in the 1960s. The United States' financial self-interest was evident during the Latin American debt crisis of the 1980s, which threatened the US banking system, and again after the Russian default in 1998, which shook financial markets. The positive side of self-interest is increasingly evident in trade and investment. Developing-country markets today account for 45 percent of US exports, up from 37 percent in 1985. Developing countries also account for 37 percent of US direct investment abroad.

Today the most immediate threat facing the United States is international terrorism. This reality should sharpen the United States' recognition that the security self-interest in global development remains vital. It would be naïve to postulate any simple link between poverty and terrorism, but it is equally implausible to maintain that the rich countries can thrive indefinitely in a world where many people are trapped in degrading and permanent poverty. Rising resentment would be inevitable, and in a globalized world this resentment could easily take a destructive form that harms Americans. In other words, the United States increasingly has a strong security interest in seeing the peoples of other countries make the

William R. Cline is a senior fellow jointly at the Institute for International Economics and the Center for Global Development. John Williamson is a senior fellow at the Institute for International Economics.

transition to prosperity that the postwar world has already witnessed in western Europe, Japan, southern Europe, Israel, and the new industrial economies of East Asia. The United States' economic and humanitarian interests in this outcome are also arguably greater than ever before.

The self-styled critics of globalization (who often seem to be objecting to capitalism rather than to globalization per se) often give the impression that poverty is not only endemic but worsening. This is simply wrong: By historical standards, the era since World War II has witnessed unparalleled progress, both economic and social. According to the World Bank, "dollar-a-day" poverty (the standard measure of what some of us would consider destitution) has been cut almost in half in little more than 20 years (from 40 percent in the early 1980s to under 21 percent now). Some analysts, such as Surjit Bhalla (2002), have argued that poverty has fallen even faster than indicated by the World Bank's figures. Moreover, the increase in world inequality that had been taking place for almost two centuries finally reversed around 1970 and certainly by the 1980s, as a result of the success of China, India, Indonesia, and other large Asian countries in getting development moving. And economic progress pales in comparison with the progress in the social indicators: Many developing countries have reached levels of infant mortality, longevity, and literacy that were achieved only at far higher income levels in the developed countries. Progress in these fields has been largely maintained even in times of economic crisis.

But this progress still leaves massive poverty in the world, especially if one measures poverty by anything better than the destitution-level figure of a dollar a day. At the $2 per day level, half of the world's population remains in poverty. The developing world to the west of Pakistan actually has done worse, not better, since 1980. Latin America, and for that matter the Middle East, experienced a Lost Decade in the 1980s, and their growth in the past dozen years has remained below the pace of the 1970s. One of the major regions, namely Africa, really is mired in the desperate sort of situation that the pessimists picture as characterizing the whole of the developing world. The spread of HIV/AIDS has brutally reversed progress in improving the social indicators in much of Africa. Most of the Millennium Development Goals to which the world's leaders solemnly committed in 2000 seem all too likely to be missed in many, maybe most, countries.

While we welcome the decision taken in 2000 to adopt the Millennium Development Goals, we also recognize that to make this more than an empty gesture will require more than has yet been done. Doubtless, many developing countries need to do more for themselves, but this chapter is about what the developed countries—and specifically the largest of them, the United States—need to do to support their efforts.

In this chapter we focus on two central issues: trade and aid. Trade is relevant to all three groups of developing countries distinguished in box

13.1. It is key in both the most rapidly growing countries and the most desperate cases of failed states, where the chance to sell on the world market what they are capable of producing offers one of the few avenues of escape from the prevailing misery. In contrast, aid is of marginal importance in the first group of countries but is key in the other two groups. However, even here there is a major difference. The second group is in a position to absorb relatively large sums of money, whereas large sums given to countries in the third group are all too likely to be wasted or diverted to the bank account of the dictator or some warlord. The report of the CGD commission advises that the donors should be ready to spend money rapidly when a promising opportunity arises, but it would be a mistake to think that throwing large sums of money at these countries will help them.

Our decision to limit this chapter to these two issues does not mean that we are blind to the fact that a wide array of other policies affect development. In fact, the CGD produces a Commitment to Development Index (CDI) that grades the performance of the donor countries in supporting development in seven dimensions (Roodman 2004). Two of these are, of course, trade and aid. The others are investment, migration, the environment, security, and technology. Investment policy is actually of far greater importance than aid to most middle-income countries. Some analysts believe that the potential gains from unrestricted movement of people exceed those from the unrestricted movement of goods, but until recently there was an almost complete absence of studies on the liberalization of migration, and there is still no consensus on what policies in the developed countries would most benefit developing countries. (The topic is discussed in Gordon Hanson's chapter in this book.)

Environmental degradation poses a threat to both developed and developing countries. Many of the latter are probably more vulnerable to degradation than most of the former. For example, global warming is likely to impose greater relative damage on developing countries than industrial countries, because typically initial temperatures are higher, agriculture constitutes a larger share of GDP, and adaptive capacity is more limited. Ironically, given that environmental sensitivity is a superior good, developed countries tend to be more concerned about environmental degradation.

The security component of the CDI reflects the fact that both internal security and freedom from external attack are indispensable to development and that rich-country policies can influence both elements.

Finally, development has taken place over substantial parts of the globe in the last quarter-millennium essentially because people learned how to produce goods better than they used to, and it will take place where it has not yet occurred to the extent that people in the rest of the globe gain access to the new technology that is so much more efficient than the old ways of producing goods and services. Hence the extent to which developed countries facilitate the access of developing countries to technology

Box 13.1 Grouping developing countries

"Developing countries" include both low- and middle-income countries. Many of them are indeed developing and can expect within a historically short time span to make the transition to developed-country income levels. But unfortunately this is not true for all the countries where living standards are still distinctly lower than those in the industrial (or developed) countries. It is necessary to distinguish at least three groups of countries and to tailor policies differently for the three groups.

The first group consists of those countries that really are on the road to development: most middle-income countries (although one worries about a few of them, like Argentina and Venezuela) plus a few low-income countries like China, India, and perhaps Indonesia. The United States has traditionally supported the development of countries in this group mainly through its backing of international financial institutions (IFIs) like the International Monetary Fund (IMF), World Bank, and regional development banks. These institutions are important to this group of countries for several reasons. They provide financial support in times of crisis. They provide loans on favorable financial terms. They give policy advice, most of which is sensible however much one may squawk in protest at their mistakes. Their traditional advice in favor of disciplined macroeconomic policies, market liberalization, and opening up to trade and foreign direct investment has in recent years been complemented by help in supervising the financial sector[1] and assistance in tackling corruption. The United States should continue to give robust support to these institutions, not surrender to the siren songs that periodically call for dismantling them. Of course, the needed policy advice changes with the times: Right now the main extra emphasis needs to be on strengthening crisis prevention (meaning anticyclical policies) and reinforcing the focus on building the human capital of the poor to ensure that growth has a propoor bias.

The second group consists of countries, primarily in Africa, that are mostly rather small and still have low incomes but are doing a reasonable job of governing themselves. These countries also have an ongoing need for IFI support: They are less likely to encounter financial crises but have even more need for the policy expertise of the IFIs. In addition, they get concessional financial support from both the IFIs and the US government (and other bilateral donors), and this is extremely important to them.

The third group consists of failed and failing states. A commission sponsored by the Center for Global Development (CGD 2004) defines these as "states that fail to ensure security, fail to meet the basic needs of citizens, and fail to maintain political legitimacy." Most of these countries are in Africa, though such countries can also be found in the Middle East (Iraq), Asia (Afghanistan and North Korea, and periodically one worries that Nepal or Pakistan may join them), Latin America (Haiti), and even Europe (parts of the former Yugoslavia). These countries not only give their own citizens a miserable life but also seem particularly likely to breed terrorists.

1. We are thinking of the Financial Sector Assessment Programs and Financial System Stability Assessments of the IMF and the Reports on the Observance of Standards and Codes now conducted for many member countries by joint IMF/World Bank teams.

is clearly important. We nevertheless limit our attention to trade and aid, because they are the two issue areas with perhaps the largest development impact (barring a radical change in migration policies) and most influenced by the policies of the United States and other industrial countries.

Trade

The tradition that international trade enhances domestic growth goes back at least to Adam Smith more than two centuries ago. Trade permits increased specialization. Specialization allows increased attainment of economies of scale, especially for countries with relatively small domestic markets. It also permits more effective utilization of a country's abundant factors of production. Imports provide competitive pressure that keeps domestic firms on their toes and may prompt them to improve their technology. Increased economic integration with the outside world also stimulates technological change through the diffusion of new technologies, especially from the more advanced countries at the technological frontier to the developing countries.[1] Imports also curb domestic monopoly power that would hold production below and prices above socially optimal levels.

Few would doubt that the traditional static specialization gains remain valid, including for developing countries. They will be able to obtain wide-bodied aircraft more cheaply by importing them from Boeing or Airbus with earnings from exports of agricultural goods or labor-intensive manufactures than by attempting to build them domestically. Most developing countries, moreover, are even more acutely dependent on the world market for economies of scale than are the larger industrial countries. Costa Rica has large export earnings from computer chips produced by its Intel plant, but it would not have the scale to produce chips efficiently if it did not have access to the external market.

Similarly, the impact of open trade in countering monopoly is likely to be even more important for developing countries than for industrial countries, again because the domestic market will tend to be smaller and

1. Grossman and Helpman (1994, 40) emphasize that integration with the world economy can help boost productivity growth: "residents of a country that is integrated into world markets are likely to enjoy access to a larger technical knowledge base than those living in relative isolation. Trade itself may help the process of technological dissemination, if foreign exporters suggest ways that their wares can be used more productively or foreign importers indicate how local products can be made more attractive to consumers in their country. . . . Whereas a firm that develops a product for a protected domestic market need only make use of technologies that are new to the local economy, one that hopes to compete in the international market-place will be forced to generate ideas that are truly innovative on a global scale."

Figure 13.1 Average annual GDP and export value growth

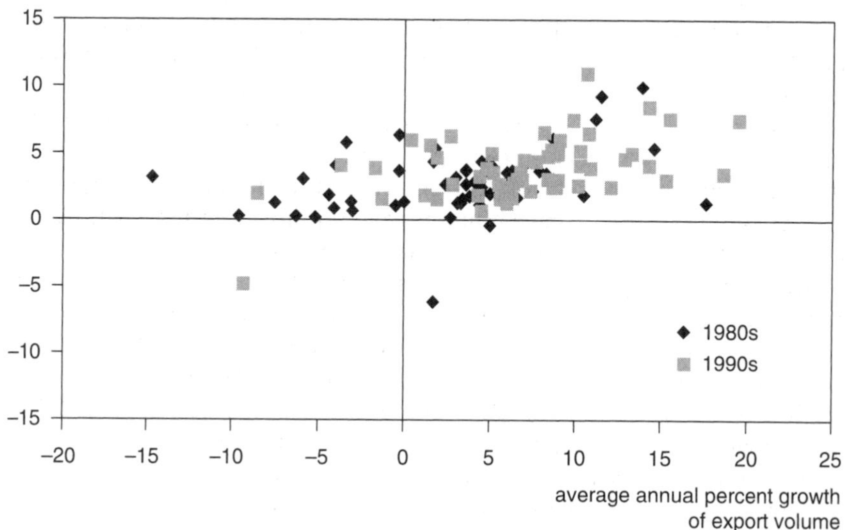

Source: Cline (2004).

hence more susceptible to monopolization. An old concern is of developing countries' being locked into monoculture-excessive dependence on a handful of traditional tropical or mineral exports. But it is worth recalling the experience of Chile, which moved from high protection in the 1950s and 1960s to open trade by the late 1970s, yet broke out of monoculture after this change. Copper as a share of Chilean exports fell from 52 percent in 1980 to 44 percent by 1990 and 30 percent in 2000 (UNCTAD 2003, 116), while new product lines such as grapes and other fruits and vegetables became major sources of export growth.

How can contact with the world market enhance total factor productivity (TFP) in an agricultural product such as cotton (West Africa) or soybeans (Brazil)? It should be kept in mind that agriculture is a sector in which technological change has been extremely important, as shown by the Green Revolution in Asia based on new seed varieties and improved practices. It is far more likely that such advances will be made by countries in close contact with global markets than by countries isolated from them.

Open trade policies in developing countries, and open markets for their exports in industrial countries, help promote export growth, which in turn helps stimulate overall growth. Figure 13.1 provides informal evidence of the positive relationship between export growth and GDP growth. For 64 countries with populations of over 10 million in 1999, export and GDP growth are shown for 1980–90 (diamonds) and 1990–99 (squares). A simple regression shows that each additional percentage point in export growth has been associated with an additional 0.15 percentage point in GDP growth. Exports contribute to growth inter alia by allowing imports of key intermediate inputs, capital goods, and technologies not available domestically and by reducing the likelihood of a foreign debt crisis.

High domestic protection is an obstacle to export growth. It tends to act as a tax on exports by creating a distorted incentive to produce for the domestic rather than the export market. In fact a formal proposition (the Lerner symmetry theorem) maintains that a uniform import tariff has an effect equivalent to a uniform export tax (Lerner 1936).

More formal empirical tests have been carried out at two levels: the relationship of growth to the "openness" of the economy and the relationship of growth to trade policy more explicitly. On the first, Cline (2004) synthesizes numerous studies on the trade-growth relationship as follows: Each 1 percent rise in the ratio of trade (imports plus exports) to GDP has been associated with a 0.5 percent rise in long-term output per capita.[2] The evidence tends to indicate that most of this addition is from an increase in TFP, but some portion is also the result of increased investment (including foreign direct investment attracted by more open economies).

Perhaps the two leading empirical studies more specifically on the relationship of growth to trade policy are by Sachs and Warner (1995) and Edwards (1998). Sachs and Warner examine growth performance for 79 countries over 1970–89. Their binary variable for trade policy is set at "closed" (zero) if *any* of the following is true: the average tariff on capital and intermediate goods is over 40 percent, nontariff barriers cover more than 40 percent of imports of capital goods and intermediates, the country has a socialist economic system, there is a state monopoly on the principal exports, or the black market premium on the official exchange rate exceeded 20 percent in the 1970s or 1980s. Their statistical regressions relating growth in real per capita income during 1970–89 to the trade policy variable and other influences (initial per capita income, investment rate, relative price of investment goods, government consumption spending relative to GDP, and variables for political stability) find that annual per capita growth was 2.2 percentage points faster in "open" economies than in "closed" economies.

Edwards uses estimates of capital and labor stocks for 93 developing and industrial countries over 1960–90 to estimate TFP growth. He then tests the relationship between TFP growth and nine alternative measures

2. The studies that lie behind this summary are Levine and Renelt (1992), Frankel and Rose (2000), Alcalá and Ciccone (2001), Dollar and Kraay (2004), Easterly (2003a), Choudhri and Hakura (2000), World Bank (2002), and OECD (2003). These studies carefully take account of the two directions of causality (from trade to growth and vice versa).

of trade policy openness.[3] In 17 of 18 regressions, the trade policy openness variable has the right sign, and in 13 of these 17 it is statistically significant. He considers the results as "quite remarkable" evidence of a "tremendous consistency of a significant positive relationship between openness and productivity growth" (p. 391).

Rodriguez and Rodrik (2000) have criticized the Sachs-Warner and Edwards studies, either by challenging the variables used or by showing that the results are sensitive to inclusion of other variables.[4] Reviewing the debate, Berg and Krueger (2003) judge that the Sachs-Warner index "represents a fairly successful effort to measure the overall importance of trade policy restrictions." Cline (2004) similarly suggests that the Rodriguez-Rodrik critique may be overdone.[5]

In sum, there is considerable evidence that more open economies achieve faster growth, and there is a strong basis in theory for expecting this result.[6] As Paul Krugman (2003, 368) has summarized:

> The raw fact is that every successful example of economic development this past century—every case of a poor nation that worked its way up to a more or less decent, or at least dramatically better, standard of living—has taken place via globalization; that is, by producing for the world market rather than trying for self-sufficiency.

The most important way that the policies of the industrial countries enhance the ability of developing countries to work their way out of poverty is by a willingness to buy the goods that they are able to make efficiently. Successive rounds of postwar multilateral trade negotiations sharply reduced protection in industrial countries for most manufactures but have

3. These nine measures include the Sachs-Warner variable, the World Bank's "outward orientation index," Edward Leamer's residual from trade flow regressions, the average black market premium, the average tariff in 1982, the average coverage of nontariff barriers, the Heritage Foundation Index of Distortions in International Trade, the Collected Trade Taxes ratio for 1980–85, and a regression-based index of import distortions in 1985.

4. For example, they argue that the black market premium is the dominant influence in the Sachs-Warner results and that it reflects macroeconomic disarray rather than protection. However, Warner (2003) provides an impressive rebuttal.

5. In particular, as shown by Sala-i-Martin (1997), the technique of decomposing some variables and adding others to remove the statistical significance of the original tests is an exercise that can bias the findings against robustness.

6. The principal contrary theory is that of "infant industry" protection. Although this may help industrial development during a "first easy stage" (Balassa and associates 1982, 40), there is widespread agreement that import-substituting industrialization behind high tariff walls becomes increasingly inefficient, as countries expand output into goods further and further removed from domestic comparative advantage. Even in the case of Korea, where intervention through "industrial policy" may have been less inefficient, it is doubtful whether it made a net contribution to industrial development (Noland and Pack 2003).

Table 13.1 Protection in agriculture (percent tariff-equivalent)

Protection	United States	Canada	European Union	Japan
Tariffs	8.8	30.4	32.6	76.4
Subsidies	10.2	16.8	10.4	3.2
Total	19.9	52.3	46.4	82.1

Source: Cline (2004).

left protection high in the politically sensitive sectors of agriculture, textiles, and apparel, which happen to be goods in which many developing countries have comparative advantage. The Uruguay Round left tariffs largely unchanged in these sectors (although it converted agricultural quotas to tariffs and promised the removal of textile and apparel quotas by 2005). The effective postponement of liberalization in these areas, together with adverse spillover from new intellectual property rules in pharmaceuticals, created a widespread impression that developing countries had not benefited much from the Uruguay Round. The current Doha Round was designated the "Development Round" to show international commitment to using the new round to permit developing countries to gain larger potential benefits. The implication is that the Doha Round should go beyond the traditional commercial deal making, whereby countries place import liberalization offers on the table solely to obtain reciprocal offers from trading partners. To live up to its title, the round will have to open new opportunities for developing countries.

Industrial-country protection against imports from developing countries is highest in agriculture. Tariffs, including the ad valorem equivalent of specific duties and taking into account the high tariffs above "tariff-rate quota" thresholds, are as high as 400 percent for rice in Japan and 250 percent for sugar in the European Union (Dimaranan and McDougall 2002). Production and export subsidies in agriculture further increase protection. Table 13.1 shows aggregate protection in agriculture for the "Quad" countries.

Protection is also relatively high in textiles and apparel, where many of the "peak tariffs" (15 percent and higher) are concentrated. In the past, under the Multi-Fiber Arrangement, quotas added further protection, but these are to be fully eliminated at the beginning of 2005. Table 13.2 shows an Aggregate Measure of Protection (AMP) against developing countries by the Quad countries after taking account of protection levels of all trade divided into four broad product categories (and including only tariff protection in textiles and apparel). As the table shows, although protection is low in manufactures outside textiles and apparel, and especially in oil and other nonagricultural raw materials, the high protection in agriculture and textiles and apparel means that trade barriers remain substantial.

Table 13.2 Aggregate Measure of Protection against developing countries (percent tariff-equivalent)

Sector	United States	Canada	European Union	Japan
Agriculture	19.9	52.3	46.4	82.1
Textiles and apparel	10.9	16.5	11.6	9.2
Other manufactures	2.1	3.5	3.2	1.5
Oil, other nonagricultural raw materials	0.9	0.9	0.6	0.3
Aggregate Measure of Protection	4.0	10.7	9.5	15.6

Source: Cline (2004).

It is often argued that protection, especially in the European Union, is lower than these "most favored nation" rates would suggest, because of preferential entry for poor countries. However, the countries eligible for the European Union's "Everything but Arms" duty-free entry account for only a small portion of imports. Even a broader group of "at-risk" countries including the heavily indebted poor countries (HIPCs), the least developed countries (LDCs), and sub-Saharan Africa (SSA) account for only 8 percent of imports from developing countries by the European Union (and 6 percent for the United States and 4 percent for Japan). So the estimates in table 13.2 accurately reflect the protection facing the great bulk of developing-country exports to these markets.

On the basis of model estimates, Cline (2004) examines how much impact the removal of protection would have on the income of developing countries and the incidence of poverty.[7] He estimates that global free trade would convey long-term economic benefits of about $200 billion annually to the developing countries. Half or more of these gains would be attributable to the removal of industrial-country protection against developing-country exports. By removing their trade barriers, the industrial countries could convey economic benefits to developing countries worth about twice the amount of annual development assistance. Helping developing countries grow through trade, moreover, would be accompanied by economic benefits for the industrial countries themselves, in the form of lower consumer costs for imports and increased economic efficiency from open trade.

Cline's study further estimates that free trade could reduce the number in poverty globally (at the $2 per day threshold) by about 500 million over 15 years, or by about one-fourth below the level that will otherwise be reached. Agricultural liberalization alone contributes about half of these gains. This suggests that the developing countries were right to risk collapse of the Doha Round at the Cancún ministerial meeting in September

7. He uses an adaptation of the computable general equilibrium model of Harrison, Rutherford, and Tarr (1996).

2003 by insisting on much deeper liberalization of agriculture than the industrial countries were then willing to offer.

The study calls for a two-track strategy. The first track is deep multilateral liberalization involving phased but complete elimination of protection by industrial countries and deep reduction of protection by at least the middle-income developing countries albeit on a more gradual schedule. The second track is immediate free entry for imports from "high-risk" low-income countries (HIPCs, LDCs, and SSA), coupled with a 10-year holiday from taxes imposed by developed countries for direct investment in the high-risk low-income countries. The head start from immediate free entry would provide an important boost to the pace of global poverty reduction.

One feature of the Uruguay Round that many developing countries have criticized was the introduction into the World Trade Organization (WTO) of disciplines on intellectual property. While the LDCs were granted a delay in implementing the agreement, all member countries of the WTO are required in principle to allow citizens from other member countries to protect their intellectual property. The general argument for protecting intellectual property is that without such rights, potential inventors will not have the incentive to take the investment risks involved. The wider the area within which such rights are protected, the greater the incentive. However, this incentive comes at the cost of ease and cheapness of diffusion. Some developing countries argue that the additional incentive to innovate coming from protection of intellectual property in developing countries, especially the poorer ones, is small and not commensurate with the increased obstacles to diffusion created by the Agreement on Trade-Related Aspects of Intellectual Property Rights (TRIPs).

The international community has accepted this argument in the specific context of developing countries' access to low-cost generic pharmaceuticals. The Doha declaration at end-2001 recognized the right to grant compulsory licenses to manufacture generic drugs to deal with HIV/AIDS, tuberculosis, malaria, and other epidemics (WTO 2001). An agreement shortly before the September 2003 Cancún ministerial meeting dealt further with the problem of poor countries without domestic capacity to manufacture generics, by permitting them to import generics from other developing countries (such as Brazil and India). The new administration needs to reaffirm this flexibility and stand ready to push it a stage further by allowing the LDCs to renew their exemption from the TRIPs agreement after their first 10-year exemption expires.

Development Assistance

While we regard import liberalization as the most important way that the industrial countries can support development, aid remains of critical importance to many of the really poor countries. Although the United States is still the largest donor in absolute terms, the country has for some years been regarded as a laggard. In recent years the United States has actually given a lower proportion of its GDP as foreign aid than any of the other members of the Organization for Economic Cooperation and Development (OECD) Development Assistance Committee (DAC), which includes all the rich industrial donor countries.[8] President George W. Bush promised a $5 billion (roughly 50 percent) increase at the Monterrey Summit in 2002, but even this may leave the United States as the least generous of the donor countries. And not only is the quantity of US aid modest in relation to the size of the US economy but also its quality has been deficient, in particular because a large proportion is tied to the purchase of US goods and services and a small proportion is given as program aid rather than to finance particular projects (and, even then, projects that are largely chosen by the donor). Fortunately the aid increase that is in the pipeline is to be distributed according to state-of-the-art principles via the new Millennium Challenge Account: untied, given to countries that are pursuing enlightened policies and have relatively good institutions for their income level, and to finance projects that the countries themselves have chosen to propose. One could not have asked for more enlightenment in choosing the underlying principles (Radelet 2003), though naturally it will not be possible to make an evaluation of how things are working out in practice for some time yet.

US politicians have customarily appealed to public opposition to increased foreign aid to explain their reluctance to sanction increased spending. Certainly it seems to be true that in the United States (in sharp contrast to Europe), the public believes that the country is giving away too much in foreign aid. But polls undertaken by the Program on International Policy Attitudes of the School of Public Affairs at the University of Maryland suggest that this is because the public is misinformed about the size of the aid program, not because Americans are less generous than Europeans. The poll evidence suggests that on average Americans believe that the government spends over 20 percent of its budget on foreign aid, whereas the true figure is about 1 percent. The average American says that he or she believes that the government ought to be spending about 10 percent of its budget on aid, which would make the United States the most, rather than the least, generous donor. Perhaps the question was framed in a way that failed to emphasize the opportunity cost of an increase in the aid program, but nevertheless there seems to be political

8. US official development assistance was 0.16 percent of GDP in 2000, compared with the DAC median of 0.38 percent. If aid through private charity is included, the US total amounted to 0.21 percent of GDP, leaving the United States still ranked last and well below the DAC median of 0.40 percent. See Roodman (2004).

space for politicians who recognize the importance of foreign aid to mobilize public support for a big increase in the aid program.

The case for a large increase in foreign aid should not blind one to the fact that aid can have perverse effects if it is given badly. Aid can permit a government to perpetuate antigrowth policies that it would otherwise be forced to abandon. It can channel resources to corrupt bureaucrats who are enabled to bid resources away from the very entrepreneurs who are the key to unlocking growth. For some years, many analysts have argued that the empirical evidence did not show any robust impact of aid on development (e.g., Boone 1994, Easterly 2003b), implying that these perverse effects are about as common as positive effects. Burnside and Dollar (2000) concluded that the evidence showed that aid could work in the presence of good policies but was ineffective otherwise, but even this conclusion was attacked as not being robust to an expanded dataset (Roodman 2003).

The latest evidence as presented in Clemens, Radelet, and Bhavnani (2004) concludes, however, that these negative views are unjustified. These authors argue that the empirical results are a consequence of jumbling together quite different forms of aid. Humanitarian aid tends to rise when a country faces a disaster that is also likely to disrupt growth, and so it produces an *inverse* association of aid and growth—but not because aid harms growth! Long-term aid (for objectives such as education) cannot reasonably be expected to promote growth over a short-run period like four years, which most of the empirical literature has focused on. When they separate out aid that could plausibly promote short-run growth (like infrastructure and budget support), they find a strong and robust positive effect of this more narrowly defined aid on growth over a four-year horizon. This positive effect implies that the unfavorable possibilities alluded to at the start of this paragraph are the exception and not the rule. Clemens, Radelet, and Bhavnani also find some evidence that the positive effects are still stronger in the presence of good policies and institutions.

The latter finding suggests, as Burnside and Dollar argued, that aid should be given with attention to the recipient's policy stance, rather than thrown at any government that declares itself willing to support a foreign policy goal (as used to happen in the days of the Cold War). It is therefore important to have a vision of the policies that are indeed likely to stimulate development. The care that was put into the design of the Millennium Challenge Account suggests that the US government has absorbed this lesson, but it will be important to make sure that it is not forgotten if and when there is a new increase in spending on aid. And one can argue for going one step beyond the Millennium Challenge Account and giving the countries that qualify for it the chance to win access to a pool of resources supplied by all the donors to finance those countries' development program as chosen by them, rather than making them jump through hoops to qualify for support for a series of projects.[9]

One prominent recent suggestion is the proposal of the British Chancellor Gordon Brown to use future aid flows as collateral to raise bonds that would permit a large increase in the aid flow in the next few years, when the world is supposed to be making a special effort to achieve the Millennium Development Goals (HM Treasury 2003). The downside of this proposal for creation of an international financing facility (IFF) is of course the reduction in the flow of aid in the longer-term future, when the bonds have to be serviced. If the mechanism could be based strictly on frontloading only the incremental portion of future aid above current ratios to donor GDP as part of a firm commitment to ramp up aid toward the long-standing (and long-unmet) target of 0.7 percent of GDP, this would not be so much of a concern. Because there is no clear way to ensure that industrial countries will raise their aid flow levels relative to GDP, the problem of taking aid from the future to boost flows today cannot safely be ignored. And if the IFF is essentially an attempt to use financial engineering to force countries to raise aid levels in the future (after their demonstrated inability to do so in the past), the proposal would seem a potential source of trouble when and if donors do not deliver.

Because in practice IFF frontloading significantly risks reducing future aid to levels below those today rather than merely moderating a hoped-for rapid buildup, it is important to think about the time profile of aid needs. It seems unlikely that the magnitudes of aid needed in 2015–25 will be sharply smaller than those needed in 2005–15. The potential time path of the AIDS pandemic alone is sufficient reason for caution in assuming that a major reduction in assistance will be appropriate after a big push in the coming years. Moreover, countries that might be strong candidates for assistance later but do not qualify now (imagine a Sudan with forceful governance reform) would be penalized by "frontloading" a quarter-century's development assistance. There are also contractual and legislative obstacles, such as the inability of legislatures (certainly the US Congress) to commit to aid flow levels for decades in advance. For these reasons, the proposal could be at best difficult to implement and at worst counterproductive.[10] In contrast, we believe that the United States should follow Britain in committing itself in principle to increase its aid progres-

9. See Kanbur and Sandler (1999) for presentation of their "Common Pool Proposal."

10. Features of the idea, however, warrant pursuit. The notion of pooling bilateral aid and eliminating the tying to donor contractors is attractive. The IFF would also allow individual donor countries to earmark funds for their favorite recipient countries, which they cannot do for their support through IDA. But pooling, untying, and earmarking could be done without frontloading.

sively in the coming years, which would permit the desired increase in aid in the short term without risking longer-term flows if they continue to be necessary. The Zedillo Report (2001) estimated that something like an extra $50 billion of aid per year would be needed to offer a reasonable chance of meeting the Millennium Development Goals, provided also that all developing countries adopted the policies that would make such an increase in aid worthwhile.

One aid area in which the Bush administration took an important initiative was in pressing for grants in place of loans for some of the operations of the World Bank's International Development Association (IDA). Many of the European countries strongly resisted this initiative on the grounds that it would reduce the return flow of money to IDA, which was intended to finance many of the future operations of IDA. This argument did not make a lot of sense, because in many cases, IDA is almost forced to make new loans to provide countries with the dollars to make their repayments. Stopping this merry-go-round can alleviate the threat of new debt problems in the poorest countries and relieve them of the need to negotiate new projects to keep the money flowing in. Up to now, only about 20 percent of IDA operations has been converted to grants, in a compromise with the Europeans.

A good initiative for the new administration would be to press for this figure to be raised. One can, admittedly, make a powerful case against converting all IDA loans into grants, because a number of the IDA countries are likely to graduate in the next few years, and it will be useful if IDA is able to draw on their repayments to finance additional operations in those countries that continue to need its support. On the other hand, it is ridiculous for the poorest countries to be receiving loans when we know perfectly well that they will need to receive yet more loans in a few years' time if they are to service the loans they are getting now! Far better that such countries receive grants until such time as they show clear evidence that their income has started to rise so that from then on they will be in a position to service loans. Hence what the World Bank needs is a third (grant-issuing) window that enables it to provide finance to the poorest countries on terms that they can responsibly accept. We suggest that the Bank reform its IDA operations based on per capita income, perhaps by placing the countries that receive money in three groups: those with per capita income below $300, those in the range of $300 to $500, and those above $500. The first group would receive all grants, the middle group might continue to receive a mix of grants and loans as at present, and the third group of less poor countries would receive all loans. If IDA continued to disburse an annual total of just over $7 billion as in 2003, and the pattern of disbursements remained the same, this would result in grants roughly doubling from $1.2 billion to $2.5 billion, of which almost $2.2 billion would go to the below-$300 countries.

Concluding Remarks

Nurturing development may not be the criterion by which commentators judge the new administration a success or failure, but in terms of its impact on the future of humanity, its achievements in this dimension may be as critical as any. The performance of the United States in this dimension in recent decades leaves much to be desired, even though for many years, when market economics was under a cloud in the rest of the world, it was the United States that kept alive the idea that a liberal economy is the road to growth. Unfortunately, the widespread acceptance of the market economy in recent years has sometimes been clouded by triumphalist advocacy of market fundamentalism instead of leading to a sober resolve to make a market economy work for the general benefit. The new administration will need to stand by the traditional US conviction that the right formula is an outward-looking market economy subject to macroeconomic discipline. But this need not prevent it from supporting initiatives to strengthen the automatic fiscal stabilizers, or improve income distribution, or encourage market-friendly interventions (e.g., to curb excessive swings in capital markets), or increase aid.

The new administration needs to make success easier for countries with governments committed to development. The most important area is trade. Developing countries need access to export markets for the goods that they are able to make efficiently. Our principal recommendations in the area of trade are the following:

- The United States should push hard for deep liberalization of trade in the current Doha Round. The United States and other industrial countries should sharply cut agricultural tariffs and tariff-rate quota protection. They should set an aggressive timetable to eliminate agricultural subsidies or strictly decouple them from production. They should sharply reduce any remaining high tariffs (e.g., 10 percent or above) in manufactures, including in textiles and apparel.
- The United States should press the middle-income countries to make relatively deep reductions in their protection as well, while acknowledging the appropriateness of longer liberalization timetables for these countries.
- The United States, other industrial countries, and middle-income countries should grant complete free entry to imports from LDCs (and perhaps HIPCs and SSA countries) as part of the Doha bargain.
- The United States and other industrial countries should ensure that the liberalization of trade in textiles and apparel through the termination in 2005 of remaining quotas under the Multi-Fiber Arrangement, agreed

in the Uruguay Round, is not thwarted by new barriers, such as unwarranted or unduly protracted "safeguards" protection.

Aid is also critically important to the poorer countries. Our principal recommendations in the area of development assistance are the following:

- The United States should build on the recent initiative of the Bush administration to substantially increase the level of its development assistance, in light of the United States' ranking as last among industrial countries in aid relative to GDP.
- The new administration should forcefully implement the new Millennium Challenge Account with its linkage of aid to policy performance by recipient countries.
- The new administration should continue strong support for the IMF and World Bank in their roles of giving policy advice, emergency financial assistance, and long-term development support to poor and emerging-market economies.
- The new administration should develop more streamlined vehicles for providing aid promptly when political conditions in "failing states" show promise of favorable change.
- The United States should continue the efforts of the Bush administration to increase the portion of IDA financing that is provided on a grant basis and should seek 100 percent grant terms for countries with incomes below $300 per capita at market exchange rates. Additional funds should also be directed to IDA, so that the grant element in its operations can be doubled without forcing a cutback in disbursements in the longer term.

With strong efforts along these lines, the new administration could make a major contribution to fostering development and reducing global poverty. Stronger prospects for international development, in turn, would contribute to a more equitable and safer world.

References

Alcalá, Francisco, and Antonio Ciccone. 2001. *Trade and Productivity*. Centre for Economic Policy Research, Discussion Paper 3095. London: CEPR.

Balassa, Bela, and associates. 1982. *Development Strategies in Semi-Industrial Countries*. Baltimore, MD: Johns Hopkins University Press for the World Bank.

Berg, Andrew, and Anne Krueger. 2003. *Trade, Growth, and Poverty: A Selective Survey*. IMF Working Paper WP/03/30. Washington: International Monetary Fund.

Bhalla, Surjit. 2002. *Imagine There's No Country: Poverty, Inequality and Growth in the Era of Globalization*. Washington: Institute for International Economics.

Boone, Peter, 1994. *The Impact of Foreign Aid on Savings and Growth.* Centre for Economic Performance Working Paper 677. London: London School of Economics.

Burnside, Craig, and David Dollar. 2000. Aid, Policies, and Growth. *American Economic Review* 90, no. 4: 847–68.

CGD (Center for Global Development). 2004. *On the Brink: Weak States and US National Security*. Washington: Center for Global Development.

Choudhri, Ehasan U., and Dalia S. Hakura. 2000. International Trade and Productivity Growth: Exploring the Sectoral Effects for Developing Countries. *IMF Staff Papers* 47, no. 1: 30–53. Washington: International Monetary Fund.

Clemens, Michael, Steven Radelet, and Rikhil Bhavnani. 2004. *Counting Chickens When They Hatch: The Short-Term Effect of Aid on Growth.* Center for Global Development Working Paper 44. Washington: Center for Global Development.

Cline, William R. 2004. *Trade Policy and Global Poverty.* Washington: Center for Global Development and Institute for International Economics.

Dimaranan, Betina V., and Robert A. McDougall, eds. 2002. *Global Trade, Assistance, and Production: The GTAP5 Data Base.* West Lafayette, IN: Center for Global Trade Analysis, Purdue University.

Dollar, David, and Aart Kraay. 2004. Trade, Growth, and Poverty. *The Economic Journal* 114, no. 493: 22–49.

Easterly, William. 2003a. *National Policies and Economic Growth: A Reappraisal.* Center for Global Development Working Paper 27. Washington: Center for Global Development.

Easterly, William. 2003b. Can Foreign Aid Buy Growth? *Journal of Economic Perspectives* 17, no. 3: 23–48.

Edwards, Sebastian. 1998. Openness, Productivity, and Growth: What Do We Really Know? *Economic Journal* 108 (March): 383–98.

Frankel, Jeffrey A., and Andrew K. Rose. 2000. *Estimating the Effect of Currency Unions on Trade and Growth.* NBER Working Paper 7857. Cambridge, MA: National Bureau of Economic Research.

Grossman, Gene, and Elhanan Helpman. 1994. Endogenous Innovation in the Theory of Growth. *Journal of Economic Perspectives* 8, no. 1: 23–44.

Harrison, Glenn W., Thomas F. Rutherford, and David G. Tarr. 1996. Quantifying the Uruguay Round. In *The Uruguay Round and Developing Economies*, ed., W. Martin and L. A. Winters. New York: Cambridge University Press.

HM Treasury. 2003. *International Finance Facility: A Technical Note.* London: UK Treasury (February).

Kanbur, Ravi, and Todd Sandler. 1999. *The Future of Development Assistance: Common Pools and International Public Goods.* Washington: Overseas Development Council.

Krugman, Paul. 2003. *The Great Unraveling: Losing Our Way in the New Century.* New York: Norton.

Lerner, Abba P. 1936. The Symmetry Between Import and Export Taxes. *Economica* 3: 306–13.

Levine, Ross, and David Renelt. 1992. A Sensitivity Analysis of Cross-Country Growth Regressions. *American Economic Review* 82, no. 4 (September): 942–63.

Noland, Marcus, and Howard Pack. 2003. *Industrial Policy in an Era of Globalization: Lessons from Asia.* Washington: Institute for International Economics.

OECD (Organization for Economic Cooperation and Development). 2003. *The Sources of Growth in OECD Countries.* Paris: OECD.

Radelet, Steven. 2003. *Challenging Foreign Aid: A Policymaker's Guide to the Millennium Challenge Account.* Washington: Center for Global Development.

Rodriguez, Francisco, and Dani Rodrik. 2000. Trade Policy and Economic Growth: A Skeptic's Guide to the Cross-National Evidence. Cambridge, MA: Harvard University. Photocopy (May). An earlier version is available as NBER Working Paper 7081 (April 1999).

Roodman, David. 2003. *The Anarchy of Numbers: Aid, Development, and Cross-Country Empirics.* Center for Global Development Working Paper 32. Washington: Center for Global Development.

Roodman, David. 2004. Ranking the Rich 2004. *Foreign Policy* (May/June): 46–56.

Sachs, Jeffrey, and Andrew Warner. 1995. Economic Reform and the Process of Global Integration. *Brookings Papers on Economic Activity* 1: 1–118. Washington: Brookings Institution.

Sala-i-Martin, Xavier X. 1997. I Just Ran Two Million Regressions. *American Economic Review* 87, no. 2 (May): 178–83.

UNCTAD (United Nations Conference on Trade and Development). 2003. *Trade and Development Report 2003: Capital Accumulation, Growth and Structural Change.* Geneva: United Nations.

Warner, Andrew. 2003. *Once More into the Breach: Economic Growth and Integration.* Center for Global Development Working Paper 34. Washington: Center for Global Development (December).

World Bank. 2002. *Global Economic Prospects and the Developing Countries 2002: Making Trade Work for the World's Poor.* Washington: World Bank.

WTO (World Trade Organization). 2001. Declaration on the TRIPS Agreement and Public Health. WT/MIN(01)/DEC/2, November 20. Geneva: World Trade Organization.

Zedillo Report. 2001. *Report of the High-Level Panel on Financing for Development.* New York: United Nations.

About the Contributors

C. Fred Bergsten has been the director of the Institute for International Economics since its creation in 1981. He is also chairman of the "Shadow G-8," which advises the G-8 countries on their annual summit meetings. He was chairman of the Competitiveness Policy Council, which was created by Congress, throughout its existence from 1991 to 1995 and chairman of the APEC Eminent Persons Group throughout its existence from 1993 to 1995. He was assistant secretary for international affairs of the US Treasury (1977–81); assistant for international economic affairs to Dr. Henry Kissinger at the National Security Council (1969–71); and a senior fellow at the Brookings Institution (1972–76), the Carnegie Endowment for International Peace (1981), and the Council on Foreign Relations (1967–68). He is the author, coauthor, or editor of 34 books on a wide range of international economic issues, including *Dollar Adjustment: How Far? Against What?* (2004), *Dollar Overvaluation and the World Economy* (2003), *No More Bashing: Building a New Japan–United States Economic Relationship* (2001), *Global Economic Leadership and the Group of Seven* (1996), and *The Dilemmas of the Dollar* (2d ed., 1996).

Jan Boyer, visiting fellow, has 20 years' experience in international finance and entrepreneurship. He has had chief executive responsibility for private equity initiatives at Softbank, FleetBoston, and Salomon Smith Barney, with committed capital in excess of $300 million and activities in seven countries. He has substantial operating, restructuring, and turnaround experience in growth and mature companies. While at Lehman Brothers, he worked on principal investing, mergers and acquisitions, corporate finance, and government advisory transactions in the United

States, Europe, Latin America, Asia, and Africa. He has served on corporate and nonprofit boards in the United States and abroad. His experience in government includes his service as senior adviser to the president at the Overseas Private Investment Corporation (OPIC), full-time participation in two US presidential campaigns (including the 2004 reelection of President George W. Bush), and working in the US Senate.

Scott C. Bradford is assistant professor at the department of economics, Brigham Young University. His research interests include international trade, political economy, and the Japanese economy. His work has appeared in *American Economic Review, Review of Economics and Statistics*, and *Journal of International Economics*. He is coauthor of *Has Globalization Gone Far Enough? The Costs of Fragmented Markets* (2004).

William R. Cline, senior fellow at the Institute since 1981 (now a joint appointment with the Center for Global Development), was on leave from the Institute during 1996–2001 while serving as deputy managing director and chief economist of the Institute of International Finance. He was a senior fellow at the Brookings Institution (1973–81), deputy director for development and trade research at the US Treasury (1971–73), Ford Foundation visiting professor in Brazil (1970–71), and assistant professor at Princeton University (1967–70). He is the author of 20 books, including *Trade Policy and Global Poverty* (2004), *Trade and Income Distribution* (1997), *Predicting External Imbalances for the United States and Japan* (1995), *International Debt Reexamined* (1995), *The Economics of Global Warming* (1992), and *The Future of World Trade in Textiles and Apparel* (2d ed., 1990).

Morris Goldstein, Dennis Weatherstone Senior Fellow since 1994, has held several senior staff positions at the International Monetary Fund (1970–94), including deputy director of its research department (1987–94). He has written extensively on international economic policy and on international capital markets. He is author, coauthor, or coeditor of *Controlling Currency Mismatches in Emerging Markets* (2004), *Managed Floating Plus* (2002), *Assessing Financial Vulnerability: An Early Warning System for Emerging Markets* (2000), *The Asian Financial Crisis: Causes, Cures, and Systemic Implications* (1998), *The Case for an International Banking Standard* (1997), *Private Capital Flows to Emerging Markets after the Mexican Crisis* (1996), and *The Exchange Rate System and the IMF: A Modest Agenda* (1995); and project director of *Safeguarding Prosperity in a Global Financial System: The Future International Financial Architecture* (1999) for the Council on Foreign Relations Task Force on the International Financial Architecture.

Paul L. E. Grieco is a research assistant at the Institute for International Economics.

Gordon H. Hanson is a professor of economics in the Graduate School of International Relations and Pacific Studies and the Department of Economics at the University of California, San Diego. He is also a research associate at the National Bureau of Economic Research and coeditor of the *Journal of Development Economics*. His current research examines the economic consequences of Mexican migration to the United States, how and why multinational firms globalize their production activities, and the factors that shape countries' export capabilities. In his recent work, he studied the impact of globalization on wages, the fiscal and labor-market consequences of immigration, and the implications of trade reform for regional economies. His most recent book is *Immigration Policy and the Welfare System* (Oxford University Press, 2002).

Gary Clyde Hufbauer, Reginald Jones Senior Fellow since 1992, was formerly the Marcus Wallenberg Professor of International Finance Diplomacy at Georgetown University (1985–92), deputy director of the International Law Institute at Georgetown University (1979–81), deputy assistant secretary for international trade and investment policy of the US Treasury (1977–79), and director of the International Tax Staff at the Treasury (1974–76). He is author or coauthor of *The Benefits of Price Convergence* (2002), *World Capital Markets* (2001), and *Western Hemisphere Economic Integration* (1994), and coeditor of *The Ex-Im Bank in the 21st Century* (2001), *Unfinished Business: Telecommunications after the Uruguay Round* (1997), *Flying High: Liberalizing Civil Aviation in the Asia Pacific* (1996), *Fundamental Tax Reform and Border Tax Adjustments* (1996), *US Taxation of International Income* (1992), *Measuring the Costs of Protection in the United States* (1994), *NAFTA: An Assessment* (rev. 1993), *North American Free Trade* (1992), and *Economic Sanctions Reconsidered* (2d ed., 1990).

Lori G. Kletzer, senior fellow, has been associated with the Institute since 2000. She is an associate professor of economics at the University of California, Santa Cruz (UCSC). Before joining UCSC, she was a faculty member at Williams College. She has also taught at the University of Washington and was a visiting fellow at the Brookings Institution. Her research has been published in a number of professional journals including the *American Economic Review*, *Journal of Economic Perspectives*, and *Industrial Relations*. She is the author or coauthor of *Workers at Risk: Job Loss from Apparel, Textiles, Footwear, and Furniture* (forthcoming) and *Job Losses from Imports: Measuring the Costs* (2001).

Nicholas R. Lardy, senior fellow since 2003, was a senior fellow in the Foreign Policy Studies Program at the Brookings Institution from 1995 to 2003 and also served as interim director of the program in 2001. He was the director of the Henry M. Jackson School of International Studies at the University of Washington from 1991 to 1995. From 1997 through the spring of 2000, he was the Frederick Frank Adjunct Professor of International Trade and Finance at the Yale University School of Management. His books include *Prospects for a US-Taiwan Free Trade Agreement* (2004), *Integrating China into the Global Economy* (Brookings Institution Press, 2002), *China's Unfinished Economic Revolution* (Brookings Institution Press, 1998), *China in the World Economy* (1994), *Foreign Trade and Economic Reform in China, 1978–1990* (Cambridge University Press, 1992; paperback, 1993), *Agriculture in China's Modern Economic Development* (Cambridge University Press, 1983), and *Economic Growth and Distribution in China* (Cambridge University Press, 1978).

Catherine L. Mann, senior fellow since 1997, held several posts at the Federal Reserve Board of Governors (1984–87 and 1989–97), including assistant director and special assistant to the staff director, International Finance Division (1994–97). She was a senior economist on the staff of the President's Council of Economic Advisers (1991–92), the principal staff member for the chief economist of the World Bank (1988–89), and a Ford Foundation Fellow at the National Bureau of Economic Research (1987). She is an adjunct professor at the Owen School of Management at Vanderbilt University and has also taught at the University of Chicago, Princeton University, University of Maryland, Georgetown University, Boston College, and Massachusetts Institute of Technology. She has written numerous articles on international trade and finance. She is the coauthor of *APEC and the New Economy* (2002) and *Global Electronic Commerce: A Policy Primer* (2000) and author of *High Technology and the Globalization of America* (forthcoming) and *Is the U.S. Trade Deficit Sustainable?* (1999).

Michael Mussa, senior fellow since 2002, served as economic counselor and director of the Department of Research at the International Monetary Fund from 1991 to 2001, where he was responsible for advising the management of the Fund and the Fund's Executive Board on broad issues of economic policy and for providing analysis of ongoing developments in the world economy. He was a member of the US Council of Economic Advisers from August 1986 to September 1988, and a member of the faculty of the Graduate School of Business of the University of Chicago (1976–91) and of the Department of Economics at the University of Rochester (1971–76). During this period, he also served as a visiting faculty member at the Graduate Center of the City University of New York, the London School of Economics, and the Graduate Institute of International Studies in Geneva, Switzerland. He is the author of *Argentina and the Fund: From Triumph to Tragedy* (2002).

J. David Richardson, senior fellow since 1991, is also professor of economics in the Maxwell School of Citizenship and Public Affairs at Syracuse University. He is the author or coauthor of *Global Forces, American Faces: US Economic Globalization at the Grass Roots* (forthcoming), *Why Global Commitment Really Matters!* (2001), *Global Competition Policy* (1997), *Competition Policies for the Global Economy* (1997), *Why Exports Really Matter!* (1995), *Why Exports Matter: More!* (1996), and *Sizing Up US Export Disincentives* (1993). He directs the Institute's Globalization Balance Sheet Project.

Howard Rosen is the executive director of the Trade Adjustment Assistance Coalition. He was a research associate at the Institute (1982–87, 1989–91), executive director of the Competitiveness Policy Council, and economist with the Bank of Israel (1987–89) and the US Department of Labor (1978–81). He is coauthor of *Trade Policy for Troubled Industries* (1986).

Jeffrey J. Schott, senior fellow, has been associated with the Institute since 1984. He was a senior associate at the Carnegie Endowment for International Peace (1982–83) and an international economist at the US Treasury (1974–82). He is the author, coauthor, or editor of *Free Trade Agreements: US Strategies and Priorities* (2004), *Prospects for Free Trade in the Americas* (2001), *Free Trade between Korea and the United States?* (2001), *The WTO after Seattle* (2000), *NAFTA and the Environment: Seven Years Later* (2000), *Launching New Global Trade Talks: An Action Agenda* (1998), *Restarting Fast Track* (1998), *The World Trading System: Challenges Ahead* (1996), *WTO 2000: Setting the Course for World Trade* (1996), *The Uruguay Round: An Assessment* (1994), *Western Hemisphere Economic Integration* (1994), *NAFTA: An Assessment* (rev. ed., 1993), *North American Free Trade: Issues and Recommendations* (1992), and *Economic Sanctions Reconsidered* (2d ed., 1990).

Edwin M. Truman, senior fellow since 2001, was assistant secretary of the Treasury for international affairs (1998–2000). He was staff director of the Division of International Finance of the Board of Governors of the Federal Reserve System (1987–98) and was director of the division from 1977 to 1987. From 1983 to 1998, he was one of three economists on the staff of the Federal Open Market Committee. He has been a member of numerous international working groups on international economic and financial issues. He is the author of *Inflation Targeting in the World Economy* (2003) and coauthor of *Chasing Dirty Money: The Fight Against Money Laundering* (2004).

Philip K. Verleger Jr., senior fellow, has been associated with the Institute since 1986. He was a staff economist at the Council of Economic Advisers (1976–77); director, Office of Domestic Energy Policy at the US Treasury (1977–79); and senior research scholar and lecturer at the School of Organization and Management at Yale University (1979–82). He is the author of numerous studies on international energy and petroleum issues, including *Adjusting to Volatile Energy Prices* (1993) and *Oil Markets in Turmoil* (1982).

John Williamson, senior fellow since 1981, was a professor of economics at Pontifícia Universidade Católica do Rio de Janeiro (1978–81), University of Warwick (1970–77), Massachusetts Institute of Technology (1967, 1980), University of York (1963–68), and Princeton University (1962–63). He also served as adviser to the International Monetary Fund (1972–74), economic consultant to the UK Treasury (1968–70), and senior economist for the South Asia Region of the World Bank (1996–99) while on leave from the Institute. He is author, coauthor, or editor of numerous studies on international monetary and development issues, including *Dollar Adjustment: How Far? Against What?* (2004), *After the Washington Consensus: Restarting Growth and Reform in Latin America* (2003), *Dollar Overvaluation and the World Economy* (2003), *Delivering on Debt Relief: From IMF Gold to a New Aid Architecture* (2002), *Exchange Rate Regimes for Emerging Markets: Reviving the Intermediate Option* (2000), *The Crawling Band as an Exchange Rate Regime: Lessons from Chile, Colombia, and Israel* (1996), *What Role for Currency Boards?* (1995), *Estimating Equilibrium Exchange Rates* (1994), and *The Political Economy of Policy Reform* (1994).

Index

Other Publications from the **Institute for International Economics**

WORKING PAPERS

94-1 **APEC and Regional Trading Arrangments in the Pacific** Jeffrey A. Frankel with Sang-Jin Wei and Ernesto Stein

94-2 **Towards an Asia Pacific Investment Code** Edward M. Graham

94-3 **Merchandise Trade in the APEC Region: Is There Scope for Liberalization on an MFN Basis?** Paul Wonnacott

94-4 **The Automotive Industry in Southeast Asia: Can Protection Be Made Less Costly?** Paul Wonnacott

94-5 **Implications of Asian Economic Growth** Marcus Noland

95-1 **APEC: The Bogor Declaration and the Path Ahead** C. Fred Bergsten

95-2 **From Bogor to Miami . . . and Beyond: Regionalism in the Asia Pacific and the Western Hemisphere** Jeffrey J. Schott

95-3 **Has Asian Export Performance Been Unique?** Marcus Noland

95-4 **Association of Southeast Asian Nations (ASEAN) and ASEAN Free Trade Area (AFTA): Chronology and Statistics** Gautam Jaggi

95-5 **The North Korean Economy** Marcus Noland

95-6 **China and the International Economic System** Marcus Noland

96-1 **APEC after Osaka: Toward Free Trade by 2010/2020** C. Fred Bergsten

96-2 **Public Policy, Private Preferences, and the Japanese Trade Pattern** Marcus Noland

96-3 **German Lessons for Korea: The Economics of Unification** Marcus Noland

96-4 **Research and Development Activities and Trade Specialization in Japan** Marcus Noland

96-5 **China's Economic Reforms: Chronology and Statistics** Gautam Jaggi, Mary Rundle, Daniel Rosen, and Yuichi Takahashi

96-6 **US-China Economic Relations** Marcus Noland

96-7 **The Market Structure Benefits of Trade and Investment Liberalization** Raymond Atje and Gary Hufbauer

96-8 **The Future of US-Korea Economic Relations** Marcus Noland

96-9 **Competition Policies in the Dynamic Industrializing Economies: The Case of China, Korea, and Chinese Taipei** Edward M. Graham

96-10 **Modeling Economic Reform in North Korea** Marcus Noland, Sherman Robinson, and Monica Scatasta

96-11 **Trade, Investment, and Economic Conflict Between the United States and Asia** Marcus Noland

96-12 **APEC in 1996 and Beyond: The Subic Summit** C. Fred Bergsten

96-13 **Some Unpleasant Arithmetic Concerning Unification** Marcus Noland

96-14 **Restructuring Korea's Financial Sector for Greater Competitiveness** Marcus Noland

96-15 **Competitive Liberalization and Global Free Trade: A Vision for the 21st Century** C. Fred Bergsten

97-1 **Chasing Phantoms: The Political Economy of USTR** Marcus Noland

97-2 **US-Japan Civil Aviation: Prospects for Progress** Jacqueline McFadyen

97-3 **Open Regionalism** C. Fred Bergsten

97-4 **Lessons from the Bundesbank on the Occasion of Its 40th (and Second to Last?) Birthday** Adam S. Posen

97-5 **The Economics of Korean Unification** Marcus Noland, Sherman Robinson, and Li-Gang Liu

98-1 **The Costs and Benefits of Korean Unification** Marcus Noland, Sherman Robinson, and Li-Gang Liu

98-2 **Asian Competitive Devaluations** Li-Gang Liu, Marcus Noland, Sherman Robinson, and Zhi Wang

98-3 **Fifty Years of the GATT/WTO: Lessons from the Past for Strategies for the Future** C. Fred Bergsten

98-4 **NAFTA Supplemental Agreements: Four Year Review** Jacqueline McFadyen

98-5 **Local Government Spending: Solving the Mystery of Japanese Fiscal Packages** Hiroko Ishii and Erika Wada

98-6 **The Global Economic Effects of the Japanese Crisis** Marcus Noland, Sherman Robinson, and Zhi Wang

99-1 **Rigorous Speculation: The Collapse and Revival of the North Korean Economy** Marcus Noland, Sherman Robinson, and Tao Wang

99-2 **Famine in North Korea: Causes and Cures** Marcus Noland, Sherman Robinson, and Tao Wang

99-3 **Competition Policy and FDI: A Solution in Search of a Problem?** Marcus Noland
99-4 **The Continuing Asian Financial Crisis: Global Adjustment and Trade** Marcus Noland, Sherman Robinson, and Zhi Wang
99-5 **Why EMU Is Irrelevant for the German Economy** Adam S. Posen
99-6 **The Global Trading System and the Developing Countries in 2000** C. Fred Bergsten
99-7 **Modeling Korean Unification** Marcus Noland, Sherman Robinson, and Tao Wang
99-8 **Sovereign Liquidity Crisis: The Strategic Case for a Payments Standstill** Marcus Miller and Lei Zhang
99-9 **The Case for Joint Management of Exchange Rate Flexibility** C. Fred Bergsten, Olivier Davanne, and Pierre Jacquet
99-10 **Does Talk Matter After All? Inflation Targeting and Central Bank Behavior** Kenneth N. Kuttner and Adam S. Posen
99-11 **Hazards and Precautions: Tales of International Finance** Gary Clyde Hufbauer and Erika Wada
99-12 **The Globalization of Services: What Has Happened? What Are the Implications?** Gary Clyde Hufbauer and Tony Warren
00-1 **Regulatory Standards in the WTO: Comparing Intellectual Property Rights with Competition Policy, Environmental Protection, and Core Labor Standards** Keith Maskus
00-2 **International Economic Agreements and the Constitution** Richard M. Goodman and John M. Frost
00-3 **Electronic Commerce in Developing Countries: Issues for Domestic Policy and WTO Negotiations** Catherine L. Mann
00-4 **The New Asian Challenge** C. Fred Bergsten
00-5 **How the Sick Man Avoided Pneumonia: The Philippines in the Asian Financial Crisis** Marcus Noland
00-6 **Inflation, Monetary Transparency, and G3 Exchange Rate Volatility** Kenneth N. Kuttner and Adam S. Posen
00-7 **Transatlantic Issues in Electronic Commerce** Catherine L. Mann
00-8 **Strengthening the International Financial Architecture: Where Do We Stand?** Morris Goldstein
00-9 **On Currency Crises and Contagion** Marcel Fratzscher
01-1 **Price Level Convergence and Inflation in Europe** John H. Rogers, Gary Clyde Hufbauer, and Erika Wada
01-2 **Subsidies, Market Closure, Cross-Border Investment, and Effects on Competition: The Case of FDI in the Telecommunications Sector** Edward M. Graham
01-3 **Foreign Direct Investment in China: Effects on Growth and Economic Performance** Edward M. Graham and Erika Wada
01-4 **IMF Structural Conditionality: How Much Is Too Much?** Morris Goldstein
01-5 **Unchanging Innovation and Changing Economic Performance in Japan** Adam S. Posen
01-6 **Rating Banks in Emerging Markets: What Credit Rating Agencies Should Learn From Financial Indicators** Liliana Rojas-Suarez
01-7 **Beyond Bipolar: A Three-Dimensional Assessment of Monetary Frameworks** Kenneth N. Kuttner and Adam S. Posen
01-8 **Finance and Changing US-Japan Relations: Convergence Without Leverage—Until Now** Adam S. Posen
01-9 **Macroeconomic Implications of the New Economy** Martin Neil Baily
01-10 **Can International Capital Standards Strengthen Banks in Emerging Markets?** Liliana Rojas-Suarez
02-1 **Moral Hazard and the US Stock Market: Analyzing the "Greenspan Put"?** Marcus Miller, Paul Weller, and Lei Zhang
02-2 **Passive Savers and Fiscal Policy Effectiveness in Japan** Kenneth N. Kuttner and Adam S. Posen
02-3 **Home Bias, Transaction Costs, and Prospects for the Euro: A More Detailed Analysis** Catherine L. Mann and Ellen E. Meade
02-4 **Toward a Sustainable FTAA: Does Latin America Meet the Necessary Financial Preconditions?** Liliana Rojas-Suarez
02-5 **Assessing Globalization's Critics: "Talkers Are No Good Doers???"** Kimberly Ann Elliott, Debayani Kar, and J. David Richardson
02-6 **Economic Issues Raised by Treatment of Takings under NAFTA Chapter 11** Edward M. Graham

03-1 **Debt Sustainability, Brazil, and the IMF** Morris Goldstein
03-2 **Is Germany Turning Japanese?** Adam S. Posen
03-3 **Survival of the Best Fit: Exposure to Low-Wage Countries and the (Uneven) Growth of US Manufacturing Plants** Andrew B. Bernard, J. Bradford Jensen, and Peter K. Schott
03-4 **Falling Trade Costs, Heterogeneous Firms, and Industry Dynamics** Andrew B. Bernard, J. Bradford Jensen, and Peter K. Schott
03-5 **Famine and Reform in North Korea** Marcus Noland
03-6 **Empirical Investigations in Inflation Targeting** Yifan Hu
03-7 **Labor Standards and the Free Trade Area of the Americas** Kimberly Ann Elliott
03-8 **Religion, Culture, and Economic Performance** Marcus Noland
03-9 **It Takes More than a Bubble to Become Japan** Adam S. Posen
03-10 **The Difficulty of Discerning What's Too Tight: Taylor Rules and Japanese Monetary Policy** Adam S. Posen and Kenneth N. Kuttner
04-1 **Adjusting China's Exchange Rate Policies** Morris Goldstein
04-2 **Popular Attitudes, Globalization, and Risk** Marcus Noland
04-3 **Selective Intervention and Growth: The Case of Korea** Marcus Noland

POLICY BRIEFS

98-1 **The Asian Financial Crisis** Morris Goldstein
98-2 **The New Agenda with China** C. Fred Bergsten
98-3 **Exchange Rates for the Dollar, Yen, and Euro** Simon Wren-Lewis
98-4 **Sanctions-Happy USA** Gary Clyde Hufbauer
98-5 **The Depressing News from Asia** Marcus Noland, Sherman Robinson, and Zhi Wang
98-6 **The Transatlantic Economic Partnership** Ellen L. Frost
98-7 **A New Strategy for the Global Crisis** C. Fred Bergsten
98-8 **Reviving the "Asian Monetary Fund"** C. Fred Bergsten
99-1 **Implementing Japanese Recovery** Adam S. Posen
99-2 **A Radical but Workable Restructuring Plan for South Korea** Edward M. Graham
99-3 **Crawling Bands or Monitoring Bands: How to Manage Exchange Rates in a World of Capital Mobility** John Williamson
99-4 **Market Mechanisms to Reduce the Need for IMF Bailouts** Catherine L. Mann
99-5 **Steel Quotas: A Rigged Lottery** Gary Clyde Hufbauer and Erika Wada
99-6 **China and the World Trade Organization: An Economic Balance Sheet** Daniel H. Rosen
99-7 **Trade and Income Distribution: The Debate and New Evidence** William R. Cline
99-8 **Preserve the Exchange Stabilization Fund** C. Randall Henning
99-9 **Nothing to Fear but Fear (of Inflation) Itself** Adam S. Posen
99-10 **World Trade After Seattle: Implications for the United States** Gary Clyde Hufbauer
00-1 **The Next Trade Policy Battle** C. Fred Bergsten
00-2 **Decision-making in the WTO** Jeffrey J. Schott and Jayashree Watal
00-3 **American Access to China's Market: The Congressional Vote on PNTR** Gary Clyde Hufbauer and Daniel H. Rosen
00-4 **Third Oil Shock: Real or Imaginary? Consequences and Policy Alternatives** Philip K. Verleger Jr.
00-5 **The Role of the IMF: A Guide to the Reports** John Williamson
00-6 **The ILO and Enforcement of Core Labor Standards** Kimberly Ann Elliott
00-7 **"No" to Foreign Telecoms Equals "No" to the New Economy!** Gary Clyde Hufbauer and Edward M. Graham
01-1 **Brunei: A Turning Point for APEC?** C. Fred Bergsten
01-2 **A Prescription to Relieve Worker Anxiety** Lori G. Kletzer and Robert E. Litan
01-3 **The US Export-Import Bank: Time for an Overhaul** Gary Clyde Hufbauer

01-4 **Japan 2001—Decisive Action or Financial Panic**
Adam S. Posen

01-5 **Fin(d)ing Our Way on Trade and Labor Standards?**
Kimberly Ann Elliott

01-6 **Prospects for Transatlantic Competition Policy**
Mario Monti

01-7 **The International Implications of Paying Down the Debt**
Edwin M. Truman

01-8 **Dealing with Labor and Environment Issues in Trade Promotion Legislation** Kimberly Ann Elliott

01-9 **Steel: Big Problems, Better Solutions**
Gary Clyde Hufbauer and Ben Goodrich

01-10 **Economic Policy Following the Terrorist Attacks**
Martin Neil Baily

01-11 **Using Sanctions to Fight Terrorism**
Gary Clyde Hufbauer, Jeffrey J. Schott, and Barbara Oegg

02-1 **Time for a Grand Bargain in Steel?**
Gary Clyde Hufbauer and Ben Goodrich

02-2 **Prospects for the World Economy: From Global Recession to Global Recovery** Michael Mussa

02-3 **Sovereign Debt Restructuring: New Articles, New Contracts—or No Change?** Marcus Miller

02-4 **Support the Ex-Im Bank: It Has Work to Do!** Gary Clyde Hufbauer and Ben Goodrich

02-5 **The Looming Japanese Crisis**
Adam S. Posen

02-6 **Capital-Market Access: New Frontier in the Sanctions Debate**
Gary C. Hufbauer and Barbara Oegg

02-7 **Is Brazil Next?**
John Williamson

02-8 **Further Financial Services Liberalization in the Doha Round?**
Wendy Dobson

02-9 **Global Economic Prospects**
Michael Mussa

02-10 **The Foreign Sales Corporation: Reaching the Last Act?**
Gary Clyde Hufbauer

03-1 **Steel Policy: The Good, the Bad, and the Ugly** Gary Clyde Hufbauer and Ben Goodrich

03-2 **Global Economic Prospects: Through the Fog of Uncertainty**
Michael Mussa

03-3 **Economic Leverage and the North Korean Nuclear Crisis**
Kimberly Ann Elliott

03-4 **The Impact of Economic Sanctions on US Trade: Andrew Rose's Gravity Model** Gary Clyde Hufbauer and Barbara Oegg

03-5 **Reforming OPIC for the 21st Century**
Theodore H. Moran and C. Fred Bergsten

03-6 **The Strategic Importance of US-Korea Economic Relations**
Marcus Noland

03-7 **Rules Against Earnings Stripping: Wrong Answer to Corporate Inversions**
Gary Clyde Hufbauer and Ariel Assa

03-8 **More Pain, More Gain: Politics and Economics of Eliminating Tariffs**
Gary Clyde Hufbauer and Ben Goodrich

03-9 **EU Accession and the Euro: Close Together or Far Apart?**
Peter B. Kenen and Ellen E. Meade

03-10 **Next Move in Steel: Revocation or Retaliation?** Gary Clyde Hufbauer and Ben Goodrich

03-11 **Globalization of IT Services and White Collar Jobs: The Next Wave of Productivity Growth**
Catherine L. Mann

04-1 **This Far and No Farther? Nudging Agricultural Reform Forward**
Tim Josling and Dale Hathaway

04-2 **Labor Standards, Development, and CAFTA**
Kimberly Ann Elliott

04-3 **Senator Kerry on Corporate Tax Reform: Right Diagnosis, Wrong Prescription** Gary Clyde Hufbauer and Paul Grieco

04-4 **Islam, Globalization, and Economic Performance in the Middle East**
Marcus Noland and Howard Pack

04-5 **China Bashing 2004**
Gary Clyde Hufbauer and Yee Wong

04-6 **What Went Right in Japan**
Adam S. Posen

04-7 **What Kind of Landing for the Chinese Economy?** Morris Goldstein and Nicholas R. Lardy

* = out of print

POLICY ANALYSES IN INTERNATIONAL ECONOMICS Series

1 **The Lending Policies of the International Monetary Fund*** John Williamson
August 1982 ISBN 0-88132-000-5

2 **"Reciprocity": A New Approach to World Trade Policy?*** William R. Cline
September 1982 ISBN 0-88132-001-3

3 **Trade Policy in the 1980s***
C. Fred Bergsten and William R. Cline
November 1982 ISBN 0-88132-002-1

4 **International Debt and the Stability of the World Economy*** William R. Cline
September 1983 ISBN 0-88132-010-2

5 **The Exchange Rate System,*** Second Edition
John Williamson
Sept. 1983, rev. June 1985 ISBN 0-88132-034-X

6 **Economic Sanctions in Support of Foreign Policy Goals***
Gary Clyde Hufbauer and Jeffrey J. Schott
October 1983 ISBN 0-88132-014-5

7 **A New SDR Allocation?*** John Williamson
March 1984 ISBN 0-88132-028-5

8 **An International Standard for Monetary Stabilization*** Ronald L. McKinnon
March 1984 ISBN 0-88132-018-8

9 **The Yen/Dollar Agreement: Liberalizing Japanese Capital Markets*** Jeffrey A. Frankel
December 1984 ISBN 0-88132-035-8

10 **Bank Lending to Developing Countries: The Policy Alternatives*** C. Fred Bergsten, William R. Cline, and John Williamson
April 1985 ISBN 0-88132-032-3

11 **Trading for Growth: The Next Round of Trade Negotiations***
Gary Clyde Hufbauer and Jeffrey J. Schott
September 1985 ISBN 0-88132-033-1

12 **Financial Intermediation Beyond the Debt Crisis*** Donald R. Lessard, John Williamson
September 1985 ISBN 0-88132-021-8

13 **The United States-Japan Economic Problem***
C. Fred Bergsten and William R. Cline
October 1985, 2d ed. January 1987
ISBN 0-88132-060-9

14 **Deficits and the Dollar: The World Economy at Risk*** Stephen Marris
December 1985, 2d ed. November 1987
ISBN 0-88132-067-6

15 **Trade Policy for Troubled Industries***
Gary Clyde Hufbauer and Howard R. Rosen
March 1986 ISBN 0-88132-020-X

16 **The United States and Canada: The Quest for Free Trade*** Paul Wonnacott, with an appendix by John Williamson
March 1987 ISBN 0-88132-056-0

17 **Adjusting to Success: Balance of Payments Policy in the East Asian NICs***
Bela Balassa and John Williamson
June 1987, rev. April 1990 ISBN 0-88132-101-X

18 **Mobilizing Bank Lending to Debtor Countries*** William R. Cline
June 1987 ISBN 0-88132-062-5

19 **Auction Quotas and United States Trade Policy*** C. Fred Bergsten, Kimberly Ann Elliott, Jeffrey J. Schott, and Wendy E. Takacs
September 1987 ISBN 0-88132-050-1

20 **Agriculture and the GATT: Rewriting the Rules*** Dale E. Hathaway
September 1987 ISBN 0-88132-052-8

21 **Anti-Protection: Changing Forces in United States Trade Politics***
I. M. Destler and John S. Odell
September 1987 ISBN 0-88132-043-9

22 **Targets and Indicators: A Blueprint for the International Coordination of Economic Policy**
John Williamson and Marcus H. Miller
September 1987 ISBN 0-88132-051-X

23 **Capital Flight: The Problem and Policy Responses*** Donald R. Lessard and John Williamson
December 1987 ISBN 0-88132-059-5

24 **United States-Canada Free Trade: An Evaluation of the Agreement***
Jeffrey J. Schott
April 1988 ISBN 0-88132-072-2

25 **Voluntary Approaches to Debt Relief***
John Williamson
Sept.1988, rev. May 1989 ISBN 0-88132-098-6

26 **American Trade Adjustment: The Global Impact*** William R. Cline
March 1989 ISBN 0-88132-095-1

27 **More Free Trade Areas?***
Jeffrey J. Schott
May 1989 ISBN 0-88132-085-4

28 **The Progress of Policy Reform in Latin America*** John Williamson
January 1990 ISBN 0-88132-100-1

29 **The Global Trade Negotiations: What Can Be Achieved?*** Jeffrey J. Schott
September 1990 ISBN 0-88132-137-0

30 **Economic Policy Coordination: Requiem or Prologue?*** Wendy Dobson
April 1991 ISBN 0-88132-102-8

31 **The Economic Opening of Eastern Europe***
John Williamson
May 1991 ISBN 0-88132-186-9
32 **Eastern Europe and the Soviet Union in the World Economy***
Susan M. Collins and Dani Rodrik
May 1991 ISBN 0-88132-157-5
33 **African Economic Reform: The External Dimension*** Carol Lancaster
June 1991 ISBN 0-88132-096-X
34 **Has the Adjustment Process Worked?***
Paul R. Krugman
October 1991 ISBN 0-88132-116-8
35 **From Soviet disUnion to Eastern Economic Community?***
Oleh Havrylyshyn and John Williamson
October 1991 ISBN 0-88132-192-3
36 **Global Warming The Economic Stakes***
William R. Cline
May 1992 ISBN 0-88132-172-9
37 **Trade and Payments After Soviet Disintegration*** John Williamson
une 1992 ISBN 0-88132-173-7
38 **Trade and Migration: NAFTA and Agriculture*** Philip L. Martin
October 1993 ISBN 0-88132-201-6
39 **The Exchange Rate System and the IMF: A Modest Agenda** Morris Goldstein
June 1995 ISBN 0-88132-219-9
40 **What Role for Currency Boards?**
John Williamson
September 1995 ISBN 0-88132-222-9
41 **Predicting External Imbalances for the United States and Japan*** William R. Cline
September 1995 ISBN 0-88132-220-2
42 **Standards and APEC: An Action Agenda***
John S. Wilson
October 1995 ISBN 0-88132-223-7
43 **Fundamental Tax Reform and Border Tax Adjustments*** Gary Clyde Hufbauer
January 1996 ISBN 0-88132-225-3
44 **Global Telecom Talks: A Trillion Dollar Deal***
Ben A. Petrazzini
June 1996 ISBN 0-88132-230-X
45 **WTO 2000: Setting the Course for World Trade** Jeffrey J. Schott
September 1996 ISBN 0-88132-234-2
46 **The National Economic Council: A Work in Progress *** I. M. Destler
November 1996 ISBN 0-88132-239-3
47 **The Case for an International Banking Standard** Morris Goldstein
April 1997 ISBN 0-88132-244-X
48 **Transatlantic Trade: A Strategic Agenda***
Ellen L. Frost
May 1997 ISBN 0-88132-228-8
49 **Cooperating with Europe's Monetary Union**
C. Randall Henning
May 1997 ISBN 0-88132-245-8
50 **Renewing Fast Track Legislation*** I. M. Destler
September 1997 ISBN 0-88132-252-0
51 **Competition Policies for the Global Economy**
Edward M. Graham and J. David Richardson
November 1997 ISBN 0-88132 -249-0
52 **Improving Trade Policy Reviews in the World Trade Organization** Donald Keesing
April 1998 ISBN 0-88132-251-2
53 **Agricultural Trade Policy: Completing the Reform** Timothy Josling
April 1998 ISBN 0-88132-256-3
54 **Real Exchange Rates for the Year 2000**
Simon Wren Lewis and Rebecca Driver
April 1998 ISBN 0-88132-253-9
55 **The Asian Financial Crisis: Causes, Cures, and Systemic Implications** Morris Goldstein
June 1998 ISBN 0-88132-261-X
56 **Global Economic Effects of the Asian Currency Devaluations**
Marcus Noland, LiGang Liu, Sherman Robinson, and Zhi Wang
July 1998 ISBN 0-88132-260-1
57 **The Exchange Stabilization Fund: Slush Money or War Chest?** C. Randall Henning
May 1999 ISBN 0-88132-271-7
58 **The New Politics of American Trade: Trade, Labor, and the Environment**
I. M. Destler and Peter J. Balint
October 1999 ISBN 0-88132-269-5
59 **Congressional Trade Votes: From NAFTA Approval to Fast Track Defeat**
Robert E. Baldwin and Christopher S. Magee
February 2000 ISBN 0-88132-267-9
60 **Exchange Rate Regimes for Emerging Markets: Reviving the Intermediate Option**
John Williamson
September 2000 ISBN 0-88132-293-8
61 **NAFTA and the Environment: Seven Years Later** Gary Clyde Hufbauer, Daniel Esty, Diana Orejas, Luis Rubio, and Jeffrey J. Schott
October 2000 ISBN 0-88132-299-7
62 **Free Trade between Korea and the United States?** Inbom Choi and Jeffrey J. Schott
April 2001 ISBN 0-88132-311-X
63 **New Regional Trading Arrangements in the Asia Pacific?**
Robert Scollay and John P. Gilbert
May 2001 ISBN 0-88132-302-0
64 **Parental Supervision: The New Paradigm for Foreign Direct Investment and Development** Theodore H. Moran
August 2001 ISBN 0-88132-313-6

65 **The Benefits of Price Convergence: Speculative Calculations**
Gary Clyde Hufbauer, Erika Wada, and Tony Warren
December 2001 ISBN 0-88132-333-0

66 **Managed Floating Plus**
Morris Goldstein
March 2002 ISBN 0-88132-336-5

67 **Argentina and the Fund: From Triumph to Tragedy** Michael Mussa
July 2002 ISBN 0-88132-339-X

68 **East Asian Financial Cooperation**
C. Randall Henning
September 2002 ISBN 0-88132-338-1

69 **Reforming OPIC for the 21st Century**
Theodore H. Moran
May 2003 ISBN 0-88132-342-X

70 **Awakening Monster: The Alien Tort Statute of 1789**
Gary C. Hufbauer and Nicholas Mitrokostas
July 2003 ISBN 0-88132-366-7

71 **Korea after Kim Jong-il**
Marcus Noland
January 2004 ISBN 0-88132-373-X

72 **Roots of Competitiveness: China's Evolving Agriculture Interests** Daniel H. Rosen, Scott Rozelle, and Jikun Huang
July 2004 ISBN 0-88132-376-4

73 **Prospects for a US-Taiwan FTA**
Nicholas R. Lardy and Daniel H. Rosen
December 2004 ISBN 0-88132-367-5

BOOKS

IMF Conditionality* John Williamson, editor
1983 ISBN 0-88132-006-4

Trade Policy in the 1980s* William R. Cline, editor
1983 ISBN 0-88132-031-5

Subsidies in International Trade*
Gary Clyde Hufbauer and Joanna Shelton Erb
1984 ISBN 0-88132-004-8

International Debt: Systemic Risk and Policy Response* William R. Cline
1984 ISBN 0-88132-015-3

Trade Protection in the United States: 31 Case Studies* Gary Clyde Hufbauer, Diane E. Berliner, and Kimberly Ann Elliott
1986 ISBN 0-88132-040-4

Toward Renewed Economic Growth in Latin America* Bela Balassa, Gerardo M. Bueno, Pedro-Pablo Kuczynski, and Mario Henrique Simonsen
1986 ISBN 0-88132-045-5

Capital Flight and Third World Debt*
Donald R. Lessard and John Williamson, editors
1987 ISBN 0-88132-053-6

The Canada-United States Free Trade Agreement: The Global Impact*
Jeffrey J. Schott and Murray G. Smith, editors
1988 ISBN 0-88132-073-0

World Agricultural Trade: Building a Consensus*
William M. Miner and Dale E. Hathaway, editors
1988 ISBN 0-88132-071-3

Japan in the World Economy*
Bela Balassa and Marcus Noland
1988 ISBN 0-88132-041-2

America in the World Economy: A Strategy for the 1990s* C. Fred Bergsten
1988 ISBN 0-88132-089-7

Managing the Dollar: From the Plaza to the Louvre* Yoichi Funabashi
1988, 2d. ed. 1989 ISBN 0-88132-097-8

United States External Adjustment and the World Economy* William R. Cline
May 1989 ISBN 0-88132-048-X

Free Trade Areas and U.S. Trade Policy*
Jeffrey J. Schott, editor
May *1989* ISBN 0-88132-094-3

Dollar Politics: Exchange Rate Policymaking in the United States*
I. M. Destler and C. Randall Henning
September 1989 ISBN 0-88132-079-X

Latin American Adjustment: How Much Has Happened?* John Williamson, editor
April 1990 ISBN 0-88132-125-7

The Future of World Trade in Textiles and Apparel* William R. Cline
1987, 2d ed. June *1999* ISBN 0-88132-110-9

Completing the Uruguay Round: A Results-Oriented Approach to the GATT Trade Negotiations* Jeffrey J. Schott, editor
September 1990 ISBN 0-88132-130-3

Economic Sanctions Reconsidered (2 volumes)
Economic Sanctions Reconsidered: Supplemental Case Histories
Gary Clyde Hufbauer, Jeffrey J. Schott, and Kimberly Ann Elliott
1985, 2d ed. Dec. 1990 ISBN cloth 0-88132-115-X
ISBN paper 0-88132-105-2

Economic Sanctions Reconsidered: History and Current Policy Gary Clyde Hufbauer, Jeffrey J. Schott, and Kimberly Ann Elliott
December 1990 ISBN cloth 0-88132-140-0
ISBN paper 0-88132-136-2

Pacific Basin Developing Countries: Prospects for the Future* Marcus Noland
January 1991 ISBN cloth 0-88132-141-9
ISBN paper 0-88132-081-1

Currency Convertibility in Eastern Europe*
John Williamson, editor
October 1991 ISBN 0-88132-128-1

International Adjustment and Financing: The Lessons of 1985-1991* C. Fred Bergsten, editor
January 1992 ISBN 0-88132-112-5

North American Free Trade: Issues and Recommendations*
Gary Clyde Hufbauer and Jeffrey J. Schott
April 1992 ISBN 0-88132-120-6

Narrowing the U.S. Current Account Deficit*
Allen J. Lenz/*June 1992* ISBN 0-88132-103-6

The Economics of Global Warming
William R. Cline/*June 1992* ISBN 0-88132-132-X
US Taxation of International Income: Blueprint for Reform* Gary Clyde Hufbauer, assisted by Joanna M. van Rooij
October 1992 ISBN 0-88132-134-6
Who's Bashing Whom? Trade Conflict in High-Technology Industries Laura D'Andrea Tyson
November 1992 ISBN 0-88132-106-0
Korea in the World Economy* Il SaKong
January 1993 ISBN 0-88132-183-4
Pacific Dynamism and the International Economic System*
C. Fred Bergsten and Marcus Noland, editors
May 1993 ISBN 0-88132-196-6
Economic Consequences of Soviet Disintegration*
John Williamson, editor
May 1993 ISBN 0-88132-190-7
Reconcilable Differences? United States-Japan Economic Conflict*
C. Fred Bergsten and Marcus Noland
June 1993 ISBN 0-88132-129-X
Does Foreign Exchange Intervention Work?
Kathryn M. Dominguez and Jeffrey A. Frankel
September 1993 ISBN 0-88132-104-4
Sizing Up U.S. Export Disincentives*
J. David Richardson
September 1993 ISBN 0-88132-107-9
NAFTA: An Assessment
Gary Clyde Hufbauer and Jeffrey J. Schott/*rev. ed.*
October 1993 ISBN 0-88132-199-0
Adjusting to Volatile Energy Prices
Philip K. Verleger, Jr.
November 1993 ISBN 0-88132-069-2
The Political Economy of Policy Reform
John Williamson, editor
January 1994 ISBN 0-88132-195-8
Measuring the Costs of Protection in the United States
Gary Clyde Hufbauer and Kimberly Ann Elliott
January 1994 ISBN 0-88132-108-7
The Dynamics of Korean Economic Development*
Cho Soon/*March 1994* ISBN 0-88132-162-1
Reviving the European Union*
C. Randall Henning, Eduard Hochreiter, and Gary Clyde Hufbauer, editors
April 1994 ISBN 0-88132-208-3
China in the World Economy Nicholas R. Lardy
April 1994 ISBN 0-88132-200-8
Greening the GATT: Trade, Environment, and the Future Daniel C. Esty
July 1994 ISBN 0-88132-205-9
Western Hemisphere Economic Integration*
Gary Clyde Hufbauer and Jeffrey J. Schott
July 1994 ISBN 0-88132-159-1
Currencies and Politics in the United States, Germany, and Japan C. Randall Henning
September 1994 ISBN 0-88132-127-3
Estimating Equilibrium Exchange Rates
John Williamson, editor
September 1994 ISBN 0-88132-076-5
Managing the World Economy: Fifty Years After Bretton Woods Peter B. Kenen, editor
September 1994 ISBN 0-88132-212-1
Reciprocity and Retaliation in U.S. Trade Policy
Thomas O. Bayard and Kimberly Ann Elliott
September 1994 ISBN 0-88132-084-6
The Uruguay Round: An Assessment*
Jeffrey J. Schott, assisted by Johanna W. Buurman
November 1994 ISBN 0-88132-206-7
Measuring the Costs of Protection in Japan*
Yoko Sazanami, Shujiro Urata, and Hiroki Kawai
January 1995 ISBN 0-88132-211-3
Foreign Direct Investment in the United States, *3d ed.*, Edward M. Graham and Paul R. Krugman
January 1995 ISBN 0-88132-204-0
The Political Economy of Korea-United States Cooperation*
C. Fred Bergsten and Il SaKong, editors
February 1995 ISBN 0-88132-213-X
International Debt Reexamined* William R. Cline
February 1995 ISBN 0-88132-083-8
American Trade Politics, 3d ed., I. M. Destler
April 1995 ISBN 0-88132-215-6
Managing Official Export Credits: The Quest for a Global Regime* John E. Ray
July 1995 ISBN 0-88132-207-5
Asia Pacific Fusion: Japan's Role in APEC*
Yoichi Funabashi
October 1995 ISBN 0-88132-224-5
Korea-United States Cooperation in the New World Order*
C. Fred Bergsten and Il SaKong, editors
February 1996 ISBN 0-88132-226-1
Why Exports Really Matter!* ISBN 0-88132-221-0
Why Exports Matter More!* ISBN 0-88132-229-6
J. David Richardson and Karin Rindal
July 1995; February 1996
Global Corporations and National Governments
Edward M. Graham
May 1996 ISBN 0-88132-111-7
Global Economic Leadership and the Group of Seven C. Fred Bergsten and C. Randall Henning
May 1996 ISBN 0-88132-218-0
The Trading System After the Uruguay Round*
John Whalley and Colleen Hamilton
July 1996 ISBN 0-88132-131-1
Private Capital Flows to Emerging Markets After the Mexican Crisis* Guillermo A. Calvo, Morris Goldstein, and Eduard Hochreiter
September 1996 ISBN 0-88132-232-6
The Crawling Band as an Exchange Rate Regime: Lessons from Chile, Colombia, and Israel
John Williamson
September 1996 ISBN 0-88132-231-8

Flying High: Liberalizing Civil Aviation in the Asia Pacific*
Gary Clyde Hufbauer and Christopher Findlay
November 1996 ISBN 0-88132-227-X
Measuring the Costs of Visible Protection in Korea* Namdoo Kim
November 1996 ISBN 0-88132-236-9
The World Trading System: Challenges Ahead
Jeffrey J. Schott
December 1996 ISBN 0-88132-235-0
Has Globalization Gone Too Far? Dani Rodrik
March 1997 ISBN cloth 0-88132-243-1
Korea-United States Economic Relationship*
C. Fred Bergsten and Il SaKong, editors
March 1997 ISBN 0-88132-240-7
Summitry in the Americas: A Progress Report
Richard E. Feinberg
April 1997 ISBN 0-88132-242-3
Corruption and the Global Economy
Kimberly Ann Elliott
June 1997 ISBN 0-88132-233-4
Regional Trading Blocs in the World Economic System Jeffrey A. Frankel
October 1997 ISBN 0-88132-202-4
Sustaining the Asia Pacific Miracle: Environmental Protection and Economic Integration Andre Dua and Daniel C. Esty
October 1997 ISBN 0-88132-250-4
Trade and Income Distribution William R. Cline
November 1997 ISBN 0-88132-216-4
Global Competition Policy
Edward M. Graham and J. David Richardson
December 1997 ISBN 0-88132-166-4
Unfinished Business: Telecommunications after the Uruguay Round
Gary Clyde Hufbauer and Erika Wada
December 1997 ISBN 0-88132-257-1
Financial Services Liberalization in the WTO
Wendy Dobson and Pierre Jacquet
June 1998 ISBN 0-88132-254-7
Restoring Japan's Economic Growth
Adam S. Posen
September 1998 ISBN 0-88132-262-8
Measuring the Costs of Protection in China
Zhang Shuguang, Zhang Yansheng, and Wan Zhongxin
November 1998 ISBN 0-88132-247-4
Foreign Direct Investment and Development: The New Policy Agenda for Developing Countries and Economies in Transition
Theodore H. Moran
December 1998 ISBN 0-88132-258-X
Behind the Open Door: Foreign Enterprises in the Chinese Marketplace
Daniel H. Rosen
January 1999 ISBN 0-88132-263-6
Toward A New International Financial Architecture: A Practical Post-Asia Agenda
Barry Eichengreen
February 1999 ISBN 0-88132-270-9
Is the U.S. Trade Deficit Sustainable?
Catherine L. Mann
September 1999 ISBN 0-88132-265-2
Safeguarding Prosperity in a Global Financial System: The Future International Financial Architecture, Independent Task Force Report Sponsored by the Council on Foreign Relations
Morris Goldstein, Project Director
October 1999 ISBN 0-88132-287-3
Avoiding the Apocalypse: The Future of the Two Koreas Marcus Noland
June 2000 ISBN 0-88132-278-4
Assessing Financial Vulnerability: An Early Warning System for Emerging Markets
Morris Goldstein, Graciela Kaminsky, and Carmen Reinhart
June 2000 ISBN 0-88132-237-7
Global Electronic Commerce: A Policy Primer
Catherine L. Mann, Sue E. Eckert, and Sarah Cleeland Knight
July 2000 ISBN 0-88132-274-1
The WTO after Seattle Jeffrey J. Schott, editor
July 2000 ISBN 0-88132-290-3
Intellectual Property Rights in the Global Economy Keith E. Maskus
August 2000 ISBN 0-88132-282-2
The Political Economy of the Asian Financial Crisis Stephan Haggard
August 2000 ISBN 0-88132-283-0
Transforming Foreign Aid: United States Assistance in the 21st Century Carol Lancaster
August 2000 ISBN 0-88132-291-1
Fighting the Wrong Enemy: Antiglobal Activists and Multinational Enterprises Edward M.Graham
September 2000 ISBN 0-88132-272-5
Globalization and the Perceptions of American Workers
Kenneth F. Scheve and Matthew J. Slaughter
March 2001 ISBN 0-88132-295-4
World Capital Markets: Challenge to the G-10
Wendy Dobson and Gary Clyde Hufbauer, assisted by Hyun Koo Cho
May 2001 ISBN 0-88132-301-2
Prospects for Free Trade in the Americas
Jeffrey J. Schott/*August 2001* ISBN 0-88132-275-X
Toward a North American Community: Lessons from the Old World for the New
Robert A. Pastor/*August 2001* ISBN 0-88132-328-4
Measuring the Costs of Protection in Europe: European Commercial Policy in the 2000s
Patrick A. Messerlin
September 2001 ISBN 0-88132-273-3

Job Loss from Imports: Measuring the Costs
Lori G. Kletzer
September 2001 ISBN 0-88132-296-2
No More Bashing: Building a New Japan–United States Economic Relationship C. Fred Bergsten, Takatoshi Ito, and Marcus Noland
October 2001 ISBN 0-88132-286-5
Why Global Commitment Really Matters!
Howard Lewis III and J. David Richardson
October 2001 ISBN 0-88132-298-9
Leadership Selection in the Major Multilaterals
Miles Kahler
November 2001 ISBN 0-88132-335-7
The International Financial Architecture: What's New? What's Missing? Peter Kenen
November 2001 ISBN 0-88132-297-0
Delivering on Debt Relief: From IMF Gold to a New Aid Architecture
John Williamson and Nancy Birdsall, with Brian Deese
April 2002 ISBN 0-88132-331-4
Imagine There's No Country: Poverty, Inequality, and Growth in the Era of Globalization
Surjit S. Bhalla
September 2002 ISBN 0-88132-348-9
Reforming Korea's Industrial Conglomerates
Edward M. Graham
January 2003 ISBN 0-88132-337-3
Industrial Policy in an Era of Globalization: Lessons from Asia
Marcus Noland and Howard Pack
March 2003 ISBN 0-88132-350-0
Reintegrating India with the World Economy
T. N. Srinivasan and Suresh D. Tendulkar
March 2003 ISBN 0-88132-280-6
After the Washington Consensus: Restarting Growth and Reform in Latin America Pedro-Pablo Kuczynski and John Williamson, editors
March 2003 ISBN 0-88132-347-0
The Decline of US Labor Unions and the Role of Trade Robert E. Baldwin
June 2003 ISBN 0-88132-341-1
Can Labor Standards Improve under Globalization?
Kimberly Ann Elliott and Richard B. Freeman
June 2003 ISBN 0-88132-332-2
Crimes and Punishments? Retaliation under the WTO Robert Z. Lawrence
October 2003 ISBN 0-88132-359-4
Inflation Targeting in the World Economy
Edwin M. Truman
October 2003 ISBN 0-88132-345-4
Foreign Direct Investment and Tax Competition John H. Mutti
November 2003 ISBN 0-88132-352-7
Has Globalization Gone Far Enough? The Costs of Fragmented Markets
Scott Bradford and Robert Z. Lawrence
February 2004 ISBN 0-88132-349-7
Food Regulation and Trade: Toward a Safe and Open Global System
Tim Josling, Donna Roberts, and David Orden
March 2004 ISBN 0-88132-346-2
Controlling Currency Mismatches in Emerging Markets
Morris Goldstein and Philip Turner
April 2004 ISBN 0-88132-360-8
Free Trade Agreements: US Strategies and Priorities
Jeffrey J. Schott, editor
April 2004 ISBN 0-88132-361-6
Trade Policy and Global Poverty
William R. Cline
June 2004 ISBN 0-88132-365-9
Bailouts or Bail-ins? Responding to Financial Crises in Emerging Economies
Nouriel Roubini and Brad Setser
August 2004 ISBN 0-88132-371-3
Transforming the European Economy
Martin Neil Baily and Jacob Kirkegaard
September 2004 ISBN 0-88132-343-8
Chasing Dirty Money: The Fight Against Money Laundering
Peter Reuter and Edwin M. Truman
November 2004 ISBN 0-88132-370-5
United States and the World Economy: Foreign Economic Policy for the Next Decade
C. Fred Bergsten
January 2005 ISBN 0-88132-380-2

SPECIAL REPORTS

1 **Promoting World Recovery: A Statement on Global Economic Strategy***
by 26 Economists from Fourteen Countries
December 1982 ISBN 0-88132-013-7
3 **Inflation and Indexation: Argentina, Brazil, and Israel*** John Williamson, editor
March 1985 ISBN 0-88132-037-4
4 **Global Economic Imbalances***
C. Fred Bergsten, editor
March 1986 ISBN 0-88132-042-0
5 **African Debt and Financing***
Carol Lancaster and John Williamson, eds.
May 1986 ISBN 0-88132-044-7
6 **Resolving the Global Economic Crisis: After Wall Street***
by Thirty-three Economists from Thirteen Countries
December 1987 ISBN 0-88132-070-6

7 **World Economic Problems***
Kimberly Ann Elliott/John Williamson, editors
April 1988 ISBN 0-88132-055-2
Reforming World Agricultural Trade*
by Twenty-nine Professionals from Seventeen Countries/*1988* ISBN 0-88132-088-9
8 **Economic Relations Between the United States and Korea: Conflict or Cooperation?***
Thomas O. Bayard and Soogil Young, editors
January 1989 ISBN 0-88132-068-4
9 **Whither APEC? The Progress to Date and Agenda for the Future***
C. Fred Bergsten, editor
October 1997 ISBN 0-88132-248-2
10 **Economic Integration of the Korean Peninsula** Marcus Noland, editor
January 1998 ISBN 0-88132-255-5
11 **Restarting Fast Track***
Jeffrey J. Schott, editor
April 1998 ISBN 0-88132-259-8
12 **Launching New Global Trade Talks: An Action Agenda** Jeffrey J. Schott, editor
September 1998 ISBN 0-88132-266-0
13 **Japan's Financial Crisis and Its Parallels to US Experience**
Ryoichi Mikitani and Adam S. Posen, eds.
September 2000 ISBN 0-88132-289-X
14 **The Ex-Im Bank in the 21st Century: A New Approach** Gary Clyde Hufbauer and Rita M. Rodriguez, editors
January 2001 ISBN 0-88132-300-4
15 **The Korean Diaspora in the World Economy**
C. Fred Bergsten and Inbom Choi, eds.
January 2003 ISBN 0-88132-358-6
16 **Dollar Overvaluation and the World Economy**
C. Fred Bergsten and John Williamson, eds.
February 2003 ISBN 0-88132-351-9
17 **Dollar Adjustment: How Far? Against What?**
C. Fred Bergsten and John Williamson, editors
November 2004 ISBN 0-88132-378-0

WORKS IN PROGRESS

New Regional Arrangements and the World Economy C. Fred Bergsten
The Globalization Backlash in Europe and the United States
C. Fred Bergsten, Pierre Jacquet, and Karl Kaiser
The United States as a Debtor Nation: Risks and Policy Reform
William R. Cline
China's Entry into the World Economy
Richard N. Cooper
American Trade Politics, 4th ed.
I. M. Destler
The ILO in the World Economy
Kimberly Ann Elliott
Reforming Economic Sanctions
Kimberly Ann Elliott, Gary C. Hufbauer, and Jeffrey J. Schott
Merry Sisterhood or Guarded Watchfulness? Cooperation Between the IMF and the World Bank Michael Fabricius
Why Does Immigration Divide America?
Gordon Hanson
Future of Chinese Exchange Rates
Morris Goldstein and Nicholas R. Lardy
NAFTA: A Ten-Year Appraisal
Gary Clyde Hufbauer and Jeffrey J. Schott
New Agricultural Negotiations in the WTO
Tim Josling and Dale Hathaway
Workers at Risk: Job Loss from Apparel, Textiles, Footwear, and Furniture
Lori G. Kletzer
Responses to Globalization: US Textile and Apparel Workers and Firms
Lori Kletzer, James Levinsohn, and J. David Richardson
The Strategic Implications of China-Taiwan Economic Relations Nicholas R. Lardy
Making the Rules: Case Studies on US Trade Negotiation, Vol. 1
Robert Z. Lawrence, Charan Devereaux, and Michael Watkins
US-Egypt Free Trade Agreement
Robert Z. Lawrence and Ahmed Galal
High Technology and the Globalization of America Catherine L. Mann
The Impact of Foreign Direct Investment on Development: New Measures, New Outcomes Theodore Moran, Edward Graham, and Magnus Blomstrom, editors
International Financial Architecture
Michael Mussa
Germany and the World Economy
Adam S. Posen
The Euro at Five: Ready for a Global Role?
Adam S. Posen, editor
Automatic Stabilizers for the Eurozone
Adam S. Posen
Global Forces, American Faces: US Economic Globalization at the Grass Roots
J. David Richardson
Curbing the Boom-Bust Cycle: Stabilizing Capital Flows to Emerging Markets
John Williamson

DISTRIBUTORS OUTSIDE THE UNITED STATES

Australia, New Zealand, and Papua New Guinea
D.A. Information Services
648 Whitehorse Road
Mitcham, Victoria 3132, Australia
tel: 61-3-9210-7777
fax: 61-3-9210-7788
email: service@adadirect.com.au
www.dadirect.com.au

Canada
Renouf Bookstore
5369 Canotek Road, Unit 1
Ottawa, Ontario KIJ 9J3, Canada
tel: 613-745-2665
fax: 613-745-7660
www.renoufbooks.com

United Kingdom and Europe
(including Russia and Turkey)
The Eurospan Group
3 Henrietta Street, Covent Garden
London WC2E 8LU England
tel: 44-20-7240-0856
fax: 44-20-7379-0609
www.eurospan.co.uk

India, Bangladesh, Nepal, and Sri Lanka
Viva Books Pvt.
Mr. Vinod Vasishtha
4325/3, Ansari Rd.
Daryaganj, New Delhi-110002
India
tel: 91-11-327-9280
fax: 91-11-326-7224
email: vinod.viva@gndel.globalnet. ems.vsnl.net.in

Japan and the Republic of Korea
United Publishers Services Ltd.
1-32-5, Higashi-shinagawa,
Shinagawa-ku, Tokyo 140-0002 JAPAN
tel: 81-3-5479-7251
fax: 81-3-5479-7307
info@ups.co.jp
For trade accounts only. Individuals will find IIE books in leading Tokyo bookstores.

Southeast Asia (Brunei, Burma, Cambodia, Malaysia, Indonesia, the Philippines, Singapore, Thailand Taiwan, and Vietnam)
APAC Publishers Services
70 Bedemeer Road #05-03
Hiap Huat House
Singapore 339940
tel: 65-684-47333
fax: 65-674-78916

Visit our Web site at:
www.iie.com
E-mail orders to:
orders@iie.com